Florian Kuhne

Die Ideologie der ersten Generation der Roten Armee Fraktion

GRIN Verlag

Bibliografische Information der Deutschen Nationalbibliothek:

Die Deutsche Bibliothek verzeichnet diese Publikation in der Deutschen Nationalbibliografie; detaillierte bibliografische Daten sind im Internet über http://dnb.d-nb.de/ abrufbar.

Impressum:

Druck und Bindung: Books on Demand GmbH, Norderstedt Germany
ISBN: 978-3-640-30956-6

Dieses Buch bei GRIN:

http://www.grin.com/de/e-book/90650/die-ideologie-der-ersten-generation-der-roten-armee-fraktion

WWU Münster, Institut für Politikwissenschaft

Standardvorlesung: „Einführung in die politische Ideengeschichte"

WS 2005/2006

Die Ideologie der ersten Generation der Roten Armee Fraktion

von

Florian Kuhne

Inhalt

Einleitung

„Immer mehr junge Menschen erwachen heute zu einem revolutionären Bewusstsein. Die Bereitschaft, konsequent und diszipliniert für die proletarische Revolution zu arbeiten, wächst. Die Einsicht, dass diese Revolution ohne eine wissenschaftliche revolutionäre Theorie nicht siegen kann, setzt sich durch; doch werden kaum Konsequenzen daraus gezogen." (Über den bewaffneten Kampf in Westeuropa (Mai 1971))

Es wurden vielleicht keine Konsequenzen gezogen von der Masse der Jugendlichen, auch nicht von den Arbeitern, sehr wohl jedoch von einer Gruppe junger Menschen, die erwuchs aus der Protestbewegung von 1967/68 und zu der Personen gehörten wie Ulrike Meinhof, Andreas Baader, Horst Mahler und Gudrun Ensslin. Diese Gruppe war die *erste Generation* der Roten Armee Fraktion (RAF).

Was wollte diese Gruppe erreichen? Welche Mittel setzte sie dafür ein? Und auf was für einer Idee fußte die RAF? Dies sind die Fragen, mit denen sich in dieser Arbeit auseinander gesetzt werden soll. Es geht darum, so etwas wie eine politische Ideologie, eine Theorie innerhalb der RAF auszumachen. Welche politischen Ideen wurden aufgenommen und durch die Gruppe weiterverarbeitet, auch diese Frage gilt es zu klären um die Ideologie der RAF verstehen zu können.

Die Arbeit befasst sich ausschließlich mit der frühen Anfangszeit des bundesdeutschen Terrorismus in den Jahren 1970/71. Aus diesen Jahren stammen auch die drei genau zu untersuchenden Dokumente der RAF, „Die Rote Armee aufbauen" vom 5. Juni 1970, „Das Konzept Stadtguerilla" vom April 1971 und „Über den bewaffneten Kampf in Westeuropa" vom Mai 1971. Diese Schriften bergen eine Fülle an Informationen und werden in jeweils eigenen Abschnitten behandelt.

Um jedoch den Fokus auf die frühen 1970er Jahre richten zu können, schien es hilfreich, eine Einführung zu der Zeit vor 1970 zu geben und außerdem die gesamten Geschehnisse bis einschließlich des „Deutschen Herbstes" 1977 zu beleuchten.

Daran anschließend werden die Dokumente der frühen RAF einzeln betrachtet und analysiert, bevor in einem dritten Teil die verschiedenen Aspekte zusammengefasst werden. Eine Schlussbetrachtung zieht dann ein kurzes Fazit zu den Bestandteilen der Ideologie der Roten Armee Fraktion.

Als Hauptquelle dient das vom ID-Verlag herausgegebene Buch „Rote Armee Fraktion. Texte und Materialien", teilweise auch für die chronologische Darstellung der Ereignisse. Zu diesem Zweck wird aber auch das dpa-Archiv herangezogen werden. Unter der Sekundärliteratur wird vornehmlich das Buch „Ideologien und Strategien", herausgegeben von Iring Fetscher und Günter Rohrmoser, benutzt werden, hinzugezogen werden außerdem „Der blinde Fleck. Die Linke, die RAF und der Staat“ und „Die alte Straßenverkehrsordnung“, herausgegeben von Klaus Bittermann.

2. Vorgeschichte

Die Geschichte der RAF beginnt vor dem 14. Mai 1970 (Befreiung Baaders) und vor den Ereignissen am 2. Juni 1967, nämlich in der Nachkriegszeit: Die Befreiung vom Faschismus weckte Hoffnung bei den Emigranten und Antifaschisten, den Sozialisten und Kommunisten auf eine „antinazistische, demokratische und sozialistische Gesellschaft“, aber die „Verdrängung der nationalsozialistischen Verbrechen, [der] Antikommunismus und [...] das ‚Wirtschaftswunder‘“, die Remilitarisierung ab den 1950er Jahren (Kampagne “Kampf dem Atomtod“) und die Notstandsgesetze zur Wahrung der „Inneren Sicherheit“ von 1960 prägten das politische Klima und ließen bei vielen die Erwartungen sinken.[1]

Unter den Studenten entwickelte sich in den 1960er Jahren eine „kulturrevolutionäre Opposition“, orientiert an „den Theoretikern des Marxismus/Leninismus [...], am Existenzialismus, der Kritischen Theorie und des Anarchismus“.[2]

Ab 1962 kam es erst unter Jugendlichen, dann verstärkt auch unter Studenten zu vermehrten gewaltsamen Aktionen. „Der Protest gegen den Vietnam-Krieg wurde zum wichtigsten Bezugspunkt für die Studentenbewegung.“ 1967 rief Rudi Dutschke zur Gründung der APO (Außerparlamentarische Opposition) auf, am 2. Juni desselben Jahres wurde der Student Benno Ohnesorg bei einer Demonstration gegen den Besuch des Schahs von Persien von einem Polizisten getötet. In den darauf folgenden Tagen kam es deutschlandweit zu ausgeprägten Demonstrationen. Im Juni 1967 wurde an der Freien Universität Berlin ein Diskussionsforum unter anderem mit Herbert Marcuse abgehalten. „Große Bedeutung hatte Marcuses ‚Kritik der repressiven Toleranz‘, in der er formulierte, ‚dass es für unterdrückte und überwältigte Minderheiten ein *Naturrecht* auf Widerstand gibt, außergesetzliche Mittel anzuwenden, sobald die gesetzlichen sich als unzulänglich herausgestellt haben.‘“ [3]

Am 2. April 1968 explodierten in Frankfurter Kaufhäusern zwei Brandsätze. Die Aktion sollte verstanden werden als ein Protest gegen „„die Gleichgültigkeit der Gesellschaft gegenüber den

[1] RAF. Texte und Materialien, S. 14
[2] ebd., S. 15
[3] vgl. RAF. Texte und Materialien, S. 16

Morden in Vietnam'".[4] Am 5. April wurden Gudrun Ensslin, Andreas Baader, Thorwald Proll und Horst Söhnlein als der Tat verdächtig festgenommen.

Nach dem Attentat auf Rudi Dutschke am 11. April und den anschließenden Demonstrationen, teilweise mit Blockaden und Straßenschlachten, rückte die „Notwendigkeit von Gegengewalt" in den Fokus der APO. Am 4. November kam es zur „Schlacht am Tegeler Weg", bei der 130 Polizisten verletzt wurden. Anlass war das Ehrengerichtsverfahren gegen Horst Mahler.

Auch außerhalb Deutschlands kam es zu Unruhen und Protesten. In Frankreich, Italien, Japan, Mexiko und Uruguay wurden Demonstrationen teilweise blutig niedergeschlagen, in Mexiko-City starben 500 Menschen, als das Militär eine Kundgebung „mit einem Massaker" beendete. Auch die Staaten des Warschauer Paktes waren betroffen. Nach der Niederschlagung des Prager Frühlings marschierten Hunderttausende durch Prag. Die Asten der Westberliner Universitäten erklärten sich solidarisch: „„Die militärische Intervention hat den Kräften des proletarischen Internationalismus erneut gezeigt, wie notwendig ihr Kampf gegen jede Form bürokratischer Herrschaft in den verschiedenen Gesellschaftssystemen ist. Es lebe die sozialistische Weltrevolution!!!'"[5]

1969 verschärften sich die militanten Auseinandersetzungen noch und wurden „zunehmend zur Aktionsform der APO". Straßenschlachten in Berlin und Frankfurt, die „Aktion Roter Punk" in Hannover, das „Knastcamp" in Bayern, Massenstreiks im Bergbau, all dies sind Beispiele dafür. Außerdem wurden 1968/69 mehrere Anschläge auf US-amerikanische Einrichtungen, Konsulate, Banken und Rathäuser verübt. Unter den Studenten diskutierte man über Werke wie Che Guevaras „Theorie und Methode des Guerilla-Krieges".[6]

Zu der „Naivität" der radikalen Linken im Anfangsstadium schrieb Til Schulz, dass die Jugendlichen „Vokabeln wie ‚Propaganda der Schüsse' (Che Guevara) oder ‚Zerschlagung des Staatsapparates' an[nahmen] – sei es von Professor Mao Tse-tung, vom Hochschullehrer Meister Guevara oder vom Sattlermeister Marcuse".[7]

---

[4] zit. n. ebd., S. 17
[5] zit. n. ebd., S. 18
[6] vgl. RAF. Texte und Materialien, S. 18
[7] Schulz, Til, „Sieg im Volkskrieg?", in: Der blinde Fleck, S. 83

3.Die RAF in den siebziger Jahren

3.1 Die Ereignisse 1970 bis 1977

Am 2. April 1970 wurde Andreas Baader in Berlin verhaftet, nachdem er seine Haftstrafe im Zuge der Brandstiftungen in Frankfurt nicht angetreten hatte. Am 14. Mai wurde er mit Waffengewalt aus dem Institut für soziale Fragen befreit, wo ein wissenschaftliches Gespräch mit Ulrike Meinhof verabredet war. Bei der Befreiungsaktion wurde ein Angestellter schwer verletzt. Am nächsten Tag wurde auch Ulrike Meinhof steckbrieflich gesucht.

Eine Woche später erschien „die erste öffentliche Erklärung der RAF“: „Die Rote Armee aufbauen“. In dieser sollte die Aktion vom 14. Mai erklärt und gerechtfertigt werden. Im April 1971 erschien „das erste Positionspapier“ der RAF unter dem Titel „Konzept Stadtguerilla“. Mit „Über den bewaffneten Kampf in Westeuropa“ wurde im Mai 1971 ein umfangreiches Papier veröffentlicht, dass sowohl die Aktionen der RAF legitimieren, als auch die sympathisierenden Volksgruppen zum Kampf bewegen sollte (s. 3.2.2 und 3.2.3).

Nach einigen Banküberfällen kam es im Mai 1972 zur „Offensive“: Es wurden Anschläge auf das Hauptquartier der US-Armee in Frankfurt am Main, auf das Polizeipräsidium in Augsburg, einen Richter des Bundesgerichtshofes und das Springer-Hochhaus in Hamburg verübt, außerdem auf das Heidelberger Hauptquartier der US-Armee, wobei drei Menschen getötet wurden.

„Gegen die RAF wurde nach der Baader-Befreiung ein bis dahin unbekannter Fahndungsaufwand betrieben.“ Nachdem im Oktober 1970 fünf Aktivisten festgenommen wurden, kam es nach einem Schusswechsel in Frankfurt am 10. Februar 1971 zur ersten großen bundesweiten Fahndungsaktion. Am 15. Juli 1971 wurde unter Aufbietung von 3000 Polizisten eine Großaktion „zur Ergreifung von neun Mitgliedern der RAF“ durchgeführt. In Hamburg wurde im Zuge dieser Maßnahme Petra Schelm erschossen. Bis zum Juni 1972 wurden sechs Menschen (davon drei Polizisten) bei weiteren Fahndungen erschossen.[8]

Seit Juli 1972 war die erste Generation der RAF inhaftiert. Baader, Holger Meins und Jan-Carl Raspe waren im Juni in Frankfurt festgenommen worden, Gudrun Ensslin ebenfalls im Juni in Hamburg, Ulrike Meinhof in Hannover. Sie studierten im Gefängnis weiterhin Guerilla-Taktik und -Strategie. Ergebnisse dieser Studien und Anweisungen wurden an die in Freiheit lebenden Aktivisten weitergegeben.

---

[8] vgl. RAF. Texte und Materialien S. 20ff

Im Sommer 1973 kam es wieder vermehrt zu „revolutionären Aktionen“, in Berlin vor allem durch die „Bewegung 2. Juni“.[9]

Ein mit „Rote Armee Fraktion, Aufbauorganisation“ unterzeichneter Brief ging im Herbst 1974 bei der Berliner Innenbehörde ein: „Bürger, Freunde, Genossen. Heute, am 4. Oktober 1974, haben wir den politisch-militärischen Kampf aufgenommen.“ Nur fünf Wochen später wurde Günter von Drenkmann, damals höchster Richter der Stadt Berlin, erschossen.

Im Februar 1975 wurde der Berliner CDU-Vorsitzende Peter Lorenz entführt. „Zum ersten Mal erpressten die Terroristen den Staat im großen Stil.“[10] Im Austausch gegen den Politiker wurden fünf von sechs Inhaftierten in den Jemen ausgeflogen, Horst Mahler weigerte sich, das Gefängnis zu verlassen. Zwei Monate später nahm das „Kommando Holger Meins“[11] in der deutschen Botschaft in Stockholm 12 Geiseln und versuchte, 26 in Deutschland inhaftierte Anarchisten freizupressen. Doch die Bundesregierung blieb hart, die Terroristen zündeten eine Bombe, 4 Menschen starben.[12]

Der Generalbundesanwalt Siegfried Buback wurde im April 1977 auf offener Straße erschossen. Bei dem Überfall sterben außerdem zwei weitere Menschen. Diese Aktion wird beschrieben als “planmäßiger Mord“, mit dem die Terroristen die „Hemmschwelle vor dem unmittelbaren Töten“ überwunden hätten. Am 30. Juli 1977 wurde Jürgen Ponto, Vorstandsvorsitzender der Dresdner Bank, bei einer misslungenen Entführung erschossen.

Am 5.9.1977 kam es zum Attentat von Köln. Bei der Entführung von Hanns Martin Schleyer, dem damaligen Arbeitgeberpräsidenten, wurden drei Polizisten und der Fahrer Schleyers erschossen. Die Entführer forderten die Freilassung von 11 Terroristen. Während die Bundesregierung versuchte, Zeit zu gewinnen, wurde am 13.10.1977 die Lufthansa-Maschine „Landshut“ entführt. Doch diese „Unterstützung“ der Schleyer-Entführer blieb wirkungslos, die Maschine wurde am 18.10. von der GSG 9 gestürmt, drei der vier Entführer starben. Am gleichen Tag starben Baader, Raspe und Ensslin in Stuttgart-Stammheim in der Haft. Die Frage nach „Selbstmord“ oder „Mord“, so wie es Sympathisanten formulierten, ist nicht geklärt. Daraufhin hatten die Schleyer-Entführer keinen Erfolg mehr in Aussicht. Sie töteten ihre Geisel mit drei Kopfschüssen.[13]

---

[9] vgl. dpa-Archiv/HG 2749, S. 4 und dpa-Archiv/HG 2751 S. 7
[10] zit. n. dpa-Archiv/HG 2749 S. 5
[11] in Anlehnung an den durch einen Hungerstreik in der Haft gestorbenen Holger Meins, der dem „harten Kern“ der RAF zugerechnet wurde
[12] vgl. dpa-Archiv/HG 2749 S. 5
[13] vgl. dpa-Archiv/HG 2749 S. 6f und dpa-Archiv/HG 2752 S. 8f

3.2 Dokumente

3.2.1 Die Rote Armee aufbauen (5. Juni 1970)

Mit der Veröffentlichung des Papiers „Die Rote Armee aufbauen" sollte die Baader-Befreiungs-Aktion erklärt werden. Allerdings „nicht den intellektuellen Schwätzern, den Hosenscheißern, den Alles-besser-Wissern [...], sondern den potentiell revolutionären Teilen des Volkes. [...] Die es satt haben!" Und weiter:

> „Denen habt ihr die Aktion zu vermitteln, die für die Ausbeutung, die sie erleiden, keine Entschädigung bekommen durch Lebensstandard, Konsum, Bausparvertrag, Kleinkredite, Mittelklassewagen. Die sich den ganzen Kram nicht leisten können, die da nicht dran hängen. [...] Denen – und nicht den kleinbürgerlichen Intellektuellen – habt ihr zu sagen, dass jetzt Schluss ist, dass es jetzt los geht, dass die Befreiung Baaders nur der Anfang ist! Dass ein Ende der Bullenherrschaft abzusehen ist! Denen habt ihr zu sagen, dass wir die Rote Armee aufbauen, das ist ihre Armee."[14]

Es sollte also so etwas wie eine „Armee des kleinen Mannes" geschaffen werden, der der Bürokratie ständig unterliegt, der dem Papier zufolge ausgebeutet wurde vom System. Darüber hinaus ist dieser erste Teil der Schrift als Ankündigung zu verstehen, als Versuch, diejenigen anzusprechen, die schon militant geworden waren.

„Was heißt: die Konflikte auf die Spitze treiben? Das heißt: sich nicht abschlachten lassen. Deshalb bauen wir die Rote Armee auf. [...] Was die Schweine mit Zensuren, Entlassungen, Kündigungen, mit Kuckuck und Schlagstock schaffen, schaffen sie damit. [...] Na und?" Diese Frage wird direkt und eindeutig beantwortet: „Macht das klar, dass die Revolution kein Osterspaziergang sein wird. [...] Um die Konflikte auf die Spitze treiben zu können, bauen wir die Rote Armee auf."[15]

Darüber hinaus ist die „Rote Armee" außerdem notwendig, um ein weiteres Ziel zu erreichen: „Ohne die Rote Armee aufzubauen, können die Schweine alles machen, können die Schweine weitermachen: einsperren, entlassen, pfänden, Kinder stehlen, einschüchtern, schießen, herrschen. Die Konflikte auf die Spitze treiben heißt: Dass die nicht mehr können, was die wollen, sondern machen müssen, was wir wollen."

Klassisch marxistische Begriffe wurden außerdem von der RAF in dieser ersten Schrift, quasi abschließend, postuliert: „Die Klassenkämpfe entfalten / Das Proletariat organisieren / Mit dem bewaffneten Widerstand beginnen / Die Rote Armee aufbauen!"[16]

---

[14] Die Rote Armee aufbauen, in: RAF. Texte und Materialien, S. 24

[15] ebd., S. 25

[16] Die Rote Armee aufbauen, in: RAF. Texte und Materialien, S. 26

3.2.2 Das Konzept Stadtguerilla (April 1971)

Mit der zweiten Veröffentlichung der RAF sollte „Das Konzept Stadtguerilla" erläutert werden. Dieses bezieht sich eindeutig auf den bewaffneten Kampf, der in den Fokus der RAF gerückt war. Man kann dieses „Positionspapier" als Rechtfertigung und Legitimationsversuch deuten. Es ist in mehrere Unterpunkte gegliedert.

I. Konkrete Antworten auf konkrete Fragen

In diesem ersten Kapitel werden zwei wichtige Voraussetzungen für den bewaffneten Kampf angesprochen. Der Satz „Eine revolutionäre politische Praxis unter den herrschenden Bedingungen – wenn nicht überhaupt – setzt die permanente Integration von individuellem Charakter und politischer Motivation voraus, d.h. politische Identität." stellt dar, was nach Meinung der RAF jeder einzelne mitzubringen hat in den Kampf: „politische Identität".[17] Der zweite Punkt spricht den richtigen Moment an und die Notwendigkeit des „bewaffneten Widerstandes": „Wir behaupten, dass die Organisierung von bewaffneten Widerstandsgruppen zu diesem Zeitpunkt in der Bundesrepublik und Westberlin richtig ist, möglich ist, gerechtfertigt ist. [...], dass es ohne das keinen antiimperialistischen Kampf in den Metropolen gibt."[18]

II. Metropole Bundesrepublik

Warum in der Bundesrepublik Deutschland genauso Widerstand stattfindet wie in Südamerika oder Südostasien, wird im zweiten Teil kurz angesprochen:

> „durch Entwicklungs- und Militärhilfe an den Aggressionskriegen der USA beteiligt, profitiert die Bundesrepublik von der Ausbeutung der Dritten Welt, ohne die Verantwortung für diese Kriege zu haben, ohne sich deswegen mit einer Opposition im Innern streiten zu müssen. Nicht weniger aggressiv als der US-Imperialismus ist sie doch weniger angreifbar."[19]

III. Studentenrevolte

Dieser dritte Teil wird dazu benutzt, die Zeit der Studentenrevolte zu analysieren und kann angesehen werden als klares Bekenntnis zur studentischen Vergangenheit der RAF.

„Es ist das Verdienst der Studentenbewegung [...], kurz: ihrer Praxis, den Marxismus-Leninismus im Bewusstsein wenigstens der Intelligenz als diejenige politische Theorie rekonstruiert zu haben, ohne die politische, ökonomische und ideologische Tatsachen und ihre Erscheinungsformen nicht auf den Begriff zu bringen sind, [...]"[20] Hier findet sich erneut ein Bezug zu Marx und Lenin, die offensichtlich tief verankert sind im Bewusstsein der RAF.

---

[17] Das Konzept Stadtguerilla, in: RAF. Texte und Materialien, S. 28
[18] ebd., S. 31
[19] ebd., S. 33
[20] Das Konzept Stadtguerilla, in: RAF. Texte und Materialien, S. 34

Der Widerspruch zwischen „Ideologie der Freiheit der Wissenschaft" und der „Realität der dem Zugriff des Monopolkapitals ausgesetzten Universität" wird angesprochen, außerdem wird noch einmal harsche Kritik geübt an der BRD:

> „Bis ihnen [den Studenten] und ihrer Öffentlichkeit klar war, dass nicht ‚Freiheit, Gleichheit, Brüderlichkeit', nicht Menschenrechte, nicht UNO-Charta den Inhalt dieser Demokratie ausmachen; dass hier gilt, was für die kolonialistische und imperialistische Ausbeutung Lateinamerikas, Afrikas und Asiens immer gegolten hat: Disziplin, Unterordnung und Brutalität für die Unterdrückten, für die, die sich auf deren Seite stellen, Protest erheben, Widerstand leisten, *den antiimperialistischen Kampf führen* [Hervorhebung d. Verf.]."[21]

Es wird ein Aktionismus eingefordert, für den Beispiele angeführt werden:

> „Die Linken wussten damals, dass es richtig sein würde, sozialistische Propaganda im Betrieb mit der tatsächlichen Verhinderung der Auslieferung der *Bild*-Zeitung zu verbinden. Dass es richtig wäre, die Propaganda bei den Gis, sich nicht nach Vietnam schicken zu lassen, mit tatsächlichen Angriffen auf Militärflugzeuge für Vietnam zu verbinden, die Bundeswehrkampagne mit tatsächlichen Angriffen auf Nato-Flughäfen. Dass es richtig wäre, die Kritik an der Klassenjustiz mit dem Sprengen von Gefängnismauern zu verbinden [...]"[22]

IV. Primat der Praxis

Im weiteren Verlauf bekennt man sich zum „Primat der Praxis": „Wir behaupten, dass ohne revolutionäre Initiative, ohne die praktische revolutionäre Intervention der Avantgarde, der sozialistischen Arbeiter und Intellektuellen, ohne den konkreten antiimperialistischen Kampf es keinen Vereinheitlichungsprozess gibt, dass das Bündnis nur in gemeinsamen Kämpfen hergestellt wird [...]."[23] Der *konkrete* Kampf wird im folgenden Dokument genau dargelegt.

Im letzten Teil werden noch zwei wichtige Aussagen zur Stadtguerilla im Besonderen gemacht: „Stadtguerilla ist eine Waffe im Klassenkampf"[24] und „Stadtguerilla machen heißt, den antiimperialistischen Kampf offensiv führen".[25]

3.2.3 Über den bewaffneten Kampf in Westeuropa (Mai 1971)

1. Bewaffneter Kampf – ein zentrales Problem der revolutionären Theorie

Die „revolutionäre Theorie" wird hier dargestellt als eine „Anleitung zum revolutionären Handeln". Sie muss Antworten geben auf die Fragen nach „den Kräften, den Zielen, den Mitteln und den Wegen der sozialistischen Revolution". Darüber hinaus muss sie „die Frage der Macht im Staate richtig lösen".

[21] ebd., S. 34
[22] ebd., S. 36
[23] ebd., S. 37
[24] ebd., S. 42
[25] ebd., S. 48

„Die notwendigen und möglichen Schritte zur *Diktatur des Proletariats* [Hervorhebung d. Verf.] müssen entwickelt werden – sonst ist die revolutionäre Theorie lückenhaft, keine Anleitung zu richtigem Handeln." Diese Aussage wird unterstützt von der sichtbaren Furcht, etwas falsch zu machen. Denn die Fehler der Vergangenheit sollen nicht wiederholt werden. Vielmehr sollen die Erkenntnisse, die man aus der Geschichte gewonnen hat, angewendet werden und somit „die Revolution voranbringen". Denn: „Erfolgreiche Klassenkämpfe der Vergangenheit sind nicht Vorbilder, die man kopieren sollte, sondern Lehrstücke."[26]

„Der bewaffnete Kampf [...] folgt aus der Tatsache, dass es den besitzenden Klassen gelungen ist, sich den bestimmenden Einfluss auf die staatlichen Machthebel zu sichern und das staatliche Monopol über die letztlich entscheidenden Gewaltinstrumente Polizei und Armee – durchzusetzen." Daher wird das „gesellschaftliche Gewaltpotential" zu einem „Herrschaftsinstrument in den Händen der besitzenden Klassen", welches nur mit Gewalt zu bekämpfen ist. Dass das „Gewaltmonopol" des Staates „Bundesrepublik Deutschland" auch in den 1970er Jahren gegen innere Feinde benutzt werden wird, davon geht die RAF aus: „Wo immer der Kapitalismus noch über reale Macht verfügt, wird er sie zu Verlängerung seiner Existenz einsetzen."[27]

„„Die zentrale Aufgabe der Revolution und ihre höchste Form ist die bewaffnete Machtergreifung, ist die Lösung der Frage durch den Krieg. Dieses revolutionäre Prinzip des Marxismus-Leninismus hat allgemeine Gültigkeit, [...]."[28]

Dieses Zitat im Text spricht zwei wichtige Aspekte für die politische Ideologie der RAF an: Zum einen drückt es aus, dass man sich in der Tradition des Marxismus-Leninismus sah, zum anderen vertrat man darüber hinaus das „revolutionäre Prinzip" des bewaffneten Kampfes, der zum „endgültigen Sieg des Proletariats" führen sollte.[29]

2. Bewaffneter Kampf und Generalstreik

Im zweiten Teil dieser Schrift wird darauf hingewiesen, dass die Organisation der Arbeiter zwar bedeutsam ist, ein Generalstreik aber am Einsatz der staatlichen Gewalt scheitert sowie am „Hunger und der Erschöpfung der Massen zugrunde geht". Es wird erkannt, dass der (bürgerliche) Staat durch die Massenbewegung geschwächt wird, jedoch nicht „vernichtend geschlagen". Dies wiederum führt laut RAF dazu, dass „das Kapital zunächst gestärkt" aus der Revolte hervorgeht und „eine faschistische Diktatur" errichtet. „Der Generalstreik lähmt zwar die Wirtschaft eines Industrielandes, er löst aber nicht automatisch die Machtfrage."[30]

---

[26] vgl. Über den bewaffneten Kampf in Westeuropa, in: RAF. Texte und Materialien, S. 49

[27] vgl. ebd., S. 50f

[28] Mao Tse Tung zit. n. Über den bewaffneten Kampf in Westeuropa, in: RAF. Texte und Materialien, S. 51

[29] vgl. ebd., S. 51f

[30] vgl. Über den bewaffneten Kampf in Westeuropa, in: RAF. Texte und Materialien, S. 53

Dies tut er auch deshalb nicht, weil die „politische Erhebung" nur die „Herstellung der ‚bürgerlichen Demokratie'" zum Ergebnis haben kann, was nach Ansicht der RAF der „präfschistischen Formation der verschleierten Diktatur der Bourgeoisie" entspricht. „Es entsteht so ein Kreislauf der verschiedenen Herrschaftsformen des Kapitals." Der „parlamentarischen Scheindemokratie" folgt die „offene, faschistische Diktatur der Bourgeoisie", welcher wiederum die parlamentarische Herrschaftsform folgt „usw., bis das Proletariat endlich begriffen hat, dass die militärische Niederringung des Klassenfeindes durch keine andere Kampfform [...] ersetzt werden kann, sondern dass alle anderen Formen des Klassenkampfes und politische Bündnisse nur eine unterstützende Bedeutung für den bewaffneten Kampf haben können."[31]

3. Proletarisches Bewusstsein, revolutionäre Theorie und die Rolle der revolutionären Intelligenz

„Jede Propaganda, die revolutionäre Ziele proklamiert, wird wirkungslos bleiben, wenn sie nicht die konkreten Wege bezeichnet, auf denen diese Ziele erreicht werden können." Hierin sieht die RAF einen entscheidenden Unterschied zur „bürgerlichen Propaganda", welche „die Massen gerade von selbständigem politischen Handeln fernhalten" soll. Die entscheidende Frage auf dem Weg zur „Verwirklichung der sozialistischen Gesellschaft" ist diese: Wie kann die „Macht des Kapitals" gebrochen werden?[32]

Außerdem wird die These vertreten, dass die Industriearbeiter anstelle der „Intelligenzschicht" (gemeint sind vor allem Studenten) die Führung übernehmen müssten, dass das Proletariat seine „tief eingeprägte Resignation" ablegen müsse und die „Lösung der Machtfrage im gesamtgesellschaftlichen Maßstab" erarbeiten solle. „Eine zeitgemäße revolutionäre Theorie kann daher nur von denen entwickelt werden, die aufgrund ihrer objektiven Klassenlage die Möglichkeit haben, die Erfahrungen und die daraus gewonnenen Erkenntnisse der Vergangenheit verstehend in ihre Überlegungen einzubeziehen [...]." Dies soll erklären, warum die sozialistischen Ideen von Menschen geprägt wurden, die ihrer Herkunft nach *nicht* dem Proletariat zuzurechnen sind. So auch in der BRD: „Nicht die Organisationen der Industriearbeiterschaft, sondern die revolutionären Teile der Studentenschaft sind heute Träger des zeitgenössischen revolutionären Bewusstseins."[33]

---

[31] vgl. ebd., S. 58
[32] vgl. ebd., S. 59
[33] vgl. ebd., S. 62ff

4. Revolutionäre Avantgarde und proletarische Klasse

„Die Notwendigkeit der proletarischen Führung beruht darauf, dass allein das Proletariat aufgrund seiner objektiven Klassenlage ein konsequentes Interesse an [...] der Überwindung des kapitalistischen Systems schlechthin in die Geschichte einbringt."[34]

Da die proletarische Führung laut RAF aber nur in der „Avantgarde-Funktion" realisiert werden kann, muss eine Avantgarde entstehen, die jedoch nicht statisch sein darf. Diese soll sich sehen als „diejenige, an deren Verhalten und Aktionen sich die revolutionären Massen orientieren". Die einzelnen Gruppen können sich also in der Avantgarde-Funktion abwechseln.[35]

„Der kollektive Widerstand ist der Keim der Revolution. Die richtige revolutionäre Theorie hat ihn zu entwickeln und zu formen." Die noch nicht involvierten Schichten des Proletariats sollen mobilisiert werden durch die Massen, die „die Fahne der Revolution bereits aufgenommen haben". Dann kann die Industriearbeiterschaft die Führung übernehmen „und die sozialistische Revolution bis zum Ende garantieren".[36]

5. Stadtguerilla als revolutionäre Interventionsmethode in den Metropolen

In diesem Kapitel wird nach der Schrift vom April erneut dargelegt, warum die RAF sich an den Methoden der Guerilla orientierte. Einer der wichtigsten Gründe scheint die „Ausschaltung des bürgerlichen Militärapparates" zu sein. Dies gelänge einer Guerilla durch „eine allmähliche Auszehrung der Kräfte des Feindes im Sinne eines moralischen Verschleißes". Außerdem muss die Guerilla vom Volk unterstützt werden. Diese Aussage wird allerdings relativiert, wenn es sich um Aktionen der Guerilla in Großstädten handelt. Dort sind „alle erforderlichen Versorgungsgüter" anzutreffen und somit ist die Stadtguerilla „von der Haltung der nicht unmittelbar beteiligten Bevölkerung weitgehend unabhängig." Darüber hinaus bietet die Großstadt eine „Massierung von Angriffszielen".

Zwei Prinzipien gelten für die Guerilla: Das Prinzip, sich selbst zu erhalten und das Prinzip, sich zu vergrößern.[37]

6. Terror gegen den Herrschaftsapparat – ein notwendiges Element der Massenkämpfe

Die „Kommandoeinheiten" der Guerilla sollen als Vorbild dienen, um den Massen die „bewaffnete Aktion als ein erfolgreiches Mittel zur Sicherung ihrer Interessen" aufzuzeigen. Dies soll zu einem „für den Feind undurchdringliche[n] Gewebe" von militanten Aktionseinheiten führen, was wiederum, in Verbindung mit der Solidarisierung der Arbeiter, dazu führt, dass

---

[34] Über den bewaffneten Kampf in Westeuropa, in: RAF. Texte und Materialien, S. 68

[35] vgl. ebd., S. 69

[36] vgl. ebd., S. 71f

[37] vgl. ebd., S. 72f

die „feindlichen Söldner“ nach und nach demoralisiert werden und sich die „Unterdrückungsstreitkräfte“ isolieren.[38]

An dieser Stelle wird der Begriff „Terror“ eingeführt, in Form einer Frage: „Aber ist das nicht ‚individueller Terror‘, das Verderben aller revolutionären Bewegungen?“ Die aufgeworfene Frage wird direkt beantwortet: „Wer hier ‚Terror‘ schreit, [...] zeigt nur, wie fürchterlich er vor der revolutionären Aufgabe erschrickt.“ Gezielte Bomben-Anschläge werden als „revolutionäre Aufgabe“ dargestellt. Hier zeigt sich deutlich, dass die von der RAF vertretene „revolutionäre Theorie“ nach Meinung der Autoren vor nichts zurückschrecken darf. Im Folgenden wird näher auf den „individuellen Terror“ eingegangen. Es wird gegen die Meinung argumentiert, Lenin hätte den „individuellen Terror“ kritisiert; Lenin hätte mit „individuell“ nicht das Opfer gemeint, sondern den Täter, der „lediglich seinem individuellen Hass gegen das volksfeindliche Regime Ausdruck gab, aber nicht den revolutionären Kampf der proletarischen Massen führte“.[39]

Der „revolutionäre Terror“, so wie ihn die RAF (unter dem Einfluss Lenins) versteht, „richtet sich ausschließlich gegen Exponenten des Ausbeutungssystems und gegen Funktionäre des Unterdrückungsapparates“ und nicht gegen das Volk. Er ist allerdings notwendig, um das System zu bekämpfen. „Will man es zerstören, muss man seine Organe ausschalten.“[40]

7. Die Kraft der Volksmassen konkret entdecken und so die Resignation in den Massen überwinden!

„In der Revolution gibt es ein oberstes Prinzip: die Kräfte des Volkes entwickeln und erhalten, die Kräfte des Feindes vernichten. Damit sind der Roten Armee Strategie und Taktik vorgegeben.“ An dieser Stelle wird eindeutig und unmissverständlich beschrieben, wie die RAF vorzugehen gedachte:

> „Wenn der Feind formiert und massiert auftritt, wird er die Guerilla nicht finden und deshalb auch nicht bekämpfen können. Wenn sich die Söldner des Feindes aber zerstreuen, wenn sie arglos und vereinzelt sind, in ihre Quartiere und Wohnungen zurückkehren, werden die Partisanen sie dort erwarten und zur Verantwortung ziehen. Die Angriffe der Guerilla sollten sich nach Möglichkeit nicht gegen die einfachen Soldaten des Feindes, wohl aber gegen seine Offiziere und leitenden Beamten richten. Für sie darf es nirgends mehr ein befriedetes Gebiet, eine ‚Etappe‘, eine friedliche Heimat, ein sicheres Privatleben geben. [...]
> Es genügt nicht, nur immer von der Kraft der Volksmassen zu reden. Es kommt darauf an, sie endlich konkret zu entdecken; die Bedingungen zu schaffen, dass die Massen nicht mehr wehrlos den Unterdrückungsfeldzügen des Kapitals ausgesetzt sind, sondern befähigt werden, ihre reale Macht konkret zu entfalten und dem Feind erfolgreich entgegenzusetzen. Hat die Auflösung der feindlichen Kräfte einen genügenden Grad erreicht, dann wird es aussichtsreich, durch koordinierte Aktionen der Massen in den Produktionsbe-

[38] vgl. Über den bewaffneten Kampf in Westeuropa, in: RAF. Texte und Materialien, S. 77
[39] vgl. ebd., S. 78f
[40] vgl. ebd., S. 83

trieben und der bewaffneten Abteilungen des Proletariats den letzten Widerstand des Feindes zu brechen und die Macht des Volkes in allen Bereichen zu festigen."[41]

Dies ist ein Teil der revolutionären Theorie der RAF. Massenmobilisierung scheint die wichtigste Stütze des Umsturzes, der Beseitigung des „faschistischen Systems". Auf die oben beschriebene Weise sollte die „Diktatur des Proletariats" eingeleitet werden.
Doch, so wird etwas weiter unten ausgeführt, wäre es falsch, „dieses Mittel erst einzusetzen, wenn die ‚Zustimmung der Massen' sicher ist; denn das hieße, auf diesen Kampf gänzlich verzichten, weil diese ‚Zustimmung der Massen' allein durch den Kampf erreicht werden kann".[42]

8. Revolution und jugendliche Gesellschaft

In diesem Kapitel wird auf die Jugend in der BRD eingegangen, die sich laut RAF einer „Ideologie der Anpassungsverweigerung" verschrieben hat. „In einer Klassengesellschaft hat diese Ideologie notwendig Klassencharakter." Sie wird verstanden als „Absage an die für den kapitalistischen Verwertungsprozess erforderten Verhaltensweisen" und ist somit „tendenziell antikapitalistisch und revolutionär". André Glucksmann wird mit dem Satz zitiert „„Der Kampf der Studenten enthält die Rebellion der modernen Produktivkräfte in ihrer Gesamtheit gegen die bürgerlichen Produktionsverhältnisse in sich und verleiht ihr öffentlichen Ausdruck.'"[43]

9. Die revolutionäre Organisation des Proletariats im und durch den bewaffneten Kampf schaffen!

„Das praktische revolutionäre Beispiel ist der einzige Weg zur Revolutionierung der Massen, die eine geschichtliche Chance zur Verwirklichung des Sozialismus beinhaltet." Auf die in Kapitel 7 beschriebene Taktik soll die „politische und organisatorische Durchdringung von Avantgarde und Masse zu einer dialektischen Einheit" folgen.[44]
„Die Bomben schmeißen wir auch in das Bewusstsein der Massen." Dies soll dann dazu führen, dass „die Massen" sich sympathisieren mit den „Revolutionären": „Aus der Quelle wird ein Bach, aus dem Bach der Fluß, aus dem Fluß der Strom, der schließlich mit seiner gewaltigen Wucht das Unterdrückungssystem wegreißen wird."[45] Diese geradezu literarische Formel ist fest verankert in der Idee der RAF.

---

41 Über den bewaffneten Kampf in Westeuropa, in: RAF. Texte und Materialien, S. 85
42 ebd., S. 86
43 vgl. ebd., S. 94f
44 vgl. ebd., S. 99
45 vgl. ebd., S. 100f

10. Die Angst vor dem Faschismus überwinden, um seine Wurzeln zu vernichten!

„Wenn der Feind seine Kräfte anstrengen muss, um die unterdrückten Klassen niederzuhalten, so ist das nicht schlecht, sondern gut; zeigt sich doch, dass das Proletariat wuchtige Schläge gegen den Klassenfeind führt, die ihn zittern machen." Das Proletariat darf allerdings nicht verzagen, sondern muss diesen „Klassenfeind" bekämpfen: „Der Faschismus ist ein großes Übel, das größte aller kapitalistischen Übel. Aber die Angst vor dem Faschismus ist schon ein Teil seiner Herrschaft."[46]

Redet nicht länger darüber, wie der Faschismus zu verhindern sei; denn er ist nicht zu verhindern – aber er ist besiegbar. Denkt darüber nach, was getan werden muss, um ihn endgültig niederzuwerfen, und handelt danach!" [47]

Was sind die nächsten Schritte?

Unter dieser Überschrift werden vier Punkte genannt: Erstens soll „umfassende Propaganda für den bewaffneten Kampf" betrieben werden. Zweitens sollen „Anleitungen für die Herstellung von Waffen, für die Kampftaktik usw." verbreitet werden. Der dritte Punkt fordert die Bildung von „Kommandogruppen" und viertens: „Den Kampf beginnen".[48]

4. Ziele und Ideologie der RAF

Aus den oben untersuchten Schriften ergibt sich eine Vielzahl von Punkten, die zu den Zielen (und den dazu zu benutzenden Mitteln) und der Ideologie der RAF etwas aussagen.

Deutlich postulierte Ziele der Gruppe waren die „Diktatur des Proletariats" und die Beseitigung von Kapitalismus, Faschismus und Imperialismus, welcher gesehen wurde als „die Politik einer globalen Expansion der Herrschaft des Monopolkapitalismus", vorangetrieben durch die USA.[49] Die Mittel, die zu diesem Umsturz des Systems eingesetzt werden sollten, wurden explizit genannt: Massenmobilisierung und die revolutionäre Organisation des Proletariats, Klassenkampf, bewaffneter Kampf. Diese militante Vorgehensweise kann als „Primat der Praxis" zusammengefasst werden, der der RAF-Ideologie zugrunde lag. Die Theorie ist zweitrangig, auch wenn man marxistisch-leninistische Ideen rezipierte und sich in der Tradition der sozialistischen Klassiker sah.[50] So kann man sagen, das unter anderem ein Prinzip aus den

---

[46] vgl. Über den bewaffneten Kampf in Westeuropa, in: RAF. Texte und Materialien, S. 104

[47] ebd, S. 106

[48] vgl. ebd., S. 107

[49] König, Alexander, Mythos RAF, in: Terror und Theologie, S. 223

[50] „ich bin aber für den umgekehrten weg: von der praxis zu den klassikern. [...] nicht die raf hat recht, weil dies alles schon bei lenin steht, sondern lenin ist gut, weil er dasselbe sagt wie die raf" Ulrike Meinhof zit. n. Fetscher/Rohrmoser, S. 75

„Marxschen Formulierungen“ übernommen wurde: „die Klasse an sich muss zur Klasse für sich werden“.[51]

Fetscher/Münkler/Ludwig (im Folgenden: Fetscher) machen zwei Voraussetzungen für den „bewaffneten Kampf“ als Mittel der Revolution aus, wenn er von den „Marxisten akzeptiert“ werden solle: Erstens müssen die Bedingungen objektiv „reif“ sein für die Revolution, Faktoren sind hier der „Reifegrad der industrie-kapitalistischen Entwicklung“ und die „Stärke der Arbeiterklasse“. Zweitens müssen alle „realen, erfolgversprechenden *demokratischen Mittel*“ ausgeschöpft sein“. Diese zweite Voraussetzung war nach Ansicht vieler nicht gegeben.[52]

Fetscher führt Wagenbach an, welcher darauf hinwies, dass unter den Studenten eher der Zufall bestimmte, wer mit den Parteiaufbauorganisationen sympathisierte und wer mit dem bewaffneten Kampf. Demzufolge „können offenbar *ideologische* Gründe für die Bildung der ‚RAF‘ kaum ausschlaggebend gewesen sein“. Er kommt zu dem Schluss: „Alle pauschalen Aussagen über ideologische Einflüsse oder gar ‚Ursachen‘ des bundesdeutschen Terrorismus greifen daneben.“[53] Dies unterstützt die Antwort von Birgit Hogefeld auf die Frage nach ihren Beweggründen, zur RAF zu gehen: Es seien „die Verhältnisse schlechthin“ gewesen.[54]

Wenn also keine pauschale Aussage getroffen werden kann, muss spezifiziert werden. Man muss davon ausgehen, dass die Ideologie der RAF nicht *nur* marxistisch oder anarchistisch, sondern wechselhaft beeinflusst wurde. So spricht auch Fetscher davon, dass die Ideologie der RAF nur ein „von inneren Widersprüchen durchsetztes, immer wieder in Teilen verworfenes Konvolut“[55] sei.

Geklärt werden muss, als welche Art des „bewaffneten Kampfes“ man die Aktionen der RAF einordnen kann. „Folgt der Guerillakrieg dem Prinzip der ‚violentia‘, der Gewalt, so der Terrorismus dem des ‚terror‘, des Schreckens.“[56] Allerdings ist der Guerillakrieg, wie mehrmals angesprochen, darauf angewiesen, Unterstützung in der Bevölkerung zu haben. Der Terror will diese Unterstützung herbeiführen durch die „psychischen Folgen“ der Gewaltanwendung. Entweder durch die Demonstration einer erfolgreichen Möglichkeit, sich zu wehren, oder aber durch die Reaktion der Staatsorgane, die die Bevölkerung auf die Seite der Terroristen ziehen soll.[57]

---

[51] vgl. Preuß, Ulrich, Rechtsstaat auf Stammtischniveau, in: Der blinde Fleck, S. 75
[52] vgl. Fetscher/Rohrmoser, Ideologien und Strategien, S. 23
[53] vgl. ebd., S. 24
[54] Reemtsma, Jan Philipp, Was heißt "die Geschichte der RAF verstehen" ?, in: Rudi Dutschke, Andreas Baader und die RAF, S. 111
[55] Fetscher/Rohrmoser, Ideologien und Strategien, S. 40
[56] ebd., S. 26
[57] vgl. ebd, S. 26f

Die RAF ging zu Beginn davon aus, einen Guerillakampf führen zu können. Die Dokumente belegen dies. Besonders in der Schrift vom Mai 1971 wird ein Guerillakampf beschrieben, der durch die ständige Ausbreitung quasi das System aushöhlt, bis dieses hinfällig geworden ist. Auch wenn darauf hingewiesen wird, dass die „Stadtguerilla" auch ohne die Hilfe der Bürger auskäme. „Als dann die mit Sicherheit erwartete Unterstützung der Bevölkerung ausblieb, waren die Mitglieder der RAF zutiefst überrascht."[58] Dies führte dazu, dass man sich abwendete von der Guerilla, und eine terroristische Strategie entwickelte.

Auch wenn man sich diese terroristische Strategie nicht eingestand, sondern sogar bestritt, und man darauf bestand, dass es sich um Guerilla-Aktionen handelte. Es wurde versucht, eine *inhaltliche* Terrorismus-Definition zu entwickeln, bei der man terroristische von nicht-terroristischen Aktionen unterschied über die Selektion der Opfer. „Aktionen die sich gegen das ‚Volk' richteten, waren terroristische Aktionen, Aktionen gegen die ‚Feinde und Unterdrücker des Volkes' dagegen waren keine terroristischen Aktionen."[59]

In jedem Fall lag der RAF die Praxis näher als die Theorien, nicht zuletzt auch deswegen, weil man sich als „reagierende Gruppierung" verstand.[60] Fetscher spricht sogar von „Theoriefeindlichkeit" innerhalb der RAF, und führt diese auch auf die Theoriediskussion unter den Linken zurück. Und so bestand die Ideologie des Terrorismus auch nicht in der Umsetzung einer von den Terroristen rezipierten politischen oder philosophischen Theorie, sondern in einer selektiven Heranziehung beliebiger Theorien zu einer „Praxis", die sich dazu noch weitgehend unabhängig von der Theorie bewegte. Allerdings sieht er auch das „Bedürfnis nach einer klaren Unterscheidung von Freund und Feind", man wollte sich seiner Meinung nach für oder gegen etwas entscheiden: „Die Dualisierung der Welt in Freund und Feind, Imperialismus und Antiimperialismus, Faschismus und Antifaschismus gehört daher zu den Grundelementen terroristischer Ideologie."[61]

So konstatiert auch Ulrich Preuß: „Es fehlte an einer Theorie, an einer rationalen Begründung der politischen Gewalt durch die Gesellschaft, weil die Gesellschaft von der Linken nie als ein Faktor, als eine Grundlage politischen Handelns anerkannt wurde."[62]

Als weiteres Grundelement ist bei der RAF der „Primat der Praxis" auszumachen. Denn durch die Praxis, durch terroristische Anschläge, soll der Bevölkerung, den potentiellen Sympathisanten gezeigt werden, dass entweder etwas erreicht werden kann durch die Gewalt, oder dass es zu einer Gegenreaktion des Staates kommt, die sich (z.B. durch verschärfte Gesetze) auf

---

[58] Fetscher/Rohrmoser, Ideologien und Strategien, S. 27
[59] vgl. ebd., S. 97
[60] König, Alexander, Mythos RAF, in: Terror und Theologie, S. 218
[61] vgl. Fetscher/Rohrmoser, Ideologien und Strategien, S. 44
[62] Preuß, Ulrich, Rechtsstaat auf Stammtischniveau, in: Der blinde Fleck, S. 75f

die Bevölkerung auswirkt und diese auf die Seite der Terroristen treibt. Damit wäre die für einen erfolgreichen Guerillakrieg benötigte Unterstützung zumindest einiger Volksteile gegeben. Die RAF sah sich als „institutionalisierter Widerstand, auf dessen sich zu steigernde Eigendynamik man in Konfrontation mit der bestehenden Ordnung setzte".[63] Im „Konzept Stadtguerilla" schreibt Ulrike Meinhof: „Ob es richtig ist, den bewaffneten Widerstand jetzt zu organisieren, hängt davon ab, ob es möglich ist; ob es möglich ist, ist nur praktisch zu ermitteln."[64]

Aber auf wen stützte sich die Hoffnung der RAF? Zu Beginn vertraute man auf die Industriearbeiterschaft, auf das Proletariat, und auf die „potentiell revolutionären Teile des Volkes"[65]. Diesen revolutionären Aufbruch wollte man mit dem „Konzept Stadtguerilla" fördern. „Bis dahin jedoch vertrauten sie auf die Unterstützung durch große Teile der Intelligenz, der Jugend und insbesondere der gesellschaftlichen Randschichten."[66] So spricht auch „Über den bewaffneten Kampf in Westeuropa" vom unter den Jugendlichen zu findendem „Potential für revolutionäre Gewaltanwendung".[67] Fetscher kommt zu dem Schluss, dass die Jugendlichen in der ersten Phase der Stadtguerilla die revolutionären Subjekte darstellen sollten, „bis auch im Proletariat die revolutionären Potentiale die Überhand gewinnen würden".[68]

Ein bedeutendes Problem bei der Formierung und Ausarbeitung einer Ideologie der RAF sieht Fetscher in dem Versuch, politische Fragen mit technischen Mitteln zu lösen:

> „Der bei der Entwicklung des ‚Konzepts Stadtguerilla' immer wieder zu beobachtende Gedanke, politische Probleme ließen sich auf technische Fragen reduzieren, die dann ihrerseits auch mit technischen Mitteln zu lösen seien, war wohl die verhängnisvollste Denkfalle bei der Entstehung der RAF und ihrer Ideologie. Konkret bedeutet das, dass eine ausgefeilte Technik des Banküberfalls die Unterstützung der Guerilla durch die Bevölkerung ersetzen sollte. Es ist eines der insgesamt bemerkenswerten Charakteristika der RAF-Ideologie, dass sie mit diesem Glauben an die Transformierbarkeit von *politischen* in *technische* Probleme Denkstrukturen verhaftet blieb, die in der Bundesrepublik heute eher konservativen als progressiven Gruppen zuzurechnen sind."[69]

Ein weiterer problematischer Gegenstand ist der Umgang mit und die Annahme von den sozialistischen Klassikern. Auch wenn es „[a]n marxistisch-leninistischer Diktion und Argumentation [...] bei der RAF nie gemangelt"[70] hat, muss man doch deutlich unterscheiden, wie viel und vor allem was Einfluss auf die RAF-Ideologie nahm.

---

[63] König, Alexander, Mythos RAF, in: Terror und Theologie, S. 223
[64] Das Konzept Stadtguerilla, in: RAF. Texte und Materialien, S. 40
[65] Die Rote Armee aufbauen, in: RAF. Texte und Materialien, S. 24
[66] Fetscher/Rohrmoser, Ideologien und Strategien, S. 63
[67] vgl. Über den bewaffneten Kampf in Westeuropa, in: RAF. Texte und Materialien, S. 94
[68] vgl. Fetscher/Rohrmoser, Ideologien und Strategien, S. 65
[69] ebd., S. 106
[70] Roth, Karl Heinz, Die historische Bedeutung der RAF, in: Die alte Straßenverkehrsordnung, S. 176

1978 sprach Horst Mahler über die Fehler der RAF und bezeichnete es als den gravierendsten, dass man den Staat nur als Unterdrückungsapparat gesehen habe, nicht aber die Identifizierung auch vieler Lohnabhängiger mit diesem Staat beachtet habe. Er beschrieb dies als Fehler, der in der sozialistischen Theorie begründet ist.[71]

Mahler schrieb im Dokument „Der bewaffnete Kampf in Westeuropa" von dem „gesellschaftlichen Gewaltpotential", das als Machtinstrument des Staates verwendet wurde (vgl. 3.2.3). Hierin kann die Grundlage gesehen werden für die Überzeugung, dass „der Übergang vom Kapitalismus zum Sozialismus nicht mit friedlichen, sondern nur mit *gewaltsamen* Mitteln möglich sei". Dies stand in der Tradition der Staatstheorien von Marx, Engels und Lenin.

Marx und Engels schrieben davon, dass alle Kämpfe in einem Staat immer auch Klassenkämpfe seien, und der Staat nicht nur der „Herrschaftsausschuss der besitzenden Klassen" sein könne, sondern immer auch ein Instrument um diesen fortdauernden Klassenkampf einigermaßen zu kontrollieren.[72] Marx folgend haben auch Kautsky und Bernstein auf die Macht der Arbeiter und Kleinbürger in einem demokratischen Staat hingewiesen. Lenin dagegen hat eine andere Meinung vom Staat, den er beschreibt als „das Produkt und die Äußerung der Unversöhnlichkeit der Klassengegensätze".[73] Lenin sah auch keine Möglichkeit des friedlichen Übergangs zum Sozialismus, und so begreift auch die RAF „den Staat als permanente Besatzungsarmee der Gesellschaft, als Okkupation und reine Willkür".[74]

Mahler vereinfachte die leninsche These zu einer so genannten „Agenturtheorie". Diese geht davon aus, dass der Staat „eine simple Agentur der herrschenden Klasse sei" (vgl. auch hier Kapitel 3.2.3). Wie oben geschildert, ist dann auch in diesem Punkt bei der RAF ein abgrenzendes Denken auszumachen: man wollte den Staat als Feind sehen. „Und wenn sich die angestrebte Legitimation der Gewaltanwendung nicht durch die Unterstützung seitens der Bevölkerung erlangen ließ, so suchte die Gruppe sie schließlich über das Bild des Feindes zu erlangen." Dies wiederum wird allerdings gedeutet als „nachgeschobene Legitimation einer Praxis, deren ursprüngliche Legitimationsinstanz, die Unterstützung durch die Bevölkerung, ausgefallen war".[75]

So entfernte sich die RAF immer weiter von der marxistischen Idee und rekurrierte immer eindeutiger auf den „Primat der Praxis". Dieser ist als zentral in der Ideologie der RAF anzusehen. Nur über die Praxis, das zeigen gerade die Dokumente, war man in der Lage, den Umsturz des Systems herbeizuführen.

---

[71] vgl. Fetscher/Rohrmoser, Ideologien und Strategien, S. 126
[72] vgl. ebd., S. 128
[73] ebd., S. 129
[74] Bruhn, Joachim, Revolution des Willens, in: Der blinde Fleck, S. 125
[75] vgl. Fetscher/Rohrmoser, Ideologien und Strategien, S. 132

Schlussbetrachtung

„Trotz aller Bezugnahmen und Hinweise auf verschiedene politische Theorien ist die Ideologie der RAF doch zutiefst theoriefeindlich.“[76] Diese Feststellung drückt zweierlei aus: Man war sich zum einen sehr wohl der klassischen sozialistischen Schriften bewusst und zitierte diese auch („Diktatur des Proletariats“), stellte aber den „Primat der Praxis“ über jede Theorie und entschied sich damit gleichzeitig gegen die Theorie.

Trotzdem entwickelte die RAF eine eigene politische Theorie, die auch jene „Praxis“ im Nachhinein legitimieren sollte. Die Gruppe ging aber sogar noch weiter und gestand ihrer nachträglich aufgestellten Theorie den Anspruch zu, „über die allein angemessene Interpretation der politischen Realität zu verfügen“.[77]

Die RAF machte sich eine Überlegung zu Eigen, die als „Dezisionismus“ beschrieben wird.[78] Das aufgeworfene Freund-Feind-Denken (Faschist - Antifaschist, Imperialist - Antiimperialist, usw) und die Parole „Wer nicht für uns ist, ist gegen uns“ bestimmten sowohl das Selbstverständnis als auch die Wahrnehmung der Umwelt. „Die stalinistische Doktrin [wonach jeder Antikommunist ein Faschist ist, d. Verf.] ist der deutschen Linken in Fleisch und Blut übergegangen, [...] Damit ging Baaders Rechnung auf; die ‚Antifaschisten‘ hielten zu ihnen.“[79]

Des Weiteren wurde „in der Ideologie der RAF die materialistische Gesellschaftstheorie durch ein subjektivistisches Geschichtsbild“ ersetzt. Man ging nicht mehr von der Analyse politischer Konstellationen aus, sondern von der Entschlossenheit und dem Mut der Guerilleros. Hierzu passt auch die Umdrehung Realität – Theorie – Praxis in die Relation Praxis – Theorie – Realität, so dass die Theorie nur noch legitimierenden Charakter besaß und als solche für die „terroristische[...] Praxis *instrumentalisiert*“ wurde.[80]

Eine grundlegende Frage, die von der frühen RAF aufgeworfen wurde, war die Frage nach dem „revolutionären Subjekt“. Man versuchte, das Industrieproletariat einzubinden, sah aber schnell ein, dass die Studenten und die „Intelligenz“ in erster Linie die Sympathisanten waren, die die RAF so dringend brauchte.

Schließlich wollte man eine Guerilla aufbauen, kein terroristisches Netzwerk. Doch dieser Versuch schlug fehl, scheiterte an der fehlenden Unterstützung durch das Volk. Die RAF musste die hohen Erwartungen zurückschrauben, so weit, dass am Ende nur die RAF als „revolutionäres Subjekt“ übrig blieb.

---

[76] Fetscher/Rohrmoser, Ideologien und Strategien, S. 179
[77] ebd., S. 179
[78] vgl. ebd., S. 180
[79] Wieland, Karin, a., in: Rudi Dutschke, Andreas Baader und die RAF, S. 97
[80] vgl. Fetscher/Rohrmoser, Ideologien und Strategien, S. 181

„Durch ihren weitgehenden Theorieverzicht und den ‚Primat der Praxis' hatte die RAF den Fraktionierungsprozess von SDS und APO überwinden wollen. Nachdem diese ‚Praxis' jedoch durch die Inhaftierung der Kerngruppe außer Vollzug gesetzt war, stellte sich zunächst die Theoriediskussion, dann die Fraktionierung und schließlich der Streit um die falschen und richtigen Zitate wieder ein. Der gordische Knoten, den die RAF mit Gewalt hatte zerschlagen wollen, hatte sich schließlich um sie selbst geschürzt."[81]

Zu bedenken bleibt aber immer, was Alexander König für die RAF als Leitmotiv herausarbeitet: „Im Hintergrund stand die Utopie einer klassenlosen Gesellschaft, die über ein ‚Interregnum' der Diktatur des Proletariats, welche den Staat selbst überflüssig werden lasse, erreicht werden könne."[82]

[81] Fetscher/Rohrmoser, Ideologien und Strategien, S. 84
[82] König, Alexande, Mythos RAF, in: Terror und Theologie, S. 225

Bibliographie

- Bittermann, Klaus (Hrsg.), Die alte Straßenverkehrsordnung, Verlag Klaus Bitterman, Berlin, 1986
- Fetscher, Iring u. Rohrmoser, Günter, Ideologien und Strategien, Westdeutscher Verlag, Opladen, 1981
- Hartung, Klaus et. al., Der blinde Fleck: die Linke, die RAF und der Staat, Neue Kritik, Frankfurt am Main, 1987
- Reemtsma, Jan Philipp (Hrsg.), Rudi Dutschke, Andreas Baader und die RAF, Hamburger Edition, Hamburg, 2005
- ID-Verlag (Hrsg.), bearb. v. Hoffman, Martin, Rote Armee Fraktion. Texte und Materialien zur Geschichte der RAF, ID-Verlag, Berlin 1997
- Deutsche Presse-Agentur (Hrsg.), dpa-Archiv. Hintergrund, Ausgabe 2749-2754, Hamburg, 1978
- Schneider, Diethelm u. Wallich, Matthias (Hrsg.), Terror und Theologie. Zur Aktualität der Apokalyptik, Röhrig UniversitätsVerlag, St. Ingbert, 2003

Lightning Source UK Ltd.
Milton Keynes UK
UKHW040040170119
335666UK00001B/237/P

Amsterdam

The Complete **Residents'** Guide

Passionately Publishing...

EXPLORER

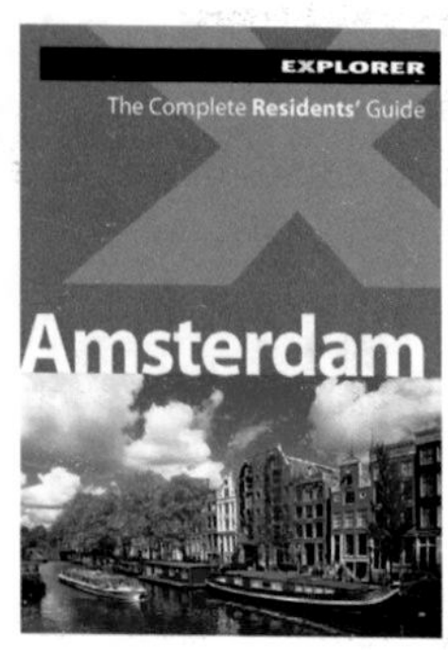

Amsterdam Explorer 1st Edition ISBN 13 - 978-9948-03-379-0 ISBN 10 - 9948-03-379-5

Front Cover Photograph: Pamela Grist

Printed and bound by Emirates Printing Press, Dubai, United Arab Emirates.

Explorer Publishing & Distribution
PO Box 34275, Dubai
United Arab Emirates
Email info@explorerpublishing.com
Web www.explorerpublishing.com

Welcome...

Living in Amsterdam will be a lot easier with this book as your guide – you'll find everything you need to know to get settled in the city as you build a new life for yourself in the Netherlands. From how to choose your electricity provider to the best place to watch a game of football, we give you all the details in six clearly defined chapters.

General Information (p.1) briefs you about the history, geography and culture of Amsterdam and the Netherlands. We provide essential information about the best places to stay and how to get around the city.

For a comprehensive insight into the day-to-day details of life in the city, the **Residents** (p.53) chapter features topics such as residency requirements and essential documentation, how to set up a bank account, and the type of health insurance you may require. There's also plenty of information on how to navigate the housing market, pick an area to live in and the education system.

For the lowdown on the key things to see in the city, **Exploring** (p.131) fills you in with everything you need to know. There are sections on museums, art galleries and other cultural activities, as well as parks, gardens and beaches. Our checklist of must-dos touches on the city's highlights.

Amsterdam's full range of recreational pastimes are covered in our **Activities** (p.183) chapter. Explorer guides you through all the social and fun-filled things you can participate in once you're settled in the city, from sports clubs and drama societies to the best spas and massage parlours – all with handy contact details so you can easily get involved.

Shopping (p.251) gives you the lowdown on the best places to indulge in retail therapy and the optimum locations for the purchase of a whole range of products. Our shopping directory gives you the multiple locations of chain stores so you can find the one that's closest to you.

The best restaurants and bars in Amsterdam are reviewed in **Going Out** (p.303). Handy, bitesize entries give you a flavour of what you can expect at each venue. Whether you're after a coffeshop to chill out in, or just fancy a trip to the cinema, this chapter has packed in all the info you need for a great night on the town.

Nearly all of the places of interest have references that correspond to the detailed **Maps** (p.363) in the back of the book , all carefully designed to help you navigate Amsterdam.

If you think we have missed something, please let us know. Go to www.explorerpublishing.com, fill in the Reader Response form, and share the knowledge with your fellow explorers.

The Explorer Team

Explorer's Amsterdam

One of Europe's finest cities, Amsterdam is conveniently compact, but jam-packed with stacks to do and see:

The cafe scene (p.332) in Amsterdam is fantastic; easy-going staff allow lazy afternoons on canal-side terraces, or watching the bustling city life around you.

The best way to explore Amsterdam is on a bicycle tour (p.164). They combine insightful commentary on the city with a cruise out of town to see countryside, cows, clogs and cheese.

For food on the go, try the famous frites (p.134), herrings, or Dutch cheese at places like Kaasland (p.267). For something more exotic, delve into Holland's colonial connection with 'rijsttafel' (rice table) at an Indonesian restaurant (p.317).

Although some expats use the holiday as a chance to escape, Queen's Day (p.46) has to be seen to be believed. The population of Amsterdam doubles for one of the best street parties anywhere, and also a good-natured, family vibe.

Andy Baker Andy is a native Texan who worked as a therapist in New York for 14 years before moving to Amsterdam to join his partner. He now teaches English, writes and works on his mastery of the Dutch language. In his spare time, he knits, sings in a church choir and enjoys watching performances at the Concertgebouw (p.360). **Best thing about living in Amsterdam:** walking or riding along the canals in the early evening. **Ultimate Amsterdam must-do:** the Anne Frank Huis (p.154).

Ann Maher Ann's most vivid memory of her first visit to Amsterdam is scoffing herrings in the office canteen while working as an editor for a Dutch media group. After a career in publishing in London, she returned. She now works as a freelance writer and editor, and has edited books including *Kidsgids English*. When not writing and researching, Ann plays backgammon and enjoys reading detective novels. **Best Amsterdam memory:** watching the fireworks from a rooftop terrace during the New Year's celebrations. **Ultimate Amsterdam must-do:** a boat trip (p.165).

Cindy Yianni Leaving her native Texas behind for a career in fashion that kept her globetrotting around Europe and the Far East, Cindy finally landed in Amsterdam 10 years ago, Following her passion for writing and travel she traded fashion for freelance journalism and now enjoys writing travel features for magazines. Her love of urban pleasures makes Amsterdam a perfect haven for her as she happily wanders around the canals looking for hidden treasures. **Best city memory:** celebrating a sunny Queen's Day (p.46) **Favourite Amsterdam cultural experience:** Museumnacht (p.133).

Elise Krentzel Elise is a professional journalist specialising in food, leisure and travel. Her latest project is a chronicle of her experiences as an expatriate, spanning 30 years in six countries. Born in New York City she left for Japan in her 20s and has been living and working in Amsterdam for the last 11 years. She's written extensive restaurant and hotel critiques for magazines and enjoys sampling the best cuisine from up-and-coming chefs. Elise's hobbies are painting and interior decorating. **Favourite Amsterdam restaurant:** Yamazato (p.325). **Favourite daytrip from Amsterdam:** Cologne in Germany (see p.180).

Having trouble navigating your way around Amsterdam? Look no further than the ***Amsterdam Mini Map,*** *an indispensable pocket-sized aid to getting to grips with the roads, areas and attractions of this picturesque city.*

Now that you've moved to Amsterdam, it won't be long before you're playing host to wave upon wave of visiting family and friends – and we've got the perfect guide to help them get the most out of their sightseeing. Packed with info on Amsterdam's shops, restaurants and tourist spots, you can't go wrong with the ***Amsterdam Mini Explorer.***

Jane Stephenson Jane has lived in the Netherlands for 20 years now and considers Amsterdam her home city. For many years she worked for a large multinational company and combined this with studying psychology. This year she took the plunge and decided to concentrate on writing and her work as a personal and business coach. She also works as a volunteer in the Amsterdam office of ACCESS on its English language helpline. Over time Jane has developed extensive knowledge of living and working in the city. **Ultimate Amsterdam must-do:** a summer picnic in the Vondelpark (p.160). **Best thing about the city:** the eclectic cultural mix.

Kim Chandler Working as the editor of a local Amsterdam magazine and as arts and culture editor for a national Dutch newspaper has provided Kim with one of the most enjoyable periods of her working life and allowed her to get to know the city extensively. She also enjoys performing poetry and writing plays. Her time in Amsterdam has included launching the Dutch chapter of the Room to Read charity, having a drink named after her: the Kimmetje (Little Kim), and hosting the online English Breakfast Radio Show. **Worst thing about Amsterdam:** the changeable weather. **Best city view:** from the top of the Post CS Tower.

Prue Duggan Prue arrived in Amsterdam for a holiday in the late 1990s and never managed to leave. She lives with her husband and their dog Fudge and is a freelance writer, editor and co-founder of international writers' collective 'wordsinhere'. When she's not writing you'll find her throwing tennis balls for Fudge, guzzling coffee and reading at one of her favourite cafes, or soaking up Amsterdam's architecture as she strolls around the city. **Best Amsterdam memory:** being on top of the ferris wheel in Dam Square when the fairground was in town. **Reason never to leave the city:** after a decade it's still full of surprises.

Thanks...

As well as our star team of authors, whose expert advice and incredible research have been invaluable, there are a number of other people who have made great contributions to this book. Big thanks go to: Anna Lysenko at ACCESS, Christian Barth at Expat Law, Constant Broeren and Kris Silvius at Amsterdam Tourism & Convention Board, Jed Payne, Mike at Mike's Bike Tours, Paul Huxley at Elynx.com and Stephen Huyton of the British Society of Amsterdam. Cheers also to our hard-working cartographers in India: Abdul Hakeem, Fathima Suhra, Mohammed Rafeeq; Ingrid for the help with Dutch translation; Jake, Pamela and Tom for proofing and fact checking; and last but not least, to Miki for her support and for holding the fort... and to Dan and Amy.

Where are we exploring next?

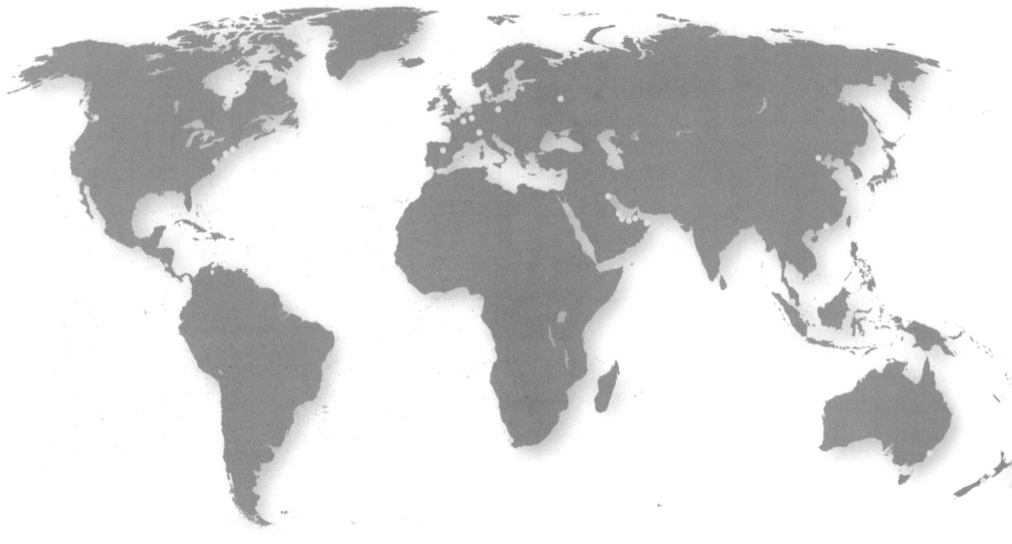

- Abu Dhabi
- Amsterdam
- Bahrain
- Barcelona
- Beijing*
- Berlin*
- Boston*
- Brussels*
- Cape Town*
- Dubai
- Dublin
- Geneva
- Hong Kong
- Kuala Lumpur*
- Kuwait
- London
- Los Angeles*
- Moscow*
- New York
- New Zealand
- Oman
- Paris
- Qatar
- San Francisco*
- Shanghai
- Singapore
- Sydney
- Tokyo*
- Vancouver*
- Washington DC*

* Available 2008

Where do you live?

Is your home city missing from our list? If you'd love to see a residents' guide for a location not currently on Explorer's horizon please email editorial@explorerpublishing.com.

Advertise with Explorer...

If you're interested in advertising with us, please contact sales@explorerpublishing.com.

Make Explorer your very own...

We offer a number of customization options for bulk sales. For more information and discount rates please contact corporatesales@explorerpublishing.com.

Contract Publishing

Have an idea for a publication or need to revamp your company's marketing material? Contact designlab@explorerpublishing to see how our expert contract publishing team can help.

www.explorerpublishing.com

Life can move pretty fast, so to make sure you can stay up to date with all the latest goings on in your city, we've revamped our website to further enhance your time in the city, whether long or short.

Keep in the know...

Our Complete Residents' Guides and Mini Visitors' series continue to expand, covering destinations from Amsterdam to New Zealand and beyond. Keep up to date with our latest travels and hot tips by signing up to our monthly newsletter, or browse our products section for info on our current and forthcoming titles.

Make friends and influence people...

...by joining our Communities section. Meet fellow residents in your city, make your own recommendations for your favourite restaurants, bars, childcare agencies or dentists, plus find answers to your questions on daily life from long-term residents.

Discover new experiences...

Ever thought about living in a different city, or wondered where the locals really go to eat, drink and be merry? Check out our regular features section, or submit your own feature for publication!

Want to find a badminton club, the number for your bank, or maybe just a restaurant for a hot first date?

Check out city info on various destinations around the world in our residents' section – from finding a Pilates class to contact details for international schools in your area, or the best place to buy everything from a spanner set to a Spandau Ballet album, we've got it all covered.

Let us know what you think!

All our information comes from residents which means you! If we missed out your favourite bar or market stall, or you know of any changes in the law, infrastructure, cost of living or entertainment scene, let us know by using our Feedback form.

ACCESS
Need help adjusting and getting more out of your life in The Netherlands?
Contact ACCESS for FREE information, advice and support
Amsterdam Helpdesk:
(020) 423 3217
helpdesk-ams@access-nl.org
The Hague Helpdesk:
(070) 346 2525
helpdesk-dh@access-nl.org
www.access-nl.org
Den Bosch 109 km
Hong Kong 9290 km
Jakarta 11358 km
228 km
Rotterdam 39 km
New York 5849 km
Singapore 10504 km
Sydney 16646 km
Utrecht 65 km
Tokyo 9297 km

Contents

Contents

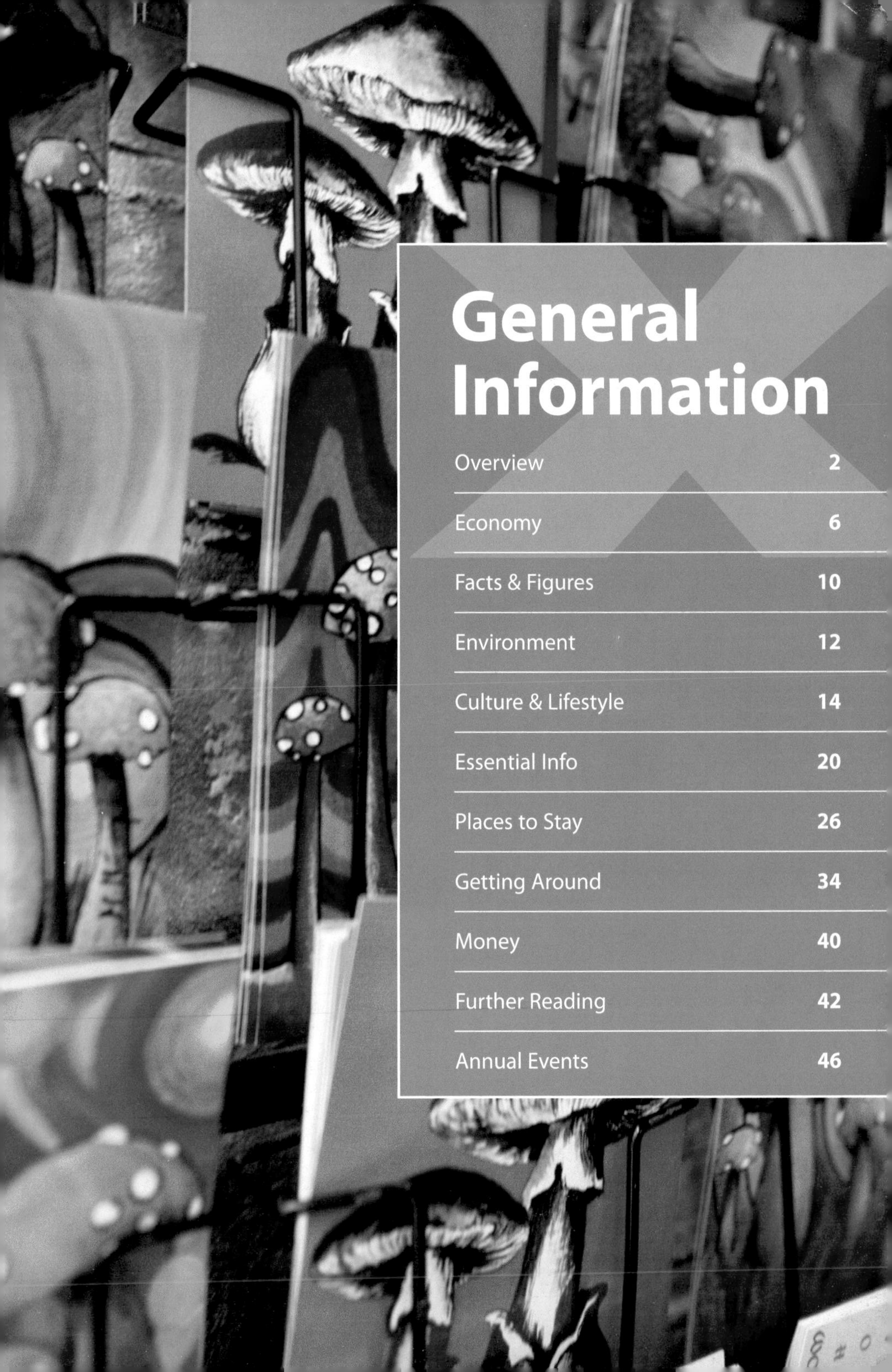

General Information

General Information

Geography

Water Point
Amsterdam's water levels are measured by a fixed point: the Normaal Amsterdams Peil (NAP) which is based on the average level of the IJ in 17th century Amsterdam. It's the basis for altitude measurements in western Europe. You can view the current NAP in the Stopera on Waterlooplein.

Located in western Europe on the North Sea and bordered by France and Germany, the Kingdom of the Netherlands is unique in being so man-made. 'While God created the earth, the Dutch created the Netherlands', goes the old saying and the landscape remains in a constant state of flux. The battles with water - a quarter of the country lies below sea level - have shaped the Dutch psyche, and the land has been developed over the centuries to meet human needs (one fifth of the country has been reclaimed from the sea).

The country comprises 41,526 square kilometres, of which 33,783 is land and 7,760 water. East to west (Enschede to Amsterdam) it measures 161 kilometres; north to south (Groningen to Maastricht) 348 kilometres. 16 million people on such a small piece of land (470 people per square kilometre) make the Netherlands the most densely populated country in Europe. People are concentrated in the cities of what is known as the Randstad – a region encompassing the provinces of North and South Holland and Utrecht. No Dutch city has yet accumulated a million inhabitants, and each has retained its unique character and architectural style.

The very neat and orderly landscape is achieved through an extensive consultation and planning process (very Dutch). Its flatness is almost unremitting – Nederland in Dutch literally translates as 'lowland'. But there are actually a few 'hills' in Limburg in the south-east, and the country's highest point is at Vaalserberg, 321 metres above sea level. Within the 13 provinces, some variety can be found in the forests of the Veluwe and the moorland in Drenthe. The Wadden Islands boast 451 kilometres of dune-filled wet and windy coastline, stretching across the north of the country. There are twenty National Parks, which are areas of outstanding beauty. Throughout the Netherlands are thousands of polders (areas of reclaimed land) surrounded by dykes (the barriers around them which keep out the water). The country's famous canals drain any water which does seep past the dykes back out to sea. This aquatic know-how derives from when windmills (such a powerful symbol of Holland) revolutionised the way water was drained from the land during the 14th century.

Netherlands Fact Box

Geographical position: between 53°33'22" and 50°45'4" latitude North; between 3°21'30" and 7°13'42" longitude East

Bordering countries: Belgium (450 km); Germany (577 km)

Coastline: 451km

Highest point: 323m Vaalserberg (Limbourg)

Lowest point: 6.7m Nieuwerkerk aan den IJssel (South Holland)

Total area: 41,526 sq km

Land: 33,883 sq km

Water: 7,643 sq km

Amsterdam Geography

The Dutch capital sits between the salt water of the North Sea and the fresh water of the IJsselmeer lake. Large parts of the city and surrounding districts lie below sea level (including Schiphol airport) with a vast system of dykes and pumps keeping the waters at bay. Amsterdam's unique landscape is intimately connected with its trading past, and much of historical Amsterdam rests on wooden pilings, driven in by hand through

the peat to a sturdy sand level about 11 metres down. The Royal Palace in Dam Square sits on 13,659 of them. Because taxes were levied on the width of houses' frontage, tall, narrow houses were the design of choice. The 17th century canal ring is another extraordinary engineering feat and in total there are 160 man-made canals stretching for 75 kilometres, with 40 sluices and a pumping station in Zeeburg enabling the water to be refreshed regularly. Some have been filled in for sanitary reasons and periodically there are campaigns to open them again. In the 18th century, the nobility built summer houses on the reclaimed land of Watergraafsmeer. Of these, it is just the elegant Frankendael house and its surrounding park that remain.
Extending for 135 kilometres around the city (and comprising of 45 forts, waterworks and floodable areas) is the Amsterdam Defence Line (afforded UNESCO heritage status) built between 1883 and 1920. In the 19th and 20th centuries detailed urban planning, such as the 1935 General Extension Plan, enabled green spaces to be integrated into the capital. The Vondelpark was on the edge of the city when it opened in 1864, but is now pretty central, and the Amsterdamse Bos was planted in 1934 – a work creation project during the Great Depression. But for the 21st century, much-needed urban expansion was limited. In north Amsterdam there is a clear boundary between the city and the Waterland – a centuries-old tract of peat meadow. To the south, the city meets the protected 'Green Heart' zone. The response has been new artificial land; in 2001 the first pile was driven in IJburg, a mixed residential environment located on eight artificial islands. These were created by spraying layer after layer of sand into the open water of the IJmeer lake.

Irrigation

The Dutch are world experts in water management and have created masterpieces of hydraulic engineering. There are 3,500 kilometres of primary flood defences (dykes and dunes) in the country and an extensive network, the Deltaworks, was completed with the opening of the Maeslant barrier in 1997. Until recently, Rhine delta river dykes were raised for flood protection, but this centuries-old policy has now been abandoned in some areas. In the 'Room for the River' policy, land will (at last) return to nature.

Royal Legs

The Dutch royal family was a fragile twosome when Queen Wilhelmina ruled, but her only daughter knew her duty. When Princess Juliana enrolled at Leiden University, a fellow student is said to have remarked that her legs were rather fat, to which she retorted, 'That's as may be, but the entire House of Orange rests upon them'.

History

For much of its early history Amsterdam was a boggy swamp. The area south of the Rhine was part of the Roman Empire (Pliny lived near Leiden) until the fifth century, and throughout the Middle Ages consisted of many separate feudal entities. Around 1270 the Amstel was dammed, and a village grew up on the site of what is now Dam Square. Aemstelledamme was granted its first charter in 1300 and by 1425 still only had a few houses and a church. In 1452 the mostly wooden city was razed by fire, and only parts of the mediaeval architecture remain, such as the Munttoren (a tower) in Muntplein. By the 1500s, when the Spanish branch of the House of Habsburg was the most potent force in Europe, the Low Countries, along with present day Belgium and Luxembourg, were part of the Holy Roman Empire of Charles V. Amsterdam prospered through trading, and by 1500 the city had grown to 9,000 inhabitants.

Eighty Years' War & Independence

Under King Philip II of Spain religious tensions came to the surface. The teachings of Calvin had taken hold and the Catholic king's persecution of Protestantism was regarded by the lowlanders as a restriction on religious freedom. Even Dutch Catholics were outraged by the antics of the Spanish Inquisition. In 1568, the northern Dutch provinces revolted under Prince William of Orange, and so began a protracted battle for independence – the Eighty Years' War. This ended in 1648 with the Peace of

Westphalia and recognition of the United Provinces as an independent state. William of Orange Nassau (Catholic, Lutheran, Father of The Fatherlands) took the position of Stadtholder (provincial governor).

Tulip Mania
The tulip, which originally arrived from Turkey, was a fashionable flower from the 1620s, but between 1636 and1637 speculation in the flowers (the world's first futures market) hit its peak. In 1636, a single tulip bulb was sold for 5,400 guilders, more than a substantial Amsterdam house cost at the time.

Golden Age

The period that followed (1585-1972) is known as the Golden Age. Goods flowed in from all over the world and people flooded into Amsterdam. The Dutch East India Company (VOC) was established in 1602 to coordinate shipping and trade with south-east Asia. Such was its global power, it could establish colonies, sign treaties and declare war. The Dutch West India Company (WIC) monopolised the seas between West Africa and the Americas and governed New Amsterdam which later became New York. William II and his son William III both married English princesses and the latter became King of England. In 1609 the Bank of Amsterdam was founded and a huge flux of skilled immigrants led to industrial diversification. Jewish workers from Spain and Portugal brought diamonds, and the religious freedom of the republic attracted many immigrants as Amsterdam became a magnet for intellectual refugees such as Spinoza and Descartes. The Dutch artists of this period – Rembrandt, Vermeer, Frans Hals – are universally known. The construction of the grachtengordel (the canal ring) began in 1613, and by 1640 Amsterdam's population had risen to 139,000.

French Occupation

As the age of enlightenment spread across the rest of Europe, the 18th century saw a period of Dutch decline. Its sea routes were under threat from the English and its lands from the French. There was a period of pro-French feeling with the Velvet Revolution and the establishment of the Batavian Republic, but the liberté, egalité and fraternité did not last long. In 1810 the Emperor Napoleon removed his brother from Amsterdam and incorporated the Netherlands into the French Empire, until its collapse in 1813.

House of Orange-Nassau

By the time the Kingdom of the Netherlands was finally established in 1815 (it initially included Belgium), Amsterdam was struggling, but philanthropists like Samuel Sarphati (banks, construction, the Amstel Hotel) and Paul van Vlissingen (steamships and engineering) got the city moving again. Trams and bicycles arrived in the 1880s, and arts and architecture in Gothic, Renaissance and Baroque-inspired styles blossomed.

Centraal Station

World Wars

During the first world war (1914-1918) the Netherlands remained neutral, but by 1940 there was no protection from the German war machine and the country was occupied throughout the second world war. Exiled in London, Queen Wilhelmina communicated with her subjects through stirring broadcasts from the BBC. The round-up of the Jewish population began in 1941 and 76% were deported to concentration camps, with few survivors. Thousands of Amsterdam residents starved to death during the 'Hunger Winter' of 1944.

Post-War Prosperity & Changing Society

The resilient Dutch bounced back after the war, abandoning neutrality by signing up to NATO, the Treaty of Rome (one of six founder members of what become the EU) and a new economic grouping, Benelux. By 1948 they were able to celebrate the coronation of one Dutch housewife, Queen Juliana, and the athletic prowess of another (Fanny Blankers-Koen at the Olympics). Former colonies became independent: Indonesia (after a struggle) in 1949; Suriname much later in 1975. Generous social legislation ensured the 60s and 70s were colourful times. Hippies camped out in Amsterdam's Vondelpark, John Lennon and Yoko Ono had a 'bed-in' for world peace at the Hilton in 1969 and homosexuals found a spiritual home (same-sex marriage was legalised in 2001). Amsterdam's population reached its peak in 1964 at almost 870,000. The government's approach to soft drugs and prostitution was 'pragmatic' and the Netherlands was seen (by its inhabitants as well as the outside world) as a glowing example of freedom and tolerance.

Immigration & Integration

The liberal image of Amsterdam has been shaken in recent years with controversial policies dealing with problems associated with rising immigration and non-integration. The murders of politician Pim Fortuyn and film director/cultural commentator Theo van Gogh shocked the world. The position of Islam and the integration of non-western foreigners into a resolutely multicultural society remains one of the Netherlands' most debated issues.

Amsterdam Timeline

50BC-400AD	The Low Countries are part of the Roman Empire.
1300	Amsterdam is granted city rights.
1533	Birth of William of Nassau, Prince of Orange, founder of the Dutch Oranje-Nassau dynasty.
1602	The East India Company is founded, coinciding with the Dutch Golden Age.
1606	Birth of Rembrandt.
1613	Digging of the grachtengordel – Amsterdam's canal ring – begins.
1635	'Tulip Mania' (inflated prices for the flowers) strikes the country.
1815	Amsterdam becomes capital of The Netherlands.
1853	Birth of Van Gogh.
1900	Ajax football club formed.
1914-1918	WW1. The Dutch remain neutral during the conflict.
1940	German troops invade the Netherlands; Rotterdam badly bombed.
1944	The Benelux agreement is signed by the Dutch, Luxembourg and Belgian governments.
1945	8th May. End of the occupation. Canadian soldiers free Amsterdam.
1947	Anne Frank's diary is published.
1948	Juliana becomes Queen.
1969	John and Yoko lie in bed for World Peace.
1976	Decriminalisation of cannabis.
1980	Beatrix becomes Queen.
1986	Stopera (city hall and Muziektheater) built.
1999	Prostitution legalised.
2001	Single-sex marriage given legal status.
2002	Introduction of the Euro. Goodbye Guilders.
2002	Right wing anti-immigration politician Pim Fortuyn is assassinated.
2005	Dutch voters reject proposed EU constitution.
2007	Jan Peter Balkenende is sworn in as head of a three-party coalition.

Netherlands Overview

The Netherlands consistently ranks as one of the best countries in the world in which to live and do business. With a GDP of €529 billion in 2006 it is ranked ninth for GDP in Europe and 16th worldwide (according to the IMF). Economic conditions are buoyant and the economy is growing strongly (2.9% in 2006 – double the rate in 2005). Inflation (1%) is also well under control. This climate for business is rated very highly by the Economist Intelligence Unit (fifth in the world rankings 2006-2010) but the World Bank thinks there's too much red tape (Netherlands is 22nd in the worldwide 2007 Doing Business rankings). A favourable tax position means the Netherlands is an attractive place to establish company headquarters and it attracts significant direct foreign investment.

Employment

The working population (7.5 million) is internationally oriented, highly educated and multilingual. Workers' rights are strongly protected, and unemployment (5% or 357,000 in the first quarter of 2007) is falling. Since October 2004, 4700 foreign nationals have gained a fast-track admission to the Netherlands as 'knowledge migrants' in IT, scientific research and industry. These new immigrants are mainly drawn from India, the USA and Japan. Other incentives for foreign workers include the 30% tax ruling. The Gross National Income (GNI) per capita is $36,620 (12th in the world rankings) compared to $43,740 for the United States (who are fifth) and $59,590 for Norway (first). The Netherlands is tenth in the United Nations Human Development Index (HDI) which ranks countries in terms of life expectancy, educational attainment and adjusted real income (Norway is top).

Major Trading Partners

Exports include machinery, chemicals, and fuels and foodstuffs, which account for 60% of GDP. The Netherlands' most important export destinations are Germany, Belgium, France and the UK. The top three import partners are Germany (17%), Belgium (9.4%) and China (8.8%).

Creative Industries

Innovative, experimental and with a sense of humour, Dutch design is recognised throughout the world. The creative industries – art, architecture, design, publishing, media – are hugely significant, even if difficult to measure on the country balance sheet. Influential architects include the iconic Rem Koolhaas, a native of Rotterdam, along with MVRDV, Erick van Egeraath, Mecanoo, West 8, Neutelings Riedijk and UN Studio. Young architects are supported by excellent training opportunities, institutions, publishers and clients with vision (HEMA, Philips, Dutch Railways) that ensure knowledge and influence is disseminated way beyond the Dutch borders. Stars in the fields of fashion, graphics and interiors include Marcel Wanders, Droog Design, Richard Hutten, Hella Jongeruis and Victor & Rolf.

Gross Domestic Product

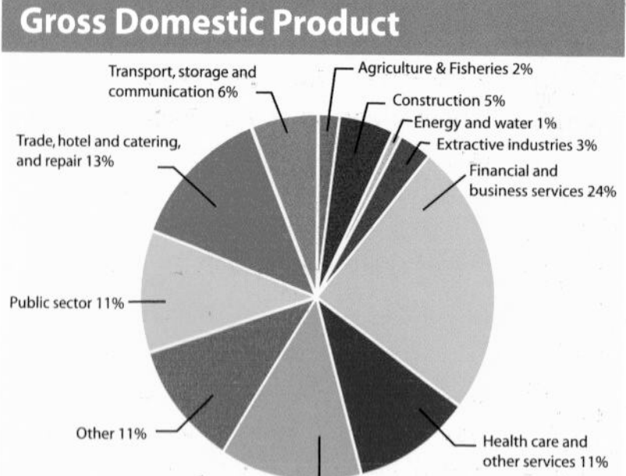

Amsterdam Overview

Amsterdam is the capital and most populous city of the Netherlands and its financial centre. Tourism, culture, education, and trade are all significant sectors.

New Developments

Amsterdam is currently a city under construction. IJburg (www. ijburg.nl), due to be completed in 2015, is an ambitious eastern archipelago of eight artificial islands which eventually will contain 18,000 homes housing 45,000 people, and creating 12,000 jobs. It has been planned as a self-contained district with offices and schools (and beach). The journey to Centraal Station on the IJ train takes 15 minutes. Two islands, Haveneiland and Steigereiland, are now occupied. The islands were created by spraying layer after layer of sand into the open water. Zuidas (www.zuidas.nl) is a new development expected to be completed by 2040. It's a housing, office and recreational development in Amsterdam South near the World Trade Centre, and aims to create employment for 50,000 people as well as 9,000 residences. ABN AMRO, ING, the Mexx Design Centre and the Rietveld Academy are already in situ. The ArenA development in the south-east of the city is the home of the famous Ajax football club, and includes extensive media and recreational facilities. The new North-South metro line is due to be completed in 2011, and aims to connect Amsterdam Noord, Centraal Station, Zuidas and the Amsterdam Zuid/WTC transport hub.

Top City

Amsterdam scores highly for logistics and labour with excellent worldwide transport connections, growing port facilities, and a multilingual, highly educated workforce. It is a popular conference destination (in 10th place worldwide) but has risen to 25th (up from 41st) in the 2007 (Mercer Human Resources) rankings of the world's most expensive cities (Moscow is top) and is 24th in the 2006 (UBS) survey of richest cities (Zurich workers are paid the most). Education is a pillar of the economy and there are 82,000 students in two universities and several colleges. Foreign investment is significant. In 2006, 86 overseas companies chose Amsterdam as their corporate HQ. Of these, 35% came from Asia including four from China. Korea and Japan also have a significant presence. Since 2004, the city has been marketed under the 'I Amsterdam' promotional motto, part of the campaign to promote the city as a place to do business.

Sectors

Economic activity is concentrated in the centre (84,000 jobs) in business services, education, government administration and tourism (turnover up 12% in first quarter of 2007). Other business districts include the western Telepoort region concentrated around Sloterdijk (telecommunications, call centres, publishing) and the Omval along the Amstel river (European HQs such as Philips and Delta Lloyd Insurance). Knowledge clusters include life sciences and IT (located in the Science Park) and medical research. Amsterdam has made significant investments in the arts ranging from workspace for artists – 'cultural incubators' – to investment in concert halls (Muziekgebouw aan 't IJ).

Development near Centraal Station

The Mayor

Job Cohen is a high profile mayor (since 2001) who has won many plaudits for his open and inclusive approach to politics and city life. He was a Time magazine 'European Hero of the Year' in 2005 and runner-up for World Mayor 2006.

Tourism

Substantial investment in city marketing and promotion has paid off for Amsterdam. After a few lacklustre years, tourism figures are beating all records. 2006 was a top year for museums and attractions, as the Rembrandt effect (400th anniversary celebrations) kicked in. There were 4,659,600 visitors in 2006, a million of them British. There was a 25% increase in the number of Spanish visitors, a 26% increase in the number of Dutch visitors and a 16% increase in visitors from Canada. An increase of 8% in the number of bed-nights spent in Amsterdam took the total to 8.6 million. The top three months for tourism are August, July and April. Tourists contribute significantly to the economy of Amsterdam and the ATCB estimate the total expenditure of visitors to be €4.5 billion. A record year is expected for 2007 with increases in visitors from Poland, Spain and Russia. Official themes are designed to attract visitors: 2006 was Rembrandt 400, 2007 is Feel the Rhythm and 2008 will be Hidden Treasures. But the real draw is the city itself. There is the charm of the canals (three million visitors take a boat trip making it the most popular 'attraction'), world-class culture (museums, the Opera, the Concertgebouw), fascinating architecture and a vibe that manages to be both cosy (*gezellig*) and contemporary. Something for everyone.

Top Development Nation

On the strength of its generous aid-giving, falling greenhouse gas emissions and support for investment in developing countries, the Netherlands is top of Foreign Policy *magazine's Commitment to Development Index 2006.*

International Relations

Dutch foreign policy is focused on international cooperation as the key to maintaining peace and promoting security, prosperity and justice. During the first world war the country was neutral, but after occupation during the second world war it took a pro-active stance in world affairs, resulting in Den Haag (The Hague) becoming the home base for almost every organisation in the field of peace and administration of justice. The Netherlands has 110 embassies and other representations, consulates and missions throughout the world. These include political and economic missions (such as within the European Union), representation in Atlantic and European organisations aimed at international peace and security (NATO, the WEU and the OSCE) and also global institutions devoted to human rights and development (the United Nations, UNESCO, the IMF and the World Bank). The Dutch have been strong advocates of European integration (they were the host country for the 1992 Maastricht and 1998 Amsterdam treaties) and the postwar economic agreements with Belgium and Luxembourg, together with the Treaty of Rome, paved the way for the European Union.

Nationaal Monument at Dam Square

Government & Politics

The Netherlands is a constitutional monarchy with a bicameral (two-chamber) parliament, called the Staten Generaal. Although Amsterdam is the capital, the Dutch parliament, government ministries and foreign embassies are all based in Den Haag (The Hague). Unusually, the monarch is part of the government, and Queen Beatrix (whose powers are mostly ceremonial) is the current head of state. The Dutch monarchy is referred to as being a 'cycling monarchy' due to its more informal relationship with the public than, for example, the British royal family. Centuries of life in the contained communities of the polders (with the constant threat of flooding if anyone undermines the defences) have resulted in the Dutch becoming known for their planning, organisation and pursuit of consensus. This is reflected in the country's political structures, where the philosophy of the 'Poldermodel' endures.

The Coalition Process

The formation of coalition governments is an elaborate process and takes months of negotiation. The record is 208 days in 1977. After the elections, the Queen appoints an 'informateur' to investigate coalition options, and then a 'formateur' to form a government. They chair the policy negotiations. If a coalition partner discontinues its support, the government falls. Balkenende's first government lasted 86 days (after being destabilised by the Lijst Pim Fortuyn Party), and his second administration fell after resignations caused by controversial immigration minister Rita Verdonk.

Constitution & Government

The constitution (mostly from 1848) describes the functions and responsibilities of institutions that have executive, legislative and judiciary power. Parliament consists of an upper chamber (eerste kamer or Senate) of 75 members elected by provincial councils every four years, and a lower chamber (tweede kamer or House of Representatives) containing 150 members elected, also every four years, by proportional representation.

There are ten political parties currently represented, and coalition cabinets – composed of two or three parties, are the norm. The last elections were in November 2006 and saw swings to the Socialist Party (SP), a drop in support for the conservative VVD (previous coalition partners) and a fragmented vote split among the smaller parties such as the Green Left (GL) and right wing Party for Freedom (PVV). The Party for Animals were the first animal rights organisation to win seats in a European parliament.

The voting age is 18. Government comprises over 1,600 organisations and bodies, including 13 ministries, 12 provincial authorities and, since 1 January 2006, 458 municipal authorities. It also includes autonomous administrative authorities, such as police regions and chambers of commerce, and public bodies for industry and the professions. Members of the cabinet cannot be members of parliament.

Cabinet

The cabinet is the main executive body of the Dutch government and consists of ministers and state secretaries. Former professor of philosophy Jan Peter Balkenende of the Christian Democratic Appeal (CDA) has been prime minister since 2002, and his current government – the fourth since coming into power – is a three party coalition with the Labour Party (PvdA) and the Christian Union (CU). Balkenende's administration also includes the first Muslim minister to achieve cabinet status.

Monarchy

The House of Orange Nassau has governed the Netherlands since 1915. William I (1772-1843), William II (1792-1849) and William III (1817-1890) were followed by the doughty Queen Wilhelmina (1880-1962) whose 50-year reign spanned two world wars and the decolonisation of Indonesia. Her only daughter Queen Juliana (1909-2004) was the cycling monarch whose unconventional views caused a few ructions. Queen Beatrix (born 1938), came to the throne in 1980 after her mother abdicated and is more formal than her mother but is widely admired for her professionalism and modern management style. She is well-educated, reasonably progressive, interested in the arts and politically ambiguous (very much the modern Nederlander). In the forming of new coalitions, Queen Beatrix has some power, but her role is mainly ceremonial, such as at the Queen's Speech that is part of the state opening of Parliament in Den Haag (Prinsjesdag). She will be succeeded by the Prince of Orange, Willem-Alexander (born 1967).

Population

The Netherlands is one of the most densely populated countries in the world with 42% of citizens concentrated in urban areas, particularly the four cities of the Randstad – Rotterdam, Amsterdam, Den Haag (The Hague) and Utrecht. The population reached 16,357,992 at the end of the first quarter of 2007, and is increasing by 80 people a day. The immigration 'waves' from former colonial territories, guest workers and asylum seekers have led to an increasingly multicultural society and this is particularly so in Amsterdam, which boasts 176 nationalities.

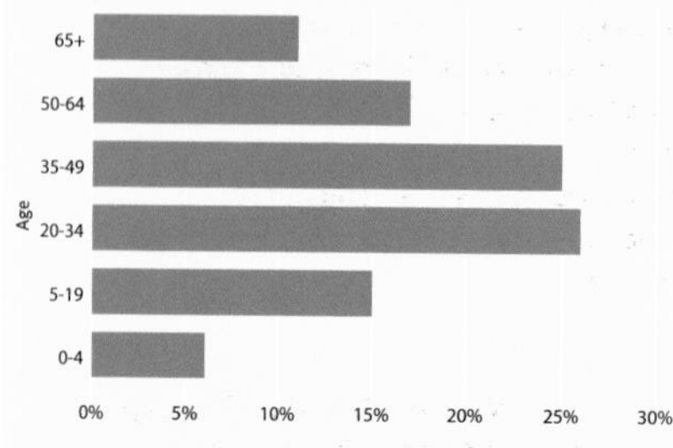

- The population of Amsterdam is 743,027 – 376,913 female and 366,114 male.
- 382,746 are 'native Dutch'; 255,169 are 'non-western foreigners' (niet-westerse allochtonen); and 105,112 are 'western foreigners'.
- Nationally, there are 3,170,406 'persons with a foreign background' who have at least one parent born abroad.
- The average household size nationally is 2.6 people.
- In Amsterdam, 54.6% households are inhabited by single people.
- Life expectancy at birth is 76.5 for men and 81.8 for women.

Sources: Centraal Bureau voor de Statistiek (www.cbs.nl); Dienst Onderzoek en Statistiek Kerncijfers Amsterdam 2007 (www.os.amsterdam.nl).

Education Levels

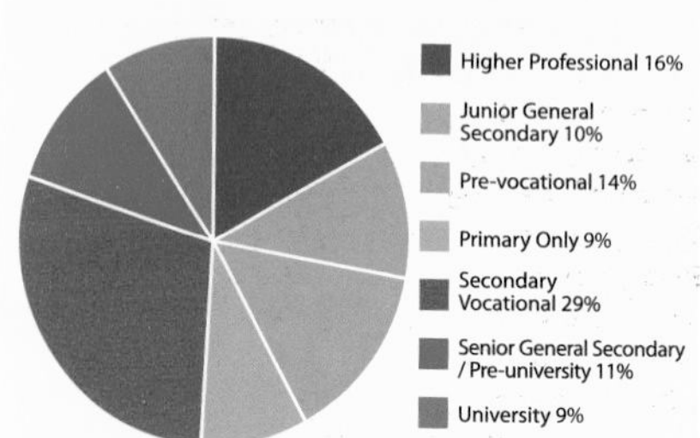

National Flag

The flag for the Kingdom of the Netherlands is a red, white and blue tricolour, one whose origins lie in the second half of the 16th century when Prince William of Orange led the revolt against the Spanish. It was officially adopted on 19 February 1937, and in 1958 the colours were precisely defined as bright vermilion and cobalt blue. There are specific days when the Dutch flag is flown from public buildings, such as Liberation Day and Armistice Day, and it is also flown on royal occasions and birthdays, when an orange pennant flies above it. Many Dutch cities and regions also have their own flags. Amsterdam's red-black-red horizontal stripes with three white St Andrew's crosses are almost as well known as the stripes of the national flag.

Local Time

Local time in the Netherlands is UTC+1 (one hour ahead of Universal Coordinated Time). The Netherlands also use Central European Summer Time, for which clocks go forward one hour on the last Sunday in March (to be UTC+2), then go back again on the last Sunday in October (returning to UCT+1). The table opposite shows local times in key cities around the world, not taking any daylight saving time into account.

Population by Nationality

Nationality	Population
Netherlands	533,636
Morocco	19,447
Turkey	10,569
United Kingdom	6,920
Germany	4,690
United States	3,740
Italy	2,903
France	2,625
Portugal	2,383
Spain	2,314
Unknown	1,399
More than One Nationality	1,109
Other	31,000

Social & Business Hours

Office hours are generally 09:00-17:30 in the Netherlands, but vary from sector to sector. Banks are open Tuesday to Friday 09:00 to 16:00, and on Mondays from 13:00. Bigger post offices are open on Saturday mornings. The working hours at embassies and consulates vary widely, with individual embassies designating specific times for different processes e.g. applying for passports and visas, or telephone-only enquiries. In terms of shopping, Amsterdam is no 24-7 environment. Shop opening hours are generally 09:00-18:00 Tuesday to Saturdays, with one late-night shopping day during the week (usually Thursday or Friday). Mondays are very quiet, with stores opening late (between 11:00 and 13:00) or not at all. Sunday shopping is certainly on the increase though, and Amsterdam, Den Haag and Rotterdam provide lots of scope to indulge this. The branches of supermarket chain Albert Heijn (p.296), which opens on Sundays, are a (relatively) safe haven from the inflated prices of nightshops.

An Hour Ahead?

If you are asked (in Dutch) to meet at 'half elf' (literally, half eleven), your appointment will be ready and waiting at 10:30. Always worth checking this...

Time Zones

Beijing	6
Dallas	-7
Denver	-8
Dubai	2
Dublin	-1
Hong Kong	6
London	-1
Los Angeles	-9
Mexico City	-7
Moscow	2
Mumbai	3.5
Munich	0
New York	-6
Paris	0
Perth	6
Prague	0
Rio de Janeiro	-5
Rome	0
Sydney	8
Toronto	-6
Wellington	11

Public Holidays

The Netherlands has the fewest national holidays in Europe, with just two official days (Queen's Day and Liberation Day) in addition to standard Christian festivals. Holidays are not pushed forward if they happen to fall on a Saturday or Sunday, but private companies sometimes compensate employees by giving them a day off on the previous Friday or following Monday. Unusually, there are two days commemorating war. Remembrance Day commemorates Dutch citizens who have died in all wars or peacekeeping missions since the second world war. It is marked with a two-minute silence at 20:00 and many other events, but is a 'working' day. Liberation Day marks the end of the German occupation and although celebrated every year, is only a public holiday once every five years (the next one is in 2010). For all Dutch citizens, Queen's Day (Koninginnedag) is the big one (see p.46 in Annual Events) – a riotous orgy of orangeness to celebrate the monarch's birthday.

There are a few additional regional variations in areas where carnavale is celebrated in February and March. The system for school holidays is one of staggered start/finish times between three regions (North, Central and South) – one year the summer holiday begins at the end of June, the next year you have to hang on until the third week of July. The timetable for international schools is different again, taking into account pupils' national holidays such as Thanksgiving. Public holidays (nationale feestdagen) are set by the Ministry for General Affairs (www.minaz.nl).

Public Holidays

Ascension (Hemelvaart)	1 May (2008)
Christmas (eerste Kerstdag)	25 Dec
Christmas (tweede Kerstdag)	26 Dec
Easter Monday (tweede Paasdag)	24 Mar
Easter Sunday (Pasen)	23 Mar
Liberation Day (Bevrijdingsdag)	5 May
New Year's Day (Nieuwjaar)	1 Jan
Queen's Day (Koninginnedag)	30 Apr (2008)
Remembrance Day (Dodenherdenking)	4 May
Whitsun (Pinksteren)	11-12 May (2008)

Photography

You won't be able to stop taking photos in scenic Amsterdam, but be alert to bicycles at all times zooming over bridges and down those cute narrow streets. The one absolute photographic no-no is the windows of the Red Light District.

Climate

Weathercams
Many Dutch cities have webcams installed at popular locations so you can check out the weather right before you go (see www.weeronline.nl).

Amsterdam has a temperate climate characterised by mild winters, cool summers, and year round precipitation (60-80cm). The extremely flat landscape means things can change very fast, but thankfully the rain tends to appear in sudden showers and disappear just as quickly. Whippy winds in the winter (1-4°C) can make cycling miserable, but when it's spring again (6-11°C) you'll be thinking tulips and sunshine and a trip to the bulb fields. Summers (14-19°C) can get hot and humid, with active mosquitoes and spectacular thunderstorms, but autumn (9-13°C) is quieter. Though there is usually snow (2005 was particularly spectacular), it doesn't hang around for long. From a long-term perspective, the weather is likely to carry on getting milder and wetter. The average temperature at Dutch weather station De Bilt was one degree Celsius higher over the last twenty years than it was at the beginning of the twentieth century.

Flora & Fauna

City planners have always taken care to incorporate space for nature into Amsterdam. Private outside space is rare, but cherished. Enormous foxgloves leap up from tiny streetside flowerbeds, herb boxes cling perilously to window ledges and exotic blooms flourish on roofterraces or houseboat decks. The great outdoors can be enjoyed in 28 parks, and for wilder landscapes (well, as wild as the neat Netherlands ever gets), the beaches and dunes are a short bike, bus, train or boat ride away.

Temperature

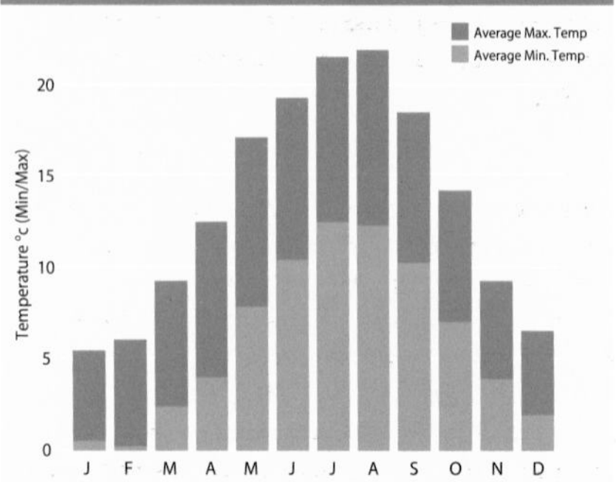

Average Max. Temp
Average Min. Temp

Temperature °c (Min/Max)

J F M A M J J A S O N D

Rainfall

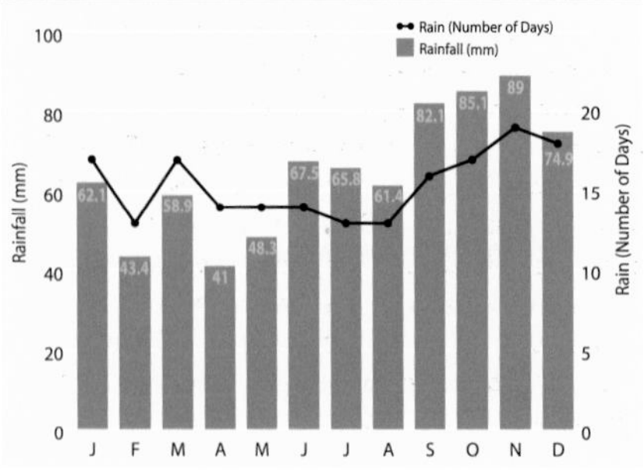

Rain (Number of Days)
Rainfall (mm)

Rainfall (mm) · Rain (Number of Days)

J 62.1 · F 43.4 · M 58.9 · A 41 · M 48.3 · J 67.5 · J 65.8 · A 61.4 · S 82.1 · O 85.1 · N 89 · D 74.9

Fauna

Over 140 bird species breed in Amsterdam, alongside 34 species of mammal, 60 species of frog and salamander, and 60 varieties of fish. The Netherlands is an important location on migration routes, and a significant destination for water birds, but Amsterdam also has its own regulars. In the trees of the Vondelpark live 1,000 green-ringed parakeets. And don't be surprised if you see a heron crossing the road – there are 7,000 of them in the city, living in three big colonies. In the country as a whole, biodiversity is decreasing, with fewer meadow birds and butterflies in particular. Common species are doing fine; since 1990, around 440 wildlife bridges, badger tunnels and other wildlife passages have been built, part of the National Ecological Network. Almost all the habitats in the Netherlands contain one or more species of higher plants, birds, mammals, butterflies, dragonflies, grasshoppers or crickets – all of international significance. Smaller explorers will love 'cuddle-hour' at one of the children's farms – kinderboerderijen (see p.167), when bunnies, guinea pigs and chickens can be stroked. Out in Amsterdamse Bos, there are pony rides and a bio-dynamic goat farm, and at Artis Zoo (p.163), which has endangered species breeding programmes, as well as wilder animals to study and courses to learn how to draw them.

Flora

200,000 trees grow in Amsterdam including the limes and elms that line every canal, and every borough has a 'trees booklet' with suggestions for enjoying local nature. There are rare varieties in the Vondelpark together with a notable rose garden. In the Plantage district, the Hortus Botanicus, founded in 1638, was originally a medicinal herb garden. Today it contains 4,000 species from all over the world, which are related to plants collected by the ships of the Dutch East India Company. One, however, is an original – the 300 year-old Eastern Cape giant cycad.

Keukenhof

Nature Links

The Netherlands Society for Nature and Environment: www.snm.nl; The National Trust for the Netherlands: www.natuurmonumenten.nl; Royal Dutch Society for Natural History: www.knnv.nl . Find your nearest natural attractions by typing in your postcode at www.natuurkaart.nl.

Environmental Issues

The environment plays a major role in politics and policy making in all cities of the Netherlands. Although not as environmentally aware as Germany, the situation is improving. Being geographically downwind and downstream from everybody else in Europe creates a unique pollution position for the Netherlands, with the potential of toxic chemicals ending up on Dutch beaches either via the Rhine or from North Sea oil drilling. Climate change is a key issue on which Dutch governments have lobbied successfully in Europe and long-term energy policy is focused on affordable, sustainable sources (including nuclear). Amsterdam's environmental policy is drawn up every four years and covers noise and air pollution, and the use of sustainable materials. Policies are also directed at ensuring people have a pleasant environment in which to live, like testing 'silencers' on the wheels of trams to make them quieter when going round corners. Amsterdam is fully implementing the Kyoto Protocol measures to reduce the annual emissions of carbon dioxide (CO^2) by 500 kilotons in 2007.

Environmental Organisations

Grassroots activism is strong – national membership of conservation organisations tripled between 1990 and 2005. Visit www.greenpeace.nl for the Dutch branch of Greenpeace and www.foei.org for Friends of the Earth. MNP (www.mnp.nl) is The Netherlands Environmental Assessment Agency. www.milieucentrumamsterdam.nl is an umbrella site for environmental groups. See www.vrom.nl for the Ministry for Housing, Spatial Planning and the Environment and www.deltawerken.com for information on the Deltaworks project. www.snm.nl is The Netherlands Society for Nature and Environment. See www.natuurmonumenten.nl for the National Trust for the Netherlands and www.knnv.nl is the website for the Royal Dutch Society for Natural History.

Amsterdam Projects

Current projects in Amsterdam include expanding the windmill park in the Westpoort (creating energy for 40,000 homes), a new waste conversion system (converting 958,962 tons of waste into energy for 161,000 homes) and using energy-efficient materials in construction activities. The city council's own fleet of cars will also be made cleaner. Fuel cell buses (using hydrogen) are in their fourth year of trials and a hydrogen boat may be on the canals later in the year. Each borough publishes a guide to local services giving details on recycling practices. Bottle, newspaper and clothing banks are numerous and conveniently placed. What's left (around 300,000 tons a year) is incinerated in an ultramodern plant on Westpoort. Although Amsterdam's canals are no longer open sewers, they are still treated as dumping grounds by some: every year, 8,000 cubic metres of rubbish are removed from the city's waters, together with 10,000 bicycles and 100 sunken boats.

Culture

Few capital cities boast a more cosmopolitan make-up than Amsterdam, with almost 150 nationalities registered in a population of under a million. Until the 1960s, society consisted of different 'pillars' (religious in origin) which co-existed side by side quite happily. But rapid secularisation and the most recent influx of immigration has triggered a huge debate about cultural identity and what it means (or could mean) to be Dutch. Traditionally egalitarian, tolerant, utilitarian, curious, trade oriented, respectful of privacy and with a sense of liberty, Dutch society is changing very rapidly and becoming increasingly consumer-driven. Like most of the world, it has been affected by international events post 9/11. There are innumerable 'dealing with the Dutch' cultural training programmes, workshops and publications, should you be wary of making a business or social gaffe. But you'll soon know, anyway.

Gezelligheid

It is a Dutch desire to make life as gezellig *(cosy, warm, companionable, comforting...) as possible. Sipping a jenever in a snug Jordaan bar while chatting to friends is very* gezellig. *Being ticked off by your boss is not at all* gezellig. *According to a popular saying,* 'gezelligheid knows no time'.

Communication is very direct. The scale of directness sometimes comes as a shock to many newcomers, but can be extremely refreshing. Mutual respect is the key. Conspicuous consumption or ostentatious, affected, or high-handed behaviour generally, will be frowned upon (though there is a Millionaires magazine...) and this is not – except on Queen's Day – a nation of exhibitionists. There is however, space to be different. 'The characteristically Dutch form of liberty', said Amsterdam Mayor Job Cohen recently, 'involves more than just the freedom to express individual integrity; it also involves freedom from interference from others'. The latter, however, is disappearing and today's Dutch are unsure about how to deal with each other's freedoms. Anti-discrimination laws to ensure equal treatment for groups (women and homosexuals) have long been part of the Netherlands' 'multidimensional liberty'. Other policies towards drugs, prostitution, religion, marriage, abortion, euthanasia and alternative lifestyles have generally added to the Dutch reputation for being relaxed but pragmatic. Rules and regulations are also a cause for moaning. Put your rubbish out in the wrong spot (or too early), for example, and you can be fined. Work and home life are kept very separate (and the Dutch definitely work to live rather than the other way round). Holidays are generous and flexible working is common for both men and women. Although open and approachable, there's a punctilious approach to social arrangements. Meals, visits and other engagements are booked in advance in an orderly way. Always carry that diary (agenda), and 'doe maar gewoon'... just act normal!

Language

Other options **Learning Dutch** p.124, **Language Schools** p.124

Dutch is one of the official languages of the European Union and is spoken by some 24 million people in the Netherlands, Belgium, Suriname, Aruba and Netherlands Antilles. The other national language is Frisian (spoken in northern province Friesland). English is widely and fluently spoken in the Netherlands, although road signs are in Dutch, so a little homework on motorway terminology is a good idea for initial forays. Almost every cafe and restaurant in Amsterdam will have a menu in English.

English language media and the internet are huge influences (films aren't dubbed) and Dutch advertising includes a smattering of English as well as 'Nederlands'. A language test has become part of the immigration procedure for residents from some countries.

Dutch Women Don't Get Depressed (But They Do Get Bossy)

Freedom of choice, a positive work/life balance and partners who help around the house are reasons why *Dutch Women Don't Get Depressed,* according to a new book by journalist and psychologist Ellen de Bruin. Ok, Dutch women aren't exactly style queens: 'We do everything by bike, which is why we don't dress very elegantly' she comments, and 'we are bossy to our men'. So do Dutch men get depressed?

Pronunciation is the key: dipthongs in 'huis' or 'muis' (like the 'i' in 'sit' followed by a 'y') are tricky to get the hang of and the clicky, gutteral sound required for a genuine rendition of seaside town Scheveningen was by repute a wartime test to catch German spies. Not surprisingly, one commentator has said 'Dutch isn't a language, it's a disease of the throat'. There are many language schools for learning Dutch as well as internet-based courses, and it is worth persisting. Efforts to integrate are always respected.

Basic Dutch

Directions	
airport	luchthaven
bank	de bank
beach	strand
close to	vlakbij
east	oost
first right/left	eerste rechts/links
hotel	hotel
how do I get to...	Hoe kom ik bij...
left	links
mountains	bergen
north	noord
petrol station	benzinestation
restaurant	restaurant
right	rechts
roundabout	rotonde
second left/right	tweede links/rechts
slow down	langzamer
south	zuid
stop	stop
straight ahead	rechtdoor
street	straat
west	west
Emergency	
accident	ongeluk
I am ill	Ik ben ziek
I need a doctor	Ik heb een dokter nodig
police	politie
road accident	wegongeluk
General	
no	nee
please	alstublieft
sorry	sorry
thank you	dank u
thanks	bedankt
yes	ja
yes, please	ja, graag
you're welcome	graag gedaan
Introductions	
I come from England	Ik kom uit Engeland
my name is...	mijn naam is / ik heet...
nice to meet you	aangenaam kennis te maken
where do you come from?	Waar komt u vandaan?
who are you?	Hoe heet u?

Greetings	
good afternoon	goedemiddag
good day	dag, goedendag
good evening	goedenavond
good morning	goedemorgen
goodbye	dag
see you later	tot ziens!
Documentation	
car insurance	autoverzekering
driver's license	rijbewijs
license plate	kenteken
Numbers	
one	een
two	twee
three	drie
four	vier
five	vijf
six	zes
seven	zeven
eight	acht
nine	negen
ten	tien
twenty	twintig
thirty	dertig
forty	veertig
fifty	vijftig
sixty	zestig
seventy	zeventig
eighty	tachtig
ninety	negentig
hundred	honderd
thousand	duizend
million	miljoen
Questions	
how	hoe
how much...?	wat kost...?
what	wat
what is the time?	hoe laat is het?
when	wanneer
where	waar
which	welk(e)
who	wie
why	waarom

Race Relations

Immigration and integration are resolutely on the political agenda in the Netherlands, particularly since the murders of anti-immigration politician Pim Fortuyn (2002) and controversial filmmaker Theo van Gogh (2004). Headlines such as 'Jihad behind the Dykes' or 'The Dutch Identity is Being Lost' do not speak of peaceful cohabitation or suggest a positive view of race relations. Although both men had expressed anti-Muslim sentiments, Fortuyn was shot during the 2002 electoral campaigns by an animal rights activist, while Van Gogh was stabbed because of a film (*Submission*) made with politician and ex-Muslim Ayann Hirsi Ali about female repression. Openly gay, Fortuyn's portrayal of Islam as a 'backward' culture (specifically with reference to treatment of women, homosexuals and the intolerances bound into Sharia law) reverberated strongly. His party (Lijst Pim Fortuijn) won 26 seats out of 150 in the elections and they were a member of the coalition cabinet. Not least because of scandal and bickering within the LPF, the government collapsed after only 86 days. In 2006 the LPF could not even muster enough votes for one seat. Following Van Gogh's death, subsequent Balkenende cabinets have introduced measures designed to improve social cohesion between 'native' Dutch and minority groups who have their own cultural and social identity. These range from the establishment of a cultural 'canon' to improve the cultural and historical knowledge of the Dutch population, to the Broad Initiative on Social Cohesion launched in 2005. Amsterdam mayor Job Cohen is also pursuing integration policies for the city of Amsterdam and favours an 'inclusive' approach to Dutch identity: 'It is possible to be Dutch, and white, black, brown or yellow. It is possible to be Dutch, and white, secular and liberal. It is just as possible to be Dutch, and black, Muslim and conservative.'

Multi-cultural Amsterdam

Religion

The oldest building in Amsterdam is a church – the 14th century Oude Kerk that was (probably) consecrated in 1306, but over the years, the Netherlands has become increasingly secular. The most popular religion is Christianity and Catholics (31%) are the biggest group. Until the 'Alteration' of 26 May 1578, Amsterdam was a Catholic city. When Protestant Calvinists took over, churches were stripped of their trappings and worship of other religions (on paper) was banned. Only members of the Dutch Reformed Church could furnish their churches with a tower, and other denominations (with the exception of the Jewish community) were forced underground in disguised venues complete with collapsible altars. The best known example of these, 'Our Lord in the Attic', is now a museum.

In reality though, tolerance and liberty of thought were the order of the day and Amsterdam became the refuge for many immigrants fleeing their countries for religious and political reasons. Before and during the second world war this included Jews escaping Hitler's anti-semitic policies in Europe. Tragically,

Population by Religion

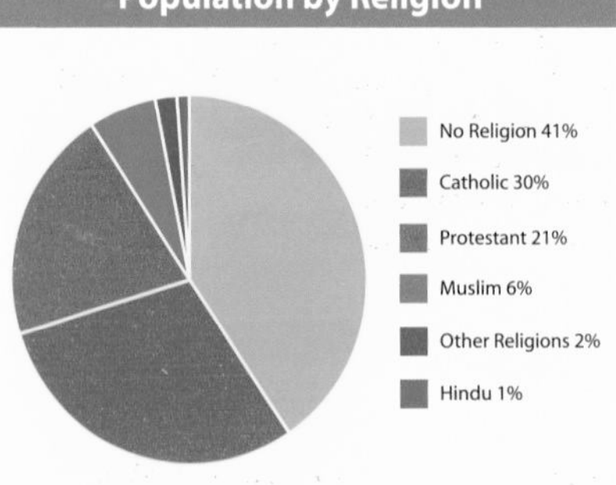

Source: Dienst Onderzoek en Statistiek www.os.amsterdam.nl

Amsterdam was no safe haven. The round up of the Jewish population began in 1941 and 76% were eventually deported to concentration camps, with few survivors. A complex of four synagogues in the centre of Amsterdam is now the Jewish Historical Museum and close by is the Portuguese Synagogue built in 1675, which astonishingly remained intact during the Nazi occupation of the city.

With over a million practising Muslims, Islam is one of the country's main religions. By 2020, it is estimated that 7% of the population will be Muslim and 10% Catholic. Turks make up 80% of the Muslim minority. In Amsterdam, the diversity of worship reflects the city's multiculturalism. Protestant groups include Dutch Reformed and Reformed, Evangelical, Quaker, Pentecostal, Methodist and Charistmatic. There are also Buddhists, humanists and members of other philosophical groups, as well as a Russian Orthodox Church.

In 2000, the Netherlands' first purpose-built Hindu temple, the Radha Krishna Mandir Hindu temple, opened its doors. In Amsterdam's Chinatown, Queen Beatrix inaugurated a new landmark, the Fo Kuang Shan Buddhist temple. Amsterdam's first mosque was opened in 1977 but proposals for a new centre have been controversial because of funding by 'radical' organisations. As this book went to press the future of the Westermoskee project was in doubt.

Places of Worship

Beit Ha'Chidush	Centrum	020 524 72 04	Jewish
Christ Church	Centrum	020 624 88 77	Anglican
Crossroads International Church	Amstelveen	020 545 14 44	Non-denominational
English Reformed Church	Centrum	020 624 96 65	English Reformed
FWBO Netherlands (Western Buddhism)	Jordaan	020 420 70 97	Buddhist
Holy Trinity	Amsterdam Zuidoost	020 691 66 02	Roman Catholic
Liberal Jewish Community Amsterdam	Rivierenbuurt	020 642 35 62	Jewish
Muslim THAIBA Islamic Cultural Centre	Amsterdam Zuidoost	020 698 25 26	Jewish
Orthodox Jewish Community Amsterdam	Amstelveen	020 646 00 46	Jewish
Parish of the Blessed Trinity	Watergraafsmeer	020 465 27 11	Roman Catholic
Salvation Army National Headquarters	Oost	020 520 84 08	Christian
Society of Friends (Quaker)	Oud Zuid	020 679 42 38	Quaker
St John and St Ursula	Centrum	020 622 19 18	Roman Catholic
St Nicholas of Myra	De Pijp	www.orthodox.nl	Russian Orthodox
Wesley Methodist Church	Amsterdam Zuidoost	06 28 172115	Methodist

National Dress

The traditional costumes and wooden shoes that the Netherlands is associated with are hardly ever seen except in tourist spots such as Volendam, where you can have your photo taken in various outfits (milkmaid etc) for a jolly folkloric-themed Christmas card (or whatever). A white cotton or lace hat with turned up triangular flaps (a 'Dutch cap') is part of the women's costume, as in Vermeer's famous painting *The Milkmaid.*

Clogs were originally used as a cheap alternative to leather shoes, and farmers, road-workers and bulb growers still wear them instead of rubber boots. The clog is of course a ubiquitous image in the souvenir industry, adorning keyrings and fridge magnets or taking the form of fluffy slippers.

Food & Drink

Other options **Eating Out** p.304

The Dutch have a hard time with their 'traditional' culinary reputation which is often represented as cheese, more cheese and variations on a theme of mashed potatoes and cabbage. In recent years however, there have been radical changes in the restaurant

Cheese shop

scene and home cooks are becoming much more adventurous. According to renowned food critic (and Amsterdammer) Johannes van Dam, things were actually fine until the 1890s but then a group of Dutch middle class women decided to set up cookery classes for the poor. Out went the herbs, rich sauces and complicated techniques of their solid bourgeois cuisine. In came cheap, simple and nourishing dishes. And because the poor did not actually attend these classes (they were out at work) it was the daughters of the middle class who warmed to food without fuss, and bang went the home cuisine. Over the years, former colonies have come to the rescue and Dutch citizens from Suriname, Indonesia and the Dutch Antilles have made their culinary mark with some surprising hybrids: Chinees-Indisch-Surinaams or Indisch-Chinees or Javaans-Surinaams, for example. Now Amsterdam's eating scene is truly international. Gourmet shops (the Haarlemmerstraat/Dijk area is a culinary hotspot) attract grateful customers and there are some great guides (try www.iens.nl and www.specialbite.nl) to local restaurants. Eet Smaakelijk!

Supermarkets & Markets

Supermarkets are not super-sized, but there are a lot of them. There's everything from the ubiquitous (but slightly expensive) Albert Heijn (www.ah.nl) to cheaper chains like Dirk van den Broek (www.dirk.nl) and no-frills operators like Aldi (www.aldi.nl) and Lidl. For anything remotely exotic, you need a toko or deli, and for organic produce the Natuurwinkel chain (www.denatuurwinkel.nl) is a supermarket option alongside individual specialists. If you want your produce to be local, seasonal, organic or more varied, markets are the place to go. For an overview of the Dutch market scene www.hollandsemarkten.nl is very useful. Notable markets in Amsterdam include the biological market at the Noordermarket on Saturdays, and the mile-long Albert Cuypstraat Markt (p.292) in De Pijp.

Cheese Fact
A mature (but unrotted) Edam was found in the South Pole in 1956, a relic of the ill-fated Scott expedition of 1912.

Dutch Delicacies

The Dutch are keen on sturdy fare and snacks are also pretty solid. Popular options in bars or in food-from-the-wall chain Febo, are kroketten (tubes of pureed meat/potato) and bitterballen (round versions) which come with mustard for dunking. Vlaamse (Belgian) chips/frites come with various toppings (satay sauce, curry ketchup, mayo, onions). Go for patatas oorlog (war potatoes) and you get the lot.

Herring (raw) is a healthier option and May and June are the months for sampling the fresh, plump fish. Its arrival is a Major Culinary Event. Vlaggetjesdag (Little Flags Day) in Scheveningen marks the beginning of the eating season. Eel is another must-try. Chocolate is an essential Dutch treat – confectioner Beune makes chocolate Amsterdammertjes (the kerbside posts) and no office canteen would be complete without little boxes of chocolate hundreds-and-thousands (hagelslag) which top a slice of bread at lunchtime (or breakfast or tea) for grown-ups as well as kids. The chunkier flakes called vlokken are even more delicious. Traditional Dutch sweets (snoepjes) include liquorice drops that comes in many guises, including both salty and sweet. Dairy (zuivel) products take up a lot of supermarket space. The Dutch dairy cow is a revered milk machine producing 35 litres of milk a day. There is even a cow museum in Friesland (www.koeienmuseum.nl). Farming methods are extremely intensive but organic options are available at butchers' and farmers' markets (there is a very limited selection in supermarkets). Delicious dairy products include sour buttermilk (karnemelk), custardy vla, which is available in many flavours, including Ajax (for the football club) and orange (around Queen's Day). The different kinds of yoghurt are also worth trying. 650 million kilograms of cheese are produced annually in the Netherlands and the Dutch population eat 15 kilograms a year each. Supermarket selections will be marked up by fat content and age – jonge kaas 48+ is young cheese with a high fat content; belegen is the tastiest.

Golden Age Blow-Outs

The Dutch have always been up for a feast. In 1703, the deacons of the guild of surgeons at Arnhem – at most seven men – got through, at one sitting, six kilograms of beef, three and a half kilograms of veal, six fowl, stuffed cabbages, apples, pears, bread, pretzels, assorted nuts, 20 bottles of red wine, 12 bottles of white wine and coffee.

Retro Recipe: Things To Do With Vla...

The Dutch population's ever increasing height has been attributed to their dairy-dependent diet. Many children grew up (literally) on a vla flip: a bottom layer of fruit, a layer of vla, a layer of yoghurt, and a dribble of fruit syrup... and voila!

Proost!

Think Dutch beer and you think Heineken – the second largest brewer in the world. However there are many other varieties of beer besides pils, including the darker bokbiers. Dutch gin (Jenever) was originally distilled for medical purposes but had a huge export market by the end of the 18th century. A special place to try some (though of course it is in ordinary bars too) is a Proeverij (tasting place). You drink it very cold whilst standing up – it's the perfect accompaniment to herring.

Seasonal Treats

In the winter, erwtensoep (split pea soup) is everywhere. Also called snert, it includes chunks of sausage and is served with rye bread. Stamppot (mashed pot) is another winter comfort food where potatoes are mashed with a green vegetable such as kale (boerenkool), or endive (andijvie) and served with smoked bacon on rye bread (this hardly complex concoction is sold in Albert Heijn's, giving some indication of the sophistication of the ready meal market). Spring delights include white asparagus which is traditionally served with ham and egg sauce. Sinterklaas and Christmas are associated with chocolate letters, speculaas (spice biscuits) and delicious banketstaaf (almond-filled pastry). New Year sees the arrival of oliebol stands. Utterly irresistible, oliebol are deep fried donuts served with tons of powdered sugar. The name can also be used as a mild form of abuse (oliebol = dummy!)

Horses carrying Heineken beer

In Emergency

112 is the emergency number for fire, police and ambulance. For medical emergencies (that are not life threatening), you can find a doctor via the central huisarts line (020 592 34 34) or get efficient accident and emergency treatment (EHBO) at one of several Amsterdam hospitals. Or simply find a local doctor via the GoudenGids (yellow pages). To report a crime, the non-emergency police line (0900 8844) will connect you to your nearest station. If your passport has been stolen, contact your embassy immediately or consult your embassy's website, which will usually provide step-by-step instructions as to what do next. ATAS Amsterdam Tourist Assistance Service (020 625 32 46) can provide practical support and help for tourist victims of crime.

Emergency Services

AMC Academisch Medisch Centrum	020 566 91 11	Hospitals
American Express	020 504 86 66	Stolen cards
Apotheek (pharmacy) helpline	0900 7244 7465	Medical
BovenIJ Ziekenhuis	020 634 63 46	Hospitals
Bureau Gevonden Vorwerpen (Lost and Found)	020 559 30 05	Lost and Found
Diners Club	020 654 55 11	Stolen cards
Discrimininatie (Discrimination)	020 638 55 51	Support
Fire, police and ambulance	112	Emergency Services
GGD STD Clinic	020 555 58 22	Medical
Huisarts (Family Doctors)	020 592 34 34	Medical
Huiselijk Geweld (Domestic Violence)	020 611 60 22	Support
M (anonymous crimeline)	0800 7000	Crimeline
Mastercard/Eurocard	030 283 55 55	Stolen cards
OLVG	020 599 91 11	Hospitals
Police (non-emergency)	0900 8844	Emergency Services
Sint Lucas Ziekenhuis	020 510 89 11	Hospitals
Slachtofferhulp (Victim Support)	020 622 84 41	Support
Slotervaartziekenhuis	020 512 93 33	Hospitals
SOS (24-hour helpline)	020 675 75 75	Support
Tandartsen (Dentists)	0900 821 2230	Medical
Visa	0800 022 3110	Stolen cards
VU	020 444 44 44	Hospitals

Women

Women travelling alone will not feel uncomfortable in Amsterdam. The sexes are unquestionably equal here and solo women travellers are a common sight. Everybody speaks English (or French or German) should some assistance be required, and public transport is safe. Really, it's just common sense. The seedier parts of town (such as the Red Light District) can be intimidating for women so solo exploration of these areas, particularly at night, is not advisable. If you want someone to leave you alone the phrase is 'laat me met rust' (leave me in peace) or simply 'ga weg!' (go away).

Gay & Lesbian

Other options **Gay & Lesbian** (Going Out, p.351)

Amsterdam is an international city with a long history of tolerance of different cultures and ways of thinking. It is argued that the city's history as a port forced its people to become accepting of other cultures and different ways of thinking. Dutch people are generally not the type to say anything degrading about gay people to their faces. Many people across the world know Amsterdam as a 'gay' city and one of the gay capitals of the world. Amsterdam is, after all, the home of the Homomonument, commemorating all the gay men and women who lost their lives in the second world war. Flowers are laid on the monument regularly and it's a great place to have your picture taken. There is no West Village like in New York City or Old Compton Street in London, but most gay establishments are in the centre.

Anyone is welcome in gay bars as long as they behave. A crowd of mixed expats would feel comfortable at any of the bars on Reguliersdwarsstraat. All of the bars are fairly mixed as far as race and nationality are concerned – even Habibi Ana (p.354), the Arab bar. The back corner of Café April (p.352) is referred to by regulars as 'Asian Corner'. In 1998, civil unions for same sex couples became legal, and in 2001 the Netherlands became the first country in the world to grant same sex couples the right to marry, enjoying the same legal rights as opposite sex couples. Since that time, thousands of gay couples have married, and some have exercised their right to divorce as well.

The oldest gay, lesbian, bisexual, and transgender organisation in the world that is devoted to advancing the social and legal position of gays and lesbians in the Netherlands (and also globally) is the COC (www.coc.nl), founded in 1946. They are still in existence and are an excellent organisation for people looking to get information or find resources. Their website has a huge assortment of activities and links. Another group devoted to changing the laws across the world is Love Exiles, based in Amsterdam (www.loveexiles.org). A love exile is someone who does not have the choice of living in his or her home country with their same sex partner. They have a political focus, but are also a great resource. HIV Vereniging (www.hivnet.org) is an organisation dedicated to helping people deal with HIV-related issues.

There are a few annual celebrations especially by and for the gay community. Rozezaterdag, or Pink Saturday (www.rozezaterdag.nl) is the last Saturday of June every year. There is a parade, food, performances, speakers and people selling a variety of goods. It's held in a different city every year, 2007 being its 30th year. Amsterdam Gay Pride (p.49), or 'Canal Pride' is held on the first Saturday in August. There's a parade through the canals and, again, lots of people selling things, performances and lots and lots of beer. Everyone is welcome. The city also has a fairly large Leather Pride Amsterdam, usually in November (fewer pink ribbons, more black leather).

The atmosphere for gay people in Amsterdam is fairly relaxed, although not everyone is okay about gay people having equal rights and being 'out', so it's not exactly a free for all. Same sex couples can regularly be seen holding hands along some streets, but not everywhere. Many other couples just go about their everyday business walking side-by-side. Just because you have the right to do something doesn't mean there are not irrational people out there who will react violently. So use your head and have fun.

Embassies & Consulates

Albania	070 427 21 01	Den Haag	p.365 A3
Argentina	070 360 51 55	Den Haag	p.365 A3
Australia	070 310 82 00	Den Haag	p.365 A3
Austria	070 324 54 70	Den Haag	p.365 A3
Belgium	070 312 34 56	Den Haag	p.365 A3
Brazil	070 302 39 59	Den Haag	p.365 A3
Canada	070 311 16 00	Den Haag	p.365 A3
China	070 306 50 91	Den Haag	p.365 A3
Cyprus	070 346 64 99	Den Haag	p.365 A3
Czech Republic	070 313 00 31	Den Haag	p.365 A3
Denmark	070 302 59 59	Den Haag	p.365 A3
Egypt	070 354 20 00	Den Haag	p.365 A3
Finland	070 346 97 54	Den Haag	p.365 A3
France	070 312 58 00	Den Haag	p.365 A3
Germany	070 342 06 00	Den Haag	p.365 A3
Ghana	070 338 43 84	Den Haag	p.365 A3
Greece	070 363 87 00	Den Haag	p.365 A3
Hungary	070 350 04 04	Den Haag	p.365 A3
Iceland	020 795 33 34	Amsterdam	p.384 A3 1
India	070 346 97 71	Den Haag	p.365 A3
Indonesia	070 310 81 00	Den Haag	p.365 A3
Ireland	070 363 09 93	Den Haag	p.365 A3
Israel	070 376 05 00	Den Haag	p.365 A3
Italy	070 302 10 30	Den Haag	p.365 A3
Japan	070 346 95 44	Den Haag	p.365 A3
Malta	076 520 90 43	Breda	p.365 A3
Mauritius	020 540 58 20	Amsterdam	p.372 C4 2
Mexico	070 360 29 00	Den Haag	p.365 A3
Monaco	070 624 52 50	Den Haag	p.365 A3
Morocco	070 346 96 17	Den Haag	p.365 A3
Nepal	020 624 15 30	Amsterdam	p.392 C3 3
New Zealand	070 346 93 24	Den Haag	p.365 A3
Norway	070 311 76 11	Den Haag	p.365 A3
Portugal	070 363 02 17	Den Haag	p.365 A3
Romania	070 354 37 96	Den Haag	p.365 A3
Russia	070 346 88 88	Den Haag	p.365 A3
Saudi Arabia	070 361 43 91	Den Haag	p.365 A3
Senegal	020 693 79 58	Amsterdam	p.365 A3
Slovakia	070 416 77 77	Den Haag	p.365 A3
Slovenia	070 310 86 90	Den Haag	p.365 A3
South Africa	070 392 45 01	Den Haag	p.365 A3
Spain	070 364 38 14	Den Haag	p.365 A3
Sweden	020 301 43 08	Amsterdam	p.367 E3
Switzerland	020 364 28 31	Amsterdam	p.384 B1 5
Thailand	070 345 20 88	Den Haag	p.365 A3
Turkey	070 360 49 12	Den Haag	p.365 A3
UK	070 427 04 27	Den Haag	p.365 A3
USA	070 310 92 09	Den Haag	p.365 A3

Efteling
Opened in 1952, Efteling (p.161) is one of the oldest theme parks in the world, and even for Disney-numbed cynics, is not without charm. Based originally on enchanting fairy tales, the park has rides for tots as well as bigger kids. Older children will enjoy the corkscrew thrills of amusement park rides like Python. The latest addition is 'de Vliegende Hollander' (The Flying Dutchman), a combination of roller coaster and water ride – with a spectacular finale. For more information on this and other Amusement Parks, see p.161.

Drive A White Car
Kids (and grown ups) will love 'driving' through 1970s Amsterdam in one of Luud Schimmelpennink's white cars now parked in the Amsterdams Historisch Museum (p.154).

Children

Amsterdam is a great city for smaller explorers. Dutch culture is family oriented and relaxed, and children are welcome pretty much everywhere. Getting around is a cinch on a bicycle or bakfiets (box bike) but public transport is also extensive, cheap and reliable, and clanging trams are an adventure. A boat trip (of some kind) is a must. Hire a canal bike, go on a tourist cruise or (for free) take one of the ferries that go back and forth to Amsterdam North (behind Centraal Station). You can also buy a ticket here for the high-speed ferry that zooms through Amsterdam port to IJmuiden and the beach. When it's raining, TunFun Speelpark (p.208) is the place to be – an enormous underground playground fashioned out of a multi-storey car park. Top 'educational' stops include interactive Science Center NEMO (p.208), housed in a giant, green ship designed by Renzo Piano, and (for pirate fanatics) the Scheepvaartmuseum (p.207) is the place to go, complete with its replica Dutch East India Company (VOC) ship moored outside. Art-loving explorers will enjoy the Van Gogh Museum's audio guide for children (see p.157). Numerous parks and playgrounds offer free entertainment and activities and a dozen or so animal farms (kinderboerderijen) often have 'cuddle hour' on Wednesday afternoons (when schools finish at midday) for bonding with bunnies (see Farm & Stable Tours on p.167). Wilder beasts can be spotted in the excellent Artis Zoo (p.163). There are restaurants with special children's menus (and colouring sheets, crayons and games), but almost every Amsterdam cafe can serve up a toasted sandwich so there will be no need for hunger tantrums. Pancakes and poffertjes (puffed up smaller versions) are top scoff. At the Kinderkookkafe in Vondelpark, children take on the whole culinary caboodle, cooking and serving up meals to family and friends. Outside Amsterdam, top attractions include theme parks such as Efteling (a Disneyesque experience with folkloric touches, see p.161) and Space Expo at Noordwijk – fascinating for budding astronauts and for miles of wild, windy (and free) beach (0900 8765 4321). Activities for children can be found in local magazines *Uitkrant* (www.uitkrant.nl) (look under jeugd), and *N20* (look under kind) and www.uitmetkinderen.nl (out with the children). The 320 page Kidsgids English guide, 'the perfect guide for the smaller explorer', provides an invaluable reference point for every aspect of life in the Netherlands when you have children. Hotels can often provide babysitting (using agencies such as Oppascentrale) and expat websites like Elynx.nl are also useful places to go to find this information. There are some creches in sportscentres, for example, but this is pretty unusual.

People With Disabilities

Amsterdam, with its narrow uneven streets and bicycles parked everywhere, isn't brilliant terrain for people with physical disabilities. But over the past few years, accessibility has improved and most museums, government offices and transport networks have been modified to accommodate visitors with special needs. The tourist board (www.holland.com) can provide details of hotels that are particularly suitable. Help is available for getting to (and through) Schiphol airport (see www.ihd-schiphol.nl) and to travel on the railways (www.ns.nl). The bureau for disabled travellers (Bureau Assistentieverlening Gehandicapten, 030 235 78 22) can also provide advice. Within Amsterdam, the newer trams have low central doors accessible for wheelchairs, but the older ones haven't (the timetable at the tramstop indicates which is which). The metro is also accessible for wheelchair users – see www.gvb.nl for further transport information. There are parking places for disabled drivers with a permit throughout the city (see www.bereikbaar.amsterdam.nl). Some taxis can take wheelchairs but it is best to book in advance. The city website (www.amsterdam.nl) has more information on facilities (in Dutch). Select 'Zorg en welzijn' (healthcare) and then 'gehandicapten'.

Dress

Amsterdam is a relaxed and informal city. Work attire is casual with juniors in suits and the bosses in sweaters. The finance industry tends to be the most conservatively dressed. Only in the swankiest of restaurants will a jacket and tie seem particularly appropriate, and the stylish-but-casual look is de rigeur at cultural events. You can wear jeans to the opera or Concertgebouw and you won't stand out a bit. In terms of the climate, there's no bad weather, only unsuitable clothing – so come prepared for rain and lots of it. If you haven't yet mastered the art of cycling with an umbrella – though many people do – pick up a rain cape at a cycling shop. Winters are getting milder but you'll need a scarf/gloves/hat combo in January.

Dos & Don'ts

Johan Cruyff (Footballer)
Ajax star of legendary status. He was famed for his 'Cruyff turn', which allowed him to speedily change direction with the ball. Named European Footballer of the Year three times, Cruyff was a member of the Ajax side of the 70s renowned for its dynamic style of open, attacking play referred to as 'Total Football'. He has also enjoyed success as both a player and manager at Barcelona.

Amsterdam is a famously laid back city where pretty much anything goes, but a bit of self control is in order. Don't smoke a joint anywhere except inside a coffeeshop. Don't buy drugs/bikes/hotel rooms off strangers in the street. Don't walk in the fietspad – that's the lane with the cute drawing of a bicycle on it. If you are on a bike, watch out for the tram lines. You'll see a lot of cycling through red lights, but the police are on the case (instant €50 fine). You can also be fined if you ride without lights at night, have no bicycle bell, or if you cycle in pedestrianised areas (like the Leidsestraat or Kalverstraat). Do enjoy Amsterdam for free: an architectural tour, a picnic in Vondelpark, a boat trip across the IJ or a Wednesday lunchtime concert at the Concertgebouw or Boekmanzaal with singers from the Netherlands Opera. Pay attention to rubbish etiquette. Get out of Amsterdam from time to time – castles, beaches, masterpieces of hydraulic engineering that keep the water out – everything is so near. One last important thing – don't take photos of the women in the windows in the Red Light District.

Crime & Safety

Other options **In Emergency** p.20

Amsterdam is a comfortably safe city provided you take sensible precautions. Burglaries and thefts (including pickpocketing) are going down and road safety is improving. Seven out of every 10 crimes reported concern theft and almost a quarter (in 2005) relate to something stolen from a car. Just as in other cities, conspicuous display of valuables is unwise. The chances of having a wallet, backpack or laptop stolen are highest on the trains travelling to and from the airport and on public transport generally. The Red Light District is not an area to carry valuables, particularly a camera. After police clean-ups, drug dealers and junkies have moved on from Zeedijk, but the area can still be threatening especially late at night. In terms of cars, 'Niets er in... Niets er uit' (nothing in, nothing out) is the police advice. Don't leave valuables in your car, not even the boot, and open the (empty) glove compartment to show there's nothing there.

Traffic Accidents & Violations

In 2005 there were 1,429 registered traffic casualties (19 deaths) compared to 2001 (2,599 casualties, 30 deaths), so road safety is improving. Cyclists, despite the wide bike lanes, are particularly at risk, and five die every year. Nationally, 23,000 children every year visit a doctor because of a biking accident. Most incidents, according to the DIVV (Organisation for Traffic and Transport) are caused by cars, and mirrors are being introduced at blackspots. Minor offences are dealt with via the Central Fine Collection Agency which automatically sends a payment slip. You will be stopped, asked for identification and told what the fine will be. The slip for payment will be sent through the post. Punishments for drink driving range from €190 to some years in prison and a driving ban for a maximum of five years (10 years for repeat offenders). See www.verkeershandhaving.nl.

Victims Of Crime

The first stage is to make a police report. You can call in at your local station. This police report is essential paperwork for applying for a new passport, contacting insurers etc. Also, contact your embassy immediately if your passport has been stolen. The non-emergency line for the police is 0900 8844. Victims of crime can obtain compensation for a loss via the court (a request to the public prosecutor), through a one-off payment from the Criminal Compensation Fund, or by initiating civil proceedings against the suspect.

If You Are Arrested

The police can hold you for six hours for questioning, but the time between midnight and 09:00 is not included (so if you are arrested at 20:00 you can be held until 11:00 the following day). The police can ask the assistant prosecutor for permission to hold you for another 72 hours. At any point you can request to speak to someone from your embassy but the police are under no obligation to grant this (though they might phone themselves). The legal aid board will appoint a lawyer if you have insufficient funds. Depending on the offence, courts can impose custodial sentences, fines or order the offender to do community service.

Bike Theft

The only type of theft actually increasing is that of bicycles (no big surprise there). The 2001 Police Monitor recorded that 80,000 bikes get stolen every year in Amsterdam. But recent research suggests it could be as high as 150,000. Statistically, the riskiest place to park your bike is outside your own home. Otherwise, theft is common at places where there are a lot of bicycles together, like at train stations, and most get stolen during the day. Bike racks and large lock-ups which are supervised are the safest option. The floating fietsenstalling (bicycle park) behind Amsterdam Centraal Station, decorated with cartoons from local artists, is a thing of beauty. Professional thieves are the main culprits but often specialise in one type of lock, so using two locks (from different manufacturers) is recommended. If you do chain your bike to a lamp post or bridge in a prohibited area, be aware that the official bike removers have chainsaws and work very fast. It's a long 'schlep' (tedious journey) to the bike pound to pick it up (see www.afac.amsterdam.nl), and there's a fine. To improve your chances of being reunited with your bike if it does get stolen, get your bike engraved with a unique number which is logged in a database. This is a free service and the engraving teams are out every week (see www.fietsendiefstal.nl).

Bicycle locker

Police

There are 5,800 police (Politie) officers in the Amsterdam-Amstelland region, which is roughly one police officer for every 170 inhabitants. Current Dutch policing policy is pro-active with a visible presence at criminal 'hot-spots' and a low tolerance approach to disturbances in public spaces. Police patrol on foot, bicycle, motorbike, horseback and when there has been some kind of incident arrive by car or van (white with blue and orange). Crime prevention is a significant part of police work and teams are assisted nationally by 4,000 uniformed 'town watchers' on patrol who help to stop anti-social behaviour and 2,000 volunteers who have the same training as regular police officers.

Alongside 25 regional police forces is the KLPD National Police Services Agency (4,500 people) which includes traffic police, railway police, water police, aviation police, mounted police and police dogs, the national criminal intelligence service and the Royal and Diplomatic Protection Service (DKDB). There is a military force (comparable to the Italian Carabinieri) that deals with national security. The Royal Military Constabulary (Koninklijke Marechaussee) has a significant team based at Schiphol Airport where there is a complete criminal justice complex that can handle 2,800 cases a year. 128 cells accommodate up to 222 people including aliens ordered to leave the Netherlands.

Standard issue for every police officer are a 9mm service pistol, a short baton, pepper spray and handcuffs. Bullet proof vests are also increasingly used. Amsterdam police officers have seen it all, so don't feel embarrassed about approaching one. They will be in uniform (white shirts with blue epaulettes, blue trousers, and black jacket) and they will be carrying ID so ask to see it. See www.politie.nl for more information.

Fake Policemen

Amsterdam police ask visitors to be on the alert for fake policemen operating in groups of two or three, who ask tourists to hand over banknotes and credit cards for 'checking' in case they are counterfeit (or some such tale). Sometimes they ask for PIN codes. After the 'check' it appears everything has been returned, but of course, it hasn't. Ask for identification – real policemen carry cards (never shiny badges); never hand over money or credit cards. If in doubt you can call the police line on 0900 8844.

Lost & Stolen Property

Lost and found objects can be dropped off at a police station, and are sent to the lost and found bureau (Bureau Gevonden Voorwerpen) once a day. This is located at 18, Stephensonstraat (Watergraafsmeer), and the telephone number is 020 559 30 05. If it is your passport that goes missing, contact your embassy straight away. You will need to get a police report before starting the replacement procedure.

Tourist Information

The VVV (Vereniging voor Vreemdelingenverkeer) is the organisation for visitors and tourists in the Netherlands and they have outposts all over the country (www.vvv.amsterdam.nl). In Amsterdam, there are two offices at Centraal Station, one at Leidseplein (see the website above for location maps) and one at the airport. There are a wide range of brochures, maps and guides for sale and the VVV can also (for a fee) book hotel accommodation. You can sometimes get a good deal if you do this because hotels submit a daily rate each morning that fluctuates wildly depending on individual hotel occupancy. The ANWB (the Dutch Automobile Association) are a very useful source of (mostly Dutch) guides and maps for cyclists and car users, with some useful route-planning and distance calculators. The city website (www.amsterdam.nl), its English version and international brand (www.iamsterdam.nl), and www.amsterdamtourist.com all provide masses of information and tips for visitors and residents. In addition to these 'official' sources, there are innumerable directories and web-based guides about the city, catering for every type of visitor.

Tourist Information			
VVV Centraal Station	Stationsplein Perron 2B 15	Centrum	020 551 25 25
VVV Leidesestraat	Leidseplein 1	Canal Belt (Grachtengordel)	020 551 25 25
VVV Stationsplein	Stationsplein 10	Centrum	020 551 25 25

Amsterdam Tourist Info Abroad

Internationally, the National Board of Tourism and Convention manages 'the destination brand Holland' (www.holland.com) and has offices in Beijing, Brussels, Cologne, London, Madrid, Milan, New York, Paris, Stockholm and Tokyo, and representative offices in Gliwice (Poland), Los Angeles, New Delhi, Seoul, Taipei and Toronto. If you want to explore Amsterdam (or other regions of the country) their website is an extremely useful starting point, with separate sites designed for visitors of different nationalities.

Places to Stay

Amsterdam has almost 350 hotels and 18,000 rooms, providing accommodation for every taste and budget. There are currently a dozen five star, 38 four star, 79 three star, 67 two star and 53 one star hotels. There are lots of other types of accommodation as well, such as campsites, hostels, B&Bs, apartments and houseboats. Business visitors and tourists are equally important for many hotels. Room rates (which are dependent on hotel occupancy) fluctuate wildly, even in high season. You should be able to negotiate a great rate on a Sunday, but some hotels are adopting a weekend three-night minimum stay. A 5% city tax may or may not be included in the price and breakfast is often extra. Many of Amsterdam's most stylish venues are (of course) by the water, ranging from elegant canal houses and mansions to floating houseboats.

Hotels

Other options **Main Hotels** p.28, **Weekend Break Hotels** p.170

Outside Amsterdam

Accommodation is no less varied in the rest of the country with castles, windmills, farms, sailing ships and lighthouses to choose from. Check out the tourist board's website www.holland.com, and the 'luxury' and 'explore' sections, or for some Dutch sources, try www.weekenddesk.com and the English version www.weekendhotel.nl

Amsterdam's hotels are mainly clustered around the centre, canals, museum area and Vondelpark. The Dutch Hotel Classification system (www.hotelsterren.nl) awards stars on a points-based system according to services and facilities available. There are no extra points for staff charm or architectural loveliness and the hotel's star rating doesn't provide an exact indicator. In a one-star hotel (the minimum rating for anything called a hotel), there'll be a basin, soap and a communal bathroom for every 10 rooms. In a two-star 'functionally equipped and middle range hotel', drinks are available and half the rooms will be en-suite and have a colour television. With three stars ('a comfortably equipped middle-range hotel'), rooms should be at least 17 square metres, there'll be information on recreational possibilities, cots are available, and there'll be an internet connection. With four stars (a 'very comfortably equipped first class hotel'), room service is available. You get a minibar and more space (a 22 square metre room). You can lock up your valuables and there will be some extra bodycare products or a sauna. In a five-star hotel ('luxurious... equipped to a high quality'), room service will be 24 hours. You'll have a restaurant, 26 square metres of room and the hotel will have at least two suites. Slippers and bathrobes are included.

The Amstel InterContinental (p.28) tops the deluxe price league in Amsterdam at €595-€4,000 a night, but there are four-star venues which deliberately don't want to be five-star, because it deters business and conference bookers. There are also some utterly charming venues with fewer stars. In the centre, canal-side hotels are situated in (one or several) 17th and 18th century residences. Elegant, cosy, full of art and antiques, these can be wonderful places to stay. Rooms vary in size, but veer towards the snug rather than spacious. The Dylan Hotel (p.28) has long been a benchmark for boutique hotels, but the last few years have seen more entrants into Amsterdam's hip list. New hotels for 2007 include the five-star Amrâth (p.29) which is housed in the 19th century Scheeepvarthuis (Shipping Office) and at the other end of the scale, Amsterdam's first budget designer hotel, the Qbic (p.30), which is located in the financial district (and development zone) of Amsterdam South.

Hotels

Five Star	Phone	Website	Map
Amstel InterContinental Amsterdam	020 622 60 60	www.amsterdam.intercontinental.com	p.394 A4 6
Amsterdam Marriott Hotel	020 607 55 55	www.marriotthotels.com	p.392 B3 7
Bilderberg Garden Hotel	020 570 56 00	www.bilderberg.nl	p.384 A2 8
Grand Hotel Amrâth Amsterdam	020 552 00 00	www.amrathamsterdam.com	p.390 A4 9
Hilton Amsterdam	020 710 60 60	www.hilton.com	p.383 F2 10
Hotel de l'Europe	020 531 17 77	www.leurope.nl	p.393 E2 11
Hotel Okura Amsterdam	020 678 71 11	www.okura.nl	p.384 C2 12
Hotel Pulitzer	020 523 52 35	www.pulitzer.nl	p.388 C4 13

Hotels

Five Star	Phone	Website	Map	
Lloyd Hotel & Cultural Embassy	020 561 36 36	www.lloydhotel.com	p.382 A2	14
NH Barbizon Palace	020 556 45 64	www.nh-hotels.com	p.389 F3	15
NH Grand Hotel Krasnapolsky	020 554 91 11	www.nh-hotels.nl	p.389 E4	16
The College Hotel	020 571 15 11	www.thecollegehotel.nl	p.384 B1	17
The Dylan	020 530 20 10	www.dylanamsterdam.com	p.392 C1	18
The Grand Amsterdam	020 555 31 11	www.thegrand.nl	p.393 E1	19
Four Star				
Ambassade Hotel	020 555 02 22	www.ambassade-hotel.nl	p.392 C1	20
Banks Mansion	020 420 00 55	www.banksmansion.com	p.392 E3	21
Bilderberg Hotel Jan Luyken	020 573 07 30	www.bilderberg.nl/hotels/janluyken	p.392 B4	22
Crowne Plaza Amsterdam City Centre	020 620 05 00	www.crowneplaza.com	p.389 E3	23
Die Port van Cleve	020 624 64 29	www.dieportvancleve.nl	p.389 D4	24
Dikker & Thijs Fenice Hotel	020 620 12 12	www.dtfh.nl	p.392 C3	25
Eden Rembrandt Square Hotel	020 890 47 47	www.edenhotelgroup.com	p.393 F2	26
Golden Tulip Amsterdam Art	020 410 96 70	www.westcordhotels.nl	p.373 F3	27
Hotel Amsterdam De Roode Leeuw	020 555 06 66	www.hotelamsterdam.nl	p.389 E4	28
Hotel Artemis	020 718 90 00	www.artemisamsterdam.com	p.382 A3	29
Hotel Estherea	020 624 51 46	www.estherea.nl	p.393 D1	30
Hotel Roemer ▶ p.45	020 589 08 00	www.hotelroemer.nl	p.392 A4	31
Hotel Toren	020 622 65 32	www.hoteltoren.nl	p.388 C3	32
Hotel Toro Amsterdam	020 6737 22 3	www.hoteltoro.nl	p.383 E1	33
Mövenpick Hotel Amsterdam	020 519 12 00	www.moevenpick-amsterdam.com	p.391 E3	34
NH Amsterdam Centre	020 685 13 51	www.nh-hotels.com	p.392 B3	35
NH Doelen	020 554 06 00	www.nh-hotels.com	p.393 E2	36
Radisson SAS Hotel Amsterdam	020 623 12 31	www.radissonsas.com	p.393 F1	37
Sofitel Amsterdam	020 627 58 00	www.accorhotels.com	p.389 E3	38
The American Hotel	020 556 30 00	www.amsterdamamerican.com	p.392 B3	39
The Gresham Memphis Hotel	020 673 31 41	www.memphishotel.nl	p.383 F1	40
Victoria Hotel	020 623 42 55	www.parkplazaamsterdam.com	p.389 F3	41
Three Star				
Botel	020 626 42 47	www.amstelbotel.nl	p.392 B3	42
Canal House Hotel	020 622 51 82	www.canalhouse.nl	p.388 C3	43
Hotel Arena	020 850 24 00	www.thehotelarena.com	p.395 D4	44
Hotel de Filosoof	020 683 30 13	www.hoteldefilosoof.nl	p.379 F4	45
Hotel Piet Hein	020 662 15 26	wwww.hotelpiethein.nl	p.392 A4	46
Hotel Savoy	020 644 74 45	www.hampshirehotels.nl/savoy	p.384 B2	47
Hotel Weichmann	020 626 63 32	www.hotelweichmann.nl	p.392 B1	48
NL Hotel Amsterdam	020 689 00 30	www.nl-hotel.com	p.393 E3	49
Qbic WTC Amsterdam	04 3321 11 11	www.qbichotels.com	p.384 A3	50
Seven One Seven ▶ p.31	020 427 07 17	www.717hotel.nl	p.392 C3	51
't Hotel	020 422 27 41	www.thotel.nl	p.388 C3	52
Two Star				
Bellington	020 671 64 78	www.hotel-bellington.com	p.392 B4	53
Hotel Belga	020 624 90 80	www.hotelbelga.nl	p.388 C4	54
Hotel Brouwer	020 624 63 58	www.hotelbrouwer.nl	p.389 D3	55
Hotel Chic and Basic Amsterdam	020 522 23 45	www.hotelnewamsterdam.nl	p.389 E2	56
Hotel Museumzicht	020 671 29 54	www.hotelmuseumzicht.nl	p.392 C4	57
Hotel Rembrandt	020 627 27 14	www.hotelrembrandt.nl	p.394 B2	58
Hotel V	020 662 32 33	www.hotelv.nl	p.385 D2	59
Hotel Weber	020 627 23 27	www.hotelweber.nl	p.392 B3	60
Seven Bridges	020 623 13 29	www.sevenbridgeshotel.nl	p.393 E3	61
One Star				
Bicycle Hotel	020 679 34 52	www.bicyclehotel.com	p.384 C1	62
Hotel van Onna	020 626 58 01	www.hotelvanonna.nl	p.388 B4	63

Main Hotels

Ambassade Hotel

Herengracht 341
Canal Belt (Grachtengordel)
Map p.392 C1 20

020 555 02 22 | *www.ambassade-hotel.nl*
A haven of opulent elegance located in 10 17th century canal houses. It's very popular with literary types who leave their signed editions in the hotel's beautiful library. In many of the 59 rooms, there is original art from the CoBrA movement and a particularly luxurious treat (Koan Float) further down the Herengracht.

Amstel InterContinental Amsterdam

Professor Tulpplein 1
Oud Zuid
Map p.394 A4 6

020 622 60 60 | *www.amsterdam.intercontinental.com*
Amsterdam's grandest and most luxurious hotel since it opened in 1867, this building has a stately presence overlooking the Amstel, and has been the location for many royal dinner dances. The hotel offers 79 rooms and suites, a swimming pool and health club, and has 180 staff, together with wonderful terraces for enjoying a brasserie lunch or drink before dinner at Michelin-starred restaurant La Rive.

The College Hotel

Roelof Hartstraat 1
Oud Zuid
Map p.384 B2 17

020 571 15 11 | *www.thecollegehotel.nl*
A training hotel set in a 19th century school building, with an award-winning interior designed by FG Stijl group (the same group that completed The Dylan refurbishment). There are 40 individualistic rooms and suites, various salons for drinks, and a stylish courtyard. A selection of modern Dutch specialities can be found on the menu.

The Dylan

Keizersgracht 384
Canal Belt (Grachtengordel)
Map p.392 C1 18

020 530 20 10 | *www.dylanamsterdam.com*
Enjoy the theatrical grandeur in one of the world's first boutique hotels, housed in 17th century surroundings. All 41 rooms and suites were individually styled by Anouska Hempel (who opened the hotel as Blakes in 1999) with public areas recently redesigned by FG Stijl. There's an equally dramatic garden courtyard for alfresco dining.

The Grand Amsterdam

Oudezijds Voorburgwal 197
Centrum
Map p.389 F4 19

020 555 31 11 | *www.thegrand.nl*
This former convent, Admiralty HQ and city hall has numerous historical associations, including being where Queen Beatrix was married. The feel is of a grand country house with 138 rooms, 35 suites, 16 apartments, and a delightful terrace and garden for taking tea. The brasserie-style 'Cafe Roux' displays Karel Appel's mural *Inquisitive Children*, a work of art which offended the Dutch burghers.

Grand Hotel Amrâth Amsterdam

Prins Hendrikkade 108
Centrum
Map p.390 A4 **9**

020 552 00 00 | *www.amrathamsterdam.com*
Amsterdam's latest five-star grand is located in the refurbished Scheepvaarthuis, the 20th century Amsterdamse School building across from the IJ, that once housed six shipping companies. The dark, dramatic interior is monumental in scale, with numerous decorative features, stained glass, a wood-panelled (but sadly out-of-bounds) paternoster lift, and 163 (huge) rooms and suites.

Hilton Amsterdam

Apollolaan 138
Oud Zuid
Map p.383 F2 **10**

020 710 60 60 | *www.hilton.com*
This is the top destination in the residential/business district part of town where many expats live, and the location for John and Yoko's 1969 'bed-in'. An attractive marina and garden are available for enjoying a drink. Five-star comfort in 271 rooms. And, of course, there is the John and Yoko Suite.

Hotel Okura Amsterdam

Ferdinand Bolstraat 333
De Pijp
Map p.384 B2 **12**

020 678 71 11 | *www.okura.nl*
There are 301 deluxe rooms and suites in this five-star tower within walking distance of Amsterdam RAI congress and exhibition centre. A health club and pool, Japanese sauna, massage, and the luxurious rooms and suites affirm its status. The French restaurant Ciel Bleu (p.315) and Japanese restaurant Yamazato (p.325) both have Michelin stars.

Hotel Pulitzer

Prinsengracht 315-331
Canal Belt (Grachtengordel)
Map p.388 C4 **13**

020 523 52 35 | *www.pulitzer.nl*
A five-star hotel made from 25 17th and 18th century houses with a peaceful, private garden. At the end of the garden is a little church, making the Pulitzer a popular wedding reception destination. It owns a classic canal boat (The Tourist) and during the Grachtenfestival (canal music festival) the performance stage is a pontoon right outside the hotel.

Hotel Roemer ▶ p.45

Roemer Visscherstraat 8-10
Oud Zuid
Map p.392 A4 **31**

020 589 08 00 | *www.hotelroemer.nl*
One of a pair of boutique hotels situated in the Oud Zuid near the park, this really comes into its own in the summer. There are chic interiors, rain showers and great outside spaces; the designer terrace and peaceful lawns are available to non-residents as well as hotel guests. A conference room is available in the garden.

Oostelijke Handelskade 34
Zeeburg
Map p.380 A2 14

Lloyd Hotel & Cultural Embassy

020 561 36 36 | *www.lloydhotel.com*
Choose from one to five-star accommodation in this 1920s building in the eastern docklands, renovated by Rotterdam architects MVRDV. There are 117 individually designed rooms styled by leading Dutch designers, with custom furniture and extraordinary bathrooms. It has several levels of gallery space and cultural happenings on Mondays (Lloydtime). Definitely not your average designer hotel.

Piet Heinkade 11
Zeeburg
Map p.391 E3 34

Mövenpick Hotel Amsterdam

020 519 12 00 | *www.moevenpick-amsterdam.com*
This is the top location in the eastern docklands for the business-oriented Mövenpick. It has stunning views over the IJ and spacious, stylish, contemporary design in 408 rooms, suites and public spaces. The dining room has a great view – be amazed (while eating breakfast) at the size of cruise ships docking at the swoopy-roofed Passenger Terminal building right next door.

Dam Square
Centrum
Map p.389 E4 16

NH Grand Hotel Krasnapolsky

020 554 91 11 | *www.nh-hotels.nl*
Amsterdam's biggest city centre hotel is located smack on Dam Square. There's non-stop bustle with extensive conference activity, and a total of 468 rooms and apartments. Architectural highlights include the 'Winter Garden' (originally an indoor tropical garden but now a stunning breakfast room), and belle epoque restaurant Reflet. This is a top spot for shoppers to stay.

WTC Amsterdam Strawinskylaan 241
Buitenveldert
Map p.384 A3 50

Qbic WTC Amsterdam

04 321 11 11 | *www.qbichotels.com*
Stay somewhere cheap and chic in Amsterdam's financial district, with a room (from €39) at the Qbic. Each 'cubi' is a practical configuration that includes a bed and Philippe Starck-designed bathroom elements, communication technology (internet access etc), and a mood changer for adjusting lighting to Mellow Yellow, Red Romance or Deep Purple Love.

Prinsengracht 717
Canal Belt (Grachtengordel)
Map p.392 C3 51

Seven One Seven

▶ p.31

020 427 07 17 | *www.717hotel.nl*
A sumptuous and elegant 'home far away from home' created in a unique canal-side house. There are eight luxurious suites decorated with a comfortable mix of antiques, artworks and deep, squashy sofas. In the winter, enjoy afternoon tea by a roaring fire, or in the summer, breakfast on the terrace.

Hotel Apartments

If you find hotels anonymous and would like more space, more privacy, or simply your own front door key, there are lots of studios and apartments. They can provide a more homely base for families on holiday and are often cheaper and friendlier than hotels for those on short-term work contracts. There is a diverse range of accommodation from serviced hotel apartments to studios on the main canals. Rental periods vary, but anything under three nights is unlikely. The apartments will be fully furnished and are usually converted from residential properties, so do bear in mind that many Amsterdam houses are tall and narrow, with precipitous staircases (and no elevator).

Houseboats

For something very different, and very Amsterdam, there are a few companies offering accommodation on houseboats. Check out the websites (in the table below) for Houseboat & Apartment Rentals and Frederic Rentabike Houseboats.

Hotel Apartments

86 sous	Canal Belt (Grachtengordel)	06 29 035956	www.86sous.nl
Amsterdam Canal Apartments	Canal Belt (Grachtengordel)	020 471 02 72	www.amsterdamcanalapartments.com
Amsterdam House	Centrum	020 626 25 77	www.amsterdamhouse.com
Apartel	Centrum	020 320 06 00	www.apartel.nl
Breaks & Butlers	Canal Belt (Grachtengordel)	020 638 99 44	www.breaksandbutlers.nl
Captain's Place	Centrum	020 419 81 19	www.meesvof.nl
City Mundo	Centrum	020 470 57 05	www.citymundo.com
De Windketel	Westerpark	na	www.windketel.nl
Frederic Rentabike Houseboats	Canal Belt (Grachtengordel)	020 624 55 09	www.frederic.nl
Houseboat & Apartment Rentals	Centrum	06 34 160580	www.houseboatrentals.nl
Ideaal II	Centrum	020 419 72 55	www.houseboats.nl
Lute	Amstelveen	020 472 24 62	www.lute.com
Old Harbour Apartments	Oost	na	www.oldharbour.nl
Prinsenhuis Design Apartments	Canal Belt (Grachtengordel)	020 521 06 10	www.prinsenhuis.nl

Bed & Breakfasts

Bed and breakfast in Amsterdam (logie en ontbijt or L&O) is not necessarily the cheapest accommodation, since the more stylish options cost the same as (or even more than) some hotels. Facilities range from the more basic (but spotlessly clean) functional bedrooms with shared bathrooms and serve-yourself breakfasts, to luxurious ensuite facilities and designer furnishings housed in Golden Age mansions. Most importantly, they offer a wide variety of accommodation and provide additional options in areas of the city not smothered in hotels. B&B portal www.bedandbreakfast.nl lists over 100, including those (rather confusingly) that don't include the breakfast element. City Mundo (www.citymundo.com) is another source of cheaper digs and www.find-an-amsterdam-bed-and-breakfast.nl gives a useful selection with innkeeper recommendations.

Bed & Breakfasts

Amsterdam Central B&B	Oudebrugsteeg 6-II	06 24 457593	www.amsterdamcentralbedandbreakfast.nl
B&B on Board	Prinsengracht 1027	06 27 408188	www.bedandbreakfastonboard.nl
Blaine's B&B	Rijnsburgstraat 24 III	06 28 771289	www.blainesamsterdam.com
Cake under my Pillow	Eerste Jacob van Campenstraat 66	020 751 09 36	www.cakeundermypillow.com
Fusion Suites	Roemer Visscherstraat 40	020 618 46 42	www.fusionsuites.com
Kamer 01	3e Weteringdwarsstraat 44	020 625 66 27	www.kamer01.nl
Marcel van Woerkom	Leidsestraat 87	020 622 98 34	www.marcelamsterdam.com
Op de Gracht	Prinsengracht 826	020 626 19 37	www.opdegracht.nl
Stay With Steel	Staalstraat 32	na	www.staywithsteel.com

Hostels

The cheapest accommodation option if not the quietest. A bed in a six to eight person dorm in the Christian Jordaan Shelter is only €16 a night, with breakfast included. There is a wide range of options around town: in the centre, Red Light District and also by the park, where the StayOkay is the best venue for families or those who would like to get some sleep. Private, ensuite accommodation is available at hostels, though most accommodation is in dorms of four to 10 beds (with shared showers) and lockers for storing backpacks securely. Some have specific age rules (only under 40s, no stag parties, no children under 5). The website www.hostelamsterdam.com includes recent reviews and www.hostels-amsterdam.nl has some some helpful info.

Budget Accommodation

High quality budget accomodation is hard to find in any city, especially one as popular as Amsterdam. Location, for many visitors, is key. Within the canal ring, the Hotel van Onna (*) on the Bloemgracht and the Hotel Brouwer (**) on the Singel offer good value for money (under €50) in top locations. Seven Bridges (**) on the Reguliersgracht and Hotel Wiechman (***) on the Prinsengracht are slightly more expensive but friendly hotels in top spots. Hotel Belga (**) on the Hartenstraat is right in the Nine Streets for shopping fiends, and you can't get closer to culture than the Hotel Museumzicht (**) which is opposite the Rijksmuseum. For families, the Stayokay Hostel (see below) in the Vondelpark is beautifully situated.

Hostels					
The Bulldog Hotel	Centrum	020 627 16 12	www.bulldoghotel.com	p.389 F4	64
The Flying Pig Hostels	Centrum	020 421 05 83	www.flyingpig.nl	p.389 E3	65
Hans Brinker Budget Hotel	Canal Belt (Grachtengordel)	020 638 20 60	www.hans-brinker.com	p.393 D3	66
The Shelter City	Centrum	020 625 32 30	www.shelter.nl	p.389 F4	67
The Shelter Jordaan	Jordaan	020 624 47 17	www.shelter.nl	p.388 A4	68
Stayokay Amsterdam	Centrum (Stadsdoelen)	020 639 10 35	www.stayokay.com	p.393 F1	69
	Oud Zuid (Vondelpark)	020 589 89 96	www.stayokay.com	p.392 B4	70

Campsites

Other options **Camping** p.192

There are several campsites with good facilities within easy reach of Amsterdam. At Amsterdamse Bos, for example, there's a launderette, shop, playground and communal kitchen, and the metro taking you to Amsterdam Centraal is just a few minutes' walk away. You don't actually have to bring a tent of course, you can rent a cabin, but checking-in facilities may not be 24 hours a day. If you decide to camp you will be not only be doing something very Dutch (as camping is hugely popular in the Netherlands) but you'll get a real feel for the landscape. Some campsites are more suitable for older visitors and families than others. In terms of price, a four-person tent at Zeeburg will cost €5 plus €5 per person, and a one to two person cabin is €40. It's 80 cents to have a shower and 20 cents for warm water.

Campsites					
Camping Amsterdamse Bos	Amstelveen	020 641 68 68	www.campingamsterdamsebos.nl	p.367 E4	71
Camping de Badhoeve	Amsterdam Noord	020 490 42 83	www.campingdebadhoeve.nl	p.367 F2	72
Camping Vliegenbos	Amsterdam Noord	020 636 88 55	www.vliegenbos.com	p.392 F1	73
Camping Zeeburg	Zeeburg	020 694 44 30	www.campingzeeburg.nl	p.381 D4	74

Getting Around

Other options **Exploring** p.132, **Transportation** p.125

Amsterdam is a compact city with excellent transport links. Schiphol airport (the fourth biggest in Europe) serves more than 200 destinations in 83 countries. There's an extensive motorway and railway network connecting the city nationally and internationally, and Amsterdam port is a significant destination for passenger liners and cargo ships. Public transport by bus, tram, metro or ferry is very reliable, and compared to London, for example, very cheap.

The best way of getting around the city centre is by bicycle (fiets). There are 400 kilometres of bike paths and a third of Amsterdam's residents use a bike to get to work. Motorists will probably find Amsterdam less convenient to negotiate. The queue for a residents' permit is measured in years, parking is expensive (there is no free parking in the centre), and drivers have to be on constant alert for bicycles and straying tourists. The ring road surrounding all of Amsterdam is the A10 and the last eastern stretch was completed in 1990. Traffic on the ring (in fact, traffic everywhere) can be heavy. The IJ tunnel (there are also tunnels east and west in the ring) connects the city centre with Amsterdam Noord. Water-based transport includes free ferries for passengers and their cycles that chug across the IJ all day, canal bikes and tour boats aimed at tourists, and water taxis for a more refined experience. Taxis can be ordered by phone or picked up at a rank and there are also taxi-cycles for an environmentally friendly trip. The North/South metro line is the city's biggest ongoing transport project made possible by developments in tunnel-digging technology, and is due to be completed in 2012. Travel information for Amsterdam, including the location of car parks, can be found on www.bereikbaaramsterdam.nl. The municipal transport authority for Amsterdam is the GVB (www.gvb.nl) and their useful website includes info about tickets and transport routes to popular destinations (e.g. museums) using trams, the metro and buses. For national travel, www.9292ov.nl (Dutch) provides a door-to-door itinerary using all transport methods including ferries. The ticket system that operates on buses, trams and the metro is the 'strippenkart'. It's a card with multiple strips that you stamp in a yellow on-board machine (it may also be stamped by a tram/bus conductor) according to the distance of the journey (one zone = two strips). This system is due to be replaced in January 2009 by the ov-chipkaart (PT Smart Card), a reloadable smart card system that will be used on all public transport. It is currently available just for the metro.

Air

There are direct flights connecting Amsterdam's Schiphol Airport with all the major cities of the world. Regional Dutch airports include Eindhoven, Rotterdam and Lelystad (owned by the Schiphol group), Groningen, Maastricht and Enschede. The national airline is KLM, which merged with Air France in 2004 to form the largest airline group in the world, servicing 250 destinations. Over 100 airlines fly into Schiphol. There are 27 budget airlines that fly to the Netherlands from the UK and Ireland, countries in eastern and western Europe and Scandinavia.

Schiphol Airport

Schiphol (www.schiphol.nl) is a sleek, highly efficient airport used by 40 million passengers each year. It is only 14 km from the city centre and easily reachable by train (15 minutes from Amsterdam Centraal Station), car or taxi. There is one terminal building, and commercial activity is centred around Schiphol Plaza. Business services include numerous airline lounges on the upper floor, a business point in the arrivals hall where chauffeurs can wait, a communication centre in departure lounges one and two, and wi-fi in several locations (and roaming), although you have to pay for this facility. Holland Casino has two mini outposts, there's an annexe of the Rijksmuseum (ten Dutch masters in the gallery plus a shop), children can be amused in special play areas between gates E and F, and there is a multi-denominational meditation room. Shopping is popular all over Schiphol Plaza and on the first floor there are duty free shops. You can even get married here, with four arrangements from the speedy Say Yes and Go (onto the plane) to Ready for Take Off. First aid and emergency medical care is available 24 hours a day, seven days a week and is provided by Airport Medical Services: 020 649 25 66 (above departure hall two). If you lose something at Schiphol the number is 0900 0141. There is a €5 administration fee for each item when you pick it up.

Airport Services

Self-service check-in is available for 25 airlines in departure halls one, two and three. Accelerated border passage is available to Privium members who, instead of going through passport control, are identified via iris recognition technology. Security checks are lengthy in most international airports, and as a major hub, Schiphol is no exception. The airport advises leaving extra time before your flight.

Airport Transport

The most efficient way of travelling to central Amsterdam from Schiphol is by train, and you can buy tickets at the yellow machines in the baggage hall and plaza (€3.60). Trains run right through the night (one an hour) and it takes approximately 15 minutes from the airport to Centraal Station, 30 minutes to Den Haag, and an hour to Rotterdam. Taxis are available at the rank outside and the fare to the city centre is approximately €40. Some hotels provide their own free shuttle bus from the airport, otherwise there is the Conexxion hotel shuttle bus (038 339 47 41) that services 100 hotels. It runs between 06:00 and 21:00 and the fee is €11 one way. And you don't have to be staying at a hotel to use it!

Airlines

Air France	020 654 57 20	www.airfrance.com
BMI	020 346 92 11	www.flybmi.com
British Airways	020 346 95 59	www.ba.com
Cathay Pacific	020 653 20 10	www.cathaypacific.com
Continental Airlines	020 346 93 81	www.continental.com
easyJet	0900 265 8022	www.easyjet.com
KLM	020 474 77 47	www.klm.nl
Lufthansa	0900 123 4777	www.lufthansa.com
Singapore Airlines	020 548 88 88	www.singaporeair.com
Transavia	0900 0737	www.transavia.com

Boat

There are no shortage of water-borne transport options for sauntering around Amsterdam's 165 canals and other waterways. Tourist-focused transport includes 110 glass-topped canal boats (a tour is the number one attraction) and boats can be picked up at several places in the city including Rokin and Centraal Station. Buy the tickets from the individual boat company kiosks. For more on these tours, see Boat Tours on p.165.

At weekends, there are canal-hoppers (small electric boats) with two routes: one covering the city centre to the Westerpark and the other heading east to KNSM and Borneo islands. Prices vary. Canal bikes (pedalos) are the most energetic option and can be picked up and dropped off at various places including Anne Frank Huis and the Rijksmuseum.

Across the IJ, ferries are essential transport for north Amsterdammers. It takes about a minute on the (free) ferries that leave regularly all day from De Ruyterkade behind Centraal Station. There are six routes in total going west to NDSM, straight across to Buiksloterweg and IJplein, and east to Java Island (which is charged at one euro a trip). Two routes run from Houthaven, to the west of Centraal Station, to NDSM and Distelweg in Amsterdam North. There's a high-speed jetfoil (run by regional operator Connexxion – see www.connexxion.nl for timetables and prices) that goes to IJmuiden. If you fancy your own boat, a permit costs around €15.50 per square metre of boat, but it can be moored pretty much anywhere (see www.binnenwaterbeheer.nl for more details).

Amsterdam's tram system

Bus

There's an extensive network of buses, which is particularly important for areas trams don't reach, such as the suburbs and Amsterdam North. Amsterdam is currently testing hydrogen (fuel cell) buses. When the trams stop, the night buses take over, with 12 routes servicing all parts of the greater Amsterdam area. You need a different 'strippenkart', available in vending machines at metro stations. A full fare 15 strip strippenkart is €6.80 (a one-zone journey is two strips) and a 45 strip version is €20.10. You can check timetables on www.gvb.nl. There are also regional Connexxion buses bringing commuters and visitors to the capital. If you have the time for leisurely gablespotting, hop on the 'Opstapper', a little bus that trundles all the way round the Prinsengracht from Centraal Station to the Stopera. Just stick out your arm, and it will stop (very Harry Potter), and then tell the driver when you want to get off.

Limos
If you fancy being flash you can hire a stretch limousine complete with natty chauffeur from Van Delden Limousines. (020 684 84 08, www.vandelden limousines.nl). Rates start at €125 per hour.

Car

Other options **Transportation** p.125

Cars in the Netherlands drive on the right hand side of the road. Vehicles coming from the right have priority and so do trams, buses pulling out, and cyclists. Take care when going around roundabouts, as you have to give way to cars entering from the right (unless they have a traffic sign telling them to wait). Seatbelts are compulsory, in both the front and back. Children under 12 must not travel in the front without a restraint. Unless otherwise marked, the speed limit is 50kph in the city, 80kph on other roads and 100/120kph on motorways.

Mobile phone use is illegal for drivers, even when you are stationary at a red light. Parking is problematic in Amsterdam with approximately 100,000 (expensive) metered parking places on the streets and ten multi-storey car parks (including seven in the centre). Meter hours are 09:00 to 24:00 Monday to Saturday and 12:00 to 24:00 on Sundays. Parking is zoned and costs €4.40 an hour in the centre, and less outside the centre. Failure to observe parking procedures will result in your car being clamped or towed away by the 'Dienst Stadstoezicht'. Amsterdam operates a park and ride scheme at four locations, with free public transport by tram, train, metro or bus into the city centre. At two of these (Sloterdijk and the Olympic stadium) you can borrow bicycles (see www.bereikbaaramsterdam.nl for more driving and parking information). Most Dutch drivers are members of the ANWB (www.anwb.nl) which provides breakdown cover *wegenwacht* at home and abroad, and fuel discounts. If you only need a car now and then, car share scheme Green Wheels (www.greenwheels.com) is an option to consider. The distinctive red and green cars are parked in bays all over the city and you can book one over the phone or internet for a minimum hire of one hour. It's a great system, but you do need a Dutch driving licence.

Hiring a Car

There is no shortage of places to hire a car, with international agencies well represented. Check Autoverhuur in the Yellow Pages (Gouden Gids) to get local quotes. It is worth shopping around as prices vary quite a lot. In terms of car models to hire, there is a complete range, from small city cars for urban driving to something more deluxe. Prices (at the small, neat end) start from around €30-€35 a day and rise to €100-plus for a seven-seater.

Car Rental Agencies

Adams Rent-a-Car	020 685 01 11	www.adamsrentacar.nl
Alamo	020 616 24 66	www.alamo.n
Avis Car Rental Amsterdam	020 683 60 61	www.avis.nl
Budget	020 612 60 66	www.budget.nl
Europcar	020 683 21 23	www.europcar.nl
Hertz	020 612 24 41	www.hertz.nl
National	0800 6284 6625	www.nationalcar-rental.com/page-nl

Harry Potter? (Prime Minister)

Much has been made of the resemblance between Dutch Prime Minister Jan Peter Balkenende and the literary and film character Harry Potter. Balkenende has borne the nickname with good humour, even posing with a 'spot the difference' photo at the 2002 general election.

Cycling

Other options **Bicycles** (Shopping, p.257), **Cycling** (Activities, p.199)

There are 750,000 people in Amsterdam and 600,000 bikes. Many residents have more than one bike – a posh one for touring, and one that inevitably gets bashed up a bit with daily use. How long your bike lasts will depend on whether it is stored outside or in: not just because of the chances of it being stolen (high) but because all that rain inevitably takes its toll. The city is keen to support cyclists, with anti-theft prevention (free registration of bikes) and more supervised lockups (there are now 25 – see www.locker.amsterdam.nl). Bike theft is pretty endemic so buy the best lock(s) you can.

Cyclists may look pretty casual in terms of their road use but the police are getting hotter on fines – cycling without lights at night or shooting through red lights (€50, thanks) are particularly common. Helmets are not common (or indeed lycra outfits or other urban cycling kit) but don't let that stop you choosing to wear one or putting one on your children (23,000 children a year are involved in accidents on bikes). The wide cycling paths and the fact that these are well observed is a critical safety issue, compared with cycling in other capital cities (London's cycle paths, where they exist, can measure just 18 inches). In accidents, it is inevitably car drivers who lose out in court.

If you want to hire a bike, see the table below. There are also numerous shops which do repairs and sell bikes, often second-hand. (For more on everything to do with

Bike Rental Companies

Beer Bike	na	06 51 850805	www.partyfiets.nl
Bike City	Jordaan	020 626 37 21	www.bikecity.nl
Conference Bike	Centrum	020 624 91 98	www.conferencebike.com
DutchBike Amsterdam	Oud West	020 683 33 69	www.dutchbikeamsterdam.nl
Frederic Rent-a-Bike	Jordaan	020 624 55 09	www.frederic.nl
Henry WorkCycles	Centrum	020 689 78 79	www.workcycles.com
Holland Rent-a-Bike Beursstalling	Centrum	020 622 32 07	www.zoekned.nl
MacBike	Centrum	020 620 09 85	www.macbike.nl
Mike's Bike Tours	Centrum	020 622 79 70	www.mikesbikeamsterdam.com
Orangebike	Centrum	020 528 99 88	www.orangebike.nl
Rent-a-Bike	Centrum	020 625 50 29	www.bikes.nl
Star Bikes Rental	Centrum	020 330 81 32	www.starbikesrental.com

bikes, see Bicycles on p.257 in Shopping). To help trace your bike if it goes missing, it is wise to get it engraved. For information on this see www.fietsendiefstal.nl. If your bike does get stolen (and it has been engraved) contact www.afac.amsterdam.nl. On a lighter note, the 20 seater Beer Bike and the Conference Bike (where you sit in a circle) are fun activities for groups visiting Amsterdam – contact details in the table on the previous page.

Taxi

Taxi Companies	
BBF SchipholTaxi	0900 900 6666
De Meerlanden Taxi Service	020 647 59 94
TCA Taxi Centrale Amsterdam	020 777 77 77

Using a taxi in Amsterdam is an ordered affair, with designated areas for taxi stands (including Centraal Station, Rembrandtplein and Leidseplein, where there are always plenty waiting) and regulations about where they might stop. You can also hail one in the street (bear in mind there are several no stopping zones) or book one over the phone or internet. Every taxi must have blue number plates, a price list visible from both inside and outside the taxi and a taxi-driver's pass on the dashboard. If they have an exemption card – meaning they have passed an exam testing their city knowledge – they can use the tram and bus lanes. You are not legally obliged to take the first taxi in the queue (although if you don't, it will not be a popular action). Taxis are metered and most include sat-nav systems so you will be able to get to your destination (somehow), but local knowledge varies considerably. The maximum basic price is €5.12 (for four or more passengers, €8.33), plus maximum price per kilometre of €1.94 (for four or more passengers, €2.23). A taxi from the airport to a central Amsterdam hotel is around €40 and from Centraal Station to Museumplein, around €13.

Train

Trains are reliable and frequent in the Netherlands and reach areas not served directly by trams or buses. Many people commute between the cities of the Randstad (they may live in Amsterdam and work in Den Haag, or the other way round). The website www.ns.nl gives info in English on routes and tickets. Train fares are reasonable and can be made even cheaper with a korting (discount) card which is well worth having. For €55 a year there's a 40% discount on all off-peak rail travel, not just for you but up to three other people with whom you are travelling. Train connections with other stations in the city, such as Amsterdam RAI exhibition centre and business zone Sloterdijk, are extremely frequent. Many trains are double deckers. You must buy (or stamp) a ticket before you board – ticket inspection is frequent and so are fines. Amsterdam has three international rail links: Belgium and France to the south, and Germany to the east.

Squeaky Wheels

Amsterdam is currently testing a lubrication system for rails in order to control the noise from the trams squeaking as they negotiate bends.

Tram

Amsterdam has 16 tramlines and 232 city trams which travel over 80 kilometres of track. Routes and timetables can be seen on the www.gvb.nl website, and you pay on the tram or stamp your strippenkart. Many trams start their journeys from Centraal Station. Unlike the bus and metro, trams travel through the main shopping streets. Recent expansion includes tram 26 to the eastern IJburg archipelago, which began operating in 2005. Newer-style trams can accommodate wheelchairs and baby buggies. Once stamped, your ticket can be used for up to one hour on other trams or alternative modes of transport. Trams stop around midnight, when night buses come into operation.

Metro

Amsterdam's metro is relatively modern and designed to connect outlying suburbs to the city, rather than transporting passengers around it. Despite this it can be extremely fast for particular journeys (Centraal Station to the Stopera, for example) and prices are reasonable. Routes and timetables can be found on the www.gvb.nl site. The first line began operations in 1977 and there are now three lines: Eastern (lines 53 and 54), Amstelveen (line 51) and Ring (line 50) with a fourth – the North/South line (line 52) – due to open in 2013. This 9.5 km route will connect Amsterdam North with Zuidas and Zuid/WTC area and there will be eight stations en route, some in the city centre. The metro is the first form of public transport to use the OV-chipkaart, a public transport smart card that will be universally used by 1 January 2009. These can be bought in either an anonymous or personalised version (you fill in an application form) from stations or the GVB offices.

Chocolate Bollards

The little posts with three crosses that line canals and pavements are known as Amsterdammertjes. At confectioner JG Beune (Haarlemmerdijk 156) you can buy chocolate versions.

Walking

Amsterdam is a compact city and easy to navigate as a pedestrian, but watch out for the bikes and bollards. It helps (some locals believe) to walk in the 'right' direction (ie. as you drive or cycle on the right hand side of the road, walk on the right hand pavement) and absolutely no wandering into the fietspad (bicycle lane), otherwise you may encounter 'whispering death' (as bikes are sometimes known in Holland). At all times watch your step – this is dog poop city. The instruction 'Hond in de gutter' (sometimes accompanied by a drawing of a dog doing its business) is often ignored by dog and owner.

Amsterdam RAI Metro station

Train

Metro

Money

Paying with a bank debit card and pin number is almost more popular than paying with cash in Amsterdam. Most machines just take Dutch bank cards. Credit cards (Visa, Mastercard, American Express and Diners Club) are widely acceptable in hotels and restaurants but not in supermarkets, bars or cafes. There's a pre-pay function on most (Dutch) debit cards where you can 'load' the card from a 'Chipknip' terminal then use the card as cash. Bills are generally paid by bank transfer either by using the yellow 'acceptgiro' attached to most bills or when paying online. Internet banking is very widely used.

Exchange Rates

Foreign Currency (FC)	1 Unit FC = €x	€1 = xFC
Australia	0.62	1.59
Bahrain	1.94	0.51
Bangladesh	0.01	93.77
Brazil	0.38	2.59
Canada	0.69	1.44
China	0.09	10.33
Cyprus	1.69	0.59
Denmark	0.13	7.44
Hong Kong	0.09	10.63
India	0.02	55
Japan	0.01	166.57
Malaysia	0.21	4.69
New Zealand	0.57	1.74
Norway	0.13	7.93
Oman	0.52	0.52
Pakistan	0.01	85.81
Philippines	0.02	62.37
Russia	0.03	34.95
Singapore	0.48	2.07
South Africa	0.11	9.5
Sri Lanka	0.01	151.5
Sweden	0.11	9.2
Switzerland	0.6	1.65
Thailand	0.02	43.2
UAE	0.2	4.99
United Kingdom	1.48	0.67
United States	0.73	1.36

Local Currency

The Netherlands has had the euro since 2002. Paper money denominations are 5, 10, 20, 50, 100, 200 and 500 euros (€). You may have problems using anything bigger than a €50 note. The coins, which have an image of Queen Beatrix on the back, come in denominations of €2, €1, 50 cents, 20 cents, 10 cents and 5 cents. The one and two cent coins remain legal tender but are no longer issued. Sums are rounded to the nearest five cents.

ABN AMRO Building

Banks

Banks are generally open Tuesday to Friday, 09:00 to 16:00, and on Mondays from 13:00, although some may open longer hours than this. Leading banks include ABN AMRO, ING and Rabobank which are among the top 20 banks in the world. Postbank is the cheapest place to convert currency. ABN AMRO have a specific expat service (www.yourexpatbank.com). See the Bank Accounts section in Residents for more information on p.71.

ATMs

ATMs, (geldautomaten) are widely available throughout Amsterdam and can dispense money in several languages 24 hours a day. They accept a wide range of credit cards and bank passes and can increasingly be found inside supermarkets.

Money Exchanges

Hotels and banks generally don't offer very good rates, but there are plenty of small exchanges in the tourist areas of Amsterdam. However, rates vary so always shop around for a good deal. The post office can be the best place to change money, and the GWK Travelex offices are also worth trying. There are 11 GWK offices around Amsterdam, including Schiphol Airport, Centraal Station and Leidseplein – for details of their locations see www.travelex.com or call 0900 0566. One thing to look out for: a 'no commission' sign may simply be cover for a poor exchange rate.

Need Some Direction?

The ***Explorer Mini Maps*** pack a whole city into your pocket and once unfolded are excellent navigational tools for exploring. Not only are they handy in size, with detailed information on the sights and sounds of the city, but also their fabulously affordable price mean they won't make a dent in your holiday fund. Wherever your travels take you, from Europe to the Middle East and beyond, grab a mini map and you'll never have to ask for directions again.

Chipknip

In response to shop owners being irritated at ATM cards being used for small purchases, the banks introduced the Chipknip, a reloadable card or chip that transfers funds immediately. The chipknip is not pin protected so should only be used for small amounts. Ask your local bank for more info.

Credit Cards

All major credit cards are accepted, but not everywhere. Hotels, restaurants, department stores, transport centres and major tourist attractions (and their shops) present no problem, but credit cards are less likely to be accepted in supermarkets (yes, no credit cards in Albert Heijn), and smaller bars and shops, as the businesses themselves pay credit card companies for the privilege of using their services. You may have to pay a few cents more if you want to use the card for transactions under a certain threshold, for example. If your card is lost or stolen, contact the card issuer immediately (see the In Emergency section p.20).

Tipping

Tax and service charges are always included in bills for everything from restaurant meals to taxis, but tipping is common, even if it is only a little extra 'rounded up' to the nearest appropriate unit. For a cup of coffee for example, it's cents, but 10% or so is pretty common for lunch and dinner. Waiting staff are paid a living wage, so this is a question of manners rather than anything else, but it is nice to show appreciation of good service, and it's best to leave the tip in cash. Although not precisely a tip, you will often pay to use the toilet in department stores and large cafes (20-50 cents). There are no public facilities in Amsterdam. If your taxi driver has been extra helpful, you may like to add another 10% or so.

Bridge to the Passenger Terminal

Newspapers & Magazines

There are seven Dutch daily newspapers, four of which are from the same publisher, PCM: *NRC Handelsblad* (liberal, intellectual, has a more populist tabloid feel), *de Volkskrant* (liberal, intellectual, younger), *Trouw* (more coverage of faith issues – where Ayaan Hirsi Ali published) and *AD Algemeen Dagblad* (extended regional coverage). In terms of circulation, the conservative *De Telegraaf* has the biggest (658,000). The specialist Dutch business newspaper is *Het Financieele Dagblad*. The local Amsterdam newspaper is *Het Parool* (circulation 89,000). Significant news magazines include *De Groene Amsterdammer*, *Vrij Nederland*, *Elsevier* and *HP/Tijd*, and the Dutch free press includes *Metro*, *Sp!ts* and quality newcomers *DAG* and *De Pers* which both launched in 2007.

Local free English language press includes award-winning cultural paper *Amsterdam Weekly* and the more news oriented *The Times*, available in Amsterdam, Den Haag (The Hague) and once a month in Rotterdam. Arts and cultural monthly *Roundabout* and quarterly *The Expat Journal* are available at bookshops or on subscription.

English language and international publications are widely available in Amsterdam. International newspapers can be bought on the day of publication from newsagents and bookshops and are included in the reading tables of grand cafes such as Café De Jaren (p.334), Café Luxembourg and Averna. Freight costs being an issue, newspapers will be more expensive than at 'home' and some international editions have fewer pages. Spui is Amsterdam's literary centre and Athenaeum Boekhandel is one of the best places to buy. There are also a few mobile newspaper stands (in the summer) around Dam Square.

Books

Other options **Books** (Shopping p.258), **Websites** p.43

As well as this residents' guide, Explorer Publishing also produce the *Amsterdam Mini Explorer* – a guidebook that is small in size, but jam-packed full of all the information visitors need to know on Amsterdam. In terms of other tourist publications, every guide book publisher does Amsterdam, with particularly good offerings from Time Out, Dorling Kindersley, Lonely Planet and Rodney Bolt's *Cadogan Guide*. Amsterdam Tourist Board publications tend to be of the hotel listings variety, but the VVV and ANWB have many helpful and comprehensive guides (at varied prices) for the regions, and Dutch publisher Mo'Media (www.momedia) provides some more design-conscious titles that are packed with ideas.

For expat life, there's a veritable library of books and you can check out many of these at www.hollandbooks.nl. The neat little *Amsterdam op zak* is a fantastically useful diary and directory that no resident should be without. It has heaps of contact information on hotels, cafes, restaurants and some thoughtful maps. For a dazzling look at the Netherlands in the Golden Age, *The Embarrassment of Riches* by Simon Schama is a racy read. Anna Pavord's (*The Tulip*) and Deborah Moggach's *Tulip Fever* give fascinating insights into the infamous bloom. *The Coffee Trader* by David Liss is set in the 17th century Jewish community. Amsterdam's Red Light District features in John Irving's *Widow for One Year*, and the city is familiar territory for policeman *Van der Valk* in the novels by Nicholas Freeling (very 1970s). Irvine Walsh featured Amsterdam (where he lived for a while) in *The Acid House*. *Amsterdam* by Geert Mak is a classic, as is *Amsterdam*

Athenaeum book shop

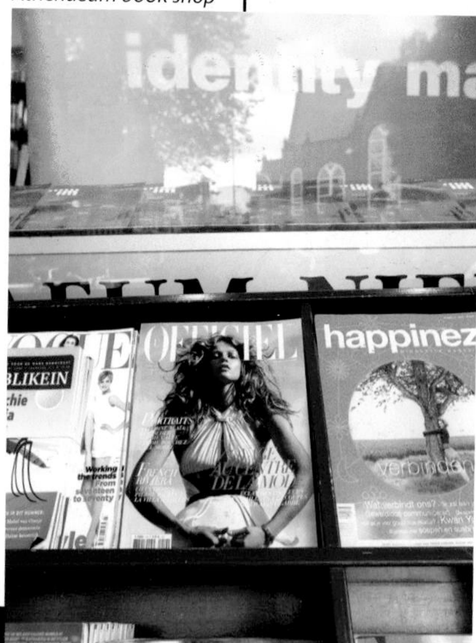

by Ian McEwan. If you can pick it up in a second-hand shop, William Hoffman's *Queen Juliana: The Story of the Richest Woman in the World* (she wasn't) is a highly-coloured account of the origins of the Dutch royal family. *Brilliant Orange: the Neurotic Genius of Dutch Football* is a great read even if you know nothing about Cruyff or that 'total football' stuff. For food guides, look no further than *Delicious Amsterdam* by Johannes van Dam and learn Dutch fast in order to tackle his fat food bible *DeDikkeVanDam*. Cultural guides include *The Low Skies* by Hans van der Horst, *Dealing with the Dutch* by KIT trainer Jacob Vossestein, *The Undutchables* by Colin White and *The Dutch I Presume* by Martijn de Rooi. *Ethnic Amsterdam* by Patricia Gosling and Fitzroy Nation is part history and part directory. *Murder in Amsterdam: The Death of Theo van Gogh and the Limits of Tolerance* by Ian Buruma and *Infidel* by Ayaan Hirsi Ali tackle recent events. Every smaller explorer should have a copy of *The Cow That Fell in the Canal* by Phyllis Krasilovsky in which Hendrika the cow takes an unexpected trip to the cheese market.

Walki-Talki

Take a guided tour of Amsterdam at your leisure after visiting www.walki-talki.com, where you can download a commentary on the key attractions onto your iPod or mp3 player.

Websites

There's no shortage of info on the web about Amsterdam or expat life, with forums where you can ask questions and learn from people who have been there before. Expatica.com is perhaps the best known – covering news, jobs and expat info, and they organise an annual expat exhibition every year, and also regular speed-dating and social events. If you want to explore the rest of the Netherlands, the official tourist board site is comprehensive and reliable, and more fun things to do can be found on www.leukedingendoen.nl.

Blogs & Pods

Amsterdam is full of travellers writing for their blogs back home. Urban site www.gridskipper.com has some nice tags and www.24oranges.nl and www.dunglish.nl highlight quirky events and linguistic mishaps. Amsterdam podcasts include englishbreakfast.podbean.com, or try www.podfeed.net or www.podcastdirectory.org. For daily musings (and a lot of knitting) there's the blog of *Amsterdam Explorer* writer Andy: www.andyinamsterdam.com.

Websites	
Business	
www.afio.amsterdam.nl	Amsterdam foreign investment site
www.hollandtrade.com	Business and investment site
City Information	
www.amsterdam.info.nl	Useful info and local links
www.amsterdamtourist.com	Non-official Amsterdam site with loads of links
www.amsterdamtourist.nl	Another official tourist board site
www.channels.nl	Virtual Amsterdam tours
www.coolcapitals.nl	Groovy site with cute graphics
www.holland.com	Tourist board site
www.iamsterdam.com	The official Amsterdam site
www.maps.google.nl	Detailed online maps of the Netherlands
www.os.amsterdam.nl	City statistics
www.simplyamsterdam.nl	Useful info and local links
Culture	
www.aub.nl	Amsterdam Uitburo for tickets
www.bimhuis.nl	Contemporary music on the IJ
www.bma.amsterdam.nl	Bureau Monuments & Archeology
www.concertgebouw.nl	Probably the best concert hall in the world
www.dno.nl	The Netherlands Opera
www.entoen.nu	The Dutch historical canon
www.evenementkalendar.nl	Event calendar
www.filmladder.nl	Film and movie theatre directory

Websites

Culture	
www.leukedingendoen.nl	Fab ideas for fun things to do
www.weekendhotel.nl	Cool hotels and B&Bs
Directories	
www.goudengids.nl	Yellow Pages
www.ikhebje.nl	Useful telephony links with images
www.overheid.nl	Central access point to government information sources
www.startpagina.nl	An extraordinarily useful multiple website link thing
Living & Working	
www.access.nl	Support organisation
www.amsterdamlive.nl	Webcams in town
www.elynx.nl	Need a cleaner or babysitter or want to find a sports club?
www.expatica.com	Biggest expat news & info site
www.expatriates.com	Expat support
www.funda.nl	Dutch property site
www.gayamsterdam.com	Amsterdam gay portal
www.globaloutpostservices.nl	Shell's expat support site
www.hetweer.nl	The weather
www.iens.nl	Restaurant reviews
www.kit.nl	Cultural training
www.koninklijkhuis.nl	The House of Oranje-Nassau (Dutch royal family)
www.mva.nl	Amsterdam estate agents property site
www.specialbite.nl	Restaurant portal
www.xpatpages.com	Need a cleaner? A babysitter? Man with a van?
News & Media	
www.amsterdamweekly.nl	Weekly cultural newspaper
www.anp.nl	Dutch press agency
www.at5.nl	Local TV. Mayor Job Cohen chats on Fridays
www.dutchnews.nl	Dutch news in English
www.englishbreakfast.nl	English language talk show 99.4FM
www.nieuwsuitamsterdam.nl	Alternative news
www.nisnews.nl	Longest running (subscription) news service
www.rnw.nl	Radio Netherlands
www.rush.nl	Website and quarterly glossy
www.wordsinhere.com	Largest international collective of writers in the Netherlands.
Nightlife	
www.amsterdamhotspots.nl	Eat, drink, lounge, smoke
www.cineac.nl	Hip nightspot
www.ilove11.nl	Great views from the Post Office Tower
www.lecool.com	Cool places in the capital
www.melkweg.nl	Premier music venue
www.panama.nl	Restaurant/nightclub/top Amsterdam hotspot
www.paradiso.nl	Top Amsterdam venue
www.partyscene.nl	Clubland
www.sugarfactory.nl	Top arty venue
www.supperclub.nl	Restaurant, club, cruise
www.the-mansion.nl	Door policy: Over 21, Dressed to Go Out
www.underwateramsterdam.nl	Amsterdam tips from one who knows
Online Shopping	
www.albert.nl	Albert Heijn online
www.susie.nl	Shop, shop, shop all over the Netherlands
www.thuisbezorgd.nl	Online takeaway for different cuisines

Amsterdam Boat Show

Amsterdam RAI
Buitenveldert
March

www.hiswa.nl

400 exhibitors and 77,000 visitors come to the annual boat show at the Amsterdam RAI exhibition centre. The 2008 dates are 4-9 March. Hundreds of boats, yachts and boat accessories. The average visitor age is 46, according to the organisers.

Miracle of Amsterdam

In 1345 a dying man in a house on the Kalverstraat vomited up the host (bread) after his last communion. As was custom, what he had brought up was thrown on the fire but the next morning the wafer was discovered undamaged. It developed healing powers, and on two occasions, miraculously made its own way back to the man's house on the Kalverstraat.

Stille Omgang

Throughout the city
March

www.stille-omgang.nl

A silent procession of Catholics commemorating the 1345 Miracle of Amsterdam. Takes place between midnight and 04:00 over a Saturday and Sunday and takes the Heiligeweg (Holy Way) pilgrims have used for centuries. It begins and ends at Spui, via Kalverstraat, Nieuwendijk, Warmoesstraat and Nes. Masses are said at local churches.

Amnesty International Film Festival

Various locations
March

773 36 21 | *www.amnesty.nl/filmfestival*

Always stimulating, this film festival brings together the finest films about issues relating to international human rights. Screenings are accompanied by a wide variety of discussions and debates. The festival's main venue is at De Balie on Leidseplein (020 553 51 51), and there are events at other theatres throughout the city as well as in Den Haag and Utrecht.

Amsterdam Fantastic Film Festival

Various locations
April

www.afff.nl

A cult annual institution with screenings of European and international thriller, cult, horror and science-fiction movies at the Filmmuseum Cinerama and the Melkweg. There's a marathon Night of Terror for nocturnal horror fans and the Silver Scream Awards for audience favourites.

National Museum Weekend

Throughout the city
April

551 29 00 | *www.museumweekend.nl*

A weekend when over 450 museums throughout the country open for free (or at least a reduced price). There are many special events at participating museums, and some get very crowded. Almost all of Amsterdam's museums take part; but be aware, it's such a popular weekend you may have to wait in line for entry to your favourite venue.

Queen's Day (Koninginnedag)

Throughout the city
30 April

www.koninginnedagamsterdam.nl

The big one! Though celebrations take place throughout the whole country, nowhere is wilder than Amsterdam. 1.5 million people gather to enjoy a chaotic and vibrant mix of street party, festival and flea market to celebrate the birthday of the monarch (actually, the monarch's mother, Queen Juliana). For one day only there is a 'free market' (vrijmarkt), enabling anyone to set up a stall and sell a stupendous variety of junk. Alongside this are parades, performers, oom pah pah bands, many stages offering some of the finest (Dutch) live music and DJs, and every manner of beer quaffing...which all provide a

Queen's Debris

All the unsold junk left on the street after Queen's Day does actually belong to the Queen, according to Dutch law, until the rubbish teams collect it.

Annual Events

Queen's Day

spectacle which must be seen to be believed. The party starts the night before (Koninginnenacht) with music and drinking. Orangeness is everywhere.

Throughout the city
May

Liberation Day

620 96 88 | *www.4en5mei.nl*

Commemorating the liberation of Holland from the yoke of its Nazi occupiers in 1945 as well as the end of the war with the Japanese, the Liberation Day celebrations take place all over the country. Amsterdam's Remembrance ceremony is centred at Dam Square and attended by thousands of the city's residents. Street parties and festivals in many of Amsterdam's parks add to the celebrations.

Various locations
May

Amsterdam Literary Festival

420 67 75 | *www.amsterdamliteraryfestival.com*

An annual book and writers international event which celebrates all that is literary in the English language always finds a great selection of events for the bookish – be they readers or writers. Filled with workshops for budding authors on how to write a bestseller, and talks by internationally renowned authors such as Kate Adie, David Mitchell and Sarah Waters, this festival is eagerly anticipated by many each year.

Amsterdam RAI
Buitenveldert
May

Art Amsterdam

www.artamsterdam.nl

Almost 18,000 visitors flock to Amsterdam RAI for a contemporary art event with work for sale from 125 galleries. An edgier version, Kunstvlaai, is held in the Westergasfabriek.

Various locations
May

National Windmill Day

www.molens.nl

On this open day 1000 windmills fly a blue pennant to show they are welcoming visitors. Many date back to the 17th and 18th centuries. Top 'molen' spotting at Kinderdijk and Zaanse Schans but this website shows many other locations.

Various locations
June

Amsterdam Roots Festival

531 81 81 | *www.amsterdamroots.nl*

A week of world music at venues such as Paradiso, Melkweg and De Balie, with some outside events at the Oosterpark. Having celebrated its 10th year in 2007, it usually attracts some 65,000 visitors. With music from Brazil, Africa, Latin America and Europe, the Amsterdam Roots Festival is a great crowd pleaser for the whole family.

Throughout the city
June

Holland Festival

788 21 12 | *www.hollandfestival.nl*

Internationally acclaimed month-long festival of opera, dance, music, film and art taking place in venues all over Amsterdam including the Muziekgebouw aan 't IJ, Muziektheater, Stadsschouwburg, Concertgebouw and Westergasfabriek. Serious culture (the 2007 theme was 'Oppression and Compassion') attracting big names and devoted international audiences.

Throughout the city
June

Open Garden Days

320 36 60 | *www.grachtenmusea.nl*

For only one weekend each year, in the third weekend of June, it is possible to discover the beautiful gardens that lie behind the stately facades of Amsterdam's canal-side homes. Around 30 gardening enthusiasts' private gardens are open for public perusal. Stroll through the stunning 17th, 18th and 19th century gardens at your own pace or collect the canal boat providing free transportation between each golden garden. Along with the garden tours, there are other activities such as music recitals, wine tastings, and canal house tours.

Various locations
July

Amsterdam Fashion Week

www.amsterdamfashionweek.com

Winter and Spring events for lowland fashionistas. The 'off-schedule inspiration program' is called Laundry Days and 100 venues participate in fashion shows, launches, events, parties and a shop window contest.

Spaarnwoude
July

Dance Valley

www.dancevalley.nl

The biggest and most popular open-air dance event held in the Netherlands. Regularly attracts 45,000 visitors to Spaarnwoude recreation area outside Amsterdam. Dancing and camping really do go together.

Various locations
July

Julidans

www.julidans.com

Two weeks of international contemporary dance in venues all over Amsterdam, including free performances at the Vondelpark Openlucht Theatre. Showcases emerging talent and dance combined with text, visual arts and film.

North Amsterdam
July

Over 't IJ Festival

www.overhetij.nl

The world is a stage but so is an old factory, shipping container, boat or Russian submarine in this eclectic cultural event in North Amsterdam. Cross the water for a dozen theatrical events, including a family programme for kids as well.

Bijlmerpark
July/August

Kwakoe Festival

www.kwakoe.nl

'It's Kwakoe time feel Kwakoe'. The Netherlands' biggest multi-cultural festival takes place every weekend in July and August. The celebration focuses on the Surinam, Antillean and African communities and cultures, with live music, dance, performances, parties, literature, sport and food. This festival, more than any other, brings Amsterdammers (who rarely leave the city centre) to the south-east Amsterdam Zuidoost neighbourhood.

Who is Kwakoe?

The name Kwakoe comes from former Dutch colony Suriname – a former slave drop during the Golden Age where the African tradition was to name males after the day on which they were born. When slavery was abolished on 1 July 1863, a statue of a freed slave was erected in commemoration. And since 1 July 1863 was a Wednesday, the statue was named Kwakoe.

Martin Luther Kingpark
Amstel
August

De Parade

www.deparade.nl

A unique travelling theatre festival with tents, fountains, a roundabout and world restaurants. Short high calibre shows (several times a night) in theatre, music, visual art, film, dance and entertainment. Performers drum up an audience with free acts in front of their stages as they did in the middle ages.

Throughout the city
August

Amsterdam Gay Pride

www.amsterdamgaypride.nl

If it walks like a duck and quacks like a duck... it's probably Gay Pride – at least if it's wearing a pink boa and dancing half-naked on a boat. One of the biggest gay and lesbian events in Europe, this event combines a party with a political message. As well as street parties and other events all weekend, the Saturday has an extravagant parade with 100 lavishly decorated boats on the Prinsengracht decked out in all their finery – this parade alone attracts 250,000 spectators each year. There are also activities centred around the Homomonument in the Jordaan. One of Amsterdam's very busiest weekends.

Various locations
August

Grachtenfestival

www.grachtenfestival.nl

The Prinsengracht concert is a truly magical event. The culmination of a nine-day classical festival, with performances taking place on a pontoon outside the Hotel Pulitzer with the audience (some 20,000) packed either side of the canal, on the bridge (with lovely twinkly lights), or sitting in loads of little boats pulled up alongside the pontoon. All kinds of musical events are on the bill, including a children's programme.

Various locations
August

Uitmarkt

020 621 13 11 | *www.uitmarkt.nl*

The Netherlands is a nation which takes pride in the variety of cultural activities produced in the country, and perhaps no city is as keen to embrace this artistic agenda as Amsterdam. The Uitmarkt is the weekend which marks the opening of the cultural season with three days to sample a taste of things to come. Previews of upcoming performances staged throughout the city on both indoor and outdoor stages, on land and on the canals (including the Dam, Nieuwmarket, Beursplein, Muziektheater and Theaterschool). Hundreds of free performances display the wide range of activities including dance, drama, opera, music, cabaret and theatre.

Jordaan
September

Jordaan Festival

www.jordaanfestival.nl

Singing has a long history in the brown cafes of the Jordaan where working-class heroes belt out sentimental ballads. Uber-crooner Johnny Jordaan is commemorated with a statue in the Elandsgraacht, but there'll be no shortage of modern day singalongers at this Jordaan knees-up.

Various locations
September

Open Monumentendag

020 422 21 18 | *www.openmonumentendag.nl*

On the second weekend of September thousands of historical and architecturally significant monuments and sites are open, free of charge, to the public as part of a European-wide Heritage Day. As in other cities, it includes architectural wonders of the 20th and 21st centuries as well, and the event is designed to encourage an interest in the preservation of buildings and sites of key national importance.

Throughout the city
September

Robodock

www.robodock.nl

A thrilling, unpredictable combination of theatre, drama, acrobatics, art, robots, fire and water. Performances take place in former docklands and wharves using recycled industrial materials. Large and small scale performances, live music and shows for a younger audience.

Through Amsterdam
October

Amsterdam Marathon

www.ingamsterdammarathon.nl

25,000 runners take the long way round Amsterdam. The route takes in the 1928 Olympic Stadium, nature reserves, Scheepvaart (Maritime) Museum, canals, Rijksmuseum and Vondelpark (twice). An elite field as well as enthusiastic amateurs take part: €57.50 to enter and you get a T-shirt.

Throughout the city
November

High Times Cannabis Cup

www.Cannabis.Cup

An annual event for marijuana aficionados. A judge's pass (€200) provides admission to all ceremonies, concerts and seminars. Oh, and three days of bus tours round Amsterdam's coffeeshops and the right to vote on the world's best cannabis too. And the T-shirt.

Throughout the city
November

Museumnacht

020 527 07 85 | www.n8.nl

One of the most popular and best attended festivals, when 40 or so of Amsterdam's museums open their doors to the public from 19:00 on Friday to 02:00 Saturday morning, with DJs, dance, music and food alongside the permanent eclectic collections. The passe-partout ticket (around €15 if you buy in advance) includes transport on buses, trams and museum boats. The Portuguese Synagogue lit by a thousand candles? Unforgettable.

Throughout the city
November/December

Sinterklaas Arrives!

www.sinterklaas.nl

From the middle of November until 'pakjesavonds' on 5 December, the Dutch go Sinterklaas mad. Chocolate letters, presents left in shoes and trillions of ginger biscuits (pepternoten), are all involved. At this big parade, Sint, as he is affectionately known, arrives from 'Spain' on a steam boat with his helper 'Zwarte Piet', his horse 'Amerigo' and a ton of other blacked-up Piets. Discussions about political correctness occur every year.

December

New Year's Eve

New Year is a particularly raucous affair in the Netherlands, involving stupendous quantities of fireworks and firecrackers, let off in scarily uncontrolled environments (like right in front of you).

December

Sinterklaas – Pakjesavonds (Presents Night!)

www.sinterklaas.nl

Dutch children get presents on 5 December rather than at Christmas, though lucky international children often get them on both occasions. Grown-ups also exchange presents accompanied by a pertinent poem. There are lots of internet Sinterklaas rhyme-generators to assist the poetically challenged.

Capoeira in Leidseplein

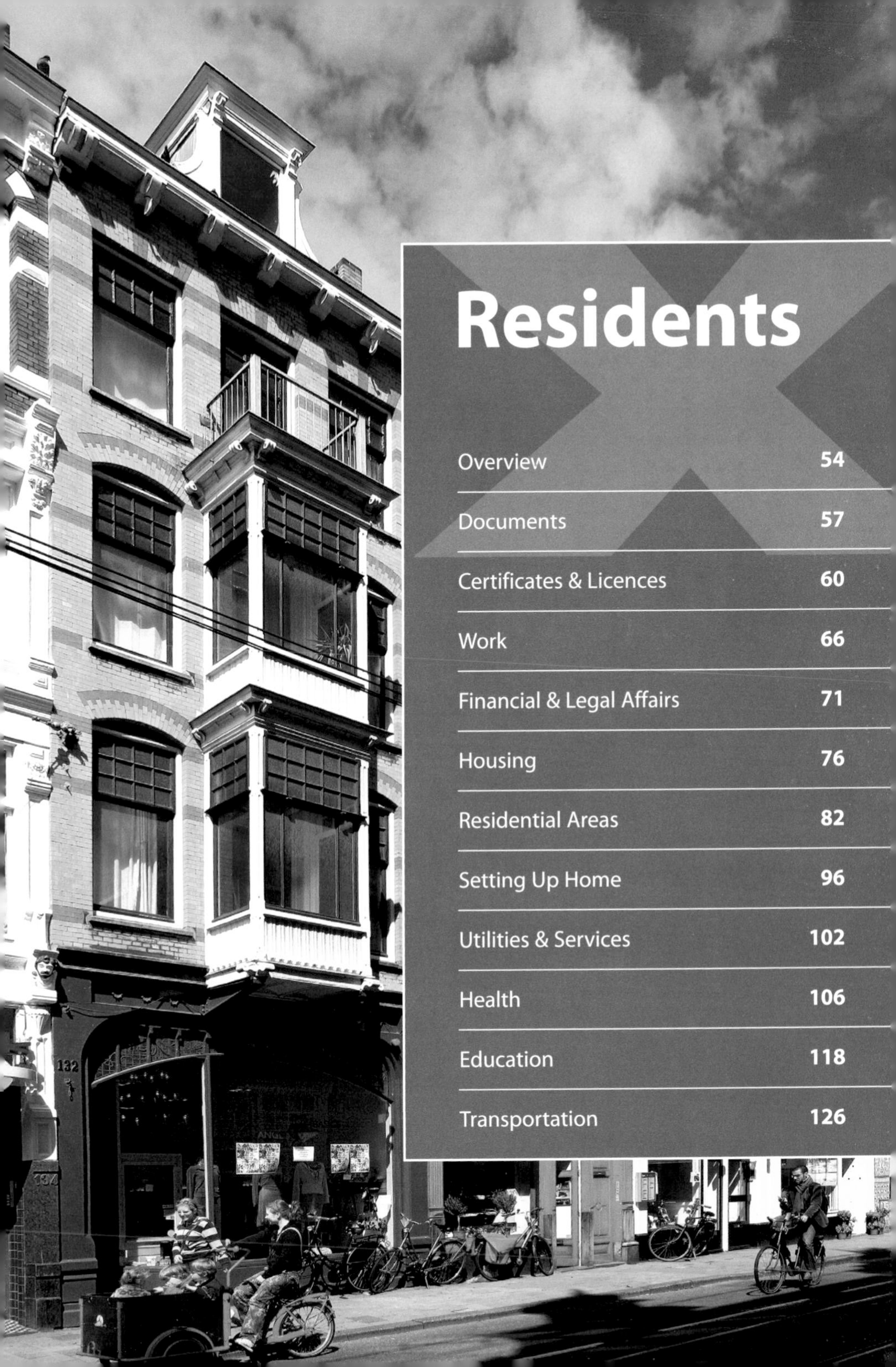

Residents

Overview

Famous in some circles and infamous in others, Amsterdam is well known to both the party crowd and the culture lover. Many visitors are struck by the beauty of the city and are surprised by how much it has to offer aside from coffeeshops and the Red Light District. It's an incredibly easy city to get around, with a great public transport system. Despite its big reputation it really is quite small. The no-nonsense attitude of the Dutch can be offputting and everyone has tales of the poor level of service in Amsterdam. Known for its culture of acceptance and tolerance, the Netherlands is a sought after destination. The Dutch economy is strong, and Amsterdam is a hotspot for those working in the creative and media industries. Many find Amsterdam crowded, but the Dutch attitude of 'keep yourself to yourself' does allay this feeling. The seasonal changes of the year are dramatic. Cold, wet and dark in winter, the city explodes in summer with people sitting on the romantic terraces along the tree-lined canals. Strict immigration regulations mean non-European Union nationals should begin the long process of applying for a visa in advance.

Get Your Bearings

A great way to get an understanding of the city when you first arrive is to take a cycle tour. You'll experience the key sights and sounds of Amsterdam as well as getting a commentary on its history and the major landmarks and attractions. For one recommended tour, see Mike's Bikes (p.164) for more details.

Considering Amsterdam

Urban Myth – 'Amsterdam Will Be Underwater By 2010'

The Netherlands is very aware of anything that may threaten the effectiveness of its impressive dams, and the water management board argues that statements like this are ridiculous and not to be taken seriously.

Amsterdam is a picturesque and lively small city with a huge amount of culture to explore. It's very easy to get around and most people love the fact they can cycle to work. Most locals speak fluent English and the cosmopolitan nature of the city makes it a very tempting destination. Aside from the booming creative industry there are also many large multinational companies in Amsterdam such as Phillips and HP (Hewlett Packard), as well as big banks like ABN AMRO and ING, all of whom employ many foreign nationals. There are a number of employment sites like www.xpatjobs.com/home.asp that will give you an idea of available employment opportunities. Living standards are high and the health and welfare systems are very strong. Finding a home can be difficult, expensive and time-consuming as space is limited in Amsterdam. The Netherlands' previously relaxed attitude towards immigration has changed a lot recently and the ongoing debate has caused obvious racial tensions. Restrictions and requirements for non-European Nationals wanting to live and work in Amsterdam have become much harsher. There are some schemes that exempt American and/or 'highly skilled migrants' from the work visa requirements but you will still need to obtain a residence visa (see p.57). In general though, if you are not a European Union national your employer will have to obtain a work visa on your behalf before you can begin to apply for your residence visa.

Before You Arrive

Moving to a new country can be incredibly stressful, but there are a few things you can do before you leave to make the transition as smooth as possible:

- **Documents** – check that all passport dates are valid for over a year to comply with visa requirements; have all the required documentation from your country of origin for your visa.
- **Property** – if you own your house you may want to consider selling (to finance your new home) or renting it out. If you decide to rent your house out make sure you

either have a reliable service to handle any problems while you're away, or a friend to check on the new tenants occasionally. Remember to cancel all utilities and tie up any waiting payments.

- **Packing** - you won't be able to bring your whole wardrobe with you when you leave so make sure you know which season you will be flying in to and pack accordingly.
- **Shipping** - if you're shipping your furniture try to do it as far in advance as you can; depending on where you are coming from it can take six to 12 weeks to arrive.
- **Finances** – contact your bank to see how they can help you accommodate your move. Check if you should close your pension plan. Make sure your taxes are in order and ensure all outstanding bills are taken care of.
- **Preparation** - before you leave you can prepare yourself for many aspects of your new life. You can research schools, housing services and jobs online. www.expatica.nl is a great site full of information on starting life in the Netherlands.

When You Arrive

When you finally reach Amsterdam it will seem like there are a million things to sort out; here's a shortlist of essentials to get you started:

- **Accommodation** – housing is expensive in Amsterdam but a good agent can help you find something quickly (see Real Estate Agents on p.77). Many apartments will be at least partly furnished and include utilities.
- **Communication** – most accommodation will not include phone or internet but that's very easy to arrange (see p.102). You may want to consider getting a mobile first if your initial housing is temporary.
- **Transport** – public transport in Amsterdam is fast, reliable and comprehensive. Try to familiarise yourself with it as soon as possible (see p.34). Amsterdam is small and very bike-friendly, so most people cycle everywhere. You will see bikes and bike shops all over and a good bike won't set you back much. Driving can be nerve-racking as you're competing with bikes, buses and trams; parking can be difficult and expensive.
- **Paperwork** – as soon as you have a fixed address you will need to register with the immigration department and start the process of obtaining your residency visa. Make sure you have all the documentation relevant to your status.
- **Meet the locals** – being in a new city can feel isolating so try and make friends as soon as possible. The internet is a great source of finding local expat communities. You can also join a gym or find out what activities in your area interest you.

Urban Myth – 'Amsterdam Is Dangerous And Full Of Junkies'

A major crackdown on criminal activity in Amsterdam has successfully seen off some of the seedier elements around town. Amsterdam has never been a city with a high violent crime rate and statistics show Amsterdam to be far safer than some US cities.

Essential Documents

Some documents you will need to obtain from your country of origin (especially if you are not a European national), so make sure you have these before you leave, as arranging this from afar can take a lot of time. Others you will have to organise once you arrive.

- Passport (valid for more than one year)
- Birth certificate
- Work permit
- Residency Permit
- Marriage or civil partnership certificate
- Proof of registration with the tax office
- Proof of employment (your employer will be asked for a reference for housing purposes)
- Proof of address (for getting a mobile, joining the library, or video store)

For non-EU nationals only:

- Legalised Birth Certificate
- Proof of sufficient funds
- Proof of health insurance coverage in the Netherlands
- 2 passport photos

Urban Myth – 'It's All Clogs, Windmills And Tulips'

Amsterdam is one of the most culturally exciting cities in the world, with over 40 museums, many more galleries, and a great live nightlife scene. Today it is one of the most innovative and creative cities in Europe.

When You Leave

Tying up loose ends is important, so when your time comes to leave Amsterdam don't forget to check up on the following:

- **Accommodation** – if you were renting make sure you give appropriate notice and have returned the space to the condition you found it in, otherwise you may forfeit your deposit. If you bought a home, make sure you have a good agent to handle everything for you (see p.77) if you won't be around for the sale. Cancel all utilities in your name and pay off any outstanding bills. (See Utilities & Services p.101).
- **Paperwork** – let your local city register know you are no longer living in the city, return your visa to the authorities, cancel all your local memberships and ensure that there will be no continuing automatic debits to your account from utilities, gym memberships and the like. You may also need to close or transfer your bank accounts. (See Bank Accounts on p.71).
- **Stuff** – You will have accumulated a lot of things while living in Amsterdam and now you'll have to decide whether to take them with you or sell them. If you choose to sell there are some great sites like www.marktplaats.nl, where you can get rid of everything from your old cushions to your new bike or car.

Rembrandtplein

Amsterdam World Trade Center

Koninklijk Paleis

Documents

The Netherlands is a bureaucratic country and proud of it. At times you may feel like you are drowning in red tape or losing valuable time waiting for documents to arrive. To ensure your visa applications run as smoothly as possible it is very important to know what documents you should have with you before you leave. If you are moving to the Netherlands with your company then your employer will help you with some parts of the process.

Entry Visa

If you are intending to come to Amsterdam to work then you will have to have applied for a work permit and a residence permit. Your employer will have to apply for the work permit on your behalf from the CWI (Centre for Work and Income) and should begin this process before you arrive. Make sure your passport is valid for longer than one year. Some foreign nationals will have to apply for a temporary entry permit - Machtiging to Voorlopig Verblijf (MVV) - before they leave their home country. If you do require an MVV your employer can apply on your behalf. Part of the application for the MVV requires that you take a Civic Integration exam before you leave your home country. You can apply for the exam with your local embassy, or on the site: http://inburgeringsformulier.minbuzamail.nl/civic/en/ or with your local embassy. Before you are eligible to take the exam you will have to pay €350 to the Ministry of Foreign Affairs.

Nationals from the EU, America, Australia, Canada, Iceland, Japan, Monaco, New Zealand, Switzerland, Liechtenstein and the Vatican City will not need to apply for an MVV. But you will have to report to the Foreign Police (Vreemdeling Politie) within three days of arriving. If your spouse, family or partner is going to join you then you will have to complete this application form: www.ind.nl/en/Images/form_ENG_M35A_tcm6-591.pdf. The fees involved are quite steep, with the initial cost of the spousal application being €830 and €188 for each accompanying family member. Two great sources of information are the Dutch Ministry of Foreign Affairs site (www.minbuza.nl/en/welcome/FAQsNL) and the Residence Wizard from Dutch Immigration (IND): www.ind.nl/EN/verblijfwijzer/ - forms and brochures are available in English, but the site itself is in Dutch.

Citizens from the European Union, Switzerland, Iceland, Norway, Liechtenstein and the Vatican City are only required to register with the Foreign Police and request a residence permit on arrival but they can begin working without this as long as they have registered with the tax office (Belastingdienst).

Visitors

If you have visitors coming from a country where the Netherlands requires them to obtain a holiday visa, before they leave you can help them out by supplying them with an invitation letter and a guarantor's declaration (if needed).

Holiday Visa

If are coming to the Netherlands for under three months, you will most likely not need to apply for a tourist or holiday visa. This type of visa (Schengen Visa or Visum Kort Verblijf) costs €60, but Americans, EU nationals, Australians and New Zealanders do not require one to enter the country. However, if you're from any other country you will need to download your visa application form from the IND site (www.ind.nl) or contact your local Dutch embassy for more information.

Residence Visa

If you are not an EU citizen you cannot apply for a residence visa (Verblijfsvergunning) for the Netherlands until you have a work permit. EU citizens do not have to apply for a work permit but should still obtain a residence card. The application for your residence visa begins with the Immigration and Naturalisation Service (IND). You will have to contact the IND to find out how to proceed with obtaining residency or extending an existing visa, or for information on how to become a Dutch citizen. The tool on their site is very helpful if you understand Dutch, and there are many forms available in Dutch and English (www.ind.nl/nl/index.asp). The Dutch Ministry of Foreign Affairs is also very informative (www.minbuza.nl/en/home). If you want to become a Dutch citizen you will have to have legally been a resident for five years and be willing to undergo inburgering (citizen education). You will also have to take an exam in Dutch to find out if you have made a good enough effort to understand and live in the Dutch culture.

Work Permit

The requirements for obtaining a residence visa vary. If you are an EU national; from Switzerland, Iceland, Norway, Liechtenstein or the Vatican City; or married to one of the aforementioned nationalities, you are automatically eligible for a residency visa and do not need a work permit to work. You must simply register with the foreign police on arrival and obtain a tax number from the Belastingdienst (tax office).

For other foreign nationals, obtaining the residence visa is dependent on whether or not you can obtain a work permit through an employer or are eligible for one of the other schemes like the Dutch American Friendship Treaty, the Highly Skilled Knowledge Migrant Scheme, Working Holiday Scheme, or if you are a student.

Studying In The Netherlands

In order to receive a residence permit to study in the Netherlands you will have to be enrolled on a full time course and fulfil all the requirements of the residence visa. For a comprehensive guide please see www.nuffic.net/immigration. And for more on studying in Amsterdam, see University & Higher Education on p.121.

Work Permit Through Employer

Your employer must apply for your work permit with the CWI (Centre for Work and Income). In order to do this they must be able to show that no one in the Netherlands or European Union is able to fulfil the position. Usually this means they have to have advertised for five weeks without finding a candidate. To fulfil the requirements for the work permit you must be between 18 and 45 years old. Once the work permit has been granted then you can proceed to file for residency with the Dutch immigration department (IND). If you fail to meet the requirements for residency (for example if you have a criminal record) then your work permit will be cancelled. When filing for a residence permit you must include the following: a €430 processing fee, an attested birth certificate (this means it must be stamped and signed by your local consulate), proof that you do not have tuberculosis, a signed declaration of background, a copy of your contract, a copy of your work permit or application, proof that you have health insurance in the Netherlands, proof of sufficient funds (usually €3000), and two passport photos. Once you have fulfilled these requirements you can submit your application and it can take anything from one to three months to process. As long as you have your work permit though, you can apply for a tax number and begin to work while waiting for your residence permit.

Dutch American Friendship Treaty

This is a special scheme for entrepreneurs. In order to be eligible you must be an American citizen under 60 years of age. Receiving a residence permit under the Dutch American Friendship Treaty means that you are free to live in the Netherlands and start your own company or represent American companies with interests in the Netherlands. You are not permitted to seek paid employment with another employer; if you wish to you will have to apply for a new work permit. When seeking to obtain a residence permit under this treaty you will have to include a comprehensive copy of your business permit. For a full outline check the IND Residence Wizard (www.ind.nl/EN/verblijfwijzer/). You will also have to pay the IND €433 to process your request. You will need valid documents like a passport and health insurance.

Highly Skilled Knowledge Migrant Scheme

This visa only applies to you if you are highly skilled in a specific area of the labour force; the burden of proof (and the majority of the paper work) is the responsibility of the employer. You will need a valid passport, health insurance that covers you in the Netherlands, a contract or declaration of employment from the employer, and be receiving a gross income of at least €46,451 or €34,130 if you're under 30. You may also need to undergo a tuberculosis test. Once this has been approved you can apply for the residence permit. Your employer should complete the paperwork but you will need to sign it. You will receive a sticker in your passport granting you the right to live, and most likely work, while you are waiting for the permit to be processed.

Working Holiday Scheme

You are only eligible for a working holiday visa if you are between the ages of 18 and 30 and are a citizen of Australia, Canada or New Zealand. If you are eligible for this visa then you will be able to live and work in the Netherlands for a period of 12 months. You can download the application form from the website of your local Dutch embassy. You will need to apply for your visa at least two weeks before your departure date. In your application you will have to include your passport, proof of medical insurance (the Netherlands has a deal with Medicare in Australia, check their website to find out details), a copy of your return air ticket, proof that you have at least €1900, (€3,800 if you do not have a return ticket), a copy of your passport signed by a Justice of the Peace who has confirmed your identity in your presence, a copy of another piece of photographic ID, two passport photos and a self - addressed envelope. You should also obtain an accredited birth certificate before you leave, as you will have to present this to the IND with your residence application. You will have 90 days to enter the Netherlands from the date of issue of the visa; if you need more time you will have to apply for your visa at the closest Dutch embassy to you while you are travelling. Check here for a full list of Dutch embassies: www.minbuza.nl. Once you arrive in Amsterdam you will have to register with the foreign police within three days. You will then have to apply for your residence permit at the town hall; they will charge you €30 and send your application to the IND for final approval. You will be given a sticker in your passport that will enable you to apply for a tax number at the tax office. You should do this as soon as possible. You will then need to return to the town hall for a temporary residence visa which will allow you to work legally while you await the permanent one from the IND, which can take months.

iAmsterdam Card

The iAmsterdam Card is a great deal for new residents of Amsterdam - it will really help you get your bearings in your new home. Over a period of 24, 48 or 72 hours, this pass gives free, or discounted admission to museums, city attractions, canal cruises, public transport and more. Visit www.iamsterdamcard.nl for more information.

Identification

Since January 2005 it is mandatory for everyone to carry valid proof of identity with them at all times. Acceptable identification is your residence permit (verblijfsvergunning), passport, Dutch or European ID card, or a driver's licence.

If you get caught without one of these you can face a fine of €50 or, if you're under 14 years old, €25.

Houseboats and canal tour

Driving Licence

Other options **Transportation** p.125

In the Netherlands you will have to be able to drive on the right side of the road, so be prepared if you're used to driving on the left. Rules for which licences are valid and how they can be exchanged in the Netherlands vary, so check carefully to ensure you don't get caught out. In the Netherlands you will incur high fines if you break any road rules. If you are not wearing your seatbelt you will be fined €75; penalties for driving under the influence of alcohol depend on how far over the limit you are (the limit is 0.5/ml) but you could get your licence suspended immediately. You must have your licence with you at all times - failure to show your licence incurs a fine of €50. If you are driving a vehicle not specified on your licence you will be fined €190. Similarly high fines apply to speeding as well, so be careful because there are cameras everywhere! See also Transportation p.73.

Exchanging Your Licence

If you are able to exchange your licence then you will have to go to your local municipal office and request and pay for a print out stating who you are and where you live (uittreksel bevolkingsregister) as well as a declaration of health form (eigen verklaring) and a form for the licence exchange. You then fill out the forms and send them with the uittreksel bevolkingsregister to the Centraal Bureau Rijvaardigheid (Central Road Aptitude Bureau). When they have processed your request, and if it's accepted, they will send you a 'certificate of fitness' or verklaring van geschiktheid (you won't need this if you are from an EU or EEA country and are exchanging your licence within a year of arriving). You will then have to take this and the following documents back to your municipal office: your original driving licence, two identical passport photos, and the licence exchange request form (completed by you and the municipal office employee). Once your application has been processed and accepted you will receive your Dutch licence in the mail. This usually takes about two to three weeks and you cannot drive during this time.

30% Ruling & Your Driving Licence

If you are benefiting from the 30% ruling (see Taxation p.73) you can exchange your licence no matter where you are from. Simply request a declaration from the tax office and include it with your application to the RDW.

Learning To Drive

You have to be over 18 years old to drive in the Netherlands. The best way to get your licence is with the help of a driving school. There are many driving schools throughout Amsterdam; you will have to register with a school and they will arrange your driving theory test for you. Usually you will have to wait six to eight weeks to take the exam. Once you have passed your theory exam you can begin taking driving lessons until your instructor thinks you're ready to take the practical exam. If you pass your practical exam you will obtain a beginner's licence (restricted) for five years. To find out more, visit: www.verkeerenwaterstaat.nl (which has an English option).

Taking The Tests

If you cannot exchange your licence you will have to take a theory exam (it is possible to do this in English: http://rijbewijs.cbr.nl/index.asp?pageid=19). You will have to contact the CBR yourself to reserve a place for the exam. The practical test will cost upwards of €150 and will have to be arranged by a driving school. If you like, a school can arrange both tests. To brush up on your Dutch highway code, log on to www.verkeerenwaterstaat.nl, and there is a PDF available to download in the English part of the site called 'Road Traffic Signs and Regulations'.

EU Citizens

If you have a licence from an EU country then you are free to drive with that licence in the Netherlands for 10 years from the date of issue, or until it expires (if it expires sooner). After that time you will have to exchange it for a Dutch driving licence. You can only exchange your licence if you have a valid residence permit.

Other Countries

You can drive on your own licence in the Netherlands for a period of six months, after which time you will have to take a theory test and a road driving test to obtain a Dutch licence. You can only do this if you are a Dutch resident and have a valid residence permit. This applies for international driving licences as well, as they are only translations of your original national licence.
The following territories are able to exchange their original licences as long as the applicant has a Dutch residence permit: Aruba, Monaco, Isle of Man, Netherlands Antilles, Jersey and Switzerland. Licences from these other countries (below) can also be exchanged for a Dutch driving licence if you have a residence permit and your home country licence allows you to drive a passenger vehicle: Taiwan, Israel, Japan and South Korea. Your licence must be valid at the time of the exchange and must have been issued during a year where you lived at least 185 days in the country of issue. See www.rijbewijs.nl for more information.

Motorcycles
If you have a car licence then you can begin taking practical motorcycle lessons immediately, but if you don't then you will have to take the road theory test before you can take lessons. Once you pass your practical test you will have a beginner's licence for five years before you can have an unrestricted licence. For more on this visit: www.verkeerenwaterstaat.nl/english/motorcycles

Driving Schools			
CBR (driving authority)	Various Locations	0900 227 0227	http://rijbewijs.cbr.nl/index.asp
Drive Right	Amstelveen	020 449 04 97	www.driveright.nl
R de Veer Autorijschool	Amstelveen	06 55 306628	www.rijschooldeveer.nl
Rijschool Amsterdam	Slotermeer	020 411 66 88	www.rijschoolamsterdam.nl
Rijschool Dragan	Centrum	020 427 41 84	www.dragan.nl

Birth Certificate & Registration

All births in the Netherlands must be registered at the town hall (gemeentehuis) of the town where the baby was born, not where you live. You have only three days to register the birth from the day after the baby was born so make sure you've narrowed down the name list in advance! To register the birth you have to have been present when the baby was born, you will also need your passport, a certified copy of the marriage licence (if applicable), proof of recognition of the baby (if applicable) and the certificate supplied by the doctor, midwife or hospital. It's usual in the Netherlands for the father of the child to handle the registration. If this isn't possible then a few extra pieces of documentation will be needed: a copy of the mother's passport and proof of address and the passport of the person registering the child. It's a good idea to check in advance what documentation the particular town hall requires as they can vary. It's worthwhile to request and pay for an international birth certificate at the same time you register for the Dutch birth certificate. This makes it much simpler for you to register the baby with your own embassy and to apply for a passport. Being born in he Netherlands does not mean your child will automatically receive Dutch nationality. This only occurs if the mother of the child is Dutch. If the father is Dutch the baby must be 'legally recognised' by him before they receive Dutch nationality. You can do this before or after birth at the town hall where you live.

Naming Baby
Despite the inordinate number of churches you see in Amsterdam, the Netherlands is a highly secular country with few of the Christian denomination actually practising. Christenings, baptisms and naming ceremonies are arranged privately through your church of choice. An alternative Humanist ceremony is another option. See www.hvo.nl for more information.

Passports

All babies and minors need their own passport to travel. If only one parent is Dutch the child can claim the nationality of both parents. You'll have to arrange this through the relevant embassies. If neither of you are Dutch then your child isn't either and you will have to apply for a passport for them from your embassy, should you want to travel. You will have to check with your country's embassy to find out the costs of this. Once you have the passport you can apply for the residence permit from the IND (Immigration and Naturalisation Service), which will cost €188. If you choose not to apply for a passport or residency then you can claim Dutch nationality for your child after three years. If you do wish to travel with your child then you will have to apply for the passport and residency, and after five years your child is eligible for Dutch naturalisation (a Dutch passport). For more details contact the IND (0900 123 4561) or visit: www.ind.nl.

Adoption

Adoption in the Netherlands is a difficult process and can take from three to five years or longer. In recent years the number of children up for adoption has been around 50, with 2000 to 2500 Dutch citizens applying for a child. Many apply to adopt a child from overseas but the same time frame applies as it is built into the structure of the process as part of vetting prospective parents. Applicants must be under 41 years of age and be Dutch nationals or have valid residence permits. Only married couples may adopt a child jointly. Although single sex marriages are legal in the Netherlands such couples cannot apply jointly for a foreign child, though they can for a Dutch child. For information in English see http://travel.state.gov/family/adoption/country/country_425.html. Although there are no adoption support groups in the Netherlands you will be able to find support and counselling services in English here: http://access-nl.org/our_services/counselling.html.

Cohabitation
If you're not quite ready to call a spade a spade and tie the knot, you can draw up a cohabitation contract instead. This is a document that requires no formal involvement from the state and is only between the two people signing it, though a notary will have to be involved if the contract involves sharing of pension rights and other legal or financial matters.

Marriage Certificate & Registration

The Paperwork

In the Netherlands to get married you must be over 18 years old (unless you are 16, female and pregnant with permission from your parents) and at least one of you must either be a Dutch national or you must both have residency. If neither of those options is applicable to you but you would still like to marry in the Netherlands you can contact the IND for a temporary visa, MVV (see Entry Visa on p.57). This can take quite a few months to arrange so make sure you begin well in advance. As same sex marriage is legal in the Netherlands many gay couples do opt to marry in Amsterdam on such a visa.

Before you begin the process of registering your marriage there is some documentation you should have. If you or your intended is not Dutch, an EU or EEA citizen, or in possession of a valid residency card you must first contact the foreign police (vreemdelingdienst) and request a declaration (M46) from them, so that they do not object to the marriage. There are several other documents you will need: a valid passport, your residence visa, attested birth certificates (if not from the Netherlands), proof that you are single, and witness forms.

The Process

You will need to have two witnesses to the marriage but you can have a total of four if you choose. The witnesses will need to supply you with a copy of their passports. Once you've gathered all the documents you must go to the town hall of the place where you live (gemeente) and enter into 'ondertrouw' which translates roughly to 'intent to marry'. There are no costs for entering into ondertrouw but there are fees depending on when and where you get married and charges for the marriage documents you receive once you are married. Once you declare your intent to marry to the city you can be married after two weeks, but no later than a year from the date of declaration. The city acts as your adviser on how to proceed, and when you enter into ondertrouw they will let you know all of your options for wedding locations and give you a book called a trouwgid (wedding guide) with information on everything from florists to honeymoon suites. If there is any documentation you don't have yet or that isn't properly attested they will let you know.

De Kritjtberg

Found The One?
Lucky you. Now you've just got to sort the invitations, the tailor-made wedding dress, the shoes, the cake, the dinner, the flowers, the music, the seating plan… But don't stress it! Turn to p.286 for information on how to get in touch with Amsterdam's finest wedding professionals.

Once you are in ondertrouw you can choose the date you wish to be married. Remember the civil ceremony can be as big or as small as you want it; if you wish to combine it with your celebrations at the same location it's possible. If you wish to have a small civil ceremony in the city hall and then organise your own religious ceremony or other celebration elsewhere it is totally up to you.

The civil ceremony is conducted by a city official and is very short, usually lasting no more than 15 minutes. Some time before the 'big day' you will meet with the person who will marry you so you can talk about what you would like him or her to say and even request that they speak in English. The cost of the civil ceremony varies and can be anything from €40 to €850 depending on the day, time and the location.

In the Netherlands you can also enter into a registered partnership, which has exactly the same legal consequences as marriage excluding parental rights. In a registered partnership the father must legally recognise the child at the city hall before he is entitled to parental rights. If you do choose to marry you can decide whether or not to change your name: this applies to husband as well as wife, but your original name must still be included on official documents.

Getting Married In Amsterdam

Amsterdam is a singularly beautiful city bursting with romantic locations and grand reception rooms. So it's no wonder that many people choose to marry there. There is a fair amount of paper work involved (see following section) but many say it is worth the trouble for the photo opportunities. Once you have performed the obligatory civil ceremony you are free to have a follow up ceremony in whichever religion, fashion or location you choose. Though the civil ceremony could be in just the location you're looking for, one site from the government covers a wide variety of locations, from bagel shops to museums, all of which are able to host your wedding: http://www.loket.amsterdam.nl:80/loket/centralestad/product/55986.

You may have to lodge a request with your local municipality office for some locations, so call and check before you make concrete plans. For more tips on how to make your wedding day in Amsterdam everything you want it to be, see Wedding Items in the Shopping section on p.286. Some residents do decide to have the civil ceremony in Amsterdam before returning to their home countries for a church or celebratory service. If you choose to do this make sure you request an international marriage certificate for a nominal fee; you may also need to have the document legalised or endorsed by the Dutch authorities if you want to use it in an official capacity.

Dying With Dignity
The Netherlands is one of the few countries in the world that has legalised euthanasia. Since April 2002 doctors who follow the strict assisted death guidelines are no longer criminally liable. See www.minbuza.nl/binaries/en-pdf/pdf/euth-amendedbill-en.pdf.

Death Certificate & Registration

In the event of a death you will need to contact the doctor of the deceased who will examine the deceased and contact the coroner on your behalf. The coroner and the doctor will determine the cause of death, and only if there is suspicion of foul play or unnatural causes will they contact the police. You will require assistance to register the death; for a list of English-speaking funeral homes who will be able to help you, you can contact the British Embassy in Den Haag (070 427 04 27, www.britishembassy.gov.uk).

Registering A Death

In the Netherlands a third party (funeral home) is always needed to complete the death registration and to help with any arrangements you need to make. Once the doctor and coroner have finished their examination they will complete the forms needed to register the death; you may be required to help with personal information and a copy of the deceased's passport. Once all the forms have been completed the undertaker will take them to the town hall to register the death and obtain the certificate (aangifte overlijden). It is important to make sure you have a copy of the death certificate as you will need to supply it to your embassy and, if applicable, to your insurance company.

Investigation & Autopsy

The police will only become involved at the request of the coroner. The police may take procession of the body and request an autopsy but the family has the right to refuse. The family may also request an autopsy through the doctor if they choose to. If an autopsy is required then the death certificate cannot be applied for until the autopsy is finished and the body released to the funeral home with the completed forms. Depending on the circumstances this can take days or longer.

Returning The Deceased To Country Of Origin

The undertaker will help you to make arrangements to return the deceased home or to bury them in the Netherlands. If you choose to transport the deceased home the undertaker will apply for a 'lijkanpass' from the town hall; you will also have to contact the embassy of the country you wish to return the body to. You will need a copy of the birth certificate, a copy of the death certificate and may need to pay a fee for a certificate from the embassy. Costs for bringing the deceased home average between €6,000 and €8,000.

Organ Donation In The Netherlands

2007 saw the Dutch TV channel, BNN, grab worldwide headlines with its spoof programme The Big Donor Show. They claimed the show was made to draw attention to the lack of organ donors. In the Netherlands as in most other countries, hundreds of people die waiting for an organ transplant. If you would like to know more about becoming a donor check here for more information: www.donorvoorlichting.nl. See also Donor Cards (p.108).

Working In Amsterdam

There is a large expat workforce in Amsterdam; recent figures show it to be around 100,000, which is over 13% of the population. The Dutch economy has been steadily strengthening over the last five years and its low unemployment rate (5.4% in 2006) is testimony to that. Amsterdam is an attractive city in which to work and not just because of the lovely views. There are several employment sectors in Amsterdam that are always actively recruiting on the international job market. Generally these are with larger multinational corporations like Cisco Systems, Phillips and KLM. There are also many opportunities with Dutch banking institutions like ABN AMRO and ING.

Be Happy
The ethics of living are just as important as those of working to the Dutch, who believe that a happy workforce is a productive one. You are legally entitled to at least four weeks off a year and you are expected to take it!

Recently Amsterdam has become known as a 'creative city', with many creative companies basing themselves here, from independent advertising agencies to new media shops like Guerilla Games. Over one quarter of the creative workforce in the Netherlands is employed in Amsterdam. With such a wide variety of employment opportunities your problem should not be finding a job but making sure you find the right one. If your company has arranged your visa for you it will be very difficult (but not impossible) to change jobs once you have arrived.

If you want to increase your desirability for Dutch companies it is advisable to learn the language; being able to speak Dutch is an asset but not a necessity as English is broadly spoken and some international companies communicate only in English. Be aware that some organisations may expect you to start taking Dutch classes when you arrive, indeed for some of you it may be an obligation of your residence permit (see Residence Visa p.57). As with anywhere else in the world the kind of jobs you can apply for will depend on your history, education and experience, so make sure your CV (resume) is up to date – see Finding Work opposite for some tips.

The Hunt

Many companies look for potential employees online. Get your name out there at:

- www.intermediair.nl
- http://monsterboard.nl
- www.dambustersrecruitment.nl
- www.jobbingmall.nl
- www.xpatjobs.com/home.asp
- www.thewhitedoor.com
- www.jobinamsterdam.com

Others want you to come to them so see these company sites for job listings:

- www.schiphol.nl
- www.jobs.heineken.nl
- www.shell.com
- www.science.uva.nl/vacatures/vacatures.cfm
- www.cisco.com/global/NL/vacatures/vacatures_home.shtml
- www.pwc.com/nl/dut/careers/main/index.html?WT.svl=0

The Dutch Work Ethic

Many expats are surprised at the relaxed work ethic of the Dutch. For the Dutch a 40 hour week means a 40 hour week and they won't willingly exceed that. Most companies operate on a five-day week from Monday to Friday; some may close early on Friday or open late on Monday but generally that is not the case. The average wage is lower than in other western countries but the demands are less. Many find that the increase in quality of life outweighs the loss of income. The standard of living in the Netherlands is also quite high, though you may find housing expensive. If you're being brought over to Amsterdam from elsewhere your company should offer to help you find accommodation or offer you something for the interim. People coming from the UK should investigate how they can benefit from the 30% tax ruling (see ahead in Taxation p.73). Depending on what deal you are able to make, a starting package could include a rental property, furniture and travel expenses.

It is standard practice in the Netherlands for employees to receive an extra month's wage for holidays, which is usually paid out in May. You should also expect to be entitled to around a month's worth of paid leave not including the usual public holidays. Health coverage is mandatory in the Netherlands and your employer should usually discuss a pension plan with you. Some international companies do not offer the same benefits, so make sure you'll be benefiting from the Netherlands 'relaxed attitude' and not just watching while everyone else does! See Working Hours (opposite).

Working Hours

The working week in the Netherlands is usually around 40 hours a week. Some companies do operate on a 36 hour week, but that is quite rare. The Dutch are quite flexible about the timings; often people will eat lunch at their desk in order to leave at 17:00 instead of 18:00. Overtime should be covered by your contract, and the rate is dependent on your employer. Those working shift hours or during the night should also expect above the minimum rate at time and a half. The public holidays in the Netherlands are dictated by the Dutch celebrations and Christian feast days, but an employer may grant a paid day off for other religious feast days. You are also entitled to leave days for anniversaries, weddings, moving house and several other occasions. For more information read this article: www.expatica.com/actual/article.asp?subchannel_id=1&story_id=30380. For more about the working culture in Holland, see Working in Amsterdam (opposite).

Business Councils & Groups

American Amsterdam Business Club	www.aabc.nl
Australian Business in Europe	www.abie.nl
Netherlands-African Business Council	www.nabc.nl
Netherlands British Chamber of Commerce	www.nbcc.co.uk
The Netherlands-India Chamber of Commerce	www.nicct.nl
Society of English-Native-Speaking Editors	www.sense-online.nl

Finding Work

The job market in the Netherlands is competitive: not overly so, but the hunt for the right job can take time. If you are not an EU or EEA citizen it is better to begin your job search before you leave, as the time it takes to find a suitable employer could be longer than you are legally allowed to stay without a visa (see Work Permit p.58). The best way to find a job these days is through the internet or a recruitment agency. Most employers prefer a short, concise CV (curriculum vitae). This should include your education, past employment and references. You should only include contact details of referees on your CV, you can supply the full reference on request. Once you have found a job you would like to apply for and have secured an interview, be aware that the process can vary from company to company and job to job. It is not unusual to be called back for several interviews and even to take a small test. The application can take time, sometimes months and you may be required to travel for your interview. Most companies will pay for your travel or reimburse you at a later date.

Anne Frank

Anne Frank was a Jewish girl who lived in hiding in Amsterdam during the German occupation of the Netherlands. Her family lived in a secret annex in her father's business premises, where she wrote her famous diaries. For two years they lived in terror of being betrayed to the Gestapo, until in 1944 the German authorities received a tip off from an informer. Anne died in Bergen-Belsen concentration camp, but her writings survive as testament to one of the darkest periods in Dutch history. For more about Anne's life, visit the Anne Frank Huis (p.154).

Finding Work Before You Come

This is undoubtably the most sensible option for those who require a visa to stay in the country for an extended period of time. The internet is your best tool for getting your CV out there. You can post your CV on any number of job sites and with recruitment agencies (see table). You can also begin perusing the local newspapers online and seeing what is on offer. A useful link for Amsterdam newspapers is www.mondotimes.com/1/world/nl/112/2796. Another way to begin your hunt is to find companies you would like to work for that are based in the Netherlands and contact them directly. You could consider ABN AMRO, Elsevier, Heineken, Shell, MEXX and Unilever to start with.

Finding Work While You're Here

Don't be afraid to call companies you're interested in and speak to HR; even stop by and introduce yourself. A little badgering goes a long way to ensuring you'll be at the top of the list when a position becomes available. Networking is also a great way to find work. There are some great ideas for making contacts on the website: www.iamsterdam.nl, under Living & Learning, then Networking & Interacting. Finding a job is a job in itself so use all the tools at your disposal; contact recruitment agencies and make an appointment to see if they can help you (see Recruitment Agencies below for more information). Post your CV on job sites and begin to familiarise yourself with the language by grabbing the Saturday papers and combing through the job section. *Het Parool*, *De Volkskrant*, and the business paper *Financieele Dagblad* are good ones to start with.

Recruitment Agencies

Recruitment agencies are big in the Netherlands - at one point or another 20% of the Dutch workforce has worked through one. They are usually very reliable and effective. Some agencies specialise in different work sectors. The largest agency in Amsterdam for 'internationals', The Undutchables, specialises in administrative and office jobs. Registering with an agency is free and they will ensure that your contract with the company adheres to the labour regulations of the Netherlands. Recruitment agencies will either help you find full-time contracted employment, fixed-term employment (you may be filling in for someone on maternity leave) or temporary work. When you are working through a recruitment agency they are your employer and you receive your wage from them. This means they are usually taking a small percentage off the wage from the company that you are hired out to. Using a recruitment agency does have some drawbacks but it is often a great way to get your foot in the door of a desired organisation.

Recruitment Agencies		
Adams' Multilingual Recruitment	020 580 03 40	www.adamsrecruit.nl
Blue Lynx	020 406 91 80	www.bluelynx.nl
Culture Works	020 420 62 91	www.culture-works-amsterdam.nl/
Kelly Services	020 607 77 20	www.dutchisnotrequired.nl
Projob International	020 573 83 83	www.projob.nl
Undutchables	020 345 51 04	www.undutchables.nl
Unique Multilingual Services	020 570 20 94	www.uniquemls.com
The White Door	06 43 903899	www.thewhitedoor.com
xpatjobs	na	www.xpatjobs.com

ACCESS
A not-for-profit organisation dedicated to supporting the needs of the English-speaking expat community in the Netherlands. Staffed by 160 volunteers they offer advice and support on all aspects of moving to live in Holland. ACCESS are always keen to hear from people who would like to volunteer to help out. (020 423 32 17, www.access-nl.org).

Voluntary & Charity Work

There are lots of opportunities for voluntary work in Amsterdam and throughout the Netherlands. In Amsterdam there is a great volunteers' centre: it's the perfect place to get advice on how you can help. (020 530 12 20: www.vwca.nl). How you can assist will depend on your skills, but there is something for everyone who has the time. Voluntary work does not help you to stay in the country without a visa but you don't need a visa to be a volunteer. If you would like to work for a non-governmental organisation there are several in the Netherlands who may be able to offer you paid employment and initiate the visa process on your behalf, if you have the skills they need. Check these sites for more information: www.fondsen.org (Dutch), and http://www.greenpeace.org/international/about/jobs. If you would just like to help or participate in a charitable cause there are hundreds of opportunities in the Netherlands; you'll find all of them here: www.allegoededoelen.nl.

Working As A Freelancer/Contractor

Many people in the Netherlands are choosing to work on a self-employed basis. Registering to become a freelancer (ondernemer) is quite easy but you will need a residence permit that is not linked to an existing work contract. The only exception to this rule is with the Dutch American Friendship Treaty (see Work Permit p.58). This is not a way to become a legal resident, you must already be one to become a freelancer. To start your own company you need to visit the tax office

(Belastingdienst) and register as a freelancer to receive a business tax number (BTW nummer) and request a Verklaringsarbeidnummer (VAR nummer). Once you have those you can go to the Chamber of Commerce (Kamer van Koophandel) and register your company name for €45. Not everyone need register a company name to legitimise their company (journalists and artists don't), but it shows the tax office you're serious. As long as you're sure you can make enough to support yourself, you'll be fine. The general rule is that you should have at least three regular clients to ensure your business is viable. You are the best judge as to whether or not you have the network (and worth) to make it work.

Employment Contracts

Employment contracts in the Netherlands are subject to strict laws set out by the collective bargaining agreement (CAO). It's important for you to be aware of what that means for you and to ensure you are receiving the benefits you're entitled to. When you are offered a job you may receive an offer letter before your contract is made; this letter will cover the basic tenets of the contract but is not a legally binding document, merely a statement that you agree to the terms mentioned and accept the job offer. You should receive your contract within one month of starting employment. Your contract should be legible to you – if you cannot read Dutch you can request an English translation of your contract. Your contract should contain all details of your employment, including your agreed benefits and anything that you have negotiated for with your employer. This may include extra paid leave, bonus or pay increases, or agreements on overtime. Your contract will also include your right to paid sick leave, health insurance and any arrangements towards a pension plan. Generally in the Netherlands there are three types of contract:

- Trial or probationary contract: can be no longer than 26 weeks and can be terminated at any point by either party.
- Fixed Term Contract: refers to either a project or time period. If referring to a time period this contract must be for two years or less, and if terminated after the probation period (which is a maximum of one month) both parties must give one month's notice.
- Permanent Contract: has a probation period of two months where either party may terminate the contract without notice; after this time the notice period is from two to four months.

Office buildings

Under Dutch law certain benefits are mandatory; for example you are entitled to 16 weeks' pregnancy leave (zwangerschapverlof) should you fall pregnant, and you do not have to tell your prospective or present employer that you are expecting a baby. See Labour Law (below) for more information. Your benefits will begin from the first day of work, including the probationary period. Generally you receive your pay at the end of every month. You'll be given a pay slip that will indicate deductions made for tax, holiday pay, health insurance and any pension plan contributions if this is part of your contract. If you choose to join a union, that's regarded as a personal matter for you and it won't be included in the contract. You can become a member at any time or contact the relevant workers' union if you need advice about your contract or treatment in the workplace.

Useful Numbers

CWI Legal department
023 751 33 30
www.werk.nl

Reputable Employment Advice Lawyers:
Noordam Advocaten
020 689 81 23
www.noordamadvocaten.nl/eng

Van Velzen C.S
016 143 72 88
www.vviworld.net

Subsidised Legal Advice:
www.rechtshulpnederland.nl

Labour Law

Under Dutch employment law you are entitled to the same benefits and protections as Dutch employees. You can contact the FNV (a Dutch trade union confederation) for detailed information in Dutch (www.fnv.nl) but generally you should not work more than 45 hours a week and you are entitled to approximately four weeks' holiday pay, an extra month's pay (paid out in May), maternity leave (16 weeks), and calamity leave. You are entitled to leave days for weddings, funerals, deaths, moving house and more. Should you fall sick you are entitled to at least two weeks' fully paid leave, and then the pay will drop to 75%. It is also compulsory in the Netherlands for the employer to share the costs of health insurance. If you feel that you have been treated unfairly by your employer you should seek legal help. Contact the FNV or www.rechtshulpnederland.nl for advice.

Changing Jobs

It's quite common to change jobs to gain promotion or just for a change of environment. Providing you honour your contract and give due notice there should be no problem with changing your job. Just make sure that you are not violating your contract by moving to a company that is actively involved in competition with your employer, or that poses a direct threat to your employer's business. Most contracts have a clause stipulating that you cannot work for such competitors for two years after your contract is terminated. The same can apply to clients of your employer. If you feel that this is preventing you from finding work you can try and overturn it in court, but if your former employer can prove a credible threat exists because of knowledge you have, it is highly unlikely a court will reverse the contract.

If you are in Amsterdam because a company hired you, your residence visa is linked to your work permit. As soon as you cease to work for the employer they have to inform the Centrum voor Werk en Inkomen (CWI), the agency responsible for work permits, who will inform the IND (Immigration and Naturalisation Service), and your residence visa will be revoked. If you are unhappy with your job you should find another company willing to take over responsibility for your work visa before you resign.

Company Closure

If your company closes and you are uncertain of your rights you should contact the legal department of the CWI (Centre voor Werk en Inkomen) see above for their number. If your company simply closes and is not bankrupt then you will be able to apply for social support or an 'uitkering' until you find new employment. The uitkering is usually 75% of your wage and is available for three months. If your company goes bankrupt then you are entitled to six months wages at 100% of your salary. If your visa is provided by a company that closes you must leave the country or find a new job as soon as possible. If you have any questions at all it is advisable to speak to an employment lawyer before you agree to anything your employer says or asks. Most importantly, do not sign any documents until you are fully informed.

Bank Accounts

The Netherlands is home to some of the biggest banking giants in the world. You should have no problem at all with being able to access your money until you are able to open an account. In order to open an account you will need to show your tax number (burgerservicenummer – used to be called sofi nummer), proof of address and occasionally a pay slip. You won't be able to open an account without these documents so make sure you have them. You will also have to choose what kind of account you would like to have: if you need a savings account, credit card and so on. In order to obtain a loan or overdraft you'll have to show proof of employment and have been receiving regular deposits for at least six months.

De Nederlandsche Bank

Chipknip

In response to shop owners being irritated at ATM cards being used for small purchases, the banks introduced the Chipknip, a reloadable card or chip that transfers funds immediately. The chipknip is not pin protected so should only be used for small amounts. Ask your local bank for more info.

The bank fees in the Netherlands are average in comparison to those with the rest of Europe. You will not be charged for using the ATMs though you can only use an ATM from another bank once a day. For a full report and comparison on banking fees in Europe go to www.bankers.asn.au/Professor-Hawtrey-report/#_Toc167086646. Cheque books are not really used in the Netherlands – there is a dedicated system for paying bills or transferring money (acceptgiro) but most banking is done online. Dutch people don't like credit and the government doesn't encourage it; though credit cards are becoming more available they are not necessarily more popular. Interest fees are not particularly high at around 5% and most banks have the system set up so that you pay off the charges swiftly and consistently. If you would like to get a credit card you will have to show proof of a regular income of more than €650 per month. Banks are open during normal business hours and all of them offer phone and internet services, though not always in English. If you're worried about the language barrier visit your bank for a tutorial about the online service. You will always be able to contact an English-speaking employee if you need advice over the phone.

Banking Comparison Table

Name	Phone	Web	Online Banking	Phone Banking
ABN AMRO	0900 0024	www.abnamro.nl	✓	✓
ASN Bank	0800 0380	www.asnbank.nl	✓	✓
De Nederlansche Bank	0800 020 1068	www.dnb.nl	✓	✓
Fortis Bank	030 226 62 22	www.fortis.com	✓	✓
ING Bank	020 541 54 11	www.inggroup.com	✓	✓
Lloyds TSB	023 516 88 00	www.lloydstsb.nl	✓	–
Postbank	0900 0933	www.postbank.nl	✓	✓
Rabobank	0900 0905	www.rabobank.com	✓	✓
SNS Bank	0900 1850	www.sns.nl	✓	✓

Financial Planning

The Netherlands is a socially conscious society and its governmental and tax policies reflect that. You may be surprised at the amount of tax you will pay – this varies from 33% to 50% depending on your salary bracket. Most people do have savings accounts in the Netherlands; the frugality of the country's Calvinist roots are still in evidence, though spending is on the increase.

One big advantage of home buying in the Netherlands is that it's not necessary to save money for a deposit as you're not required to have one to get a mortgage here. As space is always a valuable commodity in Amsterdam, property is not a bad investment idea but it's not likely you'll find any 'bargains' (See Buying Property p.79). The euro is quite strong and is predicted to remain competitive for some time. It's better to open a savings account in the Netherlands if you're going to be staying for any lengthy period. In order to fully understand your financial options and opportunities it is a good idea to hire a financial advisor. The ins and outs of the Dutch tax and banking systems are difficult enough without having to contend with the fact that they are in Dutch. Your bank will have employees who can talk to you about most aspects of finance like mortgages and savings plans, but for any more complex forms of investment you should find a reputable financial advisor to help you. A good financial advisor will also be able to advise you on offshore schemes like those in the Netherlands Antilles and Belgium (see also Buying Property on p.79).

How Much?

If the costs listed in the table opposite mean nothing to you, refer to the Exchange Rates table (p.40) to work out the equivalent in your home country's currency.

Cost Of Living	
Apples (per kg)	€2.05
Bananas (per kg)	€1.69
Bottle of house wine (restaurant)	€12.00+
Bottle of wine (off licence)	€2.99+
Burger (takeaway)	€1.25+
Bus/Tram (10km)	€1.60
Camera film (generic)	€2.59
Camera film (Kodak)	€5
Can of dog food	€0.73
Can of soft drink	€1
Cappuccino	€2.20
Car rental per day	€55+
Carrots (per kg)	€1.20
CD album	€20
Chocolate bar	€0.90
Dozen eggs	€2.05
Film developing (36 colour)	€7.99
Fresh fish (per kg)	€18
Glass of house wine	€2.70+
Golf 18 holes (weekend)	€47.50
Large takeaway pizza	€15
Loaf of bread	€1.20
Local postage stamp	€0.39
Milk one litre	€0.65
Mobile to mobile (local, prepaid per minute)	€0.24
New release DVD	€24
Orange juice one litre	€1.45
Pack of aspirin/paracetamol	€1.79
Petrol one litre	€1.49
Pint of beer	€4.80
Postcard	€0.75
Potatoes (per kg)	€1.80
Rice (1kg)	€1
Salon haircut (female)	€35+
Salon haircut (male)	€15+
Six pack of beer (off licence)	€3.59
Strawberries (punnet)	€2.50
Sugar (1kg)	€0.78
Taxi (for 10km)	€10+
Text message (local prepaid)	€0.23
Tube of toothpaste	€1.30
Water 1.5 litres (in restaurant)	€3.25
Water 1.5 litres (in supermarket)	€0.57

Pensions

Pensions are tax deductible in the Netherlands as long as they comply with the terms laid down by the tax department. If you have an existing pension plan your employer should help you find out if the plan you already have is tax deductible under Dutch law, and if so you will be able to continue paying into it and deduct it from your taxes. Your employer's contributions, if they are making any, will be tax exempt. Under EU law you should be able to continue your pension scheme once you have applied in your country of residence as long as your pension was started in either the US or one of the EEA countries. The Netherlands also has a retirement pension that everyone is entitled to if they have lived or worked in the Netherlands. For more information on social insurance and other national benefits see www.svb.nl (which has an English option).

Financial Advisors

Adams Management Service BV	020 626 25 35	www.adamsmanagement.nl
De Boer Financial Consultants ▶ p.52	070 511 87 88	www.fvbdeboer.nl
Eurofa	032 133 88 77	www.eurofa.nl
Expatax	020 403 76 80	www.expatax.nl
Finsens Planning	020 623 44 47	www.finsens.nl
Horling, Brouwer & Horlings	020 676 99 55	www.hbh.nl/index_uk.htm?

Financial Checklist

Tidying up loose ends will help you to make the most of your financial gain in Amsterdam:

- Keep your bank account in your home country topped up to cover outgoing expenses
- Build an emergency fund of about three months' salary
- Review your insurance policies (and make any necessary changes)
- Start a savings plan

Taxation

Being a social democratic country the Netherlands has a lot of taxes, as you will find out when you get your first paycheque! How much income tax you pay is dependent on which salary bracket you are in but expect to pay a minimum of 33% to the taxman. There is a goods and services tax in the Netherlands and it is usually 19%; you will see it on your receipts as BTW. If you own your own company you will be able to claim the BTW back from the Belastingdienst (tax office) for any work-related items, so hold onto those receipts. If you buy a home in the Netherlands you will also have to pay certain taxes to your local council, which do not vary from area to area. Use this site to find contact information for your area: http://amsterdam.nl/gemeente/stadsdelen; the information is in Dutch but the phone numbers are clearly visible.

You can expect to pay property tax on the value of your house as well as waste disposal tax, water tax and energy tax. You will receive a combi-anslag (combined bill) for these taxes once a year – don't be surprised if the costs run into the thousands. If you are concerned about the costs or think there is a mistake you will have to contact your local municipality. You are expected to file the previous year's tax return by the end of April – you can always contact the tax office for advice but if you are uncertain about how to proceed it's a good idea to consult an accountant either to handle your taxes for you or to teach you how to file the returns yourself. Remember to check if you're eligible for the 30% ruling, which entitles you to a 30% tax-free allowance from your employer.

To find out if you can make use of this scheme you will have to file an application jointly with your employer at the Tax Office for Non-Residents in Heerlen. If you're not in Holland long enough to file your tax forms you can do this from abroad; you can contact the Belastingdienst for details (www.belastingdienst.nl), but you'll have to have a Dutch bank account to receive any rebates.

Legal Issues

The Dutch legal system is based on the Roman system and is largely influenced by the French legal system. There are no juries and the courts are divided into four sections. The first court, the Kantongerecht, deals mostly with misdemeanours such as failure to pay fines. The next court, the Rechtbank, handles all crimes and can involve up to three judges for more complicated cases. The third court, the Gerechtshof, handles cases that are passed up from the Rechtbank. There are always three judges present in the Gerechtshof. If they wish to pass a higher sentence than one agreed upon in the Rechtbank they must agree unanimously. The fourth and final court is the Hoge Raad, which only examines cases from the other courts to determine if they were correctly handled and sentenced. This is also where appeals end up.

The courts operate in Dutch and you will have to rely on your lawyer to keep you informed. Of course, if witnesses cannot speak Dutch questions will be asked in

English or a translator may be present. Dutch law is not overly strict but it is well enforced. It is a democratic and tolerant country and this is reflected in the legal system. If you would like to read more about the Dutch legal system you will find information in English on: www.rechtspraak.nl

Herengracht

Adoption

Adopting in the Netherlands is a very long and involved process. It takes a minimum of three to five years to complete, regardless of whether you want to adopt a Dutch child or a child from abroad. If you do want to adopt a child you must request a document called a 'begintoestemming': this roughly translates into 'permit in principle from the Foundation for Adoption'. You will find more information from www.adoptie.nl.

Divorce

You can only be divorced in the Netherlands if you meet the legal requirements for the divorce to be processed. You must either both be Dutch, or have been legally residing in the Netherlands for 12 months, or one of you must be Dutch and have been living in the country for at least six months. There is also the possibility that you can petition the district court in Den Haag if one of you is Dutch but neither of you live in the country. One or both partners can file a petition for divorce at your local district court. If only one of you is filing divorce and the other does not agree, the person filing will have to prove irrevocable differences in a court of law. Under Dutch law there are four consequences of divorce that will need to be sorted out: for this you will need a mediator who will also help you to come to terms with the divorce during the process. The four consequences are: children (child support and custody), partner alimony, and division of marital property and pension rights. Under Dutch law all property within the marriage is communal and it can all be split between the partners. For more visit www.international-divorce.com.

Making A Will

A will in the Netherlands must be drawn up by a notary. You only need to create a will if you wish to deviate from the statutory provisions on succession or if you have specific personal requests. Under Dutch law children must always receive a portion of the estate. If the child is disinherited they are still entitled to one half of what they would have received had they not been so. New laws passed in 2003 state that the share can only be claimed in money and not in goods or property. If you have not made a will and die while living in the Netherlands then Dutch inheritance law applies. If you would like more information on how to make a will in the Netherlands you can find details for notaries on: www.notaris.nl/page.asp?id=361 (in Dutch).

Law Firms		
Blenheim	020 521 01 00	www.blenheim.nl
Everaert Advocaten	020 524 74 74	www.everaert.nl
Expat Law ▶ p.75	06 41 394620	www.expatlaw.nl
Noordam Lawyers	020 689 81 23	www.noordamadvocaten.nl/eng
Rosina Eising Advocaten	020 575 50 05	www.re-advocaten.nl

Housing

Amsterdam is a small city with a lot of people living in it. This makes it energetic and interesting but it also means accommodation costs are high. Some areas are less expensive than others – you may choose to live further away from the city centre so you can pay less for more space. Unless you're planning to stay in Amsterdam for over five years, or invest long term in property, it's better to rent. Read ahead for some tips on how get the best for your money in Amsterdam.

Renting In Amsterdam

The rental market in Amsterdam is costly but there are a lot of agents (makelaars) around to help you out. Your best bet is to contact a few and choose one with whom you have a good rapport. If you're lucky, your employment contract may include accommodation costs, either for the duration of your stay or for the time it should take you to get settled. Even if your company doesn't cover the rental costs they may help you out with the deposit and agent fee. This can easily run into the thousands so check with your HR department to see if they can assist. Most expats choose to live either in the city or close to it; this means the costs are higher but the streets are livelier and more attractive.

Houseboats
If you have guests coming and are looking for somewhere a little different for them to stay, there are a few companies offering accommodation on houseboats. Check out Houseboat & Apartment Rentals (www.houseboatrentals.nl) and Frederic Rentabike Houseboats (www.frederic.nl).

Finding A Home

There are a couple of ways to go about finding a rental home in Amsterdam. If you have the time you can look yourself by using the internet; local papers aren't much help as the market is competitive and the chances of being first to call are slim. Online you will find a lot of resources to help you find an apartment in the short term (a couple of months) but for the longer term it's best to choose an agency that will do the work for you. Using an agency provides you with assurances as to whether the apartment is being rented legitimately. See the list below for some reliable agents. If you are looking for shared accommodation you will have to rely on your own resources – few agents handle shared housing. The weekly papers *Amsterdam Weekly* and *Via Via* are good places to start. You can also check www.expatica.com, www.funda.nl and www.marktplaats.nl. Another option is to find your flatmates first and then contact an agent to help you. One important thing to bear in mind is that when a flat is advertised as having one kamer (room), they literally mean one room. Bedrooms are not indicated on most advertisements, so a three kamer flat will have two bedrooms or one bedroom and one small box room.

Housing Abbreviations

Excl	Excluding Utilities
G,W,E	Gas, Water, Electricity
Incl	Including Utilities
NS or NR	Non-Smoking

How Much Will It Cost?

Generally you can expect to give a deposit of two months, the first two months up front and if you've used an agent they will expect the cost of one month's rent in payment. With rental costs starting at around €1,000 you're looking at €5,000 before you've moved in. Rent is paid monthly in Amsterdam unless agreed otherwise. You'll pay either directly into the account of the landlord or managing company. A contract can be anything from a couple of months to a year depending on the property. The cost will also be influenced by whether or not the apartment is bare, partly furnished or furnished, and if utilities are included. In Amsterdam the landlord is responsible for the maintenance of the house and should keep it to a high standard. If an appliance breaks through the fault of the tenant they are responsible for repair costs. On the other hand, if it breaks down due to old age the landlord is responsible for replacing it. You can try to negotiate with the landlord to get a lower price but it is not likely to happen. Technically, there is a rent capping system in place, but this is frequently ignored due to the high demand for housing. The rental market is fierce and if you do not want to pay up someone else certainly will. See also The Lease (below).

What To Look Out For

If you find an apartment privately and the landlord wants to be paid in cash it may be an illegal sublet. This means that you won't be able register there with the city hall, belastingdienst (tax office), or foreign police. Situations like these are really best avoided as the property most likely belongs to the government and they will evict the owner and his tenants in order to give the home to someone on their very long waiting list. Waiting lists for government housing extend back a decade so illegal subletting is frowned upon. Someone with a government house can legally sublet for one year if they are going away in which case the temporary tenant can live there legally and register. If you think you're being ripped off and your rent is far too high (or your landlord isn't keeping the house in order) you can contact a 'huur team' (rent team), free of charge, to investigate (www.steunpuntwonen.nl/huurteams/). As you have read, deposits in Amsterdam are high, usually two months' rent. To ensure you get your deposit back make sure you do a thorough inventory when you arrive. This means take note of all the furniture and what state it is in, check the appliances, look at the floors and floor covers, the state of the walls and so on. If you see any damage, write it down on a list and even take a photograph. A thorough check-in makes for a smooth check-out.

Real Estate Agents

Like anywhere there are good and bad estate agents (makelaars) in the Netherlands. An honest agent will be a member of the national association of estate agents, the Nederlands Vereniging van Makelaars (NVM). The fact that they are a member doesn't necessarily make them right for you though. It's best to meet with a couple and make sure you feel they know what you're looking for. You'll be paying them well for their services and it's important you feel you're getting your money's worth. The makelaar world in Amsterdam is small so it is best not to try and 'double up' on makelaars to get the job done faster. The chances are they'll get wind of it and neither will work hard enough to find your perfect house. If you're looking for a rental property choose a makelaar with a large portfolio; some only dabble in rental on the side and may not have the network to find you a home quickly.

Real Estate Agents

Brummer & Boot	020 616 16 88	www.brummerboot.nl
Caron & Co Makelaars	020 625 11 09	www.caron-co.nl
De Groot & Compagnons	020 646 47 96	www.degrootencompagnons.nl
De Nederlanden	020 589 30 70	www.denederlanden.nl
Direct Wonen	020 616 16 66	www.directwonen.nl
Perfect Housing	020 524 11 00	www.perfecthousing.nl
Rappange	020 624 03 63	www.rappange.com
SteenKuijpers Makelaars	020 673 24 54	www.steenkuijpers.nl

The Lease

A standard rental contract should include the rental fee and what is covered by that, for example whether it includes utilities and the length of the tenancy. Check if you have the possibility to extend should you wish, and also ensure that it's not a silently extended contract where if you do not inform the landlord or agency by a certain date you are committed to another term. The contract should also include what your obligations are. If you choose to register legally at the apartment then you may have to pay the city certain taxes, such as for rubbish collection and maintaining the sewage system. If utilities are included they will remain under the name of the owner or rental company; if they are not included you will have to open accounts under your own name. The deposit and terms of its forfeit or return should also be clearly stated, as should a diplomatic clause in case you have to leave the country for unforeseen reasons. If your contract is in Dutch you can request a translation – if you get one it is still advisable to ask a native Dutch speaker to check it over as there have been cases of discrepancies in contract translations. Before you sign the contract the agency or landlord may request references from your place of employment to ensure you are able to fulfil your obligations. Contracts tend to be for six months or a year and it is standard practice to give a month's notice if you intend to terminate the contract or move out, though this can be longer if stipulated by the owner in the contract. There is a fixed cap on the amount of rent that can be charged but it is largely ignored as the market is so competitive. If you feel that the rent for your apartment is too high you can contact a Huurteam (rent team) to investigate (www.steunpuntwonen.nl/huurteams). If you have any concerns at all you must include them in the contract to ensure you have proof should any difficulties occur. Although the contracts are not held by a civic committee they are legally binding and will be of great assistance if any disputes arise.

Main Accommodation Options

Studio Apartments

A studio apartment is the cheapest option in Amsterdam. Studio really does mean studio though, and they are really only suitable for two people at most. The average studio will be between 40 and 50 square metres. You'll have an open kitchen and a (usually small) bathroom. For a studio in the centre you can expect to pay between €900 and €1,250 a month excluding gas, water and electricity. You may pay up to €200 less on the outskirts of Amsterdam.

One-Bedroom Apartments

A one-bedroom apartment will have a bedroom, a living room or dining room with both an open or separate kitchen and a bathroom. They are usually from 55 to 70m2 and will cost anything from 1000 to 1500euros per month furnished but excluding gas, water and electricity. The price variation depends on location and if the apartment has an outside space like a roof terrace or balcony.

Housing along Veenkade, on IJhaven

Larger Apartments

These are much the same as one-bedroom houses but are more often spread over two floors, with the living and kitchen area on one floor and the sleeping rooms and bathroom above. Often the second bedroom is quite tiny so make sure it's big enough if you're looking for something other than a nursery. Two-bedroom apartments should be from 70 to 90 square metres and can cost anything from €1,300 to €2,000 a month depending on proximity to the city and added extras like gardens and roof terraces. For larger apartments you will be paying upwards of €2,500 a month.

Freestanding Houses

These are not generally found in the centre so you'll be in one of the outlying suburbs like Watergraafsmeer or Amstelveen. You will have a lot more space for your money and most likely a reasonably sized garden. A two bedroom house will cost you up to €2,500 a month and a three bedroom up to €3,500. This is a great option for families who need the space and whose children may be attending an international school nearby. The extra distances you'll need to travel may mean you should look into buying a car.

Richard Krajicek (Tennis Player)

Born in Rotterdam in 1971, Krajicek is most famous for reaching the pinnacle of world tennis by winning Wimbledon in 1996, beating Pete Sampras along the way. A tall serve-volleyer, he won his first career title in Hong Kong in 1991. He now devotes his time to bringing sport to inner city children in the Netherlands and directing the ABN AMRO World Tennis Tournament (p.236).

Houseboats

There are around 2,500 houseboats in Amsterdam and most of them are occupied by their owners or rented out for short periods. If you do manage to find a houseboat for long-term rental you will be paying around €1,700-€2,500 a month. Houseboats are great for the novelty value and are usually very charming, but noise from revellers cruising the canals in the summer months can be intrusive.

Other Rental Costs

If you decide to rent in Amsterdam make sure you are aware of hidden costs. Registering your apartment, which you will invariably need to do, means you will be liable for city taxes such as sewage treatment and rubbish collection. If your contract stipulates that utilities are included you may be asked to make an advance payment. If the costs for your bills don't add up to your deposit by the time you leave, you should receive a refund. If you're renting from an agent make sure you have enough to pay their fee, usually one month's rent. Costs of parking vary throughout the city, but it's not cheap. If your new apartment claims to have available parking, unless it has a garage this will most likely mean that there are spaces on the street – but you'll still have to pay. See also Utilities & Services (p.101).

Buying Property

Property in Amsterdam is a solid investment but it is only really worthwhile if you are going to be here for five years or feel able to rent the property out after your departure. Not being a citizen won't stop you from buying a house but you will have to prove that you are financially soluble. Buying, aside from being an investment for the future, can also mean that your monthly payments will be less compared with renting a property of the same size. The market in Amsterdam is very competitive though, and you will need a good agent. Buying in Amsterdam is becoming more and more popular – favourite areas are the Oud Zuid and Oud West. Prices rose 17% between 2006 and 2007 and look set to continue doing so. If you'd like to build your own house, it is possible to buy land but only on the outskirts of the city and on the islands on the IJ. The sales are done by lottery, and the city authorities do limit what you can do with the land. A lot of properties in Amsterdam are leaseholds or 'erfpacht' and you will have to pay the yearly index to the city. This can be from €150 per annum up to €1,500, depending on the property. As the council is encouraging people to live in the city it is not believed that these costs will increase in the near future. In the case of most redevelopments the leasehold costs are paid for decades in advance so you may not have to pay anything in the short term. Other properties are freehold or 'eigen grond.' These don't require extra payments made to the council, but they are harder to find. Another bonus if you buy is that you will receive a tax rebate for the interest you pay. To be eligible for this rebate you must receive a salary in the Netherlands and the property must be your primary living address.

The Process

On paper the process of buying a property is quite straightforward. The key to keeping it that way is in the amount of preparation you do. The first step is to approach a mortgage broker and get all your finances in order. A mortgage broker will be able to advise you about how much financial assistance you can expect to receive from a bank and which documents will be needed. Usually you will have to provide an employment contract; if your contract is for a set period of time you will need a 'werkgeversverklaring' from your employer stating that they intend to keep you on at the end of the contract. You may be asked to provide tax records and proof of income for the previous year. If you're freelancing, you will be expected to show three years' worth of records. Once you know how much the bank will lend you to spend on your house it's time to start looking. Narrow down the areas you're interested in and choose an agent (see the section on real estate agents for more information). There are several sites online that enable you to search on your own: www.funda.nl is one of the largest. Some agents (makelaars) will offer a flat rate to handle the negotiations and paperwork for you when you find a house, while others will handle everything and charge from 1%-2% of the sale price. Once you've found your property you can begin negotiations to make an offer, but you'll have to be fast as the market is competitive. You may have to take part in an 'inschrijfaanbod', which is a type of silent auction with everyone who is interested simply making an offer on paper by a certain date. In Amsterdam it's important to have all the information about the house as soon as possible. There are several things to check: when the foundations were last examined, what the housing association is like, and whether all permits for garden houses and roof terraces are in order. If your offer is accepted you will sign a temporary contract that lays out all the particulars of the sale, which is for the protection of both parties. Once you sign this contract both parties have 72 hours in which to cancel the agreement. Failure to cancel during this period can mean you will forfeit the 10% of the sale price that you must arrange to be transferred to the bank within three weeks of signing the temporary contract. If you go ahead with the purchase you can inspect the property and arrange for the final contract to be drawn up by a notary, ready to be signed on the day of delivery.

Buying To Rent

The competitive rental market in Amsterdam makes buying to rent an attractive option. Although you will not benefit from the tax refund for the interest paid as it is not your primary living address, the rent you charge is 100% tax free. You will have to pay a tax for the perceived benefit of owning a house and this is 4%. It is quite common practice to buy to rent in Amsterdam. If you are living here and you already own a house you will have to consult a mortgage broker to determine if it will be possible for you to take out a second mortgage. You may have to provide a deposit of 10% or more to purchase the second house.

Selling The Property

When selling your property you can do it privately but you will have to handle all the paperwork involved and enlist the help of a notary to draw up all the agreements. It is possible to do but does mean you have to be available to show the house and handle all of the advertising. This is not too difficult as there are many housing websites to post your property on, and many people do opt to sell in this way. It is far more common – and advisable if you are not familiar with Dutch real estate law – to go through an agent. Your agent will provide you with a valuation and advise you on your asking price, as well as the market conditions. They will also advertise the property and use their network of contacts to garner further interest, guiding you through the negotiation process and the necessary contracts. Any profit made on the sale of your house is tax free.

Mortgages

When thinking about buying a house it is good to do some research in advance – the key to this is finding a good financial adviser or mortgage broker and investigating in detail what will work best for you. If you have not been in the country long it will be difficult to get a mortgage unless you have a permanent contract from your employer. Most banks in the Netherlands offer mortgages and the rates are similar; it's best to talk to your mortgage provider about what is best for you, or alternatively you could choose the provider you were using at home. Endowment mortgages are not advised for expats as it is not certain whether or not you will be in the country to benefit from the returns. Generally expats are encouraged to take on mortgages linked to an investment account, or annuity mortgages that are more transparent and also more likely to offer up benefits in the short term. It isn't necessary to pay a deposit to purchase a house in the Netherlands if your tax history and employment record is stable. Generally you can expect to get a mortgage of four times your annual salary. Most mortgage repayment periods are around 30 years, so you should investigate all offers to ensure you won't be penalised for paying off your mortgage sooner if that seems like a likely scenario.

Mortgage Providers

ABN AMRO	0900 0024	www.abnamro.nl
De Hypotheek Shop	035 646 03 30	www.hypotheekshop.nl
Europlan	070 361 17 17	www.europlanbroker.com
Expatax	020 403 76 80	www.expatax.nl
House & Hypotheek	020 616 45 00	www.huis-hypotheek.nl
ING Bank	020 541 54 11	www.inggroup.com
Postbank	0900 0933	www.postbank.nl

Other Purchasing Costs

When shopping for your house remember to add 10% on to the purchase cost to cover all taxes and expenses incurred by the sale. This will include the agent's fees, the notary costs and the mandatory government sales tax. Also find out what the housing association (huis vereniging) is like. You will be expected to contribute financially to the association for general upkeep of the building. An active association means that everyone contributes and if any big problems (like plumbing, roof repair or structural deficiencies) need sorting there is enough money in the kitty to sort it out and no-one is left with a large bill. The contribution can be anything from €25 to €150 a month. For the separate cost of utilities, if you need someone to come out to install your TV or phone line this will be included in your first bill from the relevant company. Usually a phone call is all that's needed to have the connection activated.

Real Estate Law

The land registry in the Netherlands (the Kadaster) holds all details regarding property. Your agent should check with them to ensure everything is legal in your potential new home. There are several contracts you will see throughout the process: your agreement with your chosen agent, the temporary contract that contains all the details and provides the 72 hour backout clause, and the final contract which you will sign on the day of delivery. A real estate lawyer is not needed unless something goes wrong with the contracts, but this is highly unlikely. They may become necessary if there are hidden defects in the house that were known and not disclosed by the seller. This is why it's always a good idea to ask an independent surveyor to visit the property. The survey should be done by a company other than that used by the seller; a list of surveyors will be provided by your estate agent.

Residential Areas

Other options **Amsterdam – Main Areas** (Exploring p.136)

Although Amsterdam is quite a small city, it has many distinctive areas. Some are great for young professionals who like the hustle and bustle of the city, while others are more suited to families. You may want to be part of a vibrant multicultural neighbourhood or you may prefer a more settled, relaxed community. This is a brief overview of the different areas in Amsterdam, including information on the practicalities of each and the residential make-up, but you should still explore each area for yourself to find out what's on offer – you may be surprised to find something you didn't know you were looking for.

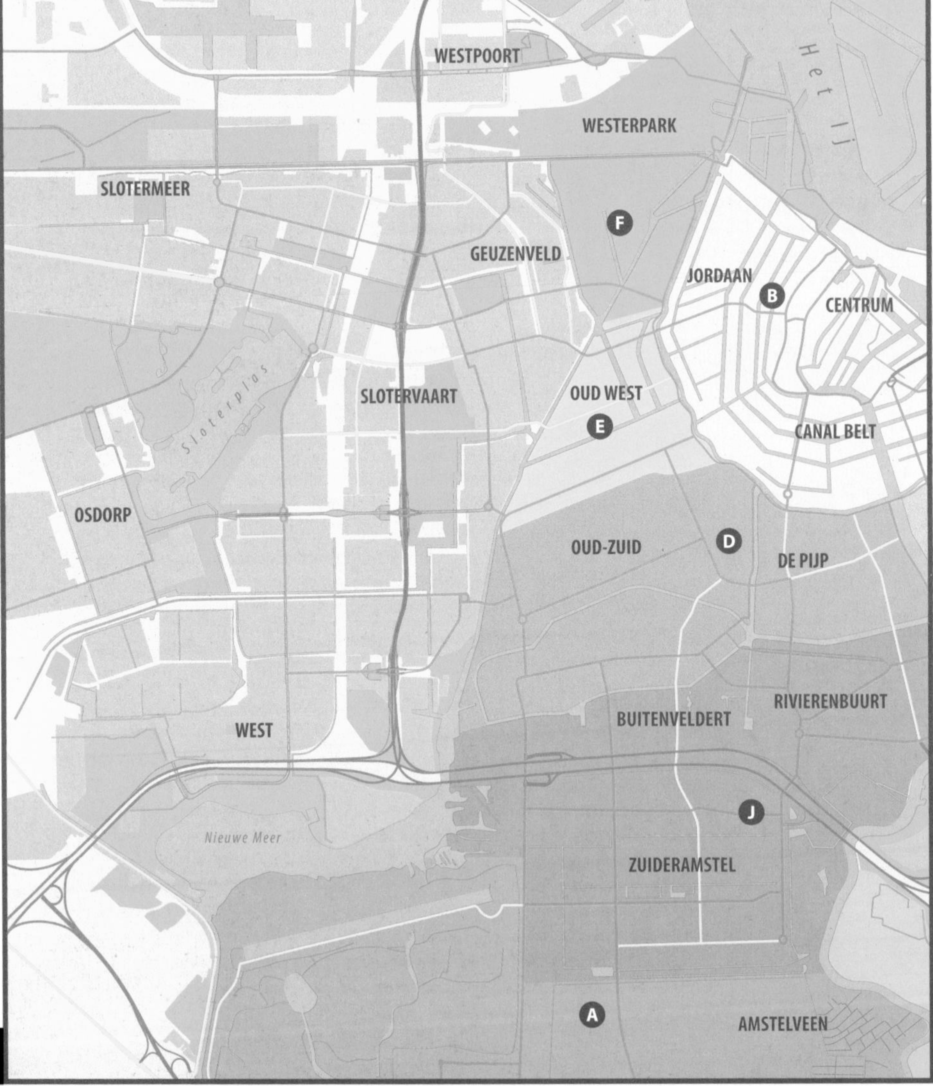

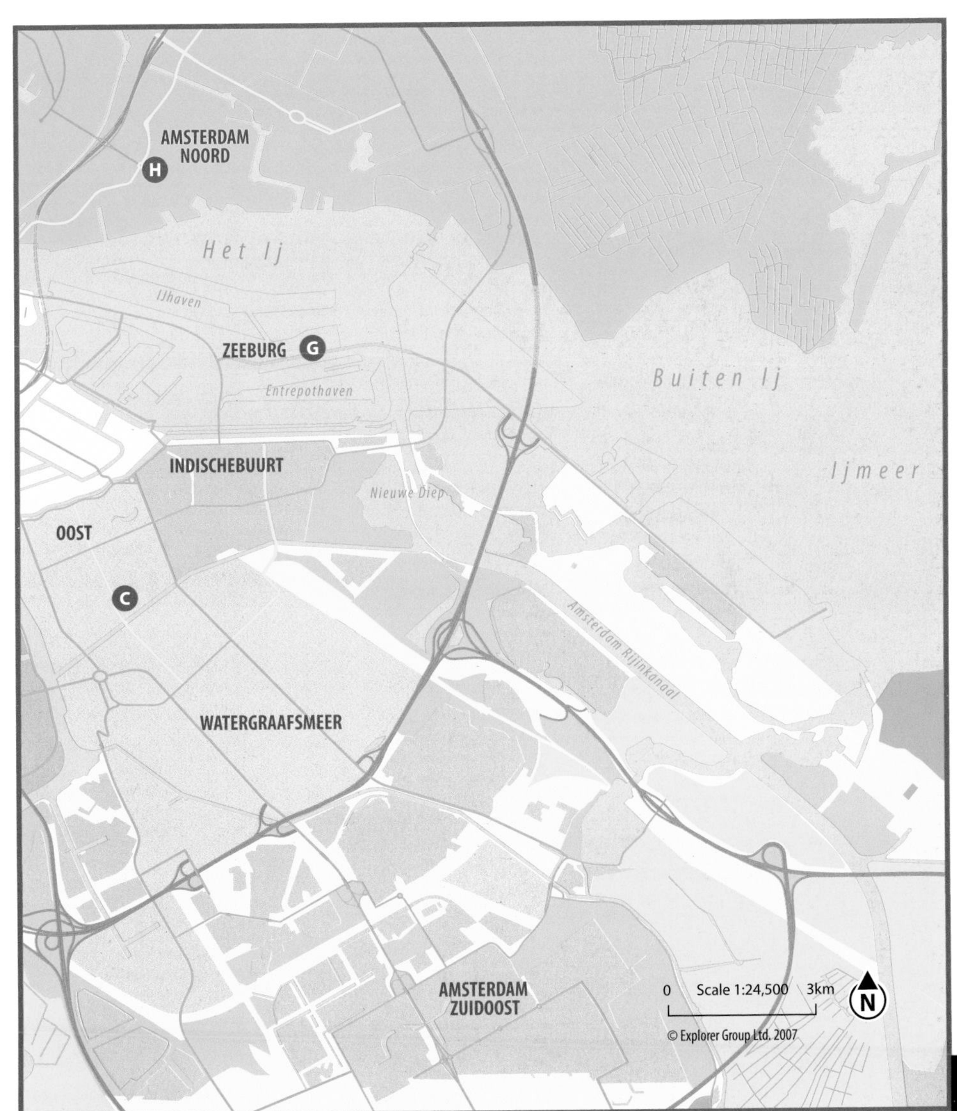

AMSTERDAM NOORD
H
Het Ij
IJhaven
ZEEBURG
G
Entrepothaven
Buiten Ij
INDISCHEBUURT
Ijmeer
Nieuwe Diep
OOST
C
Amsterdam Rijnkanaal
WATERGRAAFSMEER
AMSTERDAM ZUIDOOST
0 Scale 1:24,500 3km
N
© Explorer Group Ltd. 2007

Map p.367
Area A p.82

Amstelveen

A quiet town that's just 12 kilometres from the centre of Amsterdam, Amstelveen is very popular with families and those working for large corporations. There are quite a few expats from Japan, the US and UK living here. It has a definite suburban feel so if you're looking for edgy culture this is not the place for you. However, it was placed in the top five of the best places to live in the Netherlands. For more information on Amstelveen visit www.amstelveen.nl and click on the English language link.

Best Points

Wonderful place for children, large expat population and plenty to see and do.

Worst Points

Not for those who are looking for excitement, and commuting can be tedious.

Accommodation

Amstelveen offers a great variety of accommodation: both newer and older buildings are available, and you can find apartments as well as freestanding houses. Opportunities for renting or buying are abundant but you can expect to pay more for some of the newer developments like those in Westwijk. Other popular areas include Elsrijk, north of the town centre and known for its spacious tree-lined streets. Patrimonium is a favourite with families as it offers loads of outside space and runs alongside the peaceful Amsterdamse Bos.

Shopping & Amenities

Amstelveen is a town in itself so you'll find everything you need there. The town centre is bustling and all the major retail chains are represented. Unless there's something specific you're trying to track down you won't need to venture into Amsterdam at all.

Entertainment & Leisure

Amstelveen offers plenty to do, both indoors and outside. The proximity to Amsterdamse Bos (p.159) is great for those who want to swim or ride. The nightlife is not as good as in Amsterdam but there are plenty of great restaurants and bars. It's not lacking in international culture either; catch up on your foreign films at www.filmhuisgriffioen.nl, or ponder works of modern art at the Cobra Museum (p.154).

Healthcare

Amstelveen has a large hospital called Ziekenhuis Amstelland (www.zha.nl), which is handy in the event of any emergencies. If you need to visit the hospital for non-emergency treatment you'll first have to see your GP. Your local health insurance provider will give you a list of doctors in the area.

Mini Map

For trips around Amsterdam, the ***Amsterdam Mini Map*** is the perfect companion. Small enough for your pocket but big enough to expand your horizons – it's handy in size, has detailed information on the city, and the fabulously affordable price means it won't make a dent in your holiday fund. Keep the Mini Map handy and you'll be navigating your way around the city like a local in no time.

Education

One of the largest and most popular international schools is located in Amstelveen. The International School of Amsterdam has been open for 40 years; for more information see p.121.

Transport

Commuting can be a bit of a bother if you're not working in Amstelveen but it is in close proximity to most of the multinationals based in Amsterdam and Schiphol. The extra space means parking is not a problem and many homes have garages. There are also adequate public transport links to Amsterdam and the rest of the Netherlands.

Safety & Annoyances

Amstelveen is a safe place to live – you won't encounter many problems, but commuting by train late at night can feel unsafe.

Residential building in Amstelveen

Amstelveenweg

Offices south of Ringweg Zuid

World Trade Center

Map p.388-394
Area B p.82

Best Points
You'll have everything within two minutes from your front door as well as picturesque canal views, great bars and funky cafes.

Worst Points
The centre explodes with noisy tourists in the summer months and is overpriced all year round.

City Centre

The centre of Amsterdam is a great place to live if you like being at the heart of things. With most of the city centre being spread out over the canals you'll still be able to find tranquil hideaways within minutes of leaving your front door. Although small, the centre has several neighbourhoods within it, each with its own distinct character; the Red Light District, Jordaan and Leidsebuurt.

The Red Light District, also known as de Wallen (or de Walletjes), is the oldest and busiest part of Amsterdam. It may surprise you to know that it's a popular place to live despite its seedy reputation. There are many beautiful 17th century houses in this area, as well as converted warehouses. If you want to be at the centre of things this is the place to live, but don't be surprised to find people lounging about on your front steps in the early hours.

Originally a working class area, today the Jordaan is one of the most popular places to live in the city. The atmosphere is fantastic, communal and charming. It's full of great bars, independent galleries and antique shops. It's the least hectic part of the city centre to live in, located just west of the canal belt. Every Saturday you can stop by at the biological market on Noord Markt for your fresh fruit and veg before having a leisurely breakfast at one of the popular cafes nearby.

Almost as busy as the Red Light District, the Leidsebuurt is home to most of the retail businesses in Amsterdam and a great many of the restaurants. It's pricy, noisy and not quite as picturesque as the Jordaan, but still an attractive place to live.

Accommodation

Living in the city centre has its perks but you they will cost you. Accommodation within the canals is expensive and hard to find. The apartments also tend to be quite small or set up as shared accommodation. Mostly young professionals choose to live in the centre and families favour the outer areas. A small, attractive studio will cost you upwards of €1,100 a month. If you can spend more than €1,500 a month you shouldn't have any problem finding an apartment of a reasonable size with a gorgeous canal view.

Shopping & Amenities

Shops are everywhere in Centrum. You'll be able to find everything from antique doorknobs to Jimmy Choo's. The main clothing retail area is Kalverstraat (p.288), a pedestrian street that runs the length of the Rokin. One of Amsterdam's main malls is in Centrum, the Magna Plaza (p.294), as well as flagship store of de Bijenkorf (p.289), located just off Dam Square. If cycling isn't keeping you fit enough you'll also find a great many gyms scattered throughout the area – Fitness First (p.238) and Squash City (p.227) are two of the largest. You'll see many familiar chains around town as well; Toni & Guy and Replay have big salons in the Magna Plaza. It used to be quite difficult to find an ATM without a massive line in Amsterdam but now they are everywhere throughout Centrum, which is just as well as you'll be spending your money as soon as you get it.

Entertainment & Leisure

There's plenty to keep you busy in your leisure hours in Centrum aside from shopping. Cinema complexes are located near Rembrandtplein and Leidseplein, where you'll also find many bars, restaurants, nightclubs and theatres. These include the beautiful Stadsschouwburg theatre (p.361) and top live music venues Melkweg (p.356) and Paradiso (p.357). There are no parks in the heart of the city but there are many hidden gardens and leafy terraces that can be visited during the summer months.

Healthcare

There are chemists throughout Centrum; your doctor will advise you which one you should register with. In an emergency you should contact emergency services by dialling 112 – you will be taken to one of the city hospitals, all of which have an A&E department. If you don't need an ambulance the Onze Lieve Vrouw Gasthuis is easiest to get to. The address is Oosterpark 9, for more information go to www.olvg.nl.

Education

There are no international primary schools in the centre of Amsterdam; they are located slightly further out of town. The closest one to this area is The British School of Amsterdam (p.120) located in Oud-Zuid. Universiteit van Amsterdam (p.123) has lots of buildings throughout Centrum. Its libraries are open to the public: http://cf.uba.uva.nl/uba2006.

Transport

Parking is very expensive and there is a long wait for parking permits. Public transport is fantastic though and you should be able to get everywhere you need to very swiftly. If you're living in Centrum you'll only be a maximum of 10 or 15 minutes from Centraal Station, and from there you'll be able to get anywhere in the Netherlands.

Safety & Annoyances

The city centre is quite safe to walk around. You should take precautions in some areas, just as you would in any city. Avoid unlit alleys on your own in the Red Light District and around Nieuwmarkt. Crime is not a serious problem but these are trouble spots. Increased surveillance through CCTV and undercover policing has bought about a massive decrease in crime in these areas. Junkies standing on the street corners are more of an irritation than a threat. Bikes do get stolen frequently in this area, across all areas, so make sure you lock yours up properly.

Canal cruise on Herengracht

Reguliersgracht

Map p.394-5 & 385
Area C p.83

Best Points
Larger and more affordable houses for renters and buyers plus a developing sense of community.

Worst Points
Feels like it's out of touch with the rest of the city, some areas have an isolated, industrial feel to them.

Oost

The east of Amsterdam is one of the largest city areas and not surprisingly has a large variation in what it has to offer. There is a large ethnic community in Oost and this adds great colour and variation to the shops and restaurants. Oost is a popular choice with students due to the high number of rental properties.

Lounging at home

Accommodation

Some areas of Oost are predominantly for low-income renters and can feel a bit rough, but others, like Watergraafsmeer, which are slightly further out of town, offer more space and freestanding houses for those with families. You can expect to rent a good-sized family home for €1,800 in this area.

Shopping & Amenities

You'll be able to get all your basics covered in Oost, but for any retail therapy you'll probably want to head into the city centre. The Dapperstraat Markt (p.282) is a great market for staples and is enjoyable just to wander around. Oost is also renowned for its great Turkish bakeries.

Entertainment & Leisure

There are a smattering of good bars and restaurants around, but not too many, so you may want to head to Zeeburg, which has a little more on offer in that area. Oost does have some great sport activities available including rowing (www.berlagebrug.nl/engels/index.html).

Healthcare

Onze Lieve Vrouw Gasthuis (020 599 91 11, www.olvg.nl) is located in the Oost district, and is the best hospital in Amsterdam for any unforeseen emergencies.

Education

There are daycare centres throughout Oost, just as in other parts of the city. However, you may be quite far from any of the city's international school options.

Transport

Oost is very accessible by public transport and easy to travel around by car. You should have no problem getting a parking licence and are likely to find accommodation with private parking.

Safety & Annoyances

Some areas of Oost can be considered a bit rough – it's advisable not to leave any belongings in your car, and make sure you lock your bike up properly.

Dapperbuurt
The Dapperstraat Markt (p.292), in the centre of Dapperbuurt won the best market in the Netherlands competition. The neighbourhood itself has a lively, friendly, multicultural feel and is just beside Oosterpark.

Transvaalbuurt
Transvaalbuurt is predominantly a young ethnic neighbourhood with over 70% being under 40 years of age. This is a reasonable place to seek out if you're a student or moving to Amsterdam on a limited budget.

Map p.392 & p.383-5
Area D p.82

Best Points
Culturally fantastic, there is always something to do and see.

Worst Points
Some parts like Museumplein, Willemsparkbuurt and Stadionbuurt are very congested during peak hour.

Oud Zuid

Oud Zuid is becoming increasingly popular among residents due to its quieter streets and larger houses. It has always been an affluent area but it is slowly developing more character and you will see lively bars and restaurants scattered around. Prices are rising though so don't expect to find a bargain in this area.

Accommodation

Apartments in Oud Zuid are slightly larger but this is reflected in the price. The style of the houses comes from the Dutch School of the early 20th century. Around Vondelpark many of the homes are now businesses, as they are just too expensive for private accommodation. De Pijp is a popular area for the young and hip, while those with families may want to consider Rivierenbuurt.

Shopping & Amenities

You'll find a good variety of shopping opportunities in Oud Zuid. Upmarket and designer shoppers should go to Pieter Cornelisz Hoofstraat (p.289) and Beethovenstraat (p.287). For the biggest and most diverse market in Amsterdam head to Albert Cuypstraat (p.292). Oud Zuid is not lacking in amenities - you'll find everything you need close by. There are also many furniture and computer stores located near De Pijp.

Entertainment & Leisure

Just off the Museumplein is Zuiderbad, one of Amsterdam's few public pools. Of course, the Van Gogh Museum and Rijksmuseum are also to be found there. Just across the road is the Concertgebouw (p.360), for classical music lovers. Oud Zuid is a lovely area to wander around and the famous Vondelpark is a favourite for many throughout the year.

De Pijp

This is one of the nicest multicultural areas in Amsterdam. It's a very popular place to live among media and creative types. De Pijp is absolutely bursting with great bars, delis and restaurants. Sarphatipark (p.160) is great for barbeques, family picnics or chilling out after trawling through Albert Cuypstraat Markt (p.292).

Hoofdorppleinbuurt

Located to the south of the Vondelpark (p.160) and slightly further from the city centre then De Pijp, Hoofdorplein is becoming more popular, and as a consequence house prices are on the rise. The area is slowly transforming and is more affluent and attractive than it was even two years ago. Its proximity to great parks, schools and amenities makes it a good option for those with young families.

Healthcare

Just as in other areas of Amsterdam there are GPs and chemists throughout. Check with your local chemist to find out which chemists are open for emergencies, as the rota changes weekly. If you need to get to a hospital, Onze Lieve Vrouw Gasthuis is closest (020 599 91 11, www.olvg.nl) in the Oost district.

Education

The British School of Amsterdam (p.120) is located in Oud Zuid, as is the Amsterdam International Community School (p.120). This is a small international school which is very popular among expats. There are many day care centres throughout the area as it's popular with families. Combiwel has nurseries in five locations through Oud Zuid, for information see p.118.

Transport

Parking is easier in Oud Zuid: the streets tend to be wider, and obtaining a parking permit is not usually a problem. The area also has great public transport services and is not too far from the city centre to walk.

Safety & Annoyances

Oud Zuid is quite a safe area. You should keep an eye out for pickpockets in the busy Albert Cuypstraat Markt though. A metro line is being built through De Pijp, along Ferdinand Bolstraat, and the area is expected to be a construction site until 2011.

Map p.392, 379
Area E p.82

Oud West

Located on the other side of Vondelpark to Oud Zuid, Oud West is its younger, funkier sister. The area is popular with young families and its many cafes and restaurants are always buzzing. Helmersbuurt, just west of the Overtoom, is one of the most sought after locations in Amsterdam at the moment.

Best Points
A great community feeling and exciting vibe make it a fun neighbourhood. Just minutes from the centre of town and Vondelpark.

Worst Points
Not enough good restaurants to cope with the increase in popularity of the location. Some areas feel a bit seedy.

Accommodation

There is a lot of renovation going on in Oud West and that is expected to continue as the housing market becomes more competitive. The houses are not as spacious as those on the other side of Vondelpark but the area is a little more urban and edgy, and suited to first time homebuyers. Rent isn't as steep either and for around €1,400 you can find a decent sized two-bedroom apartment to rent. Slightly south is De Baarsjes, an area that is more affordable and becoming quite popular with younger people. It's still a bit on the shabby side but is improving.

Shopping & Amenities

The Kinkerstraat is great for fresh fruit and veg, as is the Ten Katemarkt, just off it. In the last year or so some funky boutiques have set up shop in Oud West – you'll find them nestled among other more low budget stores where bargains can be found. All the larger banks are represented in Oud West, so you'll be able to get all your errands done within a five minute radius of your home.

Entertainment & Leisure

The only gym in Amsterdam with a private pool, David Lloyd's (p.238), is just at the end of the Overtoom. Some of the most popular after work bars are located in Oud West, and there are some great restaurants. You're only minutes from Leidseplein and all of its cultural and nightlife attractions.

Healthcare

The closest hospital for emergencies is Onze Lieve Vrouw Gasthuis (020 599 91 11) located in Oost. For more information go to www.olvg.nl.

Education

There are a lot of young families in Oud West and ample childcare facilities scattered throughout. The British School of Amsterdam (p.120) and the Amsterdam International Community School (p.120) are located across the Vondelpark, just minutes from the heart of Oud West.

Transport

Proximity to the city centre means that public transport is regular and reliable, with several tram lines servicing the area. Parking isn't too hard to come by and there isn't much of a wait for parking permits.

Safety & Annoyances

The renovation work in certain parts of Oud West can be irritating, but roads aren't usually blocked, and if they arem detours are clearly indicated and don't add time to your journey.

Map p.373, 374, 379
Area F p.82

Westerpark

Westerpark is definitely one of the most up and coming areas in Amsterdam at the moment. It's located close to the city centre and is being heavily renovated by the city council. It's a lively place to live and is popular among young professionals.

Best Points
Westerpark's green space offers great concerts during the summer months. Close proximity to the Jordaan means you're not far from great food and shopping.

Worst Points
The heavy building work throughout the area will be bothersome for the next couple of years.

Accommodation

This is one of the areas set for high increases in property value over the coming years, so if you're looking to buy an investment property look here. Rental properties are quite reasonable but getting more expensive. You can expect to find a reasonably sized apartment for €1,200 a month.

Shopping & Amenities

Retail-wise there's not a lot about but you will be able to get all your basics close to home and the city centre is only 10 minutes by bike. This may change as more people invest in the area in the near future.

Entertainment & Leisure

Westerpark and Westergasfabriek are very popular hangouts for the young and hip and those with small children. There are more and more great restaurants in the area and the popular Haarlemmerstraat is only minutes away by bike, as is the Jordaan.

Healthcare

All hospitals in the Netherlands have an A&E department. If you need to find a hospital you should either call 112 or go to Onze Lieve Vrouw Gasthuis ((020 599 91 11, www.olvg.nl) or Sint Lucas Andreas (020 510 89 11, www.sintlucasandreasziekenhuis.nl).

Education

There are no international schools in Westerpark but you aren't too far from those in Oud Zuid: The British School (p.120) and Amsterdam International Community School (p.120).

Transport

Many tramlines serve Westerpark and parking is not too hard to come by. Traffic can be quite heavy along Haarlemmerweg during peak hour though.

Safety & Annoyances

Due to the large amounts of renovation (both private and city sponsored) going on throughout Westerpark there are some areas that will be a bit uncomfortable to be living in for the coming two years. Construction work tends to start and finish early, so although weekday mornings may be interrupted, your evenings and weekends shouldn't be affected.

Getting around by boat

Map p.395, 391, 380-1
Area G p.83

Best Points
Fantastic views and outdoor opportunities for families. Housing is still affordable and ripe for investment.

Worst Points
Slightly industrial feel to some areas and development is ongoing.

Zeeburg

A lot of investment has gone into the area to the east of Centraal Station. There has been the redevelopment of old shipping yards and the creation of islands to cope with Amsterdam's growing population. Some of the housing in Zeeburg is more than 100 years old while other developments are barely three years old. Other areas are still under construction. It is developing a reputation as a vibrant area and attracting many new residents.

Accommodation

The new developments in Zeeburg: those on the recently constructed islands, Java Island, KNSM and the Riet Islands, have a good range of housing for lower and upper income buyers. There are quite a few 'designer' highrises with attractive spacious apartments and views over the water, mixed with more affordable, though not unattractive, housing blocks. Most houses in Zeeburg are of good proportions. The areas closer to the city centre are more subject to the competitive housing market that is enveloping the rest of Amsterdam. The neighbourhood around Artis, for example, is one of the most expensive areas to live in Amsterdam.

Shopping & Amenities

The newer areas are not established enough yet to attract investment from many retail outlets or entrepreneurs, but you will be able to find everything you need. For serious retail therapy and other luxury services, you're best off heading into town.

Entertainment & Leisure

The nightlife in Zeeburg is catching up with the intensive developments and there are some great restaurants and plenty of cafes in the area. The Docklands are very popular for dining out, and Panama (p.357) is one of the best clubs in Amsterdam. There are also lots of outdoor opportunities, from kayaking to swimming. Flevopark is a popular summertime hangout.

Healthcare

The closest hospitals to Zeeburg are Sloteraartziekenhuis (p.110) and Onze Lieve Vrouw Gasthuis (020 599 91 11, www.olvg.nl) in Oost.

Education

There are numerous Dutch schools and childcare facilities in Zeeburg, but you can potentially be quite a long way from the international schools that are mostly located in Oud Zuid and Amstelveen.

Transport

You'll be able to reach most parts of Zeeburg with public transport, but it's not as well served as other more established parts of the city. There is ample parking though, and it's not as expensive as most of Amsterdam.

Safety & Annoyances

Crime is relatively low in Zeeburg, but residents have felt that the ethnic communities are not well integrated, so the Zeeburg area council has implemented schemes such as the creation of youth centres, designed to offset this.

De Plantage

Located close to the eastern part of the city centre, near Waterlooplein, de Plantage is a beautiful part of Amsterdam. It also contains the city zoo, Artis (p.163), which is the oldest zoo in the country and is hugely popular with families. There is also a planetarium, a geological museum and an aquarium.

Typical Amsterdam housing

Other Residential Areas

Not all areas of the city have been covered in the preceding pages, so to help you gain a fuller understanding of your options when considering Amsterdam, here is a brief overview of some alternative areas. You'll see that two of these, Haarlem and Utrecht, are actually completely different towns, but they are still valid options to consider when choosing your home. The fantastic public transport system in the Netherlands means that in journey time, the commute will be no longer than crossing from one side of the city to the other.

Map p.374-7, 390-1
Area H p.83

Amsterdam Noord

Separated from Amsterdam main by the IJ, Amsterdam Noord is not that accessible, although free ferries do run constantly from behind Centraal Station. The population is predominantly older and Dutch. Amsterdam Noord has one of the lowest percentages of foreigners and expats in the city.

Map p.366

Haarlem

Some people say that Haarlem is another suburb of Amsterdam as it's only 15 minutes by train from Amsterdam Centrum, but it has an energy all of its own and a great arty feel. Haarlem has a more relaxed atmosphere than Amsterdam and housing is far more affordable. Other benefits include the beach, which is only minutes away. Quite a few expats choose to live in Haarlem and commute to Amsterdam.

Map p.365

Utrecht

Utrecht is definitely one of the most beautiful cities in the Netherlands. It's only 20 minutes by train from Amsterdam and has much to tempt you to stay. The city centre has its own canal system which is even quainter than Amsterdam's. Bars are built into the canal walls, and terraces grace the waterside. It's a massive student town with over a quarter of the residents attending the universities. Culturally there is always something to do, and the events tend to be more intimate and progressive. It's not a cheap city though, and you may have trouble finding accommodation close to the city centre.

Map p.367
Area J p.82

Zuideramstel

A fairly popular area for expats, the population here is older than in other areas of Amsterdam, with most people being over 50. The area is quite expensive and not very attractive, though houses are larger. The Martin Luther King Park is located in Zuideramstel; it hosts De Parade (p.49) in August of every year, which is great fun. Zuideramstel is very accessible by public transport. Waiting for a parking permit can take up to six months.

Housing in Haarlem

Architectuurcentrum Amsterdam

Setting Up Home

Once you've completed the process of finding your house, it's time to start making it into a home. Having a secure and comfortable base is the key to feeling at ease in any country. There are many services in Amsterdam that will make it all happen a lot faster and be able to provide you with advice on how to go about settling in.

Smooth Moves

Do as much research as possible. Decide if you'll be renting or buying a property and if you'll be bringing furniture with you. It's much easier to plan moving house before you leave. Don't be afraid to call relocation services in Amsterdam for advice, even if you're not going to use them.

Moving Services

Moving services in the Netherlands are quite reliable but costs can vary so make sure you shop around for quotes. If you're coming from a non-EU country and are bringing household goods you will have to fill in customs forms but you won't have to pay taxes on personal goods. The moving or shipping service you are using from your point of origin should be able to assist you in this. You may also choose to use a relocation service based in the Netherlands of which there are several. It is up to you if you want to go through the cost and hassle of shipping your belongings. If you are coming for a shorter period it is likely you will rent an apartment that will be furnished. If you are only moving locally there are many options to choose from. You can hire a company to pack and move everything for you, hire a van and do it yourself, or look in the classifieds for a man with a van to help you out. Opting for a man with a van is usually cost effective but if things are broken you are unlikely to receive any compensation. However, if the job is small and you're around to supervise that should not be a problem. The *Amsterdam Weekly* has a good classifieds section that is available online: www.amsterdamweekly.nl.

Relocation Companies		
Dutch Living Services	029 728 34 55	www.dutchlivingservices.nl
Home Abroad	020 625 51 95	www.homeabroad.nl
Perfect Housing	020 524 11 00	www.perfecthousing.nl
Personal Relocation	018 362 29 03	www.personalrelocation.nl
SIRVA	020 301 23 01	www.sirvarelocation.nl
Voerman International	070 301 13 01	www.voerman.nl

Relocation Companies		
A-B Verhuizingen	020 408 14 37	www.abverhuizingen.nl
Allied Varekamp	030 247 87 47	www.alliedvarekamp.com
Atlas	020 653 02 02	www.atlas-movers.nl
Corstjens Worldwide Movers	020 426 37 77	www.corstjens.com
Passies	030 288 04 92	www.passies.nl
Peter Feitsma Verhuizingen	023 532 26 23	www.feitsma.nl
UTS Verhuizen	0800 887 6333	www.uts.nl
Verhuis Bedrijf Oma	0800 832 6662	www.vansoestbergen.nl

Furnishing Your Home

Other options **Home Furnishings & Accessories** p.271

The steps you'll need to take when furnishing your home depend on whether or not you are buying or renting. If you are renting you will have the choice of furnished, semi-furnished or unfurnished properties. Semi-furnished properties usually include a bed, table, couch, television and utilities. Unfurnished apartments often come without utilities so you will have to arrange them yourself. Finding furniture in Amsterdam will not be a problem. There are furniture and design stores throughout the city and some large wholesale outlets on the outskirts. IKEA (p.271) is a great place for getting the basics sorted out quickly. If you're lucky your company may include a furniture allowance in your salary package – check and find out if this is possible for you. Many of the smaller furniture dealers will tailor some furniture, like tables, to suit your needs. This is more expensive than buying ready-made, but still affordable. For more insider tips on where to find the best deals, check the Home and Furnishings section in the chapter on Shopping (p.271).

Second-Hand Items

Car boot sales and the like are not common in Amsterdam but you can still find good deals on second-hand items. On Monday mornings there is a furniture market at Noordermarkt in the Jordaan that usually has interesting pieces. For white goods there are several stores that offer repair and resale of items with a guarantee. You can also trawl websites like ebay and www.marktplaats.nl for decent deals. See also Second-Hand Items on p.279 in the Shopping chapter.

Tailors

Other options **Tailoring** p.283

There are many small tailors throughout the city, some of which offer curtain making services as well as repairs for clothes and dry cleaning. Specialists usually carry out re-upholstering of furniture, although in most cases it is more expensive than buying a new couch – costs for re-covering a simple sofa start around €500. Unless you're trying to save an antique, it might not be worth the time and expense.

Tailors			
Bicer Kledingreparatie	Van Hallstraat 284	De Pijp	020 686 57 05
De Gouden Schaar	Marathonweg 26	Watergraafsmeer	020 675 67 48
De Pompier	Nieuwe Nieuwestraat 30	Centrum	020 626 52 29
De Schaar	Overtoom 123	Oud West	020 685 17 67
Excellent Kledingreparatie	Kinkerstraat 49 HS	Oud West	020 412 32 18
Kalver Kledingreparatie	Voetboogstraat 129A	Centrum	020 638 78 00
The Tailor	Van Hallstraat 284	De Pijp	020 686 57 05

Household Insurance

Home thefts are not common in Amsterdam, perhaps due to the close proximity of neighbours. Still, it does happen and it is always wise to have insurance. If you own property, you should take out insurance for fire, flood, accidental damage and natural disasters. Any valuable items you have should be independently valued and added to your insurance policy as well. If you're renting you should still look into personal insurance for your belongings, as if the owner has household insurance it will only cover damage to the owner's property and not anything that you own. Most major insurance companies offer household item insurance to cover your valuable items like jewellery and electrical items. This should cost you between €20 and €50 a year. Wherever you are living you should make sure that all windows and doors lock securely to ensure you will be paid out in the event of a theft.

Household Insurance		
Aegon	070 344 32 10	www.aegon.nl
ANWB	088 269 22 22	www.anwb.nl
Centraal Beheer Achmea	055 579 88 88	www.centraalbeheer.nl
Delta Lloyd	020 594 91 11	www.deltalloyd.nl
OHRA	026 400 40 40	www.ohra.nl
Unive	072 502 45 00	www.unive.nl
Verzeker Voordelig	022 851 12 11	www.verzekervoordelig.nl

Laundry Services

Most houses have a washing machine connection and most rental properties will have one already installed. It is not customary in the Netherlands for apartment buildings to have shared laundry services and you are very unlikely to come across it. There are still laundrette and dry cleaning facilities all over Amsterdam; you won't have to look far at all to find one near your home. Usually you drop off your dirty laundry and pick it up either the same day or the following morning clean and folded. You will usually be charged a couple of euros per kilo for the service. Unfortunately, if anything goes missing in the wash you are unlikely to receive a refund or compensation. Ironing is not really offered as a service in laundrettes but you can usually have clothes pressed by those who offer dry cleaning services. The costs will depend on the item.

Domestic Help

In the Netherlands people do not have live-in maids, but it is quite common to have someone come to clean the house regularly. The best way to find help is word of mouth, via the classifieds in a paper or online. You should always ask for references and check them out. You can also advertise for help on community notice boards in your local library or supermarket. Most people offering these services will want to be paid cash in hand and costs range from €8-€15 an hour. Expat sites like www.expatica.com and www.elynx.nl are good places to look online. You can also check the website of the *Amsterdam Weekly* (www.amsterdamweekly.nl) or pick up a copy of the free paper on Thursday to make sure you're getting the latest edition.

Babysitting & Childcare

It's quite difficult to find a babysitter in Amsterdam, but there a few ways to go about it. There are some online databases which you can subscribe to and there are classifieds online at www.expatica.com, www.marktplaats.nl, www.elynx.nl and www.expatriates.com. You could approach your nursery teacher and find out if she is interested or knows someone who might be. Talk to other mothers and fathers and see if you can come to some sort of agreement about sharing childcare. Try joining some education groups and see if any parents there can offer tips or would like to share childcare. Many large hotels offer babysitting for their guests, and there are a few gyms like David Lloyd (p.238) that have a creche service. Finding a nanny can be easier and there are some agencies that will help you find the right person for your children. These agencies screen their employees carefully to ensure that your children will receive the best care.

Babysitting & Childcare		
Kriterion Opascentrale	020 624 58 48	www.kriterionoppas.org
Nanny Association	020 504 08 40	www.nanny.nl
Regel Tante	035 603 81 40	www.regeltante.nl
World Wide Au Pair & Nanny	020 411 60 10	www.worldwideaupair-nanny.com

Domestic Services

Finding reliable domestic services in Amsterdam can be difficult and time consuming. If you have a plumbing emergency you will have to locate an emergency services plumber in the phone book. For home projects like renovation you should begin looking for a contractor well in advance. Many are booked up months ahead of time. Make sure you get a few quotes and ask a lot of questions about how they will proceed and what exactly needs to be done. Try and get everything in writing with the quote. The average job will be around €50 an hour for the service and any materials/products will be added on top of that price.

Domestic Services			
AAA Alarmcentrale	Amsterdam Noord	020 492 02 21	Plumber
Aannemingsbedrijf HS de Vries	Watergraafsmeer	020 600 02 60	Builders
Aannemingsbedrijf J Van Lingen	Amstelveen	020 643 21 92	Builders
BNS Service	Watergraafsmeer	020 617 18 43	Plumber
JMB Timmerwerken	Various Location	020 348 42 32	Carpenter
Ladiges Loodgieters & Timmerbedrijf	Centrum	020 622 30 74	Carpenter/Plumber
RLKB Timmerwerken	Watergraafsmeer	020 774 35 19	Carpenter
SOS Snelservice	West	020 616 64 64	All Repairs
Witte Bouw & Annemersbedrijf	Amsterdam Noord	020 634 36 38	Builders

For emergencies there may be a call out fee depending on the day and time. If you are renting then your landlord should take care of any structural problems in the house. If you just want to change the colour of the walls you'll have to ask permission and pay for it yourself. If you do want to make improvements to the apartment you may be able to make a deal with the landlord for a rent reduction to pay for materials used. The local council deals with pest control: you can contact them for mice, cockroaches and other pests.

DVD & Video Rental

DVD & Video Rental		
Cult Videotheek	Centrum	020 622 78 43
Filmclub	De Pijp	020 671 71 11
MegaVideo	West	020 682 16 66
Movie Center	Centrum	020 421 32 59
	Oud West	020 412 05 73
	Centrum	020 627 94 44
	De Pijp	020 679 05 67
Movie Max	Oud Zuid	020 662 22 66
Super Video	Slotervaart	020 683 20 05
Video Land	Oost	020 679 90 45
Video Plaza	West	020 684 43 95

There are many DVD rental shops in Amsterdam. The best are Video Land, Movie Center and Super Video. Some still stock videos, but most have already phased them out. To become a member, you will need to provide proof of identification, proof of address and a bank statement or another official letter. You'll pay around €4 for a DVD for the first night. Some stores charge less for extra nights, but others will charge the full fee for every night you're late. There are also a number of online DVD rental services where you pay a fixed rate per month and receive a pre-set number of films. You can also opt for a package for slightly more money, around €20 a month and be entitled to an unlimited number of films. Check out www.moviemile.com, www.emmys.nl/dvd or www.interdvd.nl if you're interested, but be warned – all sites are in Dutch.

Pets

Other options **Pets** (Shopping, p.279)

Amsterdam is a very pet-friendly city. Many bars have cats wondering around, most likely to keep the mice down. Dogs are allowed almost everywhere, as long as you pick up after them. There's no problem with having a pet in your apartment as long as your landlord agrees and it is not excessively noisy. Most pet stores sell rabbits, mice, fish, birds and turtles, but not larger animals. If you do see a store that sells cats and dogs it is not advisable to buy from them. Animals kept in places like this aren't well looked after and may already be ill. There are several animal rescue shelters in Amsterdam; check www.dierenasiels.com for a full list.

Cats & Dogs

Cats and dogs are very popular pets in Amsterdam and you'll see them around everywhere. You should always buy your cat or dog from a breeder – that way you can be sure of its health and what treatments it has already had. Pets are now issued with pet passports that carry their medical history. You should also have your pet implanted with an ID chip, which is done by the vet when it is inoculated. The chip is registered to a website where your contact information can be found using the chip number. If you have a dog you will have to pay dog tax which is about €100 a year. You can contact the belastingdienst (tax office) for more information. There are plenty of parks where you can walk your dog – in some they have to be kept on a lead in certain areas, but in Vondelpark your dog is free to roam where it likes. If you want to see your pooch on the catwalk, one of the biggest dog shows in the Netherlands is the Winner Show held in November. For more information see www.winnershow.nl.

Pet Services		
Adogable	06 24 223581	Walkers
Boswandeling	06 23 689037	Walkers
De Blafferie	020 494 03 77	Walkers
De Honden Zaak	06 22 243659	Walkers
De Hooischuur Dierenhotel	020 643 39 29	Kennel
Dierenpension Amsterdam-Noord	020 636 84 42	Kennel
Ferme Vakantie Service	020 697 86 70	Kennel
Hoogendam's International Animal Hotel	020 619 41 80	Kennel

Fish & Birds

Fish and birds are for sale in most pet shops; some sell canaries and other small birds, as well as common species of fish such as goldfish. If a shop sells these pets, they will normally be able to provide you with everything you need to look after them properly.

Pet Shops

There are lots of pet shops throughout the city. They mostly sell pet products but some also sell small birds, fish, mice, rabbits, guinea pigs and rats. Generally they are very well looked after and clean. It is unlikely you will find larger pets in these stores, so if you are looking for a cat or dog to take home you should contact a breeder, visit an animal shelter, check your supermarket noticeboard for any pets looking for a new home, or ask your vet if they know of any upcoming litters. You can also look online at www.marktplaats.nl.

Vets & Kennels

Vets in Amsterdam and throughout the Netherlands offer great care for pets. The Dutch love their animals and treat them well, so the level of care is high, but costs are not exorbitant. If you are worried about affording the fees, you can insure your pet (one of the best pet insurers is www.proteq.nl). The cost does vary, but it shouldn't be more than €30 a month. There are a variety of services available in Amsterdam, such as kennels (which also take cats) and walking services (see Pet Services on p.99). You can have your dog collected and taken to a local park or woods for €10-€15 per walk. Kennels are equally well tended and you will find some around the outskirts of the city. They cost around €7-€15 a day and may ask you to have your dog inoculated against some common bacteria before it comes to stay.

Veterinary Clinics

76 Dierenkliniek	Plantage Midenlaan 76	020 622 85 67
Centrum & West Dierenartsenpraktijk	Admiraal de Ruyterweg 37	020 618 38 37
Dieren Doktors	Rozengracht 226	020 623 85 96
Dierenartspraktijk Reigersbos	Rossumplein 7	020 696 73 38
Dierenkliniek Duivendrecht	Rijksstraatweg 5	020 695 07 00
Ouderkerkerlaan Dierenartspraktijk	Dorpstraat 19	020 641 47 96
Stadion Dierenkliniek	Achillesstraat 62	020 673 87 98

Grooming & Training

If you like your pet to look its best you'll find several pet salons in Amsterdam to keep them in shape. It's essential that your dog is well socialised, as in Amsterdam they'll be coming across other dogs frequently. You can find puppy and dog training courses at several different facilities around the city. If you're at all worried about how your dog will cope with its new environment, it's a good idea to enrol in one – you may both make new friends.

Taking Your Pet Home

The procedure for taking your pet home will depend on which country you are returning to, but a Dutch vet can advise you fully on the steps you need to take.

Bringing Your Pet To Amsterdam

To bring your pet to the Netherlands you'll need to have it issued with a pet passport. A registered veterinarian in your country will have to apply for this for you. Your pet must have been vaccinated against rabies at least 30 days before departure and not more than a year previously. The pet passport will contain your pet's medical history, its breeding and physical appearance, and also its age and sex. If you enter the Netherlands without a pet passport, or outside of its rabies inoculation period, your pet will kept in quarantine for 30 days. If your pet travels without you, it will be have to be examined by a vet 24 hours before departure and again on arrival. If you fail to have your pet examined on departure it will be kept in quarantine.

Pets Grooming/Training

Arnoud Busscher	020 641 86 09	Various locations	Private Training
Boco Dierenboetiek	020 671 24 54	Henrick de Keijserstraat 32	Grooming
Dogstyle Hondentrimsalon	020 659 66 13	Roerdompstraat 15	Grooming
Hondenschool Racima	06 54 258810	Vrolikstraat 246	School
Omnia Hondenscool	020 686 07 34	Westerpark 2	School
Robbedoes	020 643 80 02	Amstelveen	Grooming
Woef Hondentrimsalon	06 25 587076	Leuvenstraat	Grooming

Electricity & Gas

In the Netherlands the electricity and gas sectors have become privatised, though the government remains a large shareholder in the original provider, Nuon. The power supply in Amsterdam is very good, and there are almost never any problems other than during severe storms. Your gas, water and electricity costs will be around €120 to €200 a month depending on how much you use. To keep electricity costs down don't leave appliances like computers and TVs on stand-by, remember to turn them off at the wall. If you're renting it's very likely utilities will be included in the cost, but make sure you check closely.

Contact one of the electricity and gas companies in Amsterdam and ask them to connect your house. If possible give them at least two weeks' notice before you move in. The largest provider is Nuon, which offers a variety of services including 'groene stroom', which is green power from renewable services. You can contact Nuon via their site, www.nuon.nl (information is in Dutch), or phone 0900 0808 from 08:00 until 20:00 Monday to Friday. Electricity plugs in the Netherlands are all the standard European two-pin plugs. You won't buy a product in the Netherlands that doesn't have the correct plug unless you specifically request it. The voltage in the Netherlands was originally 220 volts but is moving at the rate of one volt per year to 230 volts. You can expect your monthly bill to be between €120 and €250. Your gas and electricity meters are read once a year and your bill is calculated from the reading. If you've been paying too much you will be refunded, but if you've not paid enough you will be expected to cover the difference. Your monthly bill will be adjusted up or down the following year.

Electricity & Gas Suppliers		
Dong Energy Sales BV	073 616 02 00	www.dongenergy.nl
Eneco	0900 0201	www.eneco.nl
Essent	0800 0330	www.essent.nl
Green Choice	010 478 23 26	www.greeenchoice.nl
Nuon (main)	0900 0808	www.nuon.nl

Water

Cleanest Water In The World
Amsterdam has the cleanest drinking water in the world. It's drawn from the river Rhine and is filtered 14 times before it hits the pipes!

The water in the Netherlands is very clean and the service is reliable. The water companies in the Netherlands are government owned and handle everything to do with water from rivers and canals, to drinking water. Contact Waternet, the organisation responsible for Amsterdam's water, to get connected. You can reach them on 0800 1525, from 08:00 to 18:00 daily. The visiting address is Spaklerweg 16. You can also visit their website, but the information is in Dutch (www.waternet.nl). How much you must pay for your water is dependent on the amount of people registered in the house. One person costs €42.70 a year, so a family of four can expect to pay €184.37 a year including tax.

Sewerage

Amsterdam's sewerage system is a very reliable system of pipes under the city. You are taxed for maintenance of this through city council taxes that are sent to registered inhabitants. Each inhabited property must pay €115.42, irrespective of size or number of inhabitants.

Rubbish Disposal & Recycling

In Amsterdam, depending on where you live, you'll either have a collection day every week where you must put your garbage out on an indicated spot, or you'll have a large depository, mostly underground, nearby. They look a bit like juice cartons on the surface but are quite deep under the ground. You can still put out larger items that won't fit in the depository once a week for collection. Recycling bins are also all over the city. They are the same as regular bins but will have 'glas' (glass) or 'papier' (paper) printed on them. The ordinary rubbish depositories say 'rest'. Costs for garbage collection and recycling are included in your council tax bill.

Telephone

The phone lines in the Netherlands are privatised and the main provider is KPN. There are some providers who have bought up KPN lines and they offer cheaper call and internet rates but you will still have to go to KPN to get your line connected, and you will still have to pay KPN a monthly connection fee. KPN does provide reliable service. There are public phones all over the city, although few accept coins these days. You can buy a phone card from most supermarkets and news agents. If you're using a hotel phone, rates vary per hotel but they are higher than the normal fee. To get your home phone connected you'll have to contact KPN; the menu will be in Dutch but if you press # twice you will be transferred to an operator who should be able to speak English. If you find that you aren't getting the answers you need you can also go to one of their many shops called 'Primafoon'. KPN offers many services including call waiting and voicemail. To obtain more than one line you may need to have a business account. KPN has several different choices of contracts depending on how much you use your phone. You can get a certain number of calls free, and calls made over the agreement are still quite cheap at five cents per minute for local calls and 17 cents for calls to mobiles. Similar deals are available for international calls but for really cheap international calls you can subscribe to a provider like Tele2. Unfortunately, if you are receiving threatening or harassing phone calls KPN cannot block the number. You can get a phone that has a number display screen and ensure you only answer the numbers that you know. If you do manage to get the number of the person harassing you, or know them, you can file a police report. KPN will change your phone number for you and you can keep your new number from being public knowledge if you wish.

Telephone Companies

Budget Phone (Carrier)	071 581 56 00	www.budgetphone.nl
KPN	0900 0244	www.kpn.nl
Pretium (Carrier)	0900 163 7000	www.pretium-telecom.nl
Tele2 (Carrier)	0900 241 1602	www.tele2.nl

Mobile Phones

You can choose from a variety of contracts for your mobile phone and prepaid (pay-as-you-go) deals are available. If you don't have proof of address and income yet then you'll have to get a prepaid phone. The calls will cost more and you will have to pay more for your phone up front, but you'll have a phone. You can buy credit for your phone from most newsagents and supermarkets. Once you do have your address and other documents sorted out you can always cross over to a subscription. Having a subscription has several benefits: you will pay less for your calls, you can get deals on multimedia extras like the internet, cheaper texting, and if you lose your phone you can request a replacement sim card and keep your number. You also get a choice of whether or not to upgrade to a new phone at the end of your contract or pay even less for your calls. You can buy a mobile from almost anywhere these days. If you want a contract you should go to one of the phone stores throughout the city. You can check the providers' websites for locations.

Mobile Service Providers

Debitel	0900 332 4835	www.debitel.nl
KPN	06 12 001200	www.kpn.nl
Orange	0900 1480	www.orange.nl
T-Mobile	0800 7123	www.t-mobile.nl
Telfort	06 26 001200	www.telfort.nl
Vodafone	0800 200 056	www.vodafone.nl

Cheap Overseas Calls

As with the rest of the world it is possible to buy international calling cards that enable you to call home at a reduced rate - these are available here from independent call shops. These small shops are usually quite bare in appearance but have a few plywood booth constructions for you to make your call. Though they're far from comfortable and don't offer much privacy they are scattered all over Amsterdam. Call shops are less often seen in more affluent neighbourhoods. Internet telephony is becoming more popular as people become more familiar with software like Skype. Many people in the Netherlands have their calls charged through a cheaper provider. You will still have to pay your subscription fee to KPN but the calls can go through another company like Tele2 (www.tele2.nl), www.123bel.nl, or through an internet cable provider such as www.upc.nl.

All For One

Cut the number of your bills in half by choosing one provider for all of your communication needs. Most communication companies in the Netherlands (like UPC and KPN) offer deals on complete packages at a low monthly cost.

Internet

Other options **Websites** p.43, **Internet Cafes** p.338

Amsterdam is well and truly online. You can choose between having an internet connection through your phone line (ADSL) or via cable. Being online is very affordable. A high speed broadband connection will set you back no more then €50 a month. There are also a lot of internet cafes in the centre of town. Some have a few computers and charge nothing for internet use at all, others charge one or two euros for half an hour. Most people have computers at home or in the office, so internet cafes and libraries are mostly used by students or backpackers. More and more regular cafes have a wireless facility so people can work on their own laptops. When choosing your internet connection you'll have a large variety to pick from, not only which provider but which package. There's little difference in what each provider can offer these days – most include TV, phone and internet, so you should check them all and see which one suits you best; it may come down to which has the best TV programmes. You also don't need to have the same provider for everything. You may only want TV from one and phone and internet from another. If you choose an ADSL connection you'll be paying €25 a month to KPN plus the costs of the internet deal from your chosen provider, which can be anything from €16 to €50 a month. If you choose to have a cable connection you'll be paying for your usual TV costs plus the internet, which is about €15 to €60 depending on which speed of connection you need. An average connection speed is 1.5Mbps download and 256Kbps upload, and this will cost around €20 a month. With every provider you'll get an email account that will end in the name of the provider; you can choose how it begins. If you'd like to have a website you can request one from your provider for a small monthly fee.

Internet Service Providers	
KPN	www.kpn.nl
Orange	www.orange.nl
Planet	www.planet.nl
Tiscali	www.tiscali.nl
UPC	www.upc.nl
XS4ALL	www.xs4all.nl

Internet cafe

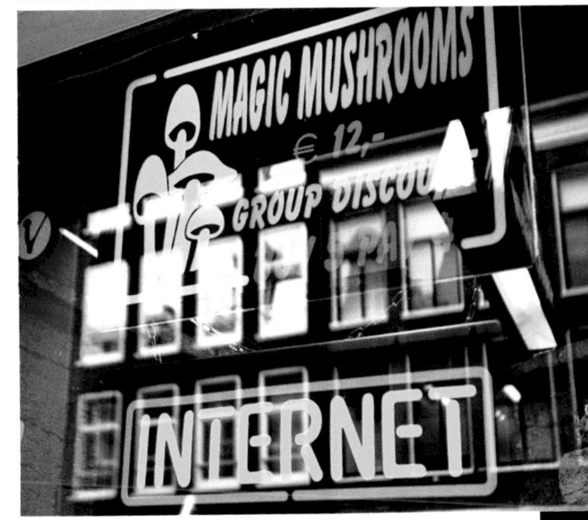

Bill Payment

Phone bills for landlines are quarterly in the Netherlands. Your landline bill will include your rent for ADSL from KPN; your internet bill will come separately and is usually monthly. The television provider, UPC, also charges quarterly. There are several choices of payment: you can arrange for the money to be automatically paid out of your account, pay online yourself, fill in the payment slip that comes with the bill and send it to your bank, or go to Postbank and pay with cash. If you miss a bill you will be sent several reminders before you are penalised. You will have to pay extra administration fees if this is the case. If you're unsure of whether or not you owe any money you can call your provider and ask to speak to the administration department. You can also request that your phone bills are itemised, which will cost a small additional fee. With some services you can now have an account online and check how much you owe.

Courier Companies

All of the major courier companies operate in the Netherlands if you need to send international packages. They are reliable and fast. You can send a package via a courier from the post office and Kinko's (Overtoom 62, 020 589 09 10) if you don't have a private account. There are also lots of smaller companies who operate nationally and offer same day or overnight delivery.

Post Services

TPG Post recently changed its name to TNT Post for competitive marketing reasons and to make it easier for its international network. The company has been private for nearly a decade. There are post offices all over the city and you can buy stamps from them as well as from newsagents and supermarkets. On the whole it's a fairly reliable system though post is delivered quite late in the day. Businesses can expect to get an early delivery in the morning and a later one in the afternoon, but private addresses should not expect to see post until early afternoon. Post is delivered to your door unless it requires a signature or is too large to fit through the mail slot, in which case if you're not home you'll receive a slip letting you know they'll come again on the next business day. If you're not there again the delivery person will leave a slip letting you know which post office to pick up your mail from; remember to take ID and the slip from the delivery person with you to claim your mail. Mail within the country is very fast, often arriving the next business day. It's also quite fast within the EU, but for countries further afield things can take a bit longer – from two to six weeks for Australia and the US. To ensure a speedy delivery you should request registered post, that way you can insure and track your mail. For packages of up two kilograms you'll pay €12.45 for most European deliveries and for Australia and the US it will cost €22.45, and still take weeks. If you need a package to arrive quickly you're better off using a courier service or finding a gift online.

Radio

The main radio stations in Amsterdam are Radio 1, 2 and 3FM. There's also Sky Radio and Radio 538. They are all local, Dutch language stations. The only station that offers news and programmes in English is Radio Netherlands International, www.rnw.nl. Many people do listen to the radio online as more stations internationally are turning digital.

Television

The standard television channels in Amsterdam offer a broad spectrum of shows in English and other languages. BBC1, 2, BBC World and CNN are included in the standard package from UPC, the main provider. Television is via cable only and the standard package costs you €16.05 a month. The Dutch use subtitles in place of dubbing and pick up most of the top shows from the UK and US which means you'll most likely see your favourite shows. Dutch channels include Veronica, Net5, SBS6 and the government-owned Ned1, 2 and 3, and RTL 4, 5 and 7. You'll find shows in English screened across all of them, though there are more on some than others. Censorship laws are not as strict as elsewhere but you won't see any extreme violence or nudity on television before 20:30. Digital television has arrived in the Netherlands and is fairly cheap. The number of channels available and the quality of the sound and image are said to be superior to that of normal television. The main provider is UPC, www.upc.nl; packages range from €3 to €45 a month. Other providers who rent cable space from UPC include www.tele2.nl and www.planet.nl.

Satellite TV & Radio

It is possible to get satellite TV and radio in Amsterdam but it is not that popular due to the availability and affordability of cable. However, should you choose to get satellite TV you will need to make sure you can fix the dish to your house or apartment. This is legal but there may be some regulations. The satellite dish will need to have an unobstructed view of the southern sky. With satellite TV you will be able to receive a lot of channels, mostly from the US.

Satellite & Cable Providers

Canal Digitaal Satellite	0900 9327	www.canaldigitaal.nl
Sky-Satellite	0049 306 549 41 25	www.sky-satellite.com
UPC	0900 19 05	www.upc.nl
Worldwide Satellite	029 946 40 56	www.tvfromhome.nu

Most people who choose satellite TV do so for the sports channels although there are several bars throughout the city that show Sky Sports. You can choose between having only free-to-air channels for which you pay no extra, or you can pay an extra monthly amount for a package of sports channels or films. The set up is similar to cable but with cable you don't need a satellite. You will need a 'media box' to enable you to receive the channels. This is free but you will have to pay a deposit. From then on you'll have digital television – costs depend on which package you have chosen. The basic package from UPC gives you 90 channels for only €5 a month.

Satellite Radio

You can also tune into radio stations with your satellite connection. What these are will depend on your package but all local stations are free to air. As radio becomes digitalised and people are able to 'tune in' with their computers this service is not prevalent in the Netherlands.

Amsterdam evening

North Sea sunset

General Medical Care

The Dutch healthcare system is a publicly funded system, offering high standards of medical care. Private healthcare is limited to private day treatment clinics specialising in eyecare, dermatology, allergies, cardiology, dentistry and plastic surgery. In the Netherlands the family doctor is central to organising your physical and mental wellbeing. Whether you need to find a specialist or arrange a hospital stay, you must always be referred by this general practitioner (GP); in Dutch: huisarts. It is mandatory to have health insurance if you are living and paying income tax here. Everyone is insured with the Basisverzekering (basic insurance) but if you would like more extensive coverage for dentistry, glasses and other services that standard insurance policies don't cover, you can pay extra and take out supplementary insurance. Generally, doctors in the Netherlands take a conservative approach when it comes to dispensing antibiotics and medicines. Most doctors here believe it's best to let the immune system fight infections by itself, so don't be surprised if you're sent home empty handed and told to get plenty of rest.

Registering With A Doctor

Huisarts
'Huisarts' means General Practitioner. You need to register with a huisarts before attempting to navigate the Dutch healthcare system. Referral is required from a huisarts to receive non-urgent medical attention from a hospital. A referral letter from them is also often required by health insurance companies if you wish to see a medical specialist.

To find a GP you need to ask your insurance company to provide you with a list of doctors in your postcode area (the idea being that a GP is only 10 minutes away in case of house calls). You can also ask around and get recommendations from friends who live in your area, but be prepared for the fact that many GPs are already full and you might have to search a little for one willing to accept patients. The Administrative Committee for the Coordination of English Speaking Services, ACCESS, is a very helpful non-profit organisation that provides free assistance to English speakers relocating to the Netherlands (www.access-nl.org, 020 423 32 17). They can also give you a list of English-speaking doctors in your area. The GP treats general, non-surgical health problems, including conducting standard gynaecological and paediatric examinations. You can ask to see a specialist for these services, but before seeking advice from any specialist you must first get a referral letter from your GP. If your GP feels it's necessary, he or she will provide an official letter and refer you to the appropriate specialist. You will also need this referral letter to organise your insurance payments. It's up to you to contact the specialist to make the appointment, and it can take weeks until one becomes available, unless it's an urgent matter. You can make an appointment with a specialist without seeing your GP first, but you must first check with your insurance company to see if they will cover the cost without a doctor's referral, or be prepared to pay the cost yourself.

Emergency Services

If you are in need of emergency assistance, whether it's fire, police or medical services, the number to call is 112. The central emergency operator will answer '112 Alarm Centre' (they will speak English). You must tell the operator which service is required: police, fire department or ambulance, and then the operator will connect you with the appropriate department. When the operator of the required service answers, say what is wrong and at which location. They will take the details and then send help, alerting any other services that might be needed. Help should arrive in five minutes. In minor emergencies, you should first contact your GP, who will either make a house call, ask you to come to the local GP surgery, or send you to hospital for treatment. If you are sent to a hospital, your GP will notify it in advance of your arrival. If you do not have a doctor's referral and your situation is not life threatening, Dutch hospitals may refuse to treat you, so be sure to call your GP first. If you need a doctor urgently and are not registered yet with a GP (or can't reach them over the phone) you can phone the Centrale Doktersdienst (Central Doctors' Service) on 020 592 34 34.

Pharmacies

Once you've registered with your GP you should find an apotheek (pharmacy/chemist) in your area that you can use regularly. The apotheek will record your family's details and enter them into their computer system for reference. Your doctor can then write or fax your prescriptions directly to the chemist for you to pick up at your convenience.

When filling in prescriptions, you can also arrange with the apotheek to charge your insurance company directly. In case you're confused about what the difference is between a drogist and an apotheek, a drogist (druggist) is only allowed to sell over-the-counter non-prescription drugs, while an apotheek dispenses prescription medicines. Pharmacists here are highly trained and are able to give medical advice for minor complaints. Many pharmacies are open Monday to Friday from 08:30 to 17:30, and some even on Saturday for half a day. There is always a pharmacy on duty in your area at the weekend, during holidays and at night. The on-duty rotation schedule for local pharmacies is displayed in the window.

Health Check-Ups

Yearly medical check-ups aren't common practice in the Netherlands, but you can request one with your GP. Doctors here generally don't feel it's necessary to check for something if you don't feel unwell. They do however have a nationwide screening programme for cervical cancer and breast cancer. All women registered at the city hall between the ages of 30 and 55 are eligible for the cervical cancer screening, with the GP or gynaecologist taking a Pap smear once every five years. If you are concerned between these screening schedules you may request another Pap smear from your doctor. Screening for breast cancer is also available at special centres nationwide. Mammograms are performed for women between the ages of 50 and 75, but if you are under 50 you can also request one. Blood tests and all other health check-ups are arranged through your GP.

Health Insurance

If you live in the Netherlands you are required to have health insurance. If you're only here temporarily or are a foreign student you may not be required to have Dutch insurance, but you must have health insurance – either some form of international insurance or cover from your home country. Once you are officially a resident, you must switch to a Dutch health insurance provider. In the past there was a difference between public and private healthcare, but as of 1 January 2006 the system was replaced by the Basisverzekering (basic insurance) for everyone, which is mandatory for all residents of the Netherlands. The government has decided that private insurance companies should provide the coverage so they can use market forces to cut healthcare costs. An insurance company is not allowed to refuse anyone the basic coverage regardless of age, employment status or general health. You are free to choose your insurance company and change insurance companies once a year.

The new basic insurance coverage is quite basic (as the name implies) and covers general medical care, hospital stay, dental care up to the age of 18, purchase of prescription medicine and short-term psychiatric treatment (under 12 months). You can also take out additional insurance (annvullende verzekering) to cover dentistry, physiotherapy and other treatments the government considers to be the individual's own responsibility. This is where the shopping around begins and where insurance companies have become very competitive, offering a range of policies from simple packages through to those that include hearing aids and a new pair of glasses each year. The approximate cost of the basic package is €1,000 to €1,100 annually, and €83 to €92 if you want to pay monthly. Children up to the age of 18 are insured for free. Those who cannot pay the premium due

Health Insurance Companies

Achmea Zorgverzekeringen	020 591 42 22	www.achmea.nl
Agis	0900 8685	www.agisweb.nl
CZ Actief in Gezondheid	0900 0949	www.cz.nl
Fortis ASR	030 257 91 11	www.fortisasr.nl
Menzis Zorg en Inkomen	010 271 61 00	www.menzis.nl
VGZ Health Insurance	0900 8490	www.vgz.nl

to a low income can apply for a compensation allowance from the tax office. As a safety net for insurers, policyholders must also pay in addition to their fixed contribution an income-related contribution of 6.25%, but usually the employer will cover this cost. Self-employed people will receive a bill for their contribution amount from the tax office. The money is used to balance out the risks between insurers with more expensive clients.

Large companies can usually strike a better deal with some offering a discount for collective health insurance policies, so it's always best to speak with your employer before deciding on an insurance company. Everyone who pays insurance premiums is also entitled to a no-claims reimbursement of a maximum of €255 if no claim is made during the year. (Doctors' appointments are not counted under the no-claims regulation).

If you are a visitor or are only here temporarily it is best to have private travel insurance which covers medical treatment in the event of emergency or non-emergency medical treatment during your stay. If you do not have travel insurance you will definitely be treated at all hospitals, but you will need to pay with a credit card or cash, and request reimbursement from your health insurance provider at home.

Donor Cards

If you would like to donate an organ for transplant after your death to help save or improve a life, you must be registered with the NIGZ (0900 821 2166, www.donorvoorlichting.nl) and carry a donor card. It is also wise to inform relatives of your wishes.

ACCESS

A not-for-profit organisation dedicated to supporting the needs of the English-speaking expat community in the Netherlands. Staffed by 160 volunteers they will offer advice and support on all aspects of moving to live in Holland. (020 423 32 17, www.access-nl.org).

Giving Blood

Donating blood saves lives and is easy to do. Usually, patients who need blood are given their own blood type, which means all types of blood are desperately needed at blood banks. However, O-negative blood is very much in demand because it's the only blood type that can be given to everyone. In emergency situations when there's no time to check a person's blood type, O-negative blood saves lives. In the Netherlands only 7% of the population have this blood type (just one in every 13 people), but relatives of O-negative types have a 30% higher chance of also being O-negative. All blood donations in the Netherlands are from unpaid volunteers. It has been proven around the world that unpaid voluntary donors are the key to a safe blood supply because they are least likely to transmit potentially life-threatening infections such as HIV and hepatitis viruses. If you are between the ages of 18 and 65 you can be a donor: telephone Sanquin Blood Supply Foundation on 020 512 30 30 for a registration card or download the donor registration form from www.sanquin.nl.

Giving Up Smoking

Smoking is the largest preventable cause of death in the Netherlands. More than 20,000 people die in the Netherlands each year from smoking-related illnesses. Thousands of people also die every year from being exposed to passive smoking. The Dutch government has finally passed a bill (that went into effect in July 2007) to ban smoking in all cafes, pubs, clubs, restaurants and hotels. Coffeeshops (that sell cannabis) are exempt from the ban except in the zone where 'soft drugs' are sold, which must be a smoke-free area. It is still possible to smoke in the places mentioned above, but the areas have to be closed off and employees are not required to serve food and drinks there.

If you need help quitting smoking there are many alternatives available, from over-the-counter nicotine substitutes (gums, patches and lozenges sold at pharmacies and druggists) to hypnotherapy, laser therapy, support groups and counselling. If you would like more information you can ask your GP or contact Stivoro, a smokers' information organisation (0900 9390, www.stivoro.nl). The website is in Dutch, but they speak English on the hotline. Another possibility is to post a notice on either Elynx (www.elynx.nl) or Expatica (www.expatica.nl), which are English websites for expats living in the Netherlands; both offer a wealth of information on current groups and activities.

Hospitals

Amsterdam has a broad range of hospitals (ziekenhuizen); most are non-profit institutions and two are university hospitals. If you or a family member require hospitalisation in a non-emergency situation, your family doctor will make the admission arrangements. The hospital will contact you with your admission date and you must notify your insurance company. The hospital administration will take insurance information and issue a hospital identity card (ponskaartje). This card will be used throughout your stay and subsequent follow-up visits to record the treatments received and the related costs incurred. During your stay you will probably be sharing a room with one to three other patients, but it's not uncommon for up to six people to share a room. You can request a private room if one is available. Hospitals do vary in the type of specialised care they provide and your family doctor will be able to decide which hospital is best for the treatment you require.

Meibergdreef 9
Amsterdam Zuidoost
Map p.367 F4

AMC Academisch Medisch Centrum

020 566 91 11 | *www.amc.uva.nl*

The AMC hospital located in south-east Amsterdam is the university hospital affiliated with the University of Amsterdam. The Academic Medical Center (AMC) is the most modern in the city and one of the largest and most prominent hospitals in the Netherlands. The AMC complex houses the university hospital and the medical faculty of the University of Amsterdam, as well as the Netherlands Institute for Brain Research, the medical department of the Royal Tropical Institute, the Dutch Ophthalmic Research Institute and a separate children's hospital called the Emma Children's Hospital. Its specialist units include neurosurgery, cardiothoracic surgery, neonatal and paediatric surgery, and intensive care and paediatric oncology.

Plesmanlaan 121
West
Map p.382 A2 2

Antoni van Leeuwenhoek Ziekenhuis – The Netherlands Cancer Institute

020 512 91 11 | *www.nki.nl*

Antoni van Leeuwenhoek Hospital – The Netherlands Cancer Institute – is an internationally renowned cancer hospital and research centre situated in Amsterdam. It maintains an important role as a national and international centre of scientific and clinical expertise, development and training in the field of oncology. It's the leading cancer hospital in the Netherlands and is solely for patients being treated for cancer.

Other Hospitals

BovenIJ Ziekenhuis	Amsterdam Noord	020 634 63 46	www.bovenij.nl
Onze Lieve Vrouw Gasthuis (OLVG)	Oost	020 599 91 11	www.olvg.nl
Prinsengracht Clinic, Onze Lieve Vrouw Gasthuis	Canal Belt (Grachtengordel)	020 599 41 00	www.olvg.nl
Sint Lucas Andreas Ziekenhuis	Slotermeer	020 510 89 11	www.slaz.nl

De Boelelaan 1117-1118
Buitenveldert
Map p.383 E4 3

Het VU Medisch Centrum (Vrije Universiteit Medisch Centrum)

020 444 44 44 | *www.vumc.nl*

The Free University Medical Center (Vrije Universiteit Medisch Centrum) or VUMC, is the university hospital affiliated with the Vrije Universiteit (Free University) of Amsterdam. Located in the Buitenveldert area of Amsterdam, it is also one of the largest and most prestigious hospitals in the Netherlands. It is a Level I trauma centre with medical emergency rescue helicopter. Its departments include advanced trauma care, paediatric and neonatal intensive care, cardiothoracic surgery, neurosurgery, and an infectious diseases section (in addition to other facilities).

Louwesweg 6
West
Map p.382 A2 4

Slotervaartziekenhuis

020 512 93 33 | *http://ziekenhuis.slz.nl*

The Slotervaart Hospital is a general hospital in Amsterdam south-west. Patients from across the Netherlands travel here to use its specialist units, including those for AIDS, geriatrics, neurosurgery, rheumatology/rheuma surgery and obstetrics. It is recognised by the Ministry of Health as the central hospital for AIDS and HIV-infected patients in the Netherlands.

Health Centres & Clinics			
Diagnostisch Centrum Amsterdam	Oud West	020 618 76 71	www.diagnostischcentrum.com
Kliniek DeLairesse	Oud Zuid	020 644 02 06	www.euroclinics.nl
Medisch Centrum Boerhaave	Oud Zuid	020 305 00 40	www.boerhaave.com
Ophthalmic Medical Center Amsterdam	Oud Zuid	020 679 71 55	www.omc-amsterdam.com
Stichting Medisch Centrum Jan van Goyen	Oud Zuid	020 305 58 00	www.medischcentrumjanvangoyen.nl

Maternity

The Netherlands has a very good record in prenatal care and safe childbirth. Traditionally it is commonplace for Dutch women to give birth at home. One-third of all births in Holland are home births, but you do have other delivery options.

Het VU Medisch Centrum

The majority of Dutch women are usually cared for by a midwife during pregnancy and childbirth. Gynaecologists or obstetricians are specialists and are usually only called in for women who have (or expect) complications in pregnancy or childbirth. Gynaecologists will also care for women who are expecting a normal delivery, but you need to ask your GP to help you arrange this. Don't forget to check with your insurance provider to see what options are covered under your policy. You can choose either to have your child with a midwife in a hospital (poliklinische bevalling), at home with a midwife (thuisbevalling), or in a hospital with a gynaecologist. Many women choose to have their child with a midwife at the hospital, which means they are in the hospital only for the delivery, and if they don't have complications can return home for the postnatal care. A woman may have her partner (or any other person she wishes) with her during delivery in the hospital. Midwives can be found either by referral from your GP or by contacting them directly – see the Gouden Gids (Yellow Pages) under Verloskundigen. You should try to interview midwives early on in your pregnancy as many are booked up and some do not attend home births.

Women in Holland tend to have their children naturally, with little medication. If you would like pain relief during your delivery, you must discuss this with your midwife or gynaecologist early in the pregnancy. Epidurals and Demerol are available in most hospitals but may not be available 24 hours a day. You should consult with your midwife or gynaecologist about this matter.

In many countries elective caesareans have become quite commonplace, but this isn't the case in Holland. A caesarean is normally only performed under emergency circumstances or in special cases. There are a number of pregnancy support groups and agencies in the Netherlands; you can get information about these from your GP or midwife, or you can contact ACCESS (020 423 32 17, www.access-nl.org). The birth must be registered at the city hall (gemeentehuis) within 48 hours, where a birth certificate will be arranged - see Birth Certificate & Registration (p. 61.) If you would like more information about pregnancy and childbirth in the Netherlands, ACCESS also regularly runs a course in English on 'Having a Baby in Holland'.

Maternity Leave

Women on maternity leave are entitled to 16 weeks' leave on full pay. Four to six weeks of the sixteen weeks is supposed to be taken as pregnancy leave before the birth and the remaining weeks as childbirth leave after the birth. If pregnancy or childbirth results in the woman being unable to work, she is eligible for benefit equivalent to 100% of her former pay for up to a maximum of one year after giving birth.

Antenatal Care

If you opt for a midwife you will have regular check-ups with her at a clinic during pregnancy and she will also aid you during the last stages of labour and delivery. If a midwife anticipates any complications she will call in a gynaecologist for a consultation. Midwives are highly trained and experienced in the Netherlands; they screen women very thoroughly to foresee any problems, referring them to hospital if necessary. If you choose to deliver with a gynaecologist you will be seen in the antenatal clinic during your pregnancy. Genetic testing is performed if the pregnant woman is in a high-risk category for foetal chromosomal defects. This applies if the mother is 36 years or older, if the father is 55 years or older, if there is a family history of chromosomal problems, or if you take epileptic medication. There are four widely available tests: The Triple Test, Echoscopie, Chorionic Villi Sampling, or Amniocentesis. Your GP will advise you concerning procedures and centres in your area.

Postnatal Care

Once your baby has arrived you will be given assistance at home by a maternity nurse (kraamverzorgster) every day for the first week. The kraamverzorgster will monitor the mother and baby's health, teach general childcare and help in setting up a daily routine. In some instances they will also help with household chores and caring for the rest of the family. Your midwife will also come by to visit you and the baby in the first week. If you were seeing a gynaecologist you will need to schedule an appointment at the office or clinic. Either the midwife or gynaeocologist does a final postnatal check-up around six weeks after the birth.

Contraception & Sexual Health

Birth control in the Netherlands is pretty much the same as it is everywhere in the western world. The birth control pill is available but there are not as many varieties prescribed here and it is not covered by health insurance. The morning after pill is available over-the-counter without a prescription at both pharmacies and druggists. Condoms can be purchased at pharmacies, druggists, supermarkets, vending machines in public toilets and at a variety of speciality condom shops in Amsterdam. For general help and information on sexual health, you can contact the Centra voor Seksuele Gezondheid (020 616 62 22). This clinic can offer advice on contraception, abortion, Pap smears, psycho-sexual problems, safer sex, sex education for teenagers, impotence and sterilisation.

If you would like to speak to someone confidentially and anonymously about sexually transmitted diseases you can contact the STI (Outpatient Clinic for Sexually Transmitted

Infections). In Amsterdam the number for HIV/AIDS information is 020 555 58 22. For treatment and information you can also contact your GP, a dermatologist (by GP referral), or a gynaecologist (after seeing a GP first). For AIDS information in Dutch and English there is a free and anonymous helpline on 0900 204 2040 (Monday to Friday between 14:00 and 22:00).

Gynaecology & Obstetrics

Gynaecology and obstetrics specialists are found in hospitals, and consultations are only by GP referral. The Dutch have a more relaxed view of childbirth than many other countries and you would normally only visit a gynaecologist or obstetrics department if complications are expected during the pregnancy – otherwise you are in the care of a midwife. However, if you feel more comfortable seeing a gynaecologist during your pregnancy, then request a referral from your GP.

Fertility Treatments

If you are having trouble starting a family there are a few available methods to try in the Netherlands. In Vitro Fertilisation (IVF) is one such procedure, but it is costly and the waiting list is long. The basic health insurance will only cover the second and third IVF treatment, but some supplemental insurance packages will also cover the first treatment. A first time fertility treatment can cost between €2,500 and €3,500 depending on whether you are using your husband's sperm or donor sperm. In order to begin treatment your GP will need to refer you to a gynaecologist. The gynaecologist will be the one to administer all the required tests. For more information on fertility treatments, please see the website www.ivfkliniek.nl (they have an English page with prices). This is the homepage of the Medisch Centrum Kinderwens (Medical Centre for Childwish), a specialised centre to help those who are involuntarily childless or infertile.

Abortion

Abortion in the Netherlands is legal up to the 24th week after conception, when the mother is in a crisis or has a 'serious need' for a termination. However, to be sure they remain within the time limit, most doctors will perform the procedure no later than 21 weeks into the pregnancy. Abortions for medical reasons may be performed in the 24th week at the latest. Although you may think the Dutch are liberal in this matter, the Netherlands has one of the lowest abortion rates in the world. You will find abortion clinics listed in the Gouden Gids under Abortus Klinieken. Women who are under 18 weeks pregnant can contact the Centrum voor Seksuele Gezondheid (020 624 54 26). For a list of English-speaking abortion clinics in your area, call ACCESS on 020 423 32 17.

Breast Cancer & Mammograms

It might be difficult for you to understand the attitude towards preventive care in the Dutch health system if you come from a country where annual breast exams from the age of 40 are routine. The Dutch health authorities feel after much research that the cost of annual routine exams is much greater than the actual benefit that these preventive exams yield. Therefore yearly breast cancer screening is limited to women between the ages of 50 and 75. However, if you feel uneasy not having regular mammograms, speak to your GP about a referral letter. You can request a referral letter from your doctor for a mammogram at an independent diagnostic clinic (see Diagnostisch Centrum Amsterdam p.110 to avoid waiting for an appointment at a hospital. If your mammogram is unclear or the clinic feels further investigation is necessary, it will give the results to your GP with the recommendation that you should be referred to a specialist at the hospital for further screening.

Paediatrics

Paediatricians are specialists in hospitals that can only be visited with a referral letter from your GP. The Consultatiebureau or baby health clinic provides basic paediatric care. The clinics are staffed with specially trained doctors and nurses who offer routine paediatric care and immunisations. They monitor the growth and development of your child from birth up to the age of 4. To use their services, you must be a member of the Stichting Thuiszorg (886 00 00), a Home Care Association that offers medical, social and preventive medical services. They will refer you to the nearest health clinic for your child's check-ups. After the age of 4, your child's records are then sent to the school health service where your child's development is monitored by your local GGD (Gemeentlijke Gezondheids Dienst) health service (020 555 59 11). The GGD will send you a card with an appointment for your child's examination or immunisations when they are due. If you would prefer your GP to administer your child's immunisations, this can also be arranged. Doctors from the GGD perform physical examinations that include eye, coordination, hearing and speech tests, and also monitor your child's growth. These GGD exams begin when the child is 5 years old and continue with two more exams between the ages of 6 and 12. During secondary school they will undergo one or two more examinations. The Consultatiebureau and GGD are no substitute for your GP, as they cannot prescribe medicine; they can only recommend non-prescription medications and treatments for minor childhood complaints. There are several stages of immunisation: DKTP (Diptheria, Whooping Cough, Tetanus and Polio) and HIB (Haemophilus Influenzae Type B) at two, three, four and 11 months; BMR (Measles, Mumps and Rubella) and Meningitis at 14 months; DTP (Diptheria, Tetanus and Polio) at 4 years; DTP (Diptheria, Tetanus and Polio) and BMR (Measles, Mumps and Rubella) at 9 years.

Immunisation Schedule

DKTP + HIB (Diptheria, Whooping Cough, Tetanus and Polio) + (Haemophilus Influenzae Type B) 2,3, 4 & 11 months.

BMR (Measles, Mumps and Rubella) + Meningitis at 14 months.

DTP (Diptheria, Tetanus and Polio) at 4 years.

DTP (Diptheria, Tetanus and Polio) + BMR (Measles, Mumps and Rubella) at 9 years.

Dentists & Orthodontists

Selecting a dentist in the Netherlands is similar to finding a doctor. You do not need a referral to make an appointment with a dentist. You can find a dentist in your area by either calling ACCESS (020 423 32 17) for a list, checking the Gouden Gids (Yellow Pages) under Tandartsen (Dentists) or by checking the website www.tandarts.nl and entering your city and postcode. To see an orthodontist you will need to ask your dentist for a recommendation and a referral letter. If you need emergency treatment you can call your dentist outside office hours and there will be a recording with the telephone number of an on-call dentist in your area. Otherwise, you can call the 24 hour emergency dental service on 020 686 11 09. Dentistry prices are quite high in the Netherlands, so it's best to check what type of supplementary insurance cover you will need to help pay for the majority of dental costs. Also, before having any major dental work done, you should check your insurance policy. Cosmetic dentistry is becoming widespread and many dentists now offer teeth whitening and cosmetic services in their practices.

Dentists & Orthodontists		
Amsterdam Dental	Oud Zuid	020 670 40 36
Amsterdamse Tandartspraktijk Leidseplein	Canal Belt (Grachtengordel)	020 625 59 30
Apollolaan Tandartsenpraktijk	Oud Zuid	020 671 38 86
Kliniek voor Cosmetische Tandheelkunde	Oud Zuid	020 662 39 14
Tandartsen aan de Herengracht	Canal Belt (Grachtengordel)	020 751 27 17

Opticians & Ophthalmologists

You do not need a referral to visit an optician, but you will need a referral from your GP to see an opthalmologist (eye specialist). Opticians can perform eye tests, fill prescriptions for glasses, sunglasses and contact lenses, but cannot give a referral to an opthalmologist – this must come from your GP. Contact lens solution can be bought either at the optician, apotheek (pharmacy) or drogist (druggist). You can either look

Opticians & Ophthalmologists		
Bril Opticien	Oud Zuid	020 676 70 50
Oogappel Optiek	Oud Zuid	020 470 93 01
Schmidt Optiek	Centrum	020 644 21 08
Specsavers Opticiens	De Pijp	020 662 54 76

one up in the Gouden Gids under 'Opticien' or just pop in to your local optician for a check-up. Laser eye surgery clinics also seem to be appearing everywhere in Amsterdam, making prices very competitive. Laser eye surgery can range from as little as €595 per eye to €1400 per eye. You do not need a referral letter from your GP or optician to have laser eye surgery. The laser clinics have optometrists in-house that will perform extensive tests to see whether or not you are a candidate for laser eye surgery. International laser eye surgery clinics in Amsterdam include Optical Express (0800 222 2100), Care Vision (0800 777 8777) and VisionClinics (0800 888 8999). For a list of opticians, see Eyewear on p.263.

Cosmetic Treatment & Surgery

Popular television shows like Extreme Makeover and Holland's Next Top Model have furthered the pursuit of physical perfection. Cosmetic treatment clinics offer a broad spectrum of beauty-enhancing treatments such as teeth whitening, Botox injections, liposuction and laser wrinkle removal. Prices vary from clinic to clinic so it's best to consult websites first and then schedule a consultation. The Medisch Centrum Boerhave is known for its dermatology specialists, and Stichting Medisch Centrum Jan van Goyen (p.110) comes highly recommended for its breast enhancement and lifting procedures. See also Health Centres & Clinics on p.110.

Cosmetic Treatment & Surgery		
The Care Industry	Oud Zuid	020 575 50 50
Esthetisch Centrum Amsterdam	Oud Zuid	020 664 32 23
Kliniek Emmastraat	Oud Zuid	020 664 94 23
Medea	Oud Zuid	020 664 35 09
Medisch Centrum Boerhaave	Oud Zuid	020 305 00 40
Medisch Laser Centrum	Oud Zuid	020 671 13 79
Qliniek	Canal Belt	020 520 00 20
Stichting Medisch Centrum Jan van Goyen	Oud Zuid	020 305 58 00

Alternative Therapies

Alternative medicine is very popular in the Netherlands, with a wide variety of treatments available such as acupuncture, Reiki, homeopathy, colour therapy and many more. Some complementary treatments are covered by additional insurance, but you should check with your insurance provider to see which treatments are included in your policy. You don't always need a referral from your family doctor to seek alternative medicine, but this will depend on your insurance company's requirements. If you need assistance with anything relating to alternative medicine you can contact the Alternatieve Geneeswijzen Infolijn (088 242 42 40, www.infolijn-ag.nl). This is a volunteer organisation that can help you find alternative therapists and organisations in your area. A wide range of alternative treatments like healing meditation and aromatherapy are offered by various practitioners at the Aurora Holistic Center (020 421 19 87, www.aurora-holistic-center.nl) situated on Prinsengracht in the city centre. Other options for relaxing and unwinding are Aromatique Amsterdam (020 624 00 44) and Classic Aromatherapy (020 668 41 30). Holistic treatments can also be found in Well-Being (p.240).

Alternative Therapies	
Aromatique Amsterdam	020 624 00 44
Aurora Holistic Center	020 421 19 87
Classic Aromatherapy	020 668 41 30
Foot Reflexology and Reiki	www.tomshanty.com

Stress Management

Stress is on the rise worldwide with workplaces becoming increasingly more competitive and employers saving costs by employing less staff, but compared to most major cities, Amsterdam is quite laid back when it comes to daily stresses like commuting in traffic or on public transport. That said, you will probably come across the term 'overspannen' once you've entered the working world in Holland. It is a uniquely Dutch phenomenon meaning 'work-related stress' that allows the employee stress leave to recover. There are countless ways in Amsterdam to relieve stress and avoid becoming 'overspannen'. Try simple, enjoyable solutions like cycling to and from work to clear your mind, or relaxing meditation to achieve inner calm. Yoga, Tai Chi and soothing massage can all be fantastic stress busters. See the Well-Being section (p.240) for more stress-relieving activities.

Acupressure & Acupuncture

Acupuncture is a traditional Chinese medical technique that has been around for thousands of years. It is performed by inserting ultra-fine metal needles at specific points on the body to unblock chi (energy) and balance the opposing forces of ying and yang. It is a popular and well-established alternative treatment for healing all sorts of pain and ailments, from migraines to nausea and even drug addiction. Only visit a properly trained acupuncturist who belongs to a reputable professional association, otherwise you could risk an infection from improperly sterilised needles. You can find reliable acupuncturists via the Nederlandse Artsen Acupunctuur Vereniging (Netherlands Doctors' Acupuncture Association), www.naav.nl. This is an association of existing healthcare professionals who have expanded their skills to include acupuncture.

Addiction Counselling & Rehabilitation

No matter what type of addiction you are dealing with, there are support groups, helplines (in English) and websites offering helpful advice and support. ACCESS (020 423 32 17) is a very good source with an extensive counselling network that can put you in touch with the support you need.

Addiction Counselling & Rehabilitation		
Alcoholics Anonymous	020 625 60 57	www.aa-netherlands.org
British Armed Forces Link (Netherlands)	060 22 22 88	www.befrienders.org
Gamblers Anonymous	0900 217 77 21	www.gamblersanonymous.org
Narcotics Anonymous Helpline Amsterdam	020 662 63 07	www.na.org

Aromatherapy

Aromatherapy is based on ancient healing methods using essential oils to heal, relax and energise the body by either inhalation or massage. Amsterdam offers a variety of possibilities for a personalised aromatherapy treatment, either at the Aurora Holistic Center, Aromatique – a beauty centre which offers aromatherapy massage, or Classic Aromatherapy. Indian Head Massage is available from Alexandra Steele, on 020 668 41 30. Some massage studios also offer aromatherapy massage, like 'doctor feelgood' in the Well-Being section (p.240).

Aromatherapy		
Aromatique Amsterdam	Canal Belt (Grachtengordel)	020 624 00 44
Aurora Holistic Center	Canal Belt (Grachtengordel)	020 421 19 87
Classic Aromatherapy	Various locations	020 668 41 30
doctor feelgood	Zeeburg	020 620 15 70

Homeopathy

There are an impressive number of homeopaths in Amsterdam and some are even doctors who couple their 'conventional' medical skills with their homeopathic knowledge. Homeopathic treatment is recognised by insurance companies in the Netherlands but some insurance companies offer more extensive coverage than others with their supplemental insurance packages. To find a good homeopath you can ask friends for a recommendation, or possibly your family doctor can recommend someone they work with. You can also check the www.nvkh.nl (Netherlands Association for Classical Homeopaths) or www.homeopathie.nl (an association for doctors who are also qualified homeopathic practitioners) to find a homeopathic practice in your area.

Reflexology & Massage Therapy

Other options **Massage** p.240

Reflexology is the use of foot massage to diagnose and cure ailments. It's based on the idea that each part of the foot corresponds to a part of the body. Practitioners of

Reflexology & Massage Therapy			
AVEDA Day Spa	Laan der Hesperiden 90	Oud Zuid	020 794 93 66
Corpus Rub	Van Breestraat 72-hs	Oud Zuid	020 416 50 55
doctor feelgood	Czaar Peterstraat 116	Zeeburg	020 620 15 70

reflexology believe they can cure a variety of complaints by massaging certain reflex points on the foot. Many massage studios, spas and centres in Amsterdam offer foot reflexology as part of their treatments, such as 'doctor feelgood' (p.244), Corpus Rub (p.244), and the AVEDA Dayspa (p.243). The Aurora Holistic Center (p.114) on the Prinsengracht usually offers courses in this field.

Rehabilitation & Physiotherapy

As work and education increasingly involve the use of computers, the hazard of developing RSI (repetitive strain injury) and the need for physiotherapy is greater. Whether you are recovering from a sports injury, muscle strain or more serious accident, Amsterdam provides a wide selection of physiotherapist and sports injury clinics to choose from. Your GP will be able to recommend a physiotherapist or rehabilitation centre in your neighbourhood. You do not need a referral letter, but check your supplemental insurance for the type of treatment you are entitled to, as the basic insurance coverage for physiotherapy is very limited. You can also check the website www.alle-fysiotherapeuten.nl or the Gouden Gids (www.goudengids.nl) under Fysiotherapeuten.

Rehabilitation & Physiotherapy		
Profysio	Canal Belt (Grachtengordel)	020 626 15 78
Revalidatiecentrum Amsterdam	Oud West	020 607 16 07
SMC Sport Medisch Centrum Amsterdam	Oud Zuid	020 662 72 44
Spits Centrum voor Fysiotherapie	Oud Zuid	020 672 00 31

Back Treatment

Other options **Massage** p.244, **Alternative Therapies** p.114, **Rehabilitation & Physiotherapy** (above)

Lower back pain is an occupational hazard, often stemming from sitting long hours in front of a computer. It is most common in people from 35 to 55 years old. More than 70% of people in developed countries will experience lower back pain at some time in their lives and approximately 30% of European workers say their occupation has resulted in them developing this affliction. With these figures it is necessary to find ways to prevent the symptoms worsening and becoming chronic. If you suffer from back pain, there are a number of chiropractic clinics, osteopaths, physiotherapy clinics and massage studios in Amsterdam. They offer various treatments such as cranio-sacral, shiatsu and deep tissue massage to help alleviate the pain. Although osteopaths and chiropractors are similar professions, a chiropractor will tend to use more diagnostic procedures such as X-rays, MRI scans, and blood and urine tests. Osteopaths use these procedures as well, but to a lesser extent. Both use movement palpation (feeling the spine as it moves) to assist in diagnosing where there are abnormalities of movement. A first consultation for both types of practioners costs between €60 and €70, and subsequent consultations €45. There are a number of reliable sources for finding accredited chiropractors in the Netherlands: www.chiropractic-ecu.org, www.chiropractie.nl or

Back Treatment		
Braund Health Chiropractie	Nieuwmarkt	020 422 29 49
Chiropractie Rodermans	West	020 671 62 60
D.C. Young Chiropractie	Oud Zuid	020 622 82 69
Osteopathy Amsterdam	Jordaan	020 620 19 00
Osteopathy Clinic	Oud Zuid	020 662 93 48

the Gouden Gids under Chiropractie. For finding osteopaths you can also look in the Gouden Gids under Osteopaten or visit www.ostepathie-nro.nl.

Nutritionists & Slimming

Although the Dutch lead a generally healthy lifestyle and are quite active, with bicycles being the most popular mode of transportation, Amsterdam still offers numerous resources for improving overall health and fitness. These include dietary support groups and places to go for advice. For more information about physical fitness see Leisure Facilities in the Activities chapter on p.237.

Nutritionists & Slimming	
Compulsive Eaters Anonymous	020 770 93 09
Health & Nutrition Counsellor	061 242 45 24
Sweet Resorts	020 573 37 00
WeightWatchers	0900 202 6060

Counselling & Therapy

Moving to a new country can be an exciting experience, but also an unsettling one when you are faced with new schools, a new house and new work (all with a foreign language, culture and customs). Everyday situations in a foreign country may be more challenging without your personal network and support system from home. In these instances, seeking professional help can ease the adjustment and integration. You can find recommendations for native English-speaking psychologists, psychiatrists and counsellors through your local consulate or embassy (see Embassies and Consulates p.21). In addition, ACCESS, a non-profit volunteer organisation set up to help the English-speaking community in the Netherlands, can provide English-speaking professional support through their counsellor network. The ACCESS Counselling Network consists of professionals with practices all over Holland. The counsellors are psychologists, mental health counsellors and social workers from a variety of different cultural backgrounds. For more information, contact ACCESS (020 423 32 17, www.access-nl.org).

Counsellors & Psychologists		
Professional Psychological Counselling - Myia Wannemiller	Canal Belt (Grachtengordel)	06 51 529959
Therapeuten Arts & Bolck - Jeanette Bolck, Psychologist	Canal Belt (Grachtengordel)	020 468 90 86
Yellow Wood Integrative Psychotherapy Practice - Debby Poort	Amstelveen	06 26 002742
Zelda Hall M. A., Psychologist and Therapist	Canal Belt (Grachtengordel)	020 683 18 92

Support Groups

Although Amsterdam has a village feel to it, it takes a little time to meet people and develop friendships in a new city, let alone a new country. Fortunately, you won't feel lonely for long, as Holland seems to have cornered the market with social groups, offering over 100 expatriate organisations across the Netherlands. There is an extensive list of social groups, sports groups, activities and support groups. If you look on www.expatica.com under Groups & Clubs you'll find nearly every nationality is represented by their own organisation. You can choose from a broad variety of groups ranging from support groups for parents with small children, to sport clubs, social societies and political groups. Another great source is www.elynx.nl, under their Activities section, or see Social Groups on p.224.

Oops!
Did we miss anything out? If you have any ideas or comments for us to include in the Residents section, drop us a line, and if your group or organisation isn't in here, let us know and we'll give you a shout in the next edition. Visit our website (www.explorerpublishing.com) and tell us whatever's on your mind.

Education

The Netherlands was ranked number one in the world in 2007 in a study which assessed general levels of children's well-being, and this is reflected in its excellent schools system. Parents may be required to meet some additional costs, but the education in publicly funded schools is free. Children can enter the Dutch education system at any time of the year, but placement of your child can be problematic due to the long waiting lists, particularly for primary schools. It is advantageous to already have an older brother or sister at the school when you're trying to enrol your child, and also to live as closely to the school as possible. Equal government financing is provided for every publicly funded school in the Netherlands, regardless of whether they are secular or religious. Often children will walk or bike to school in the Netherlands. Some Dutch schools offer English and international streams, but a range of private international schools are also available, which may be of interest to expatriate families.

Nurseries & Pre-Schools

Day nurseries (kinderdagverblijven) are available, and their rates are usually affordable. They are closely monitored by the government to ensure they provide high standards of care for your children. Waiting lists can be a problem though, so it may be a good idea to get your name down while you're pregnant. There are thousands up and down the country and they're usually available for children from several months up to 4 years old. Take a look at the Gouden Gids (www.goudengids.nl) to find a local one, contact ACCESS (020 423 32 17, www.access-nl.org), or try www.kinderopvang.net, which allows you to search for centres in your area. They're generally available between 08:00 and 18:00. Toddlers' groups (which provide activities usually several mornings or afternoons a week) after-school care, and also babysitters, can all be found in Amsterdam, through the contacts mentioned above.

Lutmastraat 81
De Pijp
Map p.384 C2 **5**

Combiwel

020 575 47 00

A large network of child care centres and after school care for children aged 4 through 12. Facilities and teachers vary from one location to another so it is important to check each one individually. There may be places for your child/children in another district. This network is Dutch and does not cater to non-Dutch speakers so if you are looking to place your child in a Dutch speaking environment for the time you are in Holland this would be a good option, if only for the reputation and large choice of locations around town. Contact Mrs. T. Burgers.

Derde Kostverlorenkade 34
Oud West
Map p.379 E4 **6**

Two Voices

020 683 33 83 | *www.xs4all.nl/~heidi/ukbro.htm*

Bilingual Dutch and English education taught to tots in a Montessori learning environment. The focus is on working together with natural materials such as hoes, rakes and buckets. Learning to care for the environment is a big focus with kids participating in the setting up and care of the facility. Many parents who have been relocated to Amsterdam and who think bilingual education is a plus send their pre-schoolers here. Between the ages of 1 and 4 (the legal age when children are required to attend school in Holland), Two Voices, although part-time, offers a stimulating environment. That said, most of the children here are not Dutch.

Primary & Secondary Schools

Primary Schools

Primary education in the Netherlands is provided by three basic types of school. Around two-thirds of 4 year olds enrol in some form of religious school, whether this is Roman

Feeling Far From Home?

Catholic, Protestant or Islamic. Around one-third attend what are referred to as public schools, which offer a secular education and are run by the local municipality. In addition, a smaller number of schools also offer teaching focused around philosophical approaches such as the Montessori method. Primary schools providing specialist teaching and care for children with disabilities and behavioural problems are also available, as are international schools which may be favoured by expat families. Subjects taught at primary level range from physical education, history and science, to languages, art and music. For more about the range of primary schools on offer in Holland visit the website www.scholenlijst.nl (in Dutch) or ring the Dutch Ministry of Education, Culture and Science on 070 412 34 56. Children aged 12 take what is known as the CITO exam, which offers information about what type of secondary school the child will be most suited to, and is combined with parental and student preference to help determine their future educational path.

Secondary Schools

There are three streams of secondary education in the Netherlands (VWO, VMBO and HAVO), but within each of the three different types of secondary school for the first three years the subject matter will be similar.

The VWO schools provide preparation for university study, and students study topics associated with their preferred 'subject cluster' for six years – clusters include economics and society, nature and technology, and culture and society. They also offer the study of Latin.

VMBO schools give children vocational skills including agricultural studies, health and personal care, and technology studies. After four years here a child will progress to MBO, the second period of vocational education, where there are courses ranging from training to be an assistant to middle management training. All are at levels of increasing difficulty until specialist training is completed and the child has the opportunity to attend a university of professional education.

The HAVO stream follows a similar curriculum to the VWO schools, but are not as academically demanding. They do however offer the possibility of more responsibility in employment than the VMBO schools, and are a middle path between the very academic VWO and the vocational VMBO schools.

Secondary schools are also divided into those which are secular and religious, and also those specialising in particular educational philosophies; some will also offer an English-speaking stream. Private international schools offer expatriate communities the choice of schooling their children in their native language and curriculum. For advice on schooling in the Netherlands contact the advice centre for the international community in Holland, ACCESS (020 423 3217, www.access-nl.org).

Prinses Irenestraat 59-60
Zuideramstel
Map p.383 F3 7

Amsterdam International Community School

020 577 12 40 | *www.aics.esprit-sg.nl*

The AICS is a Dutch government-subsidised school offering an international style of education, which may be regarded as more affordable than some of the more expensive privately run international schools. It caters for children from the ages of 3 up to 19, and prepares them for the International Baccalaureate. It is available to children of all nationalities and backgrounds, but classes are usually taught in English.

Anthonie van Dijckstraat 1
Oud Zuid
Map p.384 A2 8

British School of Amsterdam

020 679 78 40 | *www.britishschoolofamsterdam.nl*

The British School of Amsterdam's curriculum is based on that from the U.K. and services age groups from pre-school to upper school. There are four buildings scattered around Amsterdam south: a pre-school, primary, secondary and high school.

Eventually all the buildings will be housed under one roof. After school activities are not part of the school per se, although the list of clubs attended by BSA students includes football, rugby, tennis, field hockey and the British Boy and Girl Scouts. Many of the clubs are run by parents and may not exist the year you enrol your child as it is strictly voluntary. During school hours and for an extra fee, music and dance lessons are offered to boys and girls. There is very little sport offered as the school grounds are smallish. Expensive.

Sportlaan 45
Amstelveen
Map p.367 E4

The International School of Amsterdam

020 347 11 11 | *www.isa.nl*

The International School has tremendous grounds and facilities for Amsterdam. A football pitch, outdoor play area for tots, a gymnasium and stage for dramatic events and debates turn this building into a home away from home for those who appreciate the American style of education. Focused more on creativity than rote learning, children here from pre-kindergarten (age 3) up to grade 12 (age 18) are encouraged to express themselves in their own individual manner. It is home to more than 60 nationalities who are temporarily based in the Amsterdam or Randstad region. The teaching methods ready childen for the International Baccalaureate and/or an accredited American-style high school diploma. Housed in one school. Expensive.

Karel Klinkenbergstraat 137
Slotermeer
Map p.378 B3 10

The Japanese School of Amsterdam

020 611 81 36 | *www.isbi.com*

For Japanese students only; all classes are taught in Japanese. For parents who wish to maintain the same level of education as taught back home so as not to compromise their children's ability in the Japanese language, and also to foster the cultural mentality of working in a group. Many parents whose kids are at international schools also send their children here on Saturday mornings for extra study to keep up with Japanese reading and writing. The school prepares the students for re-entry back into Japanese society by keeping them up to speed with the Japanese school system.

University & Higher Education

A university degree, or a 'third level education' as it is known here, is obtainable at various universities in the Netherlands. Most expats end up going home for university, but there are some places that offer courses in English (see below for some of the most popular). The Netherlands has some universities that are popular with foreign students, although there tends to be more non-English speakers than English speakers. For students who have been through the Dutch schooling system, qualifications for entry to a university include a HAVO certificate, a pre-university certificate, VWO or a middle-management or specialist training certificate. For more information contact these websites – www.nuffic.nl

Vrije Universiteit

or www.ib-groep.nl – which can help you further in your choice of universities. Most universities now offer bilingual education and many MBA programmes are offered solely in English. Educaide, an advice office helps parents, students, teachers, schools, and authorities on a wide range of issues pertaining to international and bilingual education in the Netherlands. Contact info-educaide@xs4all.nl. ACCESS a volunteer organisation in Amsterdam, helps foreigners with any number of issues relating to settling in the area, and are knowledgeable about the education system (020 423 32 17, www.access-nl.org). Tuition fees for university are very low for Dutch students, however MBA, PhD and Master's degrees cost much more. Students under the age of 30 pay a minimal tuition of less than €5,000 per year plus expenses for books. Most students do not live on campus because accommodation is expensive. Many rent rooms in the city of the university or live at home. Unless studying engineering or IT technology, music, agriculture or a very specific line of education, most pupils do not venture to another city for their continued education, sticking close to home. In 1984 the Open University was founded for adult education without admission requirements. It offers HBO and university courses. Studielink (www.studielink.nl) is a one-stop-shop for admissions and registration to any university. Students seeking housing accommodation can visit www.come.to/kamergids.nl.

Student Life Overview

Visas For Students

In order to receive a residence permit to study in the Netherlands you will have to be enrolled on a full time course and fulfil all the requirements of the residence visa. For a comprehensive guide please see www.nuffic.net/immigration.

Studying abroad is a very appealing thought for those looking to get something extra out of the university experience; the potential for 'life education' is huge. Amsterdam is a fantastic city in which to live and the Netherlands provides a unique opportunity to experience Europe and its continental lifestyle. The political openness here creates lively public debate and the high number of English-speaking residents means that those interested can stay informed and, should they wish, get involved. However, you may find that certain aspects of Dutch life don't agree with you, so make sure you do your research about the country first. For information on being an international student in the Netherlands visit the site for 'international co-operation in higher education' (www.nuffic.nl/international-students).
There is a massive active student population and many organisations to help international students settle in. The International Student Network Amsterdam (www.isn-amsterdam.nl) and International Student Meeting Point Amsterdam (www.isma-amsterdam.org) are two great sources of information about how to prepare yourself for studying in the Netherlands.

Where To Study

Amsterdam has two major universities that offer a huge array of bachelor's and master's courses. The Universiteit van Amsterdam (p.123), and the Vrije Universiteit Amsterdam (p.124), both offer courses for international students. Between the two of them they have over 40,000 students. In a city the size of Amsterdam that's pretty massive and you can definitely feel the student vibe throughout the city. The UvA has many locations throughout the centre of Amsterdam and first opened its doors in 1632 under the name Athenaeum Illustre. It is a highly respected and well-connected university. VU is only slightly smaller than the UvA but no less prestigious. It opened its doors in 1880 as the first Protestant university and this heritage holds some influence over tuition, bringing with it an emphasis on social issues. The university grounds are situated just outside of Amsterdam centre, in the Buitenveldt area. It is easily accessible by bus, train and metro.

Student Housing

Finding somewhere to live will be your biggest challenge in Amsterdam. August and September are particularly difficult months to find accommodation as so many students

Student Work
Whether or not you can work while studying in the Netherlands depends on your work visa. There are two types available to students. One is for seasonal employment, which means you could work full time for June, July and August. The other is year round employment for 10 hours a week. If you are eligible for one of these, you will have to follow the procedure laid out in Visas for Students on the left. Some students do supplement their income by offering tutoring in their subject of expertise or by babysitting and cleaning.

are coming to the city to begin their studies. You may want to start looking well in advance of your arrival. If your course can provide you with contact details of other students, consider getting in touch with them and pooling resources. There are several student accommodation resources you can begin to investigate before you arrive. De Key works in conjunction with the universities to locate accommodation. Your university will probably subscribe for you; for more information visit the website www.shortstay.dekey.nl. There is also a 'renters' support' association that provides a great deal of information about how to rent in Amsterdam, what to expect, and a list of support services for students (www.huurders.info). Unfortunately there are a lot of people who may try and take advantage of those looking for reasonable accommodation so it's advisable to go through a recommended agency like those on the support site.

Student Money Matters

Amsterdam is not a cheap city but it's not as expensive as New York, London or Tokyo, and according to research you should be able to get by on around €1,000 a month providing you find reasonable accommodation. Depending on the type of visa you are eligible for (see Student Work on the left), you may be able to pick up some part-time work to make ends meet. You should definitely apply for an international student ID card as well as your university card. With these cards you will be able to get discounts for entry into museums, some restaurants, cinemas and youth hostels. If you are eligible for financial assistance, you should investigate this as part of your enrolment - you may qualify for discount on public transport. Even if you're not, you can go to the rail website (www.ns.nl), or in person to the train station, and apply for an Ovkaart pass, which costs €50 a year and gets you discounts on travel of up to 40%. There are also many cafes and restaurants located around the universities that offer inexpensive food.

Universities

Straatweg 25
Breukelen
Map p.365 A3

Nyenrode Business Universiteit

034 629 12 11 | *www.nyenrode.nl*

One of the top business schools churning out Holland's brightest new stars. Courses are offered in English for advanced degrees, and are a good choice for expatriates who want to continue their higher education in the Netherlands. Many of Holland's heads of industry have a degree from this prestigious school. It's still something of an old boys network when it comes to industry in Holland, based on the friendships made on the university campus – so for women trying to break through the glass social ceiling here, you may have an uphill struggle. It is located in the quaint town of Breukelen, which is just a half-hour drive outside of Amsterdam, and can easily be reached by public transportation.

Frederik Roeskestraat 96
Centrum
Map p.383 E3 12

Rietveld Academie

020 571 16 00 | *www.gerritrietveldacademie.nl*

One of the leading academies in Holland for applied arts, this institute was founded by the well-known Dutch designer and artist Gerrit Rietveld for designers and architectural students. Very recently fashion design has also been added as a discipline, as Amsterdam is trying to promote itself as an alternative fashion capital. Students graduating from this academy tend to go freelance and open their own studios or work in advertising and industrial design.

Binnengasthuisstraat 9
Centrum
Map p.393 D1 13

Universiteit van Amsterdam (UvA)

020 525 80 80 | *www.studeren.uva.nl*

For students wishing to carry on university studies in English, you may do so at the UvA. The various fields of study for BA, Master's and PhD programmes include economics and business, humanities, law, science and social and behavioural science. Many foreign students come here to study in the field of medical sciences and research. Papers published in the journals of New England Journal of Medicine and the equivalent in the UK often cite research done at the UvA.

De Boelelaan 1105
Buitenveldert
Map p.383 F4 **14**

Vrije Universiteit Amsterdam

020 598 98 98 | *www.vu.nl*

The Vrije (Free) University is one of the oldest non-religious affiliated universities in the Netherlands. Courses offered include 60 Master's courses in English, another 40 in Dutch, and PhD programmes. A liberal arts education is available here, and courses are available for adults in Dutch to top up their language skills before a course, or just to speak the local language better. Check the website for more details.

Strawinskylaan 57
Buitenveldert
Map p.384 A3 **15**

Webster University

www.webster.nl

Teaching in English only, Webster University has one campus outside Amsterdam in the suburb of in Leiden (071 516 80 01) – where Admissions is located, and a Graduate Studies Center in the World Trade Center in the south of the city (address above), where you can also study. This university is part of a global network and students can study at any one of the schools in Europe, Asia or USA. The programmes offered fall into one of four categories: communications, education, business and technology.

Special Needs Education

There are approximately 50 schools in Amsterdam that cater for children with special needs, although the process to locate just the right school for your child, depending on their needs, can be a long and drawn out one. As is the case throughout the school system, parents will have to work closely with teachers, doctors or specialists (when required) to determine the right type of school. In certain cases there may not be a special needs school in the area you live and that may impinge upon your decision as to where or how to enrol a child who has a requirement outside the norm. Categories defined as special needs are: the deaf, visually impaired, physically handicapped, severely mentally handicapped and pupils with serious behavioural problems.

Special Needs Schools
The Dutch Ministry of Education, Culture and Science website offers information about the Dutch school system (www.minocw.nl). For free advice from English-speaking volunteers, contact ACCESS (020 423 32 17, www.access-nl.org) who are ready to help with specific questions about schools in the Netherlands.

Learning Dutch

Other options **Basic Dutch** p.15, **Language Schools** p.209

While most Dutch people speak excellent English, if you plan on heading out of the Randstad area, it may benefit you to know some Dutch. For most expats in Amsterdam though, it isn't really necessary unless you are working for a Dutch organisation or with Dutch colleagues. As Dutch is a minority language and rarely spoken outside of the Netherlands, it's up to you if you'd feel better off knowing it. When you do try to speak, people do appreciate your efforts, but will most likely reply to you in English.
Dutch is taught to expatriate children at English language schools, however the level is very rarely up to par. Your child will not walk out of school speaking Dutch as lessons are too few and far between, mostly just one hour per week at most. Private language schools and teachers are the most commonly used resources to learn Dutch, although some universities offer courses for beginners.

Learning Dutch		
Berlitz	020 622 13 75	www.berlitz.nl
British Language Training School	020 622 36 34	www.bltc.nl
Institut voor Nederlands	020 525 46 42	www.intt@uva.nl
Learn Dutch	na	www.learndutch.org
Overtaal Language Services	030 242 70 02	www.overtaal.nl
Speaking Dutch	020 686 09 63	www.speakingdutch.nl
Vrije Universiteit Amsterdam (VU)	020 598 98 98	www.vu.nl

Transportation

Other options **Getting Around** p.34

Amsterdam has a great public transport system. There are trams, trains, buses and a metro, so there should be nowhere you can't get to easily. Generally though, people don't use public transport all the time. There's another way to travel in Amsterdam: pedal power! One of the first things you notice when you arrive is that bikes are everywhere. People tend to use their bikes for everyday things like going to work and going out. For more about this see Cycling in the Getting Around chapter on p.37.
Of course, if you have to commute to another city it's a different thing altogether. Most people will take the train and avoid getting stuck in traffic. For more information about the public transport network see the Getting Around section (p.34). The road system is good, but like any city, rush hour isn't pretty. Parking in Amsterdam, unless you have a permit from the council, is expensive and elusive.

Driving In Amsterdam

Owning a car in Amsterdam is not cheap. You will have to pay road tax, either quarterly or annually (it's your choice), and petrol is expensive. Parking is costly too, though you can buy a parking permit (parkeervergunning) for your municipality. The costs vary from area to area. In Centrum it is €157.50 for the six month permit, while in Zuideramstel it is only €47.88. A great alternative to worrying about having to park your own car is Green Wheels, a car share initiative. For a monthly fee you have access to several cars throughout the city. For more information visit: http://new.greenwheels.nl (in Dutch).

Centraal Station bike park

Driving Habits

Generally Dutch drivers are quite safe and getting safer. Strict enforcement of laws against dangerous driving have seen the number of fatal accidents fall 25% since 2000.

However, the number of cyclists killed on the road rose by almost 20%. The variety of other forms of transport on the roads in Amsterdam can be quite daunting for a newcomer and most drivers will not wait patiently, so make sure you understand the road rules.

Non-Drivers

Amsterdam is a highly pedestrian-oriented city, especially in the centre. It's also full of cyclists who always have the right of way. Generally pedestrians remain on the footpaths and cyclists on bike paths but sometimes it's just not possible, so keep an eye out and remember: cyclists always have right of way.

Traffic Rules & Regulations

Some basic rules to bear in mind are: the Dutch drive on the right side of the road, the speed limit is 30km/h in residential areas, 50km/h in the city, 80km/h on secondary roads and 100 to 120km/h on the motorways. Speed cameras are mostly used on the motorways and larger roads but heavy fines, up to €660, discourage speeding everywhere. For a full list of road signs and information, in English, download this pdf: www.verkeerenwaterstaat.nl/Images/RVV_UK-versie_tcm195-163061.pdf

Relax

Keep your cool in Amsterdam. Dutch drivers are impatient and won't wait around for you to figure out your next move. They will race red lights and overtake aggressively.

Accidents

If you are involved in an accident, and it is serious, it is imperative you remain at the scene until the police arrive. If you've simply had a fender bender with another driver you can decide with the other driver how best to proceed in terms of insurance - you may still want to wait for the police to arrive and file a report.

Parking

There's not a lot of parking in Amsterdam and none of it is free. It's more expensive in the inner city than it is in surrounding areas. You can expect to pay up to €4.60 an hour. You'll see ticket dispensers (parkeerautomaat) all around town. They accept coins and 'chipknip' bank passes. They also dispense day and night tickets that provide a discount of up to 40% off the hourly rate. For a full list of parking garages, and information on parking in English, see: www.bereikbaaramsterdam.nl/live/main.asp?subsite_id=23.

Petrol Stations

There are petrol stations throughout the city. Texaco, Shell and BP have stations throughout and around Amsterdam, but not in the very heart of the city. Unmanned stations are becoming popular in the Netherlands; you simply pay with your debit or credit card. Full-service stations are not common in the city, most will only offer basic services to keep you on the road. It is a whopping €1.47 per litre for unleaded and €1.08 per litre for diesel. For a gallon it is €5.73 and €4.21 respectively.

Drinking? Don't Drive!

The Netherlands has very little tolerance of drink driving. Inexperienced drivers have a limit of no more then 0.2 and experienced drivers 0.54. Fines are high and strictly enforced. They begin at €220 and increase up to €1,000 plus 10 months' suspension.

Vehicle Leasing

Vehicle leasing or rental is not necessary for travelling around in Amsterdam, as the public transport system is reliable and most people choose to use it. If you would like to rent a car for a day trip, all of the major car rental agencies like Hertz, Europe Car, Budget, and National Car Rental have locations in and outside the city. Today's competitive market means it's quite cheap to rent a car for a couple of days or even a month. Prices depend on availability but for an idea you can visit www.expedia.nl who will check all the major dealers for you. Leasing a car is not really done on a personal basis in Holland; lease companies will usually only lease cars to companies. Car dealers do provide private leasing contracts but they are very rarely called upon to do so and don't advise people to take out a lease personally as it isn't cost effective.

Company Car

In Amsterdam, businesses usually have company cars, and the car is registered to the company unless it is specifically registered to one person within the company. The employer and leasing agent will ensure all documentation is up to date and all insurance is paid. Generally companies will have several cars that can be used by employees, not just specific individuals. When using a company car you will be refunded for petrol costs as long as you provide a receipt.

Beat The Traffic

The best way to get your traffic info is online before you leave. If your Dutch is really non-existent try www.trafficnet.nl for a good visual indication of problem areas.

Buying a Vehicle

To buy a car in the Netherlands you must have a valid residence permit and driving licence. Cars are affordable: you will be able to find good deals for second-hand cars for under €3,000, and there is a good range of dealers to be found on the outskirts of the city as well. Popular brands include Volkswagens, BMWs and Peugeots. According to recent statistics, cars are not overly expensive to buy in the Netherlands, being far cheaper than in Germany and slightly more expensive than in the UK. Most major brand showrooms are concentrated south-east of the ring road and are located near each other. If you'd like to test drive a car you should call in advance to talk to the dealer personally before you visit. It's best to call at least a week in advance. Check dealer websites for deals on used cars. If you want to buy a used car make sure the dealer is a member of BOVAG (Bond Van Automobielhandelaren en Garagehouders), the car dealers' union. All cars from a BOVAG-affiliated dealer will come with a dealer's guarantee. Check here for a full list of certified dealers: www.bovag.nl.

Vehicle Finance

There are a couple of options available to help you secure the funds to purchase your car. You can approach a bank for a loan or talk to the car dealer about what sort of

New Car Dealers

Audi	Audi Centrum	020 564 64 64	www.audi.nl
BMW	BMW Amsterdam	020 460 46 90	www.bmw-amsterdam.nl
Chrysler	Eagle Motors	020 560 70 70	www.chryslerjeepamsterdam.nl
Citroen	Citroen Zuid-Oost	020 430 18 00	www.citroen.nl/CWH/nl-NL/Dealers/154-Zuidoost/
Dodge	Eagle Motors	020 560 70 70	www.chryslerjeepamsterdam.nl
Jaguar	Kimman Amsterdam BV	020 696 49 49	www.kimman.nl
Jeep	Eagle Motors	020 560 70 70	www.chryslerjeepamsterdam.nl
Lada	Garage Diamant	020 696 33 33	na
Mercedes-Benz	Stern Auto Amsterdam	020 311 36 11	www.stergam.nl
Nissan	Nissan Amsterdam BV	020 691 02 01	www.autoveeneman.nl
Porsche	A-Point BV	020 430 16 00	www.a-point.nl
Renault	Renault Amsterdam	020 561 96 11	www.renaultamsterdam.nl
Rover	Kimman Amsterdam BV	020 696 49 49	www.kimman.nl
Toyota	Louwman Amsterdam	020 565 06 10	http://louwman-amsterdam.toyota-dealers.nl/
Volkswagen	A-Point BV	020 430 16 00	www.a-point.nl
Volvo	Furness Car Amsterdam	020 452 20 20	www.furness-amsterdam.nl

deals are available. The interest on repayments can vary depending upon a number of factors. Your own credit history may also determine what kind of deal you can get.

Vehicle Insurance

You must register for third party insurance for your car as the registration is not complete without it. The cost of your insurance will depend on the type of car you drive and your driving history. If you are an experienced driver and have made no insurance claims in the past you will be able to receive a discount. If you choose to be insured by ANWB for example, your discount will begin at 35% and can increase to 80% over the years. The obligatory third party insurance (wettelijk aansprakelijkheid) generally covers damages up to €2,500.

Vehicle Insurance		
ANWB	088 269 22 22	www.anwb.nl
Autoverzekering.com	031 866 66 66	www.autoverzekering.com
Centraal Beheer Achmea	055 579 88 88	www.centraalbeheer.nl
Chrysler	030 605 92 02	www.daimlerchrysler-financialservices.com
OHRA	026 400 40 40	www.ohra.nl
Unive	072 502 45 00	www.unive.nl

Registering a Vehicle

If you buy a car from any dealer, new or used, the dealer will see that the car is registered in your name. If you buy privately, either purchase on the internet via a site called marktplaats.nl or through classifieds. You and the seller will have to go to the post office together to change the registration. You will need a valid passport, your residence permit, a bank statement less than three months old, and the record of registration from the seller. Before you buy a car privately make sure you have the car checked out fully by an inspector as advised by the ANWB, the Dutch motorists' association. All cars more than three years old must have an APK certificate as advised by the Department of Road Transport (www.rdw.nl). The APK certificate must be renewed every year - you should renew your APK at least two months before it expires. You should still have a car inspected even if it has an APK certificate, as the certificate only determines road safety, not potential mechanical faults. Once a car is registered in your name it will stay so until you sell it or you file with the RDW to have it de-registered as the car is being destroyed. Only an RDW-registered autodemontagebedriven (wrecking yard) can destroy a car; if parts can be salvaged you will be paid for the car. If you wish to bring your own car into Holland you may have to pay BPM (vehicle tax), via customs. If you've lived in another country for a year and have had the car for longer than six months you will not have to pay the import tax but you will still need to contact customs - the number is 0800 0143. Once you've paid the taxes you will be able to register the car with the RDW after paying €78 for an inspection and a €45 environment tax. You can then have Dutch number plates made. Once you've completed this process you must take out third party insurance which is mandatory in the Netherlands.

Recovery Services/Towing (24 hour)		
AA Team	018 132 44 33	na
Euro Cross	071 364 18 41	na
Route Mobiel	0800 0504	na
Wegenwacht	088 269 22 22	www.anwb.nl

Traffic Fines & Offences

Traffic regulations are strictly enforced in the Netherlands. Violating regulations can result in fines, suspension of licence and even jail. Here are some of the regulations and their fines: not wearing a seat belt: €75 per person, child not in child seat: €75, refusal to take breathalyser test: €130, expired licence or illegible licence: €50, driving without insurance or proof of insurance: €130, driving under the influence: from €220 up to €1,000 and 10 months' suspension of licence, driving with unsafe tyres: from €17 to €250, running a red light: €130, using a mobile while driving: €130, not stopping at a stop sign: €50, driving slower than 60km/hr on the motorway: €200, speeding: from €16 up to €660 (and you may have your licence suspended) depending on the speed. There isn't a points system in the Netherlands. When you are caught breaking the rules you will be given a receipt that states the particulars of the violation – this is not your ticket, you will receive this at a later date in the mail. You will be able to pay by bank transfer or cash at Postbank.

Breakdowns

If your car breaks down you should try and move it out of the path of traffic. If you cannot, or it is too dangerous to move the car you should make sure your hazard lights are on. Call for assistance immediately. If you are making a journey off the beaten track make sure you have a mobile and that you have told someone where you are going and your expected travel time. You should always have extra water in the car, for you and the car, and make sure you have a spare tyre and tyre changing kit. It's also worthwhile being a member of a roadside assistance organisation as if you're a member you'll pay less for the service should you need to call upon it.

Rutger Hauer (Actor)

Born in Breukelen, near Amsterdam, this blonde Dutch film actor shot to fame in the 1981 thriller Nighthawks, playing a villain opposite Sylvester Stallone. A year later came his most renowned role in Ridley Scott's Blade Runner, widely regarded as a science fiction masterpiece. In 1995 he was honoured by appearing on a Dutch postage stamp. 2006 saw him create his 'Film Factory', an annual series of workshops aimed at fostering young film-making talent (www.rutgerhauer.org).

Traffic Accidents

Other options **Car** p.36

According to the Dutch police, speeding, running red lights and driving while under the influence of alcohol cause most road accidents. Every year in Holland over 200 deaths are caused by driving under the influence and over 3,000 people are permanently injured. In Amsterdam, busy intersections are often the sites of accidents, so be calm and vigilant when crossing them. If you are involved in an accident that is more serious than a fender bender you must remain on the scene until the police arrive. If someone is hurt you must call emergency services. You should have your licence, car registration, and insurance papers on hand for emergencies. The Netherlands has a reputation for impatient drivers but not for road rage, though there have been isolated cases. If you feel you are involved in a situation that is raging out of control you should contact the police immediately.

Vehicle Repairs

If your car requires repairs you can take it to any garage to be repaired. You may need to show your registration and insurance papers. Depending on the type of insurance you have, the bill will be sent to the insurer. The police will not be involved unless there is a dispute over blame. You may also be restricted in which garages you can take your car to. It is best to contact your insurance provider and find out what your cover stipulates and how much of the costs they will pay for. Many garages specialise in particular models of car: this usually means they should have the correct parts on hand, which cuts down on service time.

Vehicle Repairs		
Autobedrijf West Sloterdijk	Slotermeer	020 486 55 85
Garage Oost	Oost	020 665 07 44
Gast Citroen/Peugeot Specialist	Amsterdam Noord	020 632 01 90
Schadenet ACK/Bouwman	Slotermeer	020 610 75 80
Speedy	Amstelveen	020 456 03 00
Splinter ABS Autoherstel	Amsterdam Noord	020 631 27 35
Westergarage	West	020 679 19 24

Exploring

Exploring

Amsterdam is a metropolis of the 'multi': it is multi-ethnic, multilingual, multimedia and certainly multicultural. In fact, there's a mixture of everything in this international city of business and creativity, known as the playground of Holland. The swampy piece of land which was granted a city charter by Count Floris V in 1275 was home even then to traders and seafarers. Perhaps it's because of this early, open world view that, as early as the 17th century, artisans and traders fled to Amsterdam from the Spanish rule in the south.

Trade and business continues to pulse through the heart of the nation's capital, with a myriad of international businesses here, attracted by the highly skilled, educated workforce available and, among other things, Schiphol Airport, which has links to more than 200 international cities.

The city continues to attract the artists, students, rebels and renegades looking for the tolerance that Amsterdam is famous for. There is an extremely strong community of diverse cultural and ethnic groups; perhaps the best reflection of Amsterdam's liberal ethos was the city's celebration of its first legalised same-sex civil marriages in 2001.

More than four million tourists a year are attracted to this cosmopolitan city of old world charm. They come for a variety of reasons: there are those who wish to visit the Red Light District and coffeeshops, those with 'museum mania', and people who simply want to explore the wonderfully walkable city's more than 100 canals and 1,200 bridges.

Walking is by far the easiest way to get around the city, and also one of the most enjoyable, as there are so many artistic details to be spotted on every street. Trams are convenient and cover the city extensively, but of course, the quintessential Dutch mode of transport is everywhere... the bicycle.

Recent years have seen the city authorities begin a major refurbishment of Amsterdam, which is only mid-way through as yet. Unfortunately this means that occasionally the city can seem under construction, but this won't last forever, and it is really only noticeable along the new North/South Metro line which is still being built.

The once medieval city has continued to expand and grow, most strikingly by developing the northern islands and harbour area behind Centraal Station. This area, along with housing residential developments, is also home to some of the finest new architecture and cultural institutions in the city, offering an internationally renowned selection of music, theatre, art, photography, film, festivals, dance, and museums.

Each of Amsterdam's neighbourhoods have their own particular personality, be it the slightly faded Jordaan, the concentrated grandeur of the Museum Quarter, or the drunken revelry of the Red Light District. Amsterdam is the city where freedom of expression and artistic flair reign supreme.

District Guide

We've included and Amsterdam district by each entry in this section to help you locate the museums, galleries, parks and other attractions. The map on p.368 shows which area of town each one covers.

Bring Blooms

It is considered bad form to arrive at the home of a Dutch person who has invited you over for a social occasion without a bunch of flowers or a bottle of wine. Avoid the odd glances and bring the present along, it's easier!

Walki-Talki

Take a guided tour of Amsterdam at your leisure after visiting www.walki-talki.com, where you can download a commentary on the key attractions onto your iPod or mp3 player.

Canal cruise in front of Centraal Station

Canal Cruising

With plenty of options to choose from, cruising the canals can be a lifelong adventure. Take a guided excursion with one of the many tour companies available, rent your own pedal boat, or, if you're hooked, buy your own low-lying craft and hit the water. The city will never look the same! (See Boat Tours on p.165).

A Bike Ride Along The Amstel

Riding a bike in town can be the quickest way to get around, but for the pleasure of rural riding why not head out of town along the Amstel where you can view scenes from Rembrandt's paintings, picnic along the river, or visit Amstel Park which is along the way. See Cycling (p.37) and Bicycle Tours (p.164).

Walk In Circles

Don't be a square in this town, be a circle… or at least walk in one. Amsterdam can be a bit confusing to walk around as long as you think in the grid fashion. To make things easier, remember that the city is, for the most part, built in a series of circles. To shorten distances, check your map and remember that the closer you are to the centre, the shorter the distance you'll have to walk!

Glorious Garden Weekend

Amsterdam's secret glory is its gardens hidden behind some of its stunning 17th, 18th, and 19th century canal homes. For only one weekend a year in June, these private gardens are open to the public. See Open Garden Days (p.48).

Paint Yourself Orange

Try as you might, there is no way to get away from Queen's Day (Koninginnedag), the official day celebrating the Queen's birthday, wherever you are in Holland. This is especially true in Amsterdam, which fills up with orange painted tourists from the rest of the country and around the world. Street markets, music festivals, street parties and formal ceremonies make this Holland's biggest party of the year. And the next day is the biggest clean up job! See Queen's Day (p.46).

Museumnacht p.51

Museum Night takes place each November and is the night that the city's museums open their doors to multimedia performances of theatre, dance and music, with the visitors partying with the paintings till the early morning. Always oversubscribed, so get your tickets early!

Get Proud With Pride p.49

No surprise that Amsterdam's Gay Pride weekend is a major event in the city which prides itself for its liberalism. Bridges along the inner canals are the best place to view the waterborne parade, but find your spot early, as everyone wants to feast their eyes on the fest!

Frites

Ideal food on the go while you are exploring the city, the famous Dutch frites are well worth seeking out. The best are the Vlaamse (Flemish) frites, which are freshly made from 'real potatoes', and in true Dutch style, served drowning in a choice of sauces including mayonnaise, ketchup, curry ketchup, satay sauce – and topped with chopped raw onions. Plenty of places sell them, with many claiming to offer Amsterdam's best – for one hot recommendation, try Vlaamse Friethuis on Voetboogstraat (Centrum).

Live Music

Amsterdam's two top live venues are completely tied up with the creative culture of the city, especially its music. The Paradiso (p.357) is home to, among other things, an international electronic music festival, while the Melkweg (p.356) continues to expand its space and repertoire. The stage that presented the first European gigs for U2 and The Police continues to surprise; this year hosting top acts such as Snoop Dog on the new Max Stage, along with film, dance and art exhibitions.

Amazing Acoustics

Apart from being a beautiful concert hall, the Concertgebouw (p.360) is internationally renowned by musicians and music lovers alike as having some of the finest acoustics available. Every Wednesday at 12:30 a popular free concert takes place. Arrive early as seats are coveted!

Go To An Ajax Game p.236

You can't miss the colours, and you can't miss the game. If you're in Amsterdam and it's football season (which seems to be all but six weeks of the year) then Ajax fans can't be missed. Theirs is a passion which can see grown men cry at a deserved win, and a crowd riot at a loss – deserved or not. The best place to feel the fun and the frenzy is at the ArenA itself.

World Press Photography Awards

Amsterdam is the annual host of the World Press Photography Awards (www.worldpressphoto.org); each year it is exhibited at the Oude Kerk in the city, one of the few buildings with the strength and stature to hold this most moving and provocative photographic exhibition of work by the often unsung heroes of the press.

See The City's History In The Grand Hotel p.28

Though this building is not a museum, it does hold a great deal of Amsterdam's history within its walls and courtyard. Initially a collection of convents, it later became the City Hall and Admiralty building, and holds the masterpiece which is the Wedding Room, created by Chris Lebeau. Though an international hotel, The Grand Hotel welcomes visitors and Amsterdam residents alike to come and explore and enjoy the city's history.

Street Markets p.291

Markets abound in the city, and for many local residents it is a rare occasion that finds them going into 'shops,' as everything that they might want or need can be found on the street. The biggest and best locations include the Albert Cuypstraat Markt (p.292), Waterlooplein (p.293), Dapperstraat Markt (p.292) and Noordermarkt (p.293) but there are many, many more to choose from.

Bask In A Brown Cafe p.340

Brown cafes are almost exclusively brown, the colour being formed from year upon year of tobacco stains accumulating on walls and ceilings. It might not sound appealing, but these are also centres for authentic, old-school locals. Some of the best can be found in the Jordaan. Have a coffee and Jenever (the local liquor) and try chatting to a real Amsterdammer – this is where you'll find them.

Window Shop Wandering… It Can't Be Missed

You can't avoid them, so don't try. The window women are in almost every neighbourhood of the city, and, quite frankly, most locals prefer them there to being on street corners. So get used to the idea and hey, you might end up waving hello one day... from a distance of course. See Red Light District (p.138).

View The City's Skyline From Club 11 p.355

There aren't any really majestic skyscrapers in town, but who cares when you have more than 100 canals and a medieval city layout to marvel at. Club 11, at the top of the Post CS Tower near Centraal Station, is a great place for a cocktail and a late night dance, but is also one of the finest points in the city for a panoramic view.

Find A Hof

There aren't many oases in a city as small as Amsterdam, and yet, right at the heart of the hustle and bustle is the Begijnhof (p.150), a private place of peace and quiet. Individual guests are welcome to visit the secluded courtyard just off the Spui which is also home to the 400 year-old Engelse Kerk (English church) of Amsterdam.

Museum Card

This has got to be one of the best bargains available in what is a very bargain conscious country. The museum card, for a reasonable annual fee, grants users free access to more than 400 museums in the Netherlands including almost 30 in Amsterdam alone. See also Museumnacht (p.51), and the iAmsterdam Card (p.148).

Coffee & Coffeeshops

The Dutch are addicted to coffee, and pride themselves on having discerning palates which deserve nothing but the best. This is not a land of coffee chains – this is the country of coffee connoisseurs. For reviews of some of Amsterdam's best cafes, see p.333. For more on the famous Coffeeshops (not just somewhere to go for a coffee!), see p.332.

Bring & Buy Flowers p.264

You won't be surprised by the fact that the Dutch are batty about blooms. Of course there are tulips by the tonne, but you'll be amazed at the vast array of flowers and bulbs which are available, especially on the Bloemenmarkt (p.292).

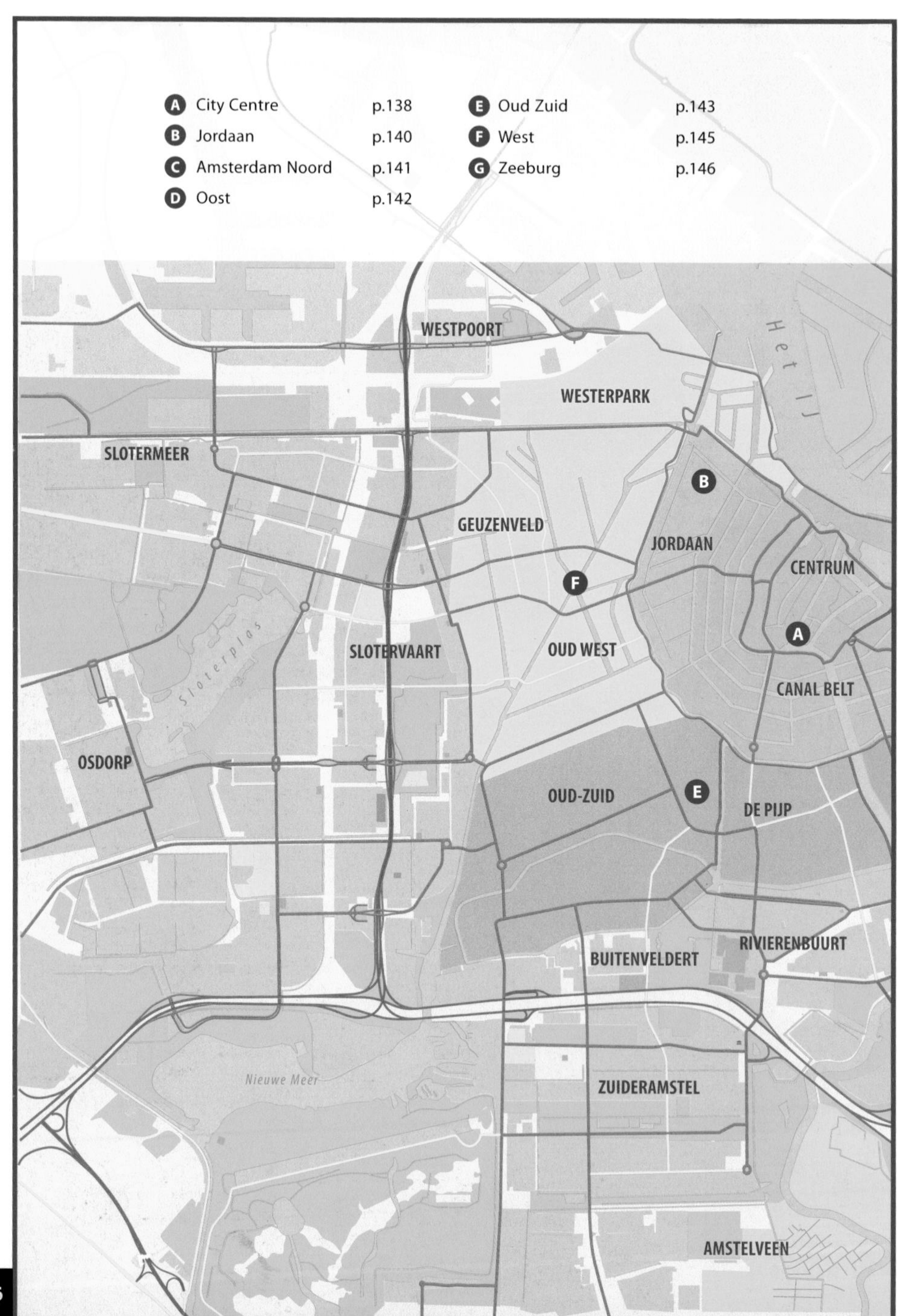
A City Centre p.138
B Jordaan p.140
C Amsterdam Noord p.141
D Oost p.142
E Oud Zuid p.143
F West p.145
G Zeeburg p.146
WESTPOORT
Het IJ
WESTERPARK
SLOTERMEER
GEUZENVELD
JORDAAN
CENTRUM
SLOTERVAART
OUD WEST
CANAL BELT
Sloterplas
OSDORP
OUD-ZUID
DE PIJP
RIVIERENBUURT
BUITENVELDERT
Nieuwe Meer
ZUIDERAMSTEL
AMSTELVEEN

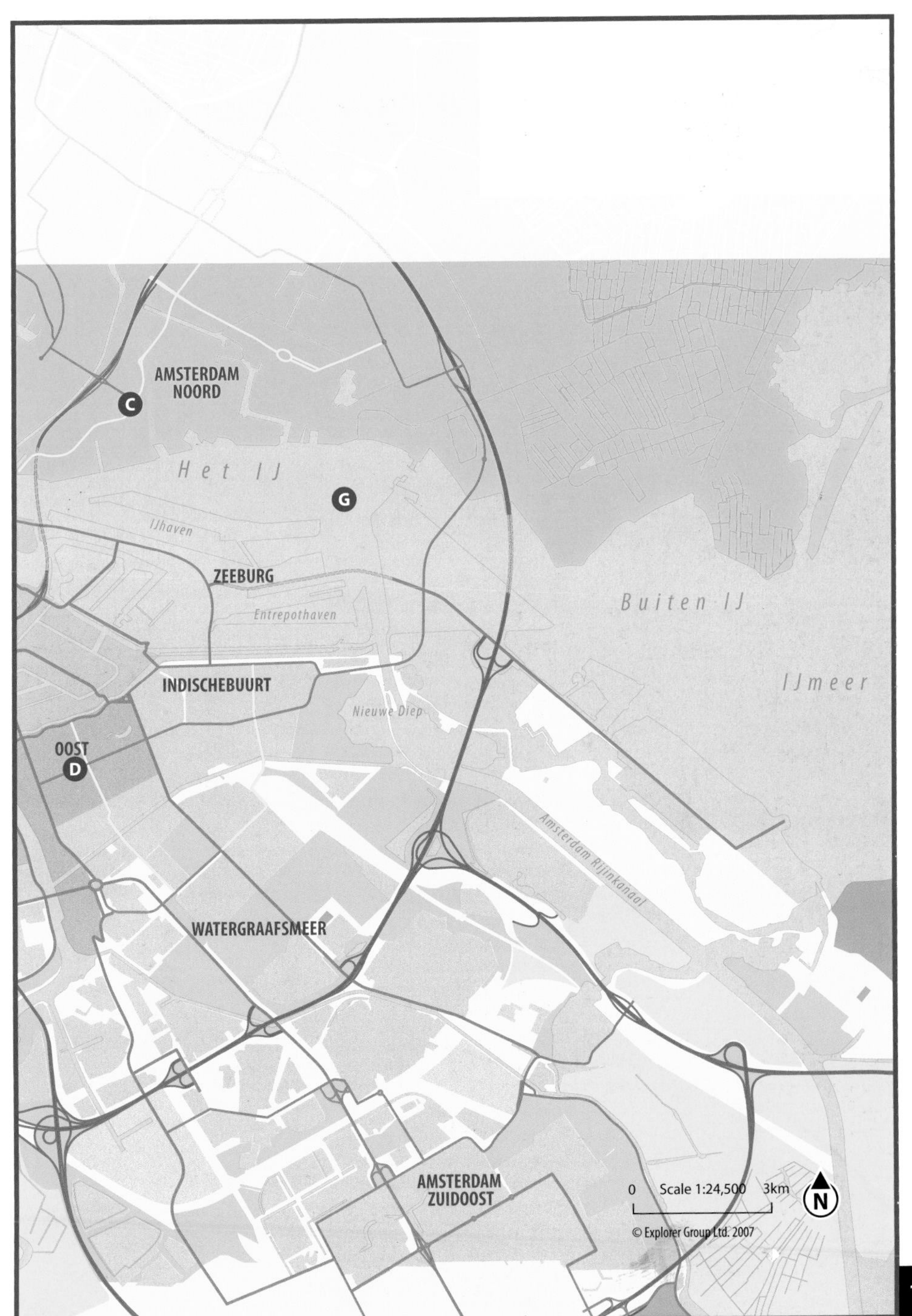
AMSTERDAM
NOORD
C
Het IJ
G
IJhaven
ZEEBURG
Entrepothaven
Buiten IJ
IJmeer
INDISCHEBUURT
Nieuwe Diep
OOST
D
Amsterdam Rijinkanaal
WATERGRAAFSMEER
AMSTERDAM
ZUIDOOST
0 Scale 1:24,500 3km
N
© Explorer Group Ltd. 2007

Map p.388-394
Area A p.136

The Lowdown
Tourist land has taken over the heart of the medieval city, but there are still great cultural sites to enjoy. You can shop for all sorts of things, from diamonds in the rough, to diamonds in the buff.

The Good
The area around Waterlooplein is fantastic to explore. Certainly the market is always full of character, and the streets around the square are filled with history. Rembrandt van Rijn's home is close by (p.156).

The Bad
You should be warned that drunken males on stag nights can be found throughout the city on any given weekend, but usually they are around the Red Light District and Rembrandtsplein.

The Must Dos
Take a seat in the tranquillity of the Begijnhof (p.150) and enjoy a rest in this exquisite spot of green in the heart of the city. Though groups are not welcome, individuals certainly are!

City Centre

If you're starting anywhere, then it's more than likely you're in the Centrum, which includes the Dam Square area, Chinatown, the Red Light District and most of the other popular tourist haunts in the city. It's a land of shopping (of all kinds), socialising, and history.

The medieval centre of the city is still the communal heart of Amsterdam: Dam Square is where you can find the Royal Palace (Koninklijk Paleis, p.155) and the Nieuwe Kerk (p.154). A five minute stroll in almost any direction can take you somewhere interesting including the Red Light District and Chinatown. A 10 minute stroll south leads you to down to Rembrandtplein, the canal belt (grachtengordel), Leidseplein and the heart of tourist land. The city centre is the area to which all out-of-towners flock, and as such, it's filled with every amenity a non-local might want.

It may look like the entire city is under renovation, but the fact is, it only feels that way. The regeneration of the city centre, southern IJ bank, new North/South Metro line and Stationplein – all of which will be under heavy construction for the next few years – continues, but the centre is still as popular a venue as ever and Centraal Station remains the most likely entry point to the city. Be aware that the taxi drivers who line up at the station are notorious for being rude and expensive. Although the city has tried to stamp down on the poor reception given to tourists, the measures have not been very effective.

Centraal Station is the land of trains, trams, metros, buses and bikes. There is a VVV Tourist Office and a GVB Bureau on site as well as hook-ups for canal boat tours. You name the form of transport, and bets are that you'll be able to find it somewhere on or near Amsterdam Centraal Station. Once you leave the station you're in the heart of tourist land, and all that entails. Monuments galore it's true, but there are also a huge number of touts trying to get your money for all sorts of tat. If you're looking for a T-shirt or 'cloggy' souvenir, this is where to find it. Having said that, the neighbourhood is chock-a-block full of culture, history, architecture, art, and fun. This area hosts such cultural and historical hotspots as the Begijnhof (p.150), the Amsterdams Historich Museum (p.154) and the Stadsschouwburg Theatre (p.361).

Whether Amsterdammers like it or not, the city is notorious for a few things: two of the most infamous are coffeeshops (p.332), which former you can find all over town and the Red Light District (see below).

Reminders of the fact that the city was once under water are everywhere. Dam Square is your first hint, but the canals come a close second. Certain areas which are now solid under foot were once sea. Spui (which rhymes with how) was one of those areas; it was underwater until 1882. It is here that you will find book markets, book stores and fantastic people-watching cafes such as Café Luxembourg (020 620 62 64).

Another central area of great interest and fun is the Nieuwemarkt, though it hasn't always been so. In the 17th century it was a harbour for ships that sailed there along the IJ to collect anchors or load and unload goods. Today it's more likely to be people who are getting 'loaded' as the square is circled by cafes, shops and popular restaurants like De Waag. Originally known as St. Anthoniespoort (St. Anthony's Gate), De Waag, dating from 1488, has had many incarnations, including that of a weigh house and also was once the home of the Surgeon's Guild which commissioned Rembrandt to paint the famous Anatomy Lesson of Dr. Tulp. It was also the home of a court where death sentences would be handed down. Public executions took place on the

Red Light District

With its women in the windows, this is an area that almost everyone has to visit, even if only once. It's most evident between the Oudezijds Achterburgwal canal in the east and Warmooesstraat in the west. Prostitution was regulated by Napoleon's forces in the early 19th century, however brothels were only completely legalised in 2000 (there is even a union for the window workers called the Red Thread).

Cracking Down
Amsterdam mayor Job Cohen announced in September 2007 that he plans to crack down on links between organised crime and the sex industry, which could result in hundreds of brothels losing their licences.

Nieuwmarkt in front of the building from the early 19th century. They were previously carried out in Dam Square, but during his rule Louis Napoleon decided it was too gory a spectacle to take place in front of his palatial home.

Happily, Amsterdam crowds now gather instead on the Nieuwmarkt to celebrate the New Year and the Chinese New Year celebrations. Though it was a fairly rough neighbourhood in the 1970s, it cleaned up its act in the mid 1980s – though there are still a few junkies around trying to sell things. North of the market is the Zeedijk, which continues its history of being a late night area catering to those looking for a little more spice. At Zeedijk you will find one of only two wooden houses from the 1500s still standing in the city; the other, older house is in the Begijnhof (p.150).

In a nutshell, the central area of the city has been given up to tourists; it is rare that an Amsterdam local who does not live in the area would spend time there. The Kalverstraat (p.288) is popular, as it is the home of high street shopping in Holland. But as such, it's also the busiest shopping street in the country and it is recommended that you should avoid it like the plague at the weekends as it is permanently congested.

Chinatown

Damrak Centrum

Red Light District

De Waag

Map p.388-392
Area B p.136

Jordaan

The Lowdown
An area concentrated with art, artists and art galleries, it's also home to numerous courtyards and brown cafes.

The Good
The Noordermarkt (p.293) has two fantastic markets each week. Monday from 09:00 to 13:00 is an overflowing flea market and Saturday from 09:00 to 16:00 offers the treat of an immensely popular organic farmers' market!

The Bad
This is probably the most crowded area of the city on Queen's Day. If you can't stand oom-pah-pah music and the joviality of drunken, orange-clad revellers, stay away from the Johnny Jordan statue in the middle of the neighbourhood.

The Must Dos
The Anne Frank Huis (p.154) commemorates the young Jewish girl and her family who hid there during the Nazi occupation of Amsterdam.

This is one of Amsterdam's trendiest areas, and it's no wonder. A neighbourhood of narrow tree-lined streets and charming canals, the Jordaan is one of the most popular places to live and have fun in the city. But it hasn't always been so.

Built in the early 17th century, the Jordaan was initially meant as an area for the working class and those who had only recently arrived in the city. Due to the comparative religious freedom found in Amsterdam, it became a mecca for many refugees, both religious and political. The Huguenots of France, Sephardic Jews of Spain and Portugal, and the Protestant Pilgrims of England all found their way here. At that time it was truly a slum with small buildings, narrow streets, open sewers and no running water – and it was crowded. At the turn of the last century there were approximately 80,000 people living in the area, only 20,000 less than at present.

As is often the case, because it cost little to live there, the Jordaan became a haven for artists. Rembrandt van Rijn, though a major success during parts of his life, was also destitute for many years. During the hard times he lived and worked in the Jordaan. The great master is buried in an unmarked grave in the Westerkerk (p153).

The area still boasts a great many artists, and art galleries, but it is no longer a low class, low rent district. Rightly proud of its artistic heritage as well as its current avant-garde residents, the district is known for its open house events. Recently the area holds the Jordaan Quarter Gallery Night which takes place every two months, and every two years there is an Open Studio event where local artists open their studios to the public.

There are more entrepreneurs than artists buying property in the area; however, there is still a tradition of providing lower rents for artists. Thus the two social groups share the quarter, along with the occasional student and expat.

Walking in this district is a pleasure as there is a never-ending variety of things to find within its charming canal side confines and courtyards. Around every corner there is an art gallery, a historic monument, a charming architectural idiosyncrasy or a fantastic place to shop. The markets are there of course, both the Saturday Lindenmarkt and its more famous neighbour the Noordermarkt (p.293). The Noorderkerk (p.151) is still in use as a Protestant church, and both it and the Westerkerk (p.153) are popular venues for classical concerts.

The area is also known for its many charming canals, many of which seem to have their own personalities. The Browersgracht (brewer's canal) is so named because historically it was the location for a great many of the city's breweries which have now been converted into some of the most coveted addresses in town. Just behind the Haarlemmerstraat it's so charming that it is almost unbelievable that a street so quaint could actually be in the middle of an international city. Another spot to discover is the Torensluis, the oldest bridge in Amsterdam still standing (and also its widest). Finished in 1648 the barred windows underneath the bridge are reminders of the prison which used to be part of the tower.

Another beautiful canal is the Egelantiersgracht, named after the eglantine plant (a member of the honeysuckle family). This canal is a stunning stroll, which will lead you to both the nearby Rockarchive (020 423 04 89) which hosts a great collection of rock photography, and the Amsterdam Tulip Museum (Prinsengracht 112, www.amsterdamtulipdepot.eu) where you can learn all you ever wanted to learn, and probably a lot more, about the nation's favourite bloom, the tulip.

Westerkerk

Map p.374-7, 390-1
Area C p.137

The Lowdown
Amsterdam Noord is the single largest autonomous borough of Amsterdam. City planners have said that Amsterdam Noord is to be the future Manhattan of the Netherlands.

The Good
The development programme for Amsterdam Noord is so promising that the European Commission has decided to support Amsterdam city with subsidy support for the projects at the NDSM site. MTV have recently moved onto the site.

The Bad
Amsterdam Noord has always felt remote from the main part of Amsterdam because of the limited public transport in and out.

The Must Dos
See if you can recognise any of the Dutch A-list celebrities who hang out at the Hotel de Goudfazant cafe-restaurant (Aambeeldstraat 10, 020 636 51 70).

Amsterdam Noord

Situated behind Centraal Station and separated by the waterways of the IJmeer, the north of Amsterdam really is a unique place. The governing council of Amsterdam Noord covers 16 neighbourhoods, with another three due to be added by the year 2015. The local population stands at around 87,000 inhabitants. Once the home of Holland's shipbuilding dockyards, Amsterdam Noord fell on hard times with the decline in the shipping industry during the 1970s, but two major factors have bought the area back out of the doldrums and into the forefront of the city planners' vision: space and the creative industries. After the closure of the shipyards, the huge empty warehouses and open landscapes along the harbour side began to attract squatters and artists in search of homes and studios. Meanwhile the network of small rural villages behind the dockyards began to attract the poor working class Amsterdammers from the cramped and overcrowded part of the inner city. A couple of decades later it had become apparent that the area would benefit from fast and intensive investment because the cultural fusion of traditional working class Dutch folk and the young squatters and artists was proving a passionate and promising mixture. This fascinating fusion has become the foundation of a completely new and exciting sort of community, which is best reflected in the section of the dockside known as the NDSM.

The NDSM site is the heart of the former shipbuilding yards and is now home to Kinetisch Noord, an umbrella organisation through which all the users of the site operate. There are monthly open air markets, which attract thousands of traders, and Skatepark, which is fast becoming a youth base for youngsters from all over the city. Warehouses on either side of the site are being converted into theatres, artists' studios and offices for small businesses. There are also clean energy-producing projects being developed to supply the new homes and offices being built around the site. Traditional and avant-garde festivals are also a feature of the area, and cultural events are held almost every week. The public transport issues are being resolved by the construction of the North/South metro service, which is due to be completed in 2012. This will complement the existing 24/7 ferry services from behind Centraal Station for foot passengers and the underground IJ tunnel for motor vehicles.

Amsterdam Noord also has its own little collection of historical monuments and buildings like the Schellingwouderkerk, which is a little white church built in 1866, and the traditional Dutch windmill Krijtmolen D'Admiraal constructed in 1792. Entire streets around the Nieuwedammerdijk are considered to be part of the country's national heritage because they reflect a variety of traditional Dutch architecture, and there are a patchwork of meadows connecting the villages using open Dutch landscape walkways. There is also 'normal' parkland like the Flora Park, and other protected green zones around Amsterdam Noord – it even has its own camping site called Vliegenbos (p.194). This modern development combined with its traditional roots, are giving Amsterdam Noord quite a special character. This is reflected in shopping malls like Boven t'Y Winkelcentrum (p.295), where you can find the latest high street fashions and consumer goods of every shape and size, as well as traditional items from communities all over the globe. Eating out in Amsterdam Noord is very easy – there are cafes and restaurants everywhere. Places like the IJ Keuken provide really traditional Dutch home cooking while Osaka does exotic Japanese fare. There are huge waterside restaurant cafes with beautiful views across the IJmeer, like the IJ Kantine and the Wilhelmina Dok, which are great places to spend an evening.

The expansion and development of Amsterdam Noord is an ongoing process and the local communities are actively taking part in it, which gives the area a great feeling of excitement and hope. As more and more new homes and buildings appear out of the dereliction of the disused industrial spaces, there is a very positive regenerative vibe to the whole place.

Oost

Map p.394-5 & 385
Area D p.137

The Lowdown
More of a residential district than tourist trove, it is still well worth a visit.

The Good
In a city that loves markets, it's quite something to be named the best market – not just in town, but in the country as a whole. That's the distinction that was given to Dapperstraat Markt!

The Bad
Every Sunday afternoon at 13:00 the Speaker's Corner in Oosterpark hosts anyone who'd like to stand on it and have their say… the only problem is that the speakers are – as one should expect in Holland – usually speaking Dutch, which means that it's very hard for non-Dutch speakers to pick up the atmosphere…and the attitude…but maybe that's not so bad after all!

The Must Dos
Take in a world music event at the KIT Tropentheater (020 568 85 00, www.tropentheater.nl) at the KIT Tropenmuseum (p.155).

Though out of the 'centre' of the city, the Oost is still an interesting and often exciting area to be. As is often the case with any area outside of the 'golden mile', it was initially set up for the working class residents of town but it has, of late, become a popular area for the young creative entrepreneurs who have flocked to the city.

In the centre of the district are the Oosterpark and the KIT Tropenmuseum (p.155), the Tropics Museum. The 19th century Oosterpark is perhaps not the most used on a daily basis, but it is the site for several annual festivals, including the Roots Festival (p.48), which makes it one of the most popular of the city's green spaces. The Tropenmuseum is in many ways one of the most important cultural spaces in the city. Firstly, it chronicles the archaeology, sociology and culture of many of the world's indigenous civilisations – especially those that were touched by the Dutch prior to, during, and following their Golden Age.

One thing that links the Oosterpark and the museum is the Slavernijmonument (Slavery Monument) in the park, which was dedicated in 2002. The Dutch are facing up to some of the unpleasant realities of their 'Golden Age', and on whose backs it was purchased.

Oost is also home to one of the city's most popular, and largest, open air markets. The Dapperstraat Markt (p.292) certainly has one of the longest stretches of stalls in the city and is an excellent example of the multiculturalism here. It is unquestionably one of the favourite spots for shopping, and is particularly popular with locals.

Though the area does date from the 19th century, it must be said that there isn't a great deal of architecture from that period still standing. The city has been extremely busy in rebuilding and remodelling the neighbourhood, so there are lots of square apartment buildings and, to be honest, it can bring to mind the square-pegged styling of the 1970s Eastern Bloc.

It is also fairly quiet in the evenings, as there really aren't a great many pubs or other places to hang out. There are two major exceptions to this rule. Firstly there is Brouwerij 't IJ (020 622 83 25) at Funenkade 7, which is the city's oldest brewery. The beer is great and the terrace is fun – added to that, it's actually in a windmill! However, be aware that it does have odd opening hours.

A more recent addition to the area is the Theater Fabriek Amsterdam (020 522 52 60, www.theaterfabriekamsterdam.nl) on Czaar Peterstraat. Though it is, for centre-dwellers, a journey to the outskirts, it's well worth the trip to this converted factory which now presents some of the city's most popular, and large scale, theatrical and musical productions.

Magere Brug

Map p.392 & 383-5
Area E p.136

The Lowdown
Entrepreneurs as well as a healthy dose of expats and artists make this area the most happening in the city. Prices for almost everything are a few percentages higher than the rest of the city, but if you don't mind paying for ambience, then the price hikes are well worth it.

The Good
One of the most sought after dinner reservations is for the French Café at Gerard Doustraat 98 (020 470 03 01, www.thefrenchcafe.nl) but it is well worth the extra effort.

The Bad
Due to the construction of the Noord Zuid metro line, a great deal of the area around the Ferdinand Bolstraat is not fully utilised. The ongoing construction has put several great stores out of business.

The Must Dos
A drink on the terrace bar of the Amstel InterContinental Hotel (p.26) on a sunny afternoon is absolutely fabulous darling!

Oud Zuid

Like it or not, this is one of 'the' places to live, work and play in Amsterdam. It is close enough to the centre of the city that nothing is more than 15 minutes away, and far enough away that it is not that difficult to escape the tourists and the noise. The area comprises some of the most interesting parts of the city, and certainly some of the most popular, such as the Museum Quarter (Museumplein), De Pijp and the Vondelpark. Though it began its life pretty much as a swamp, and remained so until the 19th century, the Museum Quarter is certainly one of the most sought after locations within Amsterdam, and is home to some of the finest cultural locations and expensive real estate on offer. This is the home of the Rijksmuseum (p.157), the Van Gogh Museum (p.157), the Concertgebouw (p.360) and, though it is temporarily in the north of the city due to renovations, it will soon be home once more to the Stedelijk Museum (p.157). Each of these international institutions borders the Museumplein park area, which offers up a great place for enjoying a sunny day. This is also the location for a great many free concerts throughout the year.

Not two minutes from Museumplein is the city's most eminent shopping street, the PC Hoofstraat (p.289). This is the land of Bulgari, Cartier and Armani, as well as several 'see and be seen' lunch spots. Though, for locals in the know, the Cornelis Schuytstraat, only a five minute walk away, is always worth a visit.

A ten minute walk from Museumplein takes you to the city's biggest and, by all accounts, most popular market, the Albert Cuypstraat Markt (p.292). With approximately 300 different stalls, there really is something for everyone at this busy, bustling bastion of commerce. Having celebrated its 100th birthday last year it certainly looks like it will continue for another hundred years. It's filled with foodstuffs and is reputedly one of the best places to buy cheese, flowers, clothes, music and a myriad of other things, up to and including the kitchen sink... well the plug, anyway. Sure, you can find most of the items elsewhere, but not at these low prices (i.e. don't buy your flowers at the Bloemenmarkt, buy them here!). The market is open every day except Sunday, from 09:00 to 17:00.

The market is the heart of the area known as De Pijp, and this former working class area which took the overflow from the 19th century Jordaan district (see p.140) is now 'the' place to be and be seen. It's hip, it's hot, and therefore it's getting expensive...but it hasn't priced out all the local flavour yet, so it's still a fantastic place to live and play. There are a few theories as to why De Pijp is so named. Some believe it's because the narrow streets are reminiscent of the stem of a pipe, others remember The Pipe gas company which used to bring supplies to the neighbourhood. Only one thing is certain, though people living in Amsterdam can call themselves Amsterdammers, people living in De Pijp shouldn't think about calling themselves 'Pijpers'...that's a horn you wouldn't want to blow, and locals will just laugh at you.

Due to its history, De Pijp, like the Jordaan, became a melting pot of different cultures and ethnicities; unlike the Jordaan, De Pijp has retained a great deal of this multicultural concentration. It is certainly an area that is historically the hideaway for artists, musicians and students. In fact, it's known as the Latin Quarter; however as per usual in these areas, it's become popular with yuppies, and prices have gone up exponentially – more than 300% – in the last few years!

Today Dutch artists such as Fabrice still live in the area, while famous painters like Mondrian made De Pijp their home. Many of the streets are named after artists (Ferdinand Bol, for example).

At the top end of the area is the Heinekenplein (where you can see some of the work of Fabrice on public display), which, as is the case with most local squares, is surrounded by bars, cafes and restaurants. What sets this square apart is the fact that the site used to be part of the old Heineken Brewery, which dominated most of the area. The Heineken Experience Museum (p.154), though it no longer brews beer, does take you through the company's nearly 250 years of brewing history, and follows the route of a bottle of the amber liquid as it takes the necessary steps to change from barley to beer. You won't get drunk on the experience, but it may inspire you into a night out on the town.

Or maybe you'd prefer a picnic in the park – the biggest open space in the city centre is in the Oud Zuid. Vondelpark (p.160) is the focus for so much and so many in the city. Apart from having acres of green open spaces, Vondelpark is also home to the Groote Melkhuis children's playground, and the Kinderkookkafe where children can cook and serve food to their friends and families on special occasions. For the adults there is the Filmmuseum (020 589 14 00, www.filmmuseum.nl), Vertigo terrace and restaurant (www.vertigo.nl) and the Blauwe Theehuis (p.335) which is great for snacks, magnificent lounge music and cocktails. The Beatrix Park is only a stone's throw away, and is a wonderful area for picnics, strolling, and for the kids with its wading pool. On a summer's day, IJssalon Venetie at Scheldestraat 68 (p.310) is extremely popular; it's perhaps not the friendliest of places, but the quality of the icecream keeps people coming back for more year after year.

Further south is an area known as Zuideramstel; recently built, it is a smaller city district which developed near to Amsterdam's World Trade Center. As such, there is a large concentration of expatriates working and living in the area. To service some of those families, the British School of Amsterdam (p.120 will move to the area in 2011. You'll find a great many fine restaurants with a wide variety of international menus. One of the central features of the area is the Olympic Stadium which was used for the 1928 Olympics held in the city (020 305 44 00, www.olympischstadion.nl). Locals in the know are less fascinated by the stadium, however, and more interested in the AVEDA Dayspa (p.243) which is one of the best pamper points in the city.

Oudebrugsteeg

Singelgracht

Map p.373-4, 379, 388
Area F p.136

The Lowdown
It must be said that the west of the city has had a pretty rough ride regarding its reputation; however, in the last few years a great deal has been done to rejuvenate the area and rewrite the reviews.

The Good
Hit The Café The Social Club at Haarlemmerplein 41 after a summer evening gig at Westergasfabriek for a great night meeting local and international musicians.

The Bad
Mercatorplein is pretty unappealing – sure there are a few shops and a terrace or two to sit out on, there are even a few trees...but that's it.

The Must Dos
A walk along Haarlemmerstraat (p.288) on a Sunday morning is the perfect spot to window shop before grabbing breakfast at Barney's on Haarlemmerstraat 98 (www.barneys.biz).

West

Granted, there are still certain parts of the district which don't have much draw, and as such, the legions of tourists that stalk the city centre are rarely seen here; but that is becoming less common as the area develops. Sure, there are neighbourhoods where it can be a bit of a walk to a decent bar, as they aren't on every corner – as is the case in De Baarsjes and Bos en Lommer, for instance. Unless you live there, there's very little reason to visit these areas. Rembrandtpark, however, which is tucked into the far side of De Baarsjes, is a nice place for jogging and walking dogs.

Within the West is an area known as Westerpark (which includes the park of the same name), and is also a residential area (see Residents p.91). Westerpark is another park worth a visit – it's at the centre of this expanding area of the city and is popular for sunbathing, enjoying a barbecue or to finish reading your latest novel. The Kinderboerderij Westerpark, in the Westerpark (p.160), is a popular children's area with a daycare centre and two playgrounds.

The west is seeing a lot of new developments, including housing, office spaces and creative arenas being provided at a pretty speedy pace. One of these developments, Westergasfabriek (020 586 0710, www.westergasfabriek.nl) – a redeveloped industrial site, is the saving grace of the Westerpark area, as it has become a venue that the entire city flocks to. It is an extremely large park and creative playground for all sorts of art, musical events and festivals. There are lots of green spaces and water features, as well as offices, event stages, bars, clubs, restaurants, a cinema and a theatre. It has become the home of open-air concerts such as the 2007 Live Earth festivities. From the park leading towards the centre of town is Haarlemmerweg, a street of funky stores, famous coffeeshops and popular pubs and bars.

Due to the burgeoning cosmopolitanism of the area, the fact that there are now a number of great places to eat is no surprise. Local favourites include the Italian Yam Yam Café on Frederik Hendrikstraat. There are loads of great Greek and Korean delis. The Haarlemmerstraat and Haarlemmerdijk (p.288) neighbourhood is also becoming much more food and fashion focused with a major increase in good restaurants, cook book and cooking equipment shops, and the now de rigueur high class delis and wine shops. The area is renowned for its specialist food outlets selling products ranging from cheese to hand-made chocolate.

Picturesque Amsterdam waterway

Map p.395, 391, 380-1
Area G p.137

The Lowdown
One of the most intense and exciting developments for the city of Amsterdam is happening in the recently created borough of Zeeburg. It is here, along with Amsterdam Noord, that the city looks to for its future expansion.

The Good
The Arts Council manages a lending service for residents of Zeeburg where they can 'borrow' works of art to hang in their homes for short periods of time.

The Bad
Though there are a multitude of new homes being built in the area, it must be noted that they are almost all sold prior to being developed. This is one of the 'hottest' areas to invest in.

The Must Dos
The Lloyd Hotel (p.30) has its own recording studio and what it calls a nomadic library which, along with its collection of random works of arts makes it an eclectic place to meet and greet.

Zeeburg

The population of Zeeburg is due to more than double by 2015 to 85,000 and it is well serviced with schools, sports facilities and youth centres. This means that there are plenty of colourful open air play parks giving the area a bright and friendly feel. With new residents arriving every day and new buildings being completed by the hour, the future for Zeeburg is safe, secure and promising.

Like the rest of Amsterdam there is no shortage of art galleries in Zeeburg, and just across the road from the Lloyd Hotel (p.30) on the KNSM-Laan is the Galerie Ahoi, which organises exhibitions and installations, not just on the premises, but also around the open public spaces in the area. Further along the same street is the SBK Amsterdam KNSM Kunstuitleen Gallery which is run by the National Arts Council (www.sbk.nl/knsm/index.php) and which not only promotes artists and their work but also manages a lending service for local residents in Zeeburg – allowing them to have works of art in their homes for short periods of time.

Linked through a simple network of roads and bridges, the Indischebuurt branches out onto the Zeeburgereiland, IJburg and along the Oostelijk Havengebied, where much of the new development is really taking effect – here the landscape changes on an almost daily basis. Some of the massive warehouses along the Oostelijk Havengebeid, like the Pakhuis Wilhelmina and De Loods, which used to house shipping freight and cargo, have been converted into studios for artists and office spaces for small creative businesses. These now proudly present diverse and combined shows, presentations and exhibitions that are simply breathtaking in size and scale and wouldn't be possible without such huge, special spaces to house them.

The local population is a balanced mixture of multicultural minorities and Dutch nationals, and although the area was once mostly made up of working class labourers it is now attracting new families and expat communities not just from the cramped and overcrowded inner city parts of Amsterdam, but also from other parts of the world. What brings the new inhabitants to Zeeburg is the incredible building of thousands of new homes, shops and businesses across the old docklands, and man-made harbour islands linked to the Indischebuurt.

The inner city gateway to Zeeburg is the main urban area called the Indische Buurt, which is a short walk from the old city centre of Amsterdam with fast and friendly public transport connections in every direction. As the oldest and most established part of Zeeburg, the Indischebuurt at the moment houses most of the inhabitants of the entire municipality. The streets and walkways here are wide and spacious and the neighbourhood has well-established shops and supermarkets, in addition to new-style shopping malls like the Brazilie, which opened in 1998. Trendy shopping streets like Javastraat and the Sumatrastraat show off the latest high street fashions, and of course there is a dizzy array of artists' studios, cafes and restaurants, including the picturesque Boulevard Café (020 693 32 99) on the Cruquiusweg.

Exhibitions, presentations, cultural events and festivals are also reinventing places like the Passenger Terminal, which used to be where long distance travellers would step off passenger ships onto Dutch soil after weeks at sea. Today this venue is a bright sparkling set of halls, shops and walkways – with fashion shows, film festivals and events for all the family. Of course there are also many large buildings along the former harbour coast that are used for other sorts of popular recreation – like Panama (p.357), which boasts a very good restaurant and an amazing nightclub. The Lloyd Hotel (p.30) is another recently opened venue along the old docklands (on the Oostelijk Handelskade) that is proving to be a local hotspot.

NEMO

Just a few minutes from Centraal Station is the giant green NEMO building. It houses a big science centre (p.208), and has a 'beach' on top (p.158), with great views over Amsterdam.

Museums, Heritage & Culture

A Click Away From Art
For a one-stop-shop for booking all your museum tickets throughout Holland, including every museum in Amsterdam, visit www.museumtickets.nl

Amsterdam is actually home to more works of art and cultural treasures per square kilometre than any other city on earth, with a stunningly comprehensive collection of masterpieces dating back to the 15th century. This is a country of collectors and long has it been so.

Art Galleries

Other options **Art** p.255, **Art Classes** p.186

The Dutch are in love with art, to a point, unfortunately however, for the average Dutchman, 'if it ain't Dutch, it ain't much.' Even so, there is an extraordinary amount of art to view in the city, and if you know where to look, some excellent art for sale as well.

The ABC Treehouse

Voetboogstraat 11
Centrum
Map p.393 D1 **1**

020 423 09 67 | *www.treehouse.abc.nl*

This gallery and community centre has been serving the expatriate community in Amsterdam since 1998 as a meeting house, as well as a performance and exhibition space. The Treehouse and its staff are dedicated to showcasing Dutch and international artists living and working in the Netherlands. As Treehouse curator Donna Ducarme notes, 'We're here for the international set. If it's open-minded and about community building we do it here!'

De Appel

Nieuwe Spiegelstr 10
Oud Zuid
Map p.393 D3 **2**

020 622 52 15 | *www.deappel.nl*

The year 2005 was the 30th anniversary of the founding of De Appel gallery, though it only moved to its current location in 1994. Initially, in the 1970s, the avante garde centre focused predominantly on live performance art installations, and has progressed and grown to include video and paintings among a huge number of other mediums. Staff say that De Appel shows anything that's 'happening now'.

Many of the artists shown in the gallery are recently discovered international finds, however, there are those rebels who've made a name for themselves that continue to show their work there, such as Jonathan Reese. This is a gallery devoted to all that is absolutely contemporary. Along with the exhibition space, De Appel also runs an eight-month international curatorial training programme.

Galerie Delaive

Spiegelgracht 23
Oud Zuid
Map p.393 D4 **29**

020 625 90 87 | *www.delaive.com*

This thriving modern and contemporary art gallery, run by Nico Delaive for more than 25 years, is only just up the road from the Reflex Gallery and is chock-a-block full of fantastic pieces. Showing artists such as Appel, Christo, Lichtenstein and Andy Warhol alongside Degas and Chagall, the gallery is only one of three of its kind in the country to display such high level international artwork. This is where to go if you really want to know about what's available on the market.

A Big Splodge Of Art

There are two major art fairs which happen annually at Amsterdam RAI, which attract the finest contemporary and classical art (from Holland and worldwide) in virtually all mediums. Taking place over a week, pAn Amsterdam takes place each November, and Art Amsterdam (formerly known as Kunst Amsterdam) takes the stage for five days each May.

Galerie Lieve Hemel

Nieuwe Spiegelstr 3
Oud Zuid
Map 393 D3 **3**

020 623 00 60 | *www.lievehemel.nl*

Conveniently located in the Spiegelhof arcade, standing proudly at the entrance of the Spiegel

Kwartier, this gallery, which has been run by Koen Nieuwendijk since 1968 (in its present location since 1996) focuses on contemporary Dutch realism and silver. Shows change at least five times a year, and the gallery window is a wonderful place to observe the myriad maze of antiquities and art on display.

iAmsterdam Card
The iAmsterdam Card is a great deal for visitors. Over a period of 24, 48 or 72 hours this pass gives free, or discounted admission to museums, city attractions, canal cruises, public transport and more. Visit www.iamsterdamcard.nl for more information.

Eerste Tuindwarsstraat 16
Jordaan
Map p.388 C3 **4**

Gallery Vassie

020 489 40 42 | *www.hughug.info*

Originally known as the Hug Gallery, Gallery Vassie is one of the only international photography galleries in Amsterdam. Owned and curated by Addie Vassie, a former curator at the Victoria and Albert Museum in London, Gallery Vassie is a reflection of the vast knowledge and contacts that Vassie has in the world of international photograpy. Representing internationally renowned artists such as Lee Miller, Antoni + Alison, Jason Oddy and Cornel Lucas, the Vassie gallery is the place to see the creme de la creme of international photography. Keep an eye out for exhibition opening dates as Vassie is one of the few curators who can virtually guarantee the attendance of the artist... and the wine is always flowing!

Spuistraat 320
Centrum
Map p.393 D1 **5**

Herman Brood Gallery

020 623 37 66 | *www.channels.nl/brood.html*

If you ask the management and die hard fans of the late and great (at least to the Dutch) rock and roll star Herman Brood, he was also the greatest artist in Dutch history. Haven't they heard of Rembrandt, Van Gogh, Appel and the rest? The Herman Brood Gallery is a homage to the man, the myth and the mystery of his art – like it or not.

Nieuwe Spiegelstr 29
Oud Zuid
Map p.393 D3 **6**

Jaski Art Gallery

020 620 39 39 | *www.jaski.nl*

This fine and friendly gallery specialises in the CoBrA movement. It isn't surprising that many Scandinavian and Benelux residents know about CoBrA considering the nationalities of the artists involved, but apparently the movement is also well known to many American visitors to the gallery due to the large CoBrA-based museum in Florida. Along with CoBrA artists such as Karel Appel, Jaski also exhibits works by renowned modern artists such as Rob Scholle, Andy Warhol, and the former enfant terrible, Herman Brood.

Kunsthandel artwork

Nieuwe Spiegelstr 13-34
Oud Zuid
Map p.393 D3 **7**

Kunsthandel Peter Pappot

020 624 26 37 | *www.pappot.com*

For all that is posh and pleasant in the art world, then you really have to visit this elegant enterprise in the heart of the antiques and art gallery sector. Inside this lush and plush gallery one can discover the finest 18th and 19th century Dutch, Belgian and French paintings, all exquisitely hung.

Keizersgracht 264
Centrum
Map p.392 C1 **8**

Montevideo/Time Based Arts

020 623 71 01 | *www.montevideo.nl*

Since 1978 those art aficionados interested in the growth, purpose and sharing of new technologies in the visual arts have found their way to the Montevideo/Time Based Arts Institute, which is renowned for ceaselessly supporting the most advanced and avant garde movements (in art installations encompassing both visual and sound-based formats). Montevideo's extensive webpage covers insights into both individual pieces and installations.

Weteringschans 79a
Oud Zuid
Map p.392 C4 **9**

Reflex Modern Art Gallery/New Art Gallery

020 627 28 32 | *www.reflex-art.nl*

This modern and contemporary art gallery mainly features photography and video installations. Conveniently located directly across the canal from the Rijksmuseum, there are six to eight different shows a year, featuring either a solo artist or group. Specialising in the CoBrA movement artists, along with international names such as Larry Sultan and Chris Verene, the gallery staff are extremely helpful, as well as being enthusiastically knowledgeable about their art and artists. Its sister, Reflex New Art Gallery is across the road; both are closed on Sundays and Mondays.

Chimes Change With Wedding Belles
The Westerkerk (p.153) was the site of the marriage between the Queen of the Netherlands, HRH Princess Beatrix, and her late husband HRH Claus on March 10, 1966. Reflecting the changing times, her eldest son and heir apparent Prince Willem-Alexander married Maxima Zorreguieta Cerruti on February 2, 2002 in a civil ceremony only then followed by a religious ceremony in De Nieuwe Kerk on the Dam.

Churches & Cathedrals

Though Amsterdam abounds with church and cathedral buildings, it must be said that most of them have been refurbished and now function as arts and exhibition centres, meeting places, clubs, and even office space. Historically, Amsterdam natives were quite adamant about following their faiths, and early in the middle ages Amsterdam was a determinedly Catholic town; but after falling into Protestant hands in 1578 many Catholic buildings, including 21 convents, were placed in the hands of Protestant groups who restored the churches to a state of plainness which was more in keeping with the style they preferred. At this time it was decreed that only Protestant churches were true churches, which inevitably led to other denominations having to disguise their appearance and hide in homes and other non-religious sites.

Hidden Churches

A wonderful example of this is the Ons' Lieve Heer op Solder museum (p.156) which houses the Our Lord in the Attic Church. When religious freedom was eventually reinstated in the city, Amsterdam became a mecca for those seeking sanctuary from the many religious conflicts raging through Europe, such as French Huguenots and Iberian Jews who brought their skills and their money to the city. It is often said of Amsterdam at that time, and this is true in the present day, that as long as you paid your taxes no one really cared what you believed.

Pilgrim's Pause

Amsterdam was also a stopping point for the Pilgrim Fathers, some of whom worshipped at the English Reformed Church in the Begijnhof (below). It must be said that the pilgrims did find the Amsterdammers slightly too risqué, and as such were quite happy to leave for Rotterdam and Leiden. In the 17th century Amsterdam was known as the city of freedom and that is a legacy which its residents are proud to maintain, even if that doesn't mean attending regular church services.

Corner of Begijnsloot and Begijensteeg
Centrum
Map p.393 D1 **10**

Begijnhof

020 622 19 18 | *www.begijnhofamsterdam.nl*

Located in a former convent, the Begijnhof spiritual centre is private property which can be found at the corner of Begijnensloot and Begijnensteeg. Visitors are asked to respect the repose, silence and the privacy of the residents. While individual guests are welcome, groups, guided tours, film shoots, cyclists and dogs are not. This is a tranquil glade of grass, trees and flowers. Within the hof is the Engelse Kerk (English Presbyterian Church) as well as the Begijnhof Kapel. The Kapel dates back to a time when the Catholic Beguines order was forced to worship secretly due to the Reformation. The last Beguine sisters died in the 1970s however there are still women living in the houses surrounding the court. House number 34 in the Begijnhof is noted as being the oldest wooden house in the Netherlands.

Prinsengracht 756
Canal Belt
(Grachtengordel)
Map p.393 E4 11

De Duif

020 520 00 70

Across from the Amstelkerk is this former Catholic church (aka The Dove), the first to be built after the French Government occupying the city declared there to be freedom of religion in Amsterdam following the Protestant Reformation. The organ in particular is breathtaking in size, as it reaches straight up to the high vaulted ceilings above. The Dove is a place of worship which is also home to many cultural events.

Dam Square
Centrum
Map p.389 D4 17

De Nieuwe Kerk

020 638 69 09 | *www.nieuwekerk.nl*

Adjacent to the Royal Palace on the Dam, the 14th century church is only 'new' in relation to the Oude Kerk which predates it by more than a century. The two were the most important churches in the city, but unlike the Oude Kerk, the Nieuwe Kerk was destroyed by fire several times. The Nieuwe Kerk is possibly the most conveniently located museum in Amsterdam.

Located on Dam Square next to the Palace, the church in famous not only for its Gothic architecture but also for the expansive exhibitions which tend to feature artefacts and glittering treasures from the different civilisations the city's own multicultural citizens reflect. As well as featuring the finest of the world's culture, the museum is also committed to reflecting the world's religions. No longer a practising church, this is an extremely popular venue – the museum has more than half a million visitors every year. Also popular are the Sunday evening organ concerts in the church which begin at 20:00.

Begijnhof 48
Centrum
Map p.393 D1 12

Engelse Kerk

020 624 96 64 | *www.ercadam.nl*

This tranquil place of contemplation is a working church (the English Reformed Church) with a community of over 400 which boasts nearly 40 different nationalities at its Sunday 10:30 services. When open to the general public, there are often organ rehearsals and community activities taking place in the well-used building. The church celebrated its 400th anniversary in February 2007 with a royal double-act attending: Queen Beatrix of the Netherlands alongside the UK's Queen Elizabeth. The stained glass window at the back of the church commemorates Amsterdam's connection with the pilgrims, by depicting them boarding the Mayflower. The sister window to this is located in Boston and shows the pilgrims disembarking from the same boat.

Noordermarkt 48
Jordaan
Map p.388 C2 13

Noorderkerk

020 626 64 36

The second church to be built to service the growing population of the Jordaan, the first being the slightly more exclusive Westerkerk, the Noorderkerk was completed in 1623. Dutch Reformed Church services are still regularly practised at the Noorderkerk which is also a popular venue for classical music performances. Located on Noordermarkt Square with its extremely popular weekend market days, the church is the site of commemoration for both the rioters killed in 1934 protesting against the government's austerity measures, and the 1941 secret meetings which were held on the square by organisers of the strike against anti-Jewish measures brought in by the Nazi occupiers.

Oudekerksplein 23
Centrum
Map p.389 F4 14

Oude Kerk

020 625 82 84 | *www.oudekerk.nl*

Built to honour the patron saint of Amsterdam, St Nicholas (who also looked out for sailors, merchants, pawn brokers and children), this gargantuan gothic glory is the oldest place of worship in the city (dating back to 1250). Visitors popping in may be lucky enough to catch an organ rehearsal on the superb Müller Organ from 1724 (which featured in John Irving's novel *Until I Find You*, that was partially based in Amsterdam). Throughout the summer months, organ recitals take place at the church and it is the site for the annual International Sweelinck Festival each October. Sunday services take place at 11:00, however the church is also often used as a venue for major art exhibitions, including the world-renowned annual World Press Photography awards (p.134).

Prins Hendrikkade 73
Centrum
Map p.390 A3 15

St Nicolaaskerk

020 624 87 49

As soon you exit Centraal Station you cannot help but notice the towers and gilded cupola of this Catholic church of the neo-Renaissance age. Located at the position where the Amstel flowed into the city, the church is well placed, because St. Nicholas is, among other things, the patron saint of seafarers. It is an impressive building, both inside and out, with art and architecture which leaves visitors with no doubt as to the reverence felt by the congregations which have paid penance in these pews. The church was the first to be built in the city following the repeal of religious restriction

St Nicolaaskerk

Nieuwe Kerk

after the Reformation, and continues to be the main place of worship for the city's Catholic community, with services taking place at 12:30 from Monday to Saturday and at 10:30 and 13:00 on Sundays.

Westermarkt
Jordaan
Map p.388 C4 16

Westerkerk

020 624 77 66

The central point of worship for Amsterdam's Dutch Reformed community, this church was the golden flagship for the 17th century rich Burghers of the city. Highlights of the church are the organ, which is covered in decorative panels, and the bell tower which is the highest in the city. The tower can be climbed, but be warned, there are more than 160 steep steps before you reach its pinnacle. Though it is unknown exactly which grave holds him, Westerkerk is also the resting place of Rembrandt van Rijn, who died nearby in October 1669. Tuesday lunchtimes find carillon recitals being performed by the 50 massive bells in the clock tower. Church services take place on Sundays at 10:30 between April and September.

Heritage Sites

Other options **Art Galleries** p.148, **Museums** p.153

Amsterdam is abundant with historical sites and treasures. There are many who would protest that the entire city centre, dating back to medieval times, is worthy of the distinction of World Heritage Site. There are a small number of reminders of the old city walls, in particular at sites such as De Waag (p.138) at Nieuwemarkt, which was a gate within the old wall, and the Munttoren (Mint Tower), also part of a medieval gate. See also Koninklijk Paleis (the Royal Palace) on p.155.

See For Yourself!
The section of the fortification closest to Amsterdam can be viewed at the Battery, near the IJ before Durgerdam.

Wall Wows The World

Certainly the ancient architecture within the old city centre is superb. Heady highlights include the Oude Kerk (Old Church, p.152) which was built in the 13th century, and the 15th century Nieuwe Kerk (New Church, p.151) situated next to the 17th century Royal Palace on Dam Square, in the very heart of the city. It was in the 17th century that the layout of the city was formalised into semicircular canal rings, and it is the 135 kilometre defence line of fortifications (built to protect Amsterdam by controlling the water) which was given a place on the UNESCO World Heritage List.

Living Easily With The Past

In a city where nearly one third of the buildings were built prior to 1850 and there are more than 6,500 national monuments, Amsterdammers have had to find a way to live with their history. Unwilling to destroy any of its past, Amsterdam has found ways to incorporate historic buildings into current lives and lifestyles.

CoBrA
The CoBrA art movement was begun by 20th century artists from the Benelux and Scandinavia. Its most famous Dutch star is Karel Appel. For more, see the Cobra Museum (p.154) and Jaski Art Gallery (p.149).

Museums

Other options **Art Galleries** p.148, **Heritage Sites** (above)

Most of the four million-plus visitors, and a majority of Amsterdam residents, make great use of the many museums in the culturally centred city. Along with the large number of exhibition spaces, there are a diverse range of exhibitions, including those exploring modern and classical art, architecture, cats, thimbles and handbags. Amsterdam's museums have long gone out of their way to make their exhibitions relevant and accessible for visitors; examples of this are the annual Museumnacht (Museum Night), and the fact that the Van Gogh and Rijksmuseum stay open until 22:00 on Friday nights.

Kalverstraat 92
Centrum
Map p.393 D1 **18**

Amsterdams Historisch Museum

_020 523 18 22_ | _www.ahm.nl_

Originally built as the city's orphanage, the museum is a superb stroll through the history of the city, from 12th century marsh to the present day and beyond. Installations include everything from chilling reminders of the cold, hard war years, through to the passion of a present day Ajax football fan. Though the main focus of the museum's art centres on the 17th century Golden Age, it's also an excellent place to find out about other art movements. There is a charming children's exhibition as well as an extremely interesting research library which is open by appointment. The sunny courtyard off Sint Luciensteeg leads to the Civic Guards' Gallery (Schuttersgallerij), showing works by hugely admired Amsterdam artists such as Govert Flinck, van der Helst and Ferdinand Bol, who all have streets in Amsterdam named after them.

Prinsengracht 267
Jordaan
Map p.388 C3 **19**

Anne Frank Huis

_020 556 71 00_ | _www.annefrankhuis.nl_

There can be few people who haven't heard of Anne Frank, which is due in no small part to the great pains the Anne Frank Foundation (founded by her father Otto in 1957) has taken to ensure that Anne's memory, and the house in which she and the rest of her family hid from the Nazis, continues to stand. It was in this house that Anne wrote her diary, famous because of the countless number of publications in more than 100 languages, as well as all the films and plays that have been produced based on it. Walking through the museum's secret rooms, climbing the impossibly tiny stairs – all these things provoke a depth of feeling and silence among visitors. However, it is an extremely popular place and as such it's best to get there as early in the day as possible.

Sandbergplein 1
Amstelveen
Map p.367 B4

Cobra Museum

_020 547 50 50_ | _www.cobra-museum.nl_

Though slightly out of Amsterdam city centre, the Cobra Museum in Amstelveen is well worth visiting as it is one of the most beautifully designed museums in the country. The CoBrA movement gathered together artists from Copenhagen, Brussels and Amsterdam, and the museum's entrance is graced with a sculpture by Karel Appel. Although it only exists to exhibit work from the CoBrA school of art on a permanent basis, it does regularly present temporary exhibits by various artists from related avant garde artistic movements.

Dam Square
Centrum
Map p.389 D4 **17**

De Nieuwe Kerk

_020 638 69 09_ | _www.nieuwekerk.nl_

The Nieuwe Kerk is possibly the most conveniently located museum in Amsterdam. Located on Dam Square next to the Royal Palace (Koninklijk Paleis), the church is famous not only for its Gothic architecture but also the expansive exhibitions which tend to feature artefacts and glittering treasures from the different civilisations the city's multicultural citizens reflect. As well as featuring the finest of the world's culture, the museum is also committed to reflecting the culture behind the world's religions. An extremely popular venue, the museum has more than half a milllion visitors every year.

Stadhouderskade 78
Oud Zuid
Map p.384 B1 **22**

Heineken Experience Museum

_020 523 96 66_ | _www.heinekenexperience.com_

Based in the old Heineken brewery, this gives an insight into the company's prestigious history. The tour follows the route of a bottle of the amber liquid as it takes the necessary steps to move from barley to beer. The experience lasts approximately one hour. The €10 charge can seem a bit steep, but you do get a couple of 'top ups' and to keep your souvenir glass. Be aware that the museum gets extremely crowded in summer.

Nieuwe Herengracht 14
Centrum
Map p.394 A2 **23**

Hermitage Amsterdam

020 530 87 55 | *www.hermitage.nl*

One of the newest museums in Amsterdam, the Hermitage Amsterdam was opened in 2004 as a satellite branch of the Hermitage Museum in St. Petersburg. With links between the two cities going back over 300 years, the Russian curators of the world famous institution felt that Amsterdam was the best place to share their immense collection, and each exhibition presented is worked on by curators from both St. Petersburg and Amsterdam. Located over three floors in the historic Amstelhof, the museum is planning to expand extensively. More room can only be a good thing as their exhibitions are generally stunning; recent shows include Greek Gold and Nicholas & Alexandra, both of which were gloriously glittering.

Nieuwe Amstelstraat 1
Centrum
Map p.394 A2 **24**

Joods Historisch Museum

020 531 03 10 | *www.jhm.nl*

The Jewish Historical Museum is a centre for the Jewish culture and religion in Amsterdam. Located across from the Portuguese Synagogue, the museum is situated within a complex embracing several buildings, including the New and Great Synagogues, which are full of collections looking at the history of the Jewish community in the city. This includes the period of the late 1600s when the Jewish community of Amsterdam was one of the most important in Europe. Several from that time became internationally renowned, such as the philosopher Spinoza. The Frits and Rita Markus Gallery houses a moving exhibition looking at the history of Jewish people in Holland from 1900 to the present, which of course includes the second world war.

Walk Back Through Time

Joods Historisch Museum (the Jewish Historical Museum) can arrange walks through the local neighbourhood, which was, prior to the second world war, Amsterdam's bustling Jewish quarter.

Linnaeusstraat 2
Oost
Map p.395 E3 **25**

KIT Tropenmuseum

020 568 82 15 | *www.tropenmuseum.nl*

You can never get bored at the KIT Tropenmuseum (the museum of the Royal Tropical Institute) with its massive collection of all that is cultural anthropology; in fact, it's the largest museum of its kind in the Netherlands. Cultures of the world, especially those that have a connection with the Netherlands are looked at, and the exhibitions are always impressively interesting. There are eight permanent exhibitions and an extensive range of temporary presentations through which visitors are given a chance to experience different cultures and living conditions. Coupled with that, the KIT Tropentheater is an excellent venue for a wide range of culturally diverse world music, dance, debates, lectures and films.

Dam Square
Centrum
Map p.389 D4 **26**

Koninklijk Paleis

020 620 40 60 | *www.koninklijkhuis.nl*

The Royal Palace, which began its life as the Amsterdam City Hall, was later to become Napoleon's residence in the city. Upon his defeat the building was given back to the city by Prince Willem of Orange, and then finally the city fathers gifted it to the Dutch royal family. When originally built in 1665 it was the largest government building in Europe, and it is still extremely impressive. Though still used by the royal family occasionally, the palace is open to the public (except on state occasions). Each summer finds exhibitions highlighting a particular feature about the building or its history, and every October the Royal Awards for Painting are presented and then put on display in the palace.

Herengracht 605
Centrum
Map p.393 F2 27

Museum Willet Holthuysen

020 523 18 22 | www.willetholthuysen.nl

This beautiful museum is Amsterdam's only fully furnished canal house which is open daily to the public. Construction was completed in 1690 and it was a fashionable home to more than 20 families until the death of its last owners Abraham Willet (1825-1888) and his wife Louisa Holthuysen, (1824-1895). Abraham was an avid collector; his collection includes a vast array of paintings, ceramics, glassworks, silver, furniture and sculpture as well as an extensive library. Louisa lived for a further seven years after Abraham and in her will, as per the pair's plan, bequeathed the house and all of its contents to the city on the proviso that it was made open and available to the public. The museum is open daily, along with the French-style garden, thus succeeding in immortalising the family.

Oudezijds Voorburgwal 40
Centrum
Map p.389 F3 28

Ons' Lieve Heer op Solder

020 624 66 04 | www.museumamstelkring.nl

Also known as the Amstelkring Museum, this is a favourite of all who find it, though it's easy to walk past, as the facade is one of a simple home. However, once you're inside, this combination of museum, house, secret church and chapel is a beautifully atmospheric trip through the art and design of the 1660s. The museum also exhibits contemporary exhibitions highlighting art and religion. Coupled with that, it houses the only secret attic church still in its original 17th century state. It was built during the Reformation when Dutch Catholics were no longer permitted to worship in public. Though secret, the museum's Our Lord in the Attic church held 150 seats and a large altar; services continued to be held in the church until 1887.

Oudekerksplein 23
Centrum
Map p.389 F4 14

Oude Kerk

020 625 82 84 | www.oudekerk.nl

Dating back to 1250, the Oude Kerk is Amsterdam's oldest place of worship. Though partially destroyed during the iconoclasm of 1566, details from this period can still be seen in the choral stalls. It was in this church that Rembrandt applied for permission to marry his first wife Saskia, who was buried here on her death in 1642, the same year that the great artist painted *The Nightwatch*. There are more than 2,500 graves in the floor of the church, and it is estimated that over 10,000 people buried are within its halls. Though there is still a Sunday service (11:00), the church is more often used as a centre for major art exhibitions including the world renowned annual World Press Photography Awards (p.134).

Jodenbreestraat 4
Centrum
Map p.394 A1 30

Rembrandthuis

020 520 04 00 | www.rembrandthuis.nl

You really can't come to Amsterdam and not visit the house where Rembrandt van Rijn lived. A huge volume of documentation and artefacts allowed the reconstruction of the home, which opened in 1999 and gives visitors an excellent window into the life and times of the artist who lived his life like a star – when he could afford to. Entering his studios and sitting at his easel is an exquisite treat for any art lover, while next door craftsmen demonstrate the etching techniques the master was renowned for. The museum has 260 of the 290 etchings Rembrandt produced, along with a great number of his paintings. Rembrandt's own wide range of collectible curios are also on display. The Rembrandt Information Centre is an excellent resource, but is available only upon appointment. Activities for children are on hand including a quiz quest through the house.

Repeat Offender

Did you know that Rembrandt's pocket-sized painting Jacob III de Cheyn (1632) is listed in the Guinness Book of Records as the world's most stolen painting as it has been stolen (and found) at least four times? Each time it has been returned anonymously, but no arrests have ever been made.

Jan Luijkenstraat 1
Oud Zuid
Map p.392 C4 31

Rijksmuseum

020 674 70 47 | www.rijksmuseum.nl

Until 2010 it may look like the Rijksmuseum is a work in progress, but in actual fact, it is still open and receiving millions of visitors. The Philips Wing of the museum displays masterpieces from the Golden Age, including exquisite Delftware ceramics, antique silver and, unsurprisingly, paintings of the Dutch masters of the 17th century such as Jan Steen, Vermeer and Rembrandt. This is the home of *The Nightwatch*, Rembrandt's most famous painting, and as such, it is hung with great pride. The painting apparently has more than 200 secrets hidden within its image. Depending on who you ask, it's either a simple depiction of the city's prominent citizens, or the J'accuse of its day, telling the story of a murder.

Click For Tix

For a one-stop-shop for booking all your museum tickets throughout Holland, including every museum in Amsterdam, visit www.museumtickets.nl.

Paulus Potterstraat 13
Oud Zuid
Map p.384 A1 32

Stedelijk Museum CS

020 573 29 11 | www.stedelijk.nl

Though its permanent home in the Museum District is temporarily under construction, the Stedelijk, one of Europe's most important venues for exhibiting modern and contemporary art, has found a temporary home in the former Post CS building near Centraal Station (see address below). Always cutting edge, the Stedelijk is continually changing its permanent presentation of works including CoBrA, Pop and Minimalist Art, as well as showcasing emerging talent which focuses on design, video and photography. The museum also looks to educate and inform, and has developed a wide range of educational tools for the vast array of visitors who come to the centre each year. Guided tours are available, but must be booked two weeks in advance. Temporary location until 2008: Post CS-building (close to Centraal Station), 2nd and 3rd floors, Oosterdokskade 5.

Paulus Potterstraat 7
Oud Zuid
Map p.384 A1 33

Van Gogh Museum

020 570 52 00 | www.vangoghmuseum.nl

Another must see is the Van Gogh Museum, home to the largest collection of paintings by Vincent van Gogh in the world. Along with providing the opportunity to see the originals of all of those postcards and coasters, it also allows visitors to put the artist into context alongside his contemporaries, through displaying works by other artists of his time. The museum is renowned for its tremendous temporary exhibitions covering the art of the 19th century. Friday nights find the museum filled with armchairs, video screens, DJs, and a bar – it stays open till 22:00 as a venue for locals to meet.

Koninklijk Paleis

Van Gogh Museum

Parks & Beaches

Rest from the high pressure lifestyle of a city environment is essential if you are to fully enjoy all a place like Amsterdam has to offer. A large selection of beautiful parks and some surprising artificial beaches allow you the time and space to return to the hustle and bustle refreshed. Whether you're lazing in Vondelpark or snoozing at the beach on top of the NEMO building, relax, sip a cool drink and enjoy watching the world go by.

Beaches

Other options **Beach Clubs** p.237, **Swimming** p.228, **Parks** p.159

Catching Kites
Get a kick out of kitesurfing? There are almost 60 spots for catching the wind and waves in the Benelux – check out Kitesurfing in the Activities chapter on p.208 or log on to www.windjunks.nl/ kitespots.

Who says you have to live beside the seaside to be able to visit the beach every day? Certainly not Amsterdam residents, who have a great selection of city beaches available to them; added to that, they are less than half an hour away from some of the country's finest and most fun seaside beaches and resorts. Travel a little further and you can enjoy exploring the coastline. There's a beach scene to suit every sunbather, whether you like it cool and happening, chilled and relaxed, nearly nude, or simply want a day out with the family. It's all here and it's all hot… Dutch weather permitting, of course!

Cool Coasting
For detailed information about the coastal areas of the Netherlands, visit the Coastal Guide to Europe website at www.coastalguide.to/netherlands which lists hotels, camping facilities, restaurants, attractions and other amenities available along Holland's coast.

Westerdokseiland
Westerpark
Map p.374 C4 34

Amsterdam Plage

06 46 016005 | *www.amsterdamplage.nl*

The Amsterdam plage is a 'created' beach, lying next to the Silodam industrial complex, behind Centraal Station. In addition to the incredibly unique location and hugely hospitable crowd, there is a tasty cafe on site serving snacks, lunch and dinner. (Take Tram 3 or Bus 48 to the Zoutkeetsgracht stop, it's only a five minute walk from the stop). There is a charge for use of the beach.

Bert Haanstrakade 2004
Zeeburg
Map p.367 F3

Blijburg aan Zee

020 416 03 30 | *www.blijburg.nl*

Part of the IJburg scene since its inception, Blijburg is both a beach and party place, and it's only a 15 minute tram ride from Centraal Station. Free entrance and a free-thinking crowd make Blijburg one of the best party places in Amsterdam's summer season. For those who know where to go, food, drinks, parties and fun are all readily available here.

Nr Zandvoort
Map p.366 A2

Bloemendaal aan Zee

www.bloemendaalaanzee.goedbegin.nl

It's not just the temperatures that are hot along this stretch of coastline; it's the spot where the hip and happening head to catch the rays and DJs on the beachfront just outside of Haarlem. During the summer months Bloemendaal is where the party starts early and finishes late… very. The two best known clubs are Republiek and Woodstock – the former is hip, the latter more hippy.

Oosterdok 2
Centrum
Map p.390 C4 21

NEMO Beach (BovenNEMO)

020 531 32 33 | *www.e-nemo.nl*

You might think it's a joke the first time you get directions to the most centrally located beach in Amsterdam. That's because it's on top of a building, and on a slant at that. On top of the NEMO science centre building (p.208), just minutes from Centraal Station, is the NEMO Beach. The bang you get for your buck is a lounge chair or bean bag, a few troughs of water, and access to a pretty steeply priced cafe. The food really isn't worth the price, but the view certainly is!

Zandvoort Beach

Noord Holland
Map p.366 B1

Wijk aan Zee

www.wijkaanzee.info

Just up the beach from Bloemendaal, Wijk aan Zee is even more trendier... perhaps because it's just that much more exclusive. It's a smaller version of the Bloemendaal beach, with a more relaxing vibe. This area is known to have some of the best surf in the country, and the best surfers. It's a relaxing place to hang out, catch a wave or check out some of the kite and windsurfing exhibitions. The place to be is Timbuktu.

Noord Holland
Map p.366 A2

Zandvoort

023 571 79 47 | *www.info-zandvoort.nl*

Zandvoort is only a 20 minute drive, or a shorter train ride, from Haarlem, but as the parking is so limited, take the train to the more than 15km of popular beaches. This beach area is set up to provide almost anything that any sunbather could want, including food, drinks, beach umbrellas, changing rooms and nude bathing sections. It's less hip than the more fashionable Bloemendaal, however, locals have let slip that quite a few of the Bloemendaal set have actually had a change of heart and are now returning to Zandvoort.

The Bos is the Boss for Green Space in Amsterdam
Amsterdamse Bos (below) has more than 130 kilometres of walking trails and 50 plus kilometres of bike paths!

Parks

Other options **Beaches** p.158

An old Dutch saying is: 'If you're working and you're sweating, stop. You're doing it wrong.' In fact, the only time you're likely to see an Amsterdammer sweat is if they're sitting in the sun. They like sitting in the sun almost as much as talking about the weather... and there's not much they like more than that. Either too warm or too cold; either way, they'll have been for a walk through the park. Parks are central to Amsterdam life: places of retreat and reflection, they provide a good location to meet and chat, or maybe just to relax with a newspaper. As so few Amsterdam homes have balconies or gardens, parks are one of the few places to have a picnic or barbeque. Green spaces have always been the lungs of cities – for Amsterdam residents, they're also a big part of the city's heart.

Totally Terrific Terrace
Every Sunday afternoon in July and August, the Hortus Botanicus (p.160) presents live classical music performances. On those evenings the gardens are open until 21:00, as is De Oranjerie cafe.

Off Amstelveenseweg
Amstelveen
Map p.367 E4

Amsterdamse Bos

020 545 61 00 | *www.amsterdamsebos.nl*

Woods, lakes and wetlands shelter a wide variety of flora and fauna just south of Amsterdam in the marvellous Amsterdamse Bos park. A favourite spot for locals to enjoy walking, cycling, canoeing, boating and horseback riding, it's the largest recreational area in the city. Activities for children include a paddling pool, adventure playground and organic goat farm. Those who are looking for a little more mature entertainment can enjoy one of the summer productions at the open air theatre.

Linnaeusstraat 89
Watergraafsmeer
Map p.386 A2 40

Frankendael

www.park-frankendael.nl

Originally the country manor of a wealthy 17th century Amsterdammer, the Frankendael ornamental park, covering seven hectares, is open to the public and provides a magnificent location for sunbathing, strolling and enjoying the sculptures on view. One section of the park has been developed into a botanical garden containing hundreds of varieties of plants and trees. Frankendael, just off of the Middenweg, is the only remaining (and preserved) country house in the city.

Plantage Middenlaan 2a
Zeeburg
Map p.394 B2 41

Hortus Botanicus

020 625 90 21 | *www.dehortus.nl*

Part of the University of Amsterdam, the Hortus Botanicus is one of the world's oldest botanic gardens, containing almost 4,000 distinct species of plants growing both in greenhouse and garden settings. Tucked into a nook on the edge of the bustling city centre, between the Artis Zoo (p.163) and Waterlooplein (p.293), stepping through the 300 year-old gates is surprisingly soothing. It was founded in 1638 as a medicinal herb garden by the City Council in the hope of creating medicines to cure the Plague. De Oranjerie, a cafe set in the midst of this city jewel, is a great place to sit, enjoy the scenery and have a great bite to eat.

Nr Albert Cuypstraat
De Pijp
Map p.384 C1 42

Sarphatipark

This park provides some respite from wandering down Albert Cuypstraat Markt (p.292), which is only two minutes away. Located in the heart of De Pijp it is extremely well used by the local population – it's a green space in a crowded space. The park is named after Samuel Sarphati – an eminent figure in the history of the city, who in his day was at the forefront of urban planning. You'll find his memorial fountain is the centrepiece of the park. Though great in the daytime, Sarphatipark is not a place to hang out in the evenings – it's dark, deserted, and (deservedly or not) doesn't have a great reputation for safety.

1e Constantijn Huygensstraat
Oud Zuid
Map p.392 A4 43

Vondelpark

020 678 16 78 | *www.vondelpark.nl*

A public space since 1865 when it was an area on the edge of the city for horseback riding and strolling, Vondelpark is now at the heart of the city and pulses with the lifestyle of its residents. Forty five hectares of greenery means a lot of room to wander, rollerskate or loll about by the water features. The park is very popular, attracting up to 10 million visitors each year, but it is rarely quiet. This is a place to people-watch rather than navel-gaze. There are six children's play areas, skate rentals, the Filmmuseum (www.filmmuseum.nl) and one of Amsterdam's best hideaways, the Het Blauwe Theehuis (p.335) terrace bar and cafe, situated smackdab in the middle of the park. The summer brings free concerts at the park's open air theatre and bandstand, and children's activities throughout the week.

Nr Haarlemmerweg
Westerpark
Map p.374 A4 44

Westerpark

Far less well known than some of Amsterdam's parks, but just as popular, this large park is located in the centre of the district of the same name – an expanding area of the city. One of the few options in the area, it is a fun place for dog walking, frisbee throwing and summer evening barbecues.

Other Attractions

Roken 78
Centrum
Map p.393 E1 45

The Amsterdam Dungeon

020 530 85 30 | www.theamsterdamdungeon.nl

Superbly sited in one of Amsterdam's treasured historic buildings, this fun and fact-filled experience incorporates live actors, special effects and a great rollercoaster ride, all of which escort you back to some gruesome chapters in Dutch history.

Max Euweplein 62
Centrum
Map p.392 C4 46

Holland Casino

020 521 11 11 | www.hollandcasino.nl

Truth be told, it's not Vegas, but it's a chance to try your hand against a Dutch dealer (cards that is). Here's a hint... it's so un-Vegas that the drinks aren't free, but if you are a fan of Casino Royale then this is your best bet.

Amusement Parks

There are no amusement centres or parks within the city centre of Amsterdam, however, as Holland is such a small country, nothing is too far away. Generally speaking the vast majority of these parks and centres are designed for families with young children (the fairytale-based Efteling for example). But the parks usually have hotels attached, and provide great weekend breaks.

Archeonlaan 1
Alphen aan den Rijn
Map p.365 B3

Archeon

0172 44 77 44 | www.archeon.nl

Easily accessible by car and train, this is both fascinating and fun. Find out what it was like to live in the Prehistoric, Roman and Middle Ages in this complex of buildings, bridges, huts, temples and more. There are loads of activities for kids to enjoy like archery, Viking games, making fire and exercising with a Roman soldier.

Duinrell 1
Wassenaar
Map p.365 A3

Duinrell Holiday & Amusement Park

0170 515 52 55 | www.duinrell.nl

A short hop, skip and a jump from Den Haag, this family fun park has loads of sports and recreation facilities in its gorgeous site in the wooded dune area along the coast. Within walking distance of Wassenaar, the park also has an amusement park, Tiki pool, overnight accommodation and a variety of themed restaurants.

Europalaan 1
Tilburg
Map p.365 B3

Efteling

0416 288 111 | www.efteling.nl

Created by much-loved Dutch designer and architect Anton Pieck, the award-winning Efteling brings to life characters from Dutch and international fairy tales. As well as a children's amusement park there are paddling pools, a boating lake, monorail and haunted castle. Those looking for more excitement will enjoy the water rides, roller coasters and other amusement park rides. The Efteling Hotel is available for overnight stays. Easily accessible by both train and car, it is located near Kaatsheuvel, 8km north of Tilburg. The park is open from 10:00 to 18:00 daily, from April until October. For more on the park, see p.22.

Arsenaalplein 1
Vlissingen
Map p.365 A4

Het Arsenaal

011 841 54 00 | www.arsenaal.com

The coastal, and historically important town of Vlissingen is home to the pirate-themed adventure park Het Arsenaal, where kids of all ages can hear tales of the treacherous deep and the pirates who ruled the waves – or sank to the dark oceanic depths. The views from the watchtower are breathtaking, as is the opportunity to touch sharks and rays as well as learn about more than 100 other underwater species.

George Maduroplein 1
Den Haag
Map p.365 A3

Madurodam

070 416 24 00 | *www.madurodam.nl*

Sure, Holland is a small country, but you still couldn't see it all in one day; that's unless you find your way to this mainstay of family entertainment near Den Haag. A miniature representation of the nation and all its highlights, Madurodam is also a venue for special events and extravaganzas throughout the year. Open September to March from 09:00 to 18:00, it closes later during the spring and summer months.

Spikweg 30
Biddinghuizen
Map p.365 C2

Walibi World

0321 329 999 | *www.walibiworld.nl*

What used to be a Six Flags amusement park is still one of Holland's most popular attractions. With over 40 rides, there's something for everyone. Queues for its most popular rides such as Goliath start early and can be very long. Coming from Amsterdam, take the train to Harderwijk to connect with the shuttle bus. Open from April to October.

Nature Reserves

Due to its location on the North Sea, the Netherlands has large swathes of protected coastal areas, not only to preserve the nation itself from being eroded, but also to safeguard the rich diversity of wildlife that inhabit the area – like the migrating birds. That said, it's a small country, so there isn't a great deal of room for reserves which are too expansive. Nonetheless, Holland offers lakes, dunes and beaches which will refresh the senses and leave you feeling reinvigorated for your return to Amsterdam.

Ruijslaan 92
Texel
Map p.365 B2

Ecomare

0222 317 741 | *www.ecomare.nl*

Ecomare is the preeminent nature centre for the Wadden and North Sea area, with a superb number of visitor centres providing information about the nature and culture of Texel, as well as seal and bird sanctuaries and aquariums. The seals are fed at 11:00 and 15:00. Each summer several sea pups are born and an adoption programme is available for visitors who would like to support Ecomare and its work.

Southwest of Naarden
Nr Huizen
Map p.365 C3

Naarder Lake

The oldest protected nature reserve in the country is the Naardermeer, which is enjoyed by walkers, cyclists and sailors alike. Though it isn't possible to take your own boat onto the lake, the local tourist information centre (VVV) will book an excursion for you, allowing you to get up close to the fantastic variety of birds and wildlife.

South-west of Lelystad
Markermeer
Map p.365 B2

Oostvaarderplassen

www.birdsnetherlands.nl

The Oostvaarderplassen is a superb wet and dry nature reserve which is extremely important internationally due to its prime location, though it was only created in 1968. It is significant in particular due to the migration of cormorants, herons, spoonbills and white-tailed eagles. There are bird watching tours available.

North of Zandvoort
West Coast
Map p.366 A2

Zuid-Kennemerland National Park

023 541 11 29 | *www.npzk.nl/*

South of the Noord Holland Dune Reserve is the stunning Zuid-Kennemerland National Park. Wander the dunes, beaches, family facilities and historic estates. With more than 350 different activities, there really is something for everyone here.

Zoos & Wildlife Parks

The Artis Express
During the summer season a special canal boat collects visitors from Amsterdam's Centraal Station and takes them to Artis Zoo. Ring 020 530 10 90 or visit www.lovers.nl for more information (p.166).

The Netherlands has several zoos and wildife parks which are well worth a day's visit. Whether it's Apenheul Primate Park Foundation which was voted the number one zoo in Holland by Dutch children and which specialises in the protection of and education about primates, or Artis Zoo which is the oldest zoo in The Netherlands, zoos here specialise in keeping animals as close to their natural environment as possible. If you prefer not to see animals in enclosures, then Beekse Bergen is a well-managed safari park, and provides an adventure which allows visitors to get up close to lions, tigers and cheetahs.

Apenheul Primate Park Foundation

J.C. Wilslaan 21
Apeldoorn
Map p.365 C3

055 357 57 57 | *www.apenheul.nl*

Recently voted the best zoo in the Netherlands by the country's children, the Apenheul provides a magnificent opportunity for visitors to learn more about primates. The park's mission is to safeguard the conservation of nature through education. Get up close and personal with the nearly 30 species of monkeys, many of which roam free in the grounds. There is a special Madagascan area devoted to the ever-playful lemur, as well as a Dayak farm introducing the culture of the Dayak tribe of Borneo, the keepers of the rainforest. A treetop walk can also be enjoyed.

Artis

Plantage Kerklaan 38-40
Centrum
Map p.394 C2 58

020 523 34 00 | *www.amsterdamzoo.nl*

This is the city zoo of Amsterdam, and it is a hugely popular institution with residents and tourists alike. The oldest zoo in the Netherlands, it had its beginnings well over 150 years ago. It has expanded to include aproximately 700 different species of animals. Get face to face with fish, birds, mammals, insects and amphibians; the zoo's impressive aquarium even brings the secret life of Amsterdam's canals to the surface. An entry ticket for Artis also provides admission to the Planetarium, the Geological Museum, the Aquarium and the Zoological Museum. Guided tours in English are now given every Sunday morning at 11:00. Open every day of the year, from 09:00 to 17:00. During the summer Artis closes at 18:00.

Beekse Bergen Safari Park

Beekse Bergen 31
Tilburg
Map p.365 B3

0900 233 573 | *www.safaripark.nl*

A superbly controlled safari park, Beekse Bergen allows visitors to get fantastic views of its lions, tigers and cheetahs. There are three ways to see the animals: either by vehicle, boat or on foot. As well as the wonderful wildlife, there is a playground for children. Nearby Speelland is a great place for camping, with its beach and boating lake.

Burgers' Zoo

Antoon van Hooffplein 1
Arnhem
Map p.365 B3

026 442 45 34 | *www.burgerszoo.nl*

This is a wonderful zoo which has a great deal to offer all visitors regardless of their age. All the animals are expertly housed in areas as close to their natural environment as possible. The aquarium section is particularly good, with the glass walkway through the largest tank providing an enthralling experience.

Rotterdam Zoo

Blijdorplaan 8
Rotterdam
Map p.365 A3

010 443 14 95 | *www.rotterdamzoo.nl*

The zoo, which celebrated its 150th anniversary in 2007, is one of the most popular attractions in the Netherlands, with more than 1.5 million visitors per year. Open every day from 09:00, the Rotterdam Zoo and Oceanarium are easily accessible from Rotterdam city centre by public transport.

Tours & Sightseeing

Other options **Out of Amsterdam** p.170, **Weekend Break Hotels** p.170

Filled to the brim with a fantastic array of things to see and do, Amsterdam has enough culture and creativity to keep any visitor busy. One of the best things about it is, however, that everything is pretty easy to get to – this is a small village in comparison with many other international cities. Amsterdam is walkable, which means that you can make up your own tour routes as you wander on foot or cycle through the city. You can grab a map or guidebook, for instance, and make your way to a museum, shopping area or famous gallery.

As well as being a wonderful city for walking around, Amsterdam is also a great city for boats and bikes, both excellent ways to see the city. As an alternative to the ubiquitious canal tours, if you want to get around under your own steam, Canal Bike pedalboats (020 623 98 86, www.canal.nl) are a fun way to combine the two. The pedal boats can be rented at four different locations, including the Rijksmuseum and Anne Frank Huis.

The city is also flooded with services for the tourist trade, including tour companies. Though there are bus tours, and even a horse and carriage available, the two most popular ways to tour town are either by canal boat or bike. There are a number of companies to choose from, and the biggest have depots throughout the city. Prices don't vary much, but service level can, so, as always, take your ticket from the tout with a smile. The following information lists some of the different types of tours on offer in Amsterdam and some of the better companies that offer them.

Diamond Tours

Amsterdam has a long history in the diamond trade, and there are numerous factories in the city which offer guided tours to demonstrate their cutting and polishing techniques during regular working hours. Try Coster Diamonds (020 305 55 55, www.costerdiamonds.com), Stoeltie Diamonds (020 623 76 01, www.stoeltiediamonds.com) or Van Moppes Diamonds (020 676 12 42, www.moppesdiamonds.com). You can also visit the Amsterdam Diamond Stock Exchange, the world's first diamond exchange (www.diamantbeurs.org).

Bicycle Tours

Cycletours Holland

Buiksloterweg 7A
Zeeburg
Map p.375 E4 77

020 521 84 90 | *www.cycletours.com*

For a tour that takes in major sights, picturesque villages and traditional tulip fields and more, Cycletours combines a wide range of Dutch scenes which are all interesting treats for tourists. They are often off the beaten track, taking in broader attractions than the 'normal' tours. Evenings are spent on the company's sailing boat which transports passengers to various morning starting points throughout the country.

Mike's Bike Tours

Kerkstratt 134
Centrum
Map p.393 D3 82

020 622 79 70 | *www.mikesbikeamsterdam.com*

Fantastic four-hour tours with friendly and knowledgeable guides. On the way through the city centre, the guides give a great overview of the history and culture of Amsterdam. Then it's out to the countryside just south of the city for a visit to a cheese farm and a clog making display. They also have a bike and boat tour, which lasts approximately five hours.

Orange Bike Rentals and Tours

Singel 233
Centrum
Map p.389 D4 83

020 528 99 90 | *www.orangebike.nl*

This friendly company has daily excursions which include beach, historical city and architectural heritage tours. Picnic and culinary jaunts, where participants stop off at cafes and sample the best of the city's cuisine are also lots of fun. A tour of Amsterdam's gay areas is also available.

Nieuwezijds Kolk 29
Centrum
Map p.389 E3 80

Yellow Bike Tours

020 620 69 40 | www.yellowbike.nl

The original bike tour company in Amsterdam, there aren't many secrets these guides aren't going to be able to fill you in on. There is a three-hour city tour and a six-hour countryside tour on offer. Tours are limited to 12 participants and are packed with information rather than pub stops. All tours are available from April to November.

Boat & Yacht Charters

Other options **Dinner Cruises** p.310

Canal cruising is one of the mainstays of the Amsterdam tourist trade. It's a rare visitor who visits the Venice of the North without taking at least one guided excursion. Of course for locals, one of the best invitations to get is to hang out on a friend's canal boat for an afternoon or evening of touring the town.

KNSM-laan 377
Zeeburg
Map p.380 B2 62

Bootnodig Boat Rentals

020 419 66 50 | www.bootnodig.nl

For the sailor in all of us there is always the opportunity to explore the Netherlands by boat, whether it's on the Amstel and Vecht rivers, or experiencing the waters of the Wadden Sea, the IJsselmeer, South-Holland or Zeeland. Boats are available to charter for private parties, company excursions and other events. Check out the selection of clippers, schooners, barges, yachts, scows, motorboats and party ships available.

Czaar Peterstr 147hs
Oost
Map p.388 A3 63

Classic Canal Charters

020 421 08 25 | www.classiccanalcharters.com

A stylish way to wind your way through the city's canals, Classic Canal Charters offer canal cruises in Amsterdam and further afield in their charmingly authentic boats. They offer dinner, group and special event trips as well.

Go Low
Though the bigger tour boats can hold a large number of people, smaller boats which sit low in the water are able to explore much more of the canal system as they can pass under some of the extremely low bridges!

Boat Tours

For the most part, the tour and excursion boats which ply their trade on the canals of Amsterdam are all quite similar. Each is set up to be able to provide an informative tour of the city. And it must be said, the city does look different from here. The tours are of varying lengths, with some lasting an hour and others providing a day-long, hop-on and hop-off feature. It's a lovely, if not wholly romantic way to see the city at night, with candlelight and cocktails. Some boats can arrange a wedding ceremony, while others give more unorthodox insights into the wetland areas, away from the conventional tours of the canal belt.

Bridges over Keizersgracht and Leidsegracht

Damrak 34
Centrum
Map p.389 F4 74

The Best of Holland

420 40 00 | www.thebestofholland.nl

This is one of Holland's largest tour companies and as such they have a wide variety of tours available including a two-hour Amsterdam by Candlelight cruise and their popular Canals and All That Jazz Cruise. A pick up service can also be arranged at various hotels in the city.

Stadhouderskade 30
Oud Zuid
Map p.392 C4 86

Blue Boat Company

020 679 13 70 | *www.blueboat.nl*

Conveniently located between the Rijksmuseum and Max Euweplein, the Blue Boat crews provide a variety of services including customised cruises and the facilities to get married on board.

Weteringschans 26
Canal Belt (Grachtengordel)
Map p.392 C4 87

Canal Bus

020 623 98 86 | *www.canal.nl*

This convenient hop-on and hop-off boat tour takes in most of the major tourist spots in the city. The Canal Bus, which has several departure points throughout the city, has three routes, 14 stops and a ticket that is valid all day. Visitors can hop on and off as they please. Adult €18, child (aged 4 to 13) €12.

Prins Henrikkade 33A
Centrum
Map p.389 F3 88

Holland International

020 622 77 88 | *www.hir.nl*

The cruises leave the harbour every 15 minutes between 09:00 to 18:00 and every half an hour from 06:00 to 21:00. It's the chain store of boat cruises but even having said that, it's still a convenient way to see the city. This is the de rigeur tourist thing to do in Amsterdam and these are the most frequented canal cruise in the city, so get to a dock early if you want to guarantee a window seat. Candlelight lunch and dinner cruises are also available.

Rokin 125
Centrum
Map p.393 E1 89

Kooij BV Rederij

020 623 38 10 | *www.rederijkooij.nl*

This is the largest boat tour company in Amsterdam and as such has the market very well covered. Commentary in eight languages is available, as is the possibility of private boat hires for groups of up to 40 people, and candlelight tours.

Damrak 26
Centrum
Map p.389 F3 79

Lindbergh

020 622 27 66 | *www.lindbergh.nl*

Daily one-hour cruises are offered each day at 30 minute intervals. Candlelight and dinner cruises are also available.

Hendrikkade 25 – 27
Centrum
Map p.389 F2 91

Lovers

020 530 10 90 | *www.lovers.nl*

Daily cruises depart every hour from 09:00. Night cruises where you can dine by candlelight are also available on a daily basis during the summer and on Wednesdays, Fridays and Saturdays during the winter months. This is the company which runs the museum boat – an excellent way to get to many of the city's excellent cultural sites.

Ruysdaelkade 174
Oud Zuid
Map p.384 B1 92

Smidtje

020 670 60 67 | *www.smidtje.nl*

These charming and comfortable canal boats generally cruise the waterways of Amsterdam's old city centre, but with prior arrangement can navigate the Amstel River and even go as far afield as Zaandam and the IJssel Lake. Though boarding is normally at the Rijksmuseum or on Ruysdaelkade, other arrangements can be made with this friendly company.

Various locations

Wetlands Safari

020 686 34 45 | *www.wetlandssafari.nl*

The Wetlands Safari uses canoes and rowing boats to explore the wetland areas outside the city. Lasting for approximately five hours, the tour takes in flora, fauna and some phenomenal views. The tour season is from 1 May to 15 September.

Bus Tours

Other options **Walking Tours** p.168

Despite Amsterdam's focus on cycling, walking and canal boats as the favoured forms of transport, city bus tours of Amsterdam will provide you with an insight into the city. Broader tours of the Netherlands are also available, allowing you to soak up the Dutch countryside, visit windmills and see clog makers at work. Whether it's Koninklijk Paleis (the Royal Palace) in Amsterdam or sampling the country's cheeses in its beautiful seaside villages, there's a perfect tour for everyone.

Damrak 34
Centrum
Map p.389 F4 74

The Best of Holland

020 420 40 00 | *www.thebestofholland.nl*

This is one of Holland's largest tour companies and as such they have a wide variety of tours available. Their various bus tours take in all of Amsterdam's most famous sights as well as tours further afield to the high points of Holland and the beauty of Belgium.

Paulus Potterstrat 8
Oud Zuid
Map p.389 F4 78

Key Tours

020 200 03 00 | *www.keytours.nl*

This is one of the largest and best established tour companies in the country. There are a wide variety of trips to choose from including exploring Edam, the fishing villages of Volendam and Marken, Delft, Den Haag, as well as places outside Holland such as Antwerp and Bruges. Of course, they also offer Amsterdam tours, including city walks and dinner cruises.

Farm & Stable Tours

There are many petting zoos throughout the city of Amsterdam. Most are open year round and have special educational programmes for children. They're a great way to teach children who may have spent their whole lives in the city about the countryside and the animals they might find on a farm.

Provincialeweg 46a
Amsterdam Zuidoost
Map p.367 F4

De Bijlmerweide

020 695 11 49 | *www.bijlmerweide.nl*

Open all year round, Bijlmerweide in the south-east of the city is a large farm with a variety of animals, a children's playground and a canteen. A nice way to teach the kids about the countryside.

Lizzy Ansinghstraat 82
Oud Zuid
Map p.384 C2 65

De Dierenpijp

020 664 83 03

This petting zoo is situated, surprisingly, next to the exclusive Hotel Okura in the Old South. There are chickens, goats and sheep to pet as well as a variety of activities to keep children entertained.

Ganzenhoefpad 8
Amsterdam Zuidoost
Map p.367 F4

De Gliphoeve

020 690 01 43

Also situated in the south-east of the city, the Gliphoeve petting zoo is stocked with the pre-requisite chickens, goats and fluffy rabbits.

Staalmeesterslaan 420
West
Map p.378 C3 67

De Uylenburg

020 618 52 35

Rembrandtpark's petting zoo is loads of fun for kids. There are animals to stroke, activities to participate in, and lots of free green areas to explore.

Amstelpark 22
Oud Zuid
Map p.367 E4

Kinderboerderij Amstelpark

_020 644 42 16_

Not far from the Amsterdam RAI conference centre, the Amstelpark petting zoo has goats and chickens, guinea pigs and rabbits running around. Added to that, there are plenty of green spaces for a kickabout or to play, there's a daycare centre and two playgrounds, and food can be purchased.

Nieuwe Meerlaan 4
Amstelveen
Map p.367 E4

Ridammer Hoeve, Geitenboerderij Amsterdamse Bos

The suburb of Amstelveen also has its own petting zoo with a goat and poultry farm, farm shop and children's playground.

Other Tours

Van IJsendijkstraat 16
Jordaan
Map p.367 E2

Amsterdam City Tours

_06 14 295174_ | _www.amsterdamcitytours.com_

This company has covered almost all the possible excursions that anyone may want to take. Examples are Daily City Walk, Cannabis Tour and Dark Amsterdam Tour, which takes you through some of the city's shadows including the Red Light District.

Veemarkt 50
Zeeburg
Map p.380 A3 71

Karos City Tours

_020 691 34 78_ | _www.karos.nl_

A thoroughly novel and nostalgic way to see the city: by horse drawn carriage. Quaint, relaxing and not as strenuous as riding a bike, this is the tour for people who want to explore Amsterdam in style.

Prins Henrikkade 94-95
Centrum
Map p.390 A3 72

Red Light District Tour

_020 623 63 02_ | _www.dewallenwinkel.nl_

This two and a half hour tour takes visitors through the past, present and possible future of the Red Light District in Amsterdam. The meeting place is at the Café Schreierstoren at Prins Henrikkade 94-95, near Centraal Station.

Meet nr Rembrandtplein
Centrum
Map p.388 A2 73

Urban Home and Garden Tours

_020 688 12 43_ | _www.uhgt.nl_

From April through to October tour the stunning 17th to 20th century homes and gardens of Amsterdam, incorporating a great deal of the lustre of the city's Golden Age. Tours last between 2.5 and 3 hours.

Walking Tours

Surprisingly, for such an immensely walkable city, Amsterdam does not have many guided walking tours. However there are many themed walks which have been devised for individuals to follow themselves, such as following Rembrandt's trail.

Damrak 34
Centrum
Map p.389 E3 74

The Best of Holland

_020 420 40 00_ | _www.thebestofholland.nl_

This is one of Holland's largest tour companies and as such they have a wide variety of tours available. Their tour of Amsterdam's Red Light District is fun, frivolous and only slightly naughty.

Tours Outside Amsterdam

It has to be said that there is a general 'tour circuit' out of Amsterdam. The best sites to be seen are the Dutch countryside with its variety of windmills, Delft and its pottery, Den Haag, and other delightful places like Scheveningen. The country's many nature reserves and wetlands provide relaxing respite from the stresses of city life. Most companies also offer trips into Belgium, hitting hotspots such as Bruges (famous for its lace), the capital Brussels, and the historic city of Antwerp.

Tour Operators		
Amsterdam City Tours (Bus)	06 14 295174	www.amsterdamcitytours.com
The Best of Holland	020 420 40 00	www.thebestofholland.nl
Blue Boat Company	020 679 13 70	www.blueboat.nl
Canal Bus	020 623 98 86	www.canal.nl
Holland International	020 622 77 88	www.hir.nl
Key Tours	020 200 03 00	www.keytours.nl
Kooij BV Rederij	020 623 38 10	www.rederijkooij.nl
Lindbergh	020 622 27 66	www.lindbergh.nl
Lovers	020 530 10 90	www.lovers.nl
Smidtje	020 670 60 67	www.smidtje.nl
Wetlands Safari	020 686 34 45	www.wetlandssafari.nl

Van IJsendijkstraat 16
Jordaan
Map p.367 E2 70

Amsterdam City Tours

06 14 295174 | www.amsterdamcitytours.com

Offering a wide range of bus tours throughout Amsterdam, Holland and Belgium, including visits to Marken, Volendam and various windmills. They also offer an eight-hour Grand Holland Tour which takes in Aalsmeer, Delft, Rotterdam and Den Haag.

Damrak 34
Centrum
Map p.389 E3 74

The Best of Holland

020 420 40 00 | www.thebestofholland.nl

Along with their Amsterdam-centred tours, The Best of Holland bus and boat tours include day tours of the Netherlands and Belgium as well as specific tours incorporating Delft, Den Haag and Madurodam.

Buiksloterweg 7a
Zeeburg
Map p.375 E4 77

Cycletours Holland

020 521 84 90 | www.cycletours.com

Bike and boat tours throughout the Netherlands including Amsterdam, a Dutch Master's Tour, an Island Hopping Tour and a Tulip Tour to the Keukenhof. In addition to these, they offer activity vacations throughout Europe including biking tours in Austria, Belgium and France; walks in Italy and Spain; and cultural tours in Estonia, Latvia and Turkey.

Paulus Potterstrat 8
Oud Zuid
Map p.389 F4 78

Key Tours

020 200 03 00 | www.keytours.nl

A wide variety of tours through Amsterdam, the Netherlands and Belgium are available with this well known and well respected tour operator.

Damrak 26
Centrum
Map p.389 F3 79

Lindbergh

020 622 27 66 | www.lindbergh.nl

Visit the Alkmaar Cheese Market; Delft, Den Haag and Madurodam; and Antwerp and Brussels. Guides speak English, French, German and Spanish.

Nieuwezijds Kolk 29
Centrum
Map p.389 E3 80

Yellow Bike Tours

020 620 69 40 | www.yellowbike.nl

This six-hour tour takes in 35 kilometres of the Waterland district north of Amsterdam. Incorporating a nature reserve, charming villages, and a vast network of waterways, this guided bike ride is full of the history and culture of the area.

Last Minute Deals

The Weekend Company at Singel 540 is a great spot for finding last minute deals at five-star hotels in Luxembourg, Antwerp, Brussels and Paris. They do have a website (0900 9335 , www.weekend company.nl) but it is not in English at this point.

Out of Amsterdam

Quite frankly, there is so much to see and do in Amsterdam, that there are those people who might just want to stay put. That said, it really is worth taking some time to explore some of the other areas of the country, as each have their own charm and particular points of interest. Holland is a coastal nation, but the coast and its islands are full of much more than just forts and fish – though there are lots of these too. The nature reserves, particularly around the dune areas, are spectacular.

Many of the towns and cities of the Netherlands owe their fortune to the sea. One reason the nation had a Golden Age was because of its trading prowess, and this was due to mastery of the world's seas and oceans. Evidence of this can be seen throughout the country, particularly in places like the Zuiderzeemuseum in Enkhuizen. For a land that was under a salty sea for so long, the Dutch have certainly managed to reclaim a great deal of it, and make it rich and ready for planting. It's a land in love with flowers, and the Keukenhof gardens (p.172) is just one example of the passion Netherlanders have for their blooms.

Cheese is another favourite and you can tour your way through the nation, nibbling its hundreds of varieties of cheese. Edam and Gouda are places well worth a visit, or indeed Alkmeer and its world famous cheese market. If you want to get really Dutch, and let's face it, fairly kitsch, how about the Clara Maria Cheese Farm and Clog Factory (Bovenkerkerweg 106, 0297 582 2 79) for a fun family day out in Amstelveen, just south of Amsterdam? While you're there, try out their new game of farmers' golf!

Weekend Break Hotels

Best Western Grand Hotel de l' Empereur	Maastricht	043 321 38 38	www.hotel-empereur.nl
Carlton Square	Haarlem	023 531 90 91	www.carlton.nl
Greenside Hotel	De Koog	022 232 72 22	www.hotelgreenside.nl
Hilton Rotterdam hotel	Rotterdam	010 710 80 00	www1.hilton.com
Hotelvilla Imhof	Bloemendaal	023 525 47 18	na
Malie Hotel	Utrecht	030 231 64 24	www.maliehotel.nl
Newport Hotel	Huizen	035 528 96 00	www.hotelnewport.nl
Residenz Stadslogement	Den Haag	070 364 61 90	www.residenz.nl
Strandhotel Zandvoort Center Parcs	Zandvoort	0900 727 5926	www.centerparcs.com

The country is so small that you can get anywhere within a few hours by either car or train. In fact, there are great areas to explore only a bike ride away, and there are quite a few hearty souls who have been known to walk out to the beach from the city for the afternoon. Let's face it, Holland is flat, so there aren't any problems with having to make it over a mountain pass. The thing to do is get out and explore; start out in any direction and you're sure to find something interesting.

Holiday chalets

Keeping Up With What's Going Down
One of the best ways to find out what's going on in Den Haag (The Hague) is by visiting the extremely popular and useful www.TheHagueOnline.com website which lists local news and events.

Knowing When To Stop
When travelling to Den Haag by train it is more convenient to go to the Den Haag Centraal Station as it is within walking distance of the city centre.

Thoughts On Thinkers
The Dutch do revere their home grown philosophers. A statue of Baruch de Spinoza (1632-77) stands outside the house where he lived and died at Paviljoensgracht 72. The city has also been the home of renowned artists Jan van Goyen (1596-56) and Jan Steen (1626-79).

Den Haag

Den Haag (The Hague) is the seat of government of the Netherlands. The city is not the capital of the country, as is often assumed, but it is where Queen Beatrix lives and works, as does the heir to the throne Crown Prince Willem Alexander, with his wife Princess Maxima and their three daughters. It is also the home of foreign embassies and consulates, the International Court of Justice (070 302 23 23, www.icj-cij.org) and The Peace Palace (070 302 42 42, www.vredespalais.nl) among many renowned international institutions and agencies. As such, it is a town of politics and political talk. Though Den Haag does profess to want to be as renowned for its current cultural life as much as for its politics, it must be said that it does tend to lag behind Amsterdam in the race for the top of the cultural heap. In recent years the city lost the North Sea Jazz Festival to Rotterdam, and it remains to be seen whether its attempts to create a smaller event will prove successful. The Anton Philips Concert Hall on Spuiplein is perhaps the most used entertainment complex in the city, housing both The Hague Philharmonic and the Lucent Dance Theatre. What Den Haag has which Amsterdam lacks, at the moment, is the superbly developed seaside suburb of Scheveningen, which is close enough to the city centre to spend a weekend afternoon with the family or enjoy an early evening cocktail.

Windmill at Keukenhoff

That said, some fantastic new cocktail bars and restaurants have opened recently. Taste – The Wine Bar, at Nieuwe Schoolstraat 19, is a good example of the change in the city. Where it once was difficult to find anything other than beer on a night out, good wine is slowly becoming not only popular, but some would say, a preoccupation. For a great night out with less than classical live music, a great bet is the Paard van Troje at Prinsengracht 12.

There are copious monuments and museums celebrating the pride of the nation. The 'must sees' include the Mauritshuis Museum on Korte Vijverberg 8, adjacent to the Binnenhof (070 302 3456, www.mauritshuis.nl) which is home to a wonderful collection of outstanding paintings by the likes of Rembrandt, Vermeer, Jan Steen, Frans Hals, Hobbema and Rubens, and the completely different, but completely captivating M.C. Escher Museum (070 427 77 30, www.escherinhetpaleis.nl) at Lange Voorhout 74, which gives a rewarding insight into the revered Dutch graphic artist and his work.

Den Haag is an extremely green city in that it is filled with parks and woodlands. In fact, many residents are delighted to boast that along with being the City of Peace and Justice, Den Haag is Holland's greenest city. The Haagse Bos near Centraal Station is an extremely popular area for walkers and cyclists as well as a location where fairs, concerts and other presentations are held. Nearby is the Clingendael Park's 133 acres of greenery, including a magnificent Japanese garden. Zuider Park to the south is better for families perhaps, as it has many recreational activities suitable for children, including mini-golf and animal centres.

Den Haag is an extremely accessible and user-friendly city, easy to get to and easy to get around in. Perhaps it doesn't have the hipster cache of Amsterdam, but it doesn't need it – Den Haag has its own personality, which its inhabitants are, rightly, proud of.

Best Bloom Times
The best time to visit Keukenhof is generally mid-April, as this tends to be the optimum time for the blooms to flower. However, do check before setting out, as the climate has a tendency to change things – just one week late, and all that'll be left are bare fields.

All Hail The Ale
The Hofje van Bakenes at Wijde Appelaarsteeg 11, which has two entrances, one at the Bakenessergracht and the other at the Wijde Appelaarsteeg, is the oldest almshouse in the Netherlands.

Haarlem & Keukenhof

Only 18 kilometres from Amsterdam, Haarlem is a small village which still retains a quaint, quiet serenity – an occasional relief from the ever-so-bustling capital nearby. It is a wonderful place for strolling and discovering its 17th and 18th century architecture, excellent art galleries, museums and historic windmills. The Grote Market is a great place to start your exploration of this gorgeous little town. Surrounding the square are a large number of eateries intermingled with its ancient architecture. You can't miss the Müller organ in the Grote Kerk which, at 30 metres tall, is one of the world's most magnificent musical instruments – this one was played by Handel and Mozart in their time.

Harsh On Haarlem
Haarlem joined many other Dutch towns in opposing its Spanish rulers, and in 1572 it was under siege for seven months. The siege only ended when Haarlem surrendered under the condition that none of its citizens would be harmed. Though the Spanish general agreed, he went back on his word, killing the Governor, Calvinist ministers and approximately 2,000 townsfolk.

The Teylers Museum (www.teylersmuseum.nl, 023 531 90 10) is the oldest museum in the Netherlands and is home to drawings by Michelangelo and Raphael among other masters. Another superb example of the city's collections is the Frans Hals Museum (www.franshalmuseum.nl, 023 511 57 75) which houses an impressive collection of Dutch Masters, including eight group portraits by Hals himself.

For those looking to stay current rather than wallow in the past, Haarlem is a very popular destination for shopping and eating out: the variety of restaurants, cafes and terraces belies the small size of the town.

It must be said that many people find their way to Haarlem on their way to the annual celebration of the Dutch mania for flowers, the Keukenhof festivities, which take place from March to May each year when the flowers are in full blossom. The Keukenhof gardens, and the blooming fields around them, are situated south of Haarlem, between the towns of Lisee and Hillegom, and are the largest flowering gardens in the world, well earning their title The Garden of Europe (0252 465 555, www.keukenhof.nl).

Grote Kerk St Bavo in Haarlem

Come To Carnival
The city is known to be the heart of the Catholic community of the Netherlands, and as such, it is home to the largest carnival celebration, which shouldn't be missed.

Superb Shopping
A favourite shopping street for clothes, jewellery, and specialty items is Wolfstraat, where the expected and unexpected can often be found side-by-side.

Marvellous Maritime Museum
The Zuiderzeemuseum in Enkhuizen is a fantastic voyage through the maritime history of this ocean-going nation. (0228 351 111, www.zuiderzeemuseum.nl).

Maastricht

Maastricht is easily accessible by both car and rail, though it's just far enough away from its northern neighbouring cities to have a personality of its own. Maastricht is a city crammed with ancient history and steeped in modern shopping. Most of the shops are to be found along narrow cobble-stoned streets, and as such, the city is much better for pedestrians than car traffic.

Internationally, the city is probably best known for being the location, in 1991, for when European politicians signed the treaty establishing the European Union. However, even in Roman times it was an important outpost and trading town. Though the historic outer walls of the city were built in 1229 it was as early as 50 BC that the Romans found good use for a town at the crossing of major trading routes. You can still see some of the city's ancient walls on the southern and eastern edges of the old town centre.

The modern city of Maastricht is a centre of culture, politics, education and shopping. With six universities in the area, it's no surprise that the city has a youthful energy, which is marvellously mixed with its old school grandeur. The city centre, deemed a 'protected area' is a fantastic location to spend the day wandering and exploring the history of this charming place. Maastricht prides itself on being 'the home of fashion' in the Netherlands, so there are a lot of shopping opportunities.

There are landmarks and historic sites galore here. One of the most ancient is the Basilica of St. Servatius (Keizer Karelplein 6) which dates from the year 1000 and is the home of the remains of the city's first bishop, St. Servatius. Another charming church to visit is Onze Lieve Basiliek (Basilica of our Beloved Lady) near the old city walls at O.L. Vrouweplein 20. The Stella Mare Chapel was a 17th century pilgrimage site, its 500 year old statue of the Madonna drawing more than 20,000 visitors a year.

Eating & Treating

The Burgundian Gastronomic Festival is a great example of the lifestyle of Maastricht residents who, allegedly, believe in eating and drinking well – rather more than their northern, Protestant countrymen.

Noord Holland

Amsterdam is part of the province of Noord Holland, and though Amsterdammers may disagree, there is actually a great deal more to do in the province than just hang out in the capital.

The many small towns and villages of the area are the heart and soul of this trading nation. Port towns like Volendam and Muidenof show us traces of life before the IJ was tamed. Hoorn and Enkhuizen provide many reminders of the Dutch East India Company, which was instrumental in bringing about Holland's Golden Age – an era still so resplendently evident in Alkmaar, Haarlem and, of course, Amsterdam.

Added to this wealth of history, the rich soil of Noord Holland is home to more than one million hectares of planted bulbs – this is equivalent to nearly 30,000 football pitches! With so many flowers sprouting up, it's no wonder that they are also the centre of many local festivities including parades, competitions and Aalsmeer's flower auction, which is the largest in the world.

Other towns which have particular interest in the area include Alkmaar with its famous cheese market that has been in existence for over four centuries. This takes place every Friday from April through to September in front of the Waagebouw (weighing house) on Wageplein. During school holidays there is also a children's cheese market.

Den Helder is at the northern end of Noord Holland and as such is often used as a departure point for exploring the northern coast and islands of the country. But Den

Helder itself is also interesting to explore. Fort Kijkduin (0223 612 366, www.fortkijkduin.nl), which was commissioned by Napoleon in 1811, is a great adventure, with the North Sea aquarium in its dungeon depths. It's also an excellent place to watch the Royal Dutch Navy during the National Fleet Days.

Another charming stop is the Zaanse Schans situated alongside the Zaan river. With its wooden homes, hump-backed bridges and historic windmills, the hamlet still retains the air of the 17th and 18th centuries. There are several museums to explore, but perhaps the best way to see the area is with a boat trip along the river.

It should come as no surprise that there is a great amount of water in the Netherlands, be it canal, river, or lake. The Dutch word 'meer' means lake, and one of the favourite recreational areas for Noord Hollanders is the IJsselmeer which can be explored not just by boat, but also by steam tram taking in Hoorn and Enkhuizen, as well as Edam, Volendam and Marken.

Though visitors may find Dutch difficult to grapple, the dialect of Fries is even more of a tongue twister. There is a Friesian area in Noord Holland where this dialect is still heard. Perhaps one of the nicest places to explore the West-Friesian culture is Schagen where summer markets focus on West-Friesian traditions.

Closer to Amsterdam are the villages of Durgerdam and Broek in the Waterland district. This is a favourite nature walk for the city's citizens. Also close by is Het Twiske recreational area which has superb children's facilities open throughout the summer months (www.wrvhettwiske.nl).

Flowers As Far As You Can See

From Monday to Friday Aalsmeer's Flower Auction sets the world's price standards for the flower trade. If you want to see the exciting auction, get up early; look to arrive by 07:30 as the flurry of flowery business is usually completed by 09:00. (0297 392 185, www.aalsmeer.nl).

A Great House

The oldest house in the Zaanstreek region is the Czaar Peterhuisje which was named after Russia's legendary ruler Czar Peter the Great, who stayed in the building for a week in 1697.

For The Fun Of The Fort

Excursions to the most famous area of Amsterdam's Defence Line, Fort Pampus Island are possible, and during the summer the fort hosts special events such as classical concerts and themed tours (0294 262 326, www.pampus.nl).

Zaan Schans

Rotterdam

Rotterdam's Own 'Thinker'
The oldest statue in the Netherlands stands in front of St. Laurenskerk on Grotekerkplein. The statue is of scholar, philosopher, and Rotterdam native Desiderius Erasmus (1469-1536).

The Pilgrim's Port
Delfshaven, which, as its name implies, was originally the port for the city of Delft, was the harbour from which the Pilgrims set off in 1620, alongside a number of Dutch sailors and workmen.

See Yourself Shopping
For those who like to see and be seen, the Witte de Withstraat is the place to be. Not only the home of some of the city's trendiest stores, it also hosts some of the finest trend-setting art galleries.

Once you arrive in Rotterdam it's easy to see why it's known as the working city of the Netherlands. The port of Rotterdam was, until recently, the largest in the world, and as such a wide variety of international products and people pass through the city. The importance of the port to the city is reflected in the number of excellent museums dedicated to its history. Harbour boat tours are an excellent way to get a taste of the city's attractions. Though only 50 miles from Amsterdam, Rotterdam, unlike the capital, was virtually destroyed during world war two and was rebuilt with a view to incorporating modern architecture – including cube houses built at a 45 degree angle, one of which is open to the public. However, there are more than 30 museums in the city, many of which display its fascinating history as well as showcasing a wonderful range of art. One of the finest is the Boijmans van Beuningen which has a splendid collection of Old Masters. And speaking of culture, Rotterdam is now the home of the North Sea Jazz Festival (www.northseajazz.nl).

The most eye-catching construction in the city is the Euromast Space Tower which, standing at 185 metres high, is the tallest structure in Rotterdam and boasts astonishing views of the city as well as a restaurant. It is also possible, for the brave, to arrange to abseil or bungee jump to the bottom. Another popular structure is the De Kuip stadium, home to the city's beloved Feyenoord football team, which has seen more European football finals played on its pitch than any other stadium.

The Coast & The Islands

Watch Your Step
This seaside area is, as one would expect, abundant with life once the tide recedes. The hobby of Wadlopen (walking the shallows) is a very popular way to explore.

Hundreds of millions of years ago the Netherlands was underwater as part of a shallow coastal sea. After the ice age and the departure of earlier cultures, including the Romans, monastic communities were the first to make dykes by combining clay, turf, seaweed and wood.

Many of the towns and cities of the Netherlands can trace their prosperity to the sea, both from trade, or strategic location during the many historic conflicts played out in their environs; this is certainly true of Amsterdam, Den Haag and Rotterdam. However, the coastline of the nation is still a thriving area filled with variety and interest. As a coastal nation, its sandy beaches, dunes and islands play host to a wide variety of birds, wildlife and vegetation as well as to the people and cultures which thrive among them. The dunes are one of the vital points of protection for this coastal country which has a quarter of its land lying below sea level. Amazingly, without them, it is likely that two-thirds of the country would occasionally be underwater. The dunes are also a large part of the water filtration system which makes

The North Sea coast

Making Friends With The Seals
One of the best ways to view the local sea population of Texel is to take a daytrip to Vlieland on the De Vriendshap (Friendship) boat which can be caught at Paal (Pole) 33.

Beach Bounty
Just to the north of Ecomare is the village of De Koog which is a superb area for seaside relaxing. There are loads of terraces to catch the sun and views of the North Sea. It is also near woodlands that are a peaceful area for walking.

Can't Beat This Retreat
The Pandhof on Domplein is a stunning garden retreat of medicinal plants and herbs enclosed by a wall on which the story of Utrecht's patron saint, St. Martin, is carved into the original stone tablets from the 15th century.

Amsterdam tap water some of the best tasting in the world. The preservation of this important habitat is a high priority for the Dutch government.

A major part of the Noord Holland coast is made up of the Noord Holland Dune Reserve which runs from Wijk aan Zee to Bergen aan Zee. This is a popular route for walkers and cyclists and has recently become a popular family visiting point since the inception of the children's Kabouter (gnome) route, which invites children to playfully search for gnomes while learning about the natural world they are exploring.

Running parallel to the Dune Reserve area are some wonderful villages and towns which capture the essence of the seaside area. Bergen aan Zee has superb beaches and an aquarium which is a popular spot for those with an aquatic bent. For those more interested in art, only five kilometres away is the charming community of Bergen which is known as an idyllic artistic retreat in the middle of stunning natural surroundings. This area is also known for the Wild Dune cycle route which was voted the best in the Netherlands.

Of course, there are forts and museums in the area to explore, including the Fort Hoek van Holland and the Zuiderzeemuseum (p.173). Added to that, there are many islands along the coastline which are wonderful places to roam, explore and have fun.

Texel is a superb example of the rich history and diversity of the nation's islands. As well as being a spot of pristine natural beauty, it is also steeped in the history of the Dutch East India Company (VOC) which used the port on Texel as a departure point to the far off places that served to boost the coffers of the Dutch Golden Age. Texel has six museums, of which its maritime museum is the best known (0222 314 956, www.texelsmaritiem.nl). The beaches on Texel are superb sand-catchers, but it must be said that they are also extremely windy. Perhaps the best and most relaxing are De Hors on the island's south side and the De Koog resort which provides pavilions and play areas.

Terschelling island is also well known, especially in the summer months when it hosts the annual Oerol Festival (0562 448 448, www.oerol.nl) of theatre and music. This festival is extraordinarily popular, not least because of the beauty of the island itself. Because of this it is extremely important that accommodation during the festival season is booked well in advance.

Utrecht

Originally a wooden Roman fort, Utrecht dates back to approximately 47AD. Today the city's beautifully preserved, medieval old centre, is now the heart of the Museum Quarter (Museumkwartier). The area is beautifully interlaced with charming canals, magnificent museums, and, unsurprisingly due to the city's status as a religious centre in the past, a number of beautiful churches. The most renowned of the pieces of religious architecture is the Domtoren (Cathedral Tower) on Domplein – at 112 metres high, it's the tallest church tower in Holland. It is possible to climb to the top to see the bells, but listening to their daily ringing is a much easier way of enjoying them. Modern Utrecht is the hub of the Dutch railway system, and its station is conveniently – or not – attached to the nation's largest shopping mall, the Hoog Catharijne.

Behind The Barricades

Though a few of the city's fortresses are open throughout the year, each September – National Fortress Month – those that are normally closed open their doors to the public. A range of activities are on offer such as tours, art exhibitions and overnight stays.

Playing For Time
Museums may not always be the most popular places for children to play; not so at the National Museum from Musical Clock to Street Organ which allows kids to compose their own music box tunes (030 231 27 89, www.museumspeelklok.nl/speelklok/uk).

Keukenhoff

Holidays from Amsterdam

Perhaps more so than any other city in Europe, Amsterdam is a hub for travel. There are more than one hundred international airlines flying in and out of Schiphol Airport to many hundreds of destinations. Added to that, its rail network is extensive and it's even easy to drive in and out of the country. There are literally hundreds of different destinations within easy reach of Amsterdam, which will provide a relaxing weekend break and an insight into the variety of fascinating cultures Europe has to offer. Alternatively, why not take a trip out of the city to another area of the Netherlands, and experience more of the varied culture available right on your doorstep? For more, see Out of Amsterdam on p.170.

Travel Agencies

Aca Latina Travel	020 663 33 79	acatravel@acanl.nl
ACO Travel	020 661 25 57	www.acotravel.nl
Ammar Company Travel Kantoor	020 669 42 11	www.ammartravel.nl
Cathay Travel Service	020 627 00 37	na
Cruisewinkel.nl	020 421 11 15	www.cruisewinkel.nl
Dostana Reizen	020 452 90 80	www.dostanareizen.nl
Free Travel Choice/Fly & Dive	020 688 60 68	www.freetravelchoice.nl
Labeto Reizen	020 618 66 33	www.labeto.nl
Maudine Travel	020 615 30 40	www.maudine.nl
Midas Reis en Vertaalburo	020 685 57 04	www.midasreizen.nl
MoveOut Georeizen	06 24 113025	www.moveout.nu
Royal Africa Travel	020 600 51 81	www.royalafrica.com
Ruskontakt	020 683 94 94	www.ruskontakt.nl
Sky International Tours	020 573 32 22	www.skytours.nl
Skyline Travels & Cargo Services	020 600 24 84	www.skylinetravels.net
Valerius Reizen BV	020 673 07 73	www.valerius.nl
World Ticket Center	020 626 10 11	www.worldticketcenter.nl

***Flight time:** 1.25 hours*
***Time difference:** None*

France

With Paris in May for romance and shopping, the French Alps in the winter months for skiing, the wine regions of the Loire, Burgundy and Champagne to name just a few, a fantastic coastline and a world famous film festival, France is a year-round treasure trove for travellers. Perhaps Paris should be avoided in August, as it is hot, humid and filled with tourists – most Parisians are off enjoying their own holidays at this time. For a touch of Dutch, Arles in the South of France is the town which inspired many artists, including Van Gogh, for hundreds of years. Fine food, wine, art and culture are part and parcel of the French lifestyle on offer to its visitors – drink it in.

Vive La Revolution!

Though the National holiday, Bastille Day, which commemorates the storming of the Bastille, is on 14 July, the best celebrations are on the night before. Look for grand fireworks displays up and down the country on the night of the 13th! Bonne fête!

***Flight time:** 50 minutes*
***Time difference:** None*

Belgium

The capital, Brussels, is often called the Capital of Europe, due to the European Union's administrative and political presence in the city. As such, it is a cosmopolitan city mixing, among other things, modern and ancient architecture, politics and culture. Filled with interesting museums, great shopping and excellent restaurants, Brussels is a tourist trove of treasures. Out of the capital there is a great deal to explore including the Market Square of Bruges, the ancient beauty of Antwerp and Ghent, and the magnificent, Romanesque Cathedral of Notre-Dame in Tournai.

Holiday Hotspots

Flight time: *2 hours*
Time difference: *None*

Italy

The different provinces of Italy each have their own distinct personalities and flavours – even their own styles of cooking. The majesty of Rome is awesome with the Colosseum, the Spanish Steps and the Vatican; Venice (Amsterdam's sister canal city) is romance personified; and Florence is awash with amazing art such as Michelangelo's *David*. Italians have a passion for life, and are overjoyed to share with their guests. One of the most welcoming of nations, it's a difficult country to leave – especially after a hearty meal!

Flight time: *1.25 hours*
Time difference: *One hour behind*

United Kingdom

Only a short hop over the English Channel, the UK (and Northern Ireland for that matter) is extremely easy to access by car, rail, ferry or flight. This is the land of Shakespeare's Stratford-on-Avon, Stonehenge, The Edinburgh Fringe Festival, draught ale and so much more. London is full of history, but be sure to get out of the capital and explore this 'green and pleasant land'.

Flight time: *1.5 hours*
Time difference: *None*

Germany

There is a lot more to Germany than just Bratwurst and beer – though the Munich beer festival in October (Oktoberfest) is always a huge draw. Further south there is a fantastic wine region to explore, while the history and grand architecture of Berlin is always fascinating.

Flight time: *1.25 hours*
Time difference: *None*

Czech Republic

Prague is one of the loveliest cities in Europe. Situated in the heart of 'Old Europe,' and thus filled with a huge range of art and architecture, the city mixes this heritage with one of the hippest and most happening cultural and clubbing spots in Europe. Outside of the capital there are a wide range of wonderful places to explore, including the Bone Church of Sedlec, and Ceske Budejovice, home of the Budweiser beer.

Flight time: *2 hours*
Time difference: *None*

Hungary

A gateway to Eastern Europe, Hungary, particularly its capital Budapest, is a glorious juxtaposition of the two versions of Europe – old and new, east and west (Buda and Pest). The city is filled with fantastic architecture and art, with the The Museum of Fine Arts being a great example of both (www2.szepmuveszeti.hu). Outside of the city highlights such as the Eger and Festetics castles are stunning and Lake Balaton is great fun for water-centred activities.

Flight time: *2 hours*
Time difference: *None*

Poland

Full of old world charm, Poland is home to a rich, proud history – and some fine vodka. Art and architecture blend beautifully in the hundreds of castles dotted around the nation, while Auschwitz gives the visitor a poignant chance to reflect.

Flight time: *2 hours*
Time difference: *None*

Austria

The hills are alive in Austria too, what with all the skiing, walking and mountain adventures available throughout this stunning country. Added to that, the charming towns, villages and cities each have their own fairytale characteristics. Visit Mozart's home in Salzburg, the impossibly dramatic Hohenwerfen Castle, and the stunning city of Innsbruck which dates back to 1180.

Flight time: *3 hours*
Time difference: *Two hours behind*

Iceland

A green land sitting on top of volcanoes is one way to describe this amazing nation. There are a multitude of natural wonders to explore, though be aware that the trekking won't be cheap – nothing is here. That said, the capital of Reykjavik is a fantastically friendly place which has become extremely popular with the young, international party set as a great place to chill out. In the land of the midnight sun (during the summer months at least) the weather can be changeable, but the welcoming nature of the locals definitely is not.

Flight time: *3.5 hours*
Time difference: *One hour ahead*

Latvia

Only recently a member of the European Union, Latvia has an attractive old world charm coupled with a dynamically young, modern feel. Young at heart, Riga is a wonderful place to explore, with its Gothic, Baroque, Classical and Art Nouveau architecture. The central part of the city was placed on the UNESCO World Heritage List in 1997. For those who want to avoid cities, the coast of the country is stunning, with beaches galore; two of the most popular are Majori and Bulduri, both of which are award winners.

Flight time: *5.25 hours*
Time difference: *One hour ahead*

Turkey

On the cusp of Europe and Asia, Turkey has long held a fascination for the traveller. The capital Istanbul – once Christendom's Constantinople – is a fascinating mix of east and west, the modern and the antiquated. The country is literally awash with antiquities. Turkey is a vast nation, and as such, there are a myriad of diverse directions a traveller can go in to discover the country. There are numerous coastlines to explore including the Aegean, Black Sea, Marmara and Mediterranean, each of which has its own stunning beauty and welcoming resorts.

Polite Prayer
If you'd like to visit a mosque, do feel welcome; however, do show respect by waiting until after prayers, removing your shoes and dressing suitably.

London

Paris

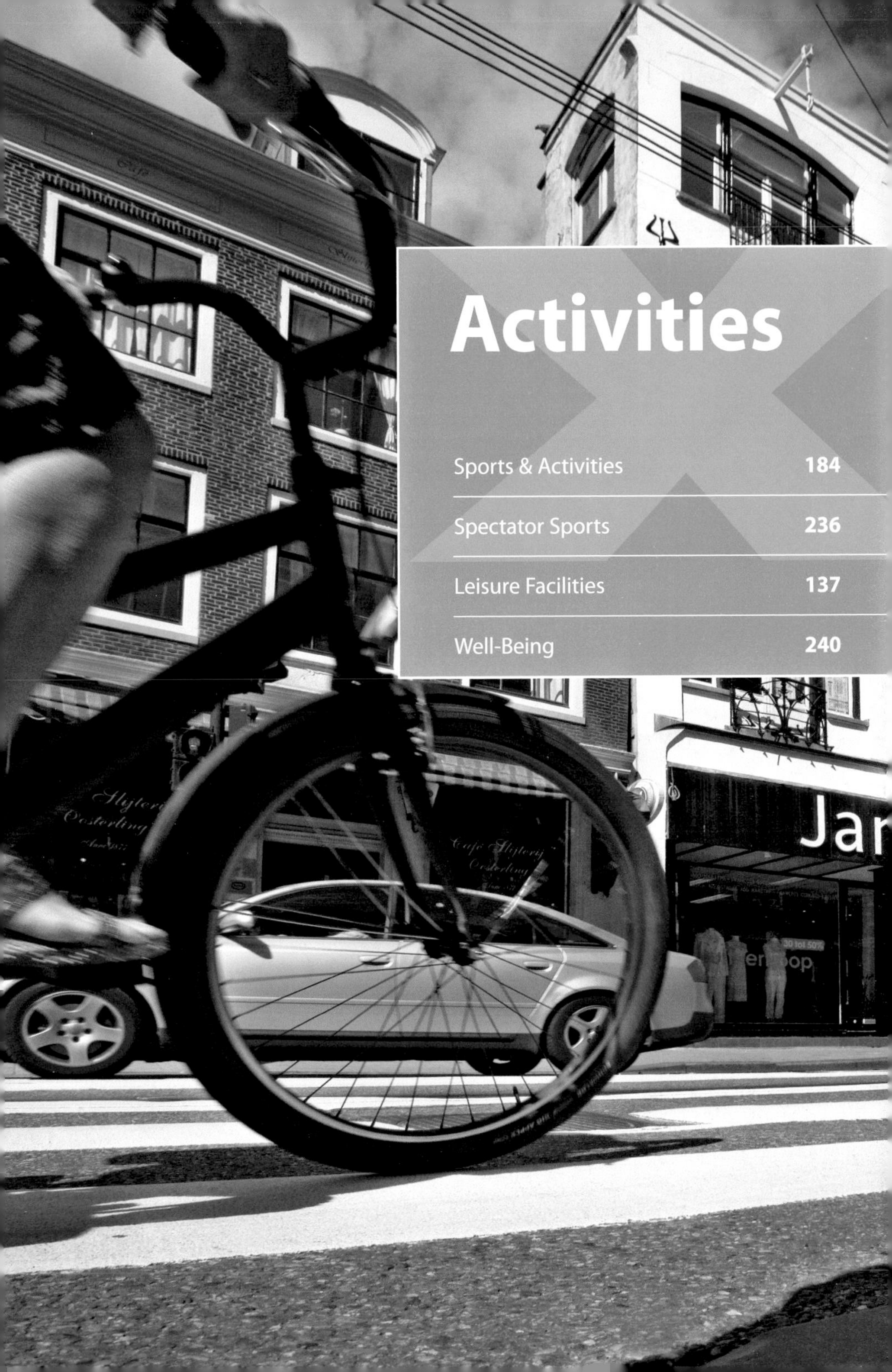

Activities

Activities

Sports & Activities

Amsterdam is a great place to find many sports and activities, both to participate in and to watch. As it is cold for half of the year, when spring comes and it's comfortable to be out without a jacket, the parks are immediately full of people playing games or enjoying the sun and warm weather. However, there are still many activities available during the winter months. The summer is rarely too hot to be outdoors, and the only thing stopping people stepping outdoors could be very wet weather. Still, when the sun is shining, people are out. One activity that goes on all around the year, rain or shine, is cycling. People in Amsterdam will ride a bike in all kinds of weather, holding an umbrella if necessary. Almost every sport you can imagine is available in Amsterdam, especially anything to do with water. Public swimming pools generally open in May, and boating, either through the canals as a sightseeing activity or in the Amsterdamse Bos as a sporting activity, is also very popular. With the sea only an hour or so away, activities such as surfing and diving are accessible, with guides and instructors if you need them. Sports teams follow the same schedules as teams around the world and the range of options is amazingly broad. One of the great things about a transient city is that people are always dropping out because they need to move, so there is always a need for new blood on most teams. If you are a sports enthusiast, you'll most likely find what you are looking for in Amsterdam.

District Guide

We've included an Amsterdam district by each entry in this section to help you locate the clubs. sports centres and spas. The map on p.368 shows which area of town each one covers.

Activity Finder

Even with football, one of the most popular sports in Amsterdam, there are teams to play in and ways to get involved either in a team focused on tournament play or a team that is just out to break a sweat before having a few beers. Exotic sports like American football, baseball and hashing are also found in Amsterdam with a smaller, but no less enthusiastic crowd.

Sports clubs can be found all around the city. They generally offer fitness rooms and facilities for indoor running, as well as group classes. Some have swimming pools and squash. Gyms are usually very friendly when dealing with expats. Some even have special deals geared to the temporary nature of expat life. Shop around for the gym that suits you as they vary greatly in price, location and offerings. A useful thing to have when researching activities on the internet is a good English-Dutch dictionary. Finding your particular activity will be simpler, and it will increase your options if you can look for it in Dutch. Instructors and staff are almost always able to speak English. The expat community, especially the English speaking expat community, is huge in Amsterdam. It's been here for a long time, hundreds of years in fact, so there are many clubs and organisations that are well-established and welcoming to new members. Of course, there is cross over in both directions with Dutch people involved in English speaking groups and English speaking people involved in Dutch organisations. Figure out what you'd like to do in Amsterdam and get out and do it. It will broaden your view of this beautiful city, help you explore new places and make it feel more like home.

Aerobics & Fitness Classes

Aerobics and keeping fit are very popular in Amsterdam, so there are quite a few gyms around. There's plenty of competition, so if one gym doesn't suit your needs you can easily find another with whatever speciality you're looking for, such as Pilates or spinning. Gyms are found all over the city. Many in Centrum are surprisingly large and well equipped, while some further out are worth the travel time. Check out the websites to find one that's right for you.

Aerobics & Fitness Classes

Name	Area	Phone	Website	Type of Class
Barry's Health Centre	Centrum	020 626 10 36	www.barrysfitness.nl	aerobics, fitness classes, yoga, Pilates
Business Health Club	West	020 681 09 96	www.businesshealthclub.nl	aerobics (various types)
Clubsportive Waterlooplein	Centrum	020 620 66 31	www.clubsportive.nl	fitness classes
Conditiecentrum Brightside	Oud Zuid	020 683 44 36	www.brightsidefitness.nl	bodyshape, powerstep, power yoga, Pilates
Fit2Fit	Centrum	020 330 31 23	www.fit2fit.nl	cardio, power training, 50+
Fitness & Aerobic Studio Jumping Feet	Noord	020 493 03 01	www.jumpingfeet.com	body pump, body, kick, body shape, spinning
Palestra Fitness Centre	West	020 615 03 14	www.palestra-amsterdam.nl	aerobics, cardio
Splash Renaissance Fitnessclub	Centrum	020 624 37 10	www.splashrenaissance.nl	body shape, step, Pilates
Sportcentrum Amstelpark	Oud Zuid	020 301 07 00	www.amstelpark.nl	na
Squash City	Various Locations	020 626 78 83	www.squashcity.com	aerobics

American Football

Other options **Football** p.185

Amsterdam has two amateur American football clubs: The Crusaders (020 617 74 50, www.amsterdam-crusaders.nl) and the Panthers (020 988 88 88, www.panthers.nl). Both clubs have quite an assortment of teams for everyone from 8 years old up to adults. There are two divisions, the youth and the seniors. They youngest players are the Peewee team (ages 8-11) and the Cubs (12-13). Both of these teams play flag football, meaning there is no tackling. There is less contact, but a lot of action. The next two teams are the Cadets (14-16) and the Juniors (16-19). The older teams tackle. The seniors are anywhere from 19 years old upwards. Seniors can choose between tackle and its friendlier cousin, flag. The Crusaders were founded in 1984 and the Panthers in 1999. They play with other American football teams in the Netherlands and against each other. Anyone who would like to know more about this surprising little sub-culture is invited to write for information and attend a practice.

Art Classes

Other options **Art & Craft Supplies** p.256, **Art Galleries** p.148

Amsterdam is a city with amazing art museums and picturesque views at every turn. Through the ages, the city has inspired many artists, both the famous and the less well known. Whether you're already an artist or you just want to learn, there are lots of opportunities to take art classes in Amsterdam. The art institutes and universities offer classes in painting, drawing, photography and much more.

Art Classes			
Barbra Jacobsen	Various Locations	020 465 42 70	www.barbra-jacobsen.com
CREA	Centrum	020 525 14 00	www.crea.uva.nl
Erna Nijman	Various Locations	020 754 91 95	www.ernanijman.nl
Impression Amsterdam	Jordaan	020 427 68 86	www.impressionshop.nl
Jet Violier	Various Locations	020 625 82 26	www.jetviolier.nl

Mauritskade 24
Oost
Map p.395 D4 1

MK24

020 692 00 93 | www.mk24.nl

MK24 (an abbreviation of the address) is one of the most important institutes offering art classes to adults. They have a wide variety of visual art classes and workshops in drawing, painting, sculpture, ceramics and photography, to name just a few. There are around 120 different classes and the teachers are experienced, often professionals in their fields. Most of the courses are 16 lessons of three hours and go from September to January or from February to June. Some courses are organised with the Volksuniversiteit Amsterdam (below). Sign up early as many of the most popular courses are booked before the summer break begins.

Ruysdaelkade 193
Oud Zuid
Map p.384 B2 2

VAK-G

020 470 87 03 | www.vak-g.com

VAK-G is an institute for visual art and design. All of the teachers have an academic degree and have been working as artists for several years. Most of the courses are related to drawing and painting. There are course names such as 'Painting like Picasso' and 'Vincent van Gogh Techniques'. There are also course offerings for children and workshops for groups.

Rapenburgerstraat 73
Centrum
Map p.394 B1 3

Volksuniversiteit Amsterdam

020 626 16 26 | www.volksuniversiteitamsterdam.nl

Along with visual art and craft classes, the Volksuniversiteit offers language and science courses. A basic knowledge of Dutch is required for the courses but if there is enough demand for courses in English they will try to organise them, so do ask. They offer everything from bookbinding to sculpture and from drawing to working with precious metals. Courses are usually between 10 and 12 weeks long, but there are also workshops of one, two or three days.

Badminton

Badminton has a dedicated following in Amsterdam and there are quite a few opportunities for people who would like to learn the game or improve their play and join a team. You can get general information about badminton in the Netherlands at www.badmintoncentral.nl. It's in Dutch, but some of the clubs have an English option for basic information.

Prins Bernhardlaan 2
Amsterdam Zuidoost
Map p.387 E4 4

Badminton Vereniging Diemen (Sporthal Diemen)

020 419 75 02 | *www.bvdiemen.org*

Badminton Vereniging Diemen was established 30 years ago and has about 90 members. They are an enthusiastic club that provides training and regular play as well as annual tournaments for young people and adults. Anyone interested in playing is encouraged to contact them and make an arrangement to take a look and possibly join up.

Lizzy Ansinghstraat 88
De Pijp
Map p.384 C2 5

Badminton Vereniging Minerva

020 642 48 22 | *www.badminton-minerva.nl*

The season of Badminton Vereniging Minerva goes from September to May. They play on Monday evenings and are located in Sportcentrum 'De Pijp' in hall 2. Membership is €140 for the year or €7.50 per session. If you are interested, go and take a look and see if this is the club for you.

Bovenkerkerweg 81
Amstelveen
Map p.367 E4

Tennis en Badmintoncentrum De Kegel

020 643 28 22 | *www.dekegel.nl*

De Kegel is a large complex housing several different sports facilities. They have eight badminton courts. Lessons and regular play are available, as are tournaments. The season lasts from September to April.

Van Musschenbroekstraat 38
Oost
Map p.394 C4 7

Universitaire Sportvereniging Badminton

020 663 19 09 | *www.us-badminton.nl*

US Badminton focuses its membership on students and recent graduates, so it's not a club for the whole family. Any member or recent graduate of a hogeschool or university can join. Fun is an important part of their programme, but they are a competitive club and they play seriously. They are coached by professional coaches and anyone who falls into this age group and is interested is encouraged to come by, take a look and participate. After your third free game, they will talk to you about joining.

Baseball

Baseball is one of the classic sports that expats, particularly from the USA, may be looking for when living in Holland. The Amsterdam Pirates are Amsterdam's local side, competing in the Dutch national league, although sadly lacking success in recent seasons (see Spectator Sports p.236). In Wassenaar, which is situated near Den Haag, an American foundation catering for English speaking people encourages active participation in the game, so for those willing to travel there are certainly opportunities to play here as well.

Ammonslaantje 1
Wassenaar
Map p.365 A3

American Baseball Foundation

070 514 65 15 | *www.abfsport.nl*

The American Baseball Foundation has provided sports programmes for all ages and nationalities for over 30 years. They are a non-profit organisation dedicated to providing opportunities to get involved in baseball, soccer and basketball for children and adults. Over 600 families are involved in the organisation. Based in Wassenaar (near Den Haag), they offer English speaking families the chance to meet new people and remain active through sports. The club offers a warm, international atmosphere and welcomes everyone.

Basketball

Basketball is a very popular sport in Amsterdam. It's not played in the street as much as football is, but there are several organisations which people can join. For English information and website links regarding Dutch basketball, check out www.internationalbasketball.com/netherlands.html. There are links to basketball camps and clubs all over the country. The basketball association for Amsterdam and North Holland is the Nederlandse Basketball Bond Noord-Holland (025 127 24 17, www.dunk.nl), which can provide more local information.

American Baseball Foundation

Ammonslaantje 1
Wassenaar
Map p.365 A3

070 514 65 15 | www.abfsport.nl

The American Baseball Foundation (ABF) has provided sports programmes for all ages and nationalities for over 30 years. They are a non-profit organisation dedicated to providing opportunities to get involved in baseball, soccer and basketball to children and adults. Over 600 families are involved in the organisation. The ABF is based in Wassenaar and offers English speaking families the chance to meet new people and remain active through sports. The club offers a warm, international atmosphere and welcomes everyone.

BV Lely Amsterdam

Dijksgracht 9a
Oud Zuid
Map p.391 D3 10

020 419 44 58 | www.bvlely.nl

BV Lely Amsterdam was founded in 1970 by pupils of the Ir Lely high school. Their homebase is the Apollohal in Oud Zuid. They now have both senior and junior teams playing in regional competitions. The senior men and women's teams are for anyone above the age of 16. There are specific email addresses on the website for each age group.

Haarlem Basketball Week

IJsbaanlaan 4a
Haarlem
Map p.366 B3

023 525 58 87 | www.basketballweek.nl

Since 1982, every year in December the Haarlem Basketball Week is organised in the Kennemer Sportcenter. Teams from all over the world participate, with an impressive list of big names making an appearance. The event attracts all kinds of people and gets quite a bit of publicity. Check out the website for specific dates and times or ring the number of the sports centre (above).

Mosquitos

Apollolaan 4
Oud Zuid
Map p.384 B2 12

020 622 89 30 | www.abvmosquitos.nl

The Mosquitos have the Apollohal in Oud Zuid as their home base. They have both junior and senior teams, but the number of junior members has recently grown rapidly. The junior division is one of the best in the Netherlands and has been very successful in recent years. In the 2004-2005 season, the boys' teams did very well in national competitions.

Nederlandse Basketball Bond

Wattbaan 31-49
Nieuwegein
Map p.365 B3

030 751 35 00 | www.basketball.nl/content.php

The Dutch national basketball union organises tournaments at various levels for recreational players as well as league players. Both men and women are welcome, as is anyone of any age. Their vision is to have 15,000 members by 2010, so if basketball is your game, they are looking for you. They also organise wheelchair basketball teams that compete in the Paralympics. Check their website for more on what they do, including dates and locations.

De Boelelaan 1105
Buitenveldert
Map p.383 F3 14

Vrije Universiteit Amsterdam

020 598 98 98 | www.vu.nl

During the VU Festival every year, the Vrije Universiteit organises street basketball. Teams are formed and there is a tournament with enthusiastic players and spectators. To get information about the event, go to the website and follow the link to 'Programma.' The festival also offers a mix of film, music, other sports and activities.

Belly Dancing

Other options **Dance Classes** p.189

The idea of belly dancing may conjure up a certain image, but the countries where it originates have very diverse styles. Additionally, each dancer has her own style dictated by taste and the way her body moves. If you're looking to get more energy and exercise in a fun and exotic way, belly dancing may be what you're looking for. When going to a class, you should wear loose-fitting clothes and possibly a wide, flowing skirt, but it's not mandatory. Some studios have a shop connected and if they don't they will be able to help you find a perfect skirt or shawl.

Various Locations

Danseres Cassandra

06 10 745127 | www.danserescassandra.nl

The studio Danseres Cassandra is run by Cassandra who is experienced in many different kinds of dance as well as body shaping exercises. She specialises in Egyptian belly dancing, and believes that any woman (all ages, all body types) can learn belly dancing and gain the benefits of making her body smoother, stronger and more elegant.

Laagte Kadijk 20
Centrum
Map p.394 C1 16

Lijfwijs

020 624 79 74 | www.lijfwijs.nl

The teachers from the studio Lijfwijs believe that anyone can benefit from belly dancing whatever your sex, age or body type. Lessons are given in short workshops or in longer, ongoing classes. A large store is available to help you find just the right look. Additionally, Pilates, yoga and other exercise classes are available through Lijfwijs.

Birdwatching

Birdwatching can be enjoyed by everyone and done practically everywhere, especially in a nature-friendly country like Holland. There are many birdwatching enthusiasts in the Netherlands. Over 450 species have been spotted around the country, almost 100 of them in Amsterdam. Of course, Amsterdam has its share of pigeons and other city birds, but there are also various water fowl that live in the canals and many others that nest in the parks. Further out, the island of Texel is a good bet, as is Oostvaardersplassen (oostvaardersplassen.biofaan.nl/scientificcd), a nature reserve just outside Amsterdam. Experienced birdwatchers can try their luck in one of the many parks in and around Amsterdam, but for anyone who would rather have someone to show them where the best spots are and which birds to look for, there are companies ready and willing to lead the way.

Various Locations

Flevo Birdwatching

www.birdsnetherlands.nl

Flevo Birdwatching can organise day trips and is run by a pair of experienced birdwatchers who will point out the birds that you'll be seeing. Based outside Amsterdam, they can also help to arrange lodging for overnight trips. Thankfully, their website is in English.

Various Locations

Vogelbescherming Nederland

030 693 77 00 | www.vogelbescherming.nl

Founded under another name in 1899, Vogelbescherming (literally: Bird Protection) Nederland's mission is to work towards the conservation of wild birds and their habitats. They are closely allied with Bird Life International, a worldwide organisation with the same mission. Based in Zeist, Vogelbescherming Nederland has many activities throughout the year and is quite politically active with a focus on ecology and keeping the world safe for wild birds.

Various Locations

Vogelgroep Amsterdam

www.vogelwerkgroepamsterdam.nl

Vogelgroep Amsterdam has a wide variety of educational opportunities and excursions available. They offer everything from archival photos of birds from the 19th century to courses on how to recognise the native birds in and around Amsterdam. Activities are available throughout the year and they are a great resource for finding any information you might need about the birds of the Netherlands.

Bowling

Bowling is no longer just the favoured pastime of suburban, middle-aged, working class folk. Yes, they enjoy it too, but Amsterdam has some great offerings for those who not only want to learn how to bowl, but also put some extra zip in their technique. People show up at all times of the day and late into the night to knock pins down, usually with self-scoring machines. If you're looking for information on competitions and events there is the Netherlands Bowling Federation (www.bowlingnbf.nl, 030 606 03 25) ready and willing to answer all of your bowling-related questions.

Borchlandweg 6-12
Amsterdam Zuidoost
Map p.327 F4 20

Amstelborgh/Borchland

020 563 33 33 | www.borchland.nl

Borchland is a conference, events and sports centre in the city's business area near Amsterdam ArenA. They have ten alleys, which were renovated in 2006. There is disco bowling with black lights every Wednesday and Saturday from 15:00 to 17:00. The alleys are equipped with screens showing clips of the music that is being played.

Scheldeplein 3
Rivierenbuurt
Map p.392 B1 21

Knijn Bowling

020 664 22 11 | www.knijnbowling.nl

Kijn Bowling is the most famous bowling alley in Amsterdam. Located close to Amsterdam RAI, they open every day at 10:00, except Saturdays when they open at 12:00. They close at 00:30 on weekdays, 01:00 on Fridays and Saturdays and 23:00 on Sundays. On Thursdays there is disco bowling (17:00 to 19:00 including snacks, and 19:00 to 20:00 including dinner). On Sundays they have a special of one hour of bowling plus dinner for a fixed price. Wednesday afternoons is kids' twilight bowling, then kids' disco bowling followed by a snack dinner. They're available for children's parties and will also organise buffet dinners. You can also rent space for parties and weddings.

Bovenkerkerweg 81
Amsteleveen
Map p.367 E4

Partycentrum De Kegel

020 64 55 57 | www.dekegel.nl

Partycentrum De Kegel offers 16 bowling lanes with a fully automated computer scoring system. A combination of bowling and dinner is available every night. This is a great place for business outings or a night out with the family. They have three dining rooms which are themed: a barn, a greenhouse and a saloon. The dining rooms have the capacity to take 96 people.

Buikslotermeerplein 4
Amsterdam Noord
Map p.376 A2 23

Pim's Bowling

020 634 00 30 | www.pimsbowling.nl

Pim's opened their doors in 1983 (although under a different name). They have 12 computerised, synthetic bowling lanes that have computerised scoring. There is also a restaurant so that you can make an evening of it. Pim's is the official home of the Bowling Vereniging Noordam (Bowling Club Noordam). The club has members from the age of 6 upwards, with about 300 members in total. They welcome not only beginners, but also experienced bowlers. Beginners have the opportunity to benefit from the advice of two official NBF A-trainers. Pim's has regular competitions in darts as well. There is disco bowling on Saturday nights at 23:00. Dinners of the very Dutch 'steengrillen' and fondue are available.

Boxing

Boxing in the Netherlands may not enjoy the support that other sports have, but there are quite a few enthusiasts all over the country and certainly in Amsterdam. It's not just the stuff of movies with swollen eyes and busted lips, it's also good for conditioning your body and building strength and muscle tone. In addition, it's good for both women and men. The Netherlands has produced quite a few champions and there is even a national boxing association, the Nederlandse Boks Bond, which is a useful resource (030 609 01 62, www.boksen.nl).

Albert Cuypstraat 241
De Pijp
Map p.384 B2 24

Albert Cuyp

020 673 45 23 | www.albertcuyp.net

The Albert Cuyp gym offers a mixture of many different disciplines, one of which is boxing. It's a large gym which has its share of champions. Training is five days a week and there are expert coaches to assist in either teaching boxing or perfecting boxing skills. In addition, the gym offers classes in capoeira, a Brazilian fighting technique. They also have a tango salon one evening a week, a singing group and a marching band.

Lauriergracht 86
Centrum
Map p.392 B1 25

Mejiro Gym Amsterdam

020 623 04 19 | www.mejirogym.com

Since 1978, Jan Plas, one of the founders of the NKBB (Dutch Kickboxing Association), has been running a gym devoted to kickboxing skills that he learned in Japan. The gym offers bag workouts as well as sparring and has a regular schedule throughout the week. There is a list of fees on the English section of the website for various activities you might be interested in.

Weesperzijde 115
Watergraafsmeer
Map p.385 E2 26

Sportcentrum Kops

www.sportcentrumkops.nl

Sportcentrum Kops offers a variety of sports activities in addition to boxing, such as conditioning, kickboxing and wrestling. Boxers are trained by a well-known boxing instructor and a world champion boxer. They teach conditioning as well as technique so that boxers are prepared whether they want to fight or just keep in shape. They pride themselves in the intensity of their training. The gym is active, full and open six days a week from 10:00. They close at 22:00 from Monday to Friday and at 14:00 on Saturdays.

Van Hallstraat 52
West
Map p.379 F1 27

Xena Sports

020 686 79 44 | www.xenasports.nl

Xena Sports is a beautiful gym that offers several training options for boxers. You can train in groups with a personal trainer. They are also proud to offer chakuriki and Thai kickboxing. Additionally, they have a full fitness room and spinning classes. They are open seven days a week and have a full staff of sports training professionals.

Bridge

Bridge is a mystery to many, but it has a large number of enthusiasts of all ages and experience levels all over the world. It's been popular in the Netherlands since about 1930. Amsterdam has several bridge clubs offering regular play as well as tournaments. The bridge organisation, Nederlandse Bridge Bond (030 275 99 99, www.bridge.nl) is useful for all kinds of information regarding bridge throughout the country.

Lijnbaansgracht 185-187
Centrum
Map p.392 B1 28

Bridge Club de Looier

020 420 69 88 | www.bridge-amsterdam.nl

Bridge Club de Looier is a group of bridge players who are committed to the game and furthering its appeal. They are open almost the entire week with competitions and tournaments being played at every level. If you need lessons, they are available and if you are already an expert bridge player you will be welcomed into the fold quickly. There are also trips planned annually to play bridge in exotic locations.

IJsbaanpad 45
Slotervaart
Map p.383 D3 29

Bridge Club Het Hok

020 776 31 75 | www.het-hok.nl

At Bridge Club Het Hok, there is open play every Monday evening beginning at 19:45. They are very open to new people and invite anyone with an interest to come and join the fun, but call before coming. Admission is free to everyone except on special evenings when there is a nominal charge to cover costs or raise money. Competitions and tournaments are held regularly.

Linneausstraat 11a
Watergraafsmeer
Map p.395 F3 30

Bridgeclub Himbuv

020 665 07 43 | www.himbuv.com

Bridgeclub Himbuv meets at Café East of Eden on the first floor. As a member of the club, you are automatically a member of the Nederlandse Bridge Bond and you get the monthly newsletter (which is in Dutch). You also get to take part, free of charge, in the 'viertallencompetitie' (set of four competition) in Amsterdam. Membership dues are €80 and the year runs from June to May.

Bungee Jumping

People who would like to experience the thrill of bungee jumping will need to travel to Scheveningen, as the jump centre in Amsterdam is no longer open. The Bungy Jump Center (070 345 36 62, www.bungy.nl) offers a jump into – or just above – the North Sea. The website has an English option and all contact information prospective jumpers will need. Jumps take place from April to October, weather permitting. Another possibility is Action Events (023 548 49 49, www.action-events.nl) based in Heemstede. They will travel and offer bungee jumping as well as other stunts and shows.

Camping

Other options **Campsites** p.227, **Outdoor Goods** p.227

The weather in the Netherlands is generally very good for camping, which should be done in designated areas when near a city. While it is sometimes a little bit wet, the spring and summer are usually perfect and very popular times to camp. The night time temperatures are great for sitting by a campfire and planning the next day's adventures. If it's been raining, mosquitoes can be pretty hungry, so bug repellant is recommended. The winter tends to be cold, so be prepared if you're camping during

Urban art

those months. Amsterdam has a lot of natural, wooded areas far from Centrum. Campsite facilities range from bars and restaurants to swimming pools and rental bikes, but there are usually some standards such as toilets and showers. There are a variety of arrangements regarding tents and campers. Reservations are sometimes only accepted for longer stays and camping permits can be obtained at the campsites. Pets may or may not be welcome, so it's best to check. It's always helpful to visit the VVV (Amsterdam Tourist Office, www.vvv.nl) to pick up any information they might have on camping. Other locations that are popular for camping are along the coastlines and north, near the island of Texel.

Kleine Noorddijk 1
Amstelveen
Map p.367 E4

Camping Amsterdamse Bos

020 641 68 68 | *www.campingamsterdamsebos.nl*

The Amsterdamse Bos (forest) is one of the best green spots in the Amsterdam area. There's a lot to do there with hiking trails, swimming and paddle boating. Or you could just stay there and camp. There are areas for tents, but you can also rent one of a variety of cabins and cottages. There is a large communal kitchen, a small supermarket and a laundrette. They are open all year long and have heated cabins for your comfort.

Uitdammerdijk 10
Amsterdam Noord
Map p.367 F2

Camping de Badhoeve

029 960 20 76 | *www.campingdebadhoeve.nl*

Camping de Badhoeve is set on the edge of Amsterdam between two lakes (the Kinselmeer and the IJsselmeer) in a nature reserve, so if you like water sports, this is a great location. There are boats and canoes available for your use, and there's also windsurfing and fishing. The camp is equipped with a bar in the clubhouse, a restaurant, snack shop and a supermarket. Tents, caravans and campers are welcome, and if you didn't bring any of these, there are facilities to rent. Toilets and shower facilities are conveniently located in the grounds.

Meeuwenlaan 138
Amsterdam Noord
Map p.375 F4 33

Camping Vliegenbos

020 636 88 55 | *www.vliegenbos.com*

Set in the middle of 62 acres of woodlands, Camping Vliegenbos is just 10 minutes from the centre of Amsterdam. If you don't have a tent, a camper or a caravan you can use one of the 'Trekkers' Cabins' (reservations recommended and bring your own linens). There are communal toilets and showers and a small store for food. Open from April to September.

Zuider IJdijk 20
Zeeburg
Map p.380 C4 34

Camping Zeeburg

020 694 44 30 | *www.campingzeeburg.nl*

Camping Zeeburg is about 15 minutes from the centre of Amsterdam. They have spaces for campers, caravans and tents, and if you really need it, they also have cabins available. For your comfort, Zeeburg has a bar and a restaurant on the premises. Additionally, they have kayak and bike rental, laundry, internet access, a small animal farm, and a swimming pool. And when you need to take a break, they will provide suggestions on things to do in nearby Amsterdam.

Loosdrechtdreef 7
Amsterdam Zuidoost
Map p.367 F4

Gaasper Camping Amsterdam

020 696 73 26 | *www.gaaspercamping-amsterdam.nl*

Gaasper is set on 166 hectares. It has a large lake, ornamental gardens and playground and lounge areas. Additionally, there is a supermarket and a restaurant, complete with takeaway food. They have no camping equipment that is available to rent and reservations must be made by letter or fax. The website has an English option.

Canal by kayak

Canoeing

Other options **Outdoor Goods** p.227

The best way to enjoy the many different waterways in and around Amsterdam is to get in the water in some sort of water craft. Amsterdam looks completely different from this perspective and, away from all the hustle and bustle of the streets, you can see things you'd never see on foot or on a bike. You can also venture out into the more natural regions of the city either with a guide or on your own. For all clubs listed, members are expected to be able to swim, although that's not supposed to be part of the outing!

Canoeing In Waterland

Waterland is a nature resort to the north of Amsterdam. It is a traditional rural landscape of grassland with cows, small villages, old farms and a lot of water. Canoeing is an excellent way of discovering the beauty it offers. Courses have been plotted and maps can be obtained at ANWB offices, the VVV tourist information centres, the visitors' centres of Staatsbosbeheer (State Organisation for Nature Preservation) or through the organisation's website: www.staatsbosbeheer.nl. Canoe maps are also available at the VVVs in the Waterland area. One of the places you can rent a canoe is the 'pontje van Ilpendam' (www.pontveer-loots.nl) at the Noordhollands Canal, the canal that connects Amsterdam to the North Sea. Canoes for one, two and three people, as well as kayaks, are available and can be rented for two hours or for the day. Reservations can be made on the website. Don't forget to bring identification.

Kanovereniging Frisia

Bleekerskade 4
Amsteleveen
Map p.367 E4

020 647 33 58 | www.kanoverenigingfrisia.nl

Founded in 1948, the club now has 130 members. It is housed in the Amsterdamse Bos, which is a beautiful part of the city. They canoe on the Bosbaan, which was used in the 1928 Olympics, and around the Amsterdamse Bos. The club owns various types of boats and organises activities throughout the year. Training is on Sunday and Wednesday evenings. They also have a competition team.

Kanovereniging Viking

Vikingpad 40
Amsterdam Noord
Map p.375 E1 37

020 633 45 36 | www.kvviking.nl

This club is very into the Viking theme, so be ready for that. They meet every Wednesday evening, with training starting at 19:00, and going on until 20:30. They organise various parties and activities throughout the year and membership is open to anyone from 5 years old upwards. There's a training camp as well as other activities such as marathons and volleyball.

Oops!

Did we miss anything? If you have any thoughts, ideas or comments for us to include in the Activities section, drop us a line, and if your club or organisation isn't in here, let us know and we'll give you a shout in the next edition. Visit www.explorerpublishing.com and tell us whatever's on your mind.

Nieuwe Vaart (Beh Veemarkt 50-78)
Zeeburg
Map p.380 A3 38

Kayak Club Zeeburg

06 17 642311 | www.kvzeeburg.nl

Located on the eastern harbour area, Kayak Club Zeeburg has unique access to the Amsterdam canals, the river Amstel, Waterland and even the IJsselmeer. You can do a trial kayaking tour during one of the regular club evenings on Wednesday if you're not sure you'll like it. There are many regularly scheduled activities on Saturday mornings. The club offers courses and there is the possibility of storing your canoe with them. They organise a lot of activities so you can meet other canoers. Members often participate in tours of more than a day and longer treks.

Chess

Chess may be just a mass of black and white squares to some people, but a lot of Amsterdammers are obsessed with the game and would rather strategise and play chess than almost anything else. Their reverence is evidenced by a giant chess board on Max Euweplein (Max Euwe was a Dutch chess champion). A group of people stand around the chessboard considering moves all day long. The pieces are mysteriously pulled out of and put into metal boxes every morning and evening. The Dutch have also been immortalised with a chess move called 'the classical Dutch,' an opening move. A great source of information for chess in the Netherlands and in Amsterdam is the Koninklijke Nederlandse Schaakbond (Royal Dutch Chess Club, www.schaakbond.nl), or visit Max Euwe-Centrum (see below).

Max Euweplein 30a 1
Centrum
Map p.392 C3 39

Max Euwe-Centrum

020 625 70 17 | www.maxeuwe.nl

In an office at the back of the first floor of Max Euweplein 30 is the Max Euwe-Centrum, dedicated to the memory of Max Euwe. The centre is part library, with books devoted to chess moves and chess history, and part museum with photographs of famous chess players and other chess memorabilia. It's a quiet place where one can sit and read, or even sit and play chess, although chess playing is not its main function. The people are welcoming and it's a nice place to be. Open Tuesday to Friday from 12:00 to 16:00.

Woestduinstraat 18
Oud West
Map p.383 D1 40

R.K. Schaakvereniging 'De Pion'

020 615 58 03 | http://home.planet.nl/~alber071/home.html

De Pion is a cosy little club that has a devoted membership and is very competitive. They play every Tuesday evening from 19:45 to midnight except for national and Christian holidays. Their home base is Woestduincentrum, at the address above. There are regular competitions within the club and at other venues.

Climbing

There are no mountains in the Netherlands and not really any hills to speak of either, so climbing enthusiasts have built climbing walls instead. It's a relatively safe activity, something you won't always find with a real mountain. It's fun and sporty and mostly indoors. For those who are into the real thing, or who would like more information, www.climbing.nl has a lot of information about climbing in the Netherlands, meeting with other climbers and possible climbing outings.

Dijksgracht 2
Amsterdam Noord
Map p.390 C3 41

De Klimmuur

020 427 57 77 | www.deklimmuur.nl

De Klimmuur has three locations in the Netherlands. Besides Klimmuur Centraal in Amsterdam, there's also one in Haarlem and Den Haag. Klimmuur, (which means 'climbing wall') will teach you to climb in four lessons, and their main focus (besides your enjoyment) is on safety. If you're already a climber, Klimmuur is still worth a visit because they can make the climbing wall more challenging, even stretching it to the height of 21 metres.

Eric de Roodestraat 16
West
Map p.378 C2 42

Klimcentrum Tussen hemel en aarde

020 412 59 94 | www.tussenhemelenaarde.nl

Klimcentrum Tussen hemel en aarde (between heaven and earth) is a great place to go for individuals, groups, adults or children. If you have a celebration or a party, this is the place to have it. Through the course of an hour, you learn to trust and make a connection with your fellow participants. Other activities include walking across a very high rope bridge or climbing a church tower.

Naritaweg 48
West
Map p.372 B4 43

Klimhal Amsterdam

020 412 59 94 | www.klimhalamsterdam.nl

Klimhal Amsterdam reportedly has the largest climbing hall in the Benelux region. They welcome individuals as well as groups and the larger the group you have, the less it costs per person. Kids and groups of kids are also welcome. Klimhal regularly organises competitions and occasionally group trips to other climbing walls nearby.

Cookery Classes

Cooking is one of those things that you can never know enough about – there's always something new to learn and there's always a new teacher. Amsterdam offers some wonderful opportunities to develop your skills in some pretty fabulous environments in Centrum - other schools based around the city may have specialisms in particular areas, so it's always worth a glance at their website to see if they offer what you're after.

Elandsstraat 169-173
Centrum
Map p.392 B3 44

Keizer Culinair

020 427 92 76 | www.keizerculinair.nl

Keizer Culinair offers cooking lessons in a old house on one of Amsterdam's most beautiful canals. Participants overlook the canal while they eat the dinner that they've just cooked. They offer lessons and workshops which have themes such as Sicilian, Moroccan or French. Classes are scheduled during the evening as well as during the day and can be arranged with your own group, or you can just take the class and make new friends. Wine tastings and wine courses are also available. Classes are available in English as well as Dutch. Don't forget to bring an apron.

James Wattstraat 75
Centrum
Map p.385 F2 45

Kookook

020 463 56 35 | www.kookook.nl

The cooking space of Kookook is divided into seven completely equipped and spacious kitchens. They offer cooking workshops with special themes such as finger foods, seasonal dishes and menu design. The cooking workshops are designed for six or more participants. They've been around for a while and have a great deal of experience cooking with groups. 'Corporate cooking' is one of their specialities.

Gerard Doustraat 46
De Pijp
Map p.384 B1 46

Kookstudio Amsterdam

020 672 39 48 | www.kookstudioamsterdam.nl

Kookstudio Amsterdam offers a basis cooking course consisting of six lessons of four hours each. This course teaches the theory and practice of cooking and each lesson deals with a theme; meat, fish or pastry, for example. You can also take a class centred around a theme like Italian or Mediterranean cuisine. For the really experienced cook, Kookstudio organises masterclasses with professional cooks showing the participants their kitchen secrets.

Warmondstraat 180
Oud Zuid
Map p.383 D1 47

La Cucina del Sole

06 54 650239 | www.cucinadelsole.nl

The owner of La Cucina del Sole, Nicoletta Tavella, offers four-week cooking courses and cooking workshops. The kitchen is, of course, Italian. During each lesson the participants cook a four course dinner with six different dishes. The lessons are on weekday evenings or on Sunday afternoons. You can participate in the workshops individually and they can also be organised for groups of eight people or more. It's also possible to organise courses or workshops in English.

Herengracht 314
Centrum
Map p.392 C1 48

La Cuisine Française

020 627 87 25 | www.lacuisinefrancaise.nl

This school is located in a 17th century house on the Herengracht. The kichen and dining room look out over the canal. They offer a wide range of activities from cooking lessons to parties. Both the Italian and French cookery courses last for four lessons and participants learn traditional recipes as well as tips for daily cooking. One unique feature of this school is the 'Table des Amis' where a group of friends can cook a fabulous dinner together and then enjoy it, leaving someone else to clean up the mess. They will also organise trips to the Cascogne area for cooking courses 'on location.'

Oudezijds Voorburgwal 219
Centrum
Map p.393 E1 49

La Cuisine Ronde

020 626 42 51 | www.lacuisineronde.com

This institute is located in an 18th century house in the oldest part of the centre of Amsterdam. It has a very large kitchen and the dining room looks out onto the canal. La Cuisine Ronde organises cooking courses eight or 10 times a year for groups. The courses consist of five evenings and start with an introduction; you then begin preparing the dishes in small groups. The recipes are from Italy, France and Holland and the food can be taken home.

KNSM laan 293
Zeeburg
Map p.380 B2 50

TIP Kookschool

020 312 09 98 | www.tipkookschool.nl

TIP is located in a new residential area by the old harbour of Amsterdam. They have a varied offering of courses for beginners as well as for more experienced cooks. There are courses in Arabic, Moroccan, Asian and Italian cooking among others. In the summer a three-day course in exotic cuisine is offered. One original idea for a child's birthday party is the Kid's Kitchen where the kids make their own birthday cake. Also offered are courses on how to make bonbons or organise a high tea, as well as wine tastings.

Cricket

Cricket is a game with a distinctively English feel. It's played all over the world and has a long, rich history. Because the Dutch love sports and being outdoors, it's not surprising that it's caught on here. There are several organisations where you can either watch or play cricket, and have teams that you can participate in. The key organisation for cricket in the Netherlands is the Koninklijke Nederlandse Cricket Bond, or Royal Dutch Cricket Organisation. They're located in Nieuwegein, but you can find a lot of information on their website (www.kncb.nl) or you can give them a call on 030 751 37 80. Alternately, you can email them at info@kncb.nl.

Opp Duinrell Amusement Park
Wassenaar
Map p.365 B3

De Kieveiten Cricket Club

06 55 377189 | www.kieviten.nl/cricket

This is a cricket club based in Wassenaar. It's an active club that offers other sports alongside cricket such as golf, hockey, tennis and squash. The club is mostly made up of expats and is always looking for new members of all ages and abilities. Theactive and friendly organisation has three men's teams and a women's team, and they travel and train regularly. If you're interested in finding out more about cricket, this may be the group for you.

Nieuwe Kalfjeslaan 21B
Amstelveen
Map p.367 D3

Volharding RAP Amstels

020 641 85 25 | www.vra.nl

The VRA has been around since 1914. They have a beautiful facility with a pavilion and a top notch playing field. The membership is mostly Dutch, but they have a good international representation. They are a social club and members can enjoy playing on one of the teams or just watching. Women's as well as men's teams are available and apparently the teams have quite a reputation for being not just fun, but very skilled.

Cycling

Other options **Sports Goods** p.383, **Cycling** (Getting Around, p.199)

The best way to see Amsterdam is on a bicycle. You can see a lot more of the city a lot quicker and there are well-marked bike paths almost everywhere, just watch out for the people who think the bike paths are footpaths. Also, you should never leave your bike unlocked, obey all traffic rules and stay out of the tram tracks! For exploring further afield, as the Netherlands is quite flat, cycling is a great way to get around the country. There are cycle paths through the countryside connecting towns and villages, as well as along the North Sea coast through the dunes and nature reserves.

If you don't have your own bike, there are many rental shops where you can get a bike for a day or a week (see the Bike Rental Companies table on p.37) and several companies offer tours in and out of the city (see Bicycle Tours on p.164). For more information on cycling in Amsterdam see Cycling in Getting Around on p.37, and for details of where to buy a bike, see Bicycles in Shopping on p.257.

Cycle path in the Zuid-Kennemerland National Park

Dance Classes

Other options **Belly Dancing** p.189, **Music Lessons** p.214

Amsterdam is a great place to take a dance class to improve your technique, or even to start from scratch. Whether your interest is ballet, salsa or modern, there is a school or class to help you along your way. Some schools even teach dance classes that are more therapeutic in nature. The type of clothing you are required to wear is dictated by the specific type of dance, but something loose and comfortable is probably a safe bet for practice. Also, be aware that several schools have other classes available, so you will have the opportunity to look in and see what you'd like to learn next.

Polanenstraat 174
Westerpark
Map p.374 A3 52

Amsterdamse Ballet-school

020 682 54 78 | http://home.tiscali.nl/balletjeannetsmit

The Amsterdamse Ballet-school teaches both classic ballet and jazz style. The students are mostly adults. Any adult is welcome and you don't have to have any experience with dance or ballet. The most important trait of a dance student is enthusiasm. An introductory lesson is only €5.

Leidsekade 68
Jordaan
Map p.392 B3 53

Balletstudio Marieke van der Heijden

020 616 87 77 | www.balletstudiomarieke.nl

Balletstudio Marieke van der Heijden has been in its current location since 2001, but has been around in other incarnations since 1979. The studio is beautifully lit and is in a central location, near the Leidseplein. It has about 220 students aged from very young (4-6) up to adult. They also have special dance and movement classes for people who would like to be active but are no longer able to wear point shoes.

De Lairessestraat 157
Oud Zuid
Map p.383 F2 54

Dansschool Kluver

020 679 00 71 | www.kluver.nl

Dansschool Kluver has been around for 65 years and the current owners took it over about 25 years ago. They have two dance studios and a unique dance system where they get people up and dancing as quickly as possible. The forms of dance they teach are ballroom and Latin American. The enthusiastic school offers various activities and shorter workshops are available. They are open from 19:30 to 22:00, Monday to Friday and on Saturdays from 14:00 to 23:30.

Columbusplein 253
Oud West
Map p.379 D3 55

Jacob Maris

020 612 25 14 | www.jacobmaris.com

Jacob Maris is an organisation that has several clubs within it. It is a large and active community with a lot going on. Along with their dance classes (ballroom, Latin American dances, street dance, country line dancing) there are occasional competitions as well as free dance evenings when the clubs get together. The other offerings of the club range from martial arts classes to music and yoga. All ages are welcome.

Staalkade 5 hs
Centrum
Map p.393 F2 56

Salsa Caliente

020 684 51 94 | www.salsacaliente.nl

Salsa Caliente has dance lessons in Salsa, Rueda de Casino, Cha-cha-cha and Bachata among others. Classes are held four days a week, and if you don't dance yet, don't worry – they have levels going from absolute beginner to experienced dancer. In addition to classes, they offer workshops and dance evenings. The workshops are available to large or small groups and instructors will travel to your location. Just provide the room and Salsa Caliente will provide the party.

Diving

With all of the water around Amsterdam, it's nice to know that there is an exciting way to explore the depths. The waters are generally clear and visibility is good. The North Sea is certainly an excellent place to explore. There are a good number of wrecks to take a look at. For a good list, go to www.getwet.nl or www.hollandsdiep.info and look for 'wrakduiken.' In the area of Hoek van Holland, there are three ships that were torpedoed in 1914 and near Bruine Bank there are also several historic wrecks. There are over 200 types of fish in the North Sea – everything from cod and mackerel to more exotic varieties that are specific to the region. There's a type of soft coral as well as many unique varieties of underwater plant life and sea life, including crabs, shrimp and sea wolves. General information about diving as well as all underwater sports can be found on the website of the Nederlandse Onderwatersport Bond (www.onderwatersport.org) the Dutch Divers' Union. Most diving schools offer training, and when a diver has reached Level 3 he attains the PADI certification.

Adm. de Ruyterweg 148
West
Map p.379 E2 57

Duikteam Manta Amsterdam

020 685 43 09 | *www.manta.nl*

Duikteam Manta was established in 1957. It is located in the Clubhuis Manta – Gebouw Westerwijk. They offer diving courses in the modular system of the Nederlandse Onderwatersport Bond. Through these courses, a participant can obtain an internationally recognised diving certificate. They are not a commercial organisation so classes are a little less expensive than at other schools. They also have a lot of their own diving equipment, so a student can borrow materials until he or she is ready to make a financial commitment. Courses range from beginner up to advanced and rescue diver level.

Jollenpad 14
Zuideramstel
Map p.383 D4 58

Groupa Diving/Aqualong

020 489 51 18 | *www.groupadiving.nl*

Groupa Diving is a small club established in 1989. They offer classes in a swimming pool so that students can learn the necessary skills and theory in a controlled environment before going out in the open water. They stress safety and enjoyment and have a number of very experienced divers around at all times. Aqualong was originally established as a part of the Amsterdam fire brigade, but has been open to membership for the general public since 1983, and fused with Groupa Diving in 2005.

Amstelveenseweg 136
Oud Zuid
Map p.383 E1 59

Holland Diving Amsterdam

070 445 00 42 | *www.holdive.nl*

Holland Diving Amsterdam is a subgroup of Holdive, which is the oldest diving organisation in the Netherlands. They offer year-round classes and outings. Some of their classes are focused on specific dive-related issues such as stress and rescue while others are based around enjoying the amazing views below the surface of the North Sea. They have their own swimming pool in an old church, where lessons are given. They welcome anyone from beginners to experienced divers and there is a store where you can get any supplies you'll need.

Dog Training

Other options **Pets** (Residents, p.99)

The Dutch are big pet lovers and you'll see lots of dogs around. The dog training schools all teach the same basic skills, but they vary in their methodology. The city has just passed a new law about picking up dog droppings and there's a pretty big fine for not doing so. You must carry a bag to pick up droppings if you're out with your dog or that's another fine.

Zeilstraat 37
Oud Zuid
Map p.383 D2 60

Dierenbescherming Afdeling Amsterdam

020 470 50 00 | www.amsterdam.dierenbescherming.nl

Dierenbescherming Afdeling Amsterdam (Animal Protection Department Amsterdam) is a non-profit agency dedicated to the protection of animals. They offer activities throughout the year, some of which are centred on training dogs. They also provide information about animal protection and care issues. Office hours are Monday to Friday from 09:00 to 17:00, and there is an emergency number on the website.

Vrolikstraat 246
Oost
Map p.367 E3

Hondenschool Racima

06 13 886101 | www.hondenschoolracima.com

Hondenschool Racima is a full service dog training school with centres in both Medemblik and Amsterdam since 2003. There are courses for puppies as well as older dogs, complete with certificates. The trainers are confident that any dog can be trained no matter what its age is or if it has ongoing behavioural problems. The school really seeks to form a community by doing activities together, such as trips to the beach and other outings with dogs and their owners.

Westerpark 2
Westerpark
Map p.374 A4 62

Omnia Hondenschool

020 686 07 34 | www.hondenschoolomnia.nl

The experienced trainers at Omnia can provide all kinds of help, such as advice on raising a dog, behaviour problems, basic training and even tips for presenting your dog. Additionally, they have a shop where you can find the appropriate lead for your pet as well as unique hand-made rope toys.

Dragon Boat Racing

Dragon Boat racing started about 2,500 years ago in China and in the last 25 years has found a place in western sports culture. The sport involves a mixture of precision rowing, drums and a lot of muscle. Races are held every year to commemorate the death of Qu Yuan, a patriotic poet who died in 278 BC. In the Netherlands, regular cup races are held throughout the year, sponsored by various clubs. The Nederlandse Drake Boot Federatie – Dutch Dragon Boat Federation (www.ndbf.nl) is the umbrella organisation for all of the dragon boat clubs in the country.

Langbroekpad 3
Oud Zuid
Map p.367 E3

Eerste Hollandse Drakenboot Club

06 51 317985 | www.ehdc.nl

There are several dragon boat clubs in the Netherlands, one of which is in Amsterdam. EHDC (First Dutch Dragon Boat Club) was established in 1989 and hosts the Amsterdam - Bosbaan International Regatta (one of the Dutch Dragon Boat Federation's cup races) every year in September. Their season lasts from March to October and members meet on Tuesday evenings from 19:30 to 21:00, and on Sundays from 11:00 to 12:30. If you're interested in seeing if dragon boat racing is for you, they offer three training sessions for free.

Drama Groups

Amsterdam has a wide range of theatre offerings, but mostly in Dutch. However, there are drama and theatre opportunities for English speakers to enjoy, and even some to participate in. Whatever type of performance you're interested in, whether it's comedy, drama, musicals or the classic plays, you can find it in Amsterdam.

Turfdraagsterpad 17
Centrum
Map p.393 E2 64

Easylaughs

020 525 14 00 | www.easylaughs.nl

Easylaughs has been in Amsterdam for more than five years putting on high energy, interactive shows. They perform every Friday night at the CREA Muziekzaal. Reservations are suggested as the shows are very popular. Courses are available in English or in Dutch for beginners or for people more experienced in improvisation. The team of professional actors is also available for corporate events and workshops. All reservations should be made via email.

Turfdraagsterpad 17 (Theater CREA)
Centrum
Map p.384 C1 65

In Players Drama and Theatre Group

020 525 14 00 | www.inplayers.org

The In Players was formed right after the second world war and is the oldest English speaking theatre company in the Netherlands. They distinguish themselves from other theatre groups with their extensive and varied range of productions from musicals and the classics through to original plays. Conveniently located in the centre of Amsterdam, they have ongoing performances throughout the year as well as opportunities to get involved in various aspects of the productions.

Various Locations

Theaterworks Amsterdam

020 471 56 36 | www.theaterworksamsterdam.nl

Originally established under another name (Theatergroep Trezoor) in 1979, Theaterworks Amsterdam came under new management in 2002. While the group initially started with readings, they are now in the process of mounting full scale productions (for example *The Crucible* by Henry Miller). They are an 'amateur' group, but the quality is high and the commitment to theatre makes it an enjoyable group not only to watch, but also to become involved in.

Fishing

Other options **Boat & Yacht Charters** p.165

To fish in the Netherlands, you have to have both a fishing licence (visakte) and a fishing permit (visvergunning). These are available at VVV offices (tourist information), at post offices, or at most of the fishing stores and clubs. There are many different kinds of fish in the eastern part of the Netherlands, in the rivers and canals, as well as in the sea. In Amsterdam, many people think very highly of the Bosbaan in the Amsterdamse Bos (Oud Zuid) for fishing. It's an artificial pond and a nice place to just hang out for a day. The Amsterdamse Hengelsport Vereniging (see below) is the major fishing organisation in Amsterdam and you can get a lot of information from their website.

Nicolaas Witsentraat 10
Canal Belt (Grachtengordel)
Map p.384 C1 67

Amsterdamse Hengelsport Vereniging

020 626 49 88 | www.ahv.nl

The Amsterdam Angler Organisation is a great resource for any questions you may have about fishing in and around Amsterdam. They provide information on the weather, news, and suggestions on good spots for certain types of fish. The website is in Dutch, but if you call, they will be able to speak enough English to answer your questions.

Flying

There is no specified level of skill one must have attained before taking flying lessons in the Netherlands, but the student pilot must be over the age of 16. No maximum age has been set, but there are some questions about the overall state of your health that have to be answered. After that, you're good to go, even if you wear glasses.

Some of the schools listed have planes to rent, most go on trips now and then, and the only requirement for membership is a love of flying. A good resource for information about all things to do with flying in the Netherlands is www.aviation.nl, which is in Dutch. It's a great starting place for anything you want to know about being in the air, including information on parachuting and ballooning. For ballooning you really have to get out of the Amsterdam area. Two reputable establishments are A3 Ballon (0573 432 755, www.ballonvaren.com) in Harfsen and 4CB Ballonvaarten (026 370 28 70, www.4cb.nl) in Arnhem.

Noodweg 43a
Hilversum
Map p.365 B3

Aeroclub Hilversum-Amsterdam

035 577 13 00 | *www.vliegclubhilversum.nl*

Hilversum is not far from Amsterdam and Vliegveld Hilversum is the home of ACHA, a group of about 400 flying enthusiasts. They are a close-knit group that meet on Wednesday evenings for club night, often with guest speakers. Lessons are available through the club, including everything from theory to practical flights. They have a whole schedule laid out. When you're finished with your lessons, or maybe before, you can join them on one of their trips around the country and the rest of Europe. The club also has planes to rent for members or non-members.

Arendweg 37
Lelystad
Map p.365 B2

Vliegclub Flevo

032 028 84 69 | *www.vliegclub-flevo.nl*

Vliegclub Flevo is based at Lelystad Airport and has seven friendly flight instructors who can teach you to fly. For a reduced fare of only €125, you can get a basic lesson on the pre-flight check, take off, a 35 to 40 minute flight and a landing. All questions asked during the flight are free, and you can bring along a friend or two for free. The club regularly organises trips around the Netherlands and to neighbouring countries such as France and Germany. You don't have to be a pilot to join the club. Non-pilots are called 'wingmembers' and can join for a reduced annual fee.

Airport Plaza 1 – Lelystad Airport
Lelystad
Map p.365 B2

Wooning Aviation

032 028 45 19 | *www.waviation.nl*

If you've always wanted to learn to fly, Wooning Aviation may be just what you're looking for. For only €105, you can spend half an hour in the air with an instructor on an introductory flight. You're shown what to look for before and after the flight, and there's a short discussion afterwards about how you found it and if you'd like to continue lessons. Wooning Aviation has a charter service if you'd just like to go on a trip, and they also offer flights in a 1942 Boeing 'Old Crow' so you can experience flying with the wind in your hair.

Football

If there's anything that gets the Dutch going, it's football. Of course Amsterdammers support their team, Ajax, but you can usually see footballs being kicked around during the spring and summer in parks and empty playing fields. Additionally, there are several teams in the Amsterdam area which play games during the season and end each year with a tournament. Since many Dutch people play football from the time they can walk, the bar is really high, but if you'd like to play, the age range of participants seems to be a little more lenient than with other sports.

Various Locations

Amsterdam Mixed Football Group

http://sports.groups.yahoo.com/group/ams_football

The Amsterdam Mixed Football Group are a group of men and women of various nationalities and soccer-playing experience who meet once a week for a friendly game.

Fortunately for some, your general skill level doesn't matter – they just play for fun. Beginners are also welcome. They play on Sundays at 11:00 in various sports halls around Amsterdam and from May they begin playing outdoors. Check out their site for more details.

De Boelelaan 50
Zuideramstel
Map p.384 A4 72

Amsterdamsche Football Club

020 661 15 13 | www.afc-amsterdam.nl

The Amsterdamsche Football Club has been around since 1895. They have a long and interesting history and continue to enjoy a lot of success. Currently located at Sportpark Goed Genoeg, they have several junior teams as well as those at senior level (men of all ages play in the senior teams). They have a great reputation and an excellent group of supporters. Anyone interested is encouraged to write for information and ask about becoming a member.

IJsbaanpad 50
Zuideramstel
Map p.383 D3 73

ASV Arsenal

020 679 42 26 | www.asvarsenal.nl

ASV Arsenal is an amalgamation of a number of other football clubs, some of which began as early as 1956.The present club has been in existence since 1998 and currently resides in the Sportpark De Schinkel. The club wears the orange of the Netherlands. They have junior and senior teams and welcome anyone who would be interested in joining their enthusiastic group.

Golf

The Dutch love being outside, so the fact that there are several golf courses in and around the city of Amsterdam is no surprise. The clubs range from being very open and welcoming to beginners and non-members, to the more exclusive establishments where you need to know someone to get an invitation to join. There are driving ranges available at all clubs listed and a par three course at Golfbaan Amsterdam. A certificate of golf proficiency is required at some courses, but not always, and an NGF (Nederlandse Golf Federatie) official handicap is rarely asked for but is occasionally required. That said, if you want to play golf, you will be able to do it easily in Amsterdam. Most clubs have a course (or baan) where they play regularly. A good website for basic information, which has an English option, is www.golf.nl.

Bauduinlaan 35
West of Slotermeer
Map p.366 C2

Amsterdamse Golf Club

020 497 78 66 | www.amsterdamsegolfclub.nl

The Amsterdamse Golf Club is a beautiful private course in the south of Amsterdam. They have golf pros, a restaurant, and an excellent golf shop. There is a specific schedule and profile for guests, the gist of it is that you have to know a member or be a member of either the Dutch greenfee-players or the foreign greenfee-players. It's outlined on the website, and that section is in English. The club holds regular competitions as well as Golf Week.

Buikslotermeerdijk 141
Amsterdam Noord
Map p.376 B1 75

Golfbaan Amsterdam – Waterland

020 636 10 10 | www.golfbaanamsterdam.nl

Golfbaan Amsterdam is a friendly, welcoming club with an 18 hole golf course as well as a nine hole, par three golf course for beginners and those who would just like to try the game. They also have a restaurant so you can have a bite to eat afterwards. Golfbaan Amsterdam is the home golf course of the Waterlandse Golf Club, which has various membership benefits including official handicap recording for the Netherlands Golf Federation (030 242 63 70, www.ngf.nl) and the right to participate in club competitions and other activities.

Golfbaan De Hoge Dijk

Abcouderstraatweg 46
Zuideramstel
Map p.367 F4

0294 281 241 | www.dehogedijk.nl

Golfbaan De Hoge Dijk is on the outskirts of Amsterdam, near scenic Abcoude. The 18 hole competition course was designed by a famous golf architect, Joan Dudok van Heel, and is an A-status course. There is also a par three course for practice. Golfbaan de Hoge Dijk is the home course of Golfclub Olympus (www.olympusgolf.nl). To play on the 18 hole course, you just need a certificate of golf proficiency. The nine hole course is open to those with a course permit. There is also a restaurant with a terrace for a snack or drink after your game.

Ice Hockey

Other options **Ice Skating** (below)

Ice hockey does have a following in the Netherlands, with the Amstel Tijgers professional hockey team being one of the top teams in the region, but there is limited access to amateur games in the immediate area. The club is, however, very welcoming and always looking for new talent.

Amstel Tijgers

Westerstraat 68
Watergraafsmeer
Map p.388 C2 77

www.amsteltijgers.nl

The Amstel Tijgers are the only ice hockey team in Amsterdam. They have been around since 1963 and they play regularly against teams in Germany, Belgium and France as well as other European countries. While they have adult teams that play at both a recreational and very competitive level, their main focus is on encouraging children to play ice hockey for exercise, amusement and fun of the game.

Ice Skating

Other options **Ice Hockey** (above)

If you were to consult pictures of Amsterdam in the 18th century, you'd think that every winter there was a party in the canals with people playing games and skating around all day long. Unfortunately, it doesn't often get that cold in Amsterdam anymore. You may have also heard about the Elfstedentocht (Eleven Cities Race). This is an ice skating race through the canals and waterways of Friesland, and it really does happen when it gets cold enough for the canals and waterways to freeze. Luckily Amsterdam has some wonderful offerings in the way of ice skating – just not in the canals.

Hardrijders Club Amsterdam

Various Locations

020 617 31 79 | www.sv-hca.nl

The Hardrijders Club Amsterdam (Speed Skaters' Club) is mostly a club for people who like to speed skate and enjoy participating in competitions. They compete and train at the Jaap Eden Ijsbanen (see below). As the club is competition based, there are a lot of younger people involved. However, the club also welcomes those who would like to learn the techniques involved in speed skating, but are not interested in competing. A temporary ice rink goes up in the Museumplein during the holiday season.

Jaap Eden Ijsbanen

Radioweg 64
Watergraafsmeer
Map p.386 B2 79

020 694 96 52 | www.jaapeden.nl

With over 400 metres of surface, Jaap Eden is a wonderful place to ice skate, and you can do it outdoors. Open from October to March every year, there is a restaurant for when you need a break as well as showers and lockers. On Saturday evenings in the winter, there's also disco skating! During the 2007-2008 season they plan to have rollerblading, fitness, spinning, and indoor skiing. The space is also available for parties, and they have some great activities for children.

Various Locations

SKITS

www.skits.nl

SKITS was formed in 2003 out of two longstanding clubs which originally had different aims. But after years of negotiations they joined forces. They do all of their skating from October to March at Jaap Eden. They have courses for people who are more recreational skaters as well as programmes for people who are interested in competitions. They do a lot of off-season training, so you can call them at any time of the year. Children are welcome. While they are serious about skating and improving their skills, SKITS is a very social club.

Kids' Activities

Occupying kids can be a challenge, particularly during the school holidays, but Amsterdam has its fair share of activities for children. Whether it's zoos, educational centres, or play parks, you'll certainly find plenty of fun things to do.

Plantage Kerklaan 38-40
Centrum
Map p.394 C2 58

Artis

020 523 34 00 | www.amsterdamzoo.nl

Artis is the oldest zoo in the Netherlands, founded in 1838. Set in the middle of Amsterdam, it has beautiful winding paths where you can view over 700 species of animals and many different species of plant life. They try to maintain a 19th century atmosphere and it's a very relaxing place to spend some time away from the noise of the busy streets. Because its focus is educational, there are a lot of exhibits geared towards children. Artis has also recently opened a new planetarium.

Koenenkade 56
Amstelveen
Map p.367 E3

Boerderij Meerzicht

020 679 27 44 | www.boerderijmeerzicht.nl

Boerderij Meerzicht (Farm With a View of The Lake) is a pancake house where you can get traditional Dutch pancakes for lunch. One of the best things about Boerderij Meerzicht is that it's right in the middle of the Amsterdamse Bos, a great place to walk around, look at nature and hike. The restaurant is also a fine place to have a party, and their website has an English option. Note that during the winter months, they are only open at the weekends.

Amstelveenseweg 264
Oud Zuid
Map p.383 E2 83

Elektrische Museumtramlijn

020 673 75 38 | www.museumtramlijn.org

This tram museum is a collection of old trams from the Netherlands and other European countries, most of them are around 50 years old. There is a tram that runs from April to October every Sunday between 10:30 and 17:00. During July and August it also runs on Tuesdays, Wednesdays, Thursdays and Saturdays. The trams depart from Haarlemmermeerstation (right by the Olympic Stadium) and go to Centraal Station.

Kattenburgerplein 1
Centrum
Map p.395 D1 84

Nederlands Scheepvaartmuseum Amsterdam

020 523 22 22 | www.scheepvaartmuseum.nl

The Scheepvaartmuseum (Maritime Museum) is comprised of the Maritime Museum and the Eastindiaman Amsterdam, a ship designed in the form of a Dutch vessel lost in 1749 after an accident. The ship is full-size and modified to accommodate visitors, but kept as much to the original design as possible. However, this museum closed for major renovations in January of 2007 and expects to reopen in 2009.

Oosterdok 2
Centrum
Map p.390 C4 85

Science Center NEMO

0900 919 1100 | www.e-nemo.nl

NEMO is a giant green building behind Amsterdam Centraal Station and it's the biggest science centre in the Netherlands. All of the exhibits in the centre are aimed at fostering enthusiasm for science and technology – they're designed to be interactive and spark a creative interest in the subject. NEMO hopes to engage all of the senses, making it ideal for kids. While people of all ages are encouraged to visit, the exhibits are largely focused on children from the ages of 6 to 16.

Mr. Visserplein 7
Centrum
Map p.394 A2 86

TunFun Speelpark

020 689 43 00 | www.tunfun.nl

TunFun is in the middle of Amsterdam and it's a place where kids can play safely without you having to worry about traffic or the weather. There are plenty of activities to keep kids occupied and entertained, such as a climbing wall, ball tank, giant slides, things to build, games to play and lots of things to jump on and off. TunFun is a large facility and welcomes children of all ages. And when it's time to get a snack, you can get that there too. School groups are welcome and it's a great place to have a party.

Kitesurfing

Other options **Beaches** p.158

Get a kick out of kitesurfing? Fortunately, just a short distance away from Amsterdam, a lot of the Dutch coastline is highly suitable for the sport. Log on to www.windjunks.nl/kitespots for information on almost 60 spots for catching the wind and waves in the Netherlands and the Benelux. Some of the easiest places to get to on the North Sea (a short train ride from Amsterdam through Haarlem) include Bloemendaal aan Zee (p.158), Wijk aan Zee (p.159) and Zaandvoort (p.159).

Various Locations

The Flying Pig Beach Hostel

071 362 25 33 | www.flyingpig.nl

The Flying Pig Beach Hostel is right on one of Holland's beautiful beaches, Noordwijk. It's a relaxed place to hang out, meet new people and do a lot of surfing of all kinds. People do board and windsurfing, but there is also a lot of kitesurfing going on. The beach is large and spacious enough to launch your own kite and it's not crowded so you'll have plenty of space to enjoy yourself. If you don't have kitesurfing equipment with you, you can rent it. And if you don't know how to kitesurf but would like to

Kitesurfing on the North Sea Coast

learn how, you can take lessons. They also have more advanced lessons for experienced kitesurfers.

Various Locations

Kitesurfschool Harry Vogelzang

06 51 323547 | www.kitesurfschool.nl

Based in Oostvoorne, Kitesurfschool is located in the Euro Fun Centre. For their kitesurfing location, they have a beach picked out (in the nature reserve) with shallow water and very few waves, so it's the perfect spot to learn. While it's not difficult, it's good to have a few lessons to learn the basics. They offer one, two and three-day courses as well as a follow up course. When you sign up for a one-day course, the rental of a wetsuit is included. For anything less, it's €5 to hire one. They start teaching in April and it's fun for everyone to try. Also, if you need a place to stay, they can recommend some places nearby the surf site.

Noordstrand 23 a
Zandvoort
Map p.366 A2

The Spot

023 571 76 00 | www.gotothespot.com

The Spot starts students out on the beach with kite control lessons. Once you can make the kite do what you want it to do, the rest is easy and you can fly over the water and feel the excitement of kite surfing. They offer courses of one, two or more days and each lesson lasts about four hours. Lessons consist of theoretical knowledge, getting to know your kite, safety and launching, landing, and steering the kite. Courses begin in May and reservations are recommended.

Language Schools

Other options **Learning Dutch** p.124

Keizersgracht 324
Centrum
Map p.392 C1 90

Amsterdam-Maastricht Summer University (AMSU)

020 620 02 25 | www.amsu.edu

Every August, the AMSU offers an intensive two week course in Dutch. Students are given a test on the first day and their level is assessed. The following day classes begin. Students learn through interactive lessons, cultural studies and a lot of homework. Through the course of the two weeks, students are offered the opportunity to go on field trips and sightseeing excursions. Slightly less intensive classes are offered throughout the year.

Rokin 87
Centrum
Map p.393 E1 91

Berlitz

020 622 13 75 | www.berlitz.nl

Berlitz is a language school located in the heart of Amsterdam in an 18th century house. The company offers private lessons, groups lessons and even online teaching for both adults and children, aimed at all levels. They use 'total immersion' – from the start you and your teacher will only use the language you are learning, even during lunches and social and cultural activities. After one to six weeks you will be comfortable conversing in the newly acquired language. During the summer special group courses lasting one week are organised.

Various Locations

Intercambio

www.intercambio-es.com/nl

As their website says, 'language exchanges are a fun way to learn a language'. The idea is that through the website, people with different native languages get together and teach each other about their native languages and cultures. You can sign up on their website, stating which language you speak and which language you want to learn.

Regina Coeli

Martinilaan 12
Hertogenbosch
Map p.365

073 684 87 90 | www.reginacoeli.nl

This language school is based in Vught. Commonly referred to as 'the nuns in Vught,' Regina Coeli was originally a boarding school for girls, founded by the Sisters of the Holy Order of St Augustine. In the 60s the nuns set up a language school that was taught intensively from the first day the students walked in. While there are no longer nuns working at the school, the way languages are taught has not changed a lot. The teachers are professional, dedicated, native speakers. At Regina Coeli, you can learn Dutch, English, French, German, Spanish and Italian.

Volksuniversiteit Amsterdam

Rapenburgerstraat 73
Centrum
Map p.394 B1 94

020 626 16 26 | www.volksuniversiteitamsterdam.nl

The Volksuniversiteit offers Dutch language courses at various levels. The courses are a preparation for the NT2 exam (Dutch as a second language for foreigners) and start in September. In January intensive courses begin that are an extension of the courses that start in September. It is possible to follow an intensive course in Basic Dutch (level one, two and three) consisting of 36 lessons. However, for this course you need to have experience of learning a foreign language, as well as the time to do homework every day. The groups have a maximum size of 15 people. The Volksuniversiteit also offers courses in 20 languages – from English (including English for the non-Dutch) to Arabic, Swedish and Greek.

Vrije Universiteit

De Boelelaan 1105
Centrum
Map p.383 F4 95

020 598 64 20 | www.taalcentrum-vu.nl

In August the NT2 (Dutch for foreigners) department of the Vrije Universiteit offers an intensive summer course in Dutch. The course takes two weeks (Monday to Friday) with five hours of lessons a day. Over and above the classes, students are expected to study independently. Certain skills are practised with the help of the computer (at home or at the university). During the course, excursions are organised including visits to museums and walks through the city.

Libraries

Other options **Books** p.258

Most of the books in Amsterdam libraries are in Dutch, but there are quite a few available in English. The selection of new material is a little hit and miss, but there's always the possibility that what you're looking for will be there, especially if it's not a recent publication. For anything really recent you could visit one of the bookshops catering for English speakers. Most libraries in Amsterdam charge a fee for a yearly membership, while some also offer a monthly rate. Both of the libraries mentioned here have multiple branches. Check the website for a location that is convenient for you.

Openbare Bibliotheek Amsterdam

Various Locations

020 523 09 00 | www.oba.nl

The public library system in Amsterdam is called the Openbare Bibliotheek Amsterdam (literally: Public Library Amsterdam) or OBA. They currently have 29 branches located throughout the city. They have a surprisingly large selection of English books including novels, classics, more recent offerings and a smattering of non-fiction books. The novels are usually in their own section, but the non-fiction books are spread throughout the library by subject. The cost of a library card for one year is €23.50. When applying, you should bring some identification (passport or Dutch driver's licence) and proof of address. The hours of each library are different, and you can find these on the website or by ringing the contact number above.

Various Locations

University of Amsterdam Library

020 566 49 92 | *http://cf.uba.uva.nl/uba2006/*

Another good resource for library books, the University of Amsterdam has many branches spread throughout the city, with subjects offered ranging from law through to humanities and zoology. The website offers a good amount of information in English. Membership is €7.50 for one month and €22.50 for a year. Non-members can't use the digital library and databases, but are able to use the online catalogue.

Martial Arts

As there are so many cultures in Amsterdam, it's not surprising that there is such a variety of martial arts available. Many sports clubs offer either a martial art or a class that is based on a martial art. There are also private facilities that focus on one form. Martial arts has quite a few benefits: participants can protect themselves, there's a commitment and a camaraderie from working with group, and there's that calming, spiritual side, which might be just what you need in a big city.

Jan den Haenstraat 41
Centrum
Map p.379 E2 98

Aikidoschool Tenchi Ryu

06 41 634716 | *www.tenchiryu.nl*

Tenchi Ryu's teaching philosophy is not to have an introductory course. You can have a free trial lesson, but after that you just go straight into the lessons and learn with the others. Men and women train together and it's a great martial art for people of all ages. The lessons begin with a short warm up and breathing exercise and then the class begins learning the techniques. It's good for all ages, but especially kids.

T.T. Melaniaweg 2
Amsterdam Noord
Map p.374 C1 99

Budoclub

06 48 820059 | *www.budoclub413.nl*

The Budoclub teaches ju-jitsu. The idea is that the person being attacked can disarm his attacker and take control of the situation in a few seconds. While it's not a real sport, there are sportier versions of ju-jitsu. The Budoclub offers self-defence courses in blocks of 10. They also offer assertiveness training courses, and courses are open to all ages.

Various Locations

Oostwest Gym

06 24 846900 | *www.oostwestgym.com*

Oostwest Gym offers training that combines Asian martial arts, Chinese medicine, Pilates and other body-shaping exercises to discipline the body and the spirit and create flexibility and emotional well being. There is a basic 10 week course that focuses on Pilates. Other courses either in groups or as an individual are available, as well as acupuncture.

IJsbaanpad 43
Oud Zuid
Map p.383 D3 101

Poekoelan Tjimindie Tulen

020 670 27 61 | *www.poekoelan.nl*

Poekoelan Tjimindie Tulen is an Indonesian martial art that is based on the movement of four animals: the crane, the monkey, the snake and the tiger. It's a playful martial art that is a form of karate. There are experienced, supportive instructors and participants. This martial art has a connection with the Netherlands through Indonesia. There are various skill levels a student can achieve by following the classes regularly.

Lizzy Ansinghstraat 88
Oud Zuid
Map p.384 C2 102

Sho Shin Aikido Dojo

020 618 27 60 | *www.shoshinaikido-dojo.nl*

Aikido is a synthesis of physical fitness and technique, mental training and controlled relaxation. It is all about redirecting the attacker's energy, as opposed to meeting force with force. Its goal is to be an art that practitioners could use to defend themselves without injuring their attacker. It's also beautiful to watch. Sho Shin occasionally offers a free introductory lesson or a set of get-to-know-aikido classes, so watch the website.

Korte Geuzenstraat 7
Centrum
Map p.379 F3 103

Sportschool van de Berg

020 618 91 46 | www.sportschoolvdberg.nl

Sportschool van de Berg has been offering judo and karate classes for four years and they remain very popular. Anybody of any age can begin classes. There is the possibility of having a trial lesson so you can check out the vibe and see if you like it. The school has special courses for children.

Abraham Kuyerplein 2
Slotermeer
Map p.367 D2

Taekwondo Academy Amsterdam

06 47 089994 | www.taekwondoacademyamsterdam.nl

One of the most widely practised martial arts in the world, taekwondo is a combat sport and a martial art that includes stretching, aerobics and lots of kicking. It comes from Korea and even made it into the Olympics. Anyone from the age of 7 can begin taking taekwondo. Apparently it's good for your flexibility and sex drive, and boosts your energy levels. The school gives lessons throughout the week and members participate in competitions on a regular basis.

Mother & Toddler Activities

The options for mothers with small children are extremely varied in Amsterdam. Not only is the city stimulating for all of your (and your child's) senses, but there is a constant influx of young professionals and young families into the city, and there are always mothers looking for ways to occupy and educate their small children. Everything is available, from formal organisations to informal groups that meet for outings. And if you start searching and don't find what you're looking for, there's always the option of organising what you think Amsterdam is missing.

Various Locations

British Society of Amsterdam

06 51 708081 | www.britishsocietyofamsterdam.org

The British Society of Amsterdam provides a range of information services to the English speaking expat community, and has a website well worth checking out. Contact the number above for advice about expat mother and toddler groups as they're a popular organisation, providing a very helpful social network.

Various Locations

Foreign Exchange

www.fexchange.net

Foreign Exchange was established in 1980 by a group of English speaking women who recognised the need to exchange information to make it easier to cope with living in a foreign country. The cost per family is €20. Along with weekly parent and child activities, there are monthly potluck suppers and events scheduled throughout the year. The group is constantly evolving and changing. New ideas are welcome, as are new members.

Henkenshage 4
Zuideramstel
Map p.367 E3

The Little Gym

020 404 07 98 | www.thelittlegym-eu.com

The Little Gym has classes geared towards children of all ages, and a special programme for children under 3. There are a variety of experiences for kids, ranging from music to colour to equipment which they can climb on and explore. Every experience has an educational twist to it so that the child's development is nurtured with each activity. Parents are encouraged to be involved at every level. Holiday camps and birthday parties are available, as is a trial session.

Jekerstraat 84
Oud Zuid
Map p.384 C3 108

Robbeburg

020 640 56 47 | www.robbeburg.com

Robbeburg began over 30 years ago when a group of parents were looking for a place for their toddlers to play. Over the years it has grown considerably and has moved from its original location in Amstelveen to Amsterdam. There are groups run in Spanish, Japanese and Swedish as well as English. The groups are all structured differently, but all generally include free time for play, a snack, a structured activity and a singalong. Mothers are encouraged to take a participatory role in their child's activities.

Mr. Visserplein 7
Centrum
Map p.394 A2 86

TunFun Speelpark

020 689 43 00 | www.tunfun.nl

While TunFun is a great place for older kids, there are also many activities geared towards toddlers, so it's a great place to spend the day and burn off a lot of energy. Located in the centre of Amsterdam, kids can run, make noise and explore new things. Jumping, falling and climbing are not a problem as that's what the place is designed for. It's inside so you won't get wet, and snacks are also not a problem since there's a cafe available for when parents or toddlers need a break.

Motorcycling

Motorcycling is quite a popular activity in the Netherlands. People from every segment of society ride motorcyles, whether you're an office worker or a Hells Angel. There are a lot of clubs, most of them divided up by the make of the motorcycle, others by region. A good resource for finding a club that might interest you is www.motorclubs.nl, which has links to clubs all over the country. And since it's such a small country, if you have a motorcycle, nothing is very far away.

Various Locations

Harley Owners' Group

020 691 79 60 | www.amsterdamchapter.nl

HOG Amsterdam was established in 2000 and has about 160 members. They are a motorcycle club with a particular enthusiasm for Harley Davidsons. An active club, they participate regularly in 'ride outs' and other activities at their clubhouse. Memberships range from Supporting Member (someone who doesn't yet have a motorcycle) of one year to Lifetime Member (motorcycle necessary).

Waterlooplein 75
Centrum
Map p.394 A2 111

Hells Angels – Amsterdam

020 330 34 70 | www.hellsangelsamsterdam.nl

The Hells Angels are no longer illegal in Amsterdam as of April 2007. Their website doesn't have a lot of information on it, but it does have the contact information for Big Red Machine (www.bigredmachine.nl), which is the Hells Angels support shop, situated on Waterlooplein 75. The Hells Angels are a good resource for getting your motorcycle repaired, and definitely a good resource for T-shirts and hats with their logo.

Wimbledonpark 2
Amstelveen
Map p.367 E4

MTC Motovatie

06 10 370900 | www.motovatie.nl

If you're old enough to legally ride a motorcycle and young enough to still move around, MTC Motovatie might be the motorcycle club for you. They enjoy road trips in and around the Netherlands as well as weekend trips to destinations a little further away – usually riding in a pack.

Music Lessons

Other options **Singing** p.221, **Dance Classes** p.200

Amsterdam has many musicians and artists, and there are performances all the time in various venues. Additionally, there is the Conservatorium van Amsterdam (020 527 75 50, www.cva.ahk.nl) where music students from all over the world come to hone their craft. For people who would merely like to learn how to play an instrument or sing, there are also quite a few opportunities, both in classes and through taking private lessons.

Harmonica Instituut

Various Locations

06 34 22 6715 | www.harmonicainstituut.nl

The Harmonica Instituut is a group of harmonica players who are experienced in various music forms: blues, country and western, classic, jazz and traditional. They have an enormous passion for the harmonica and offer activities designed to foster interest in the instrument. Among these are two-day workshops, ongoing courses, music therapy and Harmonica Heaven, a free Saturday once a month where harmonica and accordion players get together and play. The website has an English option, which has some basic information and a link to email them so they can answer your questions.

Het Muziekpakhuis

Lijnbaansgracht 164
Centrum
Map p.392 B2 114

020 627 02 02 | www.muziekpakhuis.nl

The ideology behind Het Muziekpakhuis is that learning a musical instrument should be fun. To that end, they have developed a method of teaching music where the student is encouraged to find their own unique learning style. Both adults and children are welcome. Anyone interested is encouraged to come and take a look, and most lessons can be given in English.

Muziekles Amsterdam

Hageland 117-119
Slotervaart
Map p.367 D3

020 611 63 09 | www.muzieklesamsterdam.nl

Muziekles Amsterdam (Music Lessons Amsterdam) has teachers available for guitar, piano, violin, drums, singing and more. Lessons are available for children as well as adults. They're a full service company where you can get information ranging from advice about technique to directions to the best local music stores.

Muziekschool Amsterdam

Nieuwe Kerkstraat 122
Centrum
Map p.394 B3 116

020 521 89 89 | www.muziekschoolamsterdam.nl

Muziekschool Amsterdam is a focal point for all kinds of musical experiences. It doesn't matter whether you are looking to take private lessons, join a choir or be in a band, Muziekschool Amsterdam can help you find your way. Children, young people and adults are all welcome. The address above is for the location in Centrum, but there are several branches around the city. Check the website for the one nearest you.

Orchestras & Bands

Other options **Music Lessons** p.214, **Singing** p.221

One of the great things about Amsterdam is its love of the arts, in particular, classical music. Two very different (and beautiful) buildings where one can go to hear classical music are the Concertgebouw (p.360) on the Museumplein and the Stopera on the Amstel River. Orchestras play all over the city in a variety of venues, from churches to outdoors. You can certainly hear a great deal of music during the orchestral season, but it's always easy to find throughout the year.

D.Dekkerstraat 7B
Oud West
Map p.379 F3 126

Keramiek Atelier Patty Schilder

020 618 90 06 | www.pattyschilder.com

Patty Schilder is an experienced ceramic artist with many years of experience in making art as well as teaching. Making pottery is a great way of relaxing, either on your own or in a group. Raku workshops are available for a bit of something different, and dinner is available.

Da Costakade 148
Oud Zuid
Map p.392 A2 127

Keramiek Atelier Tetterode

020 612 92 27 | www.keramiektetterode.nl

Keramiek Atelier Tetterode offers courses on Mondays, Tuesdays and Fridays. They give a lot of personal attention to the individual goals and skills of the artist. Experience is not necessary as they have courses starting from the very beginning, as well as for more experienced students. Generally, courses begin in October and end in May, but it is possible to take a block of classes at any point during the year. Each summer they organise a trip to the south of France where you can work in a natural, restful environment.

Runstraat 32
Centrum
Map p.392 C1 128

Pottery & Co

020 421 50 13 | www.pottery-and-co.nl

Pottery & Co is a unique service where you can design your own pottery with your favorite colours. Located in the heart of Amsterdam – you can paint your pottery while looking out on to the Prinsengracht. Pieces can be painted freehand or with stencils, and after everything is painted it's baked for you. All pieces are machine washable. Pottery & Co is a great idea for parties, teambuilding or just something to do with friends. There are also courses available for children.

Public Speaking

Most people put public speaking at the top of their list of fears, frequently rating it scarier than heights, spiders or even dying. But public speaking classes aren't just about giving speeches and talking in front of a large audience. They're about overcoming stress, communicating in a convincing way and using your body effectively. One might think that public speaking classes in a Dutch speaking country might be in Dutch, but not all of them are. Whatever your background, this is a useful skill to acquire.

Various Locations

The Speaker

06 46 388622 | www.thespeaker.eu

The Speaker is a one man full-service business that deals with everything you might need in the way of public speaking – but it's not just about public speaking. An Englishman living in the Netherlands for many years now, he offers leadership training, corporate coaching, workshops and a variety of other services. He's got years of experience, many happy clients and a hands-on approach that's all about gaining confidence and improving your communication skills. If an individual approach is what you're looking for, The Speaker could be for you.

Voetboogstraat 11
Centrum
Map p.393 D2 131

Toastmasters

www.toastmasters.nl/tt

Toastmasters has been around since 1924. They have a comprehensive programme that takes the student at their own pace through different exercises, with the final outcome being an effective and engaging speaker. The classes are arranged so that there is camaraderie among the participants, making the atmosphere less stressful and more conducive to learning. And it's really affordable, at only €75 for six months.

Rollerblading & Rollerskating

Other options **Beaches** p.158, **Parks** p.159

Rollerblading and rollerskating are very popular with the outdoor-loving Dutchies and their expat counterparts. One might think that it would be difficult skating on cobbles, but you just have to know where to go. A good source of information is www.inline-skate.nl which has information on events and gatherings of skaters all over the Netherlands. Two Amsterdam-specific inline skating organisations are the Friday Night Skate and Skeelers Amsterdam, both of which hold regular skates throughout the summer months.

Various Locations

Amsterdam Skeelers

www.justobjects.nl/skeeler

The Amsterdam Skeelers are a community of inline speed-skating enthusiasts. Their website provides useful information in English about where and when a skate is taking place. One of their big events is Summer Evening Skate, the oldest Dutch night-skate after the Amsterdam Friday Night Skate. Since 1996 they have been skating in packs during the evenings. The website also has information about where to buy or rent inline skates and how you go about maintaining them.

Radioweg 64
Watergraafsmeer
Map p.386 B2 133

Duosport

020 386 77 67 | *www.duosport.nl*

There are a lot of benefits to rollerblading. Not only is it good for your overall cardiovascular health and muscle conditioning, but it also prepares you for ice skating in the winter. Duosport teaches rollerblading during a 14 week summer course. However, if you can't commit to the full course, you will still be allowed to participate. They train at the Jaap Edenbaan and there's a lot of room there. Sorry kids, rollerblading courses are only for adults.

Various Locations

Friday Night Skate

06 12 124041 | *www.fridaynightskate.com*

The Friday Night Skate started quite by accident in 1997 with three friends skating in Vondelpark. Through the years, it has grown to crowds of up to 500 at times. There are occasional theme nights and now they even have a website devoted to their history, which sells T-shirts and offers advice about safety. One of the recommendations is for everyone to use helmets and other protective equipment (you never know what's going to happen as you speed along in a pack of skaters). Friday Night Skate is an amazing community of people who have a lot of fun.

Various Locations

SKITS

www.skits.nl

In the summer, when ice skating is not an option but people still have the desire to speed skate, SKITS offers rollerblading. Training generally begins in May, but new people are welcome to join any time. The price is around €15, and a little less for students. They have rollerblades which you can borrow, but you should contact them ahead of time if you would like to use them. Be aware that you have to have a helmet to train, and some running shoes, as they sometimes train by running.

Rowing

Rowing in Amsterdam is often done at the Bosbaan (although there are other locations where it takes place). The Bosbaan was built in the Amsterdamse Bos for the 1928 Olympics, and is a long strip of water that sees quite a bit of sporting activity nowadays, most notably rowing. It's well worth a trip to see this historic site and the Bos is a great place to spend a relaxing day. Rowing is a popular sport among university students, although anyone interested is certainly welcome to enquire. There are three big clubs in the area, all of which welcome prospective rowers to apply.

Bosbaan 8
Oud Zuid
Map p.367 E3

Okeanos

020 644 89 88 | www.okeanos.nl

Okeanos is open to students in either HBO or university. They generally train once or twice a week and then go for a drink afterwards, so it's a very social group as well. They train at the Bosbaan in the Amsterdamse Bos. There is an introduction period of six weeks when the trainee rows with the team and participates in other activities such as running. New rowers can apply in September or May.

Korte Ouderkerkerdijk 32
Watergraafsmeer
Map p.385 E3 137

RIC

032 692 41 40

RIC was originally started in 1930 by a group of students at Ignatius College, hence the name (Rowing team Ignatius College). While they are no longer affiliated with the college, the name has stuck. RIC is an adult organisation, but they are very much interested in getting young people enthusiastic about rowing. To this end, they hold an open day twice a year for kids between the ages of 10 and 18. They regularly compete against other rowing teams from around the country and abroad, and they have an excellent record.

Jan Vroegopsingel 4
Amsterdam Zuidoost
Map p.385 D4 138

Roei-en Zeilvereniging Poseidon

020 694 18 13 | www.rzv-poseidon.nl

The Poseidon Rowing Club was established 100 years ago and currently has a membership of 200. While rowing seems very straightforward, it's actually a very technical sport. So people new to rowing are offered lessons to acquaint them with its intricacies. After receiving a C-1 diploma certifying that you are a capable rower, you can begin with the team. Those already in possession of the C-1 diploma can write and make an appointment to demonstrate their flair.

Rugby

Rugby may not be the first game you think of when you think of Amsterdam, but there are teams that get together and play regularly. Some of the teams are more into the fun of the game and others prefer the competitive aspects of it, so choose carefully. Ages vary widely among the organisations mentioned. Some groups are for 'university' students and others are open to older members, but young people are certainly encouraged to learn the game and help foster more enthusiasm for the sport in the Netherlands.

Sportlaan 25A
Amstelveen
Map p.367 E4

Amstelveen RC 1890

020 643 89 79 | www.arcrugby.com

Amstelveen RC 1890 is located just 20 minutes south of Amsterdam city centre, in Amstelveen. It is a friendly international rugby club conveniently providing a happy, healthy environment for all who want to play, support, watch or talk rugby. There is a place for everyone, from players at the very top of their career to those at a more recreational level, and all ages are welcome. The club has been around since the early 1960s and has 13 nationalities represented. They are always keen to welcome new members.

Korverweg 3
Slotermeer
Map p.367 D2

Ascrum

06 22 261973 | www.ascrum.com

Ascrum is The Amsterdam Student Rugby Club, mainly for young men. They train on Wednesday and Friday evenings and games are always played on Sundays. The club consists of four teams. The First Team is the most competitive, serious team. The Second

Team still has good players, but they like to have more fun. The Young Dogs are the younger players, and the Amsterdam Academicals are those players who have graduated out of the other teams.

Voorlandpad 5
Watergraafsmeer
Map p.386 C3 141

DNC Rugby Amsterdam

020 663 88 94

While they are a competitive team with a good record (and getting better all the time) DNC are more concerned with being social and having a good time. They're a small club, but with a rich history. They've been around since 1973 and have their own club house. Anyone interested is welcome to come by for a practice on Thursday evenings at 20:00.

Running

Running is popular in Amsterdam, and it's one of the fastest growing sports in the country. Most of the running takes place in one of the many parks or Amsterdamse Bos, which is a pleasant place even just to take a walk. If you are a beginner just thinking about starting to run, there are clubs to help you find the motivation and gain the knowledge to do it the right way. A good website for general running information in the Netherlands is www.runnerweb.nl. If you are an experienced runner, there are organisations that can give you information and bring new vigour to your running.

Various Locations

ING Amsterdam Marathon

020 663 07 81 | *www.amsterdammarathon.nl*

Every year in October, thousands of people stream out of the Olympic Stadium and take a tour around the city that most people would rather do at a slower pace. They run alongside the Amstel River, past the Maritime Museum, along beautiful canals, by the Rijksmuseum and through Vondelpark. Anyone interested is welcome to sign up. Applications are accepted until 1 October or until the maximum number of participants is reached.

Makassarstraat 252
Zeeburg
Map p.380 B4 143

Rubik Running

020 694 06 59 | *www.rubikrunning.nl*

Rubik Running is an energetic organisation that can help you get motivated to become fitter and healthier, and to maintain that health once you attain it. They have certified trainers who can help anyone; beginner or experienced runner. They can also work with runners in groups or individually. The goal of the training is the improvement of the condition of the entire body, which includes power, speed, coordination and an overall relaxed manner of running. Running is good for boosting energy levels and much more.

Various Locations

Running Club Amsterdam

06 53 648241 | *www.runningclubamsterdam.web-log.nl*

Running Club Amsterdam is a group of people who are passionate about running. They run several times a week, in large and small groups. There is coaching available for those who are new to running. They even have a walking group for people who are not up to running or for people who have an erratic schedule and can't commit to a regular running schedule. New people are always welcome.

Sailing

Other options **Boat & Yacht Charters** p.165

Amsterdam is a harbour city with ships coming and going out all the time. A lot of these ships are commercial, but some of them are pleasure sailing vessels. Every five years, Amsterdam hosts an event called Sail Amsterdam (the last one was in 2005). Originally organised in 1975 to celebrate Amsterdam's 700th birthday, it has become a popular event with boats from all over the world. Between these events, there are plenty of opportunities to see Amsterdam from onboard various types of sailing boats, including luxury yachts.

Geldersekade

KNSM-laan 377
Zeeburg
Map p.380 B2 62

Bootnodig Boat Rentals

020 419 66 50 | *www.bootnodig.nl*

If you need a boat for a special occasion, company trip, meeting a party or just to cruise through the canals of Amsterdam, Bootnodig is a great option. They have boats, yachts and sailing vessels to suit every need, and anyone can sail. They arrange everything for you from the captain on down. Arranging a boat is easy – the website is in English and they will gladly answer any questions you have about destinations and catering.

Van Diemenkade 14
Westerpark
Map p.374 B4 146

Klipper Avontuur

020 683 88 65 | *www.avontuur.nl*

Klipper Avontuur (Clipper Adventure) offers different types of sailing outings; one is around three hours (more of a dinner cruise), others last for five or eight hours or even a whole weekend. They cater for the whole entire event and all you have to do is enjoy being on the open water. Of course the longer you are on the boat, the further away you can go and the more fun you can have. There are a variety of boats you can choose from and their website, which is mostly in English, has some great snapshots of experiences other people have had. You can book individually or as a group.

Various Locations

SailTime NL

06 18 393974 | *www.sailtime.nl*

The concept behind SailTime is 'fractional sailing', giving members access to a large fleet of beautifully maintained boats. SailTime is a worldwide organisation that lets members enjoy boating without the hassle of owning a boat, so there are no slip fees and no worries about buying or selling a boat. The cost is also a fraction of owning and maintaining a boat. There are several locations not far from Amsterdam.

Singing

Other options **Music Lessons** p.214

There are numerous opportunities to sing in Amsterdam. Most churches have a choir and there are many other choirs which are well established in the city. Music can range from classic to gospel and from chamber music to very modern styles. Most choirs require an audition of some sort, but also provide an opportunity for you to sing with them for a rehearsal or two so that you can get the feel for the group and see if you like it. A good resource is www.koorzangers.nl, which provides websites for many of the choirs.

Various Locations

Canticum Angelicum

http://come.to/canticum

Canticum Angelicum specialises in English choir music. The choir consists mostly, but not exclusively, of graduates of the University of Amsterdam. They rehearse every Wednesday from 20:00 to 22:30 and then go to a cafe for liquid refreshment. As thanks to the Vredeskerk for letting them rehearse, they sing there every third

Sunday of the month during the mass at 10:30. They give four to six concerts a year and have a large and ambitious repertoire.

Begijnhof 48
Centrum
Map p.393 D1 149

The Choir of the English Reformed Church

020 624 96 65 | www.ercadam.nl

The choir of the English Reformed Church sings in Latin and German as well as English. Rehearsals are held on Tuesdays between 19:30 and 21:30. Singing experience and the ability to read music are helpful, but not necessary. Additionally, it is preferable that members of the choir are interested in attending church, but a reverent respect is more important. The choir performs during services once a month and a few times a year with the choir community in Amsterdam. They are always looking for new members.

Camera Obscuralaan 117
Amstelveen
Map p.367 E4

Christelijke Oratorium Vereniging GrootNoord Amsterdam

020 641 67 40 | www.grootnoord.nl

This choir consists of 110 enthusiastic singers ranging from 28 to 75. They rehearse on Monday evenings from 20:00 to 22:30 in De Ark. The monthly contribution is €12. Anyone interested in the choir is invited to come and listen to them and then speak to someone about auditioning. They have a very ambitious repertoire and perform annually at the Concertgebouw. They are always looking for experienced singers who can read music.

Various Locations

Deliverance Black Gospel Choir

020 625 62 04 | www.deliverance.nl

Deliverance sings gospel music as well as other music forms. The choir sings with a beautiful, full sound and a lot of soul. Prospective members can sit through a rehearsal or two and then decide if the choir is for them. The rehearsals are every Tuesday in the Elthotokerk in Amsterdam-Oost between 20:30 and 22:00, and there is a monthly contribution of €20.50.

Pieter de Hoochstraat 78
Oud Zuid
Map p.384 B1 152

Het Amsterdams Kamerkoor

020 694 40 41 | www.amsterdamskamerkoor.nl

The Amsterdam Chamber Choir is a small mixed choir that was formed in 1945. They sing both with accompaniment and a capella. Rehearsals are on Monday evenings from 20:00 to 22:15 in the Montessori Lyceum and members are asked to provide a monthly contribution of €15. Prospective members do not have to know how to read music, although it is helpful, as is a trained voice.

Various Locations

Sweet Adelines

www.sweetadelines.nl

The Sweet Adelines are part of a worldwide organisation dedicated to women singing in the barbershop style. The organisation has existed for more than 55 years and has over 30,000 members. Workshops are organised regularly to help women learn the style and to give them the confidence to begin singing with the group. Any woman interested in joining is encouraged to get in touch via the website.

Skiing & Snowboarding

Amsterdam certainly isn't associated with a wintry climate, so perhaps you'll be surprised by the facilities the city has available. The Dutch love the outdoors and have a great sense of adventure, so it follows that they would come up with some way to experience the wintry thrills of skiing in their very flat country. Surprisingly you can learn to ski in the middle of Amsterdam or plan a skiing holiday and never leave the country. Not surprisingly, there are also many organisations who plan trips to neighbouring countries, or even further afield.

Radioweg 64
Watergraafsmeer
Map p.386 B2 154

Indoor Ski & Squash Watergraafsmeer

020 694 45 94 | www.ski-en-squash.nl

Indoor skiing and snowboarding is perhaps the best preparation you can do before setting out on a skiing holiday. At Ski & Squash, you are on the indoor ski course with just two people, so your lesson is more intense due to the personal attention. The teacher is just a couple of metres away, so they are watching and analysing your every move. Additionally, there is a mirror in front of you so that you can see what the teacher is seeing. Of course the indoor ski courses are available for you if you just need a little practice, or if you're a more experienced skier or snowboarder and you'd just like them to look over your form. They are located in Jaap Edenhal.

Baanvelden 13
Rucphen
Map p.365 B3

Ski Dome

0165 34 31 34 | www.skidome.nl

While the Ski Dome is not in Amsterdam (it's in Rucphen, in the south of the country) it's well worth mentioning as an option for people who love to ski. They have snow 365 days a year in a giant hall. The course is 21 metres high, 160 metres long and 25 metres wide. You can learn to ski or snowboard, improve your skills, learn new skills or just have a good time. There are courses for people over the age of 50, kids' courses and a lovely cafe for when you need to take a break from your ski holiday and grab something to eat. They even have hotels available so that you can make it a real vacation.

W.G. Plein 281
Oud West
Map p.379 F4 156

Ski-Inn

020 607 01 48 | www.ski-inn.nl

One of the great things about Ski-Inn is that your lesson is never going to be cancelled due to bad weather. Everything is enclosed in a wintry environment in the heart of Amsterdam while you and your personal instructor take to the course. Ski-Inn also welcomes more experienced skiers who would like to enhance their performance levels. Additionally, they regularly organise ski trips where travellers can experience skiing in the outdoors on real mountains. Groups are very welcome and it's a great place to have a party or an event.

Snooker

Snooker, pool, billiards and darts are not as popular today as they were in the past, but all of the games have loyal followings. Due to the decrease in popularity, the halls often have several of the games mentioned, which leads to a good deal of interesting crossover. There are, however, game-specific clubs and gaming halls. They are often only open in the evenings, but they do stay open late, so you can get your fill of playing before it's time to go home. Most establishments have a bar.

Jan Rebelstraat 24
Osdorp
Map p.367 D3

Biljart-en Dartcentrum Osdorp

020 610 10 51 | www.biljartendart.nl

Biljart- en Dartcentrum is open seven days a week. They are open on weekdays from 11:00 to 01:00, and on the weekends from 11:00 to 17:00. They have 12 small tables and six large tables. You can rent tables there by the hour, the month or the year. They have regular competitions, tournaments and parties. Lessons are available in blocks of five and are recommended if you have never played. Darts are played on Thursdays from 19:00 to 01:00.

Admiraal de Ruyterweg 56B
Oud West
Map p.379 E3 172

Club 8

020 685 17 03 | www.club-8.nl

Club 8 is a large establishment that includes a restaurant as well as a dancing hall. The cost of a pool table is €8.50 per hour. Membership is €20 per month – less if you pay in larger chunks, such as half a year or a year. You can get lessons if your group has between two and eight people. Anyone taking up the game of pool should realise that pool is not as difficult after a lesson, and you can get a free lesson here. They hold regular competitions and have a very comfortable, welcoming atmosphere.

Van Ostadestraat 97
Oud Zuid
Map p.384 C2 157

Pool & Snookercentrum Amsterdam-Zuid

020 676 79 03 | www.poolensnooker.com

The Pool & Snookercentrum is open every day. Sunday to Thursday they are open from 14:00 to 01:00, Friday and Saturday they are open from 14:00 to 02:00. They have regular tournaments. The cost of membership is €14 per month. Lesson are available at €15 an hour, which includes the cost of the table. If you have more than one person at a time taking lessons, it costs less per person. There are two different contact numbers for pool and snooker. The number to call for snooker information is 020 676 40 59.

Buikslotermeerplein 145
Amsterdam Noord
Map p.376 A2 158

Snooker Centrum Boven 't IJ

020 634 17 92 | www.boventij.com

Snooker Centrum Boven 't IJ is located in Winkelcentrum Boven 't IJ above Halfords. They are open from 10:00 to 01:00 on Sunday to Thursday, and from 10:00 to 03:00 on Friday and Saturday. They have teams and play tournaments on a regular basis. Pool, snooker, billiards and darts are available, with an enthusiastic crowd playing the different games. The different prices for tables and dartboards are on the website, but the basic price of a table is €5.50 a game, while for a dartboard it's €3 per game. Parking is free.

Overtoom 209
Oud West
Map p.379 F4 159

Snookervereniging The Fifth Planet

www.snookervereniging.nl

Snookervereniging was established in 1999. They are a 'vereniging' (association), for financial reasons. Cost of membership is €210 per year and there are several benefits. As a member, you are eligible for all competitions within the club and through the club in external tournaments. Also, on Sunday and Monday nights (the club nights) there is no cost for your table.

Social Groups

Other options **Support Groups** p.117

Almost any group has a social component, but there are some groups that are completely social in nature. It doesn't matter what your particular background, there is definitely one for you. Many groups are open to anyone who would like to join and other groups are more specific about their membership. But fear not, there is sure to be a group where you can find new friends and with whom you can talk about what it's like to be an expat in Amsterdam – and get help in finding what you need.

Various Locations

American Women's Club of Amsterdam

020 644 35 31 | www.awca.nl

The American Women's Club of Amsterdam is closely affiliated with groups in Den Haag and Rotterdam. Most members are American, but other nationalities are welcome. Throughout the year there are speakers, events and networking opportunities, some of which welcome partners and family. There's a varied mix of members; from stay at home mums to women running companies – a great social group to join.

Various Locations

British Society of Amsterdam

06 51 708081 | www.britishsocietyofamsterdam.org

Established in 1920, the British Society of Amsterdam (BritSoc) is open to anyone looking to socialise in the English language. Activities are planned on an ongoing basis – everything is available from yoga to book clubs to sporting events. Larger gala events occur at Christmas and in the summer. Annual membership is €30 for an individual and €55 for a couple or family.

Various Locations

Canadian Expatriates Club of Amsterdam (CECA)

www.spetz.ca/CECA.html

Canadians are often overlooked in Amsterdam, so CECA was founded in 1999 to give Canadians living in Amsterdam the opportunity to socialise informally. They meet a couple of times per month for drinks, dinner, picnics, comedy shows or other fun events. There is no annual fee and most communication is done by email. Anyone interested in Canadians and Canadian culture is welcome.

Paterswoldseweg 810
Groningen
Map p.365 C2

Connect International (Noord Holland)

050 521 4541 | www.connect-int.org

Connect NH is an organisation that serves the English-speaking expat community of North Holland. They offer support, social events and activities, relocation and business services, translation and other services related to expat living. All are welcome. Check out the website for more details.

Various Locations

Living with a Dutchie

dejarendutchies@yahoo.com

Living with a Dutchie was started by a woman who couldn't find the kind of expat social group that she felt like she needed: one for people who moved to the Netherlands to join a partner. The idea took off and now has groups all over the country. It's always good fun and they're a very social, constantly changing group of people. The group is mostly women, but anyone is welcome. Expats of all nationalities are encouraged to drop by and check out the group. There is no membership fee. The language used is English and members are requested to leave their Dutchie at home.

Various Locations

Meet in Amsterdam

www.meetin.org/city/MEETinAMSTERDAM/

Meet in Amsterdam is a group of people who enjoy having fun in a wide variety of ways on a regular basis. They enjoy eating out, dancing, movies and sports. New ideas for things to do are always encouraged. It's a great way to meet people in Amsterdam – they are a friendly group of people keen to welcome new members on board.

Nieuwe Doelenstraat 20-22
Centrum
Map p.393 E2 166

Stitch 'n Bitch Amsterdam

www.stitchnbitch.nl

As with most major cities these days, Amsterdam has a group of knitters who meet regularly to knit and talk at Café de Jaren (p.334). Not just for ladies, but usually dominated by them, this is a great group for knitters or for people who would like to learn in a cosy environment with lots of entertaining conversation. Knitters are some of the most generous, friendliest people you'll meet, so check out their website for more information, grab your needles and cast on.

Oops!

Did we miss anything out? If you have any thoughts, ideas or comments for us to include in the Activities section, drop us a line, and if your club or organisation isn't in here, let us know and we'll give you a shout in the next edition. Visit www.explorerpublishing.com and tell us whatever's on your mind.

Special Needs Activities

There is a plethora of opportunities for people with various special needs to participate in sports and all kinds of other activities in and around Amsterdam. Anything from football and tennis to judo and swimming is available, depending on the specific needs of the individual. An organisation that is a great resource for people with a disability or some sort of chronic illness is www.gehandicapten.nl, as is Fonds Gehandicaptensport (030 659 73 20, www.fondsgehandicaptensport.nl). Additionally, Stichting RESA (www.stichtingresa.nl) provides sporting activities for people who are either temporarily or permanently disabled, and the Netherlands' Special Olympics organisation (www.specialolympics.nl) is also a useful resource.

Various Locations

Amsterdam Huskies

www.amsterdamhuskies.nl

The Amsterdam Huskies was established in 1996 to offer anyone interested in the thrill of playing ice hockey in a wheelchair. The organisation has teams of men, women and children. Players who have experienced spina bifida, muscle illnesses, spinal cord injuries and amputation are encouraged to get in contact as the Huskies are always looking for players. Training will be provided.

Jozef Israelsstraat 17
Deurne
Map p.365 B4

Red Lobster Divers

049 3316375 | *www.redlobsterdivers.nl*

Based in Deurne (near Eindhoven), Red Lobster Divers is an organisation that provides disabled individuals with the opportunity to experience the underwater world. They are staffed with a group of very experienced individuals who can help anyone with a disability to enjoy and benefit from this new experience. Lessons are given so that the individual is ready for the dive. They dive at all times of the year.

Various Locations

Tennis on Wheels

www.tennisonwheels.nl

Tennis on Wheels was established a few years ago to give people in wheelchairs the opportunity to experience the thrill of chasing a ball around the court. Training is provided, as there are specific techniques that need to be employed for success in the game. The team competes against other teams in the area, as well as internationally. Specially designed wheelchairs are used as well as coaching to keep the players at the top of their game.

Various Locations

Wheelchair Rugby

06 52 367239 | *www.wheelchairrugby.nl*

The Dutch got their first wheelchair rugby team in 1991. Amsterdam's team is the Terminators (www.ideasign.demon.nl/terminators). There are also teams in Utrecht, Nijmegen and Rotterdam. The sport is rough and the team members play hard. Wheelchair rugby increases overall arm functionality, helping players get around in everyday life and giving them greater mobility. The Terminators play against local teams and also travel internationally to play against teams from all around the world. Anyone interested in learning more about either participating or supporting the teams in any way should write for information.

Squash

Other options **Leisure Facilities** p.237

Even a lot of people who would never do another sport seem to find squash engaging, probably because of the intense workout it provides. Squash courts are usually part of any good-sized gym and are all over the city – which is good news for squash lovers and for those who might like to give it a try.

Borchlandweg 6-12
Amsterdam Zuidoost
Map p.367 E4

Amstelborgh/Borchland

020 563 33 33 | *www.borchland.nl*

Borchland is a conference, events and sports centre in Amsterdam Zuidoost (near Amsterdam ArenA). There are nine squash courts. Memberships is available either privately or through a company and it is possible to reserve a court for a fixed hour for up to an entire year. Lessons are available either individually or in small groups. A 'squash evening' is available including lessons, a small competition and dinner.

IJsbaanpad 43
Oud Zuid
Map p.367 E3

Amsterdam Squash and Racket Club

020 662 87 67 | *www.asrc.nl*

The ASRC is a part of the larger Frans Otten Stadion sports centre. There are 21 courts, some of which are 'twin vue', meaning that there are glass walls and galleries on three sides. There is stadium seating for 1500 spectators. Lessons are available for both beginners and advanced players, and there are competitions held regularly.

Mini Explorer

Don't be fooled by the size of this little star – it's full of insider info, maps, contacts, tips and facts about this vibrant city. From shops to spas, bars to bargains and everything in between, the *Amsterdam Mini Explorer* helps you get the most out of your stay in Amsterdam, however long you're staying.

Koenenkade 8
Oud Zuid
Map p.383 D3 174

Sportcentrum Amstelpark

020 301 07 00 | *www.amstelpark.nl*

Sportcentrum Amstelpark has 12 competition-level squash courts. These can be reserved for a whole season or a year; prices vary depending on the hour of the day. Two types of membership, basic or full, allow different levels of access. The sauna, swimming pool, steam bath and Jacuzzi are free. Every Thursday from 18:45 to 21:00 is Ladies' Night, which comes with instruction from one of the coaches. Lessons for beginners and more experienced players are available from a professional coach.

Ketelmakersstraat 6
Centrum
Map p.374 B4 175

Squash City

020 626 78 83 | *www.squashcity.com*

Squash City is a modern sports centre for squash and also offers fitness, aerobics and Pilates. It has recently undergone a full renovation. The 13 squash courts are open daily, but it is advisable to make a reservation well ahead of time. For those with no steady squash partner or who are just looking to pick up a game, an electronic bulletin board is available. Just leave a message and your email address. Squash lessons are available and coaches from the international squash world are on hand. Lessons are available one to one, but it is also possible to take a lesson with a friend. You can buy a course of lessons and this works out to be less expensive. A bar and a restaurant are open daily.

Squash			
Indoor Ski & Squash Watergraafsmeer	Radioweg 64	020 694 45 94	www.ski-en-squash.nl
Sportcentrum De Kegel	Bovenkerkerweg 81	020 645 55 57	www.dekegel.nl
Sportcentrum Match	Sint Gilleshof 5	020 669 58 80	www.sportcentrummatch.nl
Sportcentrum Pleizier	Wisseloordplein 4	020 697 95 17	www.hennypleizier.nl
Sportsworld Amsterdam	Oranjevrijstaatkade 21	020 663 09 03	www.squashworld.nl
Squash Club Teleport	Arlandaweg 92	020 681 58 16	na
Squash Noord Oost	Zuider IJdijk 40	020 694 94 55	na
Squash Up	Floraweg 198	020 634 45 04	na

Surfing

Other options **Beaches** p.158, **Kitesurfing** p.208

While Holland is no Hawaii or Australia, the beaches here have some decent waves and there is an enthusiastic surfing community. Some people say don't bother bringing your board all the way to Holland in the hopes of catching some waves, but if you already have your board here and are looking to try it, there's fun to be had. You'll have to leave Amsterdam and go either west or south, but there are plenty of popular spots. The shops on the beaches, which are usually open during the summer months, all have a wide variety of surfing gear, lessons and people willing to help if you're thinking about trying your hand at catching some sun and hangin' ten. See also Beaches (p.158), and in particular, Wijk aan Zee (p.159).

Dfrost Surf'n Beachculture

Passage 33
Zandvoort
Map p.366 A2

023 573 00 38 | www.d-frost.nl

Based in Zaandvoort, Dfrost has surfing classes as well as anything you might need in the way of wetsuits, surfboards, swimboards and windsurfing gear. They offer instruction and their friendly staff can answer any questions you have. Haven't tried golf surfing? You can here. Open seven days a week from 12:00 to 22:00, June to September.

Hart Beach Surfshop

Vissershavenweg 55b, Scheveningen
Den Haag
Map p.365 A3

070 354 55 83 | www.hartbeach.nl

Based in Scheveningen, the Hart Beach Surfshop arranges acitivities for individuals, companies and groups. They can arrange golf surfing, canoeing, rafting and beach volleyball to go alongside your staple diet of surfing. They have a private terrace in one of the most beautiful spots in Scheveningen. You can get private tuition from experienced surf instructors, and they open every day at 10:00 and close at 18:00, except Thursdays when they close at 21:00.

Sublime Surfshop

Keizerstraat 149
Den Haag
Map p.365 A3

070 306 16 59 | www.sublimesurfshop.com

Based in Den Haag, Sublime Surfshop has a beautiful store with everything you will need for your surfing adventures. You can rent almost anything and they offer instruction so you won't be stuck out in the water wondering what to do. They offer a unique guarantee – that during your lesson you will catch a wave. Open every day from 10:00 to 18:00, except Thursdays when they are open until 21:00.

Swimming

Other options **Beaches** p.158, **Leisure Facilities** p.237

De Mirandabad

De Mirandalaan 9
Rivierenbuurt
Map p.385 D4 179

020 546 44 44 | www.zuideramstel.amsterdam.nl

De Mirandabad is owned by the city of Amsterdam. Built in 1979, it was the the first subtropical swimming pool with a wave generator. There is a 25 metre pool ideal for competitions, and a recreation pool which is under a glass roof and decorated with palm trees. Whirlpool, Jacuzzi and herbal steambaths are available. The outdoor pool is open from May to September each year. Swimming lessons and various aqua sports are available as well as

Swimming		
Bijlmerbad	020 697 25 01	Bijlmerpark 76
Familiebad Bredius	020 684 69 84	Spaarndammerdijk 306a
Flevoparkbad	020 692 50 30	Zeeburgerdijk 630
Floraparkbad Noord	020 636 81 21	Sneeuwbalweg 5
Het Marnixbad	020 524 60 00	Marnixplein 9
Sportfondsenbad Oost	020 665 08 11	Fronemanstraat 3

pregnancy swimming and swimming for babies and toddlers. Click on the link above and go to 'De Mirandabad' for more information.

President Allendelaan 3
West
Map p.378 A3 180

Sloterparkbad

020 506 35 06 | *www.optisport.nl/sloterparkbad*

This is one of the largest swimming pools in the Netherlands and was opened in 2001. The Sloterparkbad has a recreational pool, a 25 metre competition pool, diving facilities and also an outdoor pool. There is a huge lawn of five hectares and an artificial lake where you can swim as well. As with all other pools it offers swimming lessons and activities for all ages. There are also herbal steambaths, Jacuzzis, solariums and a fitness room. On Ladies' Nights the recreational pool is open only for women of 18 years and older, and they often have aquarobic lessons.

Jan van Galenstraat 315
Oud West
Map p.379 D2 181

Sportplaza Mercator

020 618 89 11 | *www.sportplazamercator.nl*

This pool has been described as the best indoor pool in Amsterdam. The outside walls of the building are covered with 50 kinds of plants and the inside is really huge. They have an outdoor pool, an indoor pool for official tournaments, and a pool for physiotherapy. There are activities for everyone, from baby swimming sessions to classes for seniors. Lessons are given every day between 16:00 and 18:30. Sauna, solariums and a fitness room are also available.

Hobbemastraat 26
Oud Zuid
Map p.384 B1 182

Zuiderbad

020 678 13 90 | *www.oudzuid.amsterdam.nl/sport_en_recreatie/zuiderbad*

Located in the shadow of the Rijksmuseum, this historic building is the indoor swimming pool for the Oud Zuid area. The building is so discreet many people aren't aware it houses a swimming pool. They offers swimming lessons for children, babies and toddlers, and also aqua jogging. Swimming lessons for women are on Wednesdays from 10:00 to 12:00 and men above the age of 55 are welcome at these lessons. Sundays from 16:30 to 17:30 is nude swimming. Every day except school holidays there is 'lunch swimming' for only €1.75. Whirlpool, steambaths and solariums are also available.

Table Tennis

Other options **Leisure Facilities** p.237

Table tennis, or ping pong, has its origins in the 1880s in England. It's been an Olympic sport since 1988. No longer just a game played by restless teenagers in the basement rec room, table tennis has quite a following in Amsterdam, and has the oldest club in the Netherlands. There isn't as much running around required as court tennis, so anyone can play. Clubs in Amsterdam are keen for you to contact them, whether you're interested in learning the game or simply want to improve your technique.

Aanloop 4
Amstelveen
Map p.367 B3

Sportpark Het Loopveld

020 645 72 48 | *www.amvj-tafeltennis.nl*

Tafeltennis Vereniging AMVJ was established in 1927 and is the oldest table tennis club in the Netherlands. They welcome anyone with an interest in table tennis. They have specific days for different age groups. Seniors have open play on Thursdays between 20:00 and 23:00, juniors on Mondays between 18:00 and 19:00, and on Wednesdays between 17:00 and 18:30. There is also an afternoon for people over 50, on Wednesdays from 15:00 to 17:00. Training is offered on Thursday evenings and afterwards there is open play. There is a restaurant and bar in the club and anyone interested in table tennis is welcome to come and look around.

Landtong 14
Amstelveen
Map p.367 B3

Tafeltennisvereniging Amstelveen

020 645 54 94 | www.ttvamstelveen.net

Tafeltennisvereniging Amstelveen is an organisation that welcomes everybody, whether you are a recreational player, a competition player, new to the game, experienced, young or old. If you have a desire to play table tennis, they will keep you busy. They have a trial month when new people can test out the club and see if it's for them. There is a large playing room with a cafe for refreshments before or after a game, and regular competitions and tournaments take place.

Various Locations

US Tafeltennis

06 16 840875 | www.ustafeltennis.nl

US was originally a student club, but many of the players are no longer students. The club maintains a youthful and unique atmosphere with about 100 members who play at all levels. There are competitions but also the possibility of recreational play. The club meets at various locations where you can play or get training with a professional coach. Anyone interested can drop by on Mondays and Wednesdays, excluding holidays. Standard membership is around €90 a year.

Team Building

Because Amsterdam is such a busy city, people are frequently forced to get together and start working with people they don't know, often from very different cultures. Occasionally it's nice to get away from the office so you can get to know your co-workers on a different level, to participate in an activity together, solve puzzles, or maybe just cook a meal. Team building helps you to see your co-workers as people, not just as the office manager or a salesman. Several companies in Amsterdam provide amazing experiences to help you and your colleagues get out of the office mentality and have fun.

WG Plein 280
Oud West
Map p.392 A3 186

The Game Company

020 589 10 10 | www.thegamecompany.nl

Through a game called De Gestolen Rembrandt (The Stolen Rembrandt) www.degestolenrembrandt.nl, participants receive instructions, a mobile telephone, advertisements in the newspaper and emails and move around the city for six hours until at the end the mystery is solved. This is a great team-building exercise, and it's an experience that people talk about for months. Many large, successful companies in Amsterdam have used De Gestolen Rembrandt to enhance their team spirit, but it's good fun for everyone to try.

Damrak 44
Centrum
Map p.389 E3 187

Mokum Events

020 427 29 09 | www.mokumevents.nl

Mokum is the Yiddish word for Amsterdam. Mokum Events is an event planning group that provides old fashioned, top quality Amsterdam experiences. The success of the company comes from the enthusiasm of the employees. In the team-building exercise, groups are sent out to find their way through Amsterdam using old maps and answering questions along the way. It seems simple, but it's not as easy as you might think. Snacks and beverages are included.

Various Locations

Weg met de Baas

020 615 41 83 | www.wegmetdebaas.nl

Weg met de Baas ('Away With The Boss') organises company trips for any purpose, but one of their specialities is team building. They help your team become a cohesive unit through trips, games, workshops and excursions. Outside of the office people begin to relate to each other in a different way and formal roles become less important. Connections are made and new ways of communicating are found. Weg met de Baas is also affiliated with Weg met de Kids and Weg met de Gezin (Family).

Tennis

Other options **Leisure Facilities** p.237

Tennis is a popular sport in Holland, with the ABN AMRO World Tennis Tournament taking place here every year since 1974. The Netherlands has had a few well-known professional tennis players, among them Richard Krajicek who won Wimbledon in 1996. Clubs in Amsterdam are open to professionals, amateurs, groups and individuals. Most offer classes, have various types of membership and are available to use on a drop-in basis.

Jaagpad 48
Slotervaart
Map p.383 D4 189

ALTC Joy Jaagpad

020 614 80 06 | *www.joyjaagpad.nl*

Joy Jaagpad was created in 1998 from two already well-established clubs. They have 13 clay courts and report a very enthusiastic membership. Tennis lessons for all ages are available, with competitions and tournaments are held annually, and a variety of membership types are available. They have a very open atmosphere and a wide variety of activities, making it easy for anyone to feel comfortable and part of the club.

Gustav Mahlerlaan 20
Buitenveldert
Map p.383 F4 190

Gold Star Tennis

020 644 54 83 | *www.goldstar.nl*

Located in the south of Amsterdam, Gold Star Tennis is equipped with 12 inside courts and 24 outside courts. They've been around for 80 years and host a number of important tennis tournaments each year. They have something for everyone – young or old, alone or with a partner, beginner or professional, the spacious facilities are open to all.

Borchlandweg 6-12
Amsterdam Zuidoost
Map p.367 E4

Laurense Tennis Academy

020 563 33 33 | *www.laurense.nl*

Located within a large sports centre near Amsterdam ArenA (Amstelborgh/Borchland, p.190), Laurense Tennis Academy is one of the best-equipped centres for tennis in Amsterdam. They specialise in tennis courses and events for professional players as well as individuals striving to play like a pro. The club has two restaurants, an event centre and caters for several other sports such as badminton, bowling, golf and squash. Tennis clinics and tournaments are also available.

Koenenkade 8
Amstelveen
Map p.367 E3

Sportcentrum Amstelpark

020 301 07 00 | *www.amstelpark.nl*

Situated on the edge of the Amsterdamse Bos, Sportcentrum Amstelpark has large modern facilities. Among their other offerings (squash, sauna, fully equipped fitness room) they have some of the best tennis facilities in the city. Their 26 outdoor courts are lit for evening play and they have an additional 16 indoor courts. Childcare is free on Mondays, Wednesdays and Fridays and they have plenty of parking. Lessons are available and tournaments are held here all year round.

Nieuw Kalfjeslaan 19a
Amstelveen
Map p.367 E4

Tennis Club Amsterdam

020 643 28 28 | *www.tcamsterdam.info*

A little further from the centre, but well worth the trip, is Tennis Club Amsterdam. The club is located in a park, which gives it a different feel from many of the tennis clubs in the Amsterdam area. Its fewer number of courts reflect its smaller facilities and membership. However, for many of the members, a smaller number of people means a tighter-knit community. Lessons are offered, showers and dressing rooms are always available and the park is open from 1 April to 1 November.

Volleyball

The Dutch national men's and women's volleyball teams have a good reputation for court volleyball as well as beach volleyball. In 2006 both teams enjoyed success at the European Championships. At the Olympics in 1996 the national men's team won the final, but at the moment they are ranked 19th in the world, and the women 10th. The Dutch beach volleyballers rank among the best in the world. Volleyball also has an enthusiastic following among amateur players.

Various Locations

Netzo

020 684 21 61 | www.netzo-amsterdam.nl

Netzo is the oldest and biggest gay and lesbian volleyball club in the Netherlands, officially established in 1988. With about 90 members in total, Netzo plays both in the gay league and the regular league. They play rougher than you might imagine and participate in tournaments in the Netherlands as well as abroad. They are famous for their 'Sinterklaastoernooi' held every year at the end of November.

Various Locations

Volleybal Vereniging Albatros

020 772 56 53 | www.albatros-amsterdam.nl

While the club has existed for 50 years, it is still relatively small. The youth division, however, has quite a few members. Training sessions are on Monday evenings in the Wethouder Verheijhal sports hall , from 19:00 to 21:00. If you want to check out the club you can join a training session for free. Once a year the club organises a party and at the end of the season there is a barbecue in the Amsterdamse Bos.

Paramaribostraat 96
Oost
Map p.379 D4 196

Volleybal Vereniging Amsterdam

06 41 764465 | www.vvamsterdam.nl

The VV Amsterdam is the largest volleyball club in Amsterdam. It is still growing and has teams playing at all levels. Both adults and children can become members. The club trains in the Blauwwit hal which is in the west part of the city (see website for details). If you are interested you can participate in two training sessions for free. There are training sessions for people who only want to play volleyball as a leisure activity. They play on Monday and Wednesday evenings. At the end of the season they organise tournaments for these recreational players.

Lizzy Ansinghstraat 88
De Pijp
Map p.384 C2 197

Volleybalclub KVA

020 642 22 32 | www.kva-amsterdam.nl

KVA means 'klaar voor actie' (ready for action) in Dutch. The club training sessions are held in Sporthal De Pijp on Mondays from 16:30 to 23:00. The club has various teams of both men and women that play in regional competitions. The organisation is run mainly by volunteers. If you want to see what training is like, just go to the training facility at 19:30 on Monday evening.

Ravenswaaipad 5
Amsterdam Zuidoost
Map p.367 E3

Volleybalvereniging Arena

020 697 72 22 | www.volleybalarena.nl

Members of Arena can play recreationally as well as in the league. At the moment there are 120 members. The location for training sessions and matches is Sporthal Gaasperdam in the modern south-east part of town (known as Bijlmermeer). The club organises monthly recreational tournaments, so-called 'mixed' tournaments, and a yearly party. They also participate in tournaments abroad.

Water Polo

Water polo is one of the most popular water sports in Amsterdam. It's a combination of swimming and handball with a little bit of football thrown in. Players are required to swim and to really love the water. Because it is such an active sport, participants are generally university age, but there are opportunities for younger players to learn and even recreational teams for people out of the median age range.

Van der Hooplaan 239
Amstelveen
Map p.367 E4

De Futen

www.defuten.nl

De Futen swims regularly at Zwembad De Meerkamp, at the address above. They have three men's teams and various other teams that include young men, girls and boys. They train throughout the week, participating in competitions throughout the season, which ends with a tournament where they compete against other Dutch teams. There are various other activities that swimmers can participate in such as the free swimming sessions and the opportunity to attain certificates. Anyone interested should make contact and try it out.

President Allendelaan 3
Osdorp
Map p.378 A2 200

Jaws Studenten Waterpolovereniging

06 54 665626 | *www.jawswaterpolo.nl*

Jaws is a fun-loving group of students (and those just past the age of being a student) who play water polo every week at Sportfondsenbad Oost in the east of Amsterdam. They train once a week during the season and play against other Dutch teams, ending the season in a tournament. After training, they like to cool down afterwards with a drink at a nearby cafe. Anyone who would like to come and see if Jaws is the kind of club they are looking for is welcome to join for a free game or two.

Various Locations

Oceanus

029 734 04 59 | *www.zsc-oceanus.nl*

Oceanus has teams for both men and women who would like to play in competition, as well as opportunities for those who would just like to play for fun. Additionally, you can get training if your ambition is to learn water polo, and there are also special classes for children.

Wine Tasting

As Amsterdam is such an international city, wines from all over the world find their way to the area and the palates of wine lovers are increasingly discriminating. Many of the best wines in the world can be found here as well as some very nice, moderately priced varieties that are good for everyday consumption. Wine sellers range from the standard Gall & Gall to an amazing array of independent distributors. No longer a pastime just for connoisseurs, wine tastings are a popular activity for everyone who wants to know more about this fascinating subject.

Haarlemmerstraat 7
Centrum
Map p.389 E2 202

Chabrol Wines

020 622 27 81 | *www.chabrol.nl*

Chabrol specialises in wines from smaller wine makers and their offerings vary from excellent house wines to fine wines. Most wines come from France, Italy and Spain. Chabrol organises an annual event each November called 'Art of Wine' in the Posthoornkerk where participants can taste different wines and finger foods. Wine tastings can be arranged for groups and businesses around particular themes. They also prepare people for recognised certificates. Check out their website for more details.

Nieuwezijdsvoorburgwal 226a
Centrum
Map p.389 E3 203

Gall & Gall

020 421 83 70 | www.gall.nl

Gall & Gall is a large and popular chain of liquor stores in the Netherlands. There are a couple of branches in every city; several in Amsterdam (for more on Gall & Gall, see p.299), and they are usually close to an Albert Heijn supermarket (they are in the same group). They don't have exclusive wines, but they do have a good selection of wines along with spirits like whisky and cognac. Gall & Gall organises monthly wine tastings in a location specifically designed for this purpose – see the address above. The tastings are free and no reservations need to be made. Additional wine tastings can be arranged with a maximum of 16 people. For reservations for these or for more details about the nearest tasting location and dates of tastings, check the website.

Fort aan de Drecht
Uithoorn
Map p.365 A3

Maison Vinocerf

0297 560 520 | www.vinocerf.nl

Vinocerf is located in the 'Fort aan de Drecht', which is part of the Stelling van Amsterdam – a line of defence surrounding Amsterdam (south of Amstelveen) built in the early 20th century. Wine can be tasted there every Saturday between 14:30 and 18:00 in a cosy atmosphere. Finger foods are also served. Please call ahead to let them know you're coming. Wine courses are organised twice a year for beginners as well as for more experienced wine lovers. Participants are taught to recognise and describe the wines and grapes, and trips are also organised.

Gierstraat 34
Haarlem
Map p.366 B3

Okhuysen

023 531 22 40 | www.okhuysen.nl

Okhuysen, based in Haarlem, was founded in 1867. The present owners bought it in the mid 70s and since then it has become one of the top addresses for wine in the Netherlands. The cellars and shop are located in the old centre of Haarlem. They have wines from all over the world, but their strength is in European wines. They organise regular tasting sessions and you can get more information about them through the website or by calling the store.

Nieuwe Herengracht 18
Centrum
Map p.394 A2 206

Tastevin Dehue

020 623 58 77 | www.tastevindehue.nl

Tastevin Dehue organises wine tastings in cooperation with Salburg Wines, usually on request. The tastings take place in the stylish cellars of the 18th century monument of Corvershof or at your own location. The minimum number of participants is 10 and tapas can also be arranged. A tasting takes around two hours and is organised around a theme, such as a particular type of grape.

Prinsengracht 411
Centrum
Map p.388 C4 207

Vyne

020 344 64 08 | www.vyne.nl

Located on one of the principal canals of Amsterdam, Vyne is long and narrow (a 'pijpenla' in Dutch). The interior has clean lines, lots of wood, no frills and has the characteristics of a normal cafe, where the beers have been replaced by wine. There is an enomatic (high tech wine storage system) against one of the walls as well as wine bottles kept in normal storage. Wines can be tasted in a 'flight' which is three half glasses of different wines. They also offer exquisite snacks. For every dish on the menu, Vyne suggests three different wines to go with it. Reservations not accepted, so show up early.

Tired of writing your insider tips…
…in a blog that nobody reads?

The Explorer Complete Residents' Guide series is growing rapidly, and we're always looking for literate, resident writers to help pen our new guides. So whether you live in Tuscany or Timbuktu, if writing's your thing, and you know your city inside out, we'd like to talk to you.

Apply online at www.explorerpublishing.com

PLORER

Spectator Sports

As with any other place in the world, spectator sports are a big part of life in Amsterdam. The biggest team of all is Ajax, Amsterdam's football team, whose form is frequently the topic of conversations across the city. Other sports also have their own enthusiastic supporters – whether it's baseball, horse riding or tennis, Amsterdammers love the thrill of live sporting action.

ABN-AMRO World Tennis Tournament

Ahoy Rotterdam
Rotterdam
Map p.365 A3

0110 293 33 00 | www.abnamrowtt.nl

From its humble beginnings in 1974, the ABN AMRO World Tennis Tournament has grown into a true world event. With initially meagre crowds and only Dutch press recording the results, now over 100,000 spectators watch the various games and the tournament is broadcast in 127 countries. If you think that you would like to go, get tickets early. Some of the biggest names in tennis play at this tournament every year in February.

Ajax

ArenA Boulevard 29
Oud Zuid
Map p.383 D3 209

020 311 14 44 | www.ajax.nl

Ajax was established in 1900 and is one of the largest and most renowned football teams in Europe. Their main rivals in the Netherlands are Feyenoord in Rotterdam and PSV in Eindhoven. If you live in the Amsterdam area, you are required to root for Ajax and be able to pronounce the name (pronounce the j like a y). Games are often sold out and are usually on television. It's worth getting tickets to a game just to see the enthusiasm of the usually laid back Dutch, particularly on European football nights.

Amsterdam Astronauts

Burgerweeshuispad 54
Oud Zuid
Map p.383 D3 210

020 423 18 18 | www.astronauts.nl

The Astronauts are one of the top teams in the Dutch basketball league. The team includes American players and they often play in international tournaments. The Astronauts also have the chance to play in the European league in 2008. You can buy a season ticket which will allow you to attend all the games played in the Sporthallen Zuid. Since the beginning of 2007 the club has had a supporters' club called 'Mokum Fire'.

Amsterdam Pirates

Sportpark Ookmeer
Osdorp
Map p.367 D3

020 612 69 69 | www.amsterdampirates.nl

The Amsterdam Pirates were established in 1959 and have been playing in the professional baseball league in the Netherlands since 1982. They are very active in getting children involved in sports through Peanutball, where the ball is set on a pole to be hit, rather than the batter receiving it from a pitch. The Pirates currently play in Sportpark Ookmeer in Osdorp. They have won the Holland Series twice, but not recently (the last time was in 1990). Still, they have a loyal fan base and a lot of fun at the games.

Jumping Amsterdam BV

Amsterdam RAI
Oud Zuid
Map p.380 B3 212

020 465 54 46 | www.jumpingamsterdam.nl

Jumping Amsterdam is an equestrian event that started in 1958. These days it takes place at the Amsterdam RAI centre, usually in January. They regularly get several thousand spectators and it's one of the leading sporting events involving horses in the country. It's got a great reputation and many fans, with some of the best riders in Europe competing in it.

Leisure Facilities

Amsterdam has a good number of facilities dedicated to sports and health. They are generally large, well equipped, and have quite a number of activities available. Membership is encouraged, but if you would like a short-term membership or to use the facilities just for a day or two they usually do have rates available. Because most of the centres are new and there is competition to get people to sign up, the facilities are usually very good. The best facilities are privately owned – some are part of fitness chains, with centres all over Holland, but a few are owned and run by the city of Amsterdam. Teenagers above the age of 16 (sometimes 15) are allowed in regularly. Most people find a club or facility near where they live. There are plenty around, so you shouldn't have to look long to find what you need in a price range you find reasonable.

Beach Clubs

Other options **Health Clubs** p.238, **Beaches** p.158

Residents of Amsterdam do not need to travel very far to get all the amenities of a luxurious beach club. There are several to choose from within the city limits. Most clubs are open to the general public, with day rates available at all of them. Along with swimming, sunbathing and all of the other activities that can be done on a beach, guests can enjoy fabulous dining, beach parties, fitness centres and also be entertained with live performances. There are a surprising array of choices, whether you want to have a great party or just sit and enjoy the atmosphere. For some other beaches worth visiting outside the city, see Beaches on p.158 in the Exploring chapter.

Blijburg aan Zee

Bert Haanstrakade 2004
Zeeburg
Map p.367 F3

020 416 03 30 | www.blijburg.nl

Blijburg is a pavilion that is set on a beautiful beach in Amsterdam. They have many options available as far as activities go. You can choose to swim or just relax, and they also have regular parties with a DJ. The restaurant serves up delicious tapas and pizzas during the day and then switches to more Asian-inspired main dishes at night. They also regularly have a barbeque and are available for parties and weddings. They are still open in the winter, but have shorter hours. Entrance is always free.

Zandvoort Beach

Stavangerweg 900
Oost
Map p.374 A3 214

Strand West

020 682 63 10 | www.strand-west.nl

Whether you're having a business dinner, a party or just want a few drinks with friends, Strand West is a great place to be. They have a large, modern facility with two lounges, a restaurant and a terrace where you can sit for as long as you want and soak up the sun. The fitness centre is open every day from 08:30 and has a huge variety of classes available as well as professional trainers. Additionally, there is a beauty salon with anything you could want regarding hair, nail and skin treatments. Kids are always welcome.

Europaplein 22
Amsterdam RAI
Rivierenbuurt
Map p.384 B3 215

Strand Zuid

020 544 59 70 | www.strand-zuid.nl

Strand Zuid has recently undergone a renovation. They have a new, larger kitchen and a beautiful outdoor cafe. The facility is also available for parties and business events. They have regular barbecues and their Mediterranean atmosphere gives visitors everything they need without having to travel to Spain or Italy.

Health Clubs

Other options **Beach Clubs** p.237

Amsterdam has many wonderful health clubs spread throughout the city. Even when part of a chain, they often try to have a distinctive feel, and to pay attention to the needs of individual clients. Membership is generally required, as it helps the club track progress and encourages the client to keep coming back, but it is usually possible to use the facility a couple of times before deciding whether it's for you. Ask about the various membership deals, as they range from a basic €60 per month upwards, depending on the amenities a club offers. Fitness rooms are the norm as well as classes in almost anything you could imagine. Saunas, steam rooms and Jacuzzis are found in most clubs and massages and physical therapy are available in some. Occasionally you will find a swimming pool. If you're looking for a personal trainer, they are looking for you too (see also Well-Being p.240).

Overtoom 557
Oost
Map p.383 E1 216

David Lloyd Sports & Health Club

020 589 71 50 | www.davidlloyd.nl

David Lloyd's is located at the end of Vondelpark. Along with regular fitness and cardio fitness facilities, they have three large rooms where they offer classes in Pilates and spinning. They also have a swimming pool, sauna and steam bath, and you can relax in the Jacuzzi. Their staff of professional trainers will keep you focused on your goals and encourage you to keep raising the bar. A creche is available for children under the age of 6.

Nieuwezijds Kolk 15
Centrum
Map p.389 E3 217

Fitness First

020 530 03 40 | www.fitnessfirst.nl

Fitness First is a worldwide chain with over a million members, but they strive to give personal attention to the members of each club. The Amsterdam branch offers a wide range of classes from BodyPump to spinning, as well as various yoga groups. Trainers are available for one-off training tips or on an ongoing basis. Their facilities are centrally located and they also offer aromatherapy, beauty therapy, saunas and sunbeds (see also Well-Being p.240). There is an area that is specifically for women and one that is for 'premium' members. Day passes are available.

Breitnerstraat 4
Oud Zuid
Map p.383 F2 218

Personal Health Club

020 470 20 67 | www.personalhealthclub.nl

The central idea of the Personal Health Club is that personal training is important. To that end, everyone is offered guidance by one of their very experienced staff so that results can be seen quickly and also maintained. Sauna and Turkish steam baths are available as well as massages and physical therapy. On top of that, they have a health check programme and nutritionist on hand to answer any questions you might have. If you're looking for an upscale health club in a beautiful neighbourhood, check this place out.

Various Locations

Splash Healthclubs

020 411 65 22 | www.splashhealthclubs.nl

Splash has three locations in Amsterdam, all of them modern, new and full of classes and activities to take part in. There are courses in spinning, yoga and aerobics. They also have sauna, steam room and sun bed facilities, alongside a staff of trainers. Splash has a 'lifestyle check' programme to help you achieve the results you are looking for. Everyone is expected to have membership and they'll chat with you about which type of membership suits you

Wisseloordplein 4
Oud Zuid
Map p.367 E3

Sportcentrum Pleizier

020 697 95 17 | www.hennypleizier.nl

Sportcentrum Pleizer has fitness facilities for everyone. Along with a giant fitness room which is equipped with the latest cardio and power equipment. They offer all sorts of classes from spinning to basic and advanced aerobics. They have a full staff of professional trainers to help you if you have any questions and there is a nursery to look after your children while you work out. When you are finished, there is also a great little restaurant with a pool table so you can relax before heading home.

Sports Centres

Other options **Health Clubs** p.238

Amsterdam has several different sports centres to choose from. Quite a few have been built in recent years, so there is a good chance that you can find an ultra-modern gym if that's what you're looking for. Trainers are generally available and some facilities have bars and restaurants.

Ijsbaanpad 43
Oud Zuid
Map p.367 E3

Frans Otten Stadion

020 662 87 67 | www.fransottenstadion.nl

The Frans Otten Stadion offers a wide variety of sports such as tennis, fitness and aerobics and more 'exotic' sports like fencing, Poekoelan (an Indonesian martial art) and Pilates. The centre is open every day from 09:00 and closes at 01:00 from Monday to Friday and 21:00 on Saturdays and Sundays.

De Boelelaan 46
Oud Zuid
Map p.384 A4 222

Universitair Sport Centrum (USC)

020 301 35 35 | www.usc.uva.nl

USC is the sports centre for students of the University of Amsterdam and the Hogeschool of Amsterdam, but anyone can use the facilities. They have an amazing assortment of classes available such as spinning, aerobics and dance. They also have boxing, martial arts and table tennis. The site has an English option and all classes are listed with prices, which vary during different times of the year.

Amsterdam ArenA

Well-Being

There are countless ways to pamper yourself in Amsterdam, whether you're looking for a spa treatment, Pilates class or bikini wax. Beauty salons abound with luxurious techniques designed to make you look and feel your very best. With the abundance of makeover shows on television, the importance of one's outward appearance seems to be a growing trend in Amsterdam, with new spas and salons popping up all the time. The holistic health sector is widespread with meditation, yoga, Reiki and other types of massage and relaxation techniques available privately or in holistic centres at affordable prices. Treatments in Amsterdam are popular so you do have to call and make an appointment with at least a week's notice at most places. Some are willing to put your name on a waiting list and call you if there's a cancellation. With all the different types of classes and treatments available here in the city, it's never been easier to maintain your overall health and appearance, so take advantage and indulge yourself at least once.

Beauty Salons

Other options **Health Spas** p.238, **Perfumes & Cosmetics** p.278

In the past many Dutch people took a casual approach to their appearance, but with the steady increase in salon openings the demand for beauty treatments for both men and women is a growing trend in Amsterdam and the Netherlands. Salons come in a variety of styles and offer a wide array of luxurious spa treatments, relaxing massages, rejuvenating facials, waxing and superb pedicures and manicures. Many beauty salons and day spas are unisex, catering for the metrosexual man. You can pretty much find a salon to suit almost every budget, depending on how extensive the treatment you want and which area of Amsterdam you choose. In posh neighbourhoods and the centre of town, prices can be a bit higher, but shop around as you can get good bargains off the beaten track (see also Well-Being p.240).

Johannes Verhulststraat 96
Oud Zuid
Map p.383 F1 223

Amsterdam Zuid Salon

020 675 95 25

Treat yourself to a gorgeous facial by one of the three highly skilled beauty therapists. A 60 minute facial will cost you €48, but you can indulge yourself with the 90 minute facial which includes a fantastic foot massage and an intensive neck massage. It's the ultimate in relaxation and well worth the extra cost. If you just need a little beauty pick-me-up there are also a variety of quick treatments like waxing (lower legs €24) and eyelash tinting (€15).

Maasstraat 145
Rivierenbuurt
Map p.383 C3 224

Face to Face

020 676 92 93 | www.facetofaceschoonheidssalon.nl

Beauty salon Face to Face offers affordable, sumptuous treatments to lavish you from head to toe. Whether you're looking for facials, full-body treatments, massages, bikini waxing, manicures, pedicures or permanent makeup, their professional beauty therapists will leave you feeling refined, refreshed and revitalised. You can also indulge that special someone with one of their gift arrangements like the 'Expectant Mother Arrangement' for €125 which includes a soothing facial, pampering pedicure and blissful leg massage designed to comfort and uplift the mother-to-be.

Minervalaan 30
Oud Zuid
Map p.383 F2 225

House of Beauty

020 664 49 88

This wonderful and friendly salon is owned and run by the English beautician Debbie Noble. She provides a range of services from moisturising, skin hydrating treatments to mild glycolic peelings for problem skin. A soothing 60 minute facial will have you glowing for €55, and pedicure, eyelash tinting, and waxing are also available. Debbie is also very helpful for new arrivals in Amsterdam; she knows everything and everyone and is always happy to dispense advice.

Runstraat 9
Canal Belt
(Grachtengordel)
Map p.392 C1 226

Skins Cosmetics

020 528 69 22 | www.skins.nl

A trendsetter in the field of beauty and cosmetics, this ultra-cool boutique located in the hip Nine Streets shopping area of Amsterdam sells unique, exclusive international perfume, cosmetics and haircare brands. In their contemporary, clinically-sleek white shop you are greeted by helpful, well-informed staff and encouraged to browse through their wide assortment of innovative makeup, skincare ranges, hair products and extraordinary fragrances. Or you can make an appointment for an uplifting professional make-up or hairstyling session, trying out some of their fabulous products.

Spuistraat 281
Centrum
Map p.393 D1 227

SOAP Treatment Store

020 428 96 60 | www.soapcompany.com

The modern, calm ambience of this luxurious day spa situated conveniently in the centre of town is fresh, clean and white, just like the name. The specialists at the SOAP Treatment Store will help you unwind and forget all the stresses of daily life with personalised, professional, rejuvenating treatments and products of the highest quality. Relax and enjoy one of their many kinds of facials.

Ceintuurbaan 145
De Pijp
Map p.384 C1 228

Venus Nails

020 673 51 88

Nail bars are not commonplace in Holland, so the recent opening of Venus Nails has caused quite a buzz in the expat community here. These Vietnamese ladies are wowing customers with this New York-style salon. Try the pedicure and foot massage. They also do solar nails and eyelash extensions.

Hairdressers

You can find almost any type of hairdresser in Amsterdam: large international chain salons like Toni & Guy, funky local hairdressers, laid-back neighbourhood barbers, or modern, sleek salons. Whatever you fancy there are many great places spread across Amsterdam, with prices varying (for a wash, cut and blow dry) for women between €40 and €65. Men should generally pay €10 or less depending on the type of place and location. You can find traditional barbers like Sjonnie Kapper (020 673 96 93), an old-fashioned barber located in Oud Zuid, where you'll get a good haircut for €18 to €20. A child's haircut can cost between €15 and €25 and isn't possible in every salon, so please ask when making your child's appointment. A walk-in blow dry service is usually only available if a hairdresser has a cancellation and a little extra time, but some do offer this service so it's worth asking. Normally, appointments should be made a week in advance but it never hurts to call spontaneously – most salons are very accommodating and will fit you right in if they have a cancellation.

Willemsparkweg 170 hs
Oud Zuid
Map p.383 F1 229

Hairstyling Adri

020 400 43 61

For a great cut or if you just need a little pampering and want an expert to wash, dry and style your hair for a special occasion, this lovely new salon conveniently located at the tram stop by the trendy Cornelis Schuytstraat shopping street is the place to go.

The talented owner Adri and skilled hairdresser Alex will tame your wild tresses and have you looking sleek and glam and ready for a little retail therapy at one of the fab boutiques on the Cornelis Schuytstraat. This friendly salon is popular in the neighbourhood with women, men and children. Standard prices for a wash, cut and blowdry for women are between €47 and €60 (depending on the hair length), €37.50 for men, and €25 for children. A wash and blow dry costs between €27.50 and €33.50. Call first for an appointment.

Elandsgracht 68
Jordaan
Map p.392 B1 230

Rob Peetoom Hair & Makeup

020 528 57 22 | *www.robpeetoom.nl*

Dutch salon chain owner Rob Peetoom has built a successful hairdressing empire with nine locations across the Netherlands and an additional two in Amsterdam at Elandsgracht 68 and the department store de Bijenkorf (p.289). He offers his clients a professional cut, colour or makeup within a beautiful, aesthetically designed, contemporary interior. Prices vary from €43 to €73, depending on the experience of the hairdresser. Athough they have a large number of employees in their salons it's still best to call in advance for an appointment.

Minervalaan 30
Oud Zuid
Map p.383 F2 231

Scalp Studio

020 673 35 82

This is one hairdressing salon you can trust completely with your precious tresses. Their aim is to have you walking out feeling drop-dead gorgeous and they succeed! The name Scalp stands for 'Scientific, Creative, Artistic, Launched Professionals' and anyone who's been to them once can vouch for it. They have a loyal clientele due to the high quality of their precision haircuts and colour expertise. The new studio has a modern, contemporary feel in clean black and white.

Prinsengracht 489
Canal Belt
(Grachtengordel)
Map p.392 C1 232

Shampoo Planet

020 420 64 12 | *www.shampooplanet.nl*

Trendy, hip Shampoo Planet is a popular hair salon in the centre of town. Situated on the Prinsengracht, this sleek, white modern salon has five immensely talented hairdressers (two are native English speakers) whose clients have been going to them faithfully for years. It might be difficult to get an appointment but all the hairdressers come very highly recommended, so if they can squeeze you in you should go give them a try. A wash, cut and blow dry for men and women is €43.50, and highlights start at €40 upwards.

Europaplein 77
Rivierenbuurt
Map p.384 C3 233

Simcha's for Hair

020 675 29 75

This cosy, unassuming salon located right across from the RAI conference centre is 'Holland's Best Kept Secret'. Royals, celebrities, locals and conference visitors all soon become regulars at this friendly, relaxed salon. A wash, cut and blow dry for women is €42.50 and for men €32.50. The superb skills and discreet manner of the staff are what make guests feel special and at ease. There are regular fashion shows and also a beauty salon in the shop.

Health Spas

Other options **Beauty Salons** p.240, **Massage** p.244

Health spas in general are a popular luxury getaway in the Netherlands, with many people enjoying a weekend retreat at an out of town spa. There are numerous health spas to choose from along the coast and also inland, with the Newport

Health & Spa in Huizen being one of the closest and most popular with people from Amsterdam. In the city itself, luxurious day spas with a vast array of treatments have recently begun to crop up – ideal for yourself or to give as a gift to someone special.

AVEDA Dayspa

Laan der Hesperiden 90
Oud Zuid
Map p.383 E3 234

AVEDA Dayspa

020 794 93 66 | www.dayspa.nl

The new AVEDA Dayspa is an oasis of tranquillity and a haven for the mind, body and spirit. Not only is this spa aesthetically beautiful with its airy, light foyer, but the friendly, highly trained staff put you in a serene state of mind from the moment you enter. Using natural products, it offers nurturing treatments for the entire body based on AVEDA's Elemental Nature philosophy. It draws from ancient plant-based healing traditions to balance five elements: infinity, air, fire, water and earth. There is a complete range of personalised treatments for the entire body.

Zaanstraat 88
Westerpark
Map p.374 A4 235

Hammam

020 681 48 18 | www.hammamamsterdam.nl

In this traditional bathhouse, women of all nationalities and cultures are welcome. In the bathing sections there are areas with different temperatures and in one of the rooms is a Turkish steam bath. There are two rooms where you can rejuvenate after bathing, a place to enjoy snacks and refreshments and other areas where you can enjoy massages or use a sunbed. The basic treatment which includes entry, soaping, scrubbing and mud pack costs only €25. Entry is €15 for those over 12 years.

Labradorstroom 75
Huizen
Map p.365 B3

Newport Health & Spa

035 523 33 04 | www.newport-health-spa.nl

Newport Health and Spa is a relaxing getaway located approximately 40 minutes south-east of Amsterdam by car in the Hotel Newport near the Gooimeer in Huizen. They offer a peaceful environment in their minimalist, luxury spa created in accordance with the principles of Feng Shui. The treatments are derived from Ayurveda, an ancient Indian philosophy based on the balance between body and soul. The spa facilities include health food bar, terrace on the harbour, solarium, steam room, whirlpool, health club and much more. A half-day spa arrangement will cost €110 and a full day is €189. Reservations are advised at least three weeks in advance even if you are staying at the Hotel Newport.

Herengracht 115
Canal Belt (Grachtengordel)
Map p.p.389 B3 237

Sauna Deco

020 623 82 15 | www.saunadeco.nl

This old-fashioned Art Deco mixed sauna, famous for its furnishings, is situated right in the heart of Amsterdam. It boasts two saunas, a Turkish steam bath, a cold water immersion pool with jet stream, hydro-massage, a tanning booth and an outdoor terrace. They provide light meals and beverages and also various beauty treatments at the beauty salon, Salon Deco (020 330 35 65). A full day beauty arrangement for €115 includes robe and towels, coffee or tea, basic facial treatment, sauna facilities, 25 minute massage and also lunch.

Sento Spa & Health Club

Marnixplein 1
Jordaan
Map p.388 B3 238

020 330 14 44 | www.sento.nl

Newly opened Sento Spa and Health Club is an exclusive addition to Amsterdam's urban surroundings. With its stunning, contemporary Japanese interior and ultramodern facilities, it's a great way of enjoying a day of pampering in the city centre. The spa offers a variety of day treatments which last four hours and include lunch, priced between €85 and €139 per person. You can choose between different combinations or separate treatments such as relaxing facials, hydro-massage, floating, hot stone massage and an array of other sublime experiences. There is also a rooftop terrace and swimming pool.

Massage

Other options **Leisure Facilities** p.237, **Health Spas** p.242

Having a massage might seem like an expensive luxury, but it's one of the easiest ways of achieving and maintaining health and well-being. It is rapidly becoming the number one treatment requested in spas, as many people use massage to unwind after a stressful day. It can also help prevent future health problems caused by tension, stress, poor posture and a common ailment nowadays for computer workers – RSI (repetitive strain injury). Endless assortments of massages are available, from shiatsu, foot reflexology and rebalancing, to floating and hot stone treatments. Some massage parlours are situated in luxury health and day spas, but others can be found in beauty salons, hammams and independent massage studios. Be prepared to pay between €50 and €80 for a 60 minute session.

Corpus Rub

Van Breestraat 72
Oud Zuid
Map p.383 F1 239

020 416 50 55 | www.corpus-rub.com

Corpus Rub is an elegant and inviting massage studio with black walls, soft, white furnishings and waxed wooden floors. As you're being massaged in the light, private, garden-facing room upstairs, lie back and listen to soft, soothing lounge music, while rain pattters on the skylight above. The studio also offers two massage rooms downstairs with a candle-lit, peaceful, subdued ambience. A 60 minute massage is €57, but you can also go for the ultimate – 90 minutes for €80.

doctor feelgood

Czaar Peterstraat 116
Zeeburg
Map p.380 A3 240

020 620 15 70 | www.doctorfeelgood.nl

Esther van der Plas, a licensed and certified massage therapist from New Mexico, USA has just opened her bright and cheerful massage store 'doctor feelgood' in Czaar Peterstraat. You can kick back and unwind in this cosy, intimate little store with its clean, calm, white and grey, stylish interior. Esther is much in demand after years of experience working with bands and celebrities from all over the world. She offers top quality therapeutic massage using natural products, aromatherapy, and hot or cold mud packs with every customised treatment. A unique highlight is her top-of-the line American massage table, where pregnant women can also fully relax and enjoy a massage on their stomachs. Don't forget to check out the thank you notes from celebrities, you might be surprised who was lying on the table just before you – maybe Bruce Springsteen, Sinead O'Connor or Hugh Grant!

The Health Company

Cornelis Schuytstraat 48
Oud Zuid
Map p.383 F1 241

020 471 07 56

The Health Company is a quaint, small shop known for its wonderful natural cosmetics, food supplements, books, aromatic candles and beautiful gifts. It now also offers various types of revitalising massage and energy therapy in the cosy little house in the back garden. On offer are bio-dynamic massages, Ayurvedic consultations and aura-soma colour therapy. A new complementary healing evaluation therapy called NES (Nutri-Energetics Systems) can scan for bodily imbalances.

Herengracht 321
Canal Belt (Grachtengordel)
Map p.392 C1 242

Koan Float Centre

020 555 03 33 | www.koan-float.com

Koan Float Centre offers a unique method of relaxation: floating on a bed of water in a womb-like, soundproof fibreglass capsule complete with light, mood music and two-way intercom. To complement your floating session you can further de-stress with one of their many massages, from relaxation massage and shiatsu, to foot reflexology and rebalancing. A 60 minute float costs €37.50 and 60 minute massage €47.50. If you take a combination of the two it will only cost you €82.50.

Meditation

As our lives become busier and more hectic with the stresses of daily life, many people are turning to meditation as a method of deep relaxation and stress management. By providing basic meditation skills such as how to breathe correctly and focus and clear the mind, meditation classes are a way to gain self-awareness and a better understanding of our true nature. Amsterdam has a number of centres that offer a variety of guided meditation courses, workshops and weekend retreats, and there is plenty of teaching available in English. Some offer classes free and rely on donations, whereas others charge a minimal amount per class.

Haarlemmerdijk 137
Jordaan
Map p.389 B2 243

Brahma Kumaris Spirituele Akademie

020 624 02 05 | www.bksa.org

A branch of the Brahma Kumaris World Spiritual University (www.bkwsu.com), an international organisation founded in India with over 7000 centres in 103 countries. Leave the busy Haarlemmerdijk and enter an oasis of serenity and peace in the centre of Amsterdam. In this calm sanctuary Raja Yoga meditation is taught, which aids your spiritual awareness. Classes are free, but donations are always appreciated and there's never any pressure. Contact the centre for a course schedule and programmes.

Centrum De Roos, P.C. Hooftstraat 183
Oud Zuid
Map p.392 B4 244

Expanding Minds

06 12 366956 | www.expandingminds.nl

Gisele Burnett gives weekly meditation classes in English at Centrum De Roos in the Vondelpark. Gisele's method of teaching is practical and grounded; she uses a western approach to what many consider an eastern practise. Her classes offer a peaceful, supportive environment for weekly meditation and reflection. Classes are held every Wednesday evening from 18:30 to 20:00 and 20:30 to 21:30, and cost €10 per class.

Brouwersgracht 157-159
Jordaan
Map p.388 C1 245

Maitreya Instituut

020 428 08 42 | www.maitreya.nl

The Maitreya Instituut is open to anyone who is interested in learning about Tibetan Buddhism and meditation. The coordinator of its Amsterdam branch teaches group classes in English to those who would like to learn to meditate as well as people who would like to further their meditation skills. The institute also offers weekend courses and other activities. Meditation classes are €2.50 per class and €22.50 for a 10 class series. See the website for the programme and course schedule.

Vondelpark
Oud Zuid
Map p.383 E1 246

Osho Laughing Meditation

020 610 43 80 | www.mysterieschool.nl

Cycle past a group of people lying on the ground in the Vondelpark, laughing and chuckling out loud, and you'd be forgiven for thinking they'd been indulging in mind-altering substances. Not so, this is a class in laughter meditation. Laughing is one of the few activities we do that involves the mind, body and soul, which makes it a natural stressbuster. When we laugh our bodies release a mixture of hormones and chemicals that have positive effects on our system. Blood pressure drops, stress levels are lowered, mood is improved and the immune system is raised. Classes run from May to September.

St Pieterspoortsteeg 29-1
Centrum
Map p.393 E1 247

Sangha Metta Meditatie Centrum

020 626 49 84 | www.xs4all.nl/~gotama

Sangha Metta means 'network of loving kindness' and this centre is devoted to those who want to practise awareness through meditation. Vipassana (or insight meditation) is said to teach you to look at your experiences with a clear mind, directly and without prejudice. The centre offers guided meditation on Monday and Wednesday evenings from 18:00 to 20:00 and on Thursdays from 18:00 to 19:30. There is no need to apply in advance and the class is given on the basis of donations only. It also offers meditation days and weekend retreats, which require reservations by phone or email.

Pilates

Other options **Yoga** p.298

Pilates is the fitness craze of the moment in the Netherlands and it's attracting people of all ages, fitness levels and body types. It's an exercise method for the entire body that focuses on breathing, strength and flexibility. It's a form of body conditioning that strengthens ligaments and joints; it also increases flexibility and coordination. The main aim of Pilates is to strengthen the back, which supports the rest of the body. Pilates is suitable for everyone because it's designed to match an individual's capabilities, making it safe for all age groups, including children and older people. In Amsterdam, Pilates is extremely popular and classes can be found in Pilates studios and most gyms. Private classes in your own home are also possible. Many Pilates studios offer both the use of studio equipment and mat classes. A one-hour private Pilates session, depending on whether it takes place in a studio or your home, will cost on average €40 to €60; a class for three will set you each back around €20 to €30 per hour.

Eerste Helmersstraat 123/III
Oud West
Map p.379 F4 250

Miss Jones Movement Practice

020 616 61 82 | www.sophiejones.nl

The Miss Jones Movement Practice is a personal training practice based on the principles and forms of Pilates, yoga, aikido and dance. Sophie Jones, who trained in competitive athletics, has been working as a personal trainer since 1993. In a private attic studio, using Pilates studio equipment and yoga techniques, her sessions offer a specific focus on body awareness, breathing, meditation and relaxation. She will conduct personal training or group work. It costs €60 for an hour and you need to phone or email to book an appointment.

Joos Banckersweg 11/1
Geuzenveld
Map p.379 D2 251

Pilates Amsterdam

06 28 932706 | www.pilatesamsterdam.nl

Pilates Amsterdam is a studio that offers only private Pilates sessions. Certified Pilates instructor Jennifer Hartnett believes that 'private sessions in a relaxed and personal atmosphere are the best way to learn, practice and perfect the Pilates Technique'. Her sessions are designed to suit a person's individual needs. A one-hour studio session will cost €40 and a lesson in the privacy of your own home €55. You can also arrange 10 one-hour sessions in the studio for €350 (paid in advance).

Borneokade 183
Zeeburg
Map p.380 B3 252

Pilates for everyBody

020 695 07 27 | *http://home.planet.nl/~helms056/*

The Pilates for everyBody studio opened its doors in 2002, founded by a teacher who has experience tutoring Pilates in both London and America. She offers mat classes, will get you using studio equipment, and gives you enthusiastic instruction. She provides various classes for beginners and intermediate students as well as workshops. Her private lessons cost €60, with reduced prices if you're a trio or quartet.

Molenpad 15-1
Canal Belt
(Grachtengordel)
Map p.392 C2 253

Smartbody

06 48 270752 | *www.smartbodystudio.com*

Founder and Director Jelena Petrovic opened this bright and spacious studio in 2006. Specialising in high quality Pilates instruction for individuals and small groups, a variety of classes are on offer, from beginner to advanced, and also private and group lessons. The group class sizes average around seven students and are split into four levels of difficulty. Beginners are encouraged to sign up for 'Introduction to Pilates', a three-week course covering the basics of Pilates. There is a new class just for men which has been specifically tailored to the male physique. It's limited to only five students, so sign up quickly.

Reiki

Reiki is a Japanese form of healing similar to faith healing. It is basically the 'laying on of hands', an ancient technique common to many spiritual traditions. Reiki practitioners say energy (Reiki translated means 'light force energy') flows through their palms to promote healing when placed above certain areas of your body. It is used to balance the body and heal a number of conditions, whether physical, emotional or mental, and is also used for deep relaxation and replenishing energy levels. Reiki can be found in Reiki centres and some massage studios offering various types of holistic therapies.

Nieuwe Spiegelstraat 11b
Canal Belt
(Grachtengordel)
Map p.393 D3 254

Aromatique Amsterdam

020 624 00 44 | *www.aromatique.nl*

Located in the charming antique shopping street Nieuwe Spiegelstraat (behind the Rijksmuseum) you'll find Aromatique Amsterdam, an exceptional shop that provides holistic body work treatments, Reiki, reflexology, aromatherapy facials and therapeutic massages. A 30 minute Reiki appointment will cost €30 and is the ideal treatment for first time or sensitive clients. You can also choose gorgeous, fragrant gifts from their luxurious range of aromatherapy products.

Prinsengracht 851
Canal Belt
(Grachtengordel)
Map p.393 D3 255

Reiki Centrum Amsterdam

020 623 87 48 | *www.reikicentrum-amsterdam.nl*

The Reiki Centrum Amsterdam is situated in the centre of town and offers the choice of either having a healing Reiki treatment for €50 (70 minutes) or taking lessons in Reiki. Reiki Master Ruth Segal teaches a two-day course of first degree Reiki instruction. On an individual basis this costs €175 (which includes a 70 minute treatment and two lunches). A second degree course of one day is also possible for €500, including one or two days of practise, if necessary. A certificate is awarded to those who complete the courses successfully. See the website for course details.

Tai Chi

Tai Chi is considered a gentle or internal form of Chinese martial art. It is a series of slow, graceful movements that can improve balance, increase flexibility, lower stress and increase energy and feelings of well-being. Because it is a low-impact type of exercise and does not put pressure on the joints, many older people also enjoy its benefits. Tai Chi classes can be found in studios, but are often held in parks.

Lijnbaansgracht 166
Jordaan
Map p.392 B1 256

ITCCA School Martin Klett

020 423 44 60 | www.itcca.nl

The ITCCA School in Amsterdam is a branch of the International Tai Chi Chuan Association, represented in seven countries in Europe. It teaches the authentic Yang style of Tai Chi Chuan, passed down from the Yang family. The school offers a free introductory lesson and a beginners' course lasts ten sessions. The course costs around €159 including membership of the ITCCA. After the beginners' course is completed, the monthly fee for practice lessons is €45. The membership fee for the ITCCA is €30 per year.

Kerkstraat 441
Canal Belt (Grachtengordel)
Map p.393 D3 257

The School of Tai Chi Chuan

020 625 96 66 | www.taichichuan.nl

The STCC Amsterdam has been in existence for 26 years and is part of an international Tai Chi Chuan organisation that has locations in more than 30 cities worldwide. Classes are taught in groups with two or more instructors in a class, giving students one teacher to follow and leaving one teacher free to observe and give instructions. They offer beginner to intermediate classes and also a week-long Kids' Camp held in Limburg during the summer holiday (see website for details). A beginner's class is €95 for 10 sessions.

Quinten Massijsstraat 22
Oud Zuid
Map p.384 A3 258

Tai Chi Ad Lakerveld

020 673 44 91 | www.lakerveld.org

Ad Lakerveld, an experienced and popular teacher of Tai Chi has been practising since 1980 and teaching for more than 12 years. Ad provides Tai Chi group lessons at his home address and at an indoor hall at Gerrit van der Veen College. A Tai Chi introduction course is held on Monday evenings from 20:00 to 21:00. You can join these lessons at any time during the course, just call or email to register. Private lessons are also available for one to two people. Professional corporate workshops are available.

Jacob Obrechtstraat 92
Oud Zuid
Map p.384 A2 259

Tai Chi School – Tai Yang

020 623 08 35 | www.taiyang.nl

Fazil Bacchus is a member of The World Taiji Boxing Association (WTBA). He is a highly trained and accomplished instructor. Fazil teaches two forms from the Yang Style Tai Chi, but has also studied the Chen style (competition routine). He gives lessons near the Concertgebouw in Oud Zuid (and the Vondelpark in good weather) and also in De Boomspijker, near the Nieuwmarkt in town. If you're a newcomer to Tai Chi you can drop by and have a look at one of his introduction lessons and get a feel for the class. He provides weekly classes (beginners are welcome). Sessions are in blocks of 10 and these cost €100. Corporate workshops and private training are €60 for a one-hour lesson. To find the class that best suits your needs, please check the schedule on the website.

Yoga

Other options **Pilates** p.246

There are a number of highly-skilled yoga instructors available in Amsterdam teaching various forms of yoga in private studios, community centres, yoga centres, health clubs and even corporate yoga in the workplace. Prices cost on average between €100 and €120 for 10 classes, or between €12 and €16 for a single lesson in a studio.

Asanaworks

Prinsengracht 512
Canal Belt (Grachtengordel)
Map p.392 C3 **260**

06 48 373262

Never feel like you have time to get to the gym after work? Well, kiss those days goodbye – now the class comes to you! Asanaworks offers a unique service to corporations who would like to bring well-being to the workplace by offering on-site yoga classes. It provides companies and their staff with high-quality yoga courses by fully trained yoga instructors. The instructors come to you so you can offer your staff the benefits of yoga while saving their time and energy. The classes can be very energising and stress-relieving at the same time, which can help employees relax and focus better.

Bikram Yoga Amsterdam

Ceintuurbaan 426
De Pijp
Map p.385 D1 **261**

020 676 70 33 | www.bikramyoga.nl

Increasing in popularity, Bikram Yoga (the hot yoga) is catching more and more devotees. Sweating through 26 yoga postures in hot rooms for a full-on 90 minute workout has a huge number of fans. One Bikram instructor puts it simply: 'You stretch, you strengthen, you get your heart rate up, you let go of stress, and you do it all in one session'. Classes are taught daily at the studio, with changing rooms, showers and a large back garden for students to enjoy in the warmer months. Classes cost €110 for 10 sessions.

Shirley Woods

Innerspace, Elandsgracht 105
Jordaan
Map p.388 B1 **262**

020 682 72 02 | www.yogapractice.nl

Shirley Woods teaches Astanga and Vijnana Yoga from beginner to intermediate levels in English and Dutch. Classes are held in the serene and intimate atmosphere of Innerspace, a centre for yoga and meditation situated in the Jordaan. She offers various types of yoga classes throughout the week, so it's best to check the schedule on her website for details. The price for a six week beginners' course is €78 and single lessons are also available for €16 per session.

The Yoga Community of Amsterdam

ABC Treehouse, Voetboogstraat 11
Centrum
Map p.393 D1 **263**

06 51 764621 | http://yoga108.org/pages/show/60

Susan Nicolas is a certified Sivananda yoga teacher and founder of The Yoga Community of Amsterdam. She has taught and practised yoga throughout America and the Bahamas, but is now settled in Amsterdam and teaches weekly Hatha yoga classes at the ABC Treehouse, as well as organising courses, retreats and workshops. Course schedules are posted on the website. Classes are €100 for a 10 lesson card or €12 for one lesson.

Yoga for Women with Ajit Kaur Sandhu

Claverhuis Elandsgracht 70
Jordaan
Map p.392 B1 **264**

020 679 87 53 | www.britsoc.nl

Ajit, a highly skilled yoga teacher, has created these classes specifically for women, as they deal mainly with women's health issues and stress management. In addition to Hatha yoga postures he puts great emphasis on improving breathing technique (Ajit is a qualified respiration therapist), learning natural ways of relaxation, and different methods of meditation and visualisation. Ajit is also an experienced healer and Reiki Master.

Yogayoga

Amaliastraat 5
Westerpark
Map p.388 A2 **265**

020 688 34 18 | www.yogayoga.nl

Sandra Kirchner and Leo Peppas, both gifted instructors with over 25 year's teaching experience between them, founded this studio in 2002. Classes are taught in Hatha yoga, the most widely known form of yoga in the west. Lessons take place in a quiet studio offering 25 classes a week, in both English and Dutch. They offer Sunday workshops, pre and postnatal yoga, private classes, and yoga for kids and teens – from 4 to 15 (in Dutch). Prices for all classes can be found on the website, but for adults it's €100 for 10 lessons.

Shopping

Shopping

Shopping in Amsterdam offers something for everyone, from the top fashion names located on the P.C. Hooftstraat to the high street chains on the Kalverstraat; from the small independent boutiques nestled in the Jordaan, to the long Albert Cuypstraat Markt, where fresh produce, household goods and textiles are all brought together in a vibrant mix of scent, sound and colour.

Prices compare well with other European cities, are cheaper than many American destinations, and just above those in Hong Kong. There is a sales tax called BTW (omzet belasting), which is usually 19%, and sometimes 6% (for consumer basics and items such as flowers and books). Many centrally located shops offer tax-free shopping to visitors from non-EU countries; look out for the sign on the shop front.

In general Amsterdam shopping is affordable and enjoyable. Sales assistants can be a bit distant unless you ask for help, but you won't be pushed into a purchase. The main annual sales start just after the Sinterklaas celebrations on 5 December, and the summer sales start in June. In the clothing sector, most shops have a quick turnover through the season collections, and many products are marked down within a few weeks of coming on the shelves. Look out for the racks marked 'uitverkoopl', 'korting' and 'kopje', or shops that offer 'kassa korting%' on selected items.

Be aware that car parks in Centrum are overflowing on busy days. It's easier to take your bike, or public transport. There are some excellent shopping centres with parking facilities on the outskirts; Boven t'Y Winkelcentrum is a mix of high street shops, open air market, and supermarkets. Woonmall Villa Arena and, next to it, ArenA Boulevard are centres for electronics, furniture and much more.

Whether tourist or resident, some items are unique to Amsterdam. The city is the centre of the diamond trade and you can buy jewellery or loose stones from one of many factories demonstrating diamond cutting. Amsterdam's wealth also came from the tulip trade; tulip bulbs and a myriad of other plants are available all year in the flower market on the Singel. Souvenir shops all over the city offer the famous Delft blue china for a few euros, but for the real thing go to the Spiegelkwartier and browse around the many specialist antique shops there.

District Guide

We've included an Amsterdam district by each entry in this section to help you locate the shops, malls and markets. The map on p.368 shows which area of town each district covers.

Online Shopping

Online shops (webwinkels) are popular in the Netherlands. The comforts of shopping from your armchair and home delivery as well as good consumer protection laws make it a logical choice for many. You can source most products online, from

Clothing Sizes

Women's Clothing							Women's Shoes						
Aust/NZ	8	10	12	14	16	18	Aust/NZ	5	6	7	8	9	10
Europe	36	38	40	42	44	46	Europe	35	36	37	38	39	40
Japan	5	7	9	11	13	15	France only	35	36	38	39	40	42
UK	8	10	12	14	16	18	Japan	22	23	24	25	26	27
USA	6	8	10	12	14	16	UK	3.5	4.5	5.5	6.5	7.5	8.5
							USA	5	6	7	8	9	10
Men's Clothing							**Men's Shoes**						
Aust/NZ	92	96	100	104	108	112	Aust/NZ	7	8	9	10	11	12
Europe	46	48	50	52	54	56	Europe	41	42	43	44.5	46	47
Japan	S	-	M	M	-	L	Japan	26	27	27.5	28	29	30
UK	35	36	37	38	39	40	UK	7	8	9	10	11	12
USA	35	36	37	38	39	40	USA	7.5	8.5	9.5	10.5	11.5	12.5

Measurements are approximate only; try before you buy

Online Shopping

Cosmetics	www.lush.nl
Department store	www.wehkamp.nl
Electronics and home appliances	www.bestsellers.nl
Flower delivery	www.interflora.nl
Online search site, for price/product comparison	www.beslist.nl
Photo developing service, department store	www.hema.nl
Supermarket	www.albert.nl
Takeaway food, links to local restaurants	www.thuisbezorgd.nl

computer equipment, to furniture, to takeaway food. One national supermarket chain, Albert Heijn (p.296), has an online shopping service which promises to deliver to your kitchen. Its registration process is simple, and part of its website is in English.

There are several ways to pay for goods ordered over the internet: credit card, using iDEAL (the online payment system via your Netherlands bank account), cash on delivery (rebours), Paypal, or payment using an Acceptgiro once you receive the goods.

It is usual for a delivery fee to be charged and many online shopping sites have the facility to bill to one address and ship to another. Most sites will also advise what shipping method is being used (courier or post) and offer the option to track and trace your package.

If ordering something from outside of the Netherlands, you will be liable to customs duties unless the item is under €22. There are also some goods that cannot be imported because they are forbidden or they require an import licence (see p.254). Full details can be obtained in English on the Netherlands tax and customs website: www.douane.nl/english/internetpurchases.

Clothing Sizes

Why oh why do they make sizes different in Europe and the US? Never mind, figuring it out isn't rocket science. Firstly, check the label international sizes are often printed on there. Secondly, check the store – it will often have a helpful conversion chart on display. And finally, do the sums yourself: aUK size is always two higher than a US size (so a UK 8 is actually a US 6), and a European size is always 30 more than a US size (so a European 38 is actually a US 8).

Refunds & Exchanges

Most shops have a clear returns policy which is displayed by the cashier. To avoid problems always keep the receipt and try to return goods in the original packaging. CDs, DVDs and video tapes which are no longer sealed will not be accepted. HEMA (p.290), with branches all over the Netherlands, has a very sympathetic returns service, and any branch will exchange an item even if bought at another location.

Most outlets will offer to exchange your unwanted item, but a shopkeeper is not obliged to give you your cash back - you may be offered other goods to the value of the item you are returning. In some stores items bought at reduced price will not be exchanged, but in the case of a faulty item you should be able to get a refund.

Shopping over the internet gives you more rights as you are not able to see the item before purchasing, so returning something because it is the wrong size, colour or quality is accepted. There is a cooling off period for internet sales, and you have seven working days s to cancel the sale after you receive the product if you do not want it. Wehkamp has a good returns policy and will pick up an unwanted article and replace it within 24 hours.

There are some exceptions to the internet cooling off period: fresh food, products with a time limit such as concert tickets, personally tailored items, travel, financial services, and, again, CDs DVDs and video tapes which are no longer sealed are usually not eligible.

Consumer Rights

As a consumer your contract is with the shop even if the item has a factory guarantee so make sure you have proof of purchase. If you make an arrangement with the salesperson, for instance the delivery date or time, make sure it is written on the receipt. Do not delay in letting the shop know if an item is faulty, or a delivery is not complete. If you are not satisfied with the shop's response there is an independent mediating body, www.geschillencommissie.nl, which can be called upon to settle disputes.

Before it comes to that, however, you can get a lot of information about your consumer rights on the website www.consuwijzer.nl, although this is in Dutch. Free legal advice is available by phone at the Rechtswinkel Amsterdam (020 673 13 11, www.rechtswinkelamsterdam.nl).

Prohibited Imports

Child pornography, weapons or ammunition, medicine, drugs, endangered plants or animals, meat products, plants and flowers, counterfeit/knock-off goods, goods that may be used to manufacture drugs (precursors), cultural goods, fireworks of any kind, substances that deplete the ozone layer, substances containing cadmium.

Shipping

Shipping within the Netherlands is often offered by big both chains and small independents; some have no charge, but it's always wise to ask. If you want to send a purchase overseas, companies with international franchises, such as Lush and Interflora, will do it for a small fee. Metz & Co (p.290) offers a sales tax-free shipping service to non-EU destinations. You can get most items from suppliers in the Netherlands, but if you are sourcing from abroad think of the shipping costs. It may be cheaper to buy books from Amazon UK than Amazon in the US, for instance, although prices of the items might vary. The national post service is fairly efficient and by far the cheapest way of sending gifts home. Couriers such as DHL and FedEx have offices throughout the city and have pick-up services available but cost significantly more. A Netherlands speciality is tulips, and the shops in Amsterdam's flower market usually arrange to ship bulbs globally so they arrive in the autumn, the perfect time for planting.

Bargaining

Bargaining is not a common practice when shopping in the Netherlands. Stores should clearly mark prices on all items. There are exceptions, however. Sales professionals have a margin for negotiation when selling items such as cars or boats, and if you are kitting out your kitchen with electrical appliances, try getting them all from one outlet and discuss discounts.

If you feel the need to practise your bargaining skills, try second-hand markets or shops. Alternatively go along late in the day to food markets, as traders will often cut prices to offload surplus goods. In the end it's a case of 'nothing ventured, nothing gained' - but be prepared for a politely worded, firm refusal.

How to Pay

The Netherlands is a member of the European Monetary Union and uses the euro. It is rare that any shop in Amsterdam would accept another currency for a cash payment. If you have a Netherlands bank account you will be able to use the PIN or chip facility in many shops. The PIN system debits your bank account when you enter a personal identification number into a machine attached to the cash register. The chip system is handy for small purchases, and acts like an electronic purse, which you load at your bank. Credit cards are accepted, but not all cards in all shops; IKEA accepts Visa but not MasterCard, for instance. It is not possible to pay for groceries at the supermarket with your credit card. Some stores have their own credit cards which offer customers extra advantages. Market stalls are normally cash only, but exceptions are found in markets aimed at the tourist trade, which may accept credit cards.

What & Where To Buy – Quick Reference

Beer kegs

Alcohol

Other options **Drinks** p.306, **On the Town** p.340

Alcohol is part of Dutch life, and is freely available in supermarkets and off licences. The only restrictions to buying alcohol are age; children under 16 cannot buy any alcohol, and if an item has an alcohol content of more than 15% of the volume, they must be over 18 years of age.

All supermarkets stock wines and beer, while spirits are usually sold in a separate off licence section. Expect to pay around €3.60 for a six pack of Heineken lager, a cheap bottle of white wine retails from about €2.20 to €5, and a 70ml bottle of vodka is approximately €15.50. You get slightly better prices at Schiphol Airport (p.34), but there's not much in it. Check out its shopping section for special offers at www.schiphol.nl.

The biggest chain of off licences is Gall & Gall (p.234), which has outlets over the whole of Netherlands. It is also possible to order online from Gall & Gall using the Albert Heijn online shopping service (www.albert.nl).

If you are looking for discounts on wine, try Aldi or Makro in Hypermarkets on p.290. On the other hand, there are some great wine dealers in Amsterdam which can source excellent bottles, and their staff are quite knowledgeable. Try Chabrol Wines (www.chabrol.nl), which also organises a wine course and wine tastings for groups. Wine dealer B.J. de Logie sells wine and spirits for consumption or investment. It also has an internet service (www.delogiedirect.nl).

Jenever is to the Dutch what whisky is to the Scots – if you're looking for a typical souvenir or are just curious about this part of Dutch culture go to Dranken Kado Shop de Vreng (www.oudamsterdam.nl). You can taste the different jenevers before you buy, and the staff are well informed about the product.

Alcohol		
Aldi	Various Locations	See p.290
B.J. de Logie	Beethovenstraat 27	020 662 62 08
Chabrol Wines	Haarlemmerstraat 7	020 622 27 81
Dranken Kado Shop de Vreng	Nieuwendijk 75	020 624 45 81
Gall & Gall	Various Locations	See p.234
Makro	De Flinesstraat 9	0900 202 5300

Art

Other options **Art & Craft Supplies** p.256, **Art Classes** p.186, **Art Galleries** p.148, **Markets** p.291

To get a flavour of Dutch contemporary art go to Arti Amicitiae on the Rokin, a prestigious art society established in 1834 which currently has 500 members. Each June, the society exhibits the new members' high-tech art installations, sculptures and paintings. All of the art is for sale and most of the artists accept commissions.

For serious art collectors the international auction houses Sotheby's and Christie's are both represented, and there are galleries and exhibitions all over the city. For example, stroll down Nieuwe Spiegelstraat and check out the Jaski Art Gallery (www.jaski.nl), Gertrude D galleries, or wander through the Negen Straatjes. For sculpture visit De Beeldenwinkel on Berenstraat, art dealer Rarekiek on Runstraat, or Varekamp on Hartenstraat.

Art		
Art Cash and Carry	Various Locations	See p.299
Arti Amicitiae	Rokin 112	020 623 35 08
Christie's	Cornelis Schuytstraat 57	020 575 52 55
De Beeldenwinkel	Berenstraat 29	020 676 49 03
Gertrude D Galleries	Nieuwe Spiegelstraat 33	020 624 76 81
Jaski Art Gallery	Nieuwe Spiegelstraat 29	020 620 39 39
Kunst Uitleen SKB	See below	na
Rarekiek	Runstraat 31	na
Sotheby's	De Boelelaan 30	020 550 22 00
Timeless Kunstuitleen	Rembrandtweg 152	020 640 60 70
Varekamp	Hartenstraat 30	na

Affordable art is to be found at Art Cash & Carry, with paintings from €25 to €1,000. There are two shops, one on the Westerstraat, and one at Woonmall Villa Arena. Alternatively, visit one of the weekly art markets in the city such as Torbecke Plein or Spui Square (p.292), both on a Sunday. Another interesting option is Kunst Uitleen (www.sbk.nl/kunstuitleen/vestigingen) where you can rent a painting from a collection for monthly payments. It works a bit like a book lending library but has paintings by Dutch artists. The paintings can be seen in the Uitleen shops, or viewed on the internet. You subscribe to the 'library', make your choice, and either pick it up, or have it delivered to you. It is an excellent solution if you want a larger painting as a focal point in the room, and if you feel like a change, just send it back and pick another one. For other options, see Spiegelkwartier in Streets/Areas to Shop on p.289.

Art & Craft Supplies

Other options **Art Classes** p.186, **Art** p.255, **Art Galleries** p.148

Whether a watercolour artist, a sculptor or scrap-booker you will find everything you need for your hobby in Amsterdam. Often basics can be found in the stationery departments of stores such as V&D (p.301). A great supplier of all types of paint, artists' paper and canvases is Cor Niekel Kunstschildermaterialen (www.corniekel.nl). It has a second shop which offers a quick framing service too. Vlieger (www.vliegerpapier.nl) is a specialist in office and art supplies, and has an incredible range of paper; artists' supplies are all housed on the first floor. De Hobbyshop Bricoleur (www.bricoleur.nl) is located in Amsterdam Noord and has a wide selection of art supplies and hobby materials for scrap-booking, designing greetings cards, soap stone carving, quilting and embroidery.

Art & Craft Supplies		
Cor Niekel Kunstschildermaterialen	Ceintuurbaan	020 672 24 98
De Hobbyshop Bricoleur	Ankerplaats 28	020 493 21 60
Quick Lijsten Lijstenmakerij	Ceintuurbaan 214	020 679 55 40
Vlieger	Amstel 34	020 623 58 34

Baby Items

Having a baby is cause for celebration and gives the opportunity to explore a whole new branch of consumerism. If you are new to parenthood, you will find a huge selection of everything you need, from baths to buggies, cuddly toys to complete baby rooms, at Prénatal (www.prenatal.nl), Maminette Baby Planet (www.babyplanet.nl) or Kids Factory Amsterdam (www.kidsfactory.nl). For those with even more money to spend, pretty specialist baby stores such as Koter & Co (www.koterenco.nl) or Sterre & Tijl (www.sterre-en-tijl.nl) are tempting. At the other end of the scale, HEMA (p.290) is a great standby for baby clothes

Baby Items		
Carla C	Blauwburgwal	020 627 36 44
Formes	Magna Plaza	020 638 91 52
HEMA	Various Locations	See p.300
Kids Factory	Ookermeerweg 404	020 610 24 90
Koter & Co	Scheldestraat 55-57	020 675 45 04
Kruidvat	Various Locations	See p.300
Maminette Baby Planet	Buikslotermeerplein 137	020 637 28 60
Prénatal	ArenA Boulevard 55	020 609 03 06
Sterre & Tijl	Beethovenstraat 5-a	020 379 22 92
V&D	Various Locations	See p.301

and accessories, and V&D (p.290) has a good range of baby items too. For the basics such as nappies, formula milk brands and baby food you will find what you need at your local supermarket, but check out branches of Etos (p.299) or Kruidvat (p.300), which sometimes have offers.
And let's not forget the expectant mother; Prénatal and Maminette both stock maternity clothing, but if you are looking for something special, go to Formes, in the Magna Plaza or the Carla C shop on Blauwburgwal in the Jordaan. This designer boutique has limited openings and it may be necessary to phone for an appointment.

Beachwear

Other options **Clothes** p.260, **Sports Goods** p.283

There is a huge selection of swimwear in many of the high street clothing stores in the early summer at very reasonable prices, but get there early as stocks dwindle towards the main summer holiday break. The lingerie store Hunkemöller (www.hunkemoller.nl) has several stores in Amsterdam and offers a great range of women's beachwear. It has an online shop too, with a handy returns service. HEMA (p.290) has a good selection for men and women (but no changing rooms), and is especially useful for children's swimwear; it has stock all year round, responding to the national practice of weekly swimming lessons. de Bijenkorf (p.289) will kit out the whole family at slightly higher prices. Decathlon (www.decathlon.nl) at the ArenA Boulevard has a full range of watersport equipment and swimwear for all the family, including maternity swimwear, wetsuits, snorkels, masks, and inflatable beach toys. Perry Sports, with one shop on ArenA Boulevard and two more in Centrum, also has a great range of swimwear (www.perrysport.nl). If you are into scubadiving (or want to get into it) you don't have to go further than Aqua Diving (www.aqua-diving.nl) for a great range of wet suits and diving paraphernalia.

Beachwear		
Aqua Diving	Haarlemmerstraat 165	020 622 35 03
de Bijenkorf	Dam 1	020 090 09 19
Decathlon	ArenA Boulevard 101	020 565 91 20
HEMA	Various Locations	See p.300
Hunkemoller	Various Locations	See p.300
Perry Sport	Various Locations	See p.300

Bicycles

The bicycle is very much part of Amsterdam culture and a near necessity within the city centre. Look closely, though, and you will see that most city bikes seem battered and uncared for, slightly old fashioned even. These are not racing bikes or mountain bikes, but standard Gazelle and Batavus models. To blend in with the crowd, select your Gazelle or Batavus city bike from one of the many bicycle dealers in Amsterdam. Kroonenberg Tweewielers or Bob Orange Bicycles are both centrally located and have good selections of new touring or mountain bikes and second-hand city bicycles; a new Batavus Flash City Bike should cost around €600. Their technicians will service and repair your bike, as will any good bike dealer in the city. In fact, should you get a puncture on the way to work, there will always be a nearby store that can repair it for you in time to pick it up on the way home.
From shops such as those mentioned above, you can get a reconditioned second-hand bike for about €300. If you would like something cheaper, there are bike dealers in Waterlooplein market; get there early in the day if you want to see a good selection.

Bicycles		
Bob Orange Bicycles	Weteringschans 195	020 421 87 54
Chopperdome Amsterdam	Admiraal de Ruyterweg	020 421 48 64
Halfords	Various Locations	See p.300
Kaptein Teewielers	Overtoom 488-490	020 612 64 93
Kroonenberg Tweewielers	Van Woustraat	020 671 64 66

Before you decide to go upmarket, make sure you have a safe place to store your bike and a really good set of locks. Wheel locks are available from €20, but are usually fitted as standard, and you will need an extra lock to fasten the bike to something solid. A good one will set you back about €120.

If you are looking for something a bit special, try Kaptein Tweewielers, which has a good selection of racing and mountain bikes. It runs Fiets Klinics for beginner racers. For a racing bike, prices start at around €720 but can run up to the thousands for a high-end model. For an eye-catching chopper bike go to the Chopperdome Amsterdam, where the colourful and cool bikes start at €400, but can cost as much as €4,000.

Once you've caught the cycling bug, having a child seat fitted front or back costs about €75 – most dealers stock these, or try Halfords, which offers a good range of accessories and new bikes for adults and children. If you feel you haven't the stamina to carry toddlers and the weekly shopping home, a cargo bike from Bob Orange cycles will set you back about €1,500 – money well spent.

Books

Other options **Books** (Further Reading, p.42), **Libraries** p.210

If you love books then the place to begin searching for your favourite author is the Spui. Not only are two of the best English bookshops located here, but there is also the prestigious Athenaeum bookshop which stages many Dutch literary events. The American Book Center supplies a wide range of American published books and press and has recently relocated to a beautiful four storey site at Spui 12. Waterstone's, also four storeys, is situated on the corner of Spui and Kalverstraat and stocks a great range of books and British press. The staff in both stores are very helpful, and both have efficient ordering systems if a book is not in stock.

Every Friday sees a book market on the Spui, a great place to go and people-watch or have a coffee on one of the terraces. Bargains are scarce but the real draw is the atmosphere. Round the corner on Koningsplein is Scheltema – the largest bookshop in Amsterdam with more than 125,000 books, as well as classical music CDs, computer

Amsterdam bookshops

Books

American Book Center	Spui 12	020 6250 55 37	www.abc.nl
Athenaeum	Spui 14	020 514 14 60	www.athenaeum.nl
De Slegte	Kalverstraat 48	020 622 59 33	www.deslegte.nl
Geografische Boekhandel Pied a Terre	Overtoom 135	020 612 23 14	www.jvw.nl
The English Bookshop	Lauriergracht 71	020 626 42 30	www.englishbookshop.nl
New English Bookstore	Various Locations	See p.300	na
Scheltema	Koningsplein 20	020 523 14 11	www.scheltema.nl
Waterstone's	Kalverstraat 152	020 638 38 21	www.waterstones.com

supplies and a coffee bar on the first floor. The English Bookshop in Jordaan is a lovely meeting place which hosts coffee mornings, story-telling events for children, and offers a good range of English books. One interesting find is Geografische Boekhandel, which is billed as the biggest travel bookshop in Europe with masses of guides and maps, including more of Explorer Publishing's guides. Sometimes however you just want to pick up a cheap paperback or something for the kids, and there are discount bookshops which fit the bill. De Slegte is located on Kalverstraat, and has many English books. The New English Bookstore also has a branch on Kalverstraat, and another store on Leidsestraat.

Camera Equipment

Other options **Electronics & Home Appliances** p.262

The advent of digital photography has revolutionised the medium, but there is still a need for specialised photography shops for both analogue and digital cameras. Electronic equipment prices in Europe never compare favourably with what may be available in Asia, but it's always a good idea to shop around in the city as some dealers may have offers on particular brands. Foto Solleveld (www.solleveld.com/foto) has two shops and supplies digital cameras and printers, offering a self-service print point (it also has an internet shop for online ordering). Henk Booms Foto + Electronicum (www.fotobooms.nl) also supplies everything for digital cameras and has a quick print shop. True enthusiasts should go to Foto Den Boer (www.fotodenboer.nl), where you will find both new and used analogue and digital camera equipment and accessories.

Camera Equipment

Henk Booms Foto + Electronicum	Van Woustraat 242	020 662 06 66
Booms Quick Print	Rijnstraat 58b	020 673 03 57
Foto Den Boer	2e Hugo De Grootstraat	020 684 45 54
Foto Solleveld	Various Locations	See p.299

Car Parts & Accessories

The number of bicycles on the road can mask the fact that there are over 200,000 private cars in Amsterdam. If you must own a car, there are a few reputable service stations throughout the city. Become a member of the ANWB (www.anwb.nl) and you receive many benefits including 24 hour roadside assistance in the Netherlands (pay for more cover and you get assistance throughout Europe) and discounts on car accessories from its shops and website. Items on sale include roof luggage boxes from €199, child car seats from €99, mini DVD players for around €200, and satellite navigation systems for €200. Another good chain supplying both car accessories and a good selection of new bicycles and cycle accessories is Halfords. The staff are very knowledgeable and helpful and there are four branches in Amsterdam. The most central is on Albert Cuypstraat (www.halfords.nl). If you have a new car it's best to go to the dealer for repairs and servicing, but a cheaper and very reliable option is one of the branches of Kwikfit (www.kwikfit.nl) in Amsterdam. It stocks and fits tyres, exhausts, windscreens and more, and offers servicing and the APK tests which are compulsory on all Netherlands registered vehicles over three years old (see p.128).

Car Parts & Accessories

ANWB	Various Locations	See p.298
Halfords	Various Locations	See p.300
Kwikfit	Various Locations	See p.300

Clothes

Other options **Beachwear** p.257, **Lingerie** p.273, **Shoes** p.280, **Tailoring** p.283, **Sports Goods** p.283

Artistic fashion display

Think fashion and the cities that spring to mind are Paris or Milan rather than Amsterdam, but Dutch designers like Viktor and Rolf have a strong presence in those two cities and bring these influences back to the Netherlands. In fact, in the liberal Dutch way, there is something for everyone available in Amsterdam. Whatever your taste, style or budget, you will find it here, from affordable family fashion to haute couture. The department stores have great clothing sections, running from the home brand designs you'll find in HEMA (p.290), to the selections of designer names you can find in de Bijenkorf (p.289). But you will find fashion throughout the city, from mode emporiums to small boutiques. European high street labels such as Mango, Zara, River Island, Replay and Noa Noa are all centrally located, but the fun of shopping is discovering the places that suit you – hopefully these suggestions will set you on your way.

Various Locations
See p.298

C&A

www.c-en-a.nl

C&A has its four-floor flagship store in Amsterdam, located between the Damrak and Nieuwendijk, and five other stores in Amsterdam and Amstelveen. It has clothes for the whole family at very affordable prices. Its aim is to provide outfits for all occasions, and during the festive season before Christmas it has a pretty range of affordable party dresses for all ages. Bonuses include great sections for maternity wear and large women.

Kalverstraat 179-181
Centrum
Map p.393 D1 2

Claudia Sträter

020 626 07 08 | *www.claudiastrater.com*

The Claudia Sträter name evokes the idea of classy ladies' fashion, and there are shops throughout the Netherlands, Belgium, Germany and Luxembourg. The hallmark of the designs is detailed tailoring using lovely fabrics which achieve a modern, stylish and refined look. The Kalverstraat store has a large seating area with comfortable chairs by the changing rooms – so long-suffering partners can rest while stylists assist the shopper.

Various Locations
See p.299

Coolcat

www.coolcat.nl

This is a great high street chain with trendy fashion aimed squarely at the under 24 age group. The absence of formal school uniforms in the Dutch education system gives this shop and others like it the chance to dictate the 'school look'. It also has great children's clothes for pre-teens who want to look older, all at very affordable prices. There are two stores in Amstelveen, and five in Amsterdam.

Zeedijk 64
Centrum
Map p.389 F4 4

DeMask

020 620 56 03 | *www.demask.com*

Located in the middle of the Red Light District, this leather specialist offers not only fetish items for men and women, but also outerwear in beautiful leathers. The store is internationally known, and includes celebrities among its clients, with branches in Barcelona, London, Munich and New York. It is said that Janet Jackson's leather 'nipplegate' dress came from this store. A leather pencil skirt goes for about €300, and men's trousers start from €500.

Various Locations
See p.300

Hennes & Mauritz

www.hm.com

Established in Sweden in 1947, this well-known European clothing chain honours its philosophy of providing quality fashion at great prices. It has a great selection of fashion for all the family; the baby and toddler's range is often irresistible. It has a nice range of accessories too – pre-teens can drool for hours over hair bands and bracelets. The stores are often very busy, and during sale time you have to queue for changing rooms, but the prices are worth it. There are 10 shops in and around Amsterdam; be aware that the centrally located store in the Kalvertoren is aimed at the young and fashionable and does not have a children's department.

Rokin 140-142
Centrum
Map p.393 E2 6

Maison de Bonneterie

020 531 34 00 | *www.debonneterie.nl*

This beautiful, light and luxurious building was one of the first fashion department stores in Amsterdam. Its original speciality was knitwear, but in the last 10 years this mode emporium has broadened its appeal, and now has up-to-date fashion for both men and women, be it the classic, suburban, or urban look. You will find top brand names here such as Hilfiger, Polo, Ralph Lauren, and Hugo Boss - and the prices to match. However, there is an outlet section on the fourth floor which is more affordable. The 'New Image' concept launched by Maison de Bonneterie recently is aimed squarely at the younger market, with brands such as Diesel, Replay and DKNY.

Various Locations
See p.300

Pauw

www.pauw.nl

These upmarket shops have beautiful women's clothing priced at the upper end of the market. Well-made tailored jackets team with sophisticated silks, and bright white cotton contrasts with sober hues. The clothing design is complemented by the subdued interiors of the stores. There are Pauw shops on Beethovenstraat, Van Bearlestraat, Leidsestraat, Heiligeweg and Gelderlandplein. The Pauw menswear range is available in the Van Bearlestraat store.

Various Locations
See p.301

Sissy Boy

www.sissy-boy.nl

The concept of this Dutch brand is to offer a lifestyle to young trendy families, as well as designing and selling attractive and wearable clothing for men, women and children. It has recently opened SB Homeland in the Magna Plaza. Sissy Boy has six stores in central Amsterdam, but due to restrictions on floor space some stores only sell the women's clothing range. The shop in Amstelveen stocks menswear and children's wear. Prices are higher than average, but you are paying for something a little bit different.

Van Ravenstein

Keizersgracht 359
Canal Belt (Grachtengordel)
Map p.392 C1 **9**

020 639 00 67 | *www.van-ravenstein.nl*

Located in the Negen Straatjes area of the grachten gordel, this is haute couture. Internationally renowned Dutch designers such as Dries van Noten and Viktor and Rolf have their collections here, as do Givenchy and Balenciaga. Don't think you can't afford this either, as the cellar has an outlet for last season's collections.

Computers

Other options **Electronics & Home Appliances** (below)

You can find computer specialists all over the city, but there is a concentration of them on the Ceintuurbaan in De Pijp, all offering different deals and expert advice on computer hardware and software. Refer to the table below for more information. Apple Mac lovers are also catered for in Amsterdam centre – try Nieuwe Mac Winkel or Mac Repair.

If you would rather compare prices in one location, get out to Mediamarkt (opposite) at the ArenA Boulevard. It has has a vast sales floor and a huge stock of computer equipment at very competitive prices. Every two months there is a 'PC Dumpdag' at the Amsterdam RAI – a discount computer fair which is a useful source of computer components. See the website for the next event (www.pcdump.com).

Prices of equipment compare well with those in countries like the US. If you are planning on going back to your home country with your new computer, ask at the store about reclaiming the sales tax before you leave the Netherlands. Warranties on equipment are standard practice. If your equipment fails within the warranty period, the goods will be returned to the manufacturer and replaced or repaired. Be aware that companies such as Dell will then reset your PC to factory settings, so do make back-ups. Outside of the warranty period, there are plenty of independent local repair businesses who will either fix on site or in a workshop – ask in advance how long the repair will take. One national service company is Guidion (www.guidion.nl). Most internet providers now offer an annual package for repair and maintenance, for example Planet Internet offers one costing €60 per year (0900 1905, www.planet.nl).

Computers		
Direct PC	Ceintuurbaan 312	020 470 00 71
Dynabyte	Ceintuurbaan 123	020 673 43 00
Guidion	na	0900 484 3466
Hardware Discount	Ceintuurbaan 135	020 423 24 23
Mac Repair	Lindengracht	020 770 18 09
Mediamarkt	ArenA Boulevard 123	020 564 16 16
Mycom	Ceintuurbaan 113	020 470 95 95
Nieuwe Mac Winkel	Weteringschans	020 626 06 84
Paradigit	Ceintuurbaan 320	020 679 10 70

Electronics & Home Appliances

Other options **Computers** (above), **Camera Equipment** p.259

For larger items such as kitchen appliances and home cinema equipment, you will get the best deals at an electronics specialist, but for smaller items such as mp3 players, mobile phones and cameras, you may find a good selection in department stores like V&D (see p.290). Blokker, the household goods chain with almost 600 branches throughout the Netherlands, is the place to go for small household appliances such as toasters, irons and coffee machines, while the Kijkshop is another alternative (for branch details see the Shopping Directory p.300). If you are looking for second hand, try www.marktplaats.nl or the classified section from www.expatica.nl. A note on prices: the government introduced a tax on the cost of recycling old electrical goods in 2000. It's called the 'verwijderings bijdrage', and the charge varies from €1 for small electrical appliances to €17 for large items – it will be shown separately on your cash receipt.

Various Locations
See p.298

BCC

www.bcc.nl

This chain has the slogan 'low prices, high service,' and its superstores price check against rival companies every day to ensure its goods remain the most competitive. It has 40 superstores in the Netherlands, six in Amsterdam and Amstelveen, as well as an online shop, www.bcc.nl. Many top brands are available alongside the store's home brand products. Sales staff are efficient and knowledgeable, and goods can be delivered and installed, and old equipment and the packing from the new goods can be taken away if requested. There is a store guarantee on all products.

Various Locations
See p.298

Blokker

www.blokker.nl

This Dutch chain specialises in household goods, and has a good range of smaller household electrical goods. There are Blokker stores on every high street. The company has a very good returns policy in which you can return an item in the original packaging with the receipt at any store in the Netherlands within 14 days of purchase. All electrical items have a store guarantee of one year from date of purchase and the receipt acts as the guarantee.

Various Locations
See p.299

Expert

www.expert.nl

Expert is a global organisation and has three branches in Amsterdam. It supplies a full range of household appliances as well as mobile phones, computers and photo equipment. It often has exchange deals, where you can hand in your old TV and upgrade to a newer model at a discounted price. The sales team are able to give excellent product advice, and service includes insurance guarantees on products over €210 as well as delivery and installation of larger items.

ArenA Boulevard 123
Amsterdam Zuidoost
Map p.367 E4 13

Mediamarkt

020 564 16 16 | *www.mediamarkt.nl*

This megastore has security on the door and you must leave bags in lockers, but once past that system you enter a treasure trove of technology. You can get everything here from household appliances to computers and cameras. Mediamarkt has a price-matching policy on all goods, and if you find the same product cheaper within 15km of the ArenA within 14 days of purchase, you will receive a gift voucher for the price difference. It also offers very good service and product guarantees.

Eyewear

Other options **Opticians & Ophthalmologists** p.113, **Sports Goods** p.283

Whether you need a pair of prescription spectacles, contact lenses, or sunglasses you won't have to look far to find what you need. There are several big chains of opticians in the Netherlands, with shops on most high streets. To find one it's best to check the company's website for an address near you. Try Hans Anders, Pearle, Specsavers or Prins Brillen. Competition is such that each chain offers different deals – often free frames, or two for the price of one offers on prescription spectacles and sunglasses. All of them sell designer sunglasses,

Disabled Access

Modern shopping centres have wide doorways, disabled toilet facilities, a great range of shops in one place and no cobbles. Easily reachable from the centre of Amsterdam, Grootgelderlandplein (p.295) in Buitenveldert has 96 shops, while Stadshart (p.295) in Amstelveen has 200. Close to the Stadshart is the Cobra Museum (p.154) for adding a little culture to consumerism.

Eyewear			
Accessorize	Various Locations	See p.298	www.accessorize.nl
Bril	Cornelis Schuytstraat	020 676 76 50	www.brilamsterdam.nl
Cityoptiek	Vijzelstraat	020 624 45 53	www.cityoptiek.nl
Etos	Various Locations	See p.299	www.etos.nl
Hans Anders	Various Locations	See p.300	www.hansanders.nl
Kidzz Eyezz	Nicolaas Berchemstraat 1	020 670 11 12	www.kidzz.nl
Optilens	Various Locations	See p.300	www.optilens.nl
Pearle Opticiens	Various Locations	See p.300	www.pearle.nl
Prins Brillen	Various Locations	See p.301	www.prinsbrillen.nl
Specsavers	Various Locations	See p.301	www.specsavers.nl

with or without prescription, and contact lenses. There are also internet services for reorders of disposable contact lenses and contact lens cleansing products.

Several independent opticians give excellent service: Cityoptiek and Bril both specialise in spectacles and sunglasses. If you want contact lenses try Optilens, with shops in Amsterdam and Amstelveen. If you're looking for glasses for kids, a great place for frames is Kidzz Eyezz near Albert Cuypstraat. For sunglasses try Etos, where you will pay from about €12, or Accessorize (with shops in Amsterdam and Amstelveen). You can also get a good cheap selection from market stalls.

Eye tests made by an optician are free of charge, and if you are insured through a Netherlands health insurance company you would normally be able to claim for a new pair of prescription spectacles once every three years.

Mini Explorer

Don't be fooled by the size of this little star – it's full of insider info, maps, contacts, tips and facts about this vibrant city. From shops to spas, bars to bargains and everything in between, the *Amsterdam Mini Explorer* helps you get the most out of your stay in Amsterdam, however long you're staying.

Flowers

Other options **Gardens** p.269

Flowers are very much a part of Dutch life; many homes are filled with both fresh flowers and house plants, and a bouquet is a customary gift when invited to someone's home for dinner. Cut flowers are sold all over the city from roadside stalls, and there are beautiful florist shops on every high street. The freshness and quality of the blooms are guaranteed to be excellent – expect to pay from €12 to €30 for a bouquet. Bouquets should last at least a week after purchase if you follow the instructions given by the florist. For very special occasions there are a few names to take note of: Gerda's (www.gerdasflowers.com) is handy for weddings and corporate events; Bloem en zo (www.bloemenzo-amsterdam.nl) offers delivery throughout the Netherlands and also designs flowers for weddings, funerals and corporate events. You could also try Art & Flowers (www.artandflowers.nl) which has a very fresh and modern approach, and collaborates with clients on short and long-term projects, supplying both flowers and plants. Chris Bloemsierkunst (www.chrisbloemsierkunst.nl) is a traditional florist and can arrange delivery of flowers through the Interflora system.

Flowers		
Art & Flowers	KNSM-laan 6	020 419 22 73
Bloem en Zo	Eerste Bloemdwarsstraat 21-23	020 320 28 08
Chris Bloemsierkunst	Jan van Galenstraat 80-82	020 618 42 66
Gerda's Flowers	Runstraat 16	020 624 29 12

Flowers at the market

Food Shopper's Guide To Holland
A comprehensive review of the finest food products in the Dutch marketplace has been written by Ada Henne Koene. It will help identify the best cuts of meat, the freshest vegetables, and guide you when searching for ingredients. It also explains the cooking methods for some traditional Dutch dishes.

Food

Other options **Health Food** p.270, **Supermarkets** p.296

The increase in supermarkets in the Netherlands has not diminished the popularity of the specialist food retailer, and people will cycle across town to pick up Italian olives from Feduzzi, or Spanish olives from Hollandaluz. Traditional butchers, bakers and fishmongers abound, as do more upmarket delicatessens. The multicultural mix of Amsterdam has seen a steady rise in speciality food shops from all four corners of the globe. In the areas around the Dapperstraat Markt and the Albert Cuypstraat Markt you will find a concentration of halal butchers and Turkish bakeries, and throughout Amsterdam there are European and Asian food stores and delicatessens.

Freshly baked bread

These suggestions are not the only specialist food shops in Amsterdam, but as a newcomer it's worth visiting some of these shops in order to understand and appreciate the variety and quality of food and service you can expect from any good specialist food shop in the Netherlands. See also Noordermarkt p.293, and Nieuwmarkt p.2925.

Haarlemerdijk 184
Oud West
Map p.374 B4 14

Bakkerij Mediterrane

020 620 35 50

The croissants here are possibly the best in Amsterdam, and it's a treat to visit in the morning and have coffee and cake in the shop itself. If you have no time for coffee, take home some of the high quality breads or pastries on offer.

Scheldestraat 63
Oud Zuid
Map p.388 C1 15

Feduzzi Mercato Italiano

020 664 63 65 | www.feduzzi.nl

This fantasic Italian delicatessen was listed as one of the top 25 in the Netherlands in 2005, and with good reason. It has an excellent selection of Italian delicacies including olive oil, honey, vinegar, fresh pasta, meat, cheese, wine and coffee. Each Wednesday a new supply of fresh buffalo milk mozzarella is imported from Naples.

The sandwiches made with freshly baked Italian bread have delicious fillings, and there are also ready made pasta salads and meals. Feduzzi has top class kitchen facilities and provides catering for functions. It also offers Italian cooking workshops.

Utrechtsestraat 98
Canal Belt (Grachtengordel)
Map p.393 F3 16

Fishes

020 626 85 00 | www.fishes.nl

This is a great wet fish shop, featured in several Dutch lifestyle magazines. Staff here can give advice on preparing fish and cooking it, as well as offering ready prepared fish dishes to be taken away. Fishes also supplies catering for functions; should you want your guests to experience the best oysters, or the real Dutch herring, this is the place to go. There is another branch in Oud Zuid on Johannes Verhulststraat 110 (6724334).

Haarlemmerstraat 71
Canal Belt (Grachtengordel)
Map p.389 E2 17

Hollandaluz

020 330 28 88 | www.hollandaluz.nl

This high quality Spanish delicatessen offers wines and tapas from the Andalucia region of Spain (Holland, Andalucia... get it?). The shop is very reminiscent of Spain, enticing you to spend more and take a flavour of the region home with you. It also caters for functions, and you can rent out the shop itself for parties with a Spanish tint.

Haarlemmerstraat 2
Centrum
Map p.389 E2 18

Kaasland

020 422 17 15 | *www.kaasland.com*

On the corner of Haarlemmerstraat and the Singel you will find a shop selling a brilliant selection of both Dutch and European cheeses. There is so much to choose from that you may feel overwhelmed, but the well informed staff can advise you and also let you sample the cheese before you buy.

Rembrandtweg 384
Amstelveen
Map p.365 B3 19

Kingsalmarkt Delicatessen

020 643 37 51 | *www.kingsalmarkt.nl*

This delicatessen specialises in American, British and Japanese products and is a boon to expats missing the comforts of home. It has a wide range of imported dry goods and delicatessen produce, as well as fresh meat, vegetables and wine. It also has ready meals to take away and the staff are very knowledgeable about their areas of speciality.

Cornelis Schuytstraat 26-28
Oud Zuid
Map p.383 F1 20

Organic Food For You

020 379 51 95 | *www.organicfoodforyou.nl*

This shop offers not only a superb range of organic food products with the simplicity of supermarket shopping, but also a selection of cookbooks, kitchen utensils and ceramics to inspire you to further enjoy the cooking experience. Specialities include delicious, fresh ready meals, fish and baked bread and pastries.

Nieuwmarkt 27
Centrum
Map p.389 F4 21

Oriental Commodities

020 626 27 97 | *www.orientalgroup.nl*

In the heart of Chinatown, this Asian supermarket stocks 4,000 items from all over Asia including China, Japan, Thailand and Indonesia. On top of great fresh fruit, vegetables and herbs, there is a terrific assortment of frozen, dried and tinned food, and a range of oriental cooking utensils. Whatever you need for an Asian meal should be available here. Established over 20 years ago, the company now has 11 shops throughout the Netherlands. There is a second shop called Oriental Enterprise (020 694 10 16) on De Flinesstraat 10.

Utrechtsestr 109
Canal Belt (Grachtengordel)
Map p.393 F3 22

Patisserie Kuyt

020 623 48 33 | *www.patisseriekuyt.nl*

This patisserie was voted the best in the Netherlands in 2006, and its hand-made cakes and pastries are works of art. In addition to its own patisserie products, you can also purchase Betjeman and Barton tea, Golden Coffee Box coffee, Vlaams Broodhuys bread and Valrhoma chocolate. Choose between buying the delicacies to take home or enjoying them in the tea salon.

Haarlemerdijk 53
Oud West
Map p.388 C1 23

Poelier H. Jonk

020 624 84 54

This is an excellent address for free range poultry and game the whole year round, but especially at Christmas time. Most poultry is either from the Netherlands or France, whereas the game in general is sourced from Scotland.

Huidenstraat 26
Canal Belt (Grachtengordel)
Map p.392 C1 24

Ron's Groenten en Fruit

020 626 16 68

This is one of the few greengrocers in the centre of town. Here you can get a fresh fruit salad to eat on a bench by the side of a canal, or a fresh fruit juice to take away. There is also a lovely selection of vegetables and salads, which are delivered fresh each day.

Various Locations
See p.301

Simon Lévelt

www.simonlevelt.nl

This firm has been supplying fine coffee and tea for almost 200 years. The scent of freshly ground coffee as you enter the shop is wonderful and you can pick from the Simon Lévelt blend of coffees and teas. There is also a good selection of coffee machines and teapots, cups and saucers. Simon Lévelt has shops all over the Netherlands and there are four branches in Amsterdam.

Haarlemmerdijk 63
Oud West
***Map p.389 D1* 26**

Slagerij Buzhu

020 625 71 37

This attractive family run butchers is in an old grocery store still fitted with some of its original hardware. Established in 1972, it sells fresh lamb, goat, veal and beef as well as salads, olives, couscous, herbs, olive oil and other Middle Eastern produce.

Johannes Verhulststraat 106
Oud Zuid
***Map p.383 F1* 27**

Slagerij Van Dam

020 662 05 32

This high quality shop has a great selection of fresh meats, salads, sandwiches and ready prepared meals to choose from. The staff are always ready to help and advise customers on the best choices and methods of preparing the meats. Its location on the corner of Johannes Verhulststraat and Cornelis Schuytstraat makes it easily accessible with a car.

Sarphatipark 114
De Pijp
***Map p.384 C1* 28**

Thomas Green's

020 673 60 61 | *www.thomasgreen.nl*

Homesick for Heinz tomato soup, PG Tips teabags, or Cadbury's Chocolate Fingers? This shop not only supplies all of these but also fresh dairy products and meat sourced from Britain. So if you crave Cumberland pork sausages or clotted cream, look no further as this shop has it all. Its online webshop is in English and it delivers to Amsterdam and Amstelveen.

Cornelis Schuytstraat 36
Oud Zuid
***Map p.383 F1* 29**

Van Avezaath Beune

020 662 08 91 | *www.vanavezaath-beune.nl*

This wonderful patisserie sells the most fantastic cakes, pastries and irresistible bonbons within the confines of a shop that could be mistaken for a work of art. There is a second shop called J.G. Beune on Haarlemmerdijk 156 -158 (6248356) and both shops will make cakes to order for weddings or parties.

Deli food

Gardens

Other options **Hardware & DIY** p.264, **Flowers** p.264

If you have an apartment in central Amsterdam, you may not have a garden, but the addition of plants to your roof terrace or balcony will give a new dimension to your living space. The most central place to look for plants is the Bloemenmarkt (p.292) on the Singel, where you are almost guaranteed enthusiastic assistance. Kees Bevaart (6258282) specialises in selling garden plants, or if you are going for a Zen feel, you can always get a bonsai tree from A.H. Abels & Zoon on the Singel (6227441). Other stalls sell a wide range of plant containers, and if you've always wanted to laze in a hammock you should go to Marañon Hangmatten (020 622 59 38). Other markets also offer garden plants, especially in and round the Albert Cuypstraat Markt (p.292).
If you are looking for a bigger selection, it's better to go to one of the big garden centres on the outskirts of Amsterdam. Tuincentrum Osdorp on Osdorperweg (020 667 60 60, www.osdorp.nl) is a family run business offering a great assortment of plants, garden furniture, tools and ornamental paving. It also has a restaurant and play area for children. The DIY chain Praxis (p.301) has two megastores with garden centres on the outskirts of Amsterdam. There are always lots of assistants who can help you load the car or arrange delivery of bulkier items.

Gifts

Finding an appropriate gift in Amsterdam is never a problem. Department stores such as de Bijenkorf (p.289) and V&D (p.290) have plenty of choice, as do the many small gift shops around the city. LEUK! (www.leukdewinkel.nl) will give you lots of ideas. What's Cooking (www.whatscooking.nl) has lovely household gifts. Chocolates are always acceptable and Leonidas in the Kalvertoren shopping mall (p.294) does lovely gift boxes from about €15. If you are thinking of cosmetics, Lush (www.lush.com) has two shops in Amsterdam, and does gift boxes from €10 up to €175, with the happy twist that none of the products were tested on animals. For ethical presents, go to the Fair Trade Shop on Heiligeweg or the Wereldwinkel ABEL on Ceintuurbaan.

Gifts		
de Bijenkorf	Dam 1	0900 0919
Fair Trade Shop	Heiligeweg	020 625 22 45
Leonidas	Various Locations	See p.300
LEUK!	Utrechtsestraat	020 638 77 68
Lush	Various Locations	See p.300
Wereldwinkel ABEL	Ceintuurbaan	020 664 10 83
What's Cooking	Reestraat	020 427 06 30

Hardware & DIY

Other options **Outdoor Goods** p.277

The big chains such as Praxis (www.praxis.nl), with nine stores in Amsterdam and Amstelveen, and Gamma (www.gamma.com), with six stores, can supply flooring, roofing and everything in between, including the correct tools. The megastores are on the outskirts but Praxis has a few smaller stores which are more centrally located.
A great place to go for interior decorating is HEMA (p.290). It has a paint mixing service, and you can't beat it for price and quality. For electric tools try Kijkshop, which has power saws from €20 and Bosch screwdrivers from €30.

Hardware & DIY		
Gamma	Various Locations	See p.300
HEMA	Various Locations	See p.300
Kijkshop	Various Locations	See p.300
Meijer	Rozengracht	020 626 37 12
Praxis	Various Locations	See p.301
Rippens	Westerstraat	020 625 23 82
Timberland Wooden Floors	Runstraat	020 421 73 67
Van Apeldoorn en Faber Hout	Utrechtsestraat	020 427 30 99
Verfmenger	Rozengracht	020 623 3140
Verfpoort	Haarlemmerdijk	020 624 56 27

As well as the big chains, there are some established smaller companies around the city. Rippens on Westerstraat and Meijer on Rozengracht both sell tools and hardware. De Verfpoort on Haarlemmerdijk is a paint specialist, as is the Verfmenger on the Rozengracht. Two good addresses for wooden flooring are Van Apeldoorn en Faber Hout on Utrechtsestraat and Timberland wooden floors on Runstraat.

Hats

There is a relaxed informality about living in Amsterdam which extends to the dress code, where hats are never obligatory but often fun. V&D (p.290) on the Kalverstraat has a good selection of affordable ladies' hats on the ground floor along with its other accessories, while de Bijenkorf (p.289) does a nice line in flattering hats. For men's headgear, go to one of the branches of The English Hatter. This traditional looking menswear shop stocks everything from an English bowler to a souwester. It also has a good range of menswear.
The upmarket ladies' fashion shop Linhard, on the corner of Van Baerlestraat (www.linhard.nl) may have something to suit you, and for original hats and caps from the designer Ans Wesseling try the Petsalon (www.petsalon.nl). But for the widest choice in fantastic hats for men and women, visit De Hoed van Tijn in Centrum (www.dehoedvantijn.nl).

Hats		
de Bijenkorf	Dam 1	0900 0919
De Hoed van Tijn	Nieuwe Hoogstraat	020 623 27 59
The English Hatter	Various Locations	See p.301
Linhard	Van Baerlestraat 50	020 679 07 55
Petsalon	Jordaan	020 624 73 85

Health Food

Other options **Food** p.266

It's not difficult to find health food in Amsterdam. Apart from the two Saturday organic markets on the Noordermarkt (p.293) and Nieuwmarkt (p.292), you can also buy organically produced products in most supermarkets; look for labels such as EKO or AH Biologisch. Supermarkets also have a selection of products especially designed for diabetics: foods produced under the Zonnatura label have been prepared with minimal processing and no additives; any sugars present occur naturally in the ingredients. They are also particularly suited to people with certain allergies.

Various Locations
See p.299

De Natuurwinkel

www.denatuurwinkel.com

There are seven of these specialist health food shops in Amsterdam and Amstelveen, selling not only organic products, both fresh and pre-packed, but also ethically produced products. Soya milk and gluten free products are also available for those suffering from specific allergies. The staff are very helpful and knowledgeable. Prices are higher than in supermarkets, however there are special offers each week.

Various Locations
See p.299

De Tuinen

www.detuinen.nl

With over 60 stores in the Netherlands (including several around Amsterdam and one in Amstelveen), this growing chain of druggist shops is aimed at keeping the mind and body in balance. Along with cosmetics, herbal teas and organic treats, there is a wide selection of vitamin supplements and herbal medicines. It's a great place to go for gifts since there are lots of reasonably priced items such as relaxation CDs and aromatherapy candles and oils.

Haarlemmerstraat 68
Centrum
Map p.389 D2 44

Leccornia Organic Delicacies

020 528 50 50 | *www.leccornia.nl*

If you want to maintain a healthy lifestyle, it is great to be able to continue to eat responsibly outside of the house. This delicatessen sells only organic produce, and you can pick up a ready made lunch or dinner knowing that the food is free of additives and artificial preservatives. Leccornia also arranges business and party catering.

Home Furnishings & Accessories

Other options **Hardware & DIY** p.269, **Markets** p.291

Dutch design is modern and functional, but that does not mean it is impossible to get classic or colonial furniture. A great place to go to get a feel for what is available is the Woonmall Villa Arena (p.295), where shops catering for all tastes are grouped together under one roof. Here you can see designer kitchens, get ideas for children's rooms, and find signature pieces. Another great place to get ideas is the Woonbeurs at the Amsterdam RAI centre, held every year in September (www.woonbeurs.nl). If you would rather have help in decision making, there are interior designers who will be happy to assist. One thing to consider is that there is often a waiting period when you order furniture; if you are in a hurry there are warehouses where you can drive away with your purchase, usually at very reasonable prices. There are also vintage furniture stores as well as antique shops which don't have delivery delays either, although the prices usually reflect their unique qualities

Elandsgracht 109
Jordaan
Map p.392 B1 32

De Looier Antiques Market

020 624 90 38 | *www.delooier.com*

This fascinating indoor antique market is a collection of dealers with stands and shops situated within a facade of houses along the Elandsgracht. There are furniture dealers, as well as porcelain, collectibles, and an auction house. It's a great place to spend some time, especially if you are looking for those special pieces to finish a room.

Haarlemmerstraat 25
Canal Belt (Grachtengordel)
Map p.389 E3 33

Het Groot Avontuur

020 626 85 97 | *www.hetgroteavontuur.nl*

This is a small shop with a colourful mix of individually designed furniture pieces and accessories. Much of the furniture is made from recycled wood, and the accessories come from all over the world. Tables and cupboards can be made to your specifications, whether full size for your home, or smaller for a child's bedroom. There is also a changing stock of second-hand furniture; it is worth browsing to see what takes your fancy. Prices are reasonable, with a table costing from about €350.

Hullenbergweg 4
Amsterdam Zuidoost
Map p.367 F4 34

IKEA

0900 235 4532 | *www.ikea.com*

This Swedish chain has a large store in Amsterdam Zuidoost, and sells everything for the home at really reasonable prices. It's a self-service set up, so if you are not familiar with the formula, allow several hours to shop here. Enjoy walking round the show rooms then take a break at the restaurant. After that, take a trolley through the huge home accessories department, probably the only place where you are tempted to impulse buy a carpet. Getting the items you want off the shelves in the huge warehouse is sometimes a challenge, but there are always yellow-shirted assistants willing to help. There is a same-day delivery service if the items you buy won't fit in the car, and a very good returns policy and customer service department. If you are driving, it's easily accessible from the A9 or, if you're using public transport take the metro in the direction of Gein and exit at station Bullewijk.

Pieter Ghijsenlaan 14
Zaandam
Map p.365 B2 35

Loods 5

0900 2355 6637 | *www.loods5.nl*

This furniture warehouse outside of Amsterdam is worth a visit. There are over 250 different suppliers under the umbrella of Loods 5, and each 'room' holds a different style and type of furniture. You can find everything here from leather armchairs to colonial tables. Prices are very reasonable, but there are no returns or exchanges possible. You can arrange delivery for larger items, but don't be surprised to see an open-top Mercedes with a two metre long hall mirror in the back seat driving out of the car park.

Rozengracht 191-193
Jordaan
Map p.388 A4 36

SPRMRKT

020 330 56 01 | *www.sprmrkt.nl*

A vintage lifestyle store selling not only furniture and accessories but clothes and music too. Some of the designer items are not cheap - an Arne Jacobsen dining table and four chairs will set you back €3,850 for instance, but other items are much more affordable. SPRMRKT also carries a large stock of furnishing fabrics from the 70s and 80s, which is priced from €12 per metre.

Beethovenstraat 10
Oud Zuid
Map p.384 A2 37

Sunny Home

020 662 00 36 | *www.sunnyhome.info*

This upmarket store will help you redesign the interior of your home completely or assist in smaller projects and design challenges. It can create storage solutions, kitchens, help bring together the soft furnishings in a room, or design the lighting needed to highlight features. The quality is top-notch, but using brands such as Arketipo, Riva1920, Art of Living, Molinari and Tonelli comes at a high price.

Various Locations
See p.301

Xenos

www.xenos.nl

These home accessories emporiums offer everything from candles, glassware and kitchen equipment through to furniture, food and reed products. If you are working with a limited budget, a few euros will go a long way here and you will be able to have pretty and colourful accessories in every room in the house. There are five branches in Amsterdam and Amstelveen.

Jewellery & Watches

PC Hooftstraat 30
Oud Zuid
Map p.392 B1 39

Boutique Cartier

020 670 34 34

The name alone implies luxury and wealth. Each Cartier piece is a work of art in platinum or gold in various tones, and both diamonds and coloured stones are used to make the pieces come alive. This jewellery can be unbelievably expensive, but if you simply must have something from the shop there are pretty charms and novelties, such as a Cartier logo phone holder, which won't break the bank.

Haarlemmerstraat 40
Canal Belt (Grachtengordel)
Map p.389 E2 40

MIO sieraden

020 624 15 17 | *www.miosieraden.nl*

This independent jewellery designer offers unique pieces made in the store's studio. As well as

ZaZare Diamonds

Amsterdam is famous for diamond trading, and there are many diamond factories and showrooms in the city. It is possible to have a guided tour of the ZaZare Diamond factory, and then select a diamond to suit your budget with a setting to suit your taste. Loose diamonds are sold with a set price per carat, but diamond factories often have stones in settings at a lower price than a retail shop. You can arrange a private tour and showroom viewing, by calling 020 626 27 98. For more information, check out www.zazarediamonds.com.

offering its own collection, there are watches from Alfex, Matteo, Thun and Paul Smith, and jewellery from Pur Swivel, which produces a unique ring design with removable stones.

Various Locations
See p.301

Siebel Juweliers

www.siebeljuweliers.nl

A traditional chain of jewellers, Siebel has addresses all over the Netherlands. Its 'Celebrate Life' campaign urges shoppers to buy jewellery for every occasion and, with its collection of designer pieces from Armani, Fossil and Tag Heuer to name but a few, there are watches and pretty pieces of jewellery to fit every occasion.

Lingerie

Other options **Beachwear** p257, **Clothes** p.260

Amsterdam's lingerie shops are quite varied and offer women every option, from comfort to pure sexiness. Hunkemoller is a high-street chain specialising in lingerie with shops all over the city. It stocks a vast range of lingerie, swimwear and night wear to suite every need, from teen sizes to G cup bras, at very reasonable prices. Staff are very helpful, and will give advice on sizes and fit. There are spacious changing rooms but at sale time it can be very busy.

All the big department stores have good quality lingerie departments, but de Bijenkorf (p.289) is really worth a visit, and with plenty of pretty and sexy brands to chose from it's very tempting to overspend. If you prefer a more exclusive shopping experience, Tony Tolo has two beautiful shops, one on Kinkerstraat and the other in Amstelveen. Top designs available include La Perla, Ravage, Mary-Jo and Aubade, as well as designer swimwear. DeDe's Underworld has exclusive lingerie and swimwear for men and women including the designer brands Antinéa, Bjorn Borg and HOM. The quiet luxury of Salon de Lingerie, on the other hand, may give the feel of stepping back in time but the luxury designs it sells are definitely of today.

For haute couture lingerie go to gorgeous Paars Lingerie. With designers such as Viktor and Rolf, John Galliano and Marlies Dekkers, you will be guaranteed lingerie and swimwear with flair and originality, but with a price tag to match.

And finally, for something that is sexy and a little naughty too, you don't need to go to the Red Light District; head to Female and Partners or Stout – two surprising little shops designed to titillate and intrigue.

Lingerie		
de Bijenkorf	Dam 1	0900 0919
DeDe's Underworld	Beethovenstraat	020 670 56 53
Female and Partners	Spuistraat	020 620 91 52
Hunkemoller	Various Locations	See p.300
Paars Lingerie	Spuistraat	020 618 28 28
Salon de Lingerie	Utrechtestraat	020 623 98 57
Stout	Berenstraat	020 620 16 76
Tony Tolo	Various Locations	See p.301

Luggage & Leather

These days, strong modern textiles often replace leather as the fabric of choice for bag manufacturers, and beautiful, practical pieces are available in every colour you desire. If you are looking for reasonably priced handbags and luggage, V&D (p.290) has a great selection which changes with the seasons; lighter fabrics and softer coloured leather goods in the summer and darker (and waterproof) stock in the winter. A pretty clutch bag can be had for as little as €20. The leather goods department on the ground floor of de Bijenkorf (p.289) has a quality selection of purses and wallets too, but expect slightly higher prices here.

Moving away from the department stores, the Australian Crumpler Store (www.crumplerbags.nl) is on Haarlemmerdijk. This affordable collection is designed to accommodate anything from your mobile phone or your laptop to your clothing for a

Luggage & Leather		
Cellarich	Haarlemmerdijk	020 626 55 26
Crumpler	Haarlemmerdijk	020 620 24 54
de Bijenkorf	Dam 1	0900 0919
Dutchies	Runstraat	020 626 30 01
Hester van Eeghen Lederwaren	Hartenstraat	020 626 92 12
Kipling	Heiligeweg	020 320 52 65
Robin en Rik Leermakers	Runstraat	020 627 89 24
Tretsom Luggage	Scheldestraat	020 662 19 57
V&D	Various Locations	See p.301

week's holiday. Kipling (www.kipling.com), the Belgium brand, now has an outlet in Amsterdam and you can find their collections in many other stores in the city. The colourful designs are squarely aimed at the modern woman's needs, be it a bag for night clubbing or a baby bag with changing mat.

Going more upmarket, but offering excellent quality and service, Tretsom Luggage sells designer handbags and luggage. You will find brands including Brics, Francesco Biasia and Claudio Ferrici for handbags as well as Rimowa, Samsonite, Eastpak, Vaude and Timberland for travel bags. Not the cheapest of options, but modern airport baggage handling systems are tough on luggage.

Of course Amsterdam also offers beautifully designed leather articles. For gorgeous ladies' handbags try Dutchies (www.dutchiesdesign.nl) or Hester van Eeghen Lederwaren. There is also Cellarich (www.cellarrich.nl) on Haarlemmerdijk which uses leather and cowhide in its own collection. For top quality leather clothing go to Robin en Rik Leermakers, bespoke leather designers to the rich and famous.

Medicine

Other options **General Medical Care** p.106

Prescription drugs in the Netherlands are only available through a doctor, but in most cases the prescription must be collected from an apotheek (chemist/pharmacy). The doctor will tell you which one to go to, as the prescription is often sent through the internet to the chemist. The many chemists in Amsterdam are often found on high streets. Along with filling prescriptions, they also dispense over-the-counter drugs medicine and advise on drug usage and whether a doctor's opinion should be sought. Most are open from 08.30 until 17.30, but for emergency and weekend cover, chemists in an area will work together to maintain a 24 hour service. To find the chemist on duty look in the local newspaper, or see if the local chemist has a notice advising the address.

Medicine		
Da	Various Locations	See p.299
Etos	Various Locations	See p.299
Kruidvat	Various Locations	See p.300
Portegies	Various Locations	See p.301

Other places to go for non-prescription medicine are the druggist stores. The biggest chains are Kruidvat and Etos, and you will find Da, Dio, and Portegies throughout the city. As well as globally recognised brands of medicine, it is often the case that these stores will suggest homeopathic or natural remedies, especially for children. If you are looking for standard painkillers supermarkets stock these too. In all cases medicines are kept behind the counter and you must be served by a sales assistant.

Mobile Telephones

Other options **Mobile Phones** p.102

There are mobile phone shops in every major shopping area, and department stores such as V&D (p.290) stock them too. Most of the major players are concentrated along the Rokin (map p.393 E1) so it's a good place to head for setting up a contract with a network or buying a pay as you go phone. It's worth remembering when

considering taking out a contract that some models of handsets are provided free. The Primafoon shop at Rokin 54 has a great selection of models of mobiles and is an outlet for KPN mobile phone contracts. The Orange shop at Rokin 64 (www.orange.nl) sells many models of phone, and you can sign up there for an Orange mobile phone contract. The BelCompany (www.belcompany.nl) at Rokin 52 is part of a national chain of phone shops which can supply all the different network contracts such as Hi, Telfort, Vodafone and T Mobile, as well as KPN and Orange, so it's easy to compare deals as well as models of phones. If you are looking for a second-hand mobile phone try www.marktplaats.nl, or www.ebay.nl. Before you buy, remember that second-hand phones are not always as good as they look online.

Music, DVDs & Videos

Fame (www.fame.nl), at the beginning of Kalverstraat, is probably the first stop for any visiting music lover. The collection of CDs, singles, vinyl, DVDs and videos, advertised as the widest range of music in the Benelux, is set out over two floors. There is a wide variety of music styles available, and the shop also has imported records not always found in the regular music chain stores.

Free Record Shop has several branches in Amsterdam and Amstelveen; the one on Kalverstraat is a great supplier of CDs, DVDs and computer games at very competitive prices. The range of music on offer appeals to a wide audience.

For the not-so-mainstream consumer, try Independent Outlet (www.outlet.nl), which aims at the skateboarding, punk, hardcore, rock, Oi! and indie loving sector of the population. At this shop you can design your ultimate dream skateboard, pick up a T-shirt or hoodie and browse the record collection for your favourite tracks.

The most famous music shop in Amsterdam, Concerto (www.concerto.nu) buys and sells CDs, DVDs and vinyl LPs. The store is spread over several shop fronts, and laid out on three floors. You can get all genres of music here, from classic through folk to indie and back again. There is a huge second-hand section at really great prices, and it's said that if you can't find it here you won't find it anywhere - definitely worth visiting.

Music, DVDs & Videos

Concerto	Utrechtsestraat	020 623 52 28
Fame	Kalverstraat 2	020 638 25 25
Free Record Shop	Various Locations	See p.299
Independent Outlet	Vijzelgracht	020 421 20 96

Musical Instruments

Other options **Music Lessons** p.214, **Music, DVDs & Videos** p.276

Most Amsterdam music shops hold both new and reconditioned stock. Many professional musicians know Dijkman Muziekinstrumenten (www.dijkmanmuziek.nl), as it buys, sells and rents an enormous range of wind, string and keyboard instruments and sound systems. Prices range from €200 for an electric guitar starter set to many thousands for a Gibson or Fender. The experienced sales staff will be happy to demonstrate an instrument for you, and help you make a choice.

Dirk Witte (www.dirkwitte.nl) is a guitar specialist, but also supplies DJ gear, keyboards and wind instruments. The shop is a treasure trove of music gear on two floors; again prices vary, but a small digital piano for a beginner is about €1,000.

In Reestraat you will

Musical Instruments

Dijkman Muziekinstrumenten	Rozengracht	020 626 56 11
Dirk Witte	Vijzelstraat	0900 040 4040
La Guitarra Buena	Reestraat	020 627 16 82
Palm Guitars	Gravelandseveer	020 422 04 45

find La Guitarra Buena (www.guitarrabuena.nl), a classic and flamenco guitar specialist that also has a big collection of sheet music and CDs and DVDs. This renowned shop has a guitar repair maintenance service too.
Located on the Binnen Amstel on Gravelandseveer is Palm Guitars (www.palmguitars.nl), a unique store trading in and renovating second-hand and antique musical instruments. This shop is only open Wednesday through to Saturday, from 12:00 until 18:00. You can get a quarter-size violin here for around €300.

Outdoor Goods

Other options **Camping** p.192, **Hardware & DIY** p.269, **Sports Goods** p.283

Although there is not much wilderness to be found in Holland, the Dutch love the outdoors, and camping and fishing are very popular, as are ski holidays and distance ice skating. In Amsterdam you will be able to kit yourself out for whichever outdoor pursuit takes your fancy.
Perry Sport (www.perrysport.nl) has three branches in Amsterdam, and the megastore on Kalverstraat has three floors of sport and outdoor equipment and clothing. Itis a good place for camping gear and snow accessories - a two-man tent can set you back as little as €100. The North Face is also centrally located on the first floor of the Kalvertoren (p.294) and has expedition tents, rucksacks, boots, sleeping bags, and clothing, all at prices that reflect the quality of the product. For the urban outdoor types Aqua Diving has an excellent range of inline skates, roller skates, skateboards, and in the winter a good range of ice skates. This shop is worth the visit for the winter ice wall alone.
Decathlon has an excellent range of equipment for outdoor pursuits such as hunting, fishing, riding and archery, as well as mountain climbing, trekking and Nordic walking. Seasonally, its winter collection includes skis and ski equipment, as well as ice skates. The prices here are very competitive; a child's safety helmet can be as little as €20. If you are going for the traditional country look an upmarket alternative to these stores is the centrally located Country Shop De Jager on the Herengracht, which supplies high quality outdoor clothing.

Outdoor Goods		
Aqua Diving	Haarlemmerstraat 165	020 622 35 03
Country Shop de Jager	Herengracht 320	020 624 71 72
Decathlon	ArenA Boulevard 101	020 565 91 20
North Face	Kalvertoren	020 689 76 86
Perry Sport	Various Locations	See p.300

Party Accessories

Other options **Parties at Home** p.358

The Dutch traditionally celebrate carnival and birthdays in style, and there are several party shops and costume hire shops throughout Amsterdam. Louis Wittenburg (www.louiswittenburg.com) is the oldest party supplies shop in Amsterdam and has a great selection of costumes for adults and children along with wigs, props and fireworks. Party Palace has two shops in Amsterdam on Utrechtsestraat and Waddenweg, and you can also order online at www.partyshop.nl; it can supply a balloon arch for the front door for €70.
Cakes for special occasions are very popular, and your local baker should have a selection of designs you can order for the celebration. These are made with fresh cream, so need to be picked up on the day and kept

Party Accessories		
Boels	Various Locations	See p.298
de Bijenkorf	Dam 1	0900 0919
HEMA	Various Locations	See p.300
Louis Wittenburg	Raadhiusstraat	020 624 68 86
Party Palace	Various Locations	See p.300

refrigerated. HEMA (p.290) does a good range of party basics for kids, such as children's champagne, petit fours and treats, but supermarkets also supply the basic items such as plastic plates and beakers, streamers and balloons. At the other end of the party spectrum, you can hire everything from marquees to bouncy castles (a reliable source of kids' entertainment). One good all-round hire company is Boels (www.boels.com), which has a couple of hire points in Amsterdam. See the website for the complete range of party items available. A bouncy castle is yours for about €98.

Christmas decorations are available in lots of department stores and household shops around the city, but de Bijenkorf (p.289) excels in stylish design. Garden centres often have a Christmas market, where you can get a fresh tree and all the lights and ornaments too.

Perfumes & Cosmetics

High street chains are the first stop for many people when it comes to affordable perfumes and cosmetics. Etos, Da, Dio, and Portegies all sell cosmetics brands such as Miss Sporty, Rimmel and Bourjois. With high-end cosmetics such as Clinique and Biodermal, de Bijenkorf (p.289) has an enviable cosmetics department. Its specialist sales staff are very helpful, and also give makeovers so you can experience the product. Men's grooming products are widely available in all these stores too. Beauty salons (p.240) also stock cosmetics; Louise Parfumerie (www.parfumerielouise.nl) supplies Estee Lauder, Sisley, La Prairie, Clarins and Kanebo, among others, and you can go there for a facial, pedicure or massage.

Perfumes & Cosmetics		
Da	Various Locations	See p.299
de Bijenkorf	Dam 1	0900 0919
Etos	Various Locations	See p.299
Louise Parfumerie	Cornelis Schuytstraat	020 662 58 76
Portegies	Various Locations	See p.301

Various Locations
See p.298

Body Shop

www.bodyshop.com

This globally recognised brand has five stores in Amsterdam and Amstelveen. The environmentally aware trail blazer is regarded by many as the greenest brand on the high street, which is a reason to shop here, but its success comes more from the quality and effectiveness of its products and the attractive pricing. Whether buying gifts or treating yourself, these stores are worth a visit.

Various Locations
See p.299

Douglas

www.douglas.nl

Douglas has eight branches around Amsterdam and Amstelveen. The light, spacious shops have trained makeup stylists who can offer expert advice on makeup and skin care. Perfume brands sold here include Chanel, Jean Paul Gaultier, Dolce&Gabanna, Cacharel, Davidoff and Dior. The Clarins and Zirh range of men's skincare products are stocked too, as well as black Up, the quality makeup for darker skinned women.

Runstraat 9
Canal Belt
(Grachtengordel)
Map p.392 C1 3

Skins Cosmetics

020 528 69 22 | *www.skins.nl*

This attractive shop has inhouse stylists and hairdressers and offers makeup master classes, and workshops. It is the Netherlands' exclusive supplier of NARS products, developed by the famous makeup stylist Francois Nars. Prices are top end; Dr Sebach's vitamin C powder cream costs €110, and a Jimmy Woo scented candle will set you back €45.

Pets

Other options **Pets** (Setting Up Home, p.99)

Pets Place and Faunaland are both national chains supplying a wide range of pet food and accessories. Pets Place (www.petsplace.nl) has a very good selection of both cold water and tropical aquarium fish and equipment. Sometimes independent pet shops, like Dierenspeciaalzaak Bello, supply more exclusive accessories.

Pet shops in Amsterdam rarely supply puppies or kittens, although they often have small animals and birds, such as rabbits, hamsters and parrots. The shop is likely to know of litters of kittens in the neighbourhood, but if you are looking for a pedigree breed of dog or cat, it's better to ask other owners to recommend a breeder.

An alternative is to take a cat or dog from one of the animal rescue centres in Amsterdam. The famous Poezenboat on Singel is a cat sanctuary for animals that need re-housing, and Dierenopvangcentrum at Polderweg 120 has both cats and dogs. The animals are all neutered and have an EU vaccination passport. Puppies cost around €155 and kittens usually cost around €105. Adult animals are cheaper.

If you get a pet remember that, before travelling with your pet outside of the Netherlands, you must get a EU passport from the vet, and your pet needs an identification chip and to be vaccinated against rabies. Some countries have further restrictions. The UK demands a blood test to be carried out on the animal, for example. It is important that you check what rules apply in your destination country before you travel. For more information on everything to do with pets, refer to Pets in the Residents chapter on p.99.

Pets		
Dieren Asiel de Poezenboat	Centrum	020 625 87 94
Dierenopvangcentrum Polderweg	Indischebuurt	020 462 23 00
Dierenspeciaalzaak Bello	Oud West	020 627 58 28
Faunaland	Rivierenbuurt	020 661 82 00
Pets Place	Amstelveen	020 641 56 80

Second-Hand Items

Other options **Markets** p.291, **Second-Hand Items** (Setting Up Home, p.97)

Thrifty Amsterdammers make good use of second-hand shops. Used Products Amsterdam buys and sells a wide range of items, and you can find all kinds of electrical goods here as well as clothes, toys and baby accessories. Not far from this location is Waterlooplein Market (p.293), which houses many second-hand and used products on the stalls. One organisation that provides work for handicapped people is the recycling company De Lokatie. It has two sales outlets, one in Distelweg in Amsterdam Noord and another in Camperstraat in Oost. There is a lot of furniture on offer at great prices and it both delivers and offers a pick-up service for unwanted items you want to donate. There are a lot of second-hand and vintage clothing stores in Amsterdam too, some with really great gear – have a look around Second Best or Ladyday. If you are getting rid of unwanted stuff, you can place adverts on supermarket noticeboards or in local newspapers. Internet sites such as www.marktplaats.nl and www.ebay.nl are simple to use too.

Second-Hand Items		
De Lokatie	Distelweg	020 463 11 15
Ladyday	Hartenstraat	020 623 58 20
Second Best	Wolvenstraat	020 422 02 74
Used Products Amsterdam	Prins Hendrikkade	020 616 61 69

Shoes

Other options **Beachwear** p.257, **Sports Goods** p.283, **Clothes** p.260

The shopping streets of Amsterdam have a shoe shop every few metres, so whether you want to spend €10 or €200, you will find something to suit your budget and taste. See below for reviews of some of the best options. If you don't wan to trawl the shops in a search for the perfect pair of shoes, de Bijenkorf (p.289), V&D (p.290) and C&A (p.260) all have goodshoe departments, as does Maison de Bonneterie (p.261). When choosing shoes, it's worth remembering that the Amsterdam cobbles can ruin a pair of stilettos in a few strides (as many have found after a night on the town). Luckily there are shoe repair points located round the city, where you can get new tips on your heels while you wait.

Rokin 9-15
Centrum
Map p.389 E4 45

Betsy Palmer

020 422 10 40

For glamour in ladies' shoes, go to this lovely shop on the Rokin. Each season's collection is irresistible. With funky and fun colours and designs, you'll feel like a child entering a sweetshop. Whether you are looking for formal businesswear, evening elegance or casual chic, you can be guaranteed to find something a little more special here. The shoes are pricey, even at sale time. Expect to pay over €100 for a pair of shoes and €150 for one of the great bags.

Various Locations
See p.298

Cinderella

www.cinderella.nl

The two stores on Kalverstraat and Leidsestraat stock lovely footwear for both men and women. The sales people are helpful and, as well as having up-to-the-minute designs, women can also come here for extra small or extra large shoes. Ladies' sizes start from European size 34, and go up to 44. They also have boots to fit extra wide or extra narrow calves, so if you have never been able to wear elegant leather boots go here - you may find you are slimmer than you thought. Prices are middle range; a pair of ladies' boots is priced around €170, and you can pay around €100 for men's business shoes.

Ultra-modern shoe shop

Various Locations
See p.299

Dolcis

www.dolcis.nl

Part of the Hoogenbosch Retail Group which also includes Manfield, Invito and PRO Sport, this shop has attractive shoes for all the family. Prices are reasonable; a pair of men's boots are priced from €80 and you can get kids' trainers from around €28. The quality of the shoes is good; Dolcis is the exclusive supplier of Hush Puppies in the Netherlands, and it also sells Wrangler brands.

Various Locations
See p.299

ECCO

www.ecco.com

This brand prides itself on providing shoes for the whole family and for a range of activities, with high technical specifications to give a high level of comfort. They also have attractive designs. Kids' shoes may seem pricey at around €60 for shoes suitable for school, but they are practical. The Leidsestraat branch only stocks the adult range of shoes. For the children's shoe department, you will have to go to Amstelveen.

Hartenstraat 1
Canal Belt
(Grachtengordel)
Map p.388 C4 49

Hester van Eeghen

020 626 92 11

Internationally known for her handbag and accessory collections, Hester van Eeghen is considered one of the most influential Dutch designers of recent times. She also has a brilliant collection of shoes for men and women. Her designs are geometric and witty, with bold contrasting colours. A visit to the shop in Hartenstraat will inspire you.

Various Locations
See p.301

Van Haren

www.vanharen.nl

This Dutch chain of shoe shops started in Rotterdam in 1924 and now has 110 stores in the Netherlands. It's a no-nonsense store with affordable footwear for all the family. The shop formula is to have the shoe boxes stacked high, with examples on display; you will get served faster if you serve yourself. There are bins full of bedroom slippers and flip flops to rummage through. Prices are low and start from €10 - and it's even cheaper at sale time.

Souvenirs

The first thing you notice as you walk up the Damrak from Centraal Station is the number of souvenir shops, all stuffed to the rafters with 'typically Dutch' souvenirs. You can grab everything you need from these shops, but there are a few other places round Amsterdam which offer souvenirs with that little extra panache.

The Bloemenmarkt (p.292) on the Singel is a great place to pick up souvenirs. From tulip bulbs to Delft Blue fridge magnets, the choice is enormous, and not expensive. If you want Dutch wooden shoes, try De Klompenboer, also known as the wooden shoe factory, just off the Nieuwemarkt. It's open everyday from 10:00 and sells not only clogs, but a great selection of cuddly toys.

If it's a really wet and miserable day, you can get your souvenirs in the luxurious surroundings of the Magna Plaza Shopping Mall (p.294). If you are

Souvenirs		
De Klompenboer	Sint Antoniesbreestraat	020 623 06 32
P.G.C. Hajenius	Rokin	020 623 74 94
Magna Plaza	Nieuwezijds Voorburgwal 182	020 626 91 99
Van Gogh Museum	Paulus Potterstraat 7	020 570 52 00

looking for good quality Dutch cheese, head to the Cheese Gift Shop, and for typically Dutch souvenirs go to Typical Dutch. Both of these shops are located on the ground floor of the shopping mall.

For classy souvenirs, go to the shop at the Van Gogh Museum (p.157). It has everything from posters to leather handbags with Vincent Van Gogh motifs. Prices are high, but you are paying for quality and originality. The tobacco trade made the Netherlands rich and you can still find top quality cigars at P.G.C. Hajenius. More than just a shop, visiting here feels like you are stepping back in time, and the shop incorporates a cigar museum.

Chocolates are another great idea, and for fresh handmade bonbons Puccini's two shops on Staalstraat (020 626 54 74) and Singel (020 427 83 41) are wonderful. The only drawback is that the sweets have a limited shelf life, and must be consumed within eight days of purchase. On the other hand, treat yourself and eat them straight away, taking the memory back as a souvenir.

Antiques and souvenirs

Sports Goods

Other options **Beachwear** p.257, **Outdoor Goods** p.277

If you are looking for sportswear a good chain is Aktie Sport (www.aktiesport.nl). It has 10 shops in Amsterdam and Amstelveen, and offers sports gear and footwear for men, women and children. It also stocks sports bags and other general accessories. The range is affordably priced, and often discounted. The well-known shoe chain Footlocker has two branches on Kalverstraat, and one on the Nieuwendijk. It stocks top brand sport and leisure shoes such as Nike, Adidas, Asics, Converse and Lacoste. If you are a dedicated runner, go to Runnersworld (www.runnersworldamsterdam.nl) and get expert advice on everything to do with running, as well as top quality running shoes and equipment.

Perry Sport (www.perrysport.nl) stores are great general sporting outlets and you will also be able to buy gym equipment here. A Kettler Giro 500 Cross trainer will set you back €279. Decathlon has a good selection of home gym equipment too, along with the rest of its great range; a basic gym would cost about €1,000. For a specialist dance and gym shop, try Papillon on the Rokin (www.lepapillon.net) for clothing and accessories.

Sports Goods		
Aktie Sport	Various Locations	See p.298
Decathlon	ArenA Boulevard 101	020 565 91 20
Footlocker	Various Locations	See p.299
Papillon	Rokin	020 623 06 42
Perry Sport	Various Locations	See p.300
Runnersworld	Vijzelgracht 7	020 420 87 00

Stationery

Other options **Art Supplies** p.256

Department stores are a good place to look for stationery whether for home, school or office use. HEMA (p.290) has a wide selection, as does de Bijenkorf (p.289). The V&D Papier Wereld on the first floor of the Kalvertoren (622 0171) has a great selection of everything school kids need, whatever their age. It also has a good stock of basic home office supplies and printer paper in different colours. Many stores in Amsterdam offer a free gift wrapping service, but if you prefer the personal touch, V&D (p.290) also sells wrapping paper, gift tags and greeting cards. For high quality and a great selection go to Cortina Geschenkartikelen, which also specialises in wedding photo albums. For office supplies at a discount try Action (www.action.nl) which has stores on Pijnackerstraat and Osdorpplein. Its stationery, wrapping paper and office supplies are surprisingly cheap; 500 sheets of A4 printer paper is under €3.

Stationery		
Action	Various Locations	See p.298
Cortina Geschenkartikelen	Reestraat	020 623 66 76
de Bijenkorf	Dam 1	0900 0919
HEMA	Various Locations	See p.300
V&D	Various Locations	See p.301

Tailoring

Other options **Textiles** p.284, **Clothes** p.260, **Souvenirs** p.281, **Tailors** p.97

While Dutch life is very informal, tailored clothing is still a thriving industry, and, in fact, a growing one. Minor alterations are often possible at dry cleaning companies, and many of the better clothing shops will alter hems and sleeves for a very small charge. More comprehensive services are offered by several companies throughout Amsterdam. For more information turn to Tailors in the Residents section on p.97.

Van Baerlestraat 50
Oud Zuid
Map p.392 B4 51

Linhard

020 679 07 55 | *www.linhard.nl*

This women's wear shop has been in the hands of the Linhard family for three generations, but looks and feels fresh and modern. It stocks pretty designer clothes, such as Just B and Avoca and Deha, but recognises that off-the-peg fashion does not always fit perfectly. It has its own tailoring department, and as well as altering new purchases, will also make adjustments to older items to bring them up to date.

Designer suit

Willemsparkweg 37-41
Oud Zuid
Map p.383 F1 52

Suit Supply

020 471 33 62 | *www.suitsupply.nl*

Suit Supply is a new company established in 1999 and growing fast. It has off-the-peg suits from €199, but also offers two custom services. With its 'cut to the bone' service a suit made to measure costs from €350, and a shirt €98. There is also a Travelling Tailor service, where a tailor comes to your home or office to measure up and the suit will be delivered within six weeks.

Maasstraat 33
Rivierenbuurt
Map p.383 C2 53

Terzi Design

020 468 76 33

This is an independent design label, with an affordable, changing collection of seasonal pieces. As well as altering its existing collection to fit you as an individual, staff are willing to discuss specific requirements with you over a cup of tea. If you have a problem finding trousers that look good on you, or if you want that special outfit, Terzi can help.

Textiles

Other options **Tailoring** p.283, **Souvenirs** p.281

Markets are your first stop for textiles and the Westerstraat (p.284) on a Monday morning has very cheap fabrics for both curtaining and dressmaking, but by far the best selection is the Albert Cuypstraat Markt (p.292). Stalls sell colourful practical fabrics for as little as €2 a metre; 'great for kids' costumes or home furnishings. Go behind the stalls and you will find wonderful shops with masses of choice and exquisite fabrics, as well as dress-making patterns and experienced staff willing to give advice. There are two shops: De Kniphal at 162 or De Hal Stoffen at 224.

If you are looking for home furnishing textiles, IKEA (p.271) has a great selection. HEMA (p.290) also has a good range of affordable fabrics and can make up curtains and blinds to your specifications. Special fabric, for a wedding dress for instance, can also be found in independent shops around the city. McLennan's Pure Silk

Textiles		
Capsicum Natuurstoffen	Oude Hoogstraat	020 623 10 16
De Hal Stoffen	De Pijp	020 679 59 73
De Kniphal	De Pijp	020 679 58 31
HEMA	Various Locations	See p.300
IKEA	Hullenbergweg 4	0900 235 4532
McLennan's Pure Silk	Hartenstraat	020 622 76 93

(www.puresilk.nl) imports silk fabric from China, Thailand and India, and has a vast collection, from chiffon to brocade. Capsicum Natuurstoffen has a great selection of furnishing fabric.

Toys, Games & Gifts

All good department stores have a toy department. For a huge selection of soft toys, don't miss de Bijenkorf (p.289), which extends its toy department at Christmas. HEMA (p.290) also has a cute range of toys suitable for babies and toddlers. There are also some very good specialist toy shops for all age ranges, from nine months to 90 years. Whether you are looking for a good selection of mass-produced toys at competitive prices, or more durable unique items you will be able to find them somewhere in Amsterdam.

Various Locations
See p.298

Bart Smit

www.bartsmit.com

A toy store chain with branches throughout the Benelux, Bart Smith has several shops around Amsterdam, mainly in shopping malls, such as Boven t'Y, Grootgelderlandplein. There is also a store in the Binnenhof in Amstelveen. This chain has a very similar product range to Intertoys and a good tip for Chistmas shoppers is to compare prices of gifts you would like online, as retail prices vary between the shops. It's also possible to order online and have everything delivered to your home.

Hartenstraat 14
Canal Belt (Grachtengordel)
Map p.388 C4 55

The Gamekeeper

020 638 15 79 | *www.gamekeeper.nl*

This little shop in the Negen Straatjes specialises in board games, jigsaws, card games, and classics such as chess, mahjong and backgammon. You can also get a traditional Dutch sjoelbak (Dutch shuffleboard) here. Probably not a shop you would go to for a gift for a young child, but a treasure trove for the serious games player, and definitely a fun place to browse.

Haarlemmerdijk 18
Westerpark
Map p.389 D2 56

Hebbes in Speelgoed

020 625 51 15

This enticing shop carries a great line of durable, quality toys for younger children. As parents, you will get a nostalgic feeling here as you are taken back to your own childhood. Some of the brands available are Thomas, Brio and New Classic Toys; not the cheapest options, but you get personal service from the owner and sales assistants.

Eyecatching ladieswear

Mystical objets d'art

Various Locations
See p.300

Intertoys

www.intertoys.nl

This national chain has several outlets in Amsterdam, including one in the Binnenhof in Amstelveen. It stocks brands including Lego, Playmobil, Barbie, Babyborn, Vtech and K'nex, as well as CDs, DVDs, videos and computers games. You are guaranteed to find something that will suit any child from babyhood upwards. The selection is really varied so you can get a budget gift for a couple of euros, or spend as much as you like. If you really cannot make a choice, you can always get a gift voucher.

Spiegelgracht 10
Canal Belt
(Grachtengordel)
Map p.392 C3 58

TinkerBell Kinderkado's en Discoveryshop

020 625 88 30 | *www.tinkerbelltoys.nl*

This great shop has a model bear outside that blows bubbles to catch your attention. You can find something for everyone here, from the smallest baby to your teenage nephew. The types of toys on offer range from wooden construction sets to microscopes and chemistry sets. Brands sold include Fisher, Brio and Schleich, but there are many others too. There are tips on what to buy for each age group, with prices ranging from €2.50 for a helicopter balloon to €350 for a go-kart.

Wedding Items

Other options **Hats** p.270, **Textiles** p.284

The popularity of the Love and Marriage Beurs (wedding fair) each January at Amsterdam RAI exhibition centre (www.trouwplannen.nl) indicates that the traditional wedding ceremony with all (or most) of the trimmings is thriving. There are plenty of bridal boutiques to choose from, whether you are looking for an off-the-peg dress or want something designed especially.

Angela Bruidsmode (www.bruidsmode.nl) is a long-established shop specialising in bridal and formal evening wear. It stocks 14 different designer collections with prices varying from €400 to €3,000. It has a great selection of wedding shoes too. If you have something special in mind this store has its own designers who can create a unique dress.

It is said that every girl in the Netherlands wants a wedding dress from Beethovenstraat, and I Do I Do Wedding Dresses (www.idoido.nl) not only carries wedding dresses and the accessories to go with them, but also offers clothing advice for the rest of the bridal party too.

Bridesmaid dresses are an important part of the ensemble and Butterfly Creations for Kids (www.butterfly-creation.nl) has dreamy dresses for little girls as it specialises in gala clothing and bridesmaid dresses for children.

Another wedding essential is the gifts, an organisational challenge in itself. Metz & Co (p.290), de Bijenkorf (p.289), Studio Bazaar (www.studiobazar.nl) and Fleur de Lys all have registries as well as English translations of their procedures to make the process as painless as possible – it's simply a case of phoning to make an appointment to discuss your wishes.

There are many printing companies in the city, so if you are after wedding stationery you won't have to look far. One address that is very central is De Posthumuswinkel (www.posthumuswinkel.nl), a printer specialising in whatever you need for the big occasion.

Wedding Items		
Angela Bruidsmode	Sarphatipark 104	020 676 27 30
Butterfly Creations for Kids	Ceintuurbaan 207	020 471 09 03
de Bijenkorf	Dam 1	020 090 09 19
De Posthumuswinkel	Sint Luciensteeg 23-26\5	020 625 58 12
Fleur de Lys	Beethovenstraat 41	020 662 17 37
I Do I Do Wedding Dresses	Beethovenstraat 103	020 676 65 40
Metz & Co	Leidsestraat 35-36	020 520 70 20
Studio Bazaar	Beethovenstraat 31	020 471 44 47

Places To Shop

Amsterdam's canals have created a unique city, but disguise the reality of a chronic land shortage. However, the main shopping streets and markets have evolved to provide for the city's every need, while charmingly still retaining the locations and formats of more than 100 years ago. Other cities may have had the heart knocked out of them and replaced with a shopping centre, but with a few exceptions, you will have to travel to the outskirts of Amsterdam if you want a shopping mall experience. The city has over 10,000 shops clustered along several main streets, each attracting huge numbers of shoppers every day.

There is a difference between areas that attract the many tourists to Amsterdam and the places where residents shop. Many shops aimed at tourists offer tax-free shopping to non-EU visitors and are outlets for international branded goods.

The shopping areas aimed at locals have a distinctly different feel to them. The Calvinistic roots of Dutch culture has created a thrifty consumerism that does not mean that goods are cheap, just that there is a value placed on conservation, and many shops resist products which exploit global resources. Vintage clothing, furniture made out of recycled products, cosmetics that have not been tested on animals, organic food and Fair Trade products are all part of the shopping scene in Amsterdam.

This section offers a guide to the shopping streets in the centre, the main shopping malls and the major department stores. It also describes the major supermarket chains, and some of the various markets, as well as touching on some of the quirkier independent shops.

Streets & Areas To Shop

The main shopping streets are spread throughout the city, each in their own neighbourhood, which to an extent determines the type of shops to be found there.

As a tourist in Amsterdam the first area to explore is around the Dam Square; Kalverstreaat running south of the palace and Nieuwendijk running north towards Centraal Station. Here you will find high street brand names in fashion, cosmetics and music with tourist shops spaced in between. It's brash and busy, so it may suit you to slip west into the Negen Straatjesd where the narrow streets hide designer stores and quaint independent shops.

If you are staying any length of time in Amsterdam, where you shop will depend on where you live. Beethovenstraat serves Oud Zuid, for instance, and you can buy almost anything you need in the area, although the prices reflect the upmarket tone of the area. If you live in Jordaan, then shopping there is naturally your first choice, while inhabitants of Oud West will find most of their needs met on Haarlemmerstraat and Haarlemmerdijk.

There are also areas which have become specialised; Spiegelstraat is renowned for art and antiques with dealers still supplying the nearby Rijksmuseum's collections. The area round the Spui is the best place to go for books, whereas collectors trade in the Nieuwezijds Voorburgwal, not only in the market but also in the dealers' shops there.

Your first stop for mobile phones could be the Rokin, south of Dam square, as several mobile phone companies are located here, and there is a concentration of computer shops on the Ceintuurbaan in the area of De Pijp.

Oud Zuid
Map p.384 A3 59

Beethovenstraat

www.beethovenstraatamsterdam.nl

This is an upmarket shopping street, located in Oud Zuid and close to the Amsterdam RAI centre and Amsterdam World Trade Center. There is a mix of shops on offer including exclusive fashion, interior furnishings, garden accessories and specialist food shops. You can equip your home with the latest Bang & Olufsen sound system, stylish

Alessi kitchen accessories, or a Villeroy & Boch dinner service. It is also possible to do your weekly grocery shopping here. Get there with tram 5 or 24, or if you go by car paid parking is available.

Nr Centraal Station
Jordaan
Map p.389 D1 60

Haarlemmerstraat & Haarlemmerdijk

Starting at the end of the Singel, where the Stubbe's herring stall stands on the bridge, these streets run west to Haarlemmerplein and have an eclectic mix of shops. Here you will find women's fashion with the tendency towards natural fabrics or vintage clothing. There is furniture from recycled wood and antique bathroom fittings. You can do your weekly shopping here, either at the supermarket, or from the many specialist food shops including delicatessens, a game butcher, cheese specialist, wet fish shop, bakeries and a patisserie. Choose gifts of hand-made chocolate or candy, pick up items for your home, or simply window shop. If you feel like lingering, there are plenty of restaurants and cafes in the neighbourhood. Take a seat on one of the terrace cafes on the Herenmarkt and watch the world go by; there may even be a wedding party entering the West Indisch Huis.

West of Canal Belt
Map p.367 E2

Jordaan

There is a village atmosphere to shopping in Jordaan, especially on a Saturday. Housewives cycle past with loaves of bread and cut flowers (through the week that same housewife is probably a high-powered business woman) and you can get your weekly shopping both from the good supermarkets on Westerstraat or Elandsgracht or from the markets on Lindengracht or Noordermarkt. These are the main streets of Jordaan, but the gems can be found on the dwaarstraatjes, the cross streets running between the main canals that dissect the neighbourhood. These narrow lanes hide designer boutiques, vintage furniture stores and gift shops. The best way to discover them is to take a cycle ride through Jordaan and stop when something takes your fancy.

Heiligeweg
Canal Belt
(Grachtengordel)
Map p.393 D1 62

Kalverstraat

020 627 69 05 | *www.kalverstraat.nl*

Kalverstraat is the most famous shopping street in Amsterdam. Originally the site of the cattle market, it runs south from the Dam to the Spui then on to the Muntplein. It is traffic free and is served by all the trams running down the Rokin and Nieuwe Zijds Voorburgwal. On weekends, there are so many people in the street that bikes are an impossibility. All the main high street stores are located here, so it's a great location for affordable fashion, shoes and accessories, as well as cosmetics, CDs and books. One entrance to the Kalvertoren Shopping Mall is on this street, opposite the entrance to V&D (p.290). Mason de Bonneterie (p.261) is close by, opposite the side street Heiligeweg, whose shops offer a slightly more exclusive tint. There are plenty of places to grab a bite to eat as you shop; Café Luna (020 622 28 05, Kalverstraat 96) is situated about halfway along, and there is also a McDonald's outlet. For a more leisurely break, slip off Kalverstraat to the cafe terraces situated on the Spui.

Nieuwendijk
Canal Belt
(Grachtengordel)
Map p.389 E3 63

Nieuwendijk

www.nieuwendijk.nl

The Nieuwendijk runs from the Dam towards the Centraal Station, and ends at the Singel. Close to the Dam, it seems to be an extension of the Kalverstraat with more high street names. C&A is located in the Passage, with the Free Record Shop close by, as well as two branches of H&M. As you get closer to the Singel there is a definite change in the type of shop, as the area is geared towards tourists coming into town from the train station. In between the ubiquitous souvenir shops selling T-shirts and

Delft blue are Amsterdam coffeeshops and outlets selling smoking paraphanalia. There are several sex shops, with erotic clothing and sex toys from the titillating to the bizarre, a few amusement arcades and plenty of fast food outlets.

Oud Zuid
Map p.392 B4 64

Pieter Cornelisz Hooftstraat

www.pchooftstrat.nl

PC Hoofstraat has the greatest collection of designer shops in Amsterdam. If you need Louis Vuitton luggage or a Mont Blanc pen, an outfit from Chanel or a Cartier watch, it's all here, sumptuously displayed. The designer names ensure a steady flow of the rich and famous strolling through and you will almost certainly find yourself rubbing shoulders with a Dutch celebrity or two should you decide to shop here. You will find it hard to park your car among the Porsches and Harley Davidsons but the nearby underground parking on the Museumplein is very convenient and almost as chic as the shopping area. At the top of the PC Hooftstraat is the Van Bearlestraat, which also has a fine selection of exclusive fashion.

Speigelgracht & Nieuwe Spiegelstraat
Canal Belt (Grachtengordel)
Map p.393 D3 65

Spiegelkwartier

www.spiegelkwartier.nl

Cross the Singel in front of the Rijksmuseum and you enter the world of antiques. This area on the Speigelgracht and Nieuwe Spiegelstraat offers art and antique lovers everything they could wish for. There are over 70 shops here and each is a specialist. Whether you collect modern art or Chinese porcelain, Louis XV furniture or rare coins, it's all here. You can browse to your heart's delight and spend to the depth of your pocket. Prices range from items in their many thousands to pretty prints of Amsterdam for a few euros. As this area is in the heart of the Canal Belt (Grachtengordel), there is no direct public transport, but you can take tram 2, 5, 6, 7, 10, 12 or bus 26, 65, 66, 170 to the Rijksmuseum and walk.

Department Stores

The first department stores were established in Amsterdam at the end of the 19th century as magnificent temples to fashion, luxury and elegance. Their goal was to rival the great fashion houses of Paris or Bussels and provide wealthy Amsterdammers with quality products. Three of these are still in existence, and today as you walk into de Bijenkorf, Maison De Bonneterie, or Metz & Co you can still feel that atmosphere of upmarket chic. Some of the services offered by these stores go way beyond your run-of-the-mill shopping, with personal shoppers, international shipping and wedding list registries. In 1923 de Bijenkorf established another chain of department stores, HEMA, aimed at the less wealthy, which is now independent and well loved. Another chain aiming at a broader public is Vroom & Dreesman (V&D, p.290). It has 70 stores throughout the Netherlands, and its central Amsterdam store is at the end of the Kalverstraat.

Dam Square
Centrum
Map p.389 E4 72

de Bijenkorf

0900 0919 | *www.debijenkorf.nl*

This Dutch institution has its flagship Amsterdam store located on the corner of the Dam Square in a beautiful building that opened in 1914. The style of de Bijenkorf is certainly not dated, however. The accent is on excellent and attractive design whether in home furnishings, children's toys or fashion. In the run up to the Sinterklaas celebrations it's an exciting place to take a child. The store is wonderfully decorated with giant parcels and model Piets climbing on ropes through the central atrium. Sint (Saint Peter) himself appears regularly on his throne and holds audience to enthralled youngsters. As soon as Sint is over, the decor takes on a Christmas theme, and you are tempted once again to spend lavishly. The Amstelveen branch is also very acccessible to Amsterdammers (Galerij 152, 020 456 77 70). The chain maintains a very loyal customer base and store card holders have many advantages including invitations to presale shopping evenings and use of a free personal shopper, but you don't have to have a card to take part in the 'drie dwaze dagen' (three crazy days) sale in the autumn where huge price reductions on certain items keep the cash tills ringing.

Various Locations
See p.300

HEMA

www.hema.nl

There are approximately 200 HEMA branches around the Benelux region offering the chain's own brand of food, fashion, and funky household items, in pleasant, well-laid out stores. The renowned HEMAworst (sausage) is sold warm at the front of the store in the winter to either take home or eat wrapped in a napkin as you shop. You can be guaranteed good quality products at low prices. It's the place to go for basics like underwear, clothes for babies and toddlers, and household textiles and kitchen utensils. It is such a household name that it also now offers insurance services and package holidays.

Leidsestraat 35-36
Canal Belt (Grachtengordel)
Map p.393 D2 74

Metz & Co

020 520 70 20 | *www.metzenco.nl*

This exclusive store, first established in 1740, was granted the title 'Purveyor to the Royal Household' in 1815. One hundred and fifty years later the company took over the former head office of the New York Life Insurance Company on the corner of Leidestraat and Kiezersgracht and the shop is still there today. From the beginning this store supplied the international elite, with exquisitely designed fashion and glassware. At the beginning of the 20th century it became the sole agent for Liberty of London in the Netherlands, Europe and Dutch overseas colonies.

Metz & Co's slogan is 'we are luxury', and on entering it's easy to see why. The prices reflect the motto however, and as a resident without the benefit of the tax-free shopping that is advertised you will find it hard to pick up a bargain. Its location in the middle of the main tourist area surrounded by other upmarket high street stores and easy access with trams 1, 2, and 5, makes it hard to resist browsing for a while however.

Various Locations
See p.301

V&D

www.vroomendreesmann.nl

This chain of department stores was established 120 years ago, and you will find a V&D (Vroom & Dreesmann) in most big shopping centres. You can be guaranteed a good selection of competitively priced products, be it kitchen utensils, household fabrics, home accessories, luggage or fashion. It has its own brand, as well as international names such as Mexx, Esprit, Benetton, Principles and Cortefiel. It has also recently launched the brand 'Fair Trade Original' and actively encourages global social responsibility.

V&D is known for its innovative 'La Place' restaurant chain. These eateries are not only found in store, but also in train stations and on motorways. The La Place formula offers fresh and healthy fast food which can be taken away or eaten in attractive surroundings. Mums shopping with babies can get a simple slice of bread with a smear of jam for toddlers while you relax with a fruit juice and salad or coffee and cake.

Hypermarkets

Sometimes it's handy to buy household articles in bulk, and there are a few shops in Amsterdam that allow you to do so. The Aldi (www.aldi.nl) supermarket chain provides high quality food and consumer goods at very competitive prices. It has a limited range, but its bulk buying policy passes excellent price savings to the customer.

Subscribe to its newsletter and find out each month what it has on offer. For branch details, see p.300.

Lidl, the giant German supermarket chain, is a newcomer to the Amsterdam shopping scene and currently has eight stores in town although this number is set to rise. The chain's philosophy is quality for the lowest price, and its format is simple with stacked pallets and overflowing bins. Although Lidl (www.lidl.nl) offers a good selection of food products, what attracts customers is its limited-period discounted items, not only on food but on consumer durables as well.

Another great place for bulk buying is Makro (www.metro-mcc.nl). To get a Makro card you must first be registered with the Chamber of Commerce. The bulk discount and huge choice of both food and none food items on offer is second to none. Makro in Amsterdam in located in an industrial area in Amsterdam Zuidoost; the address is De Flinesstraat 9.

Independent Shops

Amsterdam embraces individuality, and that is clear to see in the success of several eccentric specialist shops scattered round the city. Rejoice in Christmas World with its glittering array of Christmas decorations in stock the whole year round, or take a peek into Brilmuseum Brillenwinkel where you can buy antique or new eyeglass frames at excellent prices. On Haarlemmerdijk there is Kookboekhandel, a shop stuffed with cook books of every kind. And if you have overindulged, perhaps De Witte Tanden Winkel with its incredible assortment of toothbrushes and dental hygiene products should be your next stop. Star struck? Visit Famous on nearby Huidenstraat, and marvel at the collection of gifts and gadgets celebrating film legends, sports heroes, and top models. More collectibles are hidden in the Jordaan. For cat lovers there's Cats & Things on Hazenstraat, and for old-school toys try Mechanisch Speelgoed on Westerstraat, a toy shop with a nostalgic feel that appeals to children and adults alike.

Finally there are two addresses some visitors to Amsterdam consider essential. The Condomerie, the world's first specialist condom shop, is located on Warmoesstraat, while further along the street, Conscious Dreams Kokopelli supplies smart products like magic mushrooms, herbal ecstasies, herbs and all kinds of rare plants. They have a rather nice chill-out area with a pretty view over the canal to help you refocus after sampling the stock.

Independent Shops		
Brilmuseum Brillenwinkel	Gasthuismolensteeg 7	020 421 24 14
Cats & Things	Hazenstraat 26	020 428 30 28
Christmas World	Nieuwezijds Voorburgwal 137	020 622 70 47
Condomerie	Warmoesstraat 141	020 627 41 74
Conscious Dreams Kokopelli	Warmoesstraat 12	020 421 70 00
De Witte Tanden Winkel	Runstraat 5	020 623 34 43
Famous	Huidenstraat 17	020 528 67 06
Kookboekhandel	Haarlemmerdijk 133	020 622 47 68
Mechanisch Speelgoed	Westerstraat 67	020 638 16 80

Markets

If you enjoy shopping for bargains, you can always move away from the shopping streets and try browsing along one of the many open-air markets. Some are general markets, selling food and non-food items, open every day of the week (except Sundays), others are specialist markets frequented by dealers and enthusiasts. Some others seem at first glance to be tourist traps but, if you look past the cheap souvenirs you will often find quality goods at excellent prices.

The biggest markets are in the centre of Amsterdam, and attract crowds every day. The atmosphere, even on cold and wet days, is always friendly and open. There are plenty of cafes around where you can get a hot chocolate after you have finished shopping. The best time to visit a market depends on the type of goods on offer.

The organic market at Noordermarkt should be visited fairly early in the morning, when there is plenty of choice and the products are freshest. At the Waterlooplein Fleamarket you'll make the best discoveries early in the day; once any dealers have visited, late visitors are left with poor pickings. On the other hand, if you are looking for really cheap fresh produce, go late on a Saturday to a general market and you'll get kilos of fruit for next to nothing.

Albert Cuypstraat
De Pijp
Map p.384 C1 81

Albert Cuypstraat Markt

This is the biggest and most central of all the general markets, and the atmosphere can be described in musical terms as a mix between Andre Hazes and Shakira. Every day except Sunday you will find quality fresh fish, meat and poultry, fruit, vegetables and dairy products alongside very inexpensive clothing, household items and a range of textiles. Several tram routes take you directly to this market, including 4, 16, 24 and 25.

Off Prinsengracht
Canal Belt (Grachtengordel)
Map p.393 F4 82

Amstelveld

Located between Utrechtsestraat and Reguliersgracht, this square is very central and there are two markets held here. On Mondays there is a plant and flower market from 09:00 until 18:00, and once a month on Fridays in the summer there is and antique and collector's market which is growing in popularity. To get there by piblic transport, take tram 4 to Keizersgracht, the metro to Weesperplein, or bus 355, also to Keizersgracht.

Singel
Canal Belt (Grachtengordel)
Map p.393 E2 83

Bloemenmarkt

The famous floating flower market, with each stall on a separate barge moored on the Singel, seems like a tourist trap as you can get masses of souvenirs, blue and white china, and clogs and wooden windmills. The market is open every day, and is very busy with sightseers. The quality of the flowers and bulbs, however, is superb, and plant lovers can be guaranteed of the results when buying. This market is very central – take tram 1, 2, 4, 5, 9, 16, 24 or 25 from Centraal Station.

Nr Kalverstraat
Centrum
Map p.393 D1 84

Spui Square

The Spui is a pretty square in central Amsterdam, and there are two markets each week there. Every Friday from 10:00 to 18:00 is the book market to which traders come from all over Netherlands to sell rare and first edition volumes and prints. This specialist market is not cheap as it is aimed at serious collectors, but it's a great place to browse. Also worth a visit is the art market every Sunday from March until December, from 09:00. until 18:00, with artists exhibiting and selling original paintings, ceramics and sculptured pieces. Trams 1, 2, 4, 5, 9, 16, 24, or 25 from Centraal Station will get you there.

Off Wijttenbachstr
Indischebuurt
Map p.395 F3 86 85

Dapperstraat Markt

There are several daily general markets around Amsterdam, but this one on Dapperstraat was voted 'best market in the Netherlands' in 2006. One of the oldest markets in Amsterdam, today it is a busy and multicultural centre, with prices much lower than those in centrally located shops. Get there by taking tram 3, 7 or 10 to the Dapperstraat stop, or by bus 22, 37, 59, 120 or 126. If you're taking the train go to Muiderpoort Station.

Nr Gelderskade
Centrum
Map p.389 F4 87 86

Nieuwmarkt

Every Saturday there is an organic market in this atmospheric square in the heart of old Amsterdam, 10 minutes walk from Centraal Station. On Sundays in the summer there is a large antique market in the same square. If you don't feel like walking from the Centraal Station, take the Metro line one stop to Nieuwmarkt.

Nr Nooderkerk
Jordaan
Map p.388 C2 88 87

Noordermarkt

The organic farmer's market each Saturday seems to bring a breath of the country into the city. Twenty years ago this was the first such market in the Netherlands, and today it's easy to overspend on the great cheeses, breads, and fresh vegetables. There are other products too such as fresh cosmetics and pottery, and there is a small bird market too, so you may see live song birds, chickens or a rabbit.
On Monday mornings there is an antique/flea market on the same square. It's a pretty location to just browse, but if you are buying get there early. The Noordermarkt is on the Prinsengracht at the end of the Westerstraat. Get there through the Jordaan, or on tram 3 to Westerstraat.

Nieuwezijds Voorburgwal
Centrum
Map p.393 D1 89 88

Postzegelmarkt

This small market (the Stamp Market) specialises in stamps, coins and medals, and is open every Wednesday and Saturday afternoon. For collectors it's the place to go for new pieces, to trade items, or for browsing. Take any of trams 1, 2, 5, 6, 13 or 17 to the Dam stop.

Waterlooplein
Centrum
Map p.394 A2 90 89

Waterlooplein Market

This daily flea market is a mix of the antique, vintage, and plain second hand. There are old theatre costumes and army uniforms, prams that could have been used by Queen Wilhelmina and crockery discarded by your mother. Full of curiosities, it's a great place to browse around. Be careful not to buy upon impulse, as whatever you pick up will most probably not match the decor back home. Waterlooplein is behind the Stopera, and you can take the metro or tram 9 from Centraal Station to get there.

Nr Keizergracht
Canal Belt (Grachtengordel)
Map p.388 C4 90

Westermarkt

This market has made a specialty of textiles, although you can also get fresh market produce, clothing and accessories here. It is only open on Mondays, and best visited in the mornings as in poor weather the stall holders will pack up early. Located close to the Jordaan; tram 3 will get you there.

Curiosity shop

Sunflowers at Bloemenmarkt

Shopping Malls

There are two centrally located shopping malls in Amsterdam; the Kalvertoren and the Magna Plaza. Although they differ from each other in style and the type of shops on offer, perhaps the most accurate description for both of them is 'small but perfectly formed'. The larger malls, or 'winkel centrums' as they are known in Dutch, are located on the outskirts, and have the additional benefit of parking facilities. Here, each offers a totally different shopping experience. Stadshart and Grootgelderlandplein provide the locals with a complete spectrum of shops reflecting the economic prosperity of Amstelveen, while Boven t'Y Winkelcentrum in Amsterdam Noord has a wide range of stores at much more competitive prices. For megastores the best location is ArenA Boulevard, next to the Ajax football stadium. Adjacent to this is Woonmall Villa Arena, a huge mall with a focus on home furnishings; here you can get everything from designer furniture to a new fitted kitchen.

Shopping Malls

Shopping Malls		
Amsterdamse Poort	Amsterdam Zuidoost	p.295
ArenA Boulevard	Amsterdam Zuidoost	p.295
Boven t'Y Winkelcentrum	Amsterdam Noord	p.295
Grootgelderlandplein	Buitenveldert	p.295
Kalvertoren	Centrum	p.294
Magna Plaza	Centrum	p.295
Stadshart	Amstelveen	p.295
Woonmall Villa Arena	Amsterdam Zuidoost	p.295

Shopping Malls – Main

Kalvertoren

Kalverstraat 212-220
Centrum
Map p.393 E2 66

www.kalvertoren.nl

With entrances on Heiligeweg, Kalverstraat and the Singel, this shopping mall opened in 1997 and is an attractive airy space on four floors, with a central lift and escalators. It has a full range of interesting places to shop, from international names in fashion such as Replay, Mango, Dockers and Hilfiger Denim, to cosmetics, home furnishings, sportswear and luxury chocolates. There are small food outlets scattered throughout the mall, but the Café and Brasserie Kalvertoren is a bit more special, offering a rooftop view of the city as you eat. It's a great place to spend a couple of hours on a cold and wet Amsterdam day.

Magna Plaza

Nieuwezijds Voorburgwal 182
Centrum
Map p.389 D4 67

020 626 91 99 | *www.magnaplaza.nl*

This was the first shopping mall to be opened in Amsterdam, and is centrally situated behind the Dam Palace in the former Central Post Office building. The shops are located on three floors of galleries. With a glass roof allowing light to flood the central area, it is a beautiful setting in which to shop for designer fashion, jewellery, gifts and cosmetics. There is a lovely toy shop on the top floor called Pinokkio, and Formes offers a great selection of maternity wear. If you really want to indulge yourself you can have a massage at the Back to Life Massage Company on the top floor, or get a new hair style at the branch of Tony & Guy also located there. There is an underground car park close by (Nieuwe Zijds Kolk) but it fills up quickly on weekends. The mall is very easily reached by tram lines 1, 2, 5 and 17, which pass behind the Dam Square.

Magna Plaza

Shopping Malls – Other

Nxt Amsterdam ArenA
Amsterdam Zuidoost
Map p.367 F4

ArenA Boulevard

www.arena-boulevard.nl

ArenA Boulevard comprises four megastores open seven days a week: Prenatal (p.256), Perry Sport (p.300), Decathlon (p.257) and Mediamarkt (p.263), an electronics giant which offers huge discounts because of its bulk buy policy. Also in the area is the Heineken Music Hall, the Pathe Arena cinema and several restaurants and snack bars. If driving, take the A2 or A9 motorways and use the P1 car park under the stadium, or you can take the metro to Bijlmer Arena Station.

On the other side of the Metro line from ArenA Boulevard is Amsterdamse Poort (www.amsterdamse-poort.nl). Partly indoors, this mall serves the population of Amsterdam Zuidoost and offers high street names and many specialist shops, as well as a permanent indoor ethnic produce market in the Shopperhal. The mall is open six days a week, with a 'Koop Zondag' on the last Sunday of each month, where the shops are open from 12:00 to 17:00.

Finally there is Woonmall Villa ArenA (www.villaarena.nl), a spacious and airy indoor mall where the focus is on furniture and kitchen and bathroom design. It's a place to bring all the family, and on Saturdays you can drop off your toddler at De Blauwe Dierenparade creche on the third floor. Relax and take lunch at Grand Café Rox, or enjoy a luxury icecream at Australian Homemade. To get there, take the metro to Bijlmer Arena station and walk through ArenA Boulevard.

Buikslotermeerplein
Amsterdam Noord
Map p.367 E2

Boven t'Y Winkelcentrum

www.boventy.nl

This large shopping centre is centrally located in Amsterdam Noord, is easily accessible by buses from Centraal Station and has plenty of free parking. The shopping centre itself is only half covered and has two big supermarkets, good specialist food shops and a decent range of high street names. The department stores V&D (p.290) and HEMA (p.290) both have branches here, as does the Kijkshop. If you are looking for fashion, there are dozens of stores in the medium-price range. There is a big Babyplanet (p.256) and plenty of choice for computers and electronics, toys and music. An open-air market just off the Waddenweg sells fresh produce, flowers, plants, fabrics and clothing. There are plenty of places for a quick bite to eat, or brasserie-style restaurants if you want to linger longer.

Van Leijenberghlaan
Zuideramstel
Map p.367 E3

Grootgelderlandplein

www.grootgelderlandplein.nl

This indoor shopping mall in the south of the city boasts almost 100 shops, as well as cafes and restaurants, so it is possible to get all your grocery shopping and much more in the one place. Geared towards the local population, there is a wide selection of Dutch high street stores here, and the mall is family oriented as well as wheelchair friendly. There is a fountain in the central square and a small children's play area appealing to the under fives. Its position just off the A10 motorway means it is easily accessible by car, and parking there is free for the first 90 minutes, which ensures a quick turnover of parking places. It can get very busy here at peak times however.

Rembrandtweg 37
Amstelveen
Map p.367 E4

Stadshart

_020 426 58 00_ | _www.stadshartamstelveen.nl_

The name Stadshart means 'heart of the town', and this area is in effect three large shopping malls grouped around Amstelveen's town square, serving the growing population of the area. Two weekly markets are also held here; the organic food market on Tuesdays and the Amstelveen market on Fridays. Two of the malls, Binnenhof and Rembrandthof, are completely undercover, whereas Rembrandweg consists of a street of pleasant, upmarket shops. The major department stores are all represented here (de Bijenkorf, V&D and HEMA), along with all the high street names, supermarkets and specialist food shops.

For a few days in the summer, the town square (Stadsplein) is converted into a city beach where kids can play and adults can compete in beach sport tournaments. In the winter you can find an open air ice rink. On 'Koop Zondag' (the centre is open on the first Sunday of every month) there are often special events put on to draw in the crowds.

Such a large shopping area has many places to grab a bite to eat, or linger over lunch. Apart from the in-store cafes in stores like de Bijenkorf and V&D, there are fast food outlets including McDonald's, or for something more restful try BVLD cafe in the Binnenhof, or 8cht on the Stadsplein.

There is paid parking for 2,500 cars, but it can get very busy. Some car parks close relatively early, so make sure that you can get back to your car if you stay until later in the evening in a restaurant. A viable option is to use the public transport – tram 5 and 51 link Amstelveen with Amsterdam.

Supermarkets

Various Locations
See p.298

Albert Heijn

www.albert.nl

This is the leading supermarket chain in the Netherlands with over 700 stores. The company grades its stores by size and diversity of product. You can shop at 'AH to go' to pick up the ingredients for the evening meal and a tin of cat food, or a 'size 5 store', which are open daily until 22:00. The store's mission is to provide everyday shopping needs at a good price. There is a wide selection of branded items, and its own brand products are of excellent quality, as is the fresh produce. Many food products are organic (look for 'AH biologisch' on the label), and they have a discount pricing system called 'AH bonus'. Its internet shopping service offers the same prices and discounts as shopping in store, and charges a flat rate for delivery.

Various Locations
See p.298

C1000

www.c1000.nl

This is another big national supermarket chain, with over 400 stores. There are eight branches in Amsterdam, mostly in neighbourhood malls outside the city centre. Because of this they are rarely open on Sundays. The emphasis is on no-nonsense shopping and there is a wide choice with very competitive prices. All discounted products can be found in the first aisle as you enter the supermarket. The own brand products are good, as is the fresh produce. Organic produce can be found marked with the EKO label.

Various Locations
See p.299

Dirk van den Broek

www.dirkvandenbroek.nl

This family run supermarket chain has several stores in Amsterdam and one in Amstelveen. Located in residential areas, they do not have Sunday openings. The chain has a good product selection at very reasonable prices; recent price comparisons show that it is one of the cheapest supermarkets in the Netherlands. It also has DirckIII, the cut-price off licence chain, and Dirkx Drogist, the discount chemist chain.

Various Locations
See p.301

Spar

www.spar.nl

The Spar supermarkets are a franchise organisation, with eight small stores in Amsterdam serving local neighbourhoods. The produce is sourced centrally, however, and is of a high quality. Get to know your local Spar supermarket, and you will not be disappointed in the service offered.

Various Locations
See p.301

Super de Boer

www.superdeboer.nl

This supermarket chain, now with over 400 stores, is the result of a merger 10 years ago between the national chain Super and a regional chain named De Boer. There are several stores in Amsterdam and surrounding areas, again in neighbourhood shopping areas. The branch on the Westerstraat is open every Sunday. Super de Boer offers a very good selection of produce, organic food, fair trade products, and products endorsed by the Rain Forest Alliance (look for the green frog on the packaging). Some of the plastic packaging is produced from renewable resources.

Fresh produce

Shopping Directory

Accessorize Binnenhof 37, Amstelveen (020 345 91 48), Leidsestraat 68 (020 627 16 93)

Action Osdorpplein 806 (020 610 02 87), Pijnackerstraat 36 (020 673 96 99)

Aktie Sport Bijlmerplein 996 (020 697 15 81), Binnenhof 54 (020 441 61 32), Bos en Lommerplein 134 (020 486 22 47), Kalverstraat 180 (020 689 38 43), Kinkerstraat 227 (020 489 03 42), Leidsestraat 54 (020 624 88 31), Nieuwendijk 155-157 (020 422 16 38)

Albert Heijn ElandsGracht 13 (020 623 65 74), Haarlemmerdijk 1 (020 625 69 31), Koningsplein 6 (020 624 57 22), Nieuwmarkt 18 (020 623 24 61), Sarphatistraat 670 (020 422 12 33), Van Baerlestraat 33 (020 662 04 16), Vijzelstraat 117 (020 625 94 05), Westermarkt 21 (020 421 40 00), Westerstraat 79 (020 623 68 52)

Aldi Admiraal de Ruijterweg 56C, Baarsjesweg 269-273 W, Bijlmerplein 719-b, Bolestein 41, Gaaspstraat 41, Katrijpstraat 303, Nw Weteringstraat 24-28, Pijnackerstraat 36, Plein 40-45 12 (www.aldi.nl)

ANWB Bijlmerplein 1001 (020 691 39 96), Buikslotermeerplein 307-311 (020 636 36 60), Museumplein 5 (020 673 08 44), Osdorpplein 885 (020 610 49 05)

Art Cash and Carry Westerstraat 230, (020 330 23 70), Woonmall Villa Arena (020 330 23 70)

Bart Smit Binnenhof 5a (020 453 70 54), Buikslotermeerplein 86 (020 494 07 68), Ferdinand Bolstraat 120 (020 675 23 07), Johan Huizingalaan 187 (020 408 15 73), Kalverstraat 193-195 (020 626 29 21), Plein 40-45, J. van Weezelhof 5 Unit 4-5 (020 448 05 74), Reigerbos 31 (020 452 69 34), W.C. Bos & Lommerplein, Bos en Lommerplein 142 (020 488 39 90), W.C. Gelderlandplein, Gelderlandplein 169 (020 642 79 50), W.C. Nieuw Sloten, Kempenlaan 108-111 (020 408 52 54)

BCC Bilkerdijkstraat 91 (0900 0555), Buikslotermeerplein 721 (0900 0555), Linnaeusstraat 20 (0900 0555), Osdorpplein 138 (0900 0555)

Blokker Beethovenstraat 76 (020 471 40 68), Bilderdijkstraat 169 (020 618 23 84), Ceintuurbaan 302 (020 679 13 26), Ceintuurbaan 109 A (020 672 77 46), Damrak 28-30 (020 624 98 01), Dapperstraat 82 (020 663 10 66), Ferdinand Bolstraat 100 (020 471 50 59), Haarlemmerdijk 72-74 (020 623 97 58), Jodenbreestraat 19 (020 421 75 01), Kalverstraat 41 (020 623 44 54), Kinkerstraat 260-262 (020 618 44 07), Maasstraat 37 (020 675 07 09), Rijnstraat 64-68 (020 442 11 73)

Body Shop Binnenhof 88 (020 453 64 45), Gelderlandplein 141 (020 642 63 89), Kalverstraat 157-159 (020 623 97 89), Kinkerstraat 251 (020 412 23 58), Leidsestraat 89-91 (020 420 15 79), Magna Plaza (020 489 08 37)

Boels Johann Stiegerstr 1 (020 665 43 14), Kabelweg 52 (020 681 00 08)

C&A Beurspassage 2 (020 530 71 50), Bijlmerplein 164 (020 452 73 84), Buikslotermeerplein 298 (020 636 16 79), Osdorperplein 805 (020 410 03 23), Willem Kraanstraat 14 (020 447 11 36)

C1000 Buikslotermeerplein 52 (020 630 42 52), Ganzenpoort 96 (020 630 42 52), Oosterlijke Handelskade 1005 (020 509 50 00), Wibautstraat 80 (020 692 00 66)

Cinderella Kalverstraat 177 (020 623 36 17), Leidsestraat 86-88 (020 626 55 19)

Coolcat Bijlmerplein 110 (020 696 80 37), Buikslotermeerplein 180-182 (020 636 71 69), Nieuwendijk 188-190 (020 626 85 46)

Da Buikslotermeerplein 200 (020 494 03 30), Gruttoplein 15 (020 699 99 44), Kinkerstraat 327 (020 618 05 85)

De Lokatie Camperstraat 42 (020 463 11 15), Distelweg 85 (020 463 11 15)

De Natuurwinkel 1e Constantijn Huygensstraat 49-55 (020 685 15 36), 1e Van Swindenstraat 30-32 (020 693 59 09), Elandsgracht 118 (020 412 46 96), Haarlemmerdijk 160-164 (020 626 63 10), Heuseplein 1 (020 441 86 91), Scheldestraat 53 (020 664 11 04), Van Woustraat 80 (020 671 47 19)

De Tuinen Buikslotermeerplein 135 (020 637 37 95), Ferdinand Bolstraat 114 (020 664 90 54), Gelderlandplein 153 (020 644 09 63), Kalverstraat 11 (020 320 29 14), Kinkerstraat 190 (020 616 46 38), Leidsestraat 32 (020 420 18 63)

Dirk van den Broek 2e Nassaustraat 23 (020 686 01 32), Rijnstraat 48 (Victorieplein) (020 664 37 79), Belgieplein 137 (020 615 47 76), Bilderdijkstraat 26 (020 612 26 58), Bos en Lommerplein 1 (020 488 00 92), Marie Heinekenplein 25 (020 673 93 93), Meeuwenlaan 76 (020 632 88 08), Mercatorplein 6-12 (020 689 74 37), Sierplein 6 (020 669 65 13)

Dolcis Buikslotermeerplein 251 (020 494 03 08), Kalverstraat 117 (020 624 77 84)

Douglas Beethovenstraat 30 (020 679 07 13), Buikslotermeerplein 247 (020 637 32 84), Kalverstraat 71 (020 627 66 63), PC Hooftstraat 107 (020 679 58 22)

Ecco Leidsestraat 4 (020 423 28 68), Leidsestraat 4 (020 423 28 67), Rembrandtweg 73 (020 640 26 00)

Etos Beethovenstraat 37 (020 675 75 61), Bijlmerplein 719 (020 691 65 75), Bilderdijkstraat 45 (020 689 03 15), Buikslotermeerplein 280 (020 636 13 51), Ferdinand Bolstraat 84 (020 471 03 20), Gelderlandplein 159 (020 642 72 13), Haarlemmerdijk 81 (020 528 92 38), Kalverstraat 31 (020 528 53 66), Kinkerstraat 208 (020 612 94 70), Nieuwendijk 182 (020 626 71 44), Nieuwendijk 67 (020 420 52 73)

Expert Gelderlandplein 11 (020 442 12 99), Haarlemmerstraat 121 (020 420 21 61), Utrechtsestraat 80 (020 624 50 82)

Footlocker Kalverstraat 103 (020 620 84 30), Kalverstraat 128 (020 422 77 42), Nieuwendijk 138 (020 624 20 58)

Foto Solleveld Amstelveenseweg 214 (020 662 05 33), Kinkerstraat 187 (020 618 58 99)

Free Record Shop Buikslotermeerplein 288 (020 637 05 64), Ferdinand Bolstraat 79 (020 671 60 74), Kalverstraat 230 (020 625 30 34), Kalverstraat 32 (020 626 58 08), Leidsestraat 24 (020 638 08 38), Nieuwendijk 229 (020 622 80 34)

Gall & Gall Amstelveenseweg 174 (020 670 07 62), Beethovenstraat 78 (020 679 90 82), Bijlmerplein 719 (020 452 95 72), Nieuwezijds Voorburgwal 22 (020 421 83 70), Overtoom 468 (020 618 13 32), Rozengracht 72 (020 624 64 66), Van Bearlestraat 85 (020 679 11 22), Van Woustraat 125 (020 673 37 72)

Gamma	Klimopweg 95 (020 637 35 73), Nieuwe Hemweg (020 684 49 67), Spaklerweg 44A (020 668 53 11)
Halfords	Albert Cuypstraat 72 (020 672 24 71), Buikslotermeerplein 149 (020 636 79 66), Kinkerstraat 274-278 (020 389 20 70), Klimopweg 29 (020 636 08 25), Linnaeusstraat 237 (020 468 91 66), Spaklerweg 44C (020 694 02 46)
Hans Anders	Bijlmerplein 723 (020 696 41 72), Buikslotermeerplein 90 (020 634 09 41), Ferdinand Bolstraat 118 (020 664 18 79), Middenweg 26 (020 665 82 55)
HEMA	Buikslotermeerplein 197 (020 637 23 23), Ferdinand Bolstraat 93 (020 676 32 22), Gelderlandplein 54 (020 661 28 05), Kalverstraat 212 (020 422 89 88), Kinkerstraat 313 (020 683 45 11), Nieuwendijk 174 (020 623 41 76), Osdorpplein 626 (020 619 31 11)
Hennes & Mauritz (H&M)	Bijlmerplein 206 (0900 1988), Buikslotermeerplein 123-b (0900 1988), Kalverstraat 114-118 (0900 1988), Kalverstraat 125 (0900 1988), Kalverstraat 200, p/a Singel 457-b9, Kalvertoren (0900 1988), Nieuwendijk 141 (0900 1988), Nieuwendijk 154 A (0900 1988), Osdorpplein 128 (0900 1988), Schiphol Airport, Arrivals Area 43 (0900 1988)
Hunkemoller	Bijlmerplein 112 (020 452 81 55), Bilderdijkstraat 67 (020 618 25 03), Buikslotermeerplein 201 (020 494 58 54), Kalverstraat 162 (020 623 60 32), Osdorpplein 626 (020 410 07 61)
Intertoys	Bilderdijkstraat 135-139 (020 689 81 01), Heiligeweg 26-28 (020 638 33 56), Kinkerstraat 256-258 (020 689 87 82), Van Woustraat 163-165 (020 470 53 13)
Kijkshop	Bilderdijkstraat 81-85 (0900 9800), Buitenplein 88 (0900 9800), Burg.de Vlugtlaan 159 (0900 9800), Ferdinand Bolstraat 91 (0900 9800)
Kruidvat	Bijlmerplein 970 (020 400 28 92), Bos en Lommerplein 186 (020 684 01 35), Buikslotermeerplein 60-62 (020 636 22 01)
Kwikfit	Amstelveenseweg 88 (020 618 85 61), Ceintuurbaan 250 (020 671 21 61), Draaierweg 8 (020 494 50 08), Overtoom 36 (020 612 34 79), Wibautstraat 40 (020 668 05 05)
Leonidas	Damstraat 15 (020 625 34 97), Kalvertoren, Singel 457 (020 422 89 00), Stationsplein 15 (020 330 52 61)
Lush	Kalverstraat 98 (020 330 63 76), Leidsestraat 14 (020 423 43 15)
New English Bookstore	Kalverstraat 223 (020 624 97 89), Leidsestraat (020 623 82 83)
Optilens	Muntplein 2 (020 622 76 32), Van der Hooplaan 9 (020 641 07 94)
Party Palace	Utrechtsestraat 90 (020 620 83 04), Waddenweg 3 (020 637 17 41)
Pauw	Beethovenstraat 82 (020 671 32 99), Gelderlandplein 8 (020 644 18 80), Heiligweg 10 (020 624 47 80), Leidsestraat 16 (020 626 56 98), Van Baerlestraat 66 (020 662 62 53)
Pearle Opticiens	Beethovenstraat 35 (020 471 48 84), Bijlmerplein 872 (020 696 81 30), Ferdinand Bolstraat 95 (020 679 68 66), Kalverstraat 101 (020 528 52 52), Van Bearlestraat 36 (020 676 73 05)
Perry Sport	ArenA Boulevard (020 409 42 27), Binnenhof 7, Amstelveen (020 641 95 33), Kalverstraat 99 (020 624 71 31), Overtoom 2-8 (020 618 91 11)

Portegies	Beethovenstraat 34 (020 662 55 66), Holendrechtplein 5 (020 696 08 13), Jodenbreestraat 17 (020 420 53 20)
Praxis	Trompenburgstraat 14a (020 642 18 69), Molukkenstraat 190 (020 663 41 16), Van Slingelandtstraat 32 (020 488 99 51)
Praxis Megastore and Garden Centre	Noordzeeweg 21 (020 614 55 33), Stekkenbergweg 1 (020 342 88 88)
Prins Brillen	Banterij 10 (020 632 30 11), Buikslotermeerplein 66 (020 637 23 92), Gelderlandplein 117 (020 644 07 93)
Puccini	Singel 184 (020 427 83 41), Staalstraat 17 (020 626 54 74)
Siebel Juweliers	Binnenhof 24 (020 647 43 25), Buikslotermeerplein 196 (020 637 23 15), Kalverstraat 121-123 (020 623 85 90)
Simon Lévelt	Huidenstraat 17 (020 320 33 76), Kinkerstraat 109 (020 489 59 65), Prinsengracht 180 (020 624 08 23), Stationsplein 15, Centraal Station (020 428 58 87)
Sissy Boy	Kalverstraat 199 (020 638 93 05), Kalverstraat 210 (020 626 00 88), KNSM laan 19 (020 419 15 59), Leidsestraat 15 (020 623 89 49), Spuistraat 137 (Kelder Magna Plaza) (020 389 25 89), Van Baerlestraat 15 (020 671 51 74)
Spar	A.J. Ernststraat 183-185 (020 642 38 47), Mosplein 18 (020 492 35 59), Nieuwe Kerkstraat 65 (020 423 46 59), Planciusstraat 15 (020 626 97 09), Rapenburg 91 (020 623 15 31), Spaarndammerstraat 544 (020 686 34 41)
Specsavers	Buikslotermeerplein 286 (020 494 28 28), Ferdinand Bolstraat 130 (020 662 54 76), Joop van Weezelhof 20 (020 411 87 29), Kinkerstraat 193 (020 616 51 22), Koninginneweg 224 (020 662 26 51)
Super de Boer	Albert Camuslaan 114 (020 695 44 05), Buitenveldertslaan 184 (020 642 18 00), Waterlandplein 223 (020 637 07 92), Westerstraat 98 (020 624 59 47)
English Hatter	Binnenhof (020 641 45 92), Heiligeweg (020 626 26 05)
Tony Tolo	Binnenhof (020 453 65 85), Kinkerstraat (020 612 09 40)
V&D (Vroom & Dreesmann)	Buikslotermeerplein 123 (0900 235 8363), Buitenplein 101 (0900 235 8363), Kalverstraat 203 (0900 235 8363)
Van Haren	Buikslotermeerplein 129 (020 494 08 70), Ferdinand Bolstraat 106-108 (020 673 32 64), Kinkerstraat 125 (020 612 88 41)
Xenos	Bijlmermeerplein 698 (020 452 95 61), Kalverstraat 228 (020 422 91 63), Nieuwendijk 200 (020 427 41 53), Osdorpplein 111 (020 410 07 67)

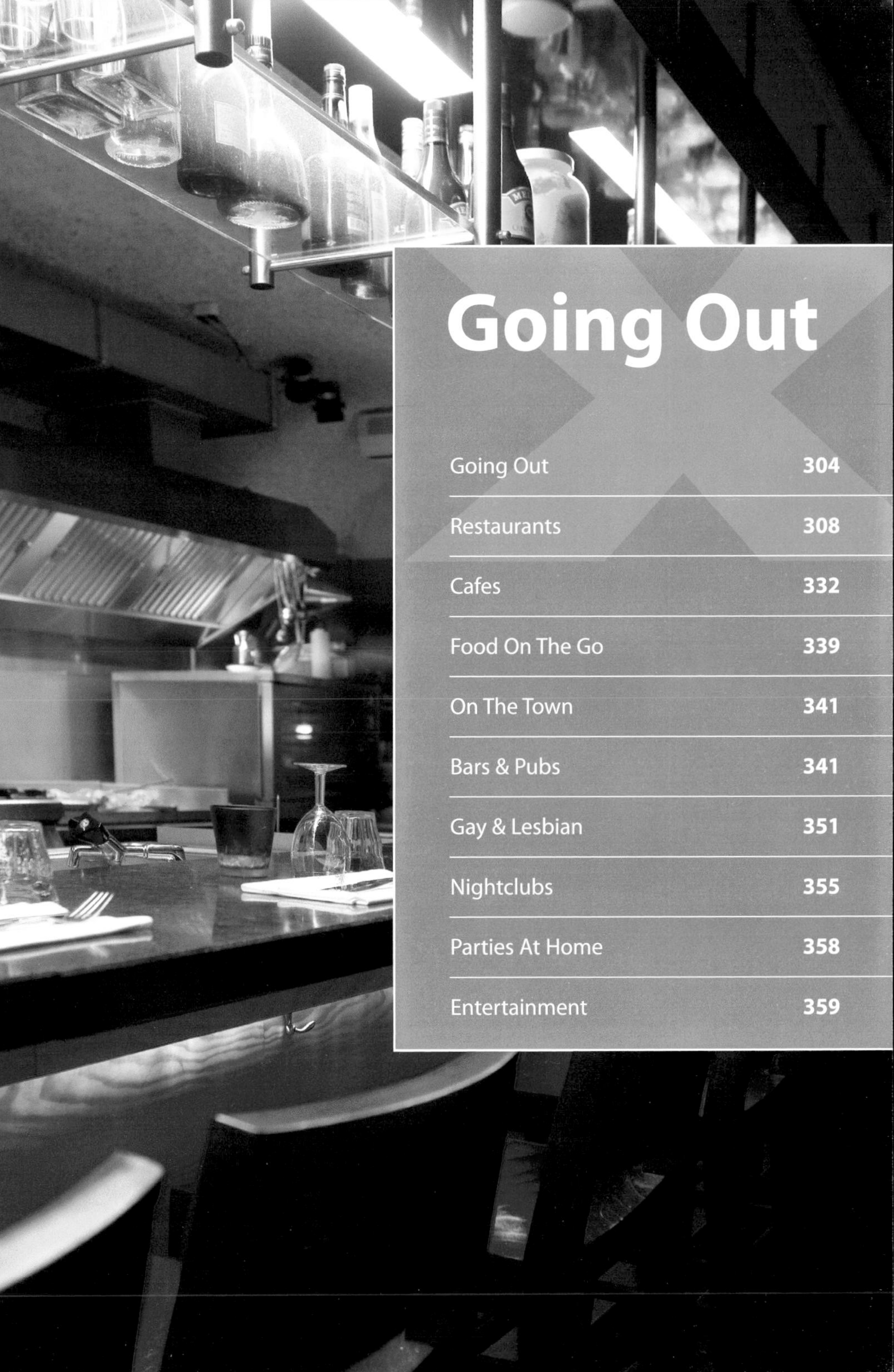

Going Out

Going Out

Amsterdam is well known for being the laid-back party capital of Europe, and not just because of the (legal) marijuana smoked at coffeeshops selling joints – not to be confused with joints selling coffee (for both, see p.332). Give the Dutch an excuse to relax at a sidewalk cafe, in a 'gezellig kroeg' (cosy pub) or with a group of friends in a restaurant, and they're in seventh heaven.

The lively cafe and bar scene is a highlight of Amsterdam for many, and venues tend to be full round the clock. Daytime can be just as buzzing as night; the large student population, sizeable part-time workforce (there are more part-time workers in Amsterdam than any other city in Europe) and regular influx of partying visitors means there's a constant crowd in search of refreshment.

The dining draw of Amsterdam may not be as strong as its hedonistic appeal, and the city would struggle to hold its own on the European culinary stage with the likes of London or Paris, but nevertheless there is good eating to be had here. And if it's quantity you're after, you'll easily be able to satisfy your appetite; many Dutch chefs like to present menus of three, four or five courses to their diners. Delicious staples typically devoured by the Dutch are salmon, sliptong (a type of sole), garlicky shrimps, home-grown lamb and all manner of stews, and there is a good range of international choice too. As well as eating more, you can now also eat for longer at many Dam establishments, as the trend for late-night opening continues to grow (see Restaurant Timings, right).

Bars abound in the city, from local-friendly low-key beer-drinking in atmospheric pubs to the more sophisticated upmarket establishments and rowdier party bars. Residents in the know, in search of a civilised evening, tend to steer clear of Leidseplein and Rembrandtplein, which are magnets for tourists and stag parties. If you're planning a full-on night on the town, prepare for things to start late, and to finish a lot later – nightclubs don't really get going until midnight.

District Guide

We've included an Amsterdam district by each entry in this section to help you locate the restaurants, cafes, bars and nightclubs. The map on p.368 shows which area of town each district covers.

No Smoke Without Fine

As of summer 2008, smoking will be banned in all establishments that serve food – and that includes bars, cafes, eating houses and all manner of restaurants. However, the Dutch are notoriously lax in adhering to laws though, so don't be surprised if after that date you find a few rebellious types lighting up in a non-smoking environment. Exactly how this ban will affect business for coffeeshops remains to be seen.

Eating Out

Although Amsterdam has been a hub of multicultural dining for many decades, based on the influence of cuisine from former Netherlands colonies such as Indonesia and Suriname, simplicity rules the roost when it comes to cooking and eating. The city is slowly catching up with other European capitals in terms of such culinary fashions as freshly grown organic food, Asian fusion and modern local cuisine, but sandwich bars and lunch/brunch cafes still rule the roost here, and can be found almost everywhere.

Cuisine List – Quick Reference

American	p.308	French	p.315	Pizzerias	p.327
Belgian	p.308	Greek	p.316	Portuguese	p.328
Cafes	p.332	Indian	p.317	Seafood	p.328
Caribbean	p.308	Indonesian	p.317	Spanish	p.329
Chinese	p.309	International	p.319	Steakhouses	p.329
Delis	p.309	Italian	p.323	Surinamese	p.330
Dinner Cruises	p.310	Japanese	p.324	Thai	p.330
Dutch	p.311	Mexican	p.325	Turkish	p.331
Eetcafe	p.312	Middle Eastern	p.325	Vietnamese	p.331
Ethiopian	p.314	Moroccan	p.327		

The king of Dutch sandwiches is the tosti, a melted affair of edam or gouda with ham. Fish stalls offering raw herring and a selection of shrimps and mackerel dot the cityscape, while the eetcafe (eating house) is still the best value in the mid-range category – expect to pay between €10 and €20 for a three-course dagschotel (daily menu) consisting of meat, veg and potato.
If you're seeking a more refined dining experience – Michelin-starred French or Japanese, say, or clever organic or fusion, you also have plenty of options in Amsterdam's burgeoning foodie scene. By European standards good restaurants in any culinary category here are slightly expensive; for an decent three-course meal, including wine, expect to pay from between €25 to €40 per person, and easily more.

Dress Code

Unless otherwise stated, there is essentially no dress code for eating and drinking out in the Netherlands – dress down is the motto. The casual Fridays that permeated the working world in the 1990s have been de rigeur here for a long time. Except for Michelin starred restaurants, casual is the fashion. Jeans and trainers are allowed in most establishments. For restaurants that are really strict at the door, look out for the 'suit' icon next to the reviews.

Local Cuisine

Other options **Street Food** p.339, **Food & Drink** p.17

Dutch food used to consist of straightforward no-nonsense grub – lamb, pork or beef, potatoes (fried or boiled) and boiled cabbage, carrot or onion. Thankfully for more adventurous diners, things have moved on somewhat, and Dutch cuisine now embraces a more innovative attitude. As well as perennial Dutch favourites (see Top Nosh, below), chefs of many restaurants are pushing boundaries and fusing cuisines. Breakfast and lunch are largely interchangeable in terms of the types of food eaten – sliced sandwiches of cheese, peanut butter (invented in Holland), jam, ham or salami are generally the order of the day until afternoon kicks in. Unique to Holland, however, is the use of chocolate or coloured sprinkles as a topping on bread. Lunch breads are served open-faced with a hearty dollop of salad, chopped into small pieces.

Top Nosh

Pannekoek (pancakes) – With a variety of toppings from sweet to savoury, favourites are syrup or powdered sugar toppings.

Maatjes haring (raw herring) – Eaten raw, topped with minced onions and sweet gherkins.

Erwtensoep (pea soup) – A thicker version than the Russian variety, with chunks of frankfurter meat, carrots, potato and ham.

Drop (liquorice candy) – From the very sweet to the dubble zout (double salt), a wealth of variety of drop can be found.

Appelgebak (apple pie) – Mums can't beat the flavour of wholesome apples with nuts and raisins, all packed inside a generous crust.

Hutspot (hotchpotch) – Boiled meat atop a bed of mash, mixed with cabbage or kohlrabi and a mountain of brown sauce (the Dutch version of shepherd's pie).

Tosti – Delectable melted cheese and ham pressed in a unique toaster that seals the sides of the bread.

Poffertjes (silver dollar pancakes) – Small pancakes puffed up to the size of silver dollars served with too much powdered sugar and wads of melted butter. Kids love them and adults, do too.

Restaurant Timings

Most places serving food generally open for dinner at 18:00 and close around 23:00. The Dutch eat quite early in the evening, although dining out later is becoming more common – you'll find that some restaurants now serve up until 01:00. Late night snack bars and avondwinkels (all night shops) are options for quick bites and lightly prepared meals.
Through the day, cafes and many restaurants open for lunch, or open between 10:00 and 11:00 and close late in the evening. Many restaurants are closed on Sundays or Mondays, so it's worthwhile making a call to check timings before you head out.

Delivery

Takeaway food is popular in Amsterdam. Pizza chains are widespread (see Pizzerias on p.327). Your average toko (takeaway) snack

Going Out

bar will serve up fastfood such as hamburgers, frikandel (a Dutch deep-fried sausage), chicken nuggets, cheese souffle and other deep-fried items, and most eating places will provide boxes or plastic containers for your do-it-yourself delivery. It's highly recommended to phone your order in if you're getting takeaway from a restaurant to avoid a lengthy wait.

Service

Service, like the prevailing general attitude in Amsterdam, is rather laid back. Waiting staff will often be students making some extra money on a part-time basis. You'll not be troubled if you want to while away a lazy afternoon in a cafe, and as staff don't rely on tips (see Tipping, right), you might have to push for service. In a restaurant, cafe, or bar, it's common to raise your index finger about eye level to indicate you are waiting to be served. Try to look the waiting staff directly in the eye and smile to get their attention. It is considered rude to raise your voice or to show impatience and anger at the speed of service – you risk not being served at all if you do.

End Of The Magic

In another clampdown announced in 2007 by what is historically known as an incredibly lenient country, the sale of the psychedelic drugs 'magic mushrooms' is to be banned by the Dutch authorities following a recent spate of incidents in the city. One of these involved an Icelandic tourist who jumped from a balcony after taking mushrooms, breaking both his legs.

Drinks

Other options **Alcohol** p.255, **On The Town**, p.340

The Netherlands is a beer-lover's delight. At the last count there were over 1,200 drinking venues in Amsterdam, not bad for a city that boasts a population of less than one million. Recently, however, something came between the Dutch and their drinks – the euro. When the guilder finally departed at the start of 2002, alcohol prices doubled in one fell swoop, triggering much crying by locals into their beer. After vociferous protest, however, peace has been restored and prices lowered; a beloved fluitje (flute of 0.25 litre) of Heineken, Amstel or Grolsch will now set you back around €2. Drinking venues range from smoke-stained old man's pubs to stylish wine bars and cocktail lounges, and as soon as there's a smidgen of sunshine, even if it's cool and windy, Amsterdam's bars and cafes put tables and chairs outside. Aside from its classic brands of beer, the Netherlands also brews a peculiar gin called Jenever. It's either oud (aged) or jong (young), just like Dutch cheese.
Unless specifically stated, most restaurants have liquor licences. Liquor can be purchased at off-licence chain Gall & Gall (p.255). Besides the independent wine and beer specialists, alcohol is sold at supermarkets and avondwinkels (night shops that open after 20:00). The legal drinking age in Holland is 16, but proof of age is hardly ever asked for when minors enter a bar or kroeg (pub).

Hygiene

The laws governing sanitation standards in restaurants and cafes are controlled at a local level. Checks are done regularly, but if you encounter problems such as food poisoning

Top Picks – Quick Reference

Romantic		Undiscovered Gem		Enjoy The View		Alfresco	
Abyssinia	p.314	Bird	p.330	Bickers a/d Werf	p.319	Baton	p.312
Ciel Bleu	p.315	Café Potgieter	p.328	Brasserie de Joffers	p.333	Brasserie de Joffers	p.333
Cilubang	p.318	De Kas	p.320	Café de Jaren	p.334	Café Cuba	p.342
d'Vijff Vlieghen	p.311	d'Vijff Vlieghen	p.311	Ciel Bleu	p.315	De Huyschkaemar	p.344
De Griekse Taverna	p.316	Greetje	p.312	Club 11	p.319	Esprit Caffe	p.335
Dinner Cruises	p.310	Kismet Eethuis	p.331	Greetje	p.312	Het Blauwe Theehuis	p.335
Mamouche	p.327	La Storia della Vita	p.323	Hard Rock Cafe	p.308	Los Pilones	p.325
Shibli Bedouin	p.326	New Draver Restaurant	p.330	Het Blauwe Theehuis	p.335	Mamouche	p.327
Visaandeschelde	p.328	Umeno	p.325	Tatin	p.316	Mucho Más	p.329
Wintertuin	p.323	Yam Yam Trattoria	p.324	Toussaint	p.337	Tatin	p.316

you can call or email the Consumentenbond (consumer affairs) hotline (www.consumentenbond.nl, 070 445 45 45). If you have a serious concern you can go to your local gemeente (city hall) to file a complaint.

When purchasing fresh food, make sure you wash it before you eat it; shop assistants in Amsterdam wear neither gloves nor caps to cover their hair, and the same holds true in many restaurant kitchens. For an insight into the hygiene standards of various individual establishments, check out TV show *De Smaakpolitie* – The Taste Police (www.sbs.nl). This weekly show features a horeca (hotel, restaurant and catering) investigator who rates the cleanliness factor of the eateries and shops he visits. He either gives the thumbs up or slaps them with an X – which forces them to change or puts them out of business.

The Yellow Star

The natty yellow star seen to the right is our way of highlighting places that we think merit extra praise. It might be the atmosphere, the food, the cocktails, the music or the crowd, but any review that you see with the star attached is somewhere that we think is a bit special.

Tipping

Tipping is rare in the hotel, restaurant and catering industries here as staff earn decent salaries that aren't dependent on tips. If you feel that the level of service you receive particularly warrants a tip, 5% to 10% of the bill in cash is a good guideline, although it is entirely at your discretion. It is common to leave a cash tip of 10 to 20% at mid-range or upmarket restaurants, but again this should only be given if you feel it's been earned.

Tax & Service Charges

Tax is included in the price of all bills. There is a 19% VAT (value added tax) for drinks, and 6% for food. There are no additional charges or hidden ones on top of this. Be prepared to pay for bottled water even when you've ordered tap – generally, tap water is not served and is mostly frowned upon when ordered. Some restaurants will refuse you outright and demand that bottled water be purchased.

Independent Reviews

All of the venues in this book have been independently reviewed by food and drink writers based in Amsterdam. The entries aim to provide informative, engaging and unbiased views of each outlet. If any of the reviews in this section have led you astray, or if your favourite local eatery doesn't grace these pages, then drop us a line at info@explorerpublishing.com.

Quick Reference Icons

- Dress Code
- Kids Welcome
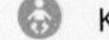
- Alfresco Option

- Cheap
- Expensive
- Unlicensed

Restaurant Listing Structure

As reviewing every restaurant, bar and cafe in Amsterdam would result in a book itself, our Going Out section features a selection of 200 places that are definitely worth a visit. Each review gives an idea of the food, service, decor and atmosphere, while those venues that really excel earn the coveted 'Explorer Recommended' star. Restaurants have been categorised by cuisine and are listed in alphabetical order. The On the Town section covers bars, pubs, nightclubs, and gay and lesbian venues. If you are planning a specific occasion, refer to the Top Picks table on p.306 for listings of romantic venues, alfresco eateries, undiscovered gems and places with great views.

Vegetarian Food

Amsterdam has a lot on offer for vegetarians. There are a number of specialist restaurants in the city (for more on these search by category online at www.iens.nl), as well as places serving all kinds of food that are particularly good for vegetarians – try De Kas, De Witte Uyl or Eat at Jo's (see the reviews for all these on p.320 in International), or Maoz Falafel (p.326). Many cafes (p.332) offer a wide range of sandwiches, salads, hearty soups served with chunks of bread and other dishes. The uitsmijter (three fried eggs served on top of slices of buttered bread) is a great alternative, as is the cheese tosti. Some ethnic cuisines can provide good options, try Indonesian restaurants (p.317) for their vegetarian rijsttafel and other dishes, or Indian (p.317), which are always great for non-meat dishes. Outside of these, practically all eateries offer at least one vegetarian option.

American

Hard Rock Cafe

Max Euweplein 59/61
Canal Belt (Grachtengordel)
Map p.392 B4 1

020 523 76 25 | www.hardrock.com

The burgers don't get any better or bigger in Amsterdam. Count on a fat juicy one done just the way you like it, with or without all the trimmings. No one will bat an eyelid if you order raw onion or extra melted cheese. If burgers aren't your thing go for a selection of Tex-Mex chicken fajitas or hot chicken wings in ranch-style sauce. Either way, adults and kids will have fun while enjoying American-sized portions. You can also get a doggy bag if you like. The views overlooking the Vondelpark and the hurly burly of the canals keep the young ones entertained, as does the sound system with flat-screen TVs screeching MTV videos. Desserts come in large portions and the fudge brownie is just too much for one person. Reservations recommended.

Belgian

Belgica

Kleine-Gartmanplantsoen 25
Canal Belt (Grachtengordel)
Map p.392 B3 2

020 535 32 90 | www.belgica.nu

Belgica is a relaxed cafe-cum-brasserie – the sort of place where you come to drink and where good food is served, as opposed to being a restaurant. Step into the spacious, beautifully lit room, decked out in marble, and the zinc bar and the antique replica espresso maker are a throwback to the days of the crooners – and Sinatra's music is what you'll hear in the background. The Belgian-style fries with mayonnaise are thickly cut, without any oily aftertaste. The shrimp croquettes are smaller than their Dutch cousins and are infused with herbs. Mash with truffle oil and chives goes down well with a salad or chilli con carne. You can order anything on the menu at any time, day or evening, so if you're in the mood for a hot plate of steak after an all-nighter, this is the place to be. The menu is small, but well chosen.

Chez George

Herenstraat 3
Canal Belt (Grachtengordel)
Map p.389 D3 3

020 626 33 32

This restaurant serves up classical Belgian food. Be audacious and order the seven course menu. If that's over the top, try the salmon or shrimp bisque, or bouillabaisse. The white asparagus with ham, chopped boiled egg and butter, and hollandaise sauce are terrific spring and summer staples. You may scratch your head and wonder how can one vegetable dish be so filling as a main course? When you find several thick stalks it becomes clear. Other standbys like Parma ham wrapped around pears are uniquely Belgian. The beer list includes many favourites and there's a decent wine list.

Caribbean

Trinbago

1e van Swindenstraat 44a
Indischebuurt
Map p.395 F3 4

020 694 58 36

Images of limes, coconuts, palm trees and hot spices come to mind when you say the words Trinidad and Tobago. This creative outpost is brand new and filled with both live bamboo trees and paintings of Caribbean scenes. The food is fresh – salads of cucumber, pineapple and mango make your mouth want to get up and dance on the table. The tender, juicy chicken with a lovely crusty batter is glazed in an orange sauce that sparkles. The chef gets his spices fresh at the import markets and changes the three-course menu every fortnight. Dasheen leaves with crab, and the crab cakes with slivers of chilli, are both spiked with innovation. The black cake (a Trinidadian speciality) and coconut icecream will make you reel with delight.

Chinese

Jan Willem Brouwersstraat 7
Oud Zuid
Map p.384 A1 5

Chang-i

020 470 17 00 | www.chang-i.nl

Step into a lavish dream of what a decadent Buddhist temple would look like if the monks let their hair grow, donned chic clothing and ate carnivorously. The deep purples and dark shaded walls glitter against the glass windows; overlooking a zigzag Zen-like garden stand several Buddha statues from all over Asia. Asian chefs serve up some eclectic food, including innovative pan-Pacific delicacies. The sashimi-type scallops are moist and tender, the US Angus beef is grilled with ginger, and Japanese wagyu is served up with shallots and melted fois gras. The baked scallops with black bean sauce in a piquant tomato base are real victors. The only downside is that portions are on the small side and may leave you hungry.

Zeedijk 111-113
Centrum
Map p.389 F4 6

Nam Kee

020 624 34 70

Amsterdammers have been raving over Nam Kee for over a decade – it's one of the top Chinese restaurants in the city. In reality, it is a good price for a quality pit stop. Noted for its Peking duck with plum sauce, you can't go wrong for €12. Most noodle plates or soups could use a dash more flavouring. Don't be shy, ask for the piquant spices the Chinese use, particularly the hot chilli oil, soy sauce and rice vinegar (which should souse up the eggrolls and prawn with vegetables). They do a decent spare rib, although at times you may have more fat than pork. Service is snappy and fast.

Scheldestraat 71/77
Rivierenbuurt
Map p.384 B3 7

Oceania

020 673 89 07 | info@restaurantoceania.nl

Make this your local Chinese hangout for lunch or dinner. This is where the local Chinese go because the food is authentic Cantonese. Conveniently situated by the Amsterdam RAI exhibition centre in the south of the city, Oceania is no nonsense and down to earth. Like so many Chinese family owned operations, you'll find the familiar black lacquer room dividers painted with birds and scrolls, as well as porcelain Buddhas. People flock here for the seafood, especially the hot pot made with generous lumps of fried tofu; the huge scallops and shrimps, and mighty portions of lobster and octopus are also a real treat. The food is not too oily, and the shitakes are fresh and juicy in soy sauce. They do banqueting and catering and if you have a special occasion such as an anniversary or birthday the owners will prepare a buffet-style arrangement.

C. Krusemanstraat 15
Oud Zuid
Map p.383 E2 8

Sing Sing

020 470 44 75 | www.sing-sing.nl

It takes an artist to get fusion cuisine right – the pan-Asian food is original, pungent and done with a perfectionist's hand. Roasting scallops sounds simple and yet it is an art not to lose the delicate flavour of the meat by overdoing it. To then top them with scallions basted in fiery lemon-scented salsa without losing the flavour of the shellfish shows how earnestly the chef approaches his craft. The crispy, hot, non-oily deep fried chicken tussled with chilli and sesame is a big hit with the crowd that isn't afraid to try 'HOT'. The oysters and Japanese ponzu sauce slide down your throat like silk. The wagyu (Japanese beef) here is grilled then served with a soy-based scented side dip.

Delis

Amsterdam's delis provide a choice range of high quality and authentic produce, catering for all tastes. You'll be able to find everything to get your taste buds tingling, whether it's sushi, Spanish ham, delicious Italian salami, smoked salmon, thick and creamy Greek yoghurt, or freshly baked French baguettes.

Delis

Feduzzi Mercato Italiano	Scheldestraat 63	020 664 63 65	For top quality Italian delicatessen items such as imported sausages with fennel from Tuscanny, freshly made pasta and gnocchi, bresaola and salami, come here. It also has an excellent assortment of wine, Italian mixers, cookies and desserts.
Frank's Smoke House	Wittenburgergracht 303	020 670 07 74	This traiteur and catering service supplies many restaurants, being one of the very few who import Alaskan wild salmon, and fewer who smoke it themselves. Besides the salmon, it offers halibut and crab, and also meats such as pastrami, wild boar and beef carpaccio.
Hollandaluz	Haarlemmerstraat 71	020 330 28 88	Holland meets Spain in this sandwich shop, caterer and traiteur. Fresh Spanish hams and chorizo, delicious combinations. Ole!
Ijssalon Venetie	Schelderstraat 68	020 662 55 60	Not a real deli in the traditional sense, this staple ice and gelati salon of Amsterdam has been serving up home-made Italian ices in 24 flavours since 1935 at this very location.
Japans Delicatessenhuis Zen	Fans Halsstraat 38	020 627 06 07	Owned and operated by the Japanese mamas who are slaving away in the kitchen, eat in or take away all sort of sushi rolls, sashimi, donburi (rice bowls with a variety of toppings) and assorted vegetarian dishes. The restaurant is simply adorned with Japanese wooden sculptures and origami designs.
Peperwortel Traiteur & Catering	Overtoom 140	020 685 10 53	An international range of delicacies, mostly Mediterranean. Known for their great quiches, which unlike the packaged variety found at most Dutch supermarkets, don't contain potato. Tapanades and dressings, olives of all varieties, lasagne and pasta mixtures are popular.
Romios Griekse Traiterie	Ceintuurbaan 350h	020 675 43 24	Home-made fresh and thick Greek yoghurts, hand-made dolmas stuffed with rice and raisins, plus all manner of excellent quality Greek takeaway food. There are some tables if you care to eat quickly, although this is more a takeaway as it is self-service.
Vlaamsch Broodhuys	Haarlemmerstraat 108	020 528 64 30	Want French-style loaves, baguettes and dark thick brown bread? This is the place! It also offers takeaway sandwiches for breakfast or lunch.

Dinner Cruises

Other options **Boat & Yacht Charters** p.165, **Boat Tours** p.165

What would tourism be in the Venice of the North if it wasn't for dinner cruises along the serene canals of Amsterdam? Passing the modestly lit stately homes along the inner rings of the city is a fascinating pastime. Only the most cynical of long-term residents would deny the beauty of the experience. Several companies are competing for your euros and all offer bespoke packages. You can rent schooners and canal boats, old sailing ships and luxury full-throttled yachts. Companies charge either per person or per hour. Some of the boat charter companies will subcontract caterers themselves.

It is also possible for you to provide your own catering. The usual food and beverage offerings include warm and cold fish platters and salads, chicken wings cooked barbecue or Indian style, borrel hapjes (bar snacks), coffee and tea and either wine or beer. Based on the type of cruise you require, you can decide whether to have buffet or sit-down dinners. The Hilton Hotel offers boats for rental with or without catering provided by the hotel's restaurants. The Blue Boat Company, Klipper Avontuur and Classic Canal Charters all provide water cruises with the option of dining onboard. For more on these companies, see Boat Tours in Exploring p.165.

Dinner Cruises		
Blue Boat Company	020 679 13 70	www.blueboat.nl
Classic Canal Charters	020 421 08 25	www.classiccanalcharters.com
Hilton Amsterdam	020 710 60 00	www.hilton.com
Klipper Avontuur	020 683 88 65	www.avontuur.nl

Dutch

Roelof Hartstraat 1
Oud Zuid
Map p.384 B2 61

The College Hotel

020 571 15 11 | www.steinhotels.com/college

The College Hotel is a fine experiment under the auspices of the ROC, an educational organisation which trains up and coming young people wishing to enter the fields of hotel management, restaurants and catering. The building houses a hotel, a lounge and bar area where lunch and snacks are served, and a more formal restaurant. The lounge has probably one of the finest BLT sandwiches this side of the Atlantic, although service can be painfully slow. The best idea is to order 15 minutes before you're ready to eat, as it takes that long to whip up a sandwich. The restaurant is a posh, subdued hangout for artists, neighbourhood locals and well-heeled travellers. The chefs create original dishes using fresh ingredients; fillet of sole with vegetable-sprinkled mash, croquettes of pheasant, and chilled fruit soups are some of the pleasures.

Spuistraat 294-302
Centrum
Map p.393 D1 10

d'Vijff Vlieghen

020 530 40 60 | www.thefiveflies.com

Foreigners and locals adore this restaurant and come back for more than just seconds because the quality just doesn't let up. New Dutch cooking at it's finest in one of the most beloved rooms in the city (The Rembrandt Room) that reeks with authenticity and old world charm. Upon entering you get a grand tour of the premises that will not disappoint. But the food is the main event here, with near to perfect service. A starter of sweetbreads with apple in an anchovy chutney, to a daily changing seasonal menu with an excellent array of wines awaits the uninitiated. A little expensive, but worth every cent.

d'Vijff Vlieghen

Damrak 93-94
Centrum
Map p.389 E4 72

De Roode Leeuw

020 555 06 66 | www.hotelamsterdam.nl

Smack in the centre of all the action, near to the Dam monument, lies a very old-fashioned Dutch institution combining a restaurant, cafe and hotel that has been serving weary travellers and hungry local residents since 1911. The art deco walls hold the secrets of deals done by stock traders in centuries past as they hungrily guzzled their lunch (it's situated close to the stock exchange). What the traders ate then, the kitchen serves today with pride. Hotchpotches of all variations can be found here such as mash filled with cabbage, kale or spinach and topped with bacon. Mussels from Zeeland known as Zeeuse oysters, which are big, orange and juicy arrive with white wine, cream and fries. Come here with the entire family – the staff are playful and patient with the little ones. The buffet breakfast is open to the public, and the quality and value is very good.

Peperstraat 23
Centrum
Map p.394 B1 11

Greetje

020 779 74 50 | www.restaurantgreetje.nl

What strikes you first is the homely atmosphere found in many of the old world, charming cafes around town. A large mahogany bar – almost too big for the reception area, with spotted, leaded glass behind the assortment of liquor bottles, is just a tease; what's to follow is original new Dutch cuisine. Take a step upstairs to the smallish room with original Delft blue tiles, or venture down into an alcove billed as 'the mayor's table' for lucky diners who can look outside through the huge glass window at the bicycles and canal boats. A typical Dutch menu may include blood sausage with apple compote, white asparagus with Hollandaise sauce, and egg white and ham. A home-made recipe of minced lamb also served with apple sauce is an excellent introduction to the brave new world of Dutch cuisine. This is a wonderful place to take your family and friends – make it a regular stop on your list of places to eat.

Oostelijke Handelskade 34
Zeeburg
Map p.380 A2 13

Lloyd Hotel

020 561 36 04 | www.lloydhotel.com

Enter this former wayward hotel for European emigrants leaving for America and step back in time. The brick facade and semi-art deco interior have been renovated to reflect a clean, modern style while keeping the elements of the past like the renaissance touches. Set apart from the dining area is a lounge section where you can work on your laptop (they have Wi-Fi), sip a coffee, read a book or people watch. When you order meat, fowl or fish you choose one of eight sauces from the sauce menu. The freshly baked baguettes are crunchy on the outside and fluffy inside, just like they should be. Beware of the size of the portions, as the side dishes alone count as a meal. Every Monday evening there are free events such as concerts, discussions, readings, art initiatives or performances.

Prinsengracht 191
Canal Belt (Grachtengordel)
Map p.388 C3 14

The Pancake Bakery

020 625 13 33 | www.pancake.nl

Pancakes were invented in Holland, and no matter what type of pancake you desire, you'll find it here. From sweet fruits, syrups or jams to savoury bacon, sausage, ham and cheese – a Dutch favourite is apple and bacon – there are more than 100 varieties to choose from. The kids love it here because they get a surprise toy to accompany their order. The location is great if you enjoy wandering along the canals at the weekend or are visiting the Anne Frank Huis nearby.

Eetcafe

Herengracht 82
Canal Belt (Grachtengordel)
Map p.389 D3 15

Baton

020 624 81 95

Sit on the cobble-stoned terrace overlooking one of the prettiest canals in town or go upstairs in this Lilliputian cafe that covers three tiny floors. A good lunch stop for a break after walking around the centre, or for when the rain comes pouring down. Ask for the oversized salads loaded with chicken and bacon, or its version of the Dutch tosti, a melted delight of cheese and ham on toasted bread. Baton's tosti is reversed with the melted cheese on the outer bread layer and is large enough for a satisfying meal. Service can be a bit on the slow side so take a magazine from the racks upstairs or delve into a good novel while waiting.

Overtoom 28/30
Oud West
Map p.392 A3 16

Bicken Eten & Drinken

020 689 39 99

Located on a busy street off the Stadhouderskade, this place has changed hands more than a dozen times over the past 10 years. At last praise can be given for the right blend of ambience, service and food. The retro 80s black interior, with touches of lilac and deep purple on the tables, is splashed against white art. Customers in bell-bottoms and tie-dye shirts look like they belong to this scene. The quest for good oysters and bouillabaisse is driving demand as more people seem to fancy fish these days and fish is what they'll find in abundance here. The tartare of tuna is unsullied. Sip the attractive asparagus soup (white or green depending on the chef's mood) out of a warmed shot glass. Eccentricity is embraced with the Portobello mushrooms.

Govert Flinckstraat 326
De Pijp
Map p.384 C1 17

Cafe Amsterdommertje

020 676 78 97 | *www.amsterdommertje.nl*

In Holland, eating at a warm, country-style Dutch eetcafe can be a memorable experience. The olive green and coral painted walls, brown wooden stools and little round tables reminiscent of toy furniture at Cafe Amsterdommertje make you feel like you're in someone's home. The atmosphere makes you feel comfortable as you settle in with a starter of French onion soup, or for the more adventurous, meatballs made of lamb in a mild curry sauce. Enjoy a full meal of halibut with caper sauce, or angler fish baked in butter. All the main courses come with overflowing bowls of potatoes (fried or boiled), a nice big serving of salad with vinaigrette, and steamed vegetables. There's also a reasonably priced kids' menu.

Watertorenplein 6
Westerpark
Map p.379 F1 18

Café-Restaurant Amsterdam

020 682 26 66 | *www.caferestaurantamsterdam.nl*

In a newly constructed area west of the city, it's housed in an old industrial warehouse, the size of which is rare in this clogged city. When you enter there's a long bar and drinks area that is swarming with kids, a pool table, and reading tables. Sit down and peruse the large menu assortment. They have a large selection from bread rolls, sweetbreads, stampot (mash with veg, some meat and a brown sauce) to grilled fish. Nibble, peck or wolf down three courses. The wine is not recommended as it comes tableside, already uncorked.

Zuidplein 22
Buitenveldert
Map p.383 F3 19

Eetwinkel Zwaan

020 442 21 12 | *www.eetwinkelzwaan.n*

Perched between the high rise office towers that make up the area around the Ringweg Zuid in the south of Amsterdam, hungry lawyers, international accountants and people not working in the area make their way to what is arguably one of the best lunch and takeaways in Amsterdam – it feels more like you're in a California lunch spot. Of course

Interior of a modern eetcafe

you can eat dinner here, but you're better off getting something to take home as the area empties after 18:00. The service is attentive and ever ready to please. The menu changes frequently so you won't get bored with the salads or sandwich offerings. The caesar salad is made beautifully with anchovies and freshly poached eggs. Trout is wonderful here. Healthy eating has left many a diner here happier and less calorie dependent. You can take the tram here even if you don't work at the World Trade Center.

Middenweg
Watergraafsmeer
Map p.386 A1 20

Elsa's Café

020 668 50 10 | www.elsascafe.nl

This is the favourite hangout of the Ajax football team. If you're a fan then it's worth the tram ride a bit out of the centre to meet the players. Most of them are ready to give an autograph or share a borrel with you so long as you're not overtly pushy. Elsa's is an archetypal local brown cafe where they speak an Amsterdam slang with an accent that other Netherlanders say is too rough. When they roll their Rs it sounds harsh. Elsa is always at your beck and call for a sandwich or a pork chop with mounds of vegetables. You can easily speak to people at the bar or the next table or watch a football game together. There's live music at night transforming it into a folksy, offbeat setting.

Amstelstraat 9
Centrum
Map p.393 F2 21

Flo Amsterdam

020 890 47 57 | www.floamsterdam.com

This is the local franchise of the famed Paris chain of brasseries. Here, just like in the French brasseries, a gold railing behind the seats allows space to put your bags. The room is warm and inviting and the unadulterated entertainment continues from morning to evening. Flo specialises in the cuisine of the Alsace region – a knockout hybrid of German and French delicacies. Highlights include the artichokes in vinaigrette, grilled quail salad with asparagus, and the choucroute – a stew of sauerkraut, loin pork, bacon, sausage and frankfurter. The sorbets will send you to the moon, as will the lemon tart with berries.

Huidenstraat 9
Canal Belt (Grachtengordel)
Map p.392 C1 22

Goodies

020 625 61 22

This miniscule spot on one of the nine cross streets of Amsterdam uses wooden outdoor picnic tables inside and on the street to foster an atmosphere of relaxation. Order a hearty lunch, soup and a chunky piece of brown bread fresh from the oven. Pastas with seafood, peppers, asparagus or broccoli are a good buy and offer vegetarians a good choice. The sandwiches topple over they're so humungous. You can bring your children – there's a family friendly ambience. The house wine at €2.75 per glass is a good deal, as are the fixed price menus.

Ethiopian

Jan Pieter Heijestraat 190
Oud West
Map p.379 E4 23

Abyssinia

020 683 07 92 | www.abyssinia.nl

The concept of sitting around a buffet either at a table or on the floor on comfy pillows appeals to the Dutch, largely because it mirrors birthday celebrations where families gather in small circles to generate a cosy feeling. Ethiopian cuisine requires you to eat with your right hand mopping up the chick peas, lentils and beef, chicken or vegetable combos with a somewhat sour pancake (think of sourdough bread) that serves as knife, fork and spoon. It comes as no surprise that the portions are tremendous and the value a real find. The interior is quite ordinary, yet couples find it an interesting experience, if only for the idea of feeding each another by hand. The banana beer served from a coconut husk is a crowd pleaser. Cash only.

French

Hotel Okura Amsterdam
De Pijp
Map p.384 B2 24

Ciel Bleu

020 678 74 50 | *www.okura.nl*

There aren't enough accolades in the dictionary to describe the ultimate in French dining at this Michelin-starred restaurant. From the moment you sit down, a footstool appears for the ladies to rest their bags, then the show begins: rice crackers dipped in squid ink, a fine filo wrap of old Amsterdam cheese dipped in a bed of sunflower seeds, and a sweet and tickly cucumber sorbet. Creations such as apple vodka with a dollop of osteria caviar leave your senses fizzing in overdrive. There are amazing feats with turbot – juicy and crunchy with white asparagus, and the deep-fried Japanese-style pigeon leg dipped in pate. If this isn't enough, the desserts will jettison you to outer space. Try sugar crystals that burst in your mouth with orange gratinee and anise cream, lollies of blood orange in a white yogurt, or the home-made white chocolate ice cream. Personable yet professional service allows you to dine at your own pace. Last but not least are the 360 degree views of the city. Downright fabulous wouldn't be an overstatement.

Westerstraat 40
Jordaan
Map p.388 C2 25

L'Olivier

020 625 27 56 | *www.l-olivier.nl*

This is one eatery that is worth the trip to even if you don't live right next door. Laid back in typical Amsterdam fashion, the owner-chef Akiko (Japanese) and his partner Richard (Malaysian) with star waiter Kodit (Nigerian) bring an intercultural cosmopolitanism right to your table. The attitude here is enjoy your meal and be relaxed, which is why after less than a year on the scene L'Olivier has regular customers more than half the time. Based on French cooking methods, chef Akiko delivers simple, well-rounded meals with international touches. The seafood salad of octopus, mussels, shrimp and rocket is fresh and tasty, while the raw salmon is infused with a pleasant wasabi-based honey sauce. The home-made lobster bisque is recommended, and the cod with sesame seeds and oil is filling, and comes with a baked potato and sour cream. Their signature dish is the pan-fried (at your table) crepe suzette with Remy Martin and Grand Marnier doused in oranges and lemons.

De Oude Molen 5
Amstelveen
Map p.367 E4

Lute

020 472 24 62 | *www.lute.com*

Once a gunpowder factory, this space has become a trend setters' paradise. A short drive from Amsterdam, it's a fashion stop for the art, design and advertising crowds. Lute's philosophy is love, taste and elegance. You can order two, three or four-course set menus or take a gastronomic journey by consuming eight smaller dishes chosen by the chef. A typical Lute staple might be goose liver with chocolate and sherry jelly that melts in your mouth while delivering a smooth punch. The scallop tartare with truffle is a distinctive take on Japanese sashimi with shallots. Order the lamb, duck, veal or fish for a memorable meal. The yellowfin sashimi is enlivened by the olive oil and lemon zest. Lunch is served to the business crowd and dinner is most certainly sold out, so reserve a table. It's worth coming just to be part of this exciting environment.

Kerkstraat 56
Canal Belt (Grachtengordel)
Map p.392 C3 12

Ron Blaauw

020 496 19 43 | *www.ronblaauw.nl*

In all categories of what makes a restaurant great Ron Blaauw deserves all the accolades he has won. A typical menu of eight courses for lunch is an outstanding testament to his ability. Scallops that are rolled like sushi and topped with a mousse of wasabi mustard and caviar will send you to heaven. Canapes made from sweet and sour cucumber have an air of delicacy. Then there's the palate pleaser of sardines – briny and thick, stuffed with shrimp scampi and lime leaf, an exotic sensation. Can you imagine bon bons made of blue cheese, so creamy and mild inside a cherry coating? The wine list is exceptional and the sommelier is female, a welcome treat in the male bastion of that world. Service here exceeds the norm; each guest is treated with respect and care. The lunch menu is reasonably priced for a restaurant of this calibre.

Borneostraat 1
Zeeburg
Map p.380 A3 28

Tatin

020 468 51 09 | *www.tatin.nl*

When you sit on the terrace to dine alfresco here and breathe in the harbour air, you'll be transported to an earlier time – maybe the golden age of Holland's seafaring adventures. As you drift, you'll be jettisoned back to earth with some of the most delicious duck or steak, brasserie style with French fries. Tatin serves French with a Mediterranean touch – you'll find foods from the Provence region, and southern delicacies like courgette flowers with olive oil. With much fanfare, a separate restaurant has been added for children, with a babysitting service and a play area. What more could parents ask for? The kids get their own menu to choose from and it's great for parties. Dinner for kids is served from 17:00 to 19:30. Reservations recommended.

Prins Hendrikkade 59
Centrum
Map p.389 F3 29

Vermeer

020 556 48 85 | *www.restaurantvermeer.nl*

From the moment you enter the front room covered in satin, cream coloured walls and the Vermeeresque squares of black and white marble on the floors, you know this restaurant doesn't pull any punches. It's serious business here, and formal. The sommelier is passionate, which sets you at ease, and the wine list is far-reaching – stretching from Holland (just one white wine) to Lebanon. Burn a hole in your pocket for a St Emilion 1994 Cheval Blanc at €675 to €2,100 for a bottle. A British chef with a heavy hand whips up single portions that are good for two. If you order the five-course menu it might be too much; safer to go for a la carte. Dishes change daily. Surprise constructions like lobster with herb-encrusted mussels, socca bread and octopus with vegetable couscous melt in your mouth. As fine dining for lunch is not yet a habit in Holland, beat the crowds and savour a refined meal for €40.

Greek

Hobbemakade 64-65
Oud Zuid
Map p.384 B1 30

De Griekse Taverna

020 671 79 23 | *www.degrieksetaverna.nl*

With their heart and soul, the staff here love what they're doing and want you too to travel with them to the glittering Adriatic where olive-skinned folk smile, dance and clap their hands to music while taking their own time to eat. The food is standard taverna, starting with a tray of mezzas. Particularly good is the olive oil swished around in yoghurt as a dip. Go for the baked feta cheese with honey and thyme or the delicious giant bean salad made with a tinge of tomato paste. The Greek tomato sauce differs from the Italian in that it's thicker and not as sweet – great over the grilled lamb chops. Don't miss the aubergines baked in a casserole with melted feta and carrots. There's live music to kick up your heels to if you're in the mood.

De Clercqstraat 106
Oud West
Map p.379 F3 31

To Ouzeri

020 618 14 12

The sign of a good restaurant is when after 10 years, it's still pulling in the crowds. Hobnobbing at the U-shaped bar, at spontaneous intervals one of the owner's family strums their ukulele. You need to shout above the din to make yourself heard and are endlessly encouraged to eat, laugh, mingle, drink, or if the mood takes you, dance on the tables. You won't mind heading out west to the edge of the city centre because this neighbourhood establishment has a great atmosphere and good Greek standbys: stuffed vine leaves, moussaka, baba ganoush or tzatziki. The ouzo oozes and the noise increases. You'll be having such a blast you may want to throw a glass against the wall, and if it's late enough you could get to do this. But before you indulge in this, reach into your pocket to pay at the cash-only bar.

Indian

Haarlemmerdijk 28
Jordaan
Map p.389 D1 32

Balraj

020 625 14 28

The owners insist that Princess Maxima ate here once. Even if she didn't, the food is fit for royalty. Indian cuisine is not that common in Amsterdam, but when it's done properly (as it is here) people flock to it like bees to pollen. With an extensive curry menu and all types of nan breads, Balraj has been in business for over 30 years, satisfying those in need of a peppery boost. You can order your curries at any degree of heat. The lamb sag is delectably cooked. The restaurant had a facelift recently, but don't come here for the room, which is a simple affair off a major high street. The silverware is bargain basement and the beer glasses advertise the logos of the breweries. Those on a budget will appreciate the prices. Cash only.

Lange Leidsedwarsstraat 56
Canal Belt (Grachtengordel)
Map p.392 C3 33

Guru of India

020 624 69 66

If you're organising an event or seminar and wish to put in some overtime at a working lunch or dinner let Guru be your inspiration. Just seconds away from Leidseplein square, which is packed with people drinking beer and wine at the numerous outdoor cafes, Guru is located off a quiet street right in the heart of the city. An easy location to get to, every tram seems to stop at this intersection. Business meetings are conducted here and private and foreign groups seem to gravitate to this spot. While it won't win any awards for its interior the restaurant has been satisfying hordes since its opening, with the generous portions of lamb, chicken or prawn sag, cauliflower and potato in curry, prawns done up with butter, and numerous vegetarian options.

Reguliersdwarsstraat 72
Canal Belt (Grachtengordel)
Map p.393 E2 34

Shiva

020 624 87 13

Cramped tables and chairs that bump up against one another force you to eat in a hurry, even though the pleasure of lingering over the yummy vegetarian bowls of lentils or spinach sag is your true desire. The service is attentive, but it's not as if you're being kicked out or asked to gobble down your Punjabi delight too speedily, it's just that the crowds at the doors (no reservations are taken) wish to eat, then take in a movie down the road. Tourists as well as locals visit Shiva because its reputation precedes it. On a street where one Indian restaurant after another has come and gone in an endless turnover, Shiva stands its ground as good value for quality food at reasonable prices.

Indonesian

Nassaukade 366
Oud West
Map p.392 B2 35

Blue Pepper

020 489 70 39 | www.restaurantbluepepper.com

The timing was right for star chef Sonja Pereira to introduce to Amsterdam a modern version of Indonesian cuisine. Rave reviews from around the world are spot on and well earned. The room is a dreamy blue, with red seating in one corner. With three categories on the menu of classic, modern and contemporary, this chef goes the whole hog with provocative pan-Pacific combinations. The lobster thermador with Indonesian spices is terrific. Or try the quail eggs served yakitori style, teasing you to dip them into a spicy pot of sambal mixed with vegetables. Monkfish charred and grilled without a trace of fatty tissue, is covered with a secret spiced dip and two long laces of asparagus. The rice table (rijsttafel) is refined and the service unabashedly understated – it's on time and very responsive to your table guests. Desserts such as the coconut icecream with black rice shouldn't be underestimated. You'll go for seconds.

Runstraat 10
Canal Belt (Grachtengordel)
Map p.392 C1 36

Cilubang

020 626 97 55 | www.cilubang.com

An intimate dining experience, at once romantic and otherworldly, as you tuck into an East Javanese selection of rice and spices – enjoy the sambal, an oriental spice that is a cross between Chinese duck sauce and chilli slivers in oil. The various assorted rice tables (rijsttafel) comprising of 15 to 28 types of dishes can be appreciated with that special someone in this rustic 16th century house located right in the city centre. Wayang Golek puppets hang on the walls and seem to sway and dance to the Gamelan music that wafts imperceptibly through the air. Some Indonesian rice table food can be overly sweet, but thank goodness that isn't the case here. While you do taste the satay and coconut shavings with the meats, chicken and fish, they aren't saturated with these flavours.

Ceintuurbaan 103
De Pijp
Map p.384 B1 37

Desa

020 671 09 79

What Indian is to London or Italian to New York, Indonesian is to Amsterdam. Too many choices, not enough time. For a mere €15 or so, you can eat your way through the broad range of dishes; they're not overly sweet or too spicy – a nice mixture. The peanut sauce and coconut icecream dessert are both sweet but worth a try, and for those who prefer savoury then why not have the strong sambal to accompany the meats and chicken? A facelift has given the place a brighter, younger appearance. You wouldn't go wrong by introducing friends and family to the cuisine here, but it's not an ideal location for business guests.

Zeilstraat 41
Oud Zuid
Map p.383 D2 38

LimZz

020 470 84 88

By day it's a breakfast place, yet by night it does a Jekyll and Hyde and becomes an Indonesian hotspot. Silk butterfly mobiles hang on the lamps; lilac doors and bric-a-brac are pushed into every available corner of this 35 seater eatery. The kitchen is tiny but used to full advantage. There's no compromise here with authentic ingredients or watering down tastes to be mild. The stark bitter herb peteh and the kemiri nuts are used with abandon, and the Gado Gado green salad is the real deal. What cannot be bought at the wholesale markets is directly imported and thus the dishes are aromatic and flavoursome – the spices used are as if you were in Indonesia yourself. There are no rice tables (rijsttafel) here, just a la carte selections.

Rijnstraat 51
Rivierenbuurt
Map p.385 D2 39

Taste of Life

020 644 77 86

Two countries that border one another meet here: Indonesia and Malaysia. This is a family run establishment that has no frills. The dark walls are aligned with glass-framed pictures of etched birds. It's rather difficult to distinguish between what is Malay and what is Indonesian as they share the same ingredients, cooking methods and presentation. Here they do three types of rice tables (rijsttafel): small, medium and large, with ascending prices to match. Local fish is presented with peanut sauce and chicken looms large on the menu. Several vegetarian dishes are popular, from salads to a type of hazelnut mixed with green vegetables.

International

Amsteldijk 25
De Pijp
Map p.385 D1 40

Altmann Restaurant & Bar

020 662 77 77 | www.altmann.nl

They ought to win a prize for literally bowling over customers with their sense of flair, refined chic, charm and service. Every item here is justifiably well above average. Tenderloin of wagyu teriyaki with julienne mango strips leave you orbiting outer space. Two soups served alongside – watercress with clumped Dutch shrimp tempura and a tangy coconut soup with lotus blossom, produce thunderbolts of flavour. Seared scallops nestled alongside slivers of grapefruit are a sparkling duet, while the popcorn sensation of the soft shell crab with spiced Asian accents reveals itself after you've sipped a Pouilly Fuisse. The ravioli of pineapple contains a hangop (Dutch creamy thick yoghurt) with a sole blueberry that bursts in your mouth. For the chocoholics try the souffle, a sticky sensation you'll want to repeat. Their wine list is superb and a four-course meal is very reasonably priced for the quality delivered.

Utrechtsedwarsstraat 141
Canal Belt (Grachtengordel)
Map p.394 A4 48

Beddington's

020 620 73 92 | www.beddington.nl

It's hard to pin down or put a label on the sublime creations you can expect here. One night you'll be blessed with a crab and asparagus entree, another with sushi of grapefruit with duck that's been braised and grilled. Diners jealously eye the next table to peek at what they decided not to order. There are no compromises here; quality and perfection are the keys to star chef Jean Beddington's continued success. Each individual order is prepared on the spot so it may take a while to be served. While waiting, ask the staff (who are very knowledgeable about the wines) to offer their admirable advice, as the wine list is far-reaching. Every week there's a new modern menu.

All You Can Eat

On the Nieuwedijk, otherwise known as Little Chinatown, you can dig into an assortment of fastfood Chinese restaurants that offer fixed price, 'all you can eat' buffets. For something more upmarket, Wintertuin at the Krasnapolsky Hotel (p.323) does a great Sunday brunch and dinner where you can eat to your heart's content, aside from the champagne and wines which are extra.

Bickerswerf 2
Westerpark
Map p.374 A4 41

Bickers a/d Werf

020 320 29 51 | www.bickersaandewerf.nl

On the planks of Bickers you have a great view of life on the IJmeer. The netting on the ceiling, and pastel walls that display all manner of nautical trinkets, remind you of Holland's illustrious past. The menu is a mixed bag of Dutch delights and international favourites. The delicate mustard soup is essential to warm the cockles on a windy day. The caesar salad has real anchovies, while the tuna sashimi is a great diet option. The portions are super and substantial. From time to time you'll find a special dish like guinea fowl with chestnuts. Lunch can be as easy as a sandwich; the high tea is also worth a nibble.

Oosterdokskade 3-5
Centrum
Map p.390 B3 42

Club 11

020 625 59 99 | www.ilove11.nl

The very reason for its existence grew out of necessity. A few years back the modern art Stedelijk museum began renovation and was moved to the former post office. Museum-goers needed somewhere to replenish their energy, thus 11 was born. Take a warehouse lift to the 11th floor then wander around a bit until you find the right door to the restaurant. There are no signs. 11 has some of the best views in the city, and you can see for miles on a clear day. A large video screen relays pop images while you sip a mint tea or a beer. At the back of the restaurant area the space becomes a dance club by night (see p.355). The food is okay, the menu is limited, but you didn't come here to take a culinary journey, you came here to be cool.

Kamerlingh Onneslaan 3
Watergraafsmeer
Map p.385 F1 104

De Kas

020 462 45 62 | www.restaurantdekas.nl

One of the first establishments to offer 100% organic vegetables, meat, poultry and fish. Expert chef Ronald Kunis cooks all the vegetables on the day they are harvested and they're served in a greenhouse-style building. Herbs are grown on the premises, while carefully selected meat (Waterland veal), poultry and fish are supplied from nearby farms. Mr. Kunis has set a trend in Holland by allowing the vegetables to take centre stage, accompanied by side dishes of meat or fish. Signature dishes are the tartin of brussels sprouts with caramel, and roasted celeriac with pancetta.

Frans Halsstraat 26
De Pijp
Map p.384 B1 201

De Witte Uyl

020 670 04 58 | www.witteuyl.com

The hanging velvet drapes and female art nouveau sculptures allow a journey inside the mind of founder Annemieke. There is a huge choice of vegetarian organic meals and free range produce. You can order two dishes and a dessert for €39.50. Wild salmon is served with horseradish soup. Mackerel, a vigorous meaty fish, is reinvented as a bitterballen (deep fried croquette filled with potato and dough and in this case shards of mackerel instead of veal). For all its praise as a top vegetarian restaurant, meat eaters won't starve, as choices of veal, lamb or sirloin grace the menu – the lamb sausage is highly recommended – and it surpasses itself with its wine list and champagne by the glass.

Keizersgracht 384
Canal Belt (Grachtengordel)
Map p.392 C1 43

The Dylan

020 530 20 10 | www.dylanamsterdam.com

Formerly Blakes Hotel, its conversion two years ago has left Amsterdam with a top dining arena and hotel with visually striking interiors and oddball ornaments. In the dining room you'll find wrought iron handles for the baker's oven because this used to be an 18th century bakery. Top chef Dennis Kuipers, former sous chef at several Michelin-starred enterprises, shines bright. His trademark anjou pigeon is succulent and lean, the sashimi of sea bass is done in the form of an orange slice drizzled oil. A wonderful wine list and desserts that are based on simple Dutch recipes are to be enjoyed in this cave-like room. Lunch is rather expensive.

Marnixstraat 209
Jordaan
Map p.388 B2 202

Eat at Jo's

020 638 33 36 | www.eatatjos.com

Mary Jo and her husband hail from deep in the American Midwest. Attached to the famous concert venue Melkweg (p.356), Eat at Jo's serves up a dedicated batch of good home-cooking to regular customers, people dining before heading nextdoor for a gig and also visiting rock stars, who lap up the finger-licking combo plates. The restaurant is a rock and roll joint with a carefree spirit and this is obvious in the alchemy of combinations available: spinach soup with cheese, burritos filled with tofu and beans and curry of cauliflower with fennel that's been battered and deep-fried. The cooks can alter the menu or ingredients as they're used to dealing with finicky rock stars, and there's plenty of choice for vegetarians. No reservations needed, just drop in and eat.

E
NL
netherlands
EXPATICA.COM
Europe's #1
helping hand
for internationals

Reguliersdwarsstraat 27
Canal Belt
(Grachtengordel)
Map p.393 D2 44

Garlic Queen

_020 422 64 26_ | _www.garlicqueen.nl_

On the so-called gay restaurant and bar street of Amsterdam sits the Queen of the castle. And what does she serve? Yes you're right, garlic. Many restaurants in China and Japan focus on one ingredient so it's a welcome novelty to enter this cosy space. In every single course, from garlic soup to the halibut with garlic oil, you really must have a fondness for the herb. In an effort to please those less enthusiastic about the herb, the chef will arrange something without it – but then, why on earth would you be here? The glittery showiness of the waiters, some more overtly camp than others, allows you to let your hair down and groove. Just don't kiss anyone after your garlic-infused icecream.

Cosy local eatery

Oude Waal 9
Centrum
Map p.390 A4 45

Hemelse Modder

_020 624 32 03_ | _www.hemelsemodder.nl_

Celestial Mud is the name of this out-of-the-way venue on one of the canals that line the Chinatown district near Centraal Station. Comfortable chairs of Scandinavian wood invite you to focus on the meal, which is served on simple tables. A well-defined changing menu of either three courses or a la carte piques the imagination. Savour the poached salmon and Dutch shrimps in a pot with white pepper sauce and a side of potatoes. Or try the tempting potato soup with leeks and fennel and a touch of cucumber puree. For the main courses there will usually be a fish, meat and vegetarian choice. Desserts here are heavenly, like the lemon and gooseberry cake with cherry coulis, or the wonderful walnut and raisin breads served fresh from the oven (delicious with the Dutch cheese). A small wine list mirrors the limited menu.

Ceintuurbaan 147
De Pijp
Map p.385 C1 46

Puyck

_020 676 76 77_ | _www.puyck.nl_

Chef de cuisine Jakob Preijde outdoes himself year after year. The superiority of his innovations and service never ebb so it's a gratifying experience to return to Puyck. The minted pea soup and scallops marinated in paprika can be relished long after that first course is devoured. Puyck charges a cork fee of €18 per bottle on top of the price. The wine list is lengthy – take your pick of fresh, fruity and dry, light and aromatic, spicy and heavy. The room isn't too ornate, with suffused lighting and background music that isn't shouting, this makes for a marvellous and relaxing meal. When the urge strikes, go next door for excellent takeaway meals.

Prinses Irenestraat 19
Buitenveldert
Map p.385 A3 47

Restaurant As

_020 644 01 00_ | _www.restaurantas.nl_

Vines and flowers grow helter skelter and napkins blow away in the wind from the French natural oak tables that line the grounds. The cylindrical building has seating indoors with a lounge feel, and grey walls adorned with gold doodles. Deep purple cushions rest along the walls. The unique 100% organic kitchen is housed during the summer months outdoors (inside a tent), allowing all the diners to watch the food being made. The cuisine is a mix of styles ranging from Italian to North African, and changes daily. Understated spaghetti with red sauce and baby octopus, or a salad of poached egg, white asparagus and bibb lettuce make lunch a delight. The free-range chicken with artichoke, potato and home-made rustic pork pate will renew your strength after a long day at the office. Order the three, four or five-course menu if you feel like splashing out.

Dam 9
Centrum
Map p.389 E4 49
€€€

Wintertuin

020 554 60 25 | *www.nh-hotels.com*

This classic old world room (the Winter Garden) at the Krasnapolsky Hotel is in a national monument. It takes you back to the end of the 19th century when wrought-iron decor and glass-covered arboretums were all the rage. The hotel was the first in Holland to offer electricity to its guests, illuminating the dark grey misty days of winter in the grandest manner. Palm trees surround the profuse buffet island, and the Sunday brunch served here is more like a Sunday dinner with every conceivable trimming. From the delectable breakfast items such as eggs benedict, to the main courses which include fillet mignon, veal cutlets, sole and steamed seasonal vegetables like white asparagus, this really is one brunch not to miss. The set-price menu includes champagne and a discreet pianist.

Italian

Other options **Pizzerias** p.327

Beethovenstraat 56
Oud Zuid
Map p.384 A2 50

€

Calzone

020 664 41 44

The twisted metal octopus-shaped tentacles that make up the base of the bar and climb to the ceiling (the restaurant's central design feature) are spirited and frolicsome. The service is amazingly forthcoming. Modern design aside, this is a straightforward trattoria with pizza and calzone selections that can be custom made. The spicy salami pizza wins the day, complemented well by the rocket and garlic. If you're looking for a hot addition, ask for the chilli oil. Lunches are packed with local business people and resident. The pastas, lasagne and some veal dishes are simple but tasty, and there is a mean tuna salad on ciabatta bread.

Weteringschans 171
Canal Belt
(Grachtengordel)
Map p.393 D4 51

La Storia della Vita

020 623 42 51 | *www.lastoriadellavita.nl*

For nine years this unassuming northern Italian gem's star has been rising. The chef is from Tuscany and all the staff are Italian. Because the store front is like a typical Amsterdam brown cafe without a trace of signage, you might miss La Storia della Vita if you're strolling by. It's worth looking hard though, because they make fresh specialities such as the ever-changing antipasti, or swordfish, tuna and shellfish delights. The courgette flowers are lightly breaded and fried to perfection. The tiramisu is made inhouse and the quality is nothing short of sublime. Reservations are a must. Parties for business and private affairs must be booked way in advance.

Hilton Hotel
Apollolaan 138
Oud Zuid
Map p.383 F2 52

Roberto's

020 710 60 25 | *www.amsterdam.hilton.com*

Roberto's stands out because it takes liberties with the menu, whipping up original yet classic dishes from all over Italy. Every season they feature a region, showering diners with the cuisine and sharing the cooking techniques of the area. New chef Franz Conde is a follower of the slow food movement and procures his products directly from Italy toensure top quality. On Sundays there is a traditional Italian tea (dinner) from noon. All the foods are served in the centre of the table in big bowls; there are three types of pasta al dente, a mixed grill of fish and meats with sides of vegetables, as well as a myriad of desserts available from the buffet. All the wine and water you can drink is included in the €38 price, which is a steal. The wine is available by the glass from a pretty good list.

Peperstraat 10
Centrum
Map p.394 B1 53

Rosario

020 627 02 80

If you missed out on a trip to Sicily or a mouthwatering episode of *The Soprano's* where Tony and crew tuck into a big steaming plate of spaghetti with marinara sauce, you've got to pay a visit here. The Sicilian owner winks at the guests, bringing out little-known Italian wines to please the clientele. The papparedelle with wild boar is a hearty, traditional offering that takes hours to prepare. The ravioli and beautifully baked and pan-fried beef tenderloin hit the spot. The menu isn't that large but it satisfies even the most discriminating palate. If you're looking for bona fide cooking you will walk away with a smile on your face.

Frederik Hendrikstraat 88-90
Westerpark
Map p.388 A4 54

Yam Yam Trattoria-Pizzeria

020 681 50 97 | *www.yamyam.nl*

Rub shoulders with the locals and dress casually in this neighbourhood trattoria. These tiny two rooms provide a cosy environment in which to indulge. Never mind that sometimes the cheerful staff forget what you've ordered – they've been known to offer free glasses of Chianti as compensation. The piece de resistance is the wood-burning oven that tosses out the crispiest pizzas with just the right touch of cheese. The tomato sauce is spiced with oregano and garlic. There are usually two types of meat on the menu; veal and lamb, several fish options and plenty of pastas. Highlights are the linguine with porcini mushrooms.

Japanese

Stadionweg 249
Oud Zuid
Map p.383 E3 55

Issa

020 662 82 24

A telltale sign of a good Japanese restaurant is one where the chef and the staff are Japanese. Too many sushi bars and teriyaki places claim authenticity but lack native chefs, so the food and customers suffer. Issa is an unpretentious, traditional neighbourhood eatery that until they changed their signage was a blind spot on the culinary trail. Offering good portions of knowledgeably sliced sushi, a fine shabu shabu, and high quality teriyaki of chicken and beef, if you want to share in the pleasure of dining here you'll need to reserve. Ask the waitress for the specials that the Japanese order because they aren't translated into English. Nameko oroshi (mushrooms with shredded radish) or yamai imo (mountain potato with a raw egg) are usually available. She'll be sure to raise an eyebrow in positive acknowledgement.

Tweede Egelantiers-dwarsstraat 24a
Jordaan
Map p.388 B3 56

Japanese Pancake World

020 320 44 47

This restaurant transports you to Osaka or Hiroshima, as the chef has been dutifully trained in the art of making okonomiyaki, often described as a Japanese pizza or pancake. They can be topped with a wide variety of ingredients including octopus, scallions, bean sprouts, potato, cheese, pork, mushrooms, spinach and onions. Watching the chef is half the fun, as he swirls the pancake and loads up the ingredients. Once cooked, they are smothered with tangy sauce and dancing bonito flakes are scattered on top. Delicious food, a great place to enjoy a meal. Plenty of options for vegetarians.

Agamemnonstraat 27
Oud Zuid
Map p.383 E3 57

Umeno

020 676 60 89

A gem tucked away in the residential quarter of Oud Zuid behind the Olympic Stadium. Shabu shabu is served with different sauces to dip your wafer thin slices of beef into. Yakitori (skewered grilled chicken in a rich sauce) and tonkatsu (tempura flaked pork on top of a rice bowl laden with fried onions and egg) are just some of the favourites that those in the know have been savouring for years. Many residents say the sushi here is just as good as at Yamazato's, and it costs less. We'll leave it up to you to decide. Reservations are mandatory because this jewel seats less than 50. Cash only.

Hotel Okura
De Pijp
Map p.384 B2 58

Yamazato

020 678 83 51 | *www.okura.nl*

Akira Oshima earned the first Michelin star ever awarded to a Japanese restaurant in Europe and maintains that position by consistently achieving high standards – fish for the sushi is flown in daily. Don't even think about eating sushi or sashimi elsewhere, even though the portions can be dainty. Several times a year Japanese festivals are celebrated, with authentic cuisine to commemorate these events. The specialities are imported specifically for these events. Whether it's cold soba noodles with king crab, hotpots of fresh clams, or a selection from over 50 delicacies, Yamazato lives up to its reputation. The room is elegant and softly spoken, just like the gorgeous kimono-clad waitresses.

Mexican

Waterlooplein 361
Centrum
Map p.394 A2 59

Agabi Santa Maria

020 412 31 83

A small outpost catering to the touristy crowd, but residents ought not to pass this up as the Argentinian steaks are grilled to perfection. The kitschy sombreros and plastic Maria figurines aside, if you concentrate on the food you'll be fine. Except for the tortilla, all the items are freshly baked on the premises. The signature dish of sliced steak or chicken fried with onions and red peppers can be done as hot as you like. The Chilaquile, a casserole of corn tortillas and melted cheese, is gooey and delicious. The chilli sauce, sour cream, guacamole and cheese toppers pack more punch than you can imagine. The deep-fried tropical fruits taste like a work of fiction.

Kerkstraat 63
Canal Belt (Grachtengordel)
Map p.392 C3 60

Los Pilones

020 320 46 51 | *www.lospilones.com*

With many Mexican restaurants you go for the food and not necessarily the decor, but at this funky and gregarious location you can have your cake and eat it too. A small place with a big reputation, Los Pilones provides some of the best dishes you'll find outside Mexico. This isn't an American version of Tex-Mex, nor will you find a watered down burrito crying out for hot chillis. The cacti fried with steak can be washed down beautifully by a Corona. Enchiladas, tacos and quesadillas leave no space for desserts. There's a kids' menu and a wide selection of cocktails to quench your thirst. Dining alfresco off the busy Leidsestraat offers some respite from the shop-till-you-drop crowds. A range of products from sauces to beans are also sold here, items very hard to find elsewhere.

Middle Eastern

Albert Cuypstraat 182
De Pijp
Map p.384 C1 61

Bazar Amsterdam

020 675 05 44 | *www.bazaramsterdam.nl*

Bazar Amsterdam is situated in a cavernous former church. You'll experience an intriguing blend of Middle Eastern and North African cultures. Souk-style lamps glitter with faux gems of purple, gold and green. The breakfast served here will satisfy the hungriest appetites. With yoghurt, ham, eggs, cheese, jams and various breads like pita and Turkish loaves, you'll leave feeling like a camel. Mosaic-adorned tables round out the colourful ambience and are a perfect backdrop for the Iranian yoghurt with walnuts and green wild spinach. All the meat (grilled and fried) is halal, and there's also a children's menu.

Bazar Amsterdam

Muntplein 1
Centrum
Map p.393 E2 203
€

Maoz Falafel

020 420 74 35

No one can beat Maoz for quality falafel. This clean little corner haven serves up healthy, 100% pure vegetarian fast food treasures. Choose from falafel on plain or whole wheat pita with an array of toppings such as olives, shredded lettuce, tomato, assorted peppers and onions. Dip into some great sauces, from plain to coriander. It can be a bit messy to eat so you should bring plenty of tissues or take it home. There are less than 10 seats inside, so be prepared to gulp down your dripping falafel quickly if it's raining.

Rozengracht 133-I
Jordaan
Map p.388 B4 62

Nomads

020 344 64 01 | *www.restaurantnomads.nl*

A magical lounge bar, restaurant and meeting place. Attracting the young and fashion conscious, rooms are split into sections where you can eat sat on high cushions. A funky blend of house music churns out Arabic lounge mixes. The cocktails reek of style: strawberry martinis or cosmopolitans in long glasses. Champagne flows like water here with a choice of Dom Perignon or Moet & Chandon. A set three-course menu is served to you as you lounge on the sofas or sit cross-legged in a meditative position. The Arabic kibbe (made from lamb) is spiced with cumin, lemon and other secret blends the chef won't reveal. The Bedouin cheese spiked with oregano tastes like feta. Best are the Iraqi and Lebanese breads that are tasty and plentiful. The mezze are smallish yet substantial.

Oudezijds Voorburgwal 236
Centrum
Map p.389 E4 63

Shibli Bedouin

020 554 60 79 | *www.shibli.nl*

The first and only replica in Europe of a Bedouin night out in the Sahara. From under the tent-like ceiling emanates music from Syria, Lebanon, the Sinai, Jordan and Egypt. The manager is half Pakistani, half Azerbaijani, while the vivacious chef is Algerian. A set five-course menu with all the wine, beer and soft drinks you can consume will set you back €60. Eat with your hands, starting with cold dishes laced with cumin, clove, cardamom, onion and carrots. Move on to strained lentil soup with spices, chunky big shrimps and sardines, and dolmas filled with minced lamb, chicken and prunes. A belly dancer graces the floor while you smoke a shisha water pipe. World peace is achievable at this love feast, negotiated through food.

Moroccan

Van der Hoopstraat 94
Westerpark
Map p.388 A1 65

El Kasbah

020 488 77 88 | www.elkasbah.nl

Rocking the kasbah isn't an option here as you unwind in a choice of two rooms, one smoke free, the other smoke filled. Puff on a water pipe while you wait, or chill on one of the homey sofas just like in Marrakech. Gaze up at the glittery lamps with diamond-shaped jewels or down to the mosaic-covered tables. You'll enjoy the tenderly prepared tajines, a speciality of the house. The chicken is drizzled with sweet scents of cinnamon and cardamom. Try some wine from Morocco, mainly dry with a hint of fruitiness. Pouches of briouts are smothered in goat's cheese or vegetables. The couscous dishes are plentiful and sweet smelling. Generous service and portions make this your one-stop shop for a Moroccan night on the town. Just don't get lost as it's located in a completely residential neighbourhood.

Quellijnstraat 104
De Pijp
Map p.384 C1 64

Mamouche

020 673 63 61 | www.restaurantmamouche.nl

A dash of striking colour – that's what Mamouche delivers in the shadows of the Albert Cuypstraat Markt. Enter a sanctuary of pure flavour. Start with the unforgettable pumpkin soup with oranges or filo filled with chicken, raisins and almonds. Glide closer to heaven with a couscous, either vegetarian or with merguez sausage. The creme brulee with almonds and chopped pistachio is memorable. You can dine outdoors when the weather is fine. Tables are ornamented with full-bodied roses and the dark walls are candlelit with long-stemmed brass candelabras. The service is timely and the staff are native or second generation Moroccans, lending a genuine touch. Parties can be booked here and reservations are recommended at the weekends.

Pizzerias

Other options **Italian** p.323

Don't expect a New York-style thick slice or a Neopolitan square laden with mozzarella and tomato sauce here, as Italian owners are scarce. The pizzerias that use brick ovens are well publicised; most use the standard steel apparatus. Generally, pizza places deliver within the immediate area. New York Pizza (www.newyorkpizza.nl) is one of the favourites,and has several outlets which deliver around the city, and the franchise Domino's (www.dominos.nl) is also very popular. Visit www.thuisbezorgd.nl (in Dutch and English) which is a website for delivery services. Companies listed on this site include New York Pizza, Domino's and a host of other places with a selection of food types - you just need to type in your postcode or click on the link to Amsterdam at the bottom of the page. Pizzeria Rossi (www.pizzeriarossi.nl) also does delivery - peruse the menu on the website before calling up. For another option try www.pizzaonline.nl, and Salvatore Pizza and Sangria Tapasbar are also worth checking out. For something a little different, Turkish pizza is to Amsterdam what curry wurst is to Berlin. It's made with a thin pita-like bread and the topping usually includes minced meat, tomato sauce and spices.

Pizzerias	
Domino's	0900 8030
New York Pizza	0900 0102
Pizzeria Rossi	020 684 57 27
Salvatore Pizza Hotlijn	020 470 60 63
Sangria Tapasbar	020 330 23 99

Portuguese

Kerkstraat 35
Canal Belt (Grachtengordel)
Map p.392 C2 66

Restaurant Portugalia

020 625 64 90 | www.portugalia.nl

Even though Portugalia is located in the area around the ultra-touristy Leidseplein, the food makes it worth a visit. It's a family-run enterprise where customers are made to feel at home. All manner of seafood is available: mussels, clams, prawns and shrimps are served in a creamy sauce. The traditional salt cod, served everywhere in Portugal, can also be found here, presented with a bechamel sauce. The lamb comes drizzled in a sauce which is tart and pepped up with chilli and lemon. Ignore the plastic lobsters and concentrate on a good solid meal.

Seafood

Potgieterstraat 35
Oud West
Map p.392 A1 67

Café Potgieter

020 612 46 62 | www.cafepotgieter.nl

It looks like an Amsterdam cafe in every way, so you'll be blown away by the realisation that you've stepped into a gourmand's paradise. Jan Naaykens, the connoisseur chef ought to win an award. Everything here is made from scratch using organic ingredients when available. Escargots, frogs' legs or silky duck rillette go nicely with the crusty bread, made fresh everyday. The fruits de mer (seafood platter) is served cold and marinated. Jan refuses Dutch beef and pork and uses Spanish produce instead. He conjures up a divine wagyu beef tartare and presents Irish or Scottish tornadoes of beef. Well worth a visit.

Schippersgracht 6
Zeeburg
Map p.394 C1 68

Eenvistweevis

020 623 28 94

The name means 'one fish two fish' and the fish are prepared without any superfluous additives, extras or condiments. Chosen daily by the chef and proprietor, Klaas de Jong, you'll get anglerfish, slit tongue (a thin type of sole fillet), trout, red snapper and whatever else is the catch of the day. The tuna steaks are hamachi rose coloured, indicating the best part of the tuna. It's aptly located right behind the Scheepvaartsmuseum (Amsterdam's Maritime Museum). Once you've found this uncomplicated nugget you'll be served by the friendly staff and the chef himself, who insists on several appearances throughout the evening. The wine list is good and vegetarians won't starve, with plenty of variations on the pasta theme.

Scheldeplein 4
Rivierenbuurt
Map p.384 B3 69

Visaandeschelde

020 675 15 83 | www.visaandeschelde.nl

The premiere haunt for fish and seafood lovers to quell those fishy needs. The smart set and business crowds who frequent this top-rated establishment shouldn't put you off, although it's best to dress well when you come here. Black and white tiles adorn the walls that are tastefully decorated with modern and abstract art. A small bar is a relief if you have to wait to be seated. Lobsters, scallops, shrimps and oysters are freshly procured every day. The exotic starters are blissful. Lobster salad with duck liver swirls and truffle dressing, or smoked mackerel with marinated Portobello mushrooms are definitely worth the investment. They're usually delivered with snow pea salad and wonderful horseradish creme. The house offers a three, four or five-course menu. Service is generally excellent although the staff could brush up on their wine knowledge, particularly as the wine list is so expansive. If you don't mind blowing a couple of hundred euros for two or need an excuse to celebrate, make a reservation.

Spanish

Andreas Bonnstraat 44-46
Oost
Map p.394 C4 70

Mucho Más

020 692 86 74 | *www.muchomasamsterdam.nl*

A quirky casa brimming over with colourful flowerpots, ad hoc pictures and paintings adoringly placed on the beige walls. A well-rounded profusion of appetisers will satisfy even the keenest appetites. Button mushrooms in sherry and pimento-filled cheese rounds add up to excellent snacks while you're popping down some beers. If you're in the mood for more substantial fillers, the turkey tapas comes as a main course, or you could enjoy grilled kebabs with a garlic dip. The triple fish and grilled meat platter is well priced. Vegetarians will have a field day with the aubergine, cheese and red pepper quiche-like tart. The three-course menu comes with delicious chocolate cake. The kids will also like it – there's a children's menu, and you can all sit on the terrace. If you want to organise an event or party here, you can chat with Juan the chef and design your own paella.

Govert Flinckstraat 308
De Pijp
Map p.384 C1 71

Vamos a Ver

020 673 69 62 | *www.vamosaver.nl*

Step into Vamos a Ver for a taste of Espana that will leave you begging for more. The hordes of starters, more than 25, can be prearranged as tapas if you'd rather take pleasure in a panorama of tastes. Paella is presented in five different flavours: fish, chicken, meat, seafood or combo dishes. Like a Swiss fondue, the crust at the bottom is the tastiest part of the meal. The fresh catch of the day is combined with prawns, shrimps and octopus in a pan streaming with spices. Uniquely, they offer a kids' menu that doesn't drench your toddler with polyunsaturated fats. The furnishings are nothing to write home about but the service is excellent.

Steakhouses

Other options **Mexican** p.325

Johannes Vermeerstraat 52
Oud Zuid
Map p.384 B1 72

Eetcafé Loetje

020 662 81 73

By day this is frequented by personnel from the American embassy and people working in and around the Rijksmuseum, who relish the huge salads and generously portioned starters. Choose from melon and ham, pate, or shrimps in garlic. If you've got the stomach for a tuna steak or veal cutlet at lunchtime, remember to make space for the home-made potatoes and a green salad on the side. By night this transforms itself into one of the city's most revered steakhouses. Steaks are grilled just as you've ordered them and staff are well versed in the subtleties and gradations of how they should be cooked. You sit chock-a-block under Tiffany-style stained glass lamps. Time and again you'll want to come back.

Spuistraat 3
Centrum
Map p.389 E3 73

Gauchos

020 625 72 72 | *www.gauchos.nl*

Gauchos is a top-class steakhouse with six locations throughout the city serving up beef that has been grazed on the Argentinian pampas. Chimichurri oil is used on the sizzling grills. Although you can't see the cooking process the aromas waft through the restaurant as you build up a manly appetite. Before you get down to some serious eating, order some ceviche, marinated shrimps or scallops as a teaser. Head on to the sumptuous salad bar for an endless round of refills or just go for broke by ordering the main course of steak – either a rump, fillet, sirloin, rib-eye or churrasco. It's all authentic stuff; sit back, relax and enjoy.

Surinamese

Tweede Oosterparkstraat 2
Oost
Map p.385 E1 74

New Draver Restaurant

020 463 12 46

This one isn't even on the radar screens of the listings websites and restaurant critics because it's so unique and authentic that the clientele consists of mainly Surinamese who know their eats. Nothing here is watered down nor does it cater to local tastes – this is the real thing! The lexicon of Surinamese dishes draws from all four ethnic groups that predominate in this former Dutch colony: Hindu, Javanese, Chinese and native Surinamese. The most famous among them is the Moksalese, a traditional array of meat (lamb or pork), rice or fish (cod) and rice whipped with coconut milk and spices. The sato soup hails from Java and consists of soy sprouts, chicken and angel hair clear noodles with a dash of black chilli oil that really stings. One drop of the stuff and you're bouncing off your chair with smoke coming out of your ears. Saving the best for last, deserts include ice cubes of mango or coconut served with hot milk and almond syrup.

Albert Cuypstraat 49
De Pijp
Map p.384 B1 75

Nieuw Albina

020 379 02 23

This combo Surinamese-Chinese hole in the wall is cheap and appetising. The nasi goreng (noodles with shrimp, pork, vegetable or a combination) have a hint of spice while the cha siu (roasted pork) is more Chinese than South American. Roti, a Surinamese delicacy, is a filled pancake with either lamb or chicken and a smattering of greens and potatoes. Choose a sauce to top off the roti; peanut (satay), curry, sweet and sour, hot or moksi. Think of the Nieuw Albina as a canteen stop between the many bars and nightly haunts of De Pijp.

Thai

Zeedijk 72-74
Centrum
Map p.389 F4 76

Bird

020 620 14 42

Make this one of your first stops for authentic Thai. A snug spot with no-nonsense service, the interior is not exactly sophisticated. Concentrate instead on the soups like the Tom Yam spicy chicken with coconut or mixed fish, and move on to the seafood. Prawns with peppers and onions will send you reeling. The beef salad with crystal clear noodles, shredded cabbage and rosettes of peanuts practically blossoms on your plate. The best deals are the northern and eastern Thai dishes such as grilled beef or Laos-style chicken, available for under €15. Bring your family here as kids are most welcome. If you're in a hurry drop into the snack bar across the street for a quick Thai bite at Snackbar Bird.

Elandsgracht 29/31
Jordaan
Map p.392 B1 77
€€€

Rakang

020 620 95 51

The King of Thailand or Queen Beatrix of the Netherlands wouldn't feel out of place here, it's so glam and chic. You feel as though you're on stage here, and the aesthetic principle manifests itself in each dish. The super-friendly waiters will guide you and explain anything you may not understand on the menu. Your water glass will never be empty. If you say you like hot, then hot it will be, signified by three icons. Try the keang pah neau – beef with ginger, bamboo shoots, Thai aubergine and basil leaves. After this your mouth will need a shower of refreshments. The vegetarian salad of cooked rice with fresh mint leaves, hot mushrooms and chilli peppers is a great alternative to the beef. For prawn lovers, the shrimps in tamarind sauce with coriander will have you jumping for more. Expensive, but worth every cent. Reservations mandatory.

Ceintuurbaan 210
De Pijp
Map p.384 B2 78

Thai Deum

020 379 07 05 | *www.thaideum.com*

You can sit down in this excellent Thai hut, but it's cramped. The woks are ablaze right near the front door and the gorgeous smells waft across the whole place – but for some the ventilation system isn't cranked up enough. Never mind, it's worth the suffering for what is ostensibly premium Thai. The portions are gratifying and if you want a takeaway this is also swiftly prepared. The best bets are the spicy noodle dishes and soups, although the garlic oyster and red curry compete for the gold medal. Ostrich cooked with black pepper and onions in a hot curry is worth the culinary journey.

Turkish

Elandsgracht 14
Jordaan
Map p.392 B1 79

Divan

020 626 82 39

The cuisine here is fit for the noblest of discriminating palates. The friendly and attentive staff will guide you through the gastronomic delights once favoured by the sultans. From aromatic mezze to the shish kebabs of rolled lamb or the moussaka-like souffle of minced lamb topped with Turkish melted cheese, you simply cannot afford to be dissatisfied. Vegetarians may have a bit of a hard time, as most of the classy dishes are full of meat. The polished wood tables set against a simplistic decor do not distract from the food.

Albert Cuypstraat 64
De Pijp
Map p.384 B1 80

Kismet Eethuis

020 671 47 68

If you have time to dine here and savour the preposterously inexpensive Turkish delights you'll be glad you did. For less than €10 you can order any number of combination meals – they all come with Turkish brown rice and potato in a tomato-like paste and a ratatouille of nightshades. Try the aubergine with minced lamb, courgette stuffed with minced lamb and rice, or the delicious beef patties and rice. Kismet serves Turkish wines and highly recommended is the Lal Kavaklidere rose, which is sharp and sparkling.

Weteringschans 93
Canal Belt (Grachtengordel)
Map p.393 D4 81

Levant Café-Restaurant

020 622 51 84 | *www.restaurantlevant.nl*

Levant's menu offers traditional cuisine as well as a great Turkish wine list. Of course you'll also find grilled meats and other modern dishes. If you're with a big group go for a platter of mezze that are fragrant and inspiring. While relaxing at your table, imagine walking the alleyways of ancient Istanbul or exploring the Bosphorus region. Glancing at the photographs on the wall not only builds up your appetite it sends shivers up your spine, a kind of homesickness for a land that isn't even yours. You'll come back here for sure.

Vietnamese

Kinkerstraat 5
Oud West
Map p.392 A2 86

Little Saigon

020 489 09 29

Little Saigon is authentic Vietnamese cuisine without a trace of Laos, Cambodia or Thailand. This efficient small restaurant is a newcomer on the block and is still proving its metal. Try the glass noodle salad with beef and chilli, the spring rolls (which come with peanut sauce), and the shrimp wrapped in rice paper. Plenty of vegetarian options are available such as tofu with garlic and ginger.

Cafes

Cafes abound in Amsterdam and throughout the Netherlands, and in a variety of styles – grand cafes, eetcafes and brown cafes, coffeeshops and regular cafes. Grand cafes have a grandiose style, architecture and ambience in the tradition of the old cafes of Vienna or Paris, and offer a dinner menu as well. Eetcafes are essentially brown cafes (called brown due to the years of tobacco smoke which have stained the walls) that serve good, basic, reasonably priced pub food. Coffeeshops in Amsterdam are not to be confused with Starbucks and Costa. Although they do serve coffee, they are licensed and controlled venues that offer customers the opportunity to buy and comfortably sit and smoke marijuana and hashish. They are not normally noted for offering food and are not allowed to serve alcohol.

So if you fancy breakfast, lunch or even just a delectable piece of homemade apple pie – head to a cafe. Cafes vary from contemporary, stylish traiteurs and delicatessens with a few small tables curbside or indoors, to those in old Dutch houses with panoramic canal views or nestled in between eclectic galleries and shops. Cafes can also be found in the parks, with huge sunny terraces amid the trees. Most specialise in home-made soups, salads and sandwiches and a few use only organic ingredients. Although international coffee chains have not managed to infiltrate the Netherlands, there are popular local franchises which offer high quality food and coffee either to eat in or take away, such as Coffee Company, Gary's Muffins, Bagels & Beans, De Bakkerswinkel and Pasta di Mamma.

Afternoon Tea
Although the tradition of afternoon tea is not customary in Amsterdam you will find a few cafes such as De Bakkerswinkel, De Taart van m'n Tante or Cafe De Vries (see Cafes on p.332) and many of the grand hotels such as the Amstel InterCon Hotel (see p.28) that offer a luxurious traditional English afternoon tea with a choice of teas, scrumptious warm scones, clotted cream and sweet jams.

Coffeeshops

Whether it's your thing or not, coffeeshops are a part of the diverse culture in Amsterdam, Europe's pot-smoking capital. Soft drugs are technically not legal, but merely 'tolerated'. At a coffeeshop, cannabis is permitted to be openly sold to the public and smoked on the premises. They are controlled and licensed by the government and are allowed to store 500 grams of marijuana, but can only sell five grams to adults over 18 (with a valid ID). In order to deter young people from smoking pot, some coffeeshops have recently raised the age limit to 21 with the assumption that few 21 year-olds will hang out with minors. Coffeeshops aren't allowed to advertise so they either have a menu in booklet form with photos, or a chalkboard under the counter listing items. *High Times* magazine, a popular cannabis publication, presents carefully selected Amsterdam coffeeshops with their prestigious *High Times* Cannabis Cup award (p.51) for the best pot in the world. Coffeeshops come in a variety of styles: touristy, 70s style, mellow, hip, dark, or typically Dutch.

Coffeeshops			
Bulldog Palace	Leidseplein 17	020 626 51 85	The most well-known coffeeshop in Amsterdam. Big, loud and the first stop for most coffeeshop tourists.
Bluebird	St Antoniebreestraat 71	020 622 52 32	Seventies-style, cosy, friendly atmosphere.
De Dampkring	Handboogstraat 29	020 638 07 05	Large, pub-style coffeeshop that can get very crowded. A scene from the movie *Ocean's Twelve* was filmed here.
De Rokerij	Lange Leidsedwarsstraat 41		Very mellow, low tables and lounge seating, candles, incense, dimly lit. Tibetan feel with Nepalese and Hindu artwork.
Grey Area	Oude Leliestraat 2	020 420 43 01	Tiny, hip, with a friendly American owner Jon. Third place in the prestigious 2007 Cannabis Cup award presented yearly by *High Times* magazine for the best pot in the world. Popular with American tourists
Rusland	Rusland 16	020 627 94 68	Large multi-level coffeeshop, some claim was Amsterdam's first.

Veemkade 368
Zeeburg
Map p.380 A2 87

Bagels & Beans

020 419 46 22 | *www.bagelsbeans.nl*

The newest location for Bagel & Beans is a welcome addition to the up and coming docklands area of Amsterdam. The light and spacious waterfront cafe packs them in for their yummy homemade bagels (the warm cinnamon raisin bagel smothered in butter is to die for), lush muffins and sensational freshly squeezed juices. Prices are reasonable with most bagels and toppings for under €5 and healthy juices priced between €2 and €4. With its waterside terrace and cheerful staff this has already become a hotspot for young families and professionals living on the islands. For details of their other nine locations in Amsterdam, see the website.

Willemsparkweg 163
Oud Zuid
Map p.383 F1 88

Brasserie de Joffers

020 673 03 60

Although often difficult to find a place to sit at this cherished cafe in stylish Oud Zuid it's worth the visit. It has an enchanting old-fashioned French bistro flair. Whether you're in the mood for a yummy scrambled egg and bacon breakfast, buttery croissant and cafe au lait, or light fresh tuna salad lunch, Joffers never disappoints with its high quality cuisine and friendly service. Dinners are also a delight, as the crowds seem to disperse in the afternoon leaving the cafe with a wonderfully relaxed evening atmosphere, perfect for enjoying an early alfresco dinner with a glass of wine. You can even relish your drink on the attractive front terrace in the colder months as they have wonderfully toasty outdoor heaters and blankets to keep the chill out. Frequented by Oud Zuid locals and trendy fashionistas. Due to its prime location prices are a little higher than in other areas of Amsterdam.

Herengracht 309
Canal Belt
(Grachtengordel)
Map p.392 C1 89

Buffet van Odette

020 423 60 34 | *www.buffet-amsterdam.nl*

Those looking for a healthy, delicious meal using traditional and primarily organic products from some of the finest food suppliers need look no further. Charming owner Odette conjures up a scrumptious scrambled egg or omelette breakfast served with the best croissants in Amsterdam. Her delicious sandwiches under €5, quiche, salads, home-made cakes, apple pie and brownies make this a favourite stop for both locals and tourists. It has a lovely canal-side picture window. The mouthwatering roasted tomato soup with basil oil accompanied by mustard bread is simply divine and will keep you dreaming of coming back for more. Although it can get a little cosy when busy, you never have to worry about second-hand smoke in this rare (for Amsterdam)

Classic Dutch Eetcafe

Warming homecooking

smoke-free haven. Odette also caters for special occasions such as private dinner parties (up to 30 people).

Nieuwe Doelenstraat 20-22
Centrum
Map p.393 E2 90

Café de Jaren

020 625 57 71 | *www.diningcity.nl/cafedejaren*

An institution in Amsterdam, this spacious grand cafe and restaurant on the Amstel river is housed in a magnificent old three-storey bank building, which has been lovingly restored emphasising light and space. Take time out with a newspaper at the cafe's communal reading table or treat yourself to a light lunch from the healthy salad bar upstairs in the restaurant. But what most people come to de Jaren for is to relax on the splendid waterfront terrace. The cost of lunch is average, but dinner prices are a bit steeper with an entree running at €17. De Jaren attracts an eclectic mix of patrons; arty, trendy types, students from the nearby university, and tourists.

Roelofhartstraat 68
Oud Zuid
Map p.384 B2 91

De Bakkerswinkel

020 662 35 94 | *www.debakkerswinkel.nl*

The bright and cheerful Bakkerswinkel in South Amsterdam is a magnificent cafe and bakery, ideal for a heavenly breakfast, lunch or lazy Sunday brunch. Glorious freshly baked cakes and pies with crumbly, fruity, devilishly chocolatey or tangy fillings are crying out to be eaten. The hearty, wholesome sourdough, pesto, lemon or nut breads will make you soon forget you ever considered going on a low-carb diet – they're all superb. Enjoy a relaxing cup of tea and scones fresh from the oven – they're decadent, sweet and full of real butter just like Grandma used to make. De Bakkerswinkel has two other charming shops in Amsterdam: in the centre at the Warmoestraat (020 489 80 00) and a new location at the Westergasfabriek (020 688 06 32). Classical concerts are also arranged in the cafes, see the website for concert dates and times.

Ferdinand Bolstraat 10
Amstelveen
Map p.384 B1 92

De Taart van m'n Tante

020 776 46 00 | *www.detaart.com*

Fabulously kitsch cake shop and cafe located in a late 19th century merchant's house. Famous for its wonderfully wacky cake creations and funky decor – picture the mismatched retro tables and chairs and plastic flamingo ornaments. In this fantasyland parlour you can choose from an assortment of sweet and savoury cakes baked for any occasion. The 'Totally Zen' Buddha cake with a fat Buddha is a classic. Not only will they bake you a one-of-a-kind extraordinary wedding cake, but you can also tie the knot here. The Taart van m'n Tante is also an official municipal marriage office. As if that wasn't enough, you can even spend your honeymoon in their charming bed and breakfast upstairs called Cake Under My Pillow (020 751 09 36, www.cakeundermypillow.nl).

Haarlemmerdijk 108a
Jordaan
Map p.388 C1 93

De Vries

020 427 05 75 | *www.devriesamsterdam.nl*

This sleek yet classic cafe with its floral black and cream wallpaper, black furnishings and red wall accents has been generating a bit of buzz. Young Dutch Indonesian owner Anthony de Vries likes to offer traditional Dutch classics like a home-made meatball and gravy sandwich, but with a twist. Popular items are the in-house salted roast beef and sauerkraut sandwich and the tuna salad sandwich with apples and capers. Light quiches, fresh salads, wholesome soups and traditional desserts complete this menu full of contemporary Dutch comfort food. Prices are on a par with cafes around town and this is quickly becoming a favourite spot for locals and weekend shoppers on the Haarlemmerdijk.

Spui 10
Centrum
Map p.393 D1 94

Esprit Caffe

020 622 19 67 | www.caffeesprit.nl

A longstanding favourite in Amsterdam, the Esprit Caffe never disappoints when it comes to quality. This crowd-pleasing cafe was the brainchild of the original Californian owners of the Esprit clothing brand, which has a large retail shop adjacent to the cafe. It's known for tasty American cuisine like juicy hamburgers, but also does chicken and avocado wraps, a variety of healthy salads, tummy-warming tomato soup with dill and creme fraiche, frothy cafe latte served in bowls, and mouthwatering moist carrot cake with cream cheese icing. There's something for everyone and then some more. The portions are good-sized and prices are reasonable. The choice is immense, but that's just fine since you'll keep on coming back. If you're lucky enough to snag a table outside on Spui Square you'll find this is a great place to chill out.

Beukenplein 18h
Oost
Map p.385 E1 95

Gewoon eten en meer...

020 665 50 75 | www.gewoonmeer.nl

Gewoon in Dutch means 'usual', but this gorgeous traiteur/delicatessen/cafe/shop is anything but. You can relax on turquoise cushions and modern dark wood furniture in the tiny hip lounge corner of their shop and enjoy their delicious pumpkin, feta, coriander and nut salad. Or if the mood takes you, munch on a heavenly chicken wrap with coriander mayonnaise and chives. If these don't take your fancy then choose from 22 different daily dishes presented mouthwateringly in their glass vitrine. As if that wasn't enough, the patisserie offers an immense selection of decadent desserts: lemon yoghurt cheesecake, chocolate orange pie, apple crumble and many more temptations. With plenty of corporate event catering experience, their food styling talents have also been featured in spreads in several glossy magazines.

Vondelpark
Oud Zuid
Map p.383 F1 96

Het Blauwe Theehuis

020 662 02 54 | www.blauwetheehuis.nl

Situated right in the heart of Amsterdam's most popular park the Vondelpark (p.160), this funky 1930s blue flying saucer-shaped building is completely surrounded by towering green trees. You can spend a relaxing afternoon in the tranquil atmosphere of the teahouse with its stained glass windows and panoramic views of the park. On sultry summer evenings, enjoying drinks and tapas sitting outside is a real treat. The terrace turns into a late night bar with lounge music. It draws a mixed crowd of students, bohemians, locals and tourists escaping the sightseeing frenzy. Various reasonably priced sandwiches and rolls are available for lunch, tapas snacks during the cocktail hour, and a small dinner menu in the evening. It can also be hired for weddings and private parties.

Prinsenstraat 3
Canal Belt (Grachtengordel)
Map p.389 D3 97

Letting

020 627 93 93 | www.letting.nl

This hip cafe situated in one of the coolest shopping streets in Amsterdam serves breakfast, lunch and dinner in a pleasant, friendly atmosphere. Locals and visitors alike appreciate the warm welcome they receive whenever they pop in for a bite to eat, or a quick coffee and slice of one of their exquisite cakes or yummy fresh fruit shakes. Letting has an extensive menu where all dishes can be ordered throughout the day, including a wide variety of breakfast combos complete with coffee or tea and juice.

Anyone For Croquette?

The croquette is often called the quintessential Dutch dish – it's their equivalent of the American hamburger or German frankfurter...and like these it has its better and worse varieties. Those 'in the know' recognise that for Amsterdam's best crusty croquette they need look no further than Cafe Luxembourg (020 620 62 64) at Spui 24.

An elaborate champagne breakfast is available for a mere €14.80. Regulars swear the burgers are the best; check the chalkboard for specials. The menu is packed with delicious sandwiches, heartwarming soups like Provencal lentil, and pasta and meat dishes.

Czaar Peterstraat 174
Zeeburg
Map p.380 A3 98

Mondo Mediterraneo

020 421 20 25 | *www.mondomediterraneo.com*

Off the beaten track in the up and coming Czaar Peterstraat neighbourhood you'll find this upmarket Italian cafe and delicatessen that insiders already know warrants more than one visit. Drop in for a heavenly home-made lunch, or a foamy cappuccino and freshly baked cookie outside on one of their sunny alfresco tables. Their clientele ranges from young local city dwellers to media and creative types. The chefs prepare fresh pastas, simple yet enticing main courses like grilled tuna steak, soup, salads, and delightful desserts – either to go or devour on the spot. They can cater for exclusive dinners or large-scale banquets. Prices are reasonable and only the finest products are used.

Van Leijenberglaan 216
Buitenveldert
Map p.367 E3

Gusto di Casto

020 644 89 03 | *www.gustodicasto.nl*

Formerly a franchise of Pasta di Mamma, owner Ermanno Casto has branched out on his own and renamed his solo venture Gusto di Casto (The Flavour of Casto). Still located in the Grootgelderlandplein mall, this incredibly popular traiteur and cafe has been serving contented customers for years. The convenient location and friendly staff make it a perfect stop for a real cappuccino injection and scrumptious food. Sandwiches on freshly baked olive, sun-dried tomato, whole-grain or natural ciabatta bread come with an abundant choice of fillings – homemade pesto, mozzarella, Romano tomatoes, mortadella, tuna, Parma ham, rucola, tapenade – the options are endless. There is also a luxurious selection of imported Italian products and appetising homemade delicacies for takeaway or to enjoy on the spot. Prices are a little high, but portions are large and very satisfying. Catering is also a possibility for any occasion, small or large.

Huidenstraat 12
Jordaan
Map p.392 C1 100

Pompadour

020 623 95 54 | *www.patisseriepompadour.com*

This charming patisserie, chocolatier and tearoom has been serving delighted customers in their nostalgia-themed salon since 1963. It is famed locally for serving the best croissants in town and supplies many of the local cafes. Soak up the grand surroundings and select from an exquisite array of beautiful cakes, hand-made chocolate bon bons and petit fours. In stark contrast the new branch on Kerkstraat (020 330 09 81) has a contemporary lounge feel, with sleek modern furnishings. In addition to delectable sweet offerings there is a selection of savoury toasted sandwiches using choice ingredients. The WLT (Wagyu beef bacon with lettuce and tomato) is scrumptious. Ideal for a bite after perusing the shops and galleries in the Nieuwe Spiegelstraat and surrounding canals.

Staalstraat 21
Centrum
Map p.393 F2 101

Puccini

020 620 84 58 | *www.puccini.nl*

Sunday mornings in this sunny, modern Italian cafe kitchen are a sheer delight. The smiley staff greet you warmly as you're met by the aromatic scent of freshly baked Pompadour croissants and rich, Italian brewed coffee. The fluffy scrambled eggs with fresh herbs, toast and salad are served with salmon or warm ham – all for a mere €7.50. A huge flaky croissant with jam and butter will be around €3. Their sandwiches like the 'Vegetariano' (grilled vegetables on fresh Italian bread) are a feast for the eyes as well as the palate. The clientele is mixed, with regulars who appear like clockwork every morning, as well as the city visitors and families exploring the canals. They are also open late when there's a concert on at the nearby Stopera.

Binnen Oranjestraat 14
Jordaan
Map p.388 C1 102

Small World Catering

020 420 27 74 | www.smallworldcatering.nl

This tiny deli-style traiteur and cafe tucked away in a Jordaan side street is not to be missed. Hop up on a barstool along the window counter and enjoy a frothy cafe latte with a choice of cheesecake, moist muffins, sinfully delicious pies or huge, extremely Belgian chocolatey cookies. Feast on one of the amazing sandwiches like the fresh tuna carpaccio. Sandwich prices might seem a bit on the high side but these aren't normal creations, they're taste sensations. Portions are large, so it might even be wise to share with a friend, if you can bear to part with half. There's also a wide selection of pasta, couscous or other vegetarian and non-vegetarian salads. You can pick up a scrumptious takeaway, or engage Small World Catering for corporate or private events.

Piet Heinkade 1
Zeeburg
Map p.390 C3 103

Star Ferry

020 788 20 90 | www.starferry.nl

This architectural gem is a must-visit destination in Amsterdam. Situated on the IJ harbour the new Muziekgebouw houses the stunning contemporary glass Star Ferry cafe. With incredible views in every direction, relax watching the harbour traffic and enjoy a cool aperitif or snack. The day menu offers breakfast items, plus a wide selection of sandwiches, soups and salads. The dinner menu features an eclectic mix of world cuisines such as Armenian red lentil soup with dried apricots or Szechuan marinated duck breast. Prices aren't cheap, but you're here for the ambience and it's well worth it. It has an urban cool atmosphere with a mixed crowd of architects, city visitors and trendy urbanites.

Europaplein 22
Rivierenbuurt
Map p.384 B3 215

Strand Zuid

020 544 59 70 | www.strand-zuid.nl

Tired of traffic jams on the way to the Dutch beaches? This hip urban beach is the place to be for a late breakfast, laid-back lunch or romantic dinner. The lunch menu offers a variety of fresh salads and various panini sandwiches. In the evening the dinner menu expands to include home-made pasta dishes and an array of meat and fish entrees for €14 to €20. The salad of goat's cheese, apple and walnuts is perfect on a hot summer afternoon. The kids' menu for €7.50 is just another bonus point for this super-cool hotspot. As it's situated just behind Amsterdam RAI conference centre, if you do drive and park at the RAI, be sure to pay your parking ticket at the cafe – otherwise instead of €8 you will be charged €12.

Bosboom Toussaintstraat 26
Oud West
Map p.392 A2 105

Toussaint

020 685 07 37 | www.bosboom-toussaint.nl

This lively neighbourhood cafe has a French bistro flair, with wooden decor and candlelight making this cosy retreat a favourite with some. In a tiny kitchen the chef creates tasty sandwiches for €4 and home-made soups and salads. The dinner menu has plenty of healthy vegetarian options. There's a pretty pavement terrace for their clientele to enjoy the friendly village-like atmosphere of the street outside. During the cocktail hour between 16:00 and 18:00 customers can enjoy the speciality tapas dishes.

Cornelis Schuytstraat 8
Oud Zuid
Map p.383 F1 106

Van Dam Brasserie

020 670 65 70 | www.vandamcatering.nl

Newcomers and neighbourhood regulars are all made to feel right at home by Van Dam's friendly and professional staff. Situated along the super-chic shopping street Cornelis Schuytstraat in Amsterdam's posh neighbourhood of Oud Zuid. Van Dam's speciality is a scrumptious vitello tonnato sandwich, or one of the beloved tosti combos like ham and cheese on farmer's bread. The brasserie offers an array of delicious fresh salads, luxurious sandwiches, hearty soups and changing daily specials listed on the chalkboard. Prices are what you would expect for this neighbourhood. It's impossible to leave Van Dam without picking up a little something on the way out from the beautifully tempting traiteur, whether it's one of their spectacular rosemary roast chickens or a tub of the decadently rich chocolate mousse.

Internet Cafes		
't Nes-cafe	Centrum	020 623 42 50
easyInternetcafe	Centrum	www.easyinternetcafe.com
The Internet Cafe	Centrum	www.internetcafe.nl
Internet Cafe Freeworld	Centrum	020 620 09 02
The MAD Processor	Oud West	020 612 18 18
UnderWorld C@fe	Centrum	020 638 13 88

Internet Cafes

Amsterdam is full of internet cafes for those wishing to keep in touch via cyberspace. You can choose from game cafes, coffeeshops that offer a smoke while checking emails, and high-tech cafes with wireless internet access. The standard rate is around €1 per half hour, but some have a compulsory drink policy. Others offer a free internet service as long as you buy a drink. Many are good for just hanging out, relaxing and having a few drinks or a coffee, while others are quite busy and strictly for online access – like the easyInternetcafe with its 144 terminals, located conveniently near Centraal Station.

The variety of Amsterdam's eateries

Bakeries

Dutch bread is soft on the inside and a bit crustier around the edges. Most bakeries order the dough then pop it in their ovens so it is baked fresh but not freshly made. The same holds true for supermarkets, all of whom have bakery sections. The explosion of French-style bakeries has added a new dimension to the Dutch landscape. Bakken met Passie (see right) offer original breads baked in French ovens under the supervision of master bakers, while Vlaamsch Broodhuys offer great bread and sandwiches (see Delis on p.310). On the Vijzelstraat you can find a few lovely bakeries, and wholesome organic loaves are sold on the Noordermarkt on Saturdays.

Bakken Met Passie

The owner went all the way to France to convince a young baker to loan him his secret recipes. After much cajoling and persuading he got what he wanted: the secrets of how to make real baguettes, loaves with seeds and that lovely crust. Expensive yet well worth it. You can find it Albert Cuypstraat 51, De Pijp (020 670 13 76).

Brunch

A plethora of cafes (p.332) serve breakfast way past lunchtime, qualifying them as brunch spots especially for those with a late night hangover. Sandwiches, eggs, soups, pancakes or salads are typical options while some cafes offer traditional English breakfasts as brunch. Most hotels offer a version of Sunday brunch. At the Hilton, Roberto's (p.324) offers an Italian take on this in-between meal, while another hotel brunch that is not to be missed is at Wintertuin (p.323). There are a few locales that have jazz music. Bagels with cream cheese and salmon and other toppings are as commonplace as the tosti. Gary's Muffins (020 637 36 43) is a good place to head to on Sundays, where they offer blueberry pancakes and freshly made bagels.

Fruit Juices

There are many juices bars scattered around town offering freshly made juices and smoothies. Juicetera is right across the street from Magna Plaza inbetween Nieuwe Kerk and the optician, convenient if you're shopping on Kalverstraat or visiting Dam Square. Another renowned juice bar sits cosily at the centre of the Olympic Stadium health club but you don't have to be a member to drink a healthy lunch alternative. Frood Fresh Fruit Juices (06 510 3752) on the Korte Lijnbaansteeg in the centre sells wheatgrass juice, among other things. You can also get juices from many one stop shops and cafes (p.332).

Street Food

The ubiquitous patat (French fries) are best eaten from a paper cone and topped with mayonnaise, ketchup or satay sauce. Of numerous places offering them around Amsterdam, one of the very best places is Vlaamse Friethuis on Voetboogstraat. Vis (fish) stalls are dotted around the city and offer maatjes haring (raw herring), sliced and topped with sweet gherkins, Hollandse garnalen (Dutch shrimps) and crawfish. Makarel (mackerel) is a fish stall staple as is raw paling (eel), tuna, fried kibbeling (cod) and mussels. The counter assistant will ask you what kind of sauce you want with your fish – garlic, whisky or cocktail. It's served in a plain or buttered bread roll, or in a plastic dish. FEBO is an Amsterdam institution. It's dubious fastfood served from all-day vending machines where you plunk a coin in and out of the wall comes a frikandel (offal posing as frankfurter), bitterballen (croquettes of doughy mash and beef), cheese souffles (deep-fried breaded cheese) and other sordid snacks. Do avoid vendors selling hot dogs as none are made with beef and the lack of stringent laws allows for unorthodox sanitation.

On The Town

__Drinking & Driving__
Drink driving in the Netherlands isn't tolerated. The legal limit is 0.2 and the fines and restrictions if you are over the limit escalate in proportion to your intoxication, ranging from €220 to €1,000 and suspension of your licence. Luckily there are now plenty of taxis in Amsterdam. You'll see taxis queueing by all the major squares and you can also flag them down as they pass. They're not cheap though, with the average ride across town setting you back at least €15. Of course, this being Amsterdam you could jump on your trusty bike and get yourself anywhere just as quickly without worrying about traffic.

Amsterdam has a great variety of drinking venues; from the traditional 'brown cafe' to the swanky lounge bar, the funky local to the English-style beer and football pub, you won't have to look far to find the one that suits you for every or any night of the week. The city centre has the highest concentration of bars, but every suburb has its fair share too – once you move into an area you'll no doubt find a little gem around the corner from you that hasn't made it on to this list, but our selection of bars and pubs should certainly get you started. Beer is the main tipple of choice for locals – Grolsch, Amstel and Heineken are all brewed in Holland – and you can pretty much guarantee a good glass in most venues. Less reliable, however, are the cocktails; they have generally been slow to catch on in Amsterdam, although they are now gaining popularity. Unfortunately not everyone who sells them knows how to make them properly. Most bars will have one or two cocktails on the menu but they may not have time to make them if they're busy. For the best cocktails in town go to Hotel de L'Europe (020 531 17 77) at the top of the Rokin; they're pricey but worth it. Good cocktail bars to start the night off are Harry's (p.345), Gespot (p.345) or Café Cuba (p.342).

A popular member of the Amsterdam nightlife is the lounge bar. These places attract the young professionals and trendsetters, with the atmosphere falling somewhere between decadent design and attractive functionality. One of the first lounge bars in the city, and still considered one of the best, is Club NL (p.355).

There's plenty of choice too for those who want to drink or dance the night away, with late bars and clubs scattered around town (see Nightclubs, p.355), and the city also has a thriving gay bar and club scene (see p.351).

The Amsterdam nightlife may be synonymous in the eyes of many with its Red Light District (p.138), but this notorious part of town is far from the den of iniquity it was even five years ago. An aggressive clean-up policy from the city council has seen much of the seedier element off, and the streets are now paved and lit. You can safely wander the district's streets, have a great meal and experience some of Amsterdam's oldest drinking houses. You're still advised not to take unsolicited pictures of those plying the world's oldest trade though.

Door Policy

Most bars in Amsterdam don't have bouncers, but clubs do. If you're heading to a club make sure you look the part (that mainly means men shouldn't be wearing trainers or shorts). Large groups of women should have no problem getting into clubs, but men should get in early if going out en masse. You'll also encounter problems if the bouncer thinks you've had a few too many – it's no use arguing or coming back later, just move on.

Dress Code

There are no official dress codes as such in Amsterdam, but you should always dress smartly to be on the safe side when going out on the tiles. Every now and then there will be a themed club night that requires a certain dress, such as all white or all black, but this is not usually strictly enforced. Regulations do vary from club to club, of course; you'll have to have your finger on the fashion pulse to get into Jimmy Woo's (p.356), for example, whereas Club 11 (p.355) is far more relaxed. It's worth calling ahead to check if you are intending to go to a particular venue.

Sports Bars
The best place to watch international sports is on the Leidseplein – the Bulldog and the Satellite Sports Café both screen international games. If you're after European football, rugby or Aussie rules, most of the Irish bars screen the games. The Tig Barra, Tara and O'Reilly's are all good, friendly venues (see p.351).

Bars

Other options **Pubs** p.349, **Nightclubs** p.355

Brown Cafes

Known in Dutch as 'bruine kroegs, and sometimes referred to as brown bars, these are a real institution. A real kroeg is likely to be around 200 years old and have walls plastered with posters dating back almost as far. They get their name from their dark appearance, richly coloured wood and minimal lighting. Some standout brown cafes are Café Hoppe (p.342), Café Chris (p.341), Elsa's Café (p.314) and Café de Oranjerie (p.342).

Leidsekruisstraat 6-8
Canal Belt (Grachtengordel)
Map p.392 C3 108

Bourbon St Blues

020 623 34 40 | www.bourbonstreet.nl

Despite the rather kitsch appearance the place feels old and authentic. It's been around since 1990 and has attracted some big names from Sting to the Rolling Stones. Budding musicians are welcome to join the jam nights on Sundays, Mondays and Tuesdays. The crowd tends to be a bit older and quite Dutch but very ready to let their hair down and make some noise on the floorboards. The entry fee is free before 23:00 and around €5 or €10 after that. The drinks are pricey, but that is normal for this tourist-saturated area.

Nes 37
Centrum
Map p.393 E1 109

Bubbles & Wines

020 422 33 18 | www.bubblesandwines.com

A secret cave of bottled treasures that caters to the discerning pallet, Bubbles and Wines is tucked away behind the Rokin on the theatre-rich Nes. The interior is very tasteful and doesn't interrupt the soothing atmosphere. The long, thin bar serves up a wonderful assortment of wines and champagnes by the glass or bottle. You can also order up some snacks, but don't be shocked at the prices – aside from the €175 for Iranian caviar, they are quite reasonable for the quality served. The service is fast, professional and knowledgeable. Bubbles and Wines is worth a visit for anyone interested in wines or in simply enjoying a pleasant experience.

Bloemstraat 42
Jordaan
Map p.388 B4 110

Café Chris

020 624 59 42

Café Chris came into existence when the Westerkerk was being built back in 1624. The workers used to come to the cafe to get lunch and collect (and spend) their wages. The place itself is small and dark, just like a good brown cafe should be. It's rumoured that Rembrandt used to stop by for schnapps on his way home from his studio on Bloemgracht to his then home on Rozengracht. If you sit at the bar long enough the wonderful staff and owners will be happy to tell many stories of this calibre. Whether or not you believe them, Café Chris is definitely worth a visit. The crowd is a good mix of locals and regulars, with the occasional tourist thrown in. In warmer months you can enjoy your beer (or schnapps) on one of the outside benches. Cash only.

Leidseplein's bars and cafes

Nieuwmarkt 3
Centrum
Map p.389 F4 111

Café Cuba

020 627 49 19

Located on the ever fashionable Nieuwmarkt, Café Cuba is incredibly popular in summer. It has a large terrace, decent service and affordable prices. They offer a good range of cocktails by glass or pitcher; try the strawberry margaritas. The crowd tends to be Dutch students and after work drinkers. The dark and dusty interior makes a strangely schizophrenic attempt to create an atmosphere indicative of its name. For whatever reasons it seems to work and after a few drinks you won't notice the beady eyes of the mounted wildlife glaring at you. There's no food available but if you're peckish you can munch on corn chips. The area has a lot of great restaurants nearby so Café Cuba is a great place for pre or post-dinner drinks.

Binnen Oranjestraat 15hs
Jordaan
Map p.388 C1 112

Café de Oranjerie

020 623 43 11 | www.oranjeriejoure.nl

West of Centraal Station and in the north of Jordaan you'll find Café de Oranjerie, a quintessential brown cafe dating from the mid 19th century. The walls are inches thick with posters and the atmosphere is thickened by history. The beautiful bar stands out as a deco-esque art piece and is propped up by locals, who could be nearly as old as the bar. De Oranjerie has a simple kitchen that produces good quality pub food. For under €20 you'll get a mouthwatering steak, some icecream or apple pie, and quite a few beers. When you've finished eating, ask for one of the board games behind the bar (the collection is impressive), and settle in to soak up the atmosphere. The kitchen is open from 18:00 and reservations are not accepted, but it's unlikely you'll need one. The electronic age hasn't reached de Oranjerie yet so make sure you've got enough money on you as bank and credit cards are not accepted.

Prinsengracht 124
Jordaan
Map p.388 C3 113

Café de Prins

020 624 93 82 | www.deprins.nl

Café de Prins is conveniently located centrally on the Prinsengracht just across from Anne Frank Huis and makes a great meeting place in the summer months with its canal-side terrace. The kitchen is open all day and offers a good variety of meals from salads and pastas to steaks and outstanding uitsmijters (a Dutch breakfast favourite). There are also daily changing specials and vegetarian options. The portions are a good healthy size for the price and the ingredients fresh and tasty. The atmosphere is relaxed and friendly with helpful staff who are happy to chat when they're not too busy. De Prins is simply decorated with wooden tables and booths and art from local artists for sale on the walls. The canal house itself dates from the 1700s and De Prins has been inhabiting it since 1960. Every other month you can enjoy live jazz on the canal.

Spuistraat 18-20
Centrum
Map p.393 D1 114

Café Hoppe

020 420 42 20 | www.cafe-hoppe.nl/

Undeniably one of the best known of Amsterdam's brown cafes, Hoppe has been serving beers since 1680. In the older half of the bar (half of Hoppe was a hotel for a hundred years before it was converted to a bar) you'll find sand covering the old wooden floor, a few tables and a couple of older Dutch gentlemen serving at the bar with nothing but the sound of jovial conversations dancing on the air. In the 'younger' side of the bar there are quite a few more tables, music playing and a couple of lads wiping down the bar. The two bars are connected and customers are welcome to wander between them. The staff refer to the two bars as the zitcafe (sit cafe) and the staancafe (standing cafe). Café Hoppe is a great place to begin your night out but don't be surprised if you end up whiling the evening away drinking beers and watching the city pass by.

Veemkade 576
Zeeburg
Map p.380 A2 115

Café Pakhuis Wilhelmina

020 419 33 68 | www.cafepakhuiswilhelmina.nl

Part of the redevelopment of the warehouse district by Centraal Station, Pakhuis Wilhelmina has been devoted to promoting culture in Amsterdam. The building houses several artists and studios as well as the cafe. It is a great space and you'll find some great upcoming talent. The prices are very reasonable as it's a subsidised initiative and some of the events are wonderfully offbeat; check out the Hard Rock Karaoke night! The crowd is young, hip and arty but not at all pretentious. If you're looking for something different and energetic you should definitely give it a visit.

Prinsengracht 424
Canal Belt (Grachtengordel)
Map p.392 B2 116

Café Pieper

020 626 47 75

A true Amsterdam institution, Café Pieper has been serving up beer and jenevers since 1665. The atmosphere is comfortingly old; the decor feels dusty though it isn't, the glass in the windows appears ancient and the pictures of an older Amsterdam on the walls add to the effect. In the summer months you can enjoy the breeze and simple pub nibbles like cheese and sausage on the canal-side terrace, while watching boats pass by. The staff are very friendly and happy to talk about the history of both the bar and Amsterdam. A real place for locals, Café Pieper celebrates with its regulars every year and springs for outings like bowling. You'll have to be a regular customer for over a year to merit an invite but that is very likely if you're living in the area. Cash only.

Amstelveensweg 126
Oud Zuid
Map p.383 E1 117

Café Rouleau

020 671 95 09 | www.rouleau.nl

Café Rouleau nestles just behind the Vondelpark on Amstelveenseweg. Although it's only been open for four years the cafe has become a local favourite with its full windows, simple decor and reasonably priced, tasty food. The new owners have returned it to its original, understated art deco appearance and this compliments the atmosphere well. The food is a cut above normal Dutch cafe cuisine, bringing a modern international twist to well known favourites like goat cheese salad and lamb tenderloin. The menu does change regularly but there are always enough options for all tastes. A three-course meal and glass or two of wine should set you back no more then €35. Don't miss the homemade chocolate truffle pie. It's best to reserve for Friday and Saturday evenings. The clientele are mostly young professionals and locals stopping by for an end of day beer or two. In the summer months the nicely sized terrace draws people from the park. Rouleau is open for lunch at the weekend and the comfy couch in the front of the cafe is a perfect place for reading the papers.

Herengracht 319
Canal Belt (Grachtengordel)
Map p.392 C2 118

De Admiraal

020 625 43 34 | www.de-ooievaar.nl/proeven.html

De Admiraal is a beautiful restaurant and tasting house (proef lokaal). Come here for over 60 liqueurs and around 20 jenevers made by Amsterdam's last working independent distillery, A. Van Wees distillery de Oolievaar. The food is traditionally rich Dutch cuisine which is a little on the pricey side but typical for the area. Expect to pay at least €40 a head; the atmosphere though, is worth it. The restaurant is around 35 years old but the building was a distillery before that, and previously was a horse and coach station. The stone floor and dark bar are made to feel warm and welcoming by the traditional ceramic distillery pots and wine barrels. The staff are highly professional and will be able to answer all your queries about the history of Dutch jenever making. It's best to make a reservation, as the restaurant is often booked for group tastings or celebrations.

Rapenburgerplein 83
Zeeburg
Map p.394 C1 119

De Druif

020 624 45 30

De Druif is a tiny brown cafe situated at the end of the Herengracht to east of Centraal Station. De Druif means The Grape and could hark back to its days as a distillery, although it never made wine. Dating back to either 1585 or 1630 depending on who you're talking to, it's every bit as old as it feels with, layers and layers of beer and jenever memorabilia covering the walls. The locals are friendly and chatty, especially if it's warm enough to sit outside and enjoy the peace and the view. De Druif is a quiet place to visit away from the bustling city centre, but don't come here if you're looking for a lively atmosphere, it's much more of a Sunday papers, lazy afternoon kind of place. Cash only.

Utrechtesraat 137
Canal Belt (Grachtengordel)
Map p.393 F4 120

De Huyschkaemar

020 627 05 75

A wonderful discovery on the 'find-filled' Utrechtestraat, De Huyschkaemer is located towards the end of the street. It's a small split level bar and restaurant and is very popular on Friday and Saturday evenings and for a few after work drinks during the week. The cocktails are well mixed and, unlike most bars in Amsterdam, you won't have to wait too long for them. The staff are friendly and swift, ensuring the crowd stays relaxed. Not the place for a quiet meal but a drink on the small outside terrace on a lazy Saturday afternoon is a must. The name is a sort of slang that translates into 'living room' so don't be afraid to be put your feet up and relax.

Nieuwezijds Voorburgwal 256
Centrum
Map p.389 D4 121

Diep

020 420 20 20

Located centrally with plenty of other places to bar hop to, this great little venue is an Amsterdam staple. The crowd feels refreshingly local, friendly and young. Your eyes will be drawn to features like the giant shark hung on the wall. The cocktails are nothing to write home about but aren't too shoddy. The DJs play an eclectic range of music to keep you bopping and occasionally they'll manage to squeeze a band into the tiny space by the toilets.

Overtoom 50
Oud West
Map p.392 A3 122

Ebeling

020 689 48 58

Located in an old bank (you'll find the toilets in the safe), the Ebeling has long been a popular hangout on the Overtoom. It predates most of the new popular bars in Oud West and will probably outlive a few of them too. A year or two ago it went through drastic cosmetic changes and traded its pool table and a little bit of its friendly atmosphere for a funky lounge and club feel. The extension and DJ tables at the back were well thought out though and the Ebeling continues to be a popular nightspot. The food is simple; steaks, pastas and the like, but some things are fantastically done, such as the goats cheese salad. Ebeling is a good option for an afternoon drink but may have you crawling home much later then you had intended.

Ruysdaelstraat 48
Oud Zuid
Map p.384 B1 123

En Pluche

020 471 46 95 | *www.enpluche.nl*

A dark and seductive atmosphere, perfect if you're looking for a romantic hideaway, En Pluche serves appetising finger foods like oysters, lamb racks and other nibbles with an Asian influence, alongside their terrific cocktails. En Pluche's sister restaurant next door (Le Garage) serves more substantial meals, so if you have an appetite go there. The staff at En Pluche are a little snooty but quite professional, and though they struggle with the tightness of the space they'll get you everything you need eventually. Generally it is perfect for small, intimate evenings but does have a reputation for pretentiousness.

Flex Bar

Pazzanistraat 1
Westerpark
Map p.374 A4 124

020 486 21 23 | *www.flexbar.nl*

More of a club then a bar really, Flex Bar is the new, hip venture from the minds behind the refurbishment of the Westergasfabriek area in Amsterdam's west. The interior is a cut beyond the cutting edge and the sound system is phenomenal. The venue itself is flexible and can become two separate spaces, one clubby, the other more of a bar. The sharp, sleek lines and bold colours make it the perfect background for the hard, shiny media faces that frequent it. Surprisingly the vibe is quite relaxed and not at all intimidating, perhaps because the Westergasfabriek site is all about art and cultural promotion and doesn't take itself too seriously. The music varies and the venue is booked out by event organisers so check the website for up to date information.

Gespot

Prinsengracht 422
Canal Belt (Grachtengordel)
Map p.392 B2 125

020 320 37 33 | *www.restaurant-gespot.nl*

Beneath Gespot the restaurant you'll find a little gem of a bar. Small but cosy and beautifully designed, the bar is a great place for a pre-dinner drink or, if the terrace is open, an afternoon by the canal. The service is great and the cocktails better, try the apple martini. The restaurant serves lunch and dinner and there are also snacks available for those who only want to nibble. It's a fairly upmarket place and you may spot a few well-known Dutch faces sipping their cocktails or sucking on lobster claws.

The Getaway

Nieuwezijds Voorburgwal 250
Centrum
Map p.389 E4 126

020 627 14 27

Formerly the infamous late bar Seymour Likely's, The Getaway had some big shoes to fill and less hours in which to do it. Nonetheless it's still a great place for a few drinks and a dance. Split over two levels with some booths and the bar on ground level, a few tables on the mezzanine and a fireman-style staircase winding up to the toilets, Getaway does a lot with little space. The clientele is edgy, arty or like to think they are; either way it makes for great people watching. The drinks are overpriced but nothing extraordinary for this part of town.

Gollem

Ramsteeg 4
Centrum
Map p.393 D1 127

020 676 71 17

Gollem is a true haven for beer lovers. Tucked away between Spuistraat and Singel in a building that's over 400 years old, Gollem itself isn't quite so old, but 33 years ago it was the first specialised beer cafe in Amsterdam. Today, it is still one of the best, with over 200 beers to choose from. If you'd like to try something from the tap, the knowledgeable staff will be happy to give you a tester and the history of the beer before you commit to a full glass. The crowd is varied with a good bunch of regulars who know how to appreciate a good beer and a bad joke. The bar is large and takes up most of the space at the front of the cafe, but there's a mezzanine at the back with a few tables and chairs. Should you want to make a night of it you can organise a beer tasting tailored to your needs.

Harry's

Spuistraat 285
Centrum
Map p.393 D1 128

06 21 558300 | *www.harrysbaramsterdam.com*

Harry's is a small cocktail bar located just near Spuiplein. Styled after cocktail bars in New York, it's small but well decorated with a large table at the front and a few small tables at the back and upstairs. The staff are impeccably dressed and service is professional. The cocktails are fantastic but pricey, beginning around €8. Attention to detail means orders can take a while to appear and if the place is busy, which it often is on a Friday and Saturday, your wait could be up to 20 minutes for a cocktail.

Jazzcafé Alto

Korte Leidsedwarsstraat 115
Canal Belt (Grachtengordel)
Map p.392 C3 129

020 626 32 49 | www.jazz-cafe-alto.nl

The place to go for jazz fans, don't expect the old school stuff though. It's a very popular venue so if you want to grab a seat, get there early – you'll probably not be the only one waiting for the doors to open. The interior is in the style of a simple brown cafe, with a few tables and chairs and posters on the wall, but you're not there for the decor. The crowd is very mixed with a liberal sprinkling of different nationalities and young and old. Prices are reasonable for the area and you won't be put out of pocket by a door fee. All in all, a safe bet for a pleasant night out if you like jazz.

Kamer 401

Marnixstraat 401
Canal Belt (Grachtengordel)
Map p.392 B3 130

020 620 06 14

Just around the corner from Leidseplein, this is one of a trio of popular bars on Marnixstraat. 401's interior is intended to feel like a lounge room and in the early hours it does. On Friday and Saturday nights it feels more like a game of sardines in a sweatbox, but in a good kind of way. It's a well-known stomping ground for Amsterdam media expats but manages to maintain an unpretentious atmosphere. The DJs can be relied upon for good music but whether or not space will be available for dancing depends on your own personal space hang-ups. Price wise it's reasonable for the part of town and if you stick to beers you won't have an ache in your wallet the next day.

Kingfisher

Ferdinand Bolstraat 23
De Pijp
Map p.384 B1 131

020 671 23 95

This is a real local bar that manages to be as inviting and relaxed during the day as it is hip and happening in the evening. Large windows and a sense of space complement its corner position in De Pijp. Its simple decor feels like a less-suffocating brown cafe. Good food and snacks are available and dishes change daily. You should be able to fill yourself completely for €20 or so. Friday and Saturday evenings often include a DJ and the locals say goodbye to the week. The staff are relaxed, friendly and not bad to look at either!

Kletskop

Zeedijk 10
Centrum
Map p.389 F4 132

020 622 57 28

Close to Centraal Station on the edge of the Red Light District, this building is over 300 years old and has been in its present incarnation as Kletskop for over 20 years. The wooden interior is minimally lit but on a summer evening the large windows let plenty of light in so you can admire the ancient Marylyn Monroe posters on the walls. What type of clientele you'll be drinking with depends on the time and the day but there are always a few ageing locals sitting at the bar. Every second Sunday of the month there's an acoustic music session and you can sit in one of the wooden booths and listen while drinking a glass of Lachouffe or Palm (strong beers), both of which are on tap. There's no kitchen but you can ask for a Tosti (a toasted ham/cheese/tomato sandwich) for only €1.70. Cash only.

Lime

Zeedijk 104
Centrum
Map p.389 F4 134

020 639 30 20

A great little bar tucked just inside the Red Light District, Lime is a good choice for a pre-boogie drink or after work gossip session. They specialise in vodka and white beers but also make awesome cocktails. The service is always friendly and copes well when it gets busy. The decor doesn't strive for the uber cool of other overstylised bars, which makes it all the more comfortable. The retro lamps and other details create a funky, relaxing atmosphere that suits the vibe. Prices are reasonable and the crowd is friendly. Don't go too early if you're looking to strike up conversations with handsome strangers as it doesn't really get going until around 22:00.

Marnixstraat 403
Canal Belt (Grachtengordel)
Map p.392 B3 134

LUX

020 422 14 12

This fairly funky, arty bar is massively popular at the weekends, and most other nights too. Its slightly later opening hours may have something to do with its popularity or it maybe the relaxed atmosphere, sexily seedy interior design, reasonably priced drinks and retro films screened above the bar. Whatever it is, if you want to get your foot in the door, arrive before 22:00.

Lijnbaansgracht 163
Canal Belt (Grachtengordel)
Map p.392 A1 135

Maloe Melo

020 420 45 92 | www.maloemelo.com

The live blues, rock, punk or rockabilly experience at Maloe Melo is like no other. The venue consists of two rooms, the front room being the main bar with tables and chairs and great posters, the back room being the stage. You're not likely to get this up close and personal with a band anywhere else and if you love raw, live music you won't find anywhere better. It's old and it's dusty but that's what happens when you rock away the night, every night. The relaxed crowd is there to dance and throw themselves around until their clothes drip. The staff are friendly, burly rockabilly boys who are happy to chat. With the entrance fee rarely over €5, you can't usually get a livelier night out for less.

Hobbemastraat 2
Oud Zuid
Map p.392 B4 136

The Mansion

020 616 66 64 | www.the-mansion.nl

The three cocktail bars in The Mansion are almost as intoxicating to look at as they are to sit in. It's best to arrive early as the doormen can be a bit heavy-handed. Once inside you'll find the bars on the ground floor, a dim sum club in the basement and fine dining rooms serving Chinese cuisine on the top floor. If you're out for a drink, you should stop on the ground floor and enjoying some truly magnificent cocktails – the range is staggering and the mixing perfect. The staff are almost as icy as their shakers though and The Mansion tends to attract those who are trying to be seen, but that shouldn't stop you from going there to see.

Ferdinand Bolstraat 178
De Pijp
Map p.384 B2 137

Pur

020 471 55 44 | www.pur-amsterdam.nl

Popular among locals in De Pijp, the beautifully designed interior is eyecatching without being intrusive. Pur has created different areas within its walls; the brasserie and bar area at the front is the perfect place for a pre-dinner cocktail – whether you move on to another restaurant for dinner is up to you, but the dining room is also hard to beat. The crowd at Pur is varied – early in the evening you will have more distinguished diners sharing space with the usual young and hip Pijp crowd, later on, the atmosphere becomes even more low key and relaxed thanks to the amazing cocktails.

Rokin 81-83
Centrum
Map p.393 E1 138

Subterraneo

020 612 39 35 | www.subterraneo.nl

A new location in the centre of Amsterdam, Subterrano is a stunningly designed bar in an 18th century house on the Rokin. The inspiration for the bar comes from Barcelona and you'll find tasty tapas snacks are available late into the night. The extensive drinks menu offers a selection of beers, wines, champagnes, cavas and cocktails to choose from. Prices are a bit steep with cocktails starting at €8 and, unless you're sticking to beer, don't expect to come out on top. The staff are attentive, friendly and fit in well with the attractive clientele. A great sound system and constantly changing DJs put thump in your rump. Subterraneo is a successful compromise between a club and a lounge, definitely worth checking out if you can't decide what you're up for or feel like being surprised.

Pijlsteeg 37
Centrum
Map p.389 E4 139

Wynand Fockink

020 639 26 95 | *www.wynand-fockink.nl*

What began as a local distillery for liqueurs, jenever and other traditional Dutch tipples is now one of Amsterdam's best loved 'proeflokaals', or tasting rooms. Wynand Fockink is a time machine full of magic potions; they have been distilling in exactly the same way for over 350 years and they do it very well. The tasting area consists of two cosy rooms with a few seats. The walls are covered in traditional brown shelves holding mysteriously coloured bottles and items of jenever history. A window behind the bar opens onto the pedestrian-only Pijlsteeg so you can order your drink while you are outside mingling with other tasters of the proeflokaal's delights. The helpful staff are chatty and relaxed, and after a glass or two of 'Bride's Tears' (Bruidstranen) or 'Walk in the Forest' (Boswandeling) you will be feeling much the same. The old distillery is still operating next door and if you are interested you can stop by for a tour or even a workshop in how the best Dutch jenever is made.

Pubs

Other options **Bars** p.341

Max Euweplein 73
Canal Belt
(Grachtengordel)
Map p.392 C4 140

Aran Pub

020 461 72 48 | *www.aranpub.com*

Just beside the Hard Rock Café on Max Euweplein at the beginning of Vondelpark, Aran suffers a bit in comparison with other pubs in Amsterdam as it's contained in a new development that doesn't quite lend itself the 'ye olde' feel of other locations. The big terrace on the canal certainly adds some points, but if you are looking for something approaching the real thing this isn't it. However, the food here is far more reasonably priced than at some other bars. It's also one of the only places in Amsterdam you can get a full fry up at 09:00 before the hangover really kicks in.

Amstel 100
Centrum
Map p.393 E2 141

Mulligan's Irish Music Bar

020 622 13 30 | *www.mulligans.nl*

In the modern tradition of a 'real' Irish pub, Mulligan's is something else altogether. It doesn't need the 'real', the black pudding or cod & chips – and just as well because you won't find any of that here. It's a small, simple bar that prides itself on being the first Irish bar in Amsterdam and pulling perfect Guinness. The decor is worn and tired, with smoke-stained walls covered with instruments. This is not the place to head to if you're about to go out on the town but it's worth wandering into in the afternoon… just for the craic!

Ferdinand Bolstraat 5
De Pijp
Map p.384 B1 142

O'Donnell's Irish Pub

020 676 77 86

On the corner of the Heinekenplein in De Pijp, looking slightly out of place with all the new, funky additions that have popped up around it, O'Donnell's is a quintessential Irish pub complete with snug. A popular venue with sport fans, O'Donnell's doesn't quite have the same atmosphere that the others muster but it still fits the bill. The staff are chatty and friendly and the clientele a

Live Music

Live music can be hard to find in Amsterdam, but look hard enough and you'll discover it is out there. Aside from the larger venues like the Heineken Music Hall (p.360), Paradiso (p.357) and the Melkweg (p.356) there are a couple of options for people who like to get off the beaten track and hear something new (or old for that matter). These live music venues all have a bit of character: Maloe Melo (p.348), Bourbon St Blues (p.341), Jazzcafé Alto (p.346) and Café Pakhuis Wilhelmina (p.343). For listings of all types of gigs and concerts, and who's playing every week, pick up a copy of the free *Amsterdam Weekly*.

bit older than in some of the other, more central pubs. As with other pubs the food is hearty and simple and you can expect to shell out around €25 for three courses.

Paleisstraat 103
Centrum
Map p.389 E4 143

O'Reilly's

020 624 94 98 | *www.oreillys.com*

O'Reilly's is hugely popular with tourists and is often packed, due to its location and recognisable brand. The atmosphere is buzzing on the weekends and for sporting events. The terrace is usually packed, keeping the staff on their toes while they invariably handle the busy times well and maintain their friendly composure. The food is good and the beers many but it's very expensive for pub fare. You'll be paying almost €5 for a pint.

Rokin 89
Centrum
Map p.393 E1 144

The Tara

020 421 26 54 | *www.thetara.com*

One of the largest bars in Amsterdam, The Tara has been around for over a decade and has undergone three extensions in that time. They have managed to maintain a cosy atmosphere and the place is riddled with nooks and crannies to sip your pint in. The decor is eclectic with tables and chairs, big squishy armchairs around open fires and long tables with benches. Very popular during football tournaments, the pub has several screens on which to watch any major sporting event. The food is good, hearty and costs what you would expect to pay in the centre of town. Many European, English and Irish beers are available for you to sample. The crowd is a good mix of Dutch, expats and tourists, as well as young and old. Expect to spend around €30 on a three-course meat and potatoes bender.

Overtoom 31
Oud Zuid
Map p.392 A3 145

Tig Barra

020 412 22 10 | *www.tigbarra.com*

The Tig is a favourite for expats. Many who don't actually live close to it will forgo other, closer pubs, to come here. It does have a nice, relaxed atmosphere and the staff are great. The kitchen churns out all the Irish and English favourites. Several screens around the pub show sporting events and you can make your own at the ping pong table down the back. The decor is very simple and a little shabby, but the terrace out the front is popular for afternoon drinks in the sun. There is a slew of regulars propping up the bar who are happy to strike up a chat with everyone and the Sunday roast is incredibly tasty.

Designer bars

Gay & Lesbian

Other options **Gay & Lesbian** (General Information, p.20)

The gay scene in Amsterdam is spread throughout the centre of the city. Some bars are clustered together in areas such as Reguliersdwarsstraat, but others can be found all over town, which is nice when you're out and about. Most gay bars are separate. However, anyone is welcome. Women can be found in most places except for the really leathery ones. Best to send in a scout if you're in doubt to see if there are already women in the bar. Straight men are always welcome too, as long as they behave. Mixed crowds would feel comfortable at any of the bars on Reguliersdwarsstraat. All of the bars are fairly mixed as far as race and nationality, and the back corner of Café April (p.352) is referred to by regulars as 'Asian Corner'. A couple of places that are recommended for mixed crowds are Prik (p.354), and Pub Soho (p.354), which have well-established 'mixed' scenes with a big gay twist. Dutch law allows gay marriage, and evidence of gay coupling can be seen all over the city. However, no law can do away with prejudice and bigotry, so when you're out, be aware that not everyone is celebrating your gay pride.

Amstel 54
Centrum
Map p.393 E2 146

Amstel Taveerne

020 623 42 54 | www.amsteltaveerne.nl

The Amstel Taveerne may have seen better days (they're planning a renovation), but it is still standing and is a regular drinking spot for many gay Amsterdammers. It's got a rustic atmosphere with old beer steins hanging from the ceiling and lots of wood. The mood is friendly, easy and unpretentious, and there are songs playing with words you can actually understand – lots of tunes from the days when the bar was in its heyday.

Reguliersdwarsstraat 44
Canal Belt (Grachtengordel)
Map p.393 D2 147

ARC

020 689 70 70 | www.bararc.com

ARC is a very modern, sleek bar with a hip young crowd and 'cute' bar staff. They serve mainly cocktails, but finger foods are available. The crowd is mixed almost to a fault, but the ARC is still clearly gay. It's often very busy and if you arrive early, you can grab a seat looking out onto the small garden (where patrons are not permitted). Failing that, you can look for a seat on one of the many low couches or go out onto the pavement with many of the other patrons to enjoy your drinks.

Warmoesstraat 85
Centrum
Map p.389 F4 148

Argos

020 622 65 95 | www.argosbar.com

Argos is dark, leathery, smokey and very claustrophobic. There are chains hanging from the ceiling and various other objects of interest hanging from the walls, all of which lend to a cluttered feeling, which the management is probably going for. One bar on each level makes getting another beer convenient. Screens at the back of the bar makes not getting sucked in by the TV a bit easier. The clientele and bar staff are very much of the 'bear' variety and while they are pretty serious, they are not unfriendly. Men only.

Reguliers-dwarsstraat 105
Canal Belt (Grachtengordel)
Map p.393 E2 149

Cafe 't Leeuwtje

020 622 25 77 | www.cafehetleeuwtje.nl

One of the newest offerings in Amsterdam is the very small, but bustling, 't Leeuwtje (pronounced "uht" Leo-chuh). It's a very female friendly place and the crowd often overflows out onto the street. With a very 'old Amsterdam', friendly, party atmosphere and anyone is welcome. There is free soup on Tuesdays and free coffee on Sundays. Closed on Wednesdays, but there's a regular following the rest of the week.

Café April

Reguliersdwarsstraat 37
Canal Belt (Grachtengordel)
Map p.393 D2 150

020 625 95 72 | *www.cafeapril.eu*

By far the most popular Sunday afternoon happy hour is at Café April where the lively crowd spills out onto the street in the summer. April's most notable feature is the rotating bar at the back, so people can sit while they cruise and not waste energy walking around. There is another large bar at the front that is manned by bar staff with a bit of attitude. The clientele is mostly men, with the occasional woman here and there. The atmosphere is relaxed, the music is poppy and the decor is slightly dated. A regular gay bar that could be almost anywhere in the world.

Café Rouge

Amstel 60
Centrum
Map p.393 E2 151

020 420 98 81 | *www.caferouge.nl*

Just off the beaten path, this is a friendly, kitschy bar with plenty of pictures lining the walls. One wall holds pictures of celebrities, old turn-of-the-century photos in gilded frames grace another, while in the back, several pictures of the royal family, especially the beloved Juliana, round things out. This is a consummate locals' bar. A barmaid stands in front of a huge vase of red roses while a DJ spins old Dutch pop music and a few customers sing along. The atmosphere is very comfortable, sort of like stepping back a bit in time.

Club Cockring

Warmoesstraat 96
Centrum
Map p.389 F4 152

020 623 96 04 | *www.clubcockring.com*

While the name implies a leather scene, that's not the only thing you'll find at Club Cockring. The €5 cover gives you entry to plenty of cruising space, there's a disco in the basement, and there are even small rooms available, if necessary. It attracts a fairly diverse crowd, but maintain a mellow atmosphere. There are regular strip shows and it really gets going around 01:00 at the weekends. Absinthe is available at the bar downstairs.

Cuckoo's Nest

Nieuwezijds Kolk 6
Centrum
Map p.389 E3 153

020 627 17 52 | *www.cuckoosnest.nl*

Cuckoo's Nest has the feel of a small city leather bar. The lighting is probably a bit brighter than usual and the crowd is very normal, not at all strictly leather. Poppy music perfectly accompanies the several screens of run-of-the-mill porn. There's a cop at the door, who also checks coats. The main room is a good size and there's a cellar with darkrooms and a regular stream of men going in and out. It's a place you might want to visit while on an Amsterdam bar crawl, but maybe not end the night at. They do offer free condoms though.

Eagle

Warmoesstraat 86-90
Centrum
Map p.389 F4 154

020 627 86 34

Despite the name, the Eagle isn't strictly leather anymore. The clientele is more everyman; tourists not only new to Amsterdam, but also to the 'scene'. There's a buzzer to get in and once you do, you'll feel like you're in a shack or barn, albeit with a coat check and lots of things hanging from the walls and ceiling. Techno and trance music fills the space and if you get bored while cruising, there's a video game. Friendlier than Argos, but still men only.

Getto

Warmoesstraat 51
Centrum
Map p.389 F3 155

020 421 51 51

Getto is the typical shape of an Amsterdam bar – long and thin. The interior is kitschy-hip, with plenty of stuff from eras gone by hanging from the walls and ceiling. A DJ spins funky music that complements the inviting, open front. At the back, the restaurant serves up everything from burgers to full dinners. At the front, there's a bar that is very big on cocktails, although they do have beer. It's a very tourist-friendly place, so anyone can pop in for a drink.

Drag Queen Olympics

Leidsedwarstraat 4-6
Canal Belt
(Grachtengordel)
Map p.392 C3 156

Habibi Ana

06 21 921686 | www.habibiana.nl

Billed as 'the first and only Arabic gay bar in the world,' Habibi Ana is an unsuspecting little bar off Leidseplein. The small, Middle Eastern-style sitting area creates a cosy environment perfect for the friendly, multilingual bar staff. Arabic music and shisha pipes round out the theme and attract a good number of Arabic patrons. That shouldn't stop non-Arabs from coming, all of whom are welcome. The bar gets going around 23:00 and it's busiest on Friday and Saturday night.

Spuistraat 109
Canal Belt
(Grachtengordel)
Map p.389 D4 157

Prik

020 320 00 02 | www.prikamsterdam.nl

Prik is a cute, small bar with tables out front and plenty of inside seating. There are two rooms: a large front room with a bar and a friendly staff, and a smaller, cosier room at the back with an aquarium, where the seating is not quite so easily available. There's an overall attempt at creating an eclectic atmosphere. They have snacks available and poppy tunes play at a reasonable volume. The mixed crowd still retains a very gay atmosphere and Prik is the only bar in Amsterdam where you can get a T-shirt that says, 'I love…'

Reguliersdwarsstraat 36
Canal Belt
(Grachtengordel)
Map p.393 D2 158

Pub Soho

020 422 33 12 | www.pubsoho.eu

Designed to look like a London pub, Soho is a large but crowded bar with two floors. The first floor has a bar with plenty of seating and a nice ring for cruising. The cut-glass lighting fixtures cast a warm glow on the dark wood and red embossed wallpaper. A red carpeted stairway leads to a loungy second floor where a fake fireplace and large, comfortable chairs create a library feel. The crowd is mixed with the great majority being men in their 30s and 40s, although anyone is welcome.

Zeedijk 20
Centrum
Map p.389 F3 159

The Queen's Head

020 420 24 75 | www.queenshead.nl

Situated at the beginning of the busy Zeedijk, in the oldest part of Amsterdam, this small bar provides a cosy venue to sip drinks and look out of the back windows onto the canal while listening to hip music. They have regular bingo with Amsterdam's most famous transvestite, Dolly Bellefleur. The well-worn decor is the perfect setting for the friendly bar staff and regular crowd. Well worth stopping in for a biertje.

Elandsstraat 119
Canal Belt
(Grachtengordel)
Map p.392 B1 160

Saarien2

www.saarein.nl

Saarein2 looks like a traditional Dutch neighbourhood bar, but it's actually the first 'women-only' bar, with a history going to back to 1978 and an interior going back to the 19th century. Since 1999 it has been open to all queer-minded people, but the clientele is still mostly women. Saarein2 hosts the Transgender Cafe every third Sunday of the month at 17:00. Every Friday afternoon from 17:00 to 19:00 is happy hour and bingo starts at 19:00. It's open every day from noon and there is a working kitchen, so stop in for lunch.

Amstelstraat 7
Canal Belt
(Grachtengordel)
Map p.393 F2 161

Vivalavie

020 624 01 14 | www.vivelavie.net

Vivalavie is certainly a women's bar, but that's not to say it isn't a friendly place in a great location. Open to anyone who's up for a good time, it's been around for 26 years. Conveniently located close to Rembrandtplein, the walls of the bar are lined with photographs of famous women and the lighting fixtures are art deco. The outside seating is great for when the weather is good, while for rainy days the inside plays host to a friendly, inviting crowd.

Nightclubs

The club scene in Amsterdam is not what it used to be but you can still have a great night out. There is a good amount of variety, but prices are high so it's best to do your research and find out what's going on where so you are not disappointed. A few clubs do draw big names but tickets can sell out quickly so keep an eye on the free weekly and monthly publications around town (such as *Amsterdam Weekly*) or sign up to a mailing list. Design is important in Amsterdam and most of the clubs have cutting edge interiors to entertain your eyes while your ears are buzzing. Door policies are not that strict but large groups of men sometimes have problems. Security is quite strict so don't be surprised at having to walk through a metal detector or having your bag searched on entry. There are not as many clubs in Amsterdam as there used to be. This is attributed to the rise of the lounge bars that offer relaxed surroundings, good music and no cover charge. Amsterdam also has a lot of late bars which stay open until 03:00 or 04:00 on weekends and feature local DJs.

Spuistraat 2
Canal Belt
(Grachtengordel)
Map p.389 E3 162

Bitterzoet

020 521 30 01 | *www.bitterzoet.com*

A short walk from Centraal Station, Bitterzoet offers more then the usual club night. It began with the philosophy of providing a space for up-and-coming DJs, bands and artists. Downstairs houses a comfy, funky bar and dance floor, upstairs there's a theatre. The music is predominantly hip hop and funk, though other music does get a look in. Check the website if you're after a specific style of music. The crowd is young and urban and you may feel out of place if you're lacking the latest trainers. The doormen can be intimidating but if you're early you'll have no problems getting in. The door price is far less than at most clubs, and the average night's entry fee is under €10.

Oosterdokskade 3-5
Centrum
Map p.390 B3 42

Club 11

020 625 59 99 | *www.ilove11.nl*

Located on the top floor of the industrial looking ex-post office building to the right of Centraal Station, Club 11 has spectacular views of Amsterdam. The space is around the size of two basketball courts with windows on all sides. The venue is open for lunch and dinner all week (see 319) and transforms into a club on Friday and Saturday evenings from 22:30. The music varies so check the website for what's going on. The crowd is young, hip and urban but fairly relaxed, with everyone out to have a good time. The door code isn't strict but aims for 'edgy cool'. The entry fee depends on what's going on but a usual club night should cost around €12.

Nieuwezijds Voorburgwal 169
Centrum
Map p.389 D4 164

Club NL

020 622 75 10 | *www.clubnl.nl*

One of Amsterdam's plushest and most decadent lounge clubs has a rich, ambient interior that urges you to sink back into the cushions and let yourself melt into the music. Open every night of the week, it's more lounge bar during the week. Come Thursday, however, and the mellow tunes disappear and the dancing shoes come out. Despite its high prices, NL is a good place to start or end your night. Depending on which day and how early you arrive you may not have to pay the €5-€10 entry fee, but you'll certainly pay and pay for your drinks.

Club 11

Rembrandtplein 11
Canal Belt (Grachtengordel)
Map p.393 F2 165

Escape

020 231 15 77 | www.escape.nl

Escape is one of the biggest and best-known clubs in Amsterdam. Located on the Rembrandtplein, you will see the queue for Escape before you make it to the square. Inside, the innovative lighting revolves around a giant LED screen that covers the whole ceiling of one of the rooms. Although it can get crowded, dancers can find space to take a breather. The crowd caters towards young, mainstream clubbers and the music usually isn't the only thing making them move. Escape is definitely worth checking out – you may not become a regular, but it should be on your 'to do' list. Depending on the night, entry is between €10 and €20.

Korte Leidsedwarsstraat 18
Canal Belt (Grachtengordel)
Map p.392 C3 166

Jimmy Woo

020 626 31 50 | www.jimmywoo.com

A feat in design and elegance, Jimmy Woo is the ultimate in chic. It's difficult to get into, so call ahead and try get on the guest list. Inside you'll find a world of mob-like decadence – not surprising since the name comes from a fictitious Hong Kong mobster. The dark ambience is dotted with lounges and sleek furniture, while the bar serves fabulous (pricey) cocktails. Downstairs is a dance floor with amazing lighting. The strict door policy ensures only the uber cool find their way in, and consequently the club is full of beautiful girls and sharp media types. The music varies so check the website for details.

Lijnbaansgracht 161
Canal Belt (Grachtengordel)
Map p.392 A1 167

Korsakoff

020 625 78 54 | www.korsakoffamsterdam.nl

Amsterdam's alternative music club is about as grungy as they get, but that can be a good thing. There's no door fee here and no dress code but there are some scary looking doormen who, thankfully, are not called upon often. There are two floors but the second floor is only open on Friday and Saturday and the music is usually more dance orientated than that playing below. The ground floor is alternative grooves only. The mixed, all age crowd is very laid back.

Lijnbaansgracht 234a
Canal Belt (Grachtengordel)
Map p.392 B3 168

Melkweg

020 531 81 81 | www.melkweg.nl

Another Amsterdam staple, Melkweg has been around since 1970 and continues to deliver the goods. Similar to Paradiso, this venue is not just about clubbing but also draws fantastic (international) bands, art exhibitions and media installations. Inside you'll find three large dance rooms, a cafe and a few smaller spaces that are used mostly for small installations or when the venue is involved in one of the many cultural festivals that take place throughout the city. It's a little bit on the scruffy side but, like Paradiso, the crowd largely depends on what's happening. You can expect to pay from €5 to €50 depending on what you're going to see or hear. Club nights are usually €10. You'll have to pay an extra €3 for the compulsory membership fee but it's valid for a month if you remember to hold onto the ticket.

Singel 460
Centrum
Map p.393 D2 169

Odeon

020 521 85 55 | www.odeontheater.nl

Recently re-opened, The Odeon is a multi-faceted venue with a restaurant, bar and club. The club is only open from Thursday to Saturday and the music is mostly comfortable classics; so if you want to take a step back in time, this is the place. It has been beautifully refurbished and it's worth taking a look at the building itself. The crowd is mostly conservative Dutch letting their hair down. It's a club that works for large groups of varying ages and tastes, if you're entertaining relatives or less adventurous types. The door cover ranges from €10 to €30 depending on what's going on.

Oostelijke Handelskade
Zeeburg
Map p.380 A2 170

Panama

020 311 86 86 | www.panama.nl

A bit of a trek from the centre of town, Panama is a large club in what used to be the port centre of Het IJ. It's worth the journey though, as it attracts some of the world's hottest DJs like Dave Angel, Carl Craig and John Digweed. It's best to check the site for who's coming and reserve tickets, which for feature nights are usually around €40. The normal club nights will set you back around €10. Panama also has a restaurant and theatre so you can easily spend your entire evening there. The decor is minimal but attractive; you wouldn't mistake the club area for being anything else. The dance space is great and you'll rarely feel too squashed – if you do, you can retire to one of the booths in the spacious balcony. The crowd, usually young and hip, varies depending on the night but if there's nothing special planned it can be a bit of a meat market.

Weteringschans 6-8
Canal Belt (Grachtengordel)
Map p.392 C4 171

Paradiso

020 626 45 21 | www.paradiso.nl

Disguised as a church just off Leidseplein, Paradiso is a cultural icon in Amsterdam and shows run the gamut from punk and poetry to hard house. Although quite small, Paradiso attracts some of the world's biggest and best bands. Opening times vary depending on the show but club nights usually start around 23:00 and finish around 05:00. Entry costs from €5 to €25 and you can expect to pay an extra €2.50 compulsory membership fee as well. Tickets sell out fast, so if there's a show you'd like to catch, then get your tickets as soon as possible. Inside there are two stages or dance rooms. The large lower floor, originally the mass area, is surrounded by a balcony that's great for dancing if you need some breathing room. The smaller space at the top of the club can feel claustrophobic but is usually used for smaller events like poetry readings or small name artists.

Rembrandtplein 44
Canal Belt (Grachtengordel)
Map p.393 F2 172

Rain

020 626 70 78 | www.rain-amsterdam.com

One of the new breed of clubs that isn't happy being just one thing, Rain is a restaurant, club and bar. The club side of things happens mostly on Friday and Saturday evenings. Its location on Rembrandtplein makes it quite popular and a queue can form quickly from around 23:00. The dress code isn't strict but you will be frisked on your way in. The space occupies two floors but the upper floor is used for dining except for the last Friday of every month. The overall is look is very subtle, with a modern lounge style and an oriental influence. The crowd is mostly Dutch people letting off some steam after a long week's work. The prices are average for a club in this area. Beers are a couple of euros and mixed drinks €5 and up. This is not a club for the hard-core dancer but remains a good option for an after-work cocktail.

Lijnbaansgracht 238
Canal Belt (Grachtengordel)
Map p.392 B3 173

Sugar Factory

020 624 10 12 | www.sugarfactory.nl

In contrast to other nightclubs, Sugar Factory bills itself as a night theatre and every night is crazier, stranger and more beautiful then the last. It's only a couple of years old but is already a favourite. Sugar Factory is easy to find, it's just down from Leidseplein and across from Melkweg. Club nights vary from disco to Brazilian beats and the cultural shows cover everything from cabaret to supercharged poetry sessions. Check the website for what's coming up and for ticket sales, which cost between €5 and €15. The interior is small but space is maximised. The bar stretches the length of the dance floor and the large stage is great for boogying if there's no band. You can also chill on the spacious balcony and watch the madness below if you're danced out. The staff are friendly and have fun behind the bar. The crowd is varied in age, gender and orientation, and makes for great people watching.

Parties At Home

Entertaining at home in a damp cold climate such as Holland's is how the Dutch like to have fun. All manner of dinner parties abound – from pot luck (bring your own dish) to formal sit-downs with name cards and seating arrangements. Birthdays are celebrated with much fanfare in Holland – preferably on the exact date of birth, and with family and close friends all invited.

Kids' Parties

Kids' parties among the expat community are usually themed. Beware though, the selection of character and famous movie-based party decorations and tableware is dismally too non-existent; many families have them sent from websites overseas. Clowns, balloon makers, makeup artists, magicians, puppet theatres and child minders who oversee arts and crafts activities are all for hire for parties in or outside the home. A good reference is *Kids Gids* (www.kidsgids.nl) which is a guidebook for children in Holland, in English. Good party locations include The Little Gym (020 404 07 98, www.thelittlegym-eu.com) Race Planet (020 611 11 20, www.raceplanetforkids.nl) and Konijn Bowling (020 664 22 11, www.knijnbowling.nl) to name just a few.

Themed Nights

Apart from Halloween, where people dress up in spooky costumes, themed nights aren't that common. Most bars do cater for Dutch football even when lacking a TV screen, by covering the interior in orange crepe paper. Ladies' nights are more common at bars that are full of tourists and expats. Happy hour is short, usually from 17:00 to 18:00, as the Dutch eat early. There is usually no bar food to accompany a happy hour. St. Patrick's Day is well represented at Irish pubs, while American Thanksgiving dinners are served at the major hotels. Christmas dinner is served mostly everywhere in Holland on the first Christmas day (5 December), referred to as 'Sinterklaas' day – the birthday of St Nicholas. The Dutch also have another special festive day, their second Christmas day, on 26 December.

Caterers

Caterers provide all-in services for everything from gala events, corporate soirees, on-site dinner parties and on-location celebrations to arranging a romantic dinner for two at home. The listings website www.kies.com/netwijzer/catnhams.htm is good beginners' resource if you wish to customise a party or event. You can find every type of catering outlet, from those who rent tableware to ones specialising in a particular cuisine. Alternatively, you can walk into any restaurant or hotel and the food and beverage manager will only be too pleased to plan your party in the comfort of their venue. Since the Dutch are addicted to their agendas it is a wise strategy to plan at least three months ahead if you're going to have a big bash.

Melkweg

Cabaret & Strip Shows

Amsterdam is well known for its tolerant attitude towards the sex industry. It's perhaps due to prostitution being legal that there aren't many strip clubs. One which opened recently in Amsterdam, The Zebra Lounge, was forced by the city to close and re-open as a nightclub, with no strippers. There are plenty of brothels scattered around town and the three Red Light Districts (p.138) where you will see women presenting themselves in windows. The main one is close to Centraal Station, the other two are to be found running parallel to Singel and on the edge of De Pijp. Although there are no 'real' strip shows there are a few venues that offer erotic entertainment and sex shows. They tend to focus on the theatre aspect of sex and many find them humorously exaggerated.

Oudezijds Achterburgwal 37
Centrum
Map p.389 F4 174

Banana Bar

020 622 76 40

The Banana Bar is one of the oldest erotic venues in Amsterdam. You pay a €45 entrance fee for one hour of unlimited drinks inside, and while you're there you are entertained by the ladies who will perform the special 'trick' that gives the bar its name. This is one is not comfortable for both sexes to enjoy.

Oudezijds Achterburgwal 106-108
Centrum
Map p.389 F4 175

Casa Rosso

020 627 89 54 | *www.casarosso.com*

The same company owns Casa Rosso and Banana Bar but Casa Rosso is more of a staged affair and prefers to be known as a theatre. It's more enjoyable for both sexes and you can catch a male strip show as well as female perfomers. They also exhibit live couple sex and more erotic tricks. Be warned, you may be asked to participate in the theatre. Entry is €30 per person or €45 including four drinks.

Bethlehemsteeg 23
Centrum
Map p.389 E4 176
€€€

La Vie en Proost

020 626 16 35 | *www.lavieenproost.com*

La Vie en Proost has been in business for 20 years and is the only topless dancing bar in Amsterdam. The girls are energetic, beautiful and strong and have no problem generating a frenzy around the bar to ensure you don't notice how much you're paying for your drinks. Ouch. You can also get a lap dance for a fee. Don't confuse 'Proost' with La Vie en Rose next door, as the latter is a brothel.

Oudezijds Achterburgwal 5-7
Centrum
Map p.389 F4 177

Moulin Rouge

020 625 13 78 | *www.moulinrougeamsterdam.nl*

Moulin Rouge is similar to Casa Rosso and bills itself as a sex theatre. The crowd is not as boisterous as that of the others and there is a good mix of men and women. The stage is quite small, and entry is €25 including two drinks. There are four acts repeated on rotation. If you're curious about erotic theatre and don't want something over the top this is the place to head to.

Cinemas

Amsterdam has quite a few cinemas. Pathe has several large multiplexes in and around the city. The largest being Pathe Arena where there is an Imax. There are also a good number of independent cinemas that show art house flicks and golden oldies. Films are always shown in their original languages with Dutch subtitles which is great, but if you're going to see a foreign film make sure your Dutch is up to

Cinemas

Film Museum	Vondelpark 3	020 589 14 00	www.filmmuseum.nl
Het Ketel Huis	Pazzanistraat 13	020 684 00 90	www.ketelhuis.nl
Kriterion	Oost	020 623 17 08	www.kriterion.nl
The Movies	Centrum	020 638 60 16	www.themovies.nl
Pathe	Various Locations	0900 1458	www.pathe.nl
Rialto	De Pijp	020 676 87 00	www.rialtofilm.nl
Uitkijk	Centrum	020 623 74 60	www.uitkijk.nl

Casinos
Gambling is not overly popular in the Netherlands, not surprising given the frugal, Calvinistic nature of the Dutch. There is only one legal casino chain, Holland Casino. The Amsterdam branch is located on Max Euweplein. See p.161 for more information.

scratch. Occasionally you'll find a film in the video store before it makes it to the cinemas as the film release date is so far behind the release date in the original country; this doesn't usually happen with the blockbusters though. The facilities in the cinemas are quite good but vary from location to location. You can't always get popcorn but you can always get a beer or wine to carry into the theatre. The Tuchinski, now part of the Pathe chain, is one of the oldest and most beautiful cinemas. It was recently refurbished and is well worth checking out. To find out film times you can check the Pathe website for any big name movies or go to www.biosagenda.nl, which has the information from independents as well.

Concerts

Amsterdam is a great city for music, and just about everything rolls through town. Some venues are quite small though, and tickets go fast, so it's a good idea to keep an eye on publications such as the free *Amsterdam Weekly*, or more in advance on websites like www.aub.nl to make sure you don't miss out. Paradiso (p.357) and Melkweg (p.356), both in the nightclub section, are popular for rock and pop performances and often pull big names. They also get some great up and coming acts and the tickets are quite affordable. Throughout the year there are several cultural and music festivals like the Roots Festival (p.48), the North Sea Jazz Festival, 5 Days Off, Uitmarkt (p.50), Grachten Festival (p.50) and the Holland Festival. You'll find an overview of these events here" www.amsterdam.info/events.

ArenA Boulevard
Amsterdam Zuidoost
Map p.367 F4

Amsterdam ArenA

020 311 13 33 | www.amsterdamarena.nl

Easily reached by metro, Amsterdam ArenA is the largest performance ground around. It's also the Ajax home stadium. When it's not being skipped across by footballers it's being stomped on by happy dancers. Occasionally massive raves are held here but you will also catch performances by some of the world's biggest artists like Madonna, U2 and The Rolling Stones. Check the website for upcoming events.

Pietheinkade 3
Zeeburg
Map p.390 C2 179

Bimhuis

020 788 21 88 | www.bimhuis.nl

A great little venue that's been around since 1973, Bimhuis attracts local and international artists. it's predominantly a jazz venue but they also present more mainstream acts and world music.

Concertgebouwplein 2
Oud Zuid
Map p.384 A1 180

Concertgebouw

020 671 83 45 | www.concertgebouw.nl

Another venue worthy of its own applause, the Concertgebouw was opened in 1888. There are two auditoriums, with the large one seating more then 2,000 people. The Concertgebouw shows classical performances from artists around the world. It also features contemporary music, vocal concerts and concerts just for children.

ArenA Boulevard 590
Amsterdam Zuidoost
Map p.367 F4

Heineken Music Hall

0900 300 1250 | www.heineken-music-hall.nl

Located on the edge of the city, the Heineken Music Hall is easily accessible by metro but don't dilly dally too long after your concert or you may miss the last one and end up joining the scrum for cabs. It's a fairly soulless venue but very smoothly run and the sound system is excellent. You can see big names such as Kraftwerk, Chemical Brothers and Joss Stone. There are also theatre and dance shows like Riverdance, and festivals and raves.

Amstel 3
Centrum
Map p.394 A2 182

Het Muziektheater

020 625 54 55 | *www.hetmuziektheater.nl*

It's hard to miss Het Muziek Theater if you're travelling along the Amstel for an evening. It is a startling modern structure that looks chunky during the day but at night lights up beautifully. Het Muziek Theater is the home of the Netherlands Opera and National Ballet, and it also draws similar quality troupes from around the world.

Amstel 112-125
Centrum
Map p.394 A3 183

Konnilijk Theater Carre

0900 252 5255 | *www.theatercarre.nl*

It's worth going to a concert here just to see the building. It is amazing. The Carre first opened its doors in 1887 and after a rocky road it is still one of the most charismatic places to enjoy a performance in. It attracts a variety of performers including James Taylor, Jewel, The Buena Vista Social Club, Van Morrison and Lou Reed to name just a few.

Boom Chicago

Boom perform a special blend of improvisational comedy and social commentary – a ticket costs around €20 and they have been entertaining the Amsterdam expat community since 1993. There are nightly shows at their 300 seat Leidseplein Theater, where you can also enjoy a hearty meal along with the performance. The shows are based on improvisation and involve audience suggestions and audience participation. Group sales are possible or you can buy tickets individually. Classes in improvisation are also available. You can get drinks during the show including beer, wine and cocktails (020 423 01 01, www.boomchicago.nl).

Fashion Shows

One of the most innovative fashion shows in the world is held in Amsterdam. The international fashion week is a recent invention, and 2007 marked its third year in existence. This international show provides a stage for upcoming and established brands twice a year in January and July. For more information on this international fashion bonanza go to www.amsterdamfashionweek.com.

Theatre

Other options **Drama Groups** p.202

Finding quality English entertainment in Amsterdam can be difficult. Although you probably won't get to see an English production of Shakespeare, there are some opportunities to enjoy smaller contemporary productions if you keep an eye out for them. Of course language is not a barrier to enjoying a classical recital or opera and you won't be short of options to view either of those. Amsterdam does have a few great comedy productions. Boom Chicago presents a show every night in its own 300 seat theatre on Leidseplein (see above). There's also a great improvisation company in Amsterdam, Easylaughs (p.203), that does shows and provides workshops and courses. If you prefer a more serious amateur venture, then In Players (p.203) could be for you. It's Amsterdam's oldest English-speaking theatre company, and it stages productions and holds workshops. You can also check out Theater Works (p.203), a younger company that presents classics and contemporary retakes.

Leidseplein 26
Canal Belt
(Grachtengordel)
Map p.392 B3 184

Stadsschouwburg

020 624 23 11 | *www.ssba.nl*

The Stadsschouwburg is an Amsterdam institution that dominates Leidseplein. It is a stunning building that combines classic and contemporary, not only in its programme, but also in its presentation. In the basement you'll find Cafe Cox, a funky little bar/cafe worth a visit if you're waiting for the show to start. Stadschouwburg is the home of the Amsterdam Theatre group and often shows modern interpretations of classics. Unfortunately most of the performances are in Dutch. The space is also used by international theatre and ballet troupes as well as orchestras, so keep an eye on the agenda.

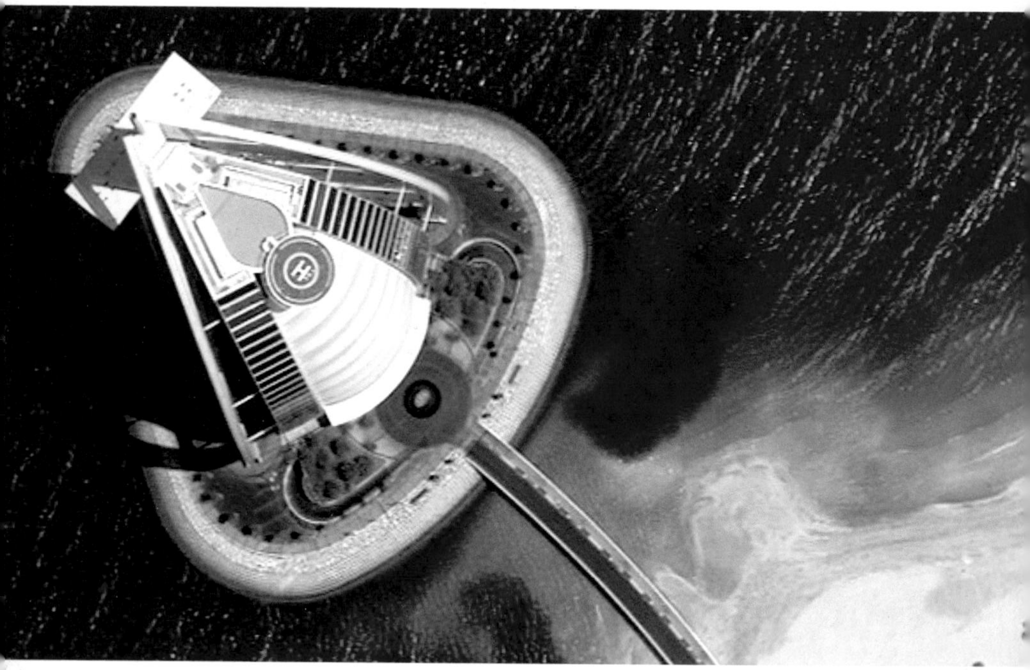

Maps

Maps

User's Guide

This section of the book has twelve detailed map spreads of Amsterdam - these include four of the city centre (p.388-395) and eight covering the greater city area (p.372-387). They are intended to help you get your bearings when you first arrive, and give you an idea of the location of all the places mentioned throughout the main chapters of the book. The Sheet Index & District Map on p.368-9 shows which part of the city each spread covers, and outlines the areas covered by the individual districts of Amsterdam. All are big, and in full detail; the city centre maps are drawn at a 1:15,000 scale (1cm = 150m) and the maps of the rest of Amsterdam are 1:7,500 (1cm = 75m). Many of the places mentioned in the guide have map references, like this: Map p.000 A1 XXX. The page number (p.000) refers to the page that the map is on, the grid reference (A1) reads horizontally then vertically, and the annotation XXX shows exactly where the place is. Annotations in different colours show items from different chapters. Green numbers are from General Information, red numbers are restaurants, bars, cafes and nightclubs from Going Out chapter, blue are from Exploring, and so on. See the map margins for a full key. You'll also find a country map of the Netherlands on p.365, and a map of the area around Amsterdam on p.366.

More Maps

Beyond the maps in this section and the very nifty Amsterdam Mini Map *(see right for details) there are a number of street directories and maps available in Amsterdam's bookshops. One very useful guide is Falk's Amsterdam Stratengids (Street Guide), which lists all streets in the city.*

Need More?

This residents' guide is a pretty big book. It needs to be, to carry all the information you need about living in Amsterdam. But, unless you've got the pockets of a clown, it's unlikely to be carried around with you on day trips. With this in mind, Explorer Publishing also produce the *Amsterdam Mini Map* as a more manageable alternative. This packs the whole city into your pocket and, once unfolded, is an excellent navigational tool. It's part of a series of Mini Maps that includes cities as diverse as Dubai, London, New York and Singapore. For details of how to pick one up, visit www.explorerpublishing.com or nip into any good bookshop.

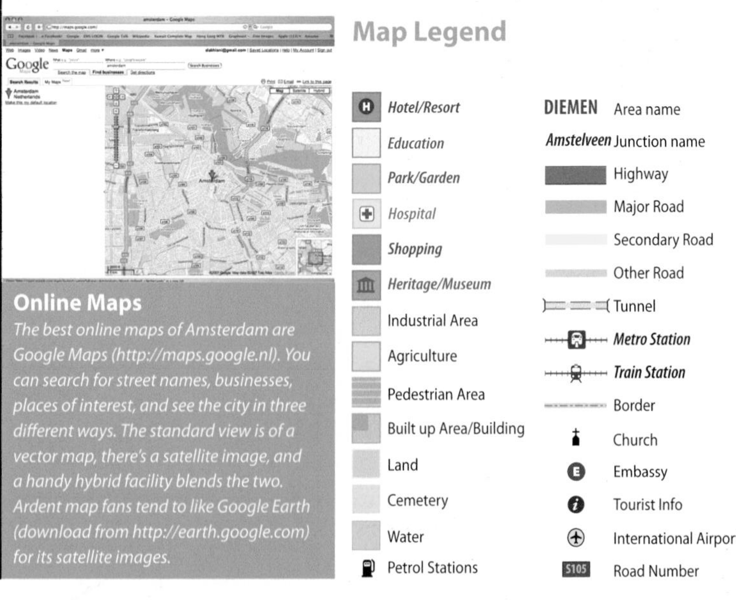

Online Maps

The best online maps of Amsterdam are Google Maps (http://maps.google.nl). You can search for street names, businesses, places of interest, and see the city in three different ways. The standard view is of a vector map, there's a satellite image, and a handy hybrid facility blends the two. Ardent map fans tend to like Google Earth (download from http://earth.google.com) for its satellite images.

Map Legend

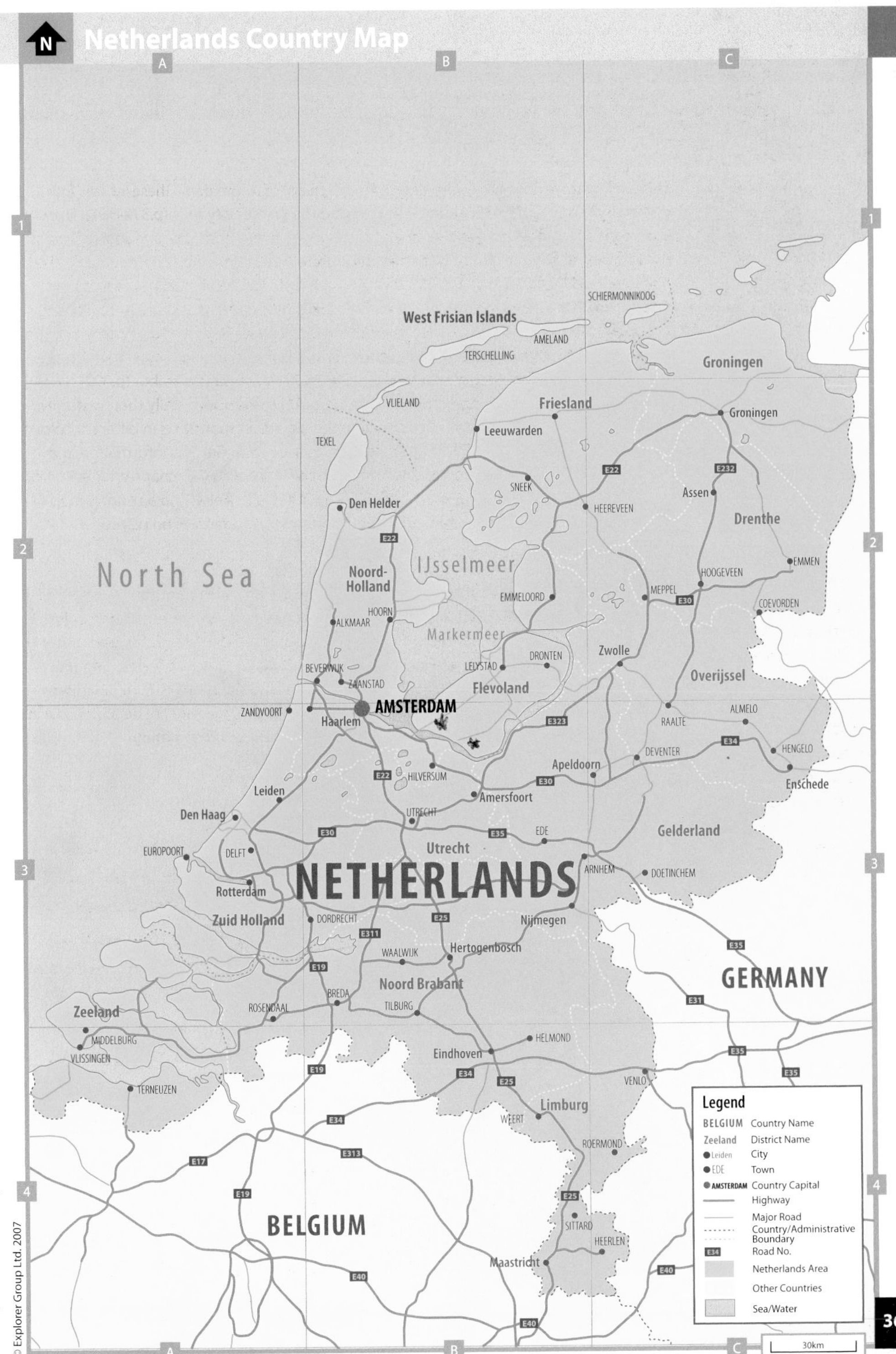
Netherlands Country Map
N
A
B
C
1
2
3
4
North Sea
West Frisian Islands
SCHIERMONNIKOOG
AMELAND
TERSCHELLING
VLIELAND
TEXEL
Groningen
Friesland
Leeuwarden
Groningen
E22
E232
SNEEK
HEERENVEEN
Assen
Drenthe
Den Helder
E22
Noord-
Holland
IJsselmeer
EMMELOORD
MEPPEL
HOOGEVEEN
EMMEN
E30
COEVORDEN
HOORN
ALKMAAR
Markermeer
DRONTEN
LELYSTAD
Zwolle
Overijssel
BEVERWIJK
ZAANSTAD
Flevoland
ZANDVOORT
AMSTERDAM
Haarlem
E323
RAALTE
ALMELO
E34
DEVENTER
HENGELO
Apeldoorn
Enschede
E22
HILVERSUM
E30
Leiden
Amersfoort
Den Haag
UTRECHT
E30
E35
EDE
Gelderland
EUROPOORT
DELFT
Utrecht
ARNHEM
DOETINCHEM
NETHERLANDS
Rotterdam
Zuid Holland
DORDRECHT
E25
Nijmegen
E311
WAALWIJK
Hertogenbosch
E35
E19
GERMANY
BREDA
Noord Brabant
Zeeland
ROSENDAAL
TILBURG
E31
MIDDELBURG
VLISSINGEN
HELMOND
Eindhoven
E35
E19
E34
E25
VENLO
E35
TERNEUZEN
Limburg
WEERT
E34
ROERMOND
E17
E313
E19
E25
BELGIUM
SITTARD
HEERLEN
Maastricht
E40
E40
E40
Legend
BELGIUM Country Name
Zeeland District Name
Leiden City
EDE Town
AMSTERDAM Country Capital
Highway
Major Road
Country/Administrative Boundary
E34 Road No.
Netherlands Area
Other Countries
Sea/Water
30km

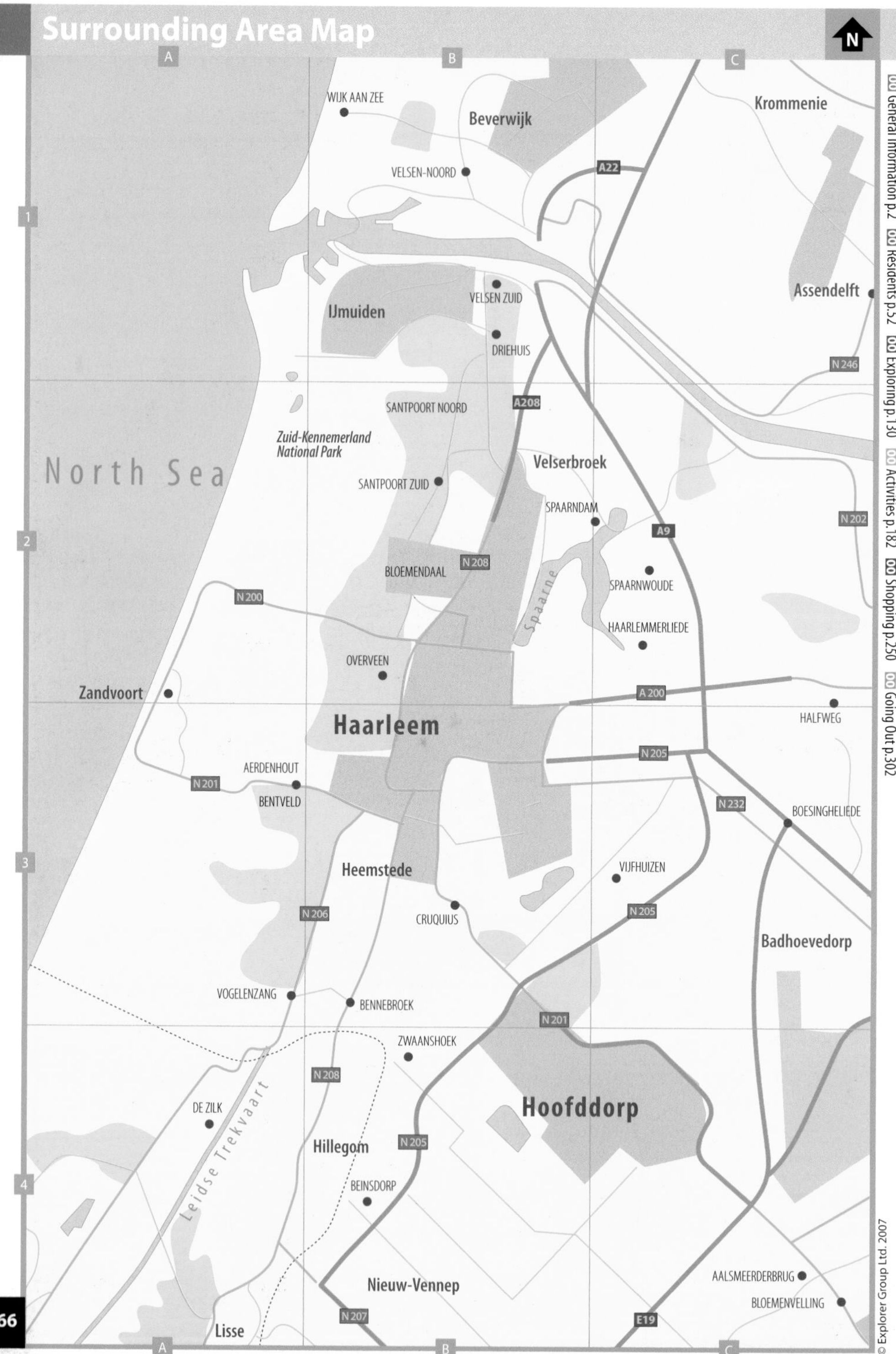

General Information p.2 Residents p.52 Exploring p.130 Activities p.182 Shopping p.250 Going Out p.302

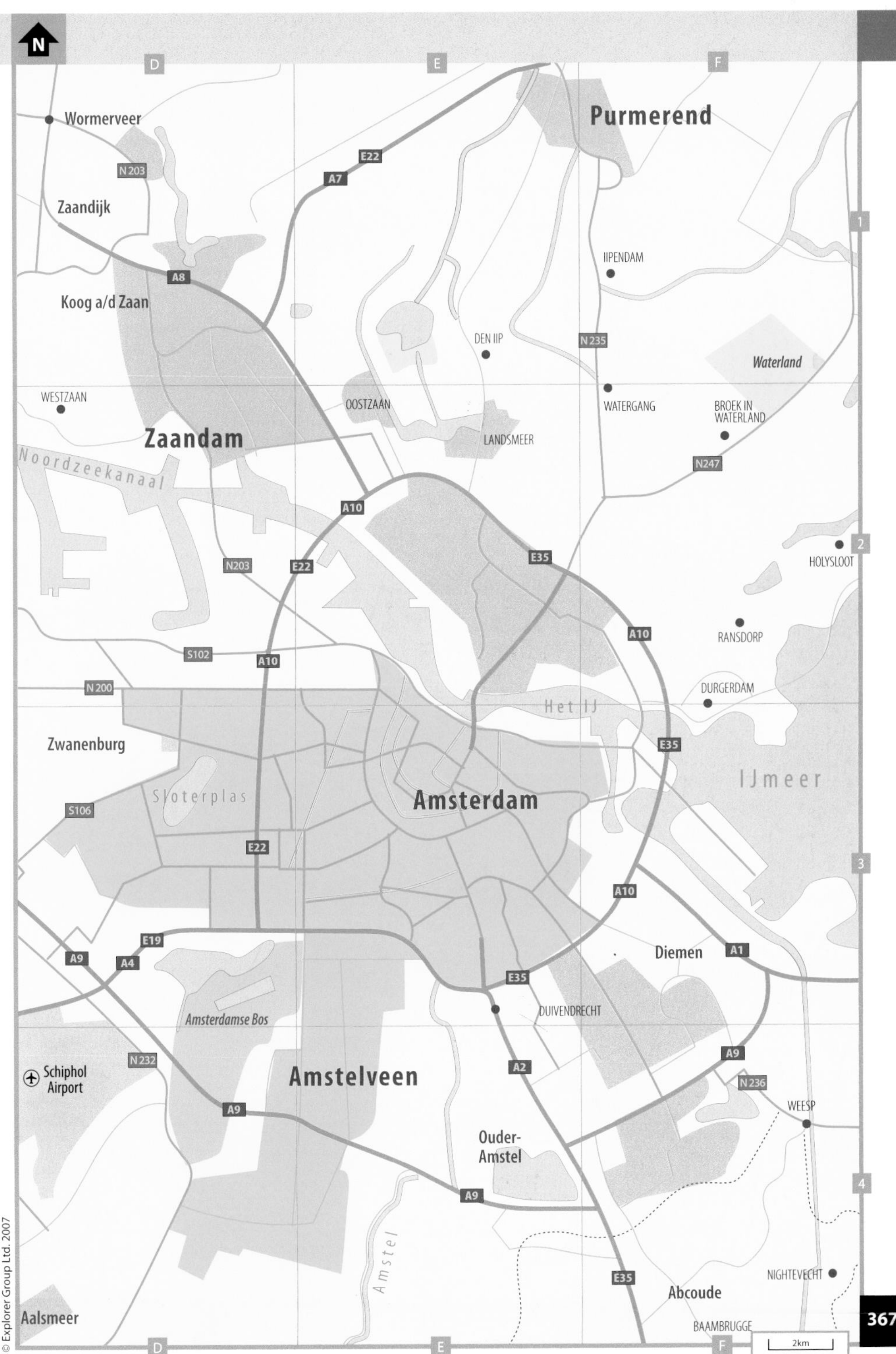
N
D
E
F
1
2
3
4
Wormerveer
N 203
Zaandijk
A8
Koog a/d Zaan
WESTZAAN
Zaandam
Noordzeekanaal
E22
A7
Purmerend
IIPENDAM
DEN IIP
N 235
Waterland
OOSTZAAN
WATERGANG
BROEK IN WATERLAND
LANDSMEER
N247
A10
E35
N203
E22
HOLYSLOOT
A10
RANSDORP
S102
A10
DURGERDAM
N 200
Het IJ
Zwanenburg
E35
IJmeer
Sloterplas
Amsterdam
S106
E22
A10
E19
A9
A4
Diemen
A1
E35
Amsterdamse Bos
DUIVENDRECHT
N 232
Schiphol Airport
A2
A9
Amstelveen
N 236
A9
WEESP
Ouder-Amstel
A9
Amstel
E35
NIGHTEVECHT
Abcoude
Aalsmeer
BAAMBRUGGE
2km

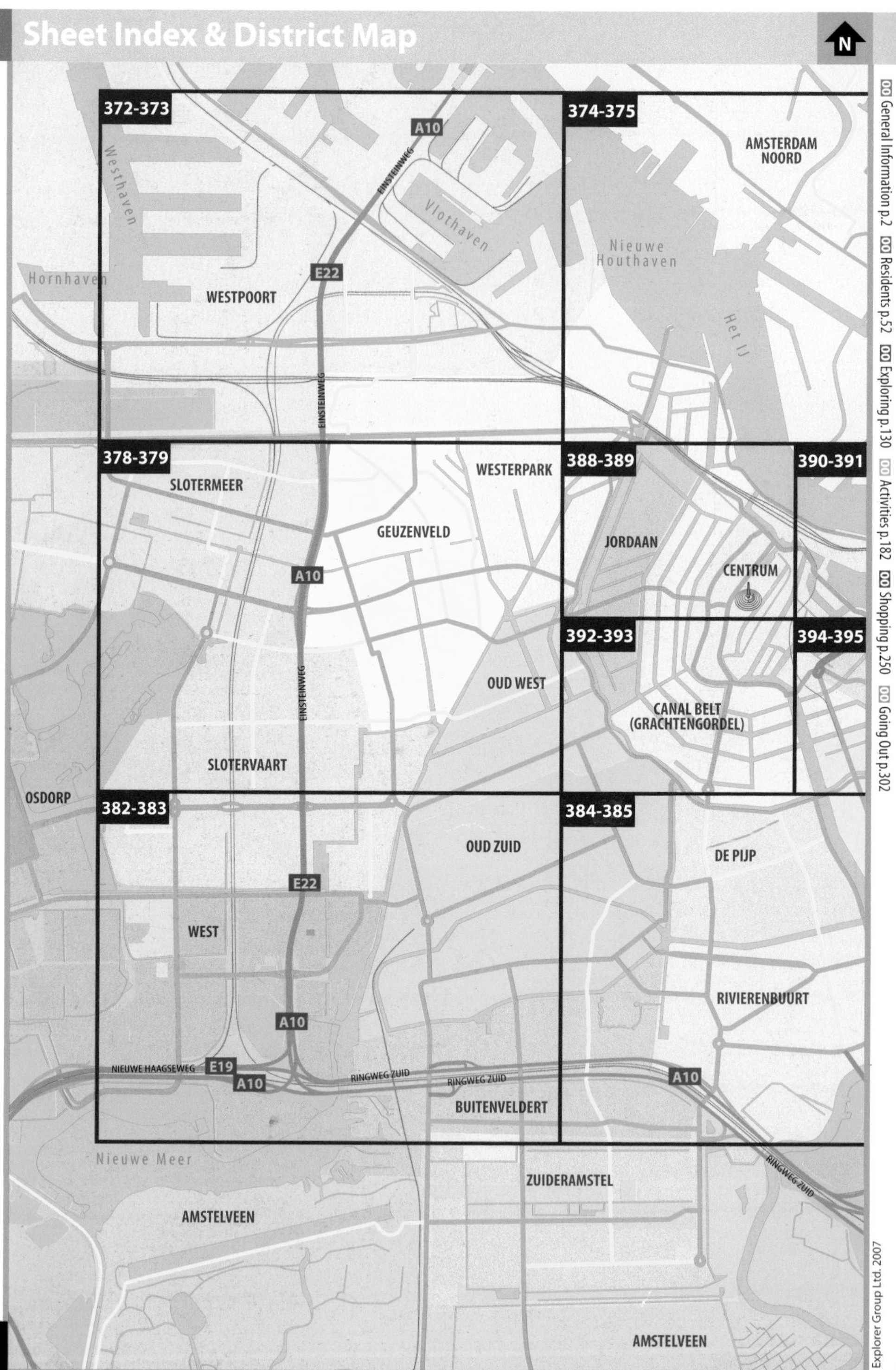

General Information p.2 Residents p.52 Exploring p.130 Activities p.182 Shopping p.250 Going Out p.302

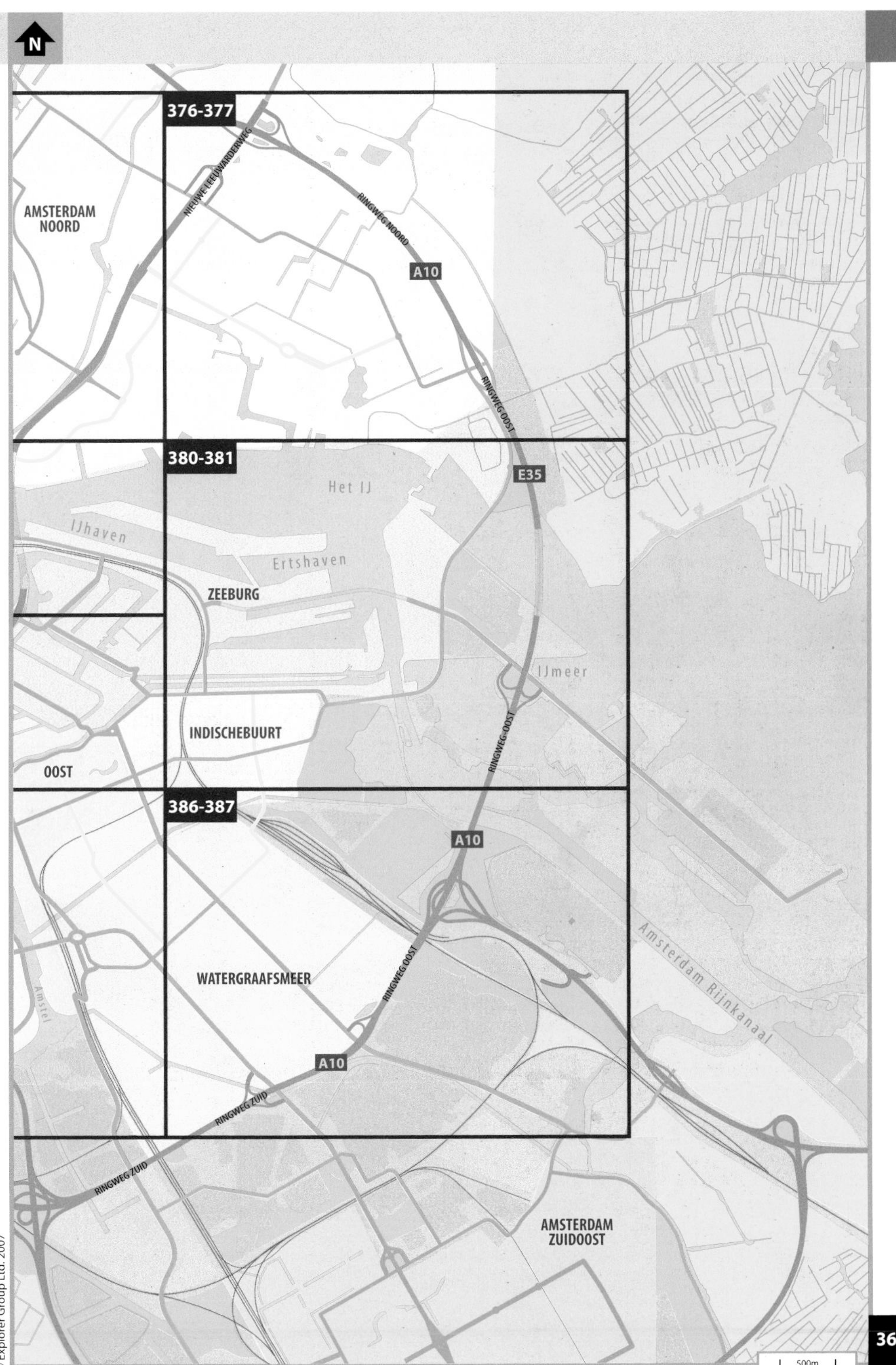
N
376-377
380-381
386-387
AMSTERDAM
NOORD
NIEUWE LEEUWARDERWEG
RINGWEG NOORD
A10
RINGWEG OOST
E35
Het IJ
IJhaven
Ertshaven
ZEEBURG
IJmeer
INDISCHEBUURT
OOST
RINGWEG-OOST
A10
Amsterdam Rijnkanaal
WATERGRAAFSMEER
Amstel
RINGWEG OOST
A10
RINGWEG ZUID
RINGWEG ZUID
AMSTERDAM
ZUIDOOST
500m

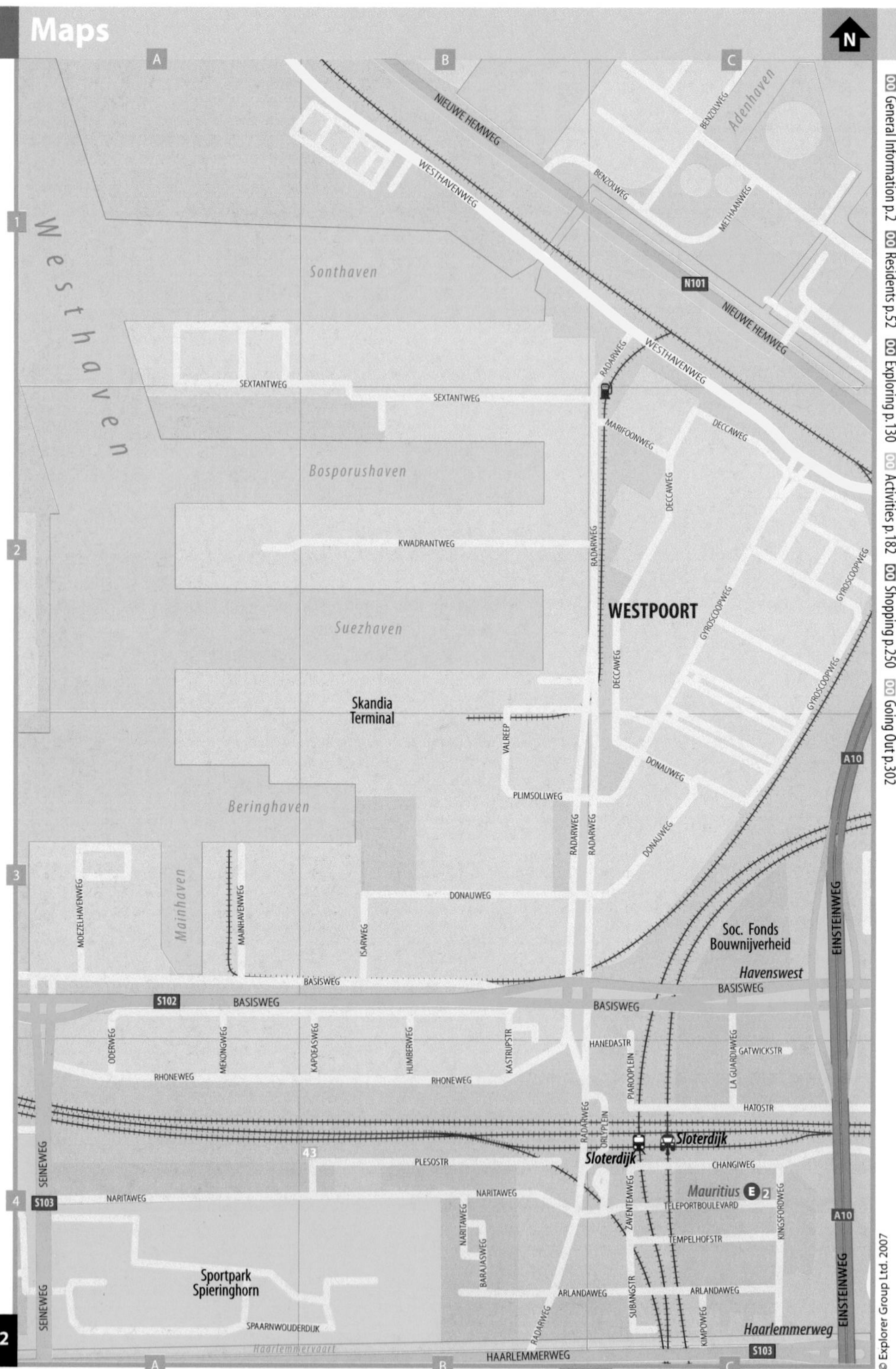

General Information p.2 Residents p.52 Exploring p.130 Activities p.182 Shopping p.250 Going Out p.302

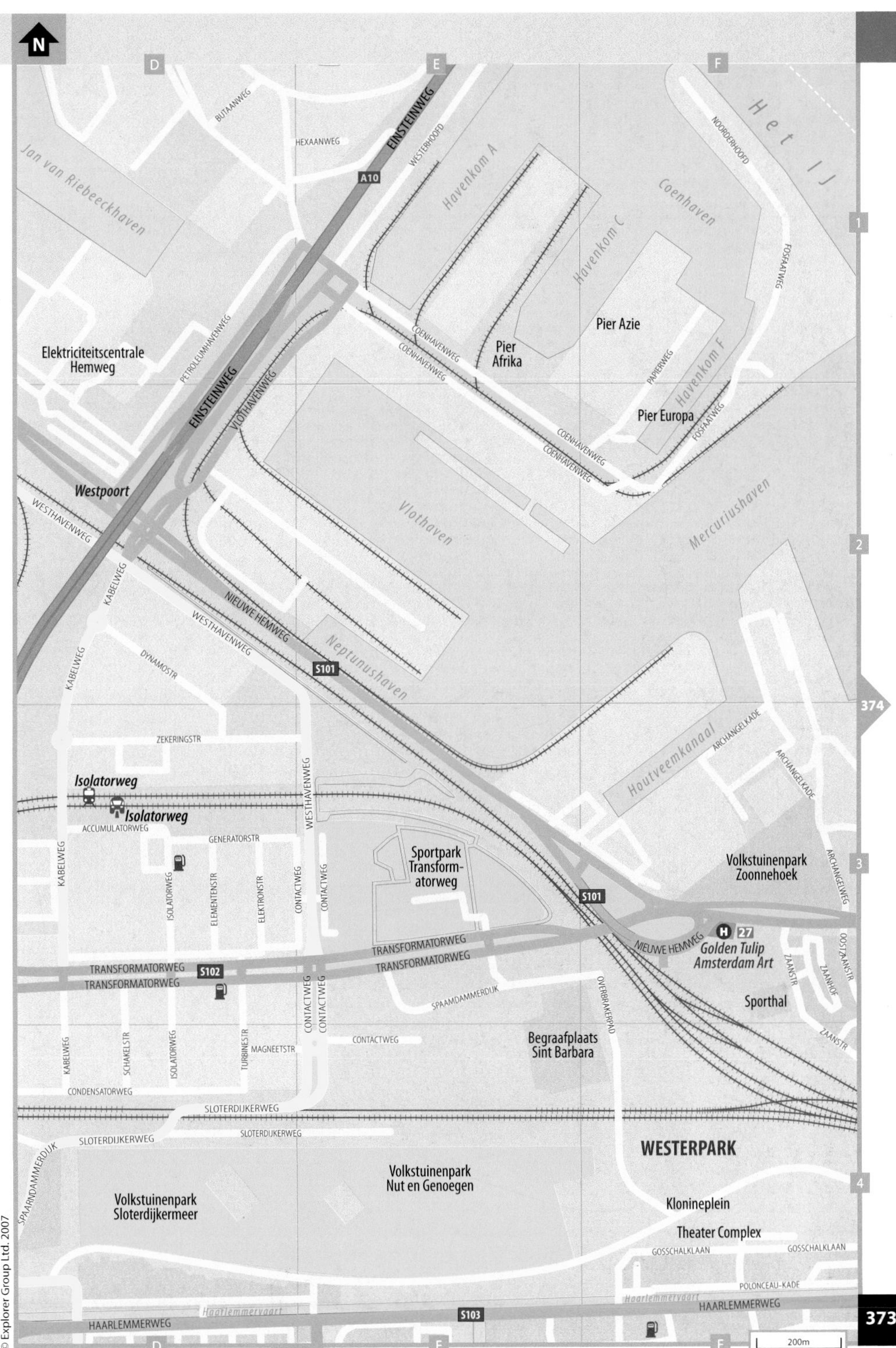
N
Het IJ
Jan van Riebeeckhaven
Havenkom A
Havenkom C
Coenhaven
Pier Azie
Pier Afrika
Havenkom F
Pier Europa
Elektriciteitscentrale Hemweg
Westpoort
Vlothaven
Mercuriushaven
Neptunushaven
Houtveemkanaal
Isolatorweg
Isolatorweg
Sportpark Transformatorweg
Volkstuinenpark Zoonnehoek
Golden Tulip Amsterdam Art
Sporthal
Begraafplaats Sint Barbara
WESTERPARK
Volkstuinenpark Sloterdijkermeer
Volkstuinenpark Nut en Genoegen
Klonineplein
Theater Complex
EINSTEINWEG
A10
S101
S102
S103
NIEUWE HEMWEG
WESTHAVENWEG
TRANSFORMATORWEG
SLOTERDIJKERWEG
HAARLEMMERWEG
Haarlemmervaart
200m

374
379

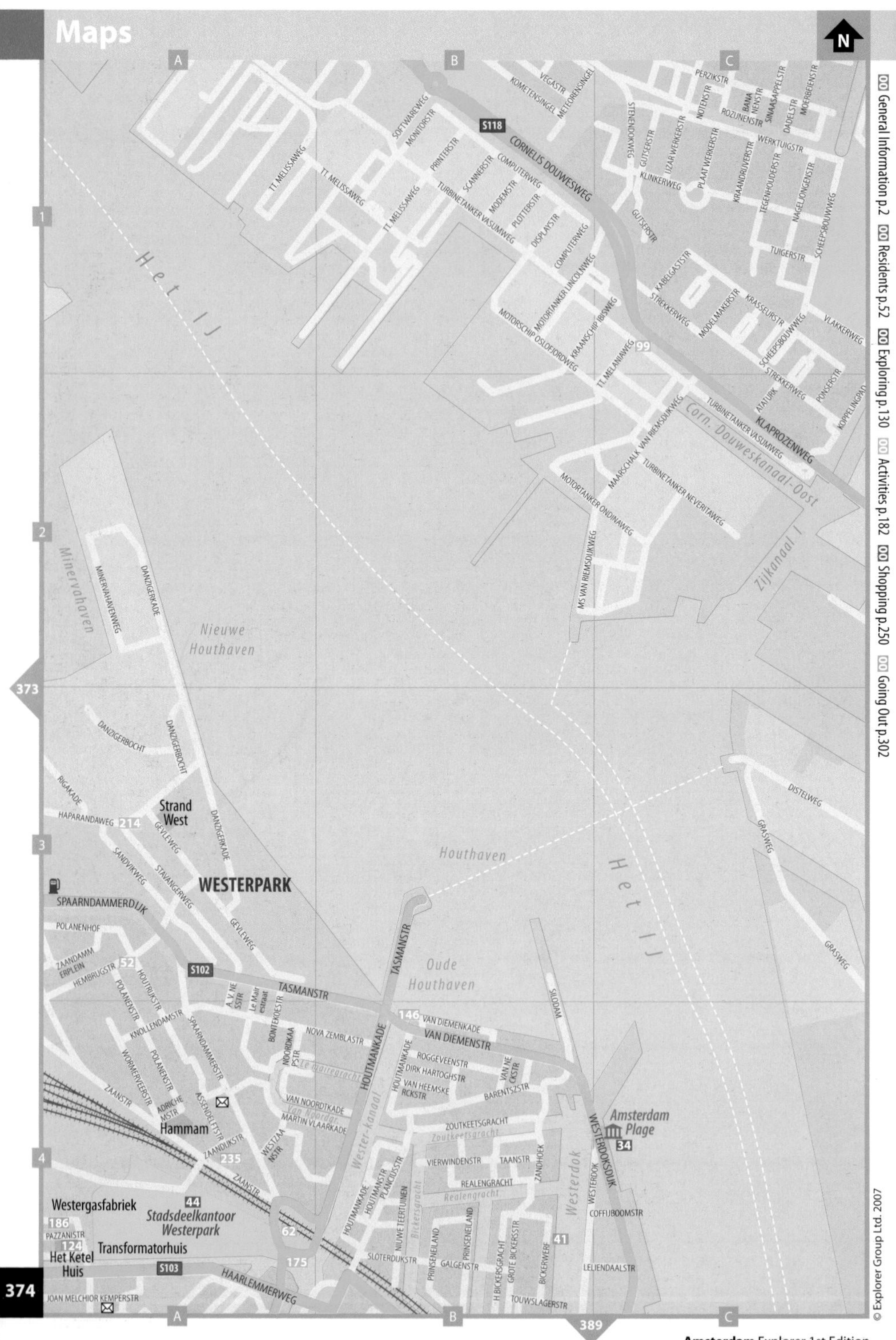

General Information p.2 Residents p.52 Exploring p.130 Activities p.182 Shopping p.250 Going Out p.302

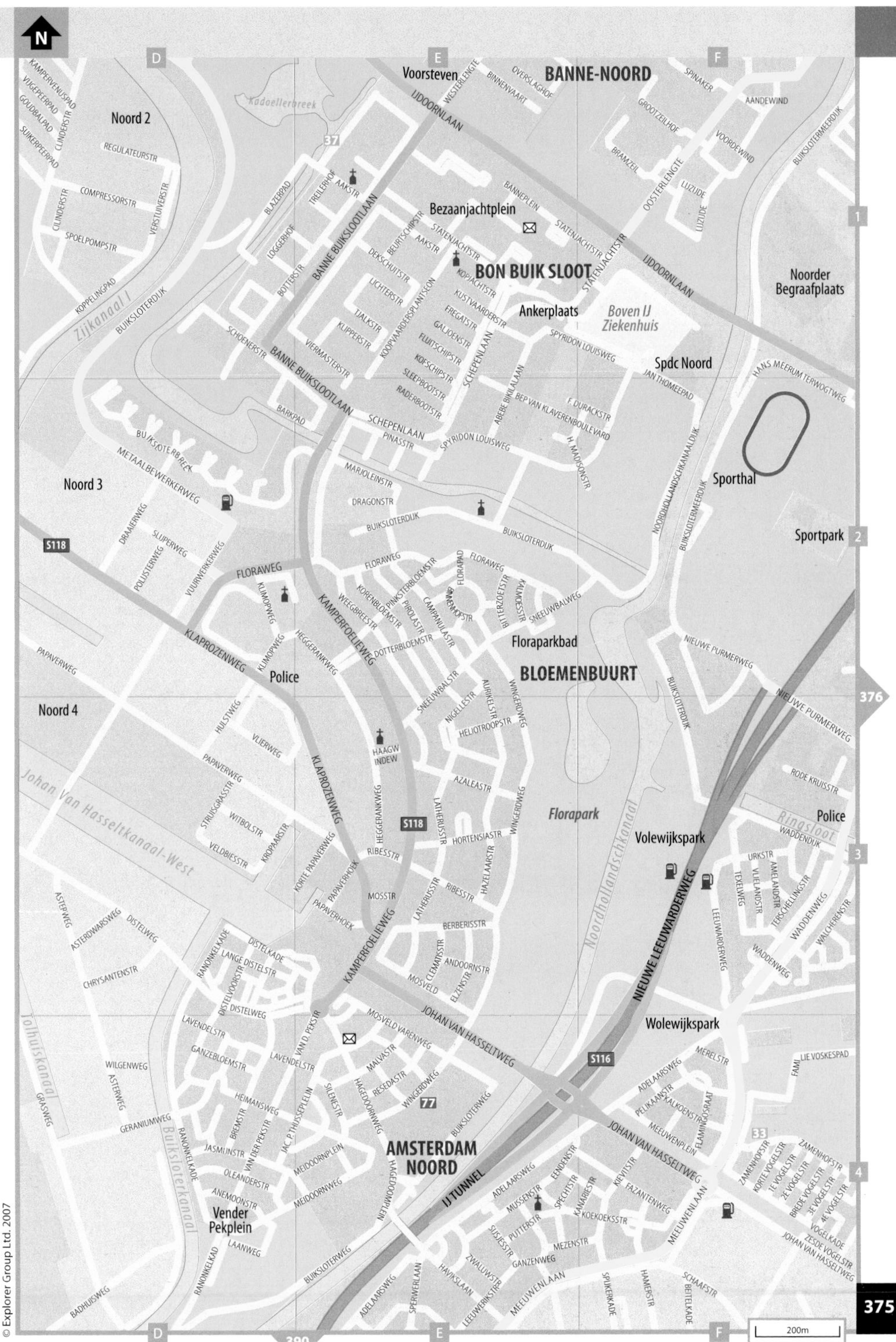
BANNE-NOORD
BON BUIK SLOOT
BLOEMENBUURT
AMSTERDAM NOORD
Noord 2
Noord 3
Noord 4
Voorsteven
Bezaanjachtplein
Ankerplaats
Boven IJ Ziekenhuis
Spdc Noord
Noorder Begraafplaats
Sporthal
Sportpark
Floraparkbad
Police
Florapark
Volewijkspark
Wolewijkspark
Vender Pekplein
IJ TUNNEL
NIEUWE LEEUWARDERWEG
JOHAN VAN HASSELTWEG
KLAPROZENWEG
KAMPERFOELIEWEG
BANNE BUIKSLOOTLAAN
IJDOORNLAAN
S118
S116
200m

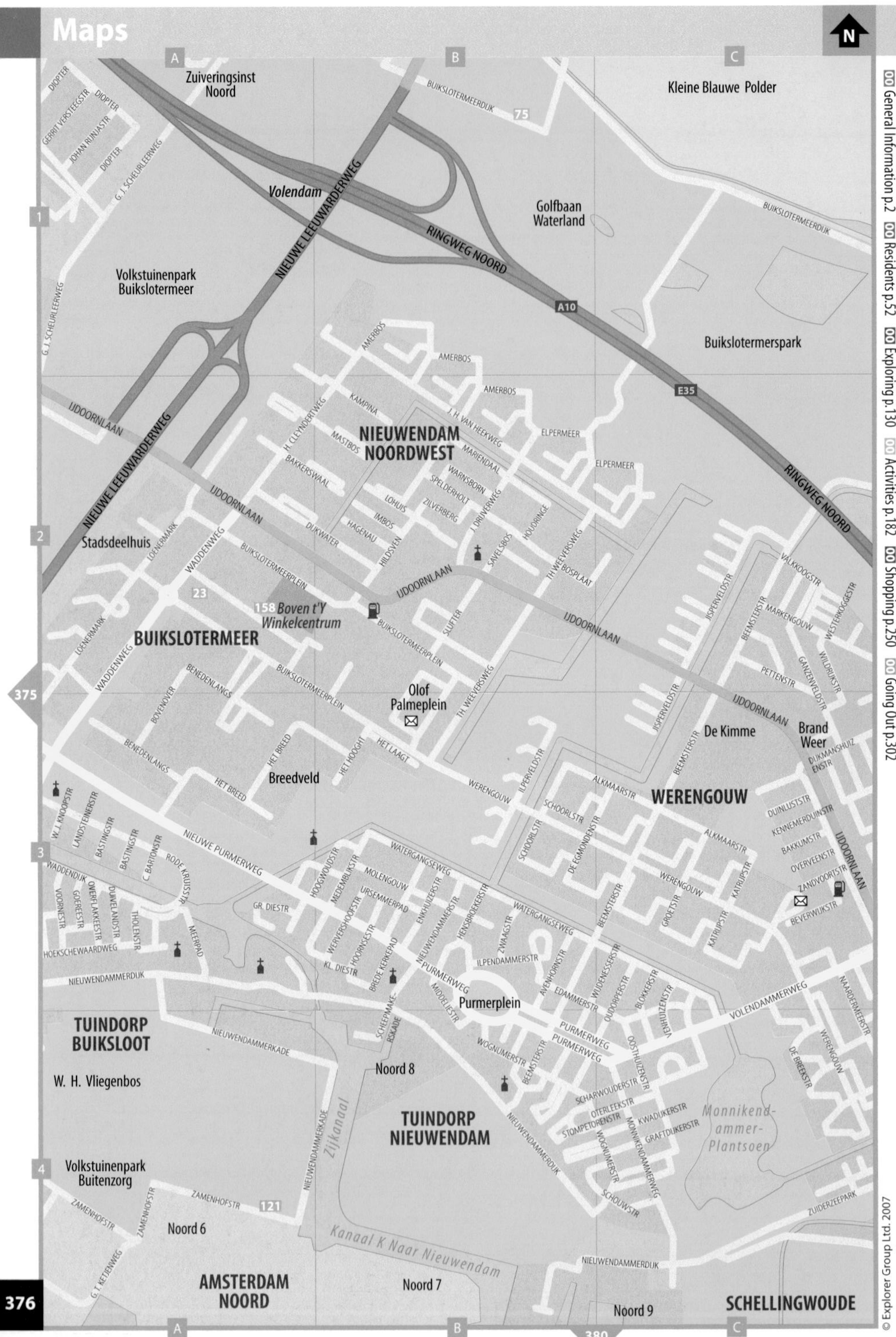

General Information p.2 Residents p.52 Exploring p.130 Activities p.182 Shopping p.250 Going Out p.302

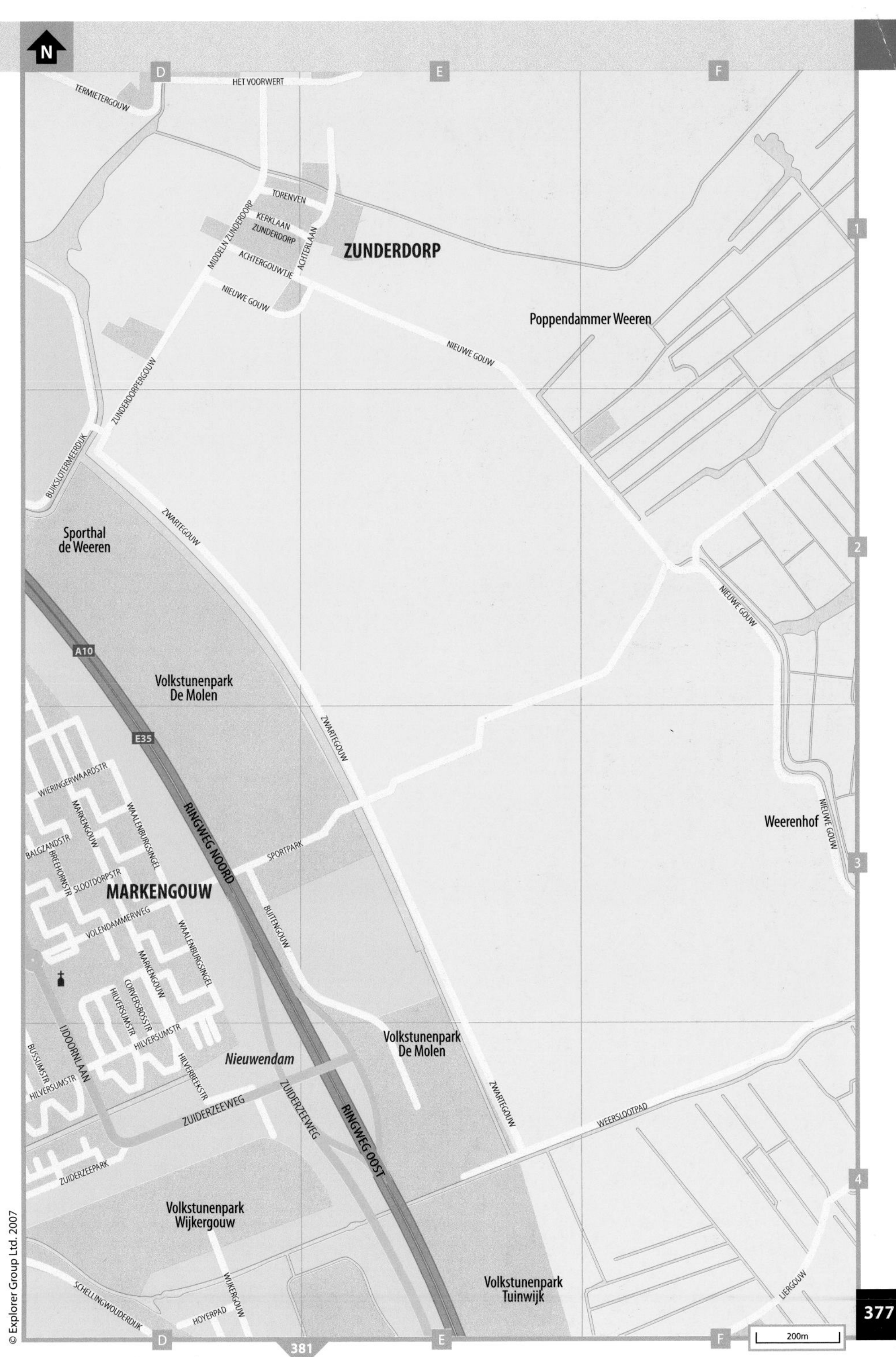
N
D
E
F
HET VOORWERT
TERMIETERGOUW
TORENVEN
KERKLAAN
ZUNDERDORP
MIDDELN ZUNDERDORP
ACHTERLAAN
ACHTERGOUWTJE
ZUNDERDORP
NIEUWE GOUW
Poppendammer Weeren
NIEUWE GOUW
ZUNDERDORPERGOUW
BUIKSLOTERMEERDIJK
1
Sporthal
de Weeren
ZWARTEGOUW
2
NIEUWE GOUW
A10
Volkstunenpark
De Molen
E35
ZWARTEGOUW
WIERINGERWAARDSTR
MARKENGOUW
WAALENBURGSINGEL
RINGWEG NOORD
Weerenhof
NIEUWE GOUW
BALGZANDSTR
BREEHORNSTR
SLOOTDORPSTR
SPORTPARK
3
MARKENGOUW
BUITENGOUW
VOLENDAMMERWEG
WAALENBURGSINGEL
MARKENGOUW
CORVERSBOSSTR
HILVERSUMSTR
HILVERSUMSTR
Volkstunenpark
De Molen
IJDOORNLAAN
BUSSUMSTR
Nieuwendam
HILVERBEEKSTR
HILVERSUMSTR
ZUIDERZEEWEG
ZUIDERZEEWEG
RINGWEG OOST
ZWARTEGOUW
WEERSLOOTPAD
ZUIDERZEEPARK
4
Volkstunenpark
Wijkergouw
SCHELLINGWOUDERDIJK
HOYERPAD
WIJKERGOUW
Volkstunenpark
Tuinwijk
LIERGOUW
200m
381

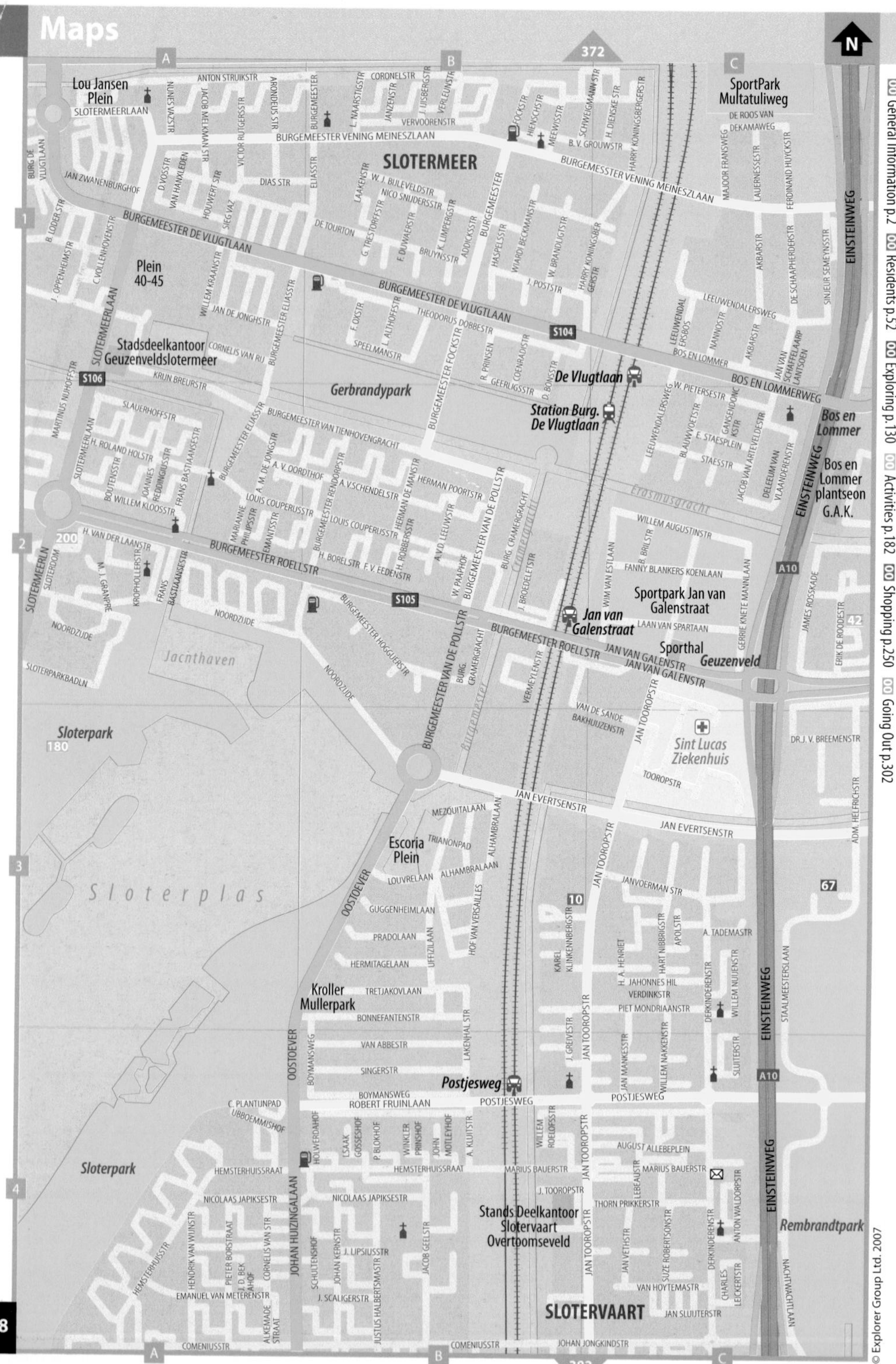

General Information p.2 · Residents p.52 · Exploring p.130 · Activities p.182 · Shopping p.250 · Going Out p.302

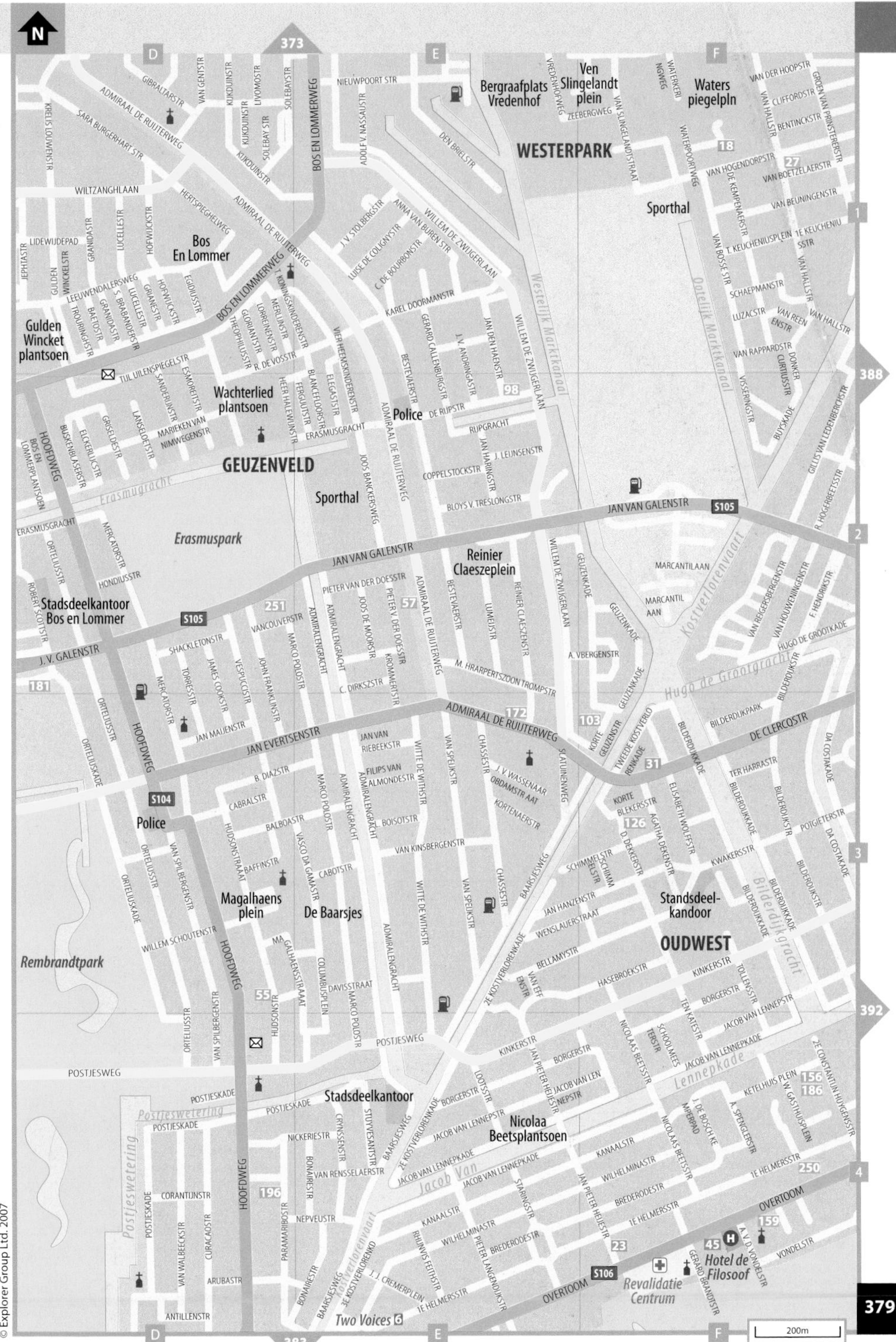
N
373
383
388
392
D
E
F
1
2
3
4
Ven Slingelandt plein
Bergraafplats Vredenhof
Waters piegelpln
WESTERPARK
Sporthal
Bos En Lommer
Gulden Wincket plantsoen
Wachterlied plantsoen
Police
GEUZENVELD
Erasmuspark
Reinier Claeszeplein
Stadsdeelkantoor Bos en Lommer
Magalhaens plein
De Baarsjes
Rembrandtpark
Standsdeel-kandoor
OUDWEST
Stadsdeelkantoor
Nicolaa Beetsplantsoen
Revalidatie Centrum
Hotel de Filosoof
Two Voices
Westelijk Marktkanaal
Oostelijk Marktkanaal
Kostverlorenvaart
Hugo de Grootgracht
Bilderdijkgracht
Lennepkade
Jacob Van
Postjeswetering
Erasmusgracht
BOS EN LOMMERWEG
ADMIRAAL DE RUIJTERWEG
JAN VAN GALENSTR
J. V. GALENSTR
JAN EVERTSENSTR
HOOFDWEG
POSTJESWEG
DE CLERCQSTR
KINKERSTR
OVERTOOM
WILLEM DE ZWIJGERLAAN
BAARSJESWEG
NIEUWPOORT STR
WILTZANGHLAAN
S105
S104
S106
200m

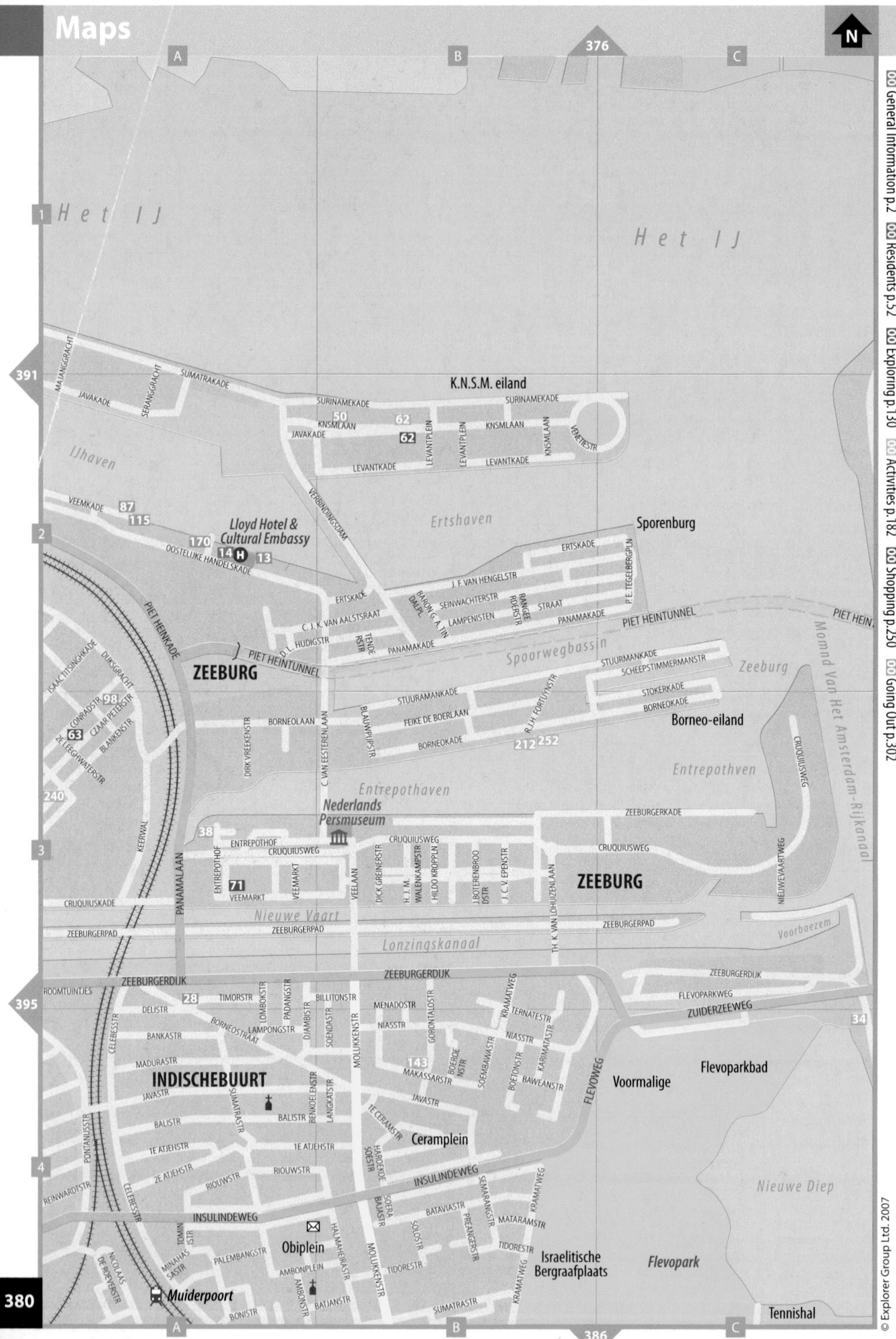

General Information p.2 Residents p.52 Exploring p.130 Activities p.182 Shopping p.250 Going Out p.302

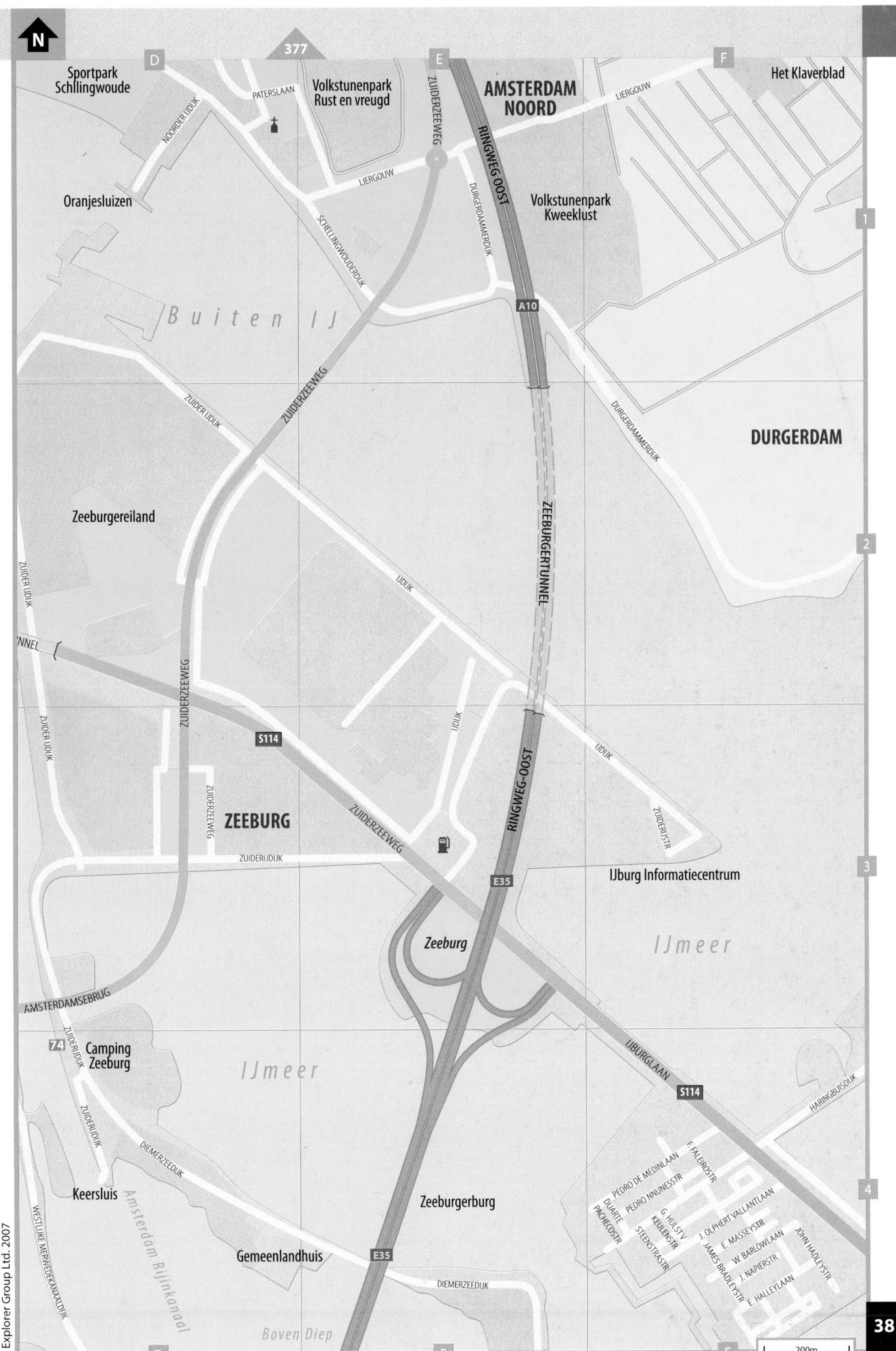

N
377
D
E
F
Sportpark Schllingwoude
Volkstunenpark Rust en vreugd
AMSTERDAM NOORD
Het Klaverblad
PATERSLAAN
NOORDER IJDIJK
ZUIDERZEEWEG
LIERGOUW
RINGWEG OOST
Oranjesluizen
DURGERDAMMERDIJK
Volkstunenpark Kweeklust
SCHELLINGWOUDERDIJK
A10
Buiten IJ
ZUIDERZEEWEG
ZUIDER IJDIJK
DURGERDAMMERDIJK
DURGERDAM
ZEEBURGERTUNNEL
Zeeburgereiland
IJDIJK
ZUIDER IJDIJK
ZUIDER IJDIJK
ZUIDERZEEWEG
S114
IJDIJK
IJDIJK
RINGWEG-OOST
ZUIDERZEEWEG
ZEEBURG
ZUIDERZEEWEG
ZUIDERIJSTR
ZUIDERIJDIJK
E35
IJburg Informatiecentrum
Zeeburg
IJmeer
AMSTERDAMSEBRUG
74
ZUIDERIJDIJK
Camping Zeeburg
IJmeer
IJBURGLAAN
S114
HARINGBUISDIJK
ZUIDERIJDIJK
DIEMERZEEDIJK
F. FALEIROSTR
PEDRO DE MEDINLAAN
PEDRO NNUNESSTR
DUARTE PACHECOSTR
G. HULSTV
KEULENSTR
STEENSTRASTR
J. OLPHERT VALLANTLAAN
E. MASSEYSTR
W. BARLOWLAAN
JOHN HADLEYSTR
J. NAPIERSTR
JAMES BRADLEYSTR
E. HALLEYLAAN
Keersluis
Amsterdam Rijnkanaal
Zeeburgerburg
WESTLIJKE MERWEDEKANAALDIJK
Gemeenlandhuis
E35
DIEMERZEEDIJK
Boven Diep
200m
387
1
2
3
4

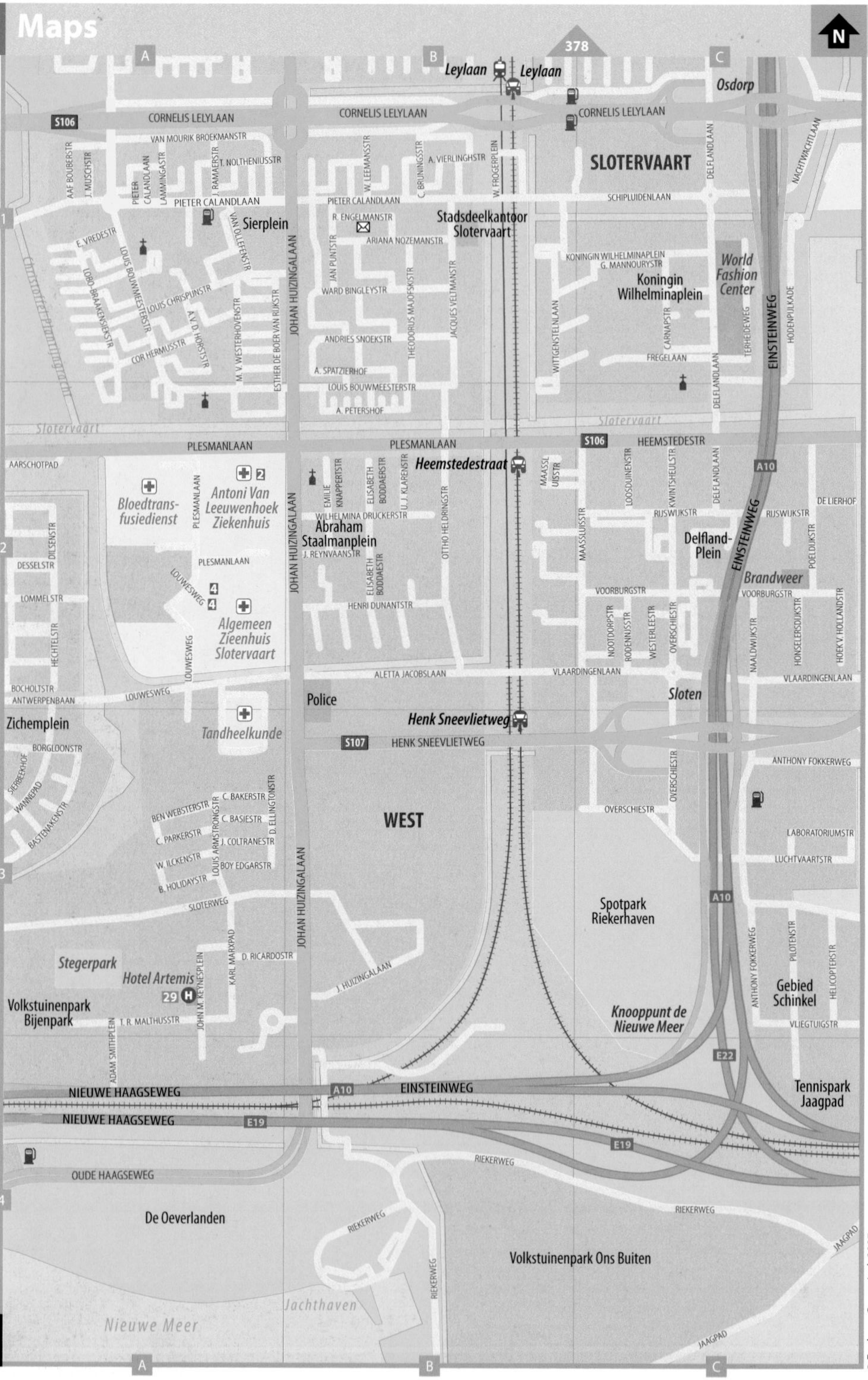

N

378

A B C

1 2 3 4

Leylaan
Leylaan
Osdorp
S106
CORNELIS LELYLAAN
CORNELIS LELYLAAN
CORNELIS LELYLAAN
VAN MOURIK BROEKMANSTR
T. NOLTHENIUSSTR
AAF BOUBERSTR
J. MUSCHSTR
PIETER CALANDLAAN
LAMMINGASTR
J. RAMAERSTR
W. LEEMANSSTR
A. VIERLINGHSTR
C. BRUININGSSTR
W. FROGERPLEIN
SLOTERVAART
DELFLANDLAAN
NACHTWACHTLAAN
PIETER CALANDLAAN
PIETER CALANDLAAN
SCHIPLUIDENLAAN
Sierplein
R. ENGELMANSTR
ARIANA NOZEMANSTR
Stadsdeelkantoor Slotervaart
E. VREDESTR
VAN OLLEFENSTR
LOUIS BOUWMEESTERSTR
LOBO BRAAKENSIEKSTR
LOUIS CHRISPIJNSTR
A.V.D. HORSTSTR
COR HERMUSSTR
M. V. WESTERHOVENSTR
ESTHER DE BOER VAN RIJKSTR
JOHAN HUIZINGALAAN
JAN PUNTSTR
WARD BINGLEYSTR
THEODORUS MAJOFSKISTR
JACQUES VELTMANSTR
ANDRIES SNOEKSTR
A. SPATZIERHOF
LOUIS BOUWMEESTERSTR
A. PETERSHOF
KONINGIN WILHELMINAPLEIN
G. MANNOURYSTR
Koningin Wilhelminaplein
World Fashion Center
WITGENSTEINLAAN
CARNAPSTR
FREGELAAN
TERHEIDEWEG
HODENPIJLKADE
EINSTEINWEG
Christoffel Plantijngracht
Slotervaart
Slotervaart
PLESMANLAAN
PLESMANLAAN
S106
HEEMSTEDESTR
A10
AARSCHOTPAD
Heemstedestraat
Bloedtransfusiedienst
PLESMANLAAN
Antoni Van Leeuwenhoek Ziekenhuis
2
EMILIE KNAPPERTSTR
ELISABETH BODDAERSTR
U. J. KLARENSTR
MAASSL UISSTR
LOOSDUINENSTR
KWINTSHEULSTR
DELFLANDLAAN
DE LIERHOF
WILHELMINA DRUCKERSTR
Abraham Staalmanplein
J. REYNVAANSTR
OTTHO HELDRINGSTR
MAASSLUISSTR
RIJSWIJKSTR
RIJSWIJKSTR
EINSTEINWEG
Delfland-Plein
DILSENSTR
DESSELSTR
PLESMANLAAN
LOUWESWEG
4
4
Algemeen Zieenhuis Slotervaart
ELISABETH BODDAESTR
POELDIJKSTR
Brandweer
VOORBURGSTR
VOORBURGSTR
LOMMELSTR
HENRI DUNANTSTR
HECHTELSTR
LOUWESWEG
NOOTDORPSTR
RODENRIJSSTR
WESTERLEESTR
OVERSCHIESTR
NAALDWIJKSTR
HONSELERSDIJKSTR
HOEK V. HOLLANDSTR
ALETTA JACOBSLAAN
VLAARDINGENLAAN
VLAARDINGENLAAN
BOCHOLTSTR
ANTWERPENBAAN
LOUWESWEG
Police
Sloten
Zichemplein
Henk Sneevlietweg
Tandheelkunde
S107
HENK SNEEVLIETWEG
BORGLOONSTR
ANTHONY FOKKERWEG
SIERBEEKHOF
WANNEPAD
BASTENAKENSTR
C. BAKERSTR
D. ELLINGTONSTR
BEN WEBSTERSTR
C. BASIESTR
C. PARKERSTR
J. COLTRANESTR
LOUIS ARMSTRONGSTR
W. ILCKENSTR
BOY EDGARSTR
B. HOLIDAYSTR
WEST
OVERSCHIESTR
OVERSCHIESTR
LABORATORIUMSTR
LUCHTVAARTSTR
SLOTERWEG
JOHAN HUIZINGALAAN
Spotpark Riekerhaven
A10
Stegerpark
KARL MARXPAD
D. RICARDOSTR
Hotel Artemis
29
J. HUIZINGALAAN
JOHN M. KEYNESPLEIN
ANTHONY FOKKERWEG
PILOTENSTR
HELICOPTERSTR
Gebied Schinkel
Volkstuinenpark Bijenpark
T. R. MALTHUSSTR
ADAM SMITHPLEIN
Knooppunt de Nieuwe Meer
VLIEGTUIGSTR
E22
NIEUWE HAAGSEWEG
A10
EINSTEINWEG
Tennispark Jaagpad
NIEUWE HAAGSEWEG
E19
E19
RIEKERWEG
OUDE HAAGSEWEG
De Oeverlanden
RIEKERWEG
RIEKERWEG
JAAGPAD
Volkstuinenpark Ons Buiten
RIEKERWEG
Jachthaven
Nieuwe Meer
JAAGPAD

General Information p.2 Residents p.52 Exploring p.130 Activities p.182 Shopping p.250 Going Out p.302

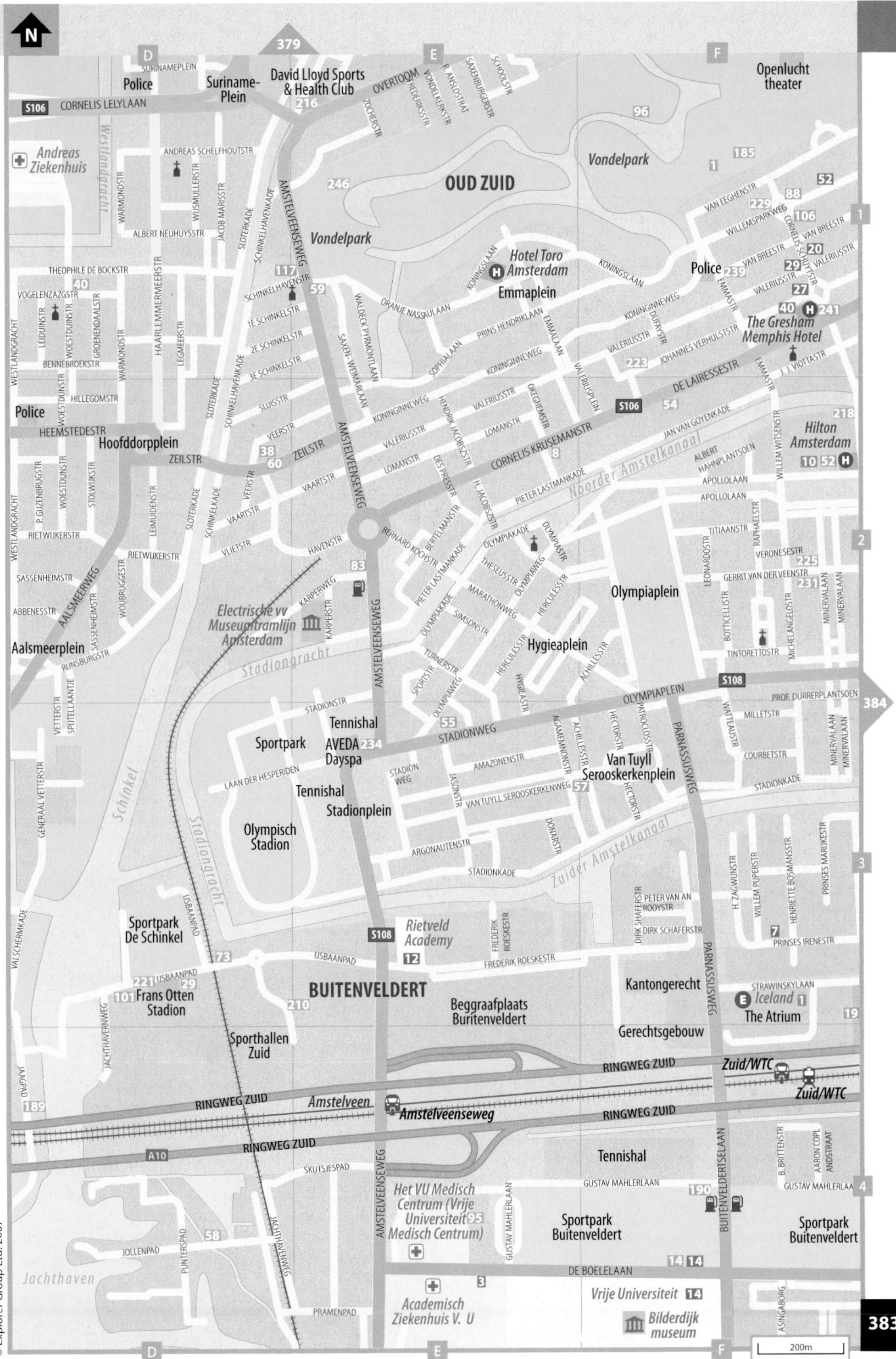
OUD ZUID
BUITENVELDERT
Vondelpark
Police
Suriname-Plein
David Lloyd Sports & Health Club
Openlucht theater
Andreas Ziekenhuis
Hotel Toro Amsterdam
Emmaplein
The Gresham Memphis Hotel
Hoofddorpplein
Hilton Amsterdam
Electrische vv Museumtramlijn Amsterdam
Aalsmeerplein
Olympiaplein
Hygieaplein
Tennishal
Sportpark
AVEDA Dayspa
Van Tuyll Serooskerkenplein
Stadionplein
Olympisch Stadion
Sportpark De Schinkel
Rietveld Academy
Frans Otten Stadion
Beggraafplaats Buritenveldert
Kantongerecht
Iceland
The Atrium
Gerechtsgebouw
Sporthallen Zuid
Zuid/WTC
Amstelveen
Amstelveenseweg
Het VU Medisch Centrum (Vrije Universiteit Medisch Centrum)
Sportpark Buitenveldert
Academisch Ziekenhuis V. U
Vrije Universiteit
Bilderdijk museum
Jachthaven
RINGWEG ZUID
AMSTELVEENSEWEG
PARNASSUSWEG
BUITENVELDERTSELAAN
DE BOELELAAN
GUSTAV MAHLERLAAN
STADIONWEG
OLYMPIAPLEIN
CORNELIS LELYLAAN
DE LAIRESSESTR
CORNELIS KRUSEMANSTR
Noorder Amstelkanaal
Zuider Amstelkanaal
Stadiongracht
Schinkel
200m
379
384
© Explorer Group Ltd. 2007

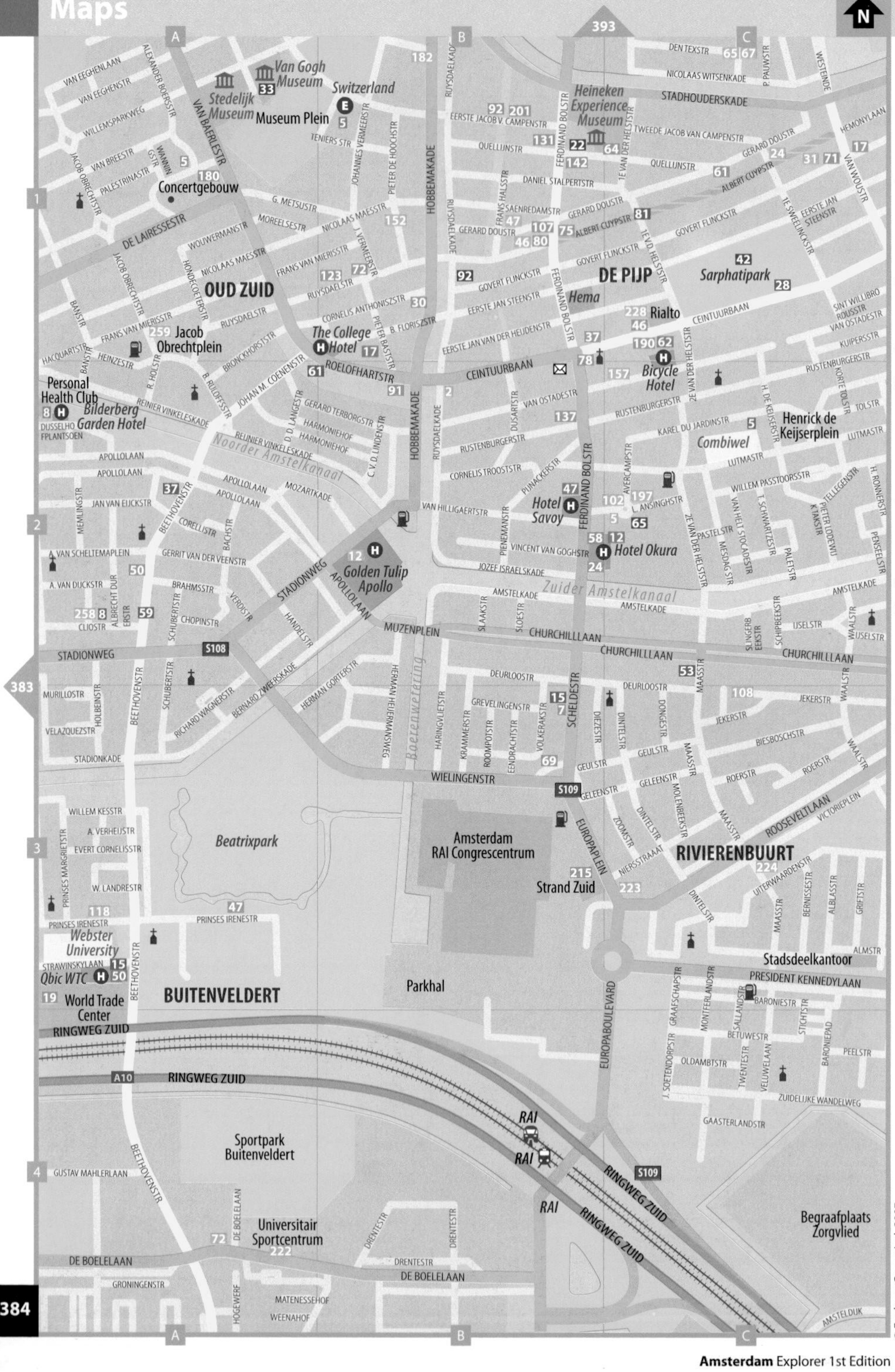

General Information p.2 Residents p.52 Exploring p.130 Activities p.182 Shopping p.250 Going Out p.302

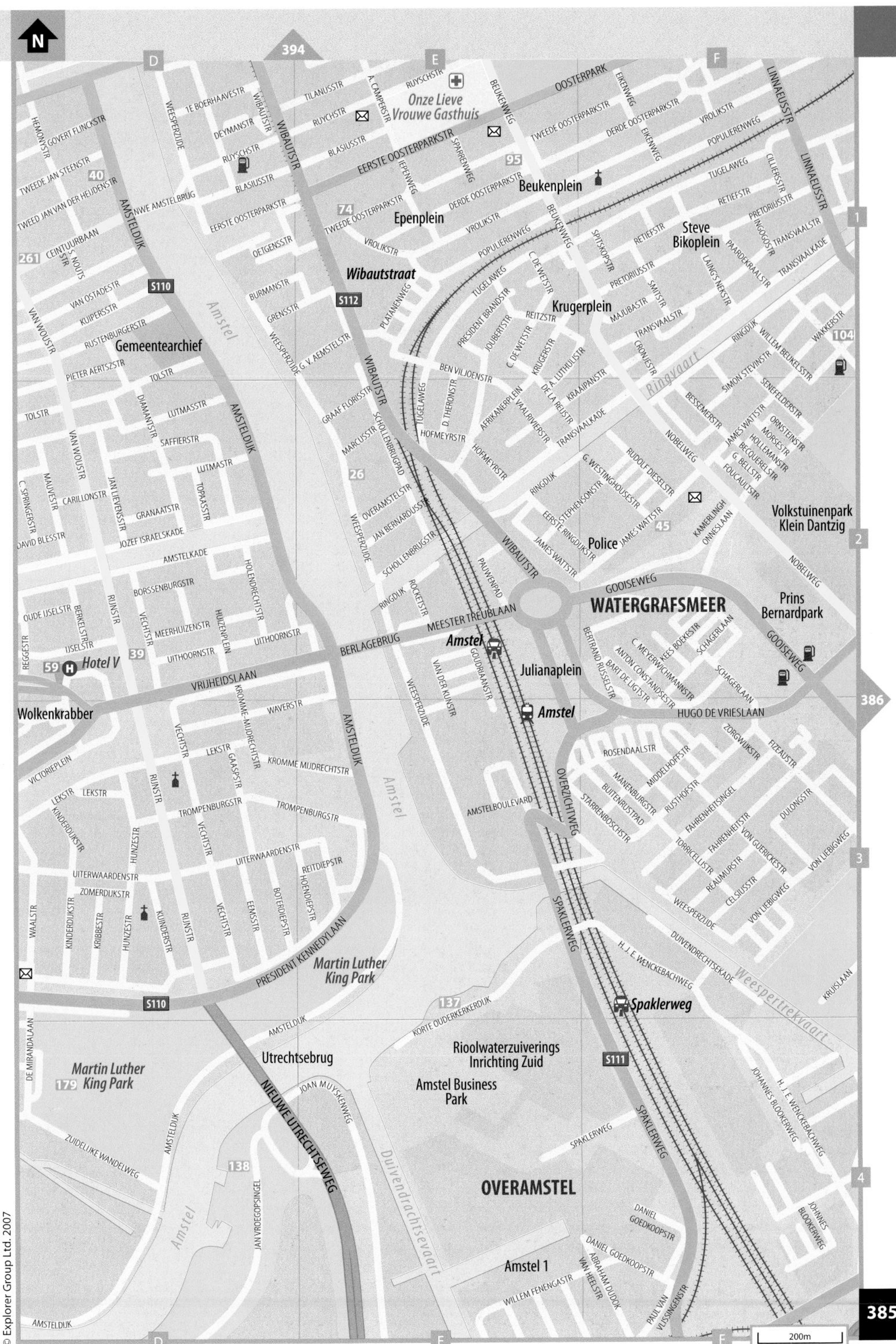

N
394
386
WATERGRAFSMEER
OVERAMSTEL
Onze Lieve Vrouwe Gasthuis
Beukenplein
Epenplein
Steve Bikoplein
Krugerplein
Wibautstraat
Gemeentearchief
Volkstuinenpark Klein Dantzig
Prins Bernardpark
Police
Julianaplein
Amstel
Hotel V
Wolkenkrabber
Martin Luther King Park
Utrechtsebrug
Rioolwaterzuiverings Inrichting Zuid
Amstel Business Park
Spaklerweg
Amstel 1
200m

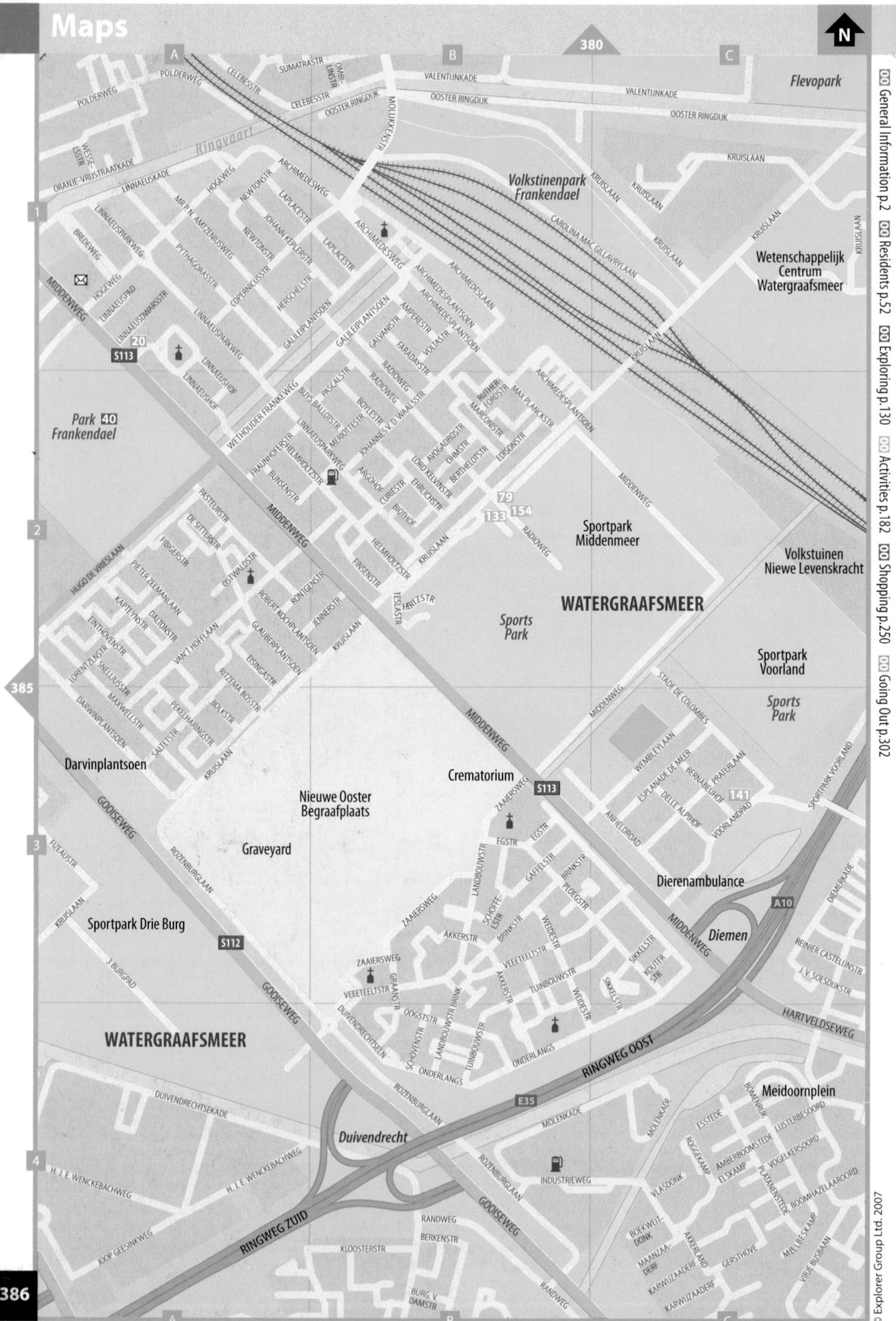

General Information p.2 · Residents p.52 · Exploring p.130 · Activities p.182 · Shopping p.250 · Going Out p.302

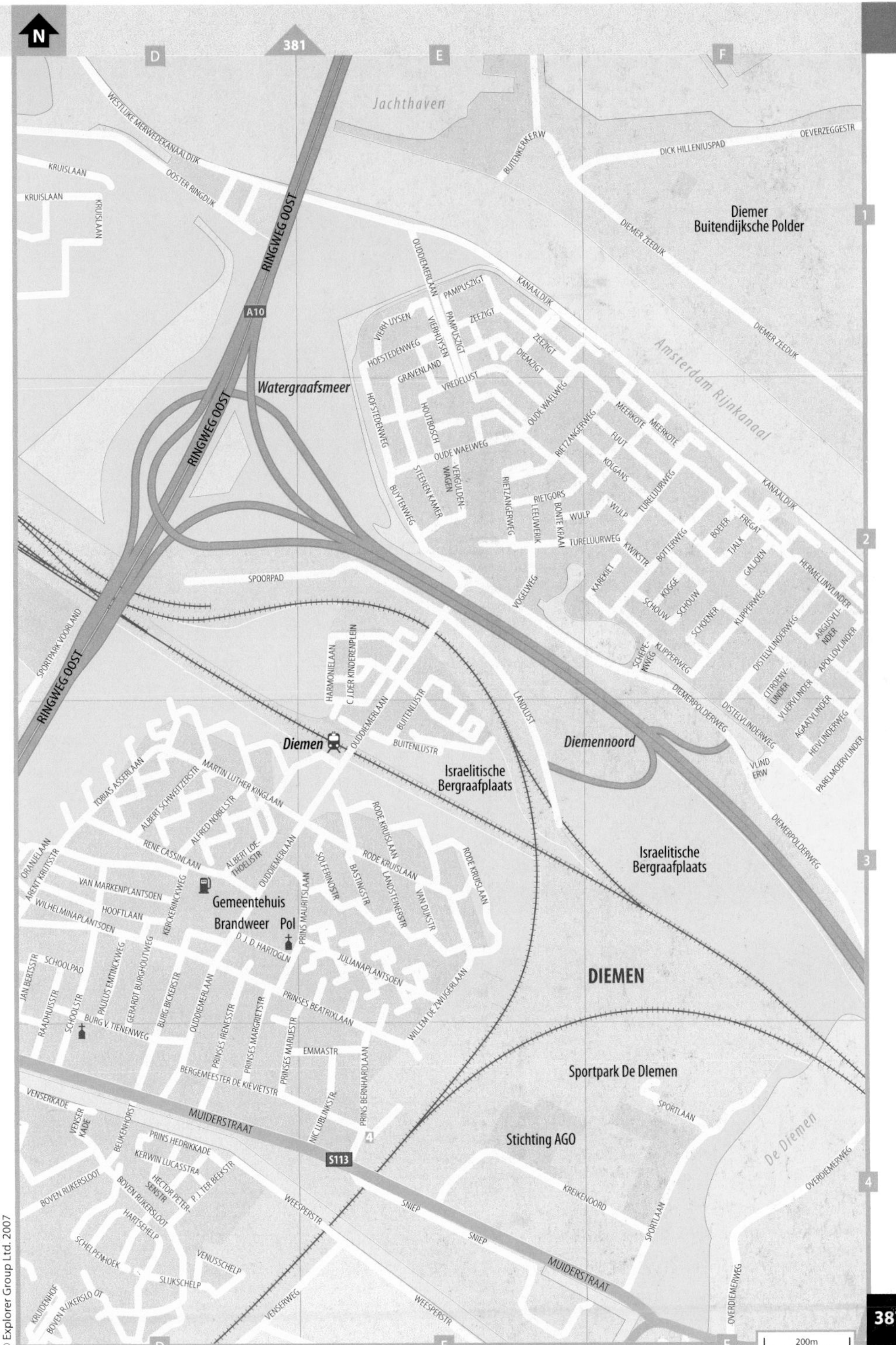
N
381
D
E
F
Jachthaven
Diemer Buitendijksche Polder
Watergraafsmeer
RINGWEG OOST
A10
Amsterdam Rijnkanaal
Diemen
Israelitische Bergraafplaats
Diemennoord
Israelitische Bergraafplaats
Gemeentehuis
Brandweer
Pol
DIEMEN
Sportpark De Dlemen
Stichting AGO
De Diemen
MUIDERSTRAAT
S113
200m
1
2
3
4

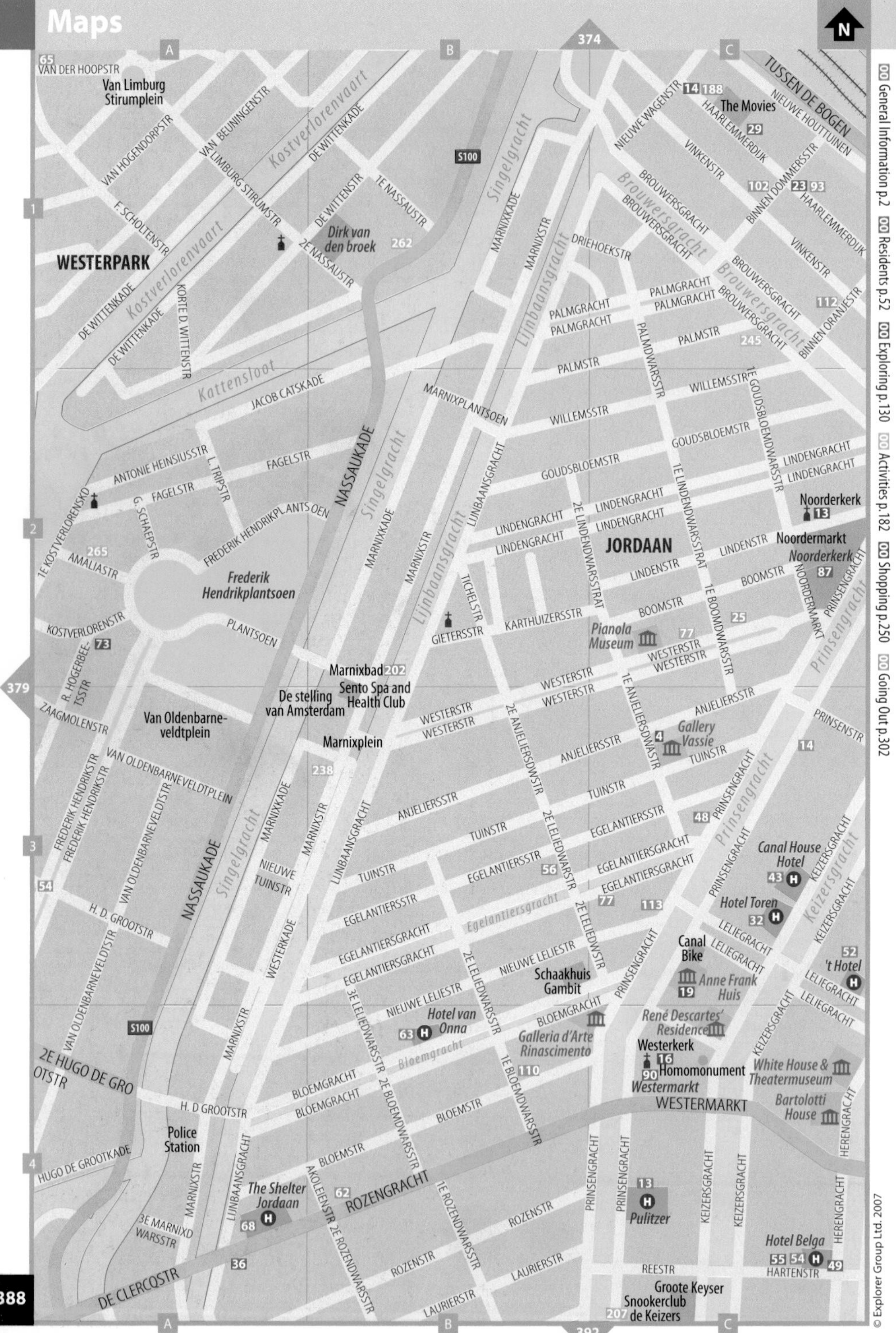

General Information p.2 Residents p.52 Exploring p.130 Activities p.182 Shopping p.250 Going Out p.302

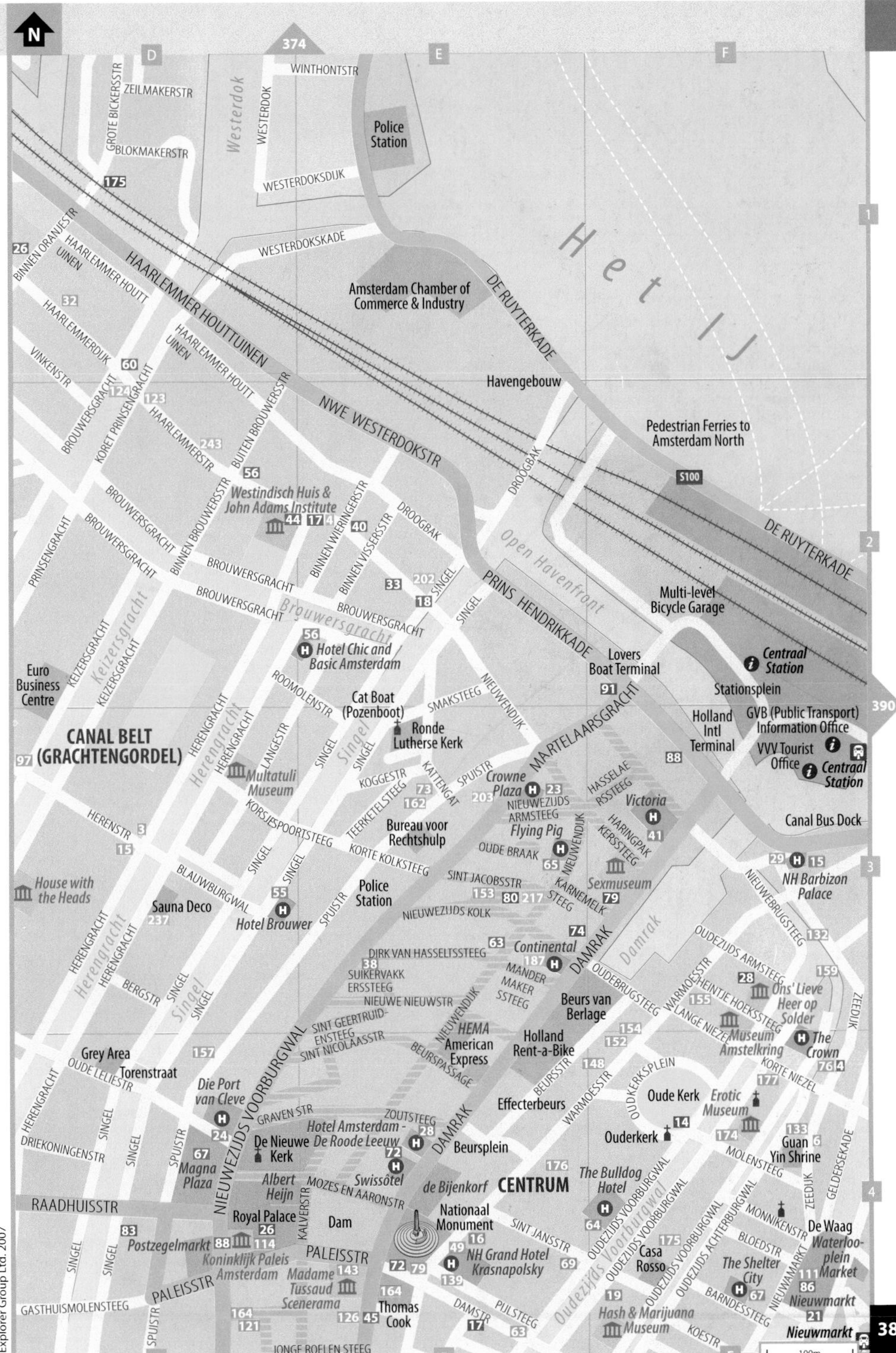
Het IJ
Police Station
Amsterdam Chamber of Commerce & Industry
Havengebouw
Pedestrian Ferries to Amsterdam North
Multi-level Bicycle Garage
Open Havenfront
Lovers Boat Terminal
Centraal Station
Stationsplein
Holland Intl Terminal
GVB (Public Transport) Information Office
VVV Tourist Office
Canal Bus Dock
Westindisch Huis & John Adams Institute
Hotel Chic and Basic Amsterdam
Cat Boat (Pozenboot)
Ronde Lutherse Kerk
Euro Business Centre
CANAL BELT (GRACHTENGORDEL)
Multatuli Museum
Bureau voor Rechtshulp
Crowne Plaza
Victoria
Flying Pig
Sexmuseum
NH Barbizon Palace
House with the Heads
Sauna Deco
Hotel Brouwer
Police Station
Continental
Beurs van Berlage
Holland Rent-a-Bike
HEMA
American Express
Ons' Lieve Heer op Solder
Museum Amstelkring
The Crown
Grey Area
Torenstraat
Die Port van Cleve
Effecterbeurs
Oude Kerk
Erotic Museum
Ouderkerk
Guan Yin Shrine
De Nieuwe Kerk
Hotel Amsterdam - De Roode Leeuw
Beursplein
Magna Plaza
Albert Heijn
Swissôtel
de Bijenkorf
CENTRUM
The Bulldog Hotel
Royal Palace
Dam
Nationaal Monument
De Waag
Waterlooplein Market
Postzegelmarkt
Koninklijk Paleis Amsterdam
Madame Tussaud Scenerama
NH Grand Hotel Krasnapolsky
Casa Rosso
The Shelter City
Nieuwmarkt
Thomas Cook
Hash & Marijuana Museum
100m
© Explorer Group Ltd. 2007

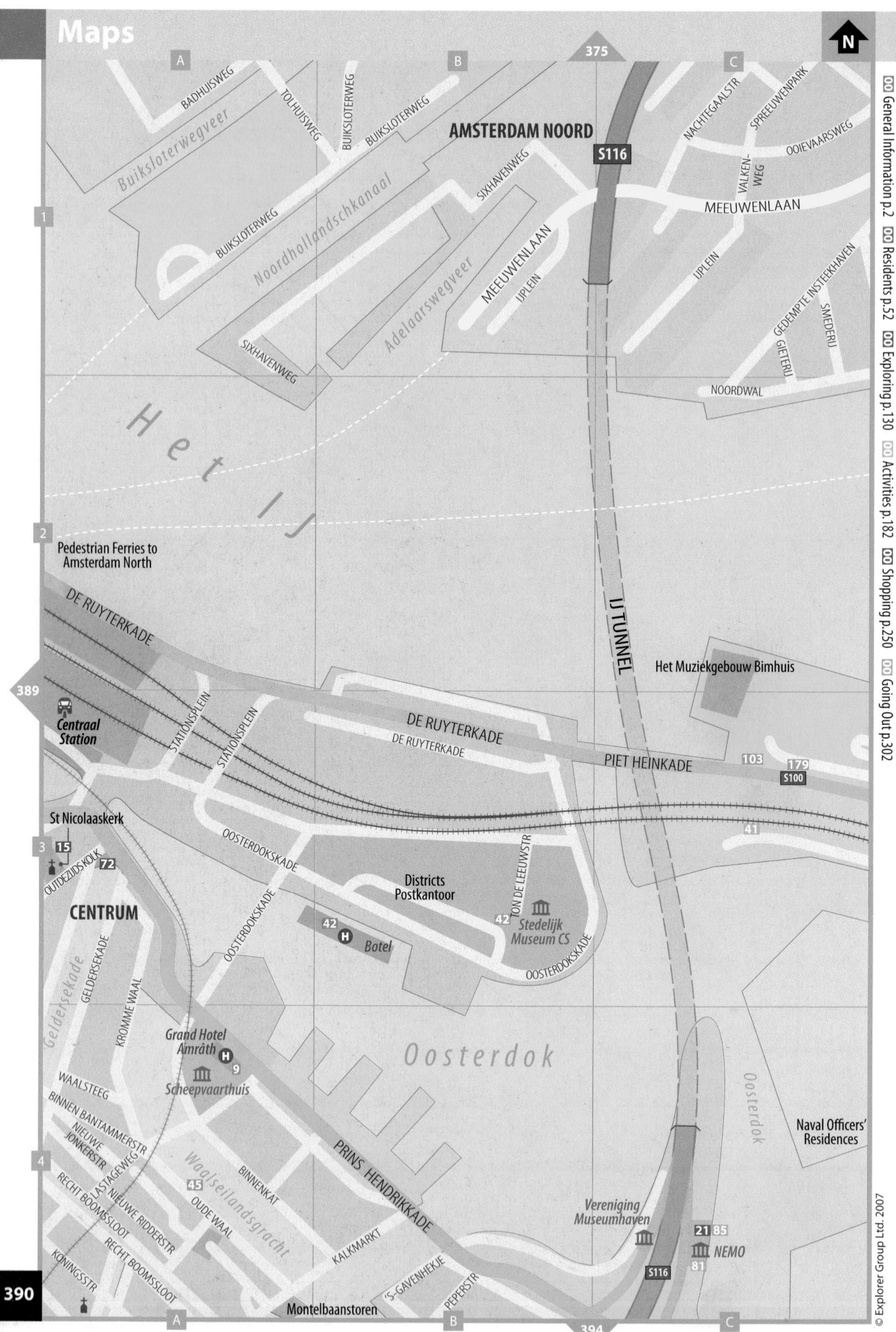

General Information p.2 Residents p.52 Exploring p.130 Activities p.182 Shopping p.250 Going Out p.302

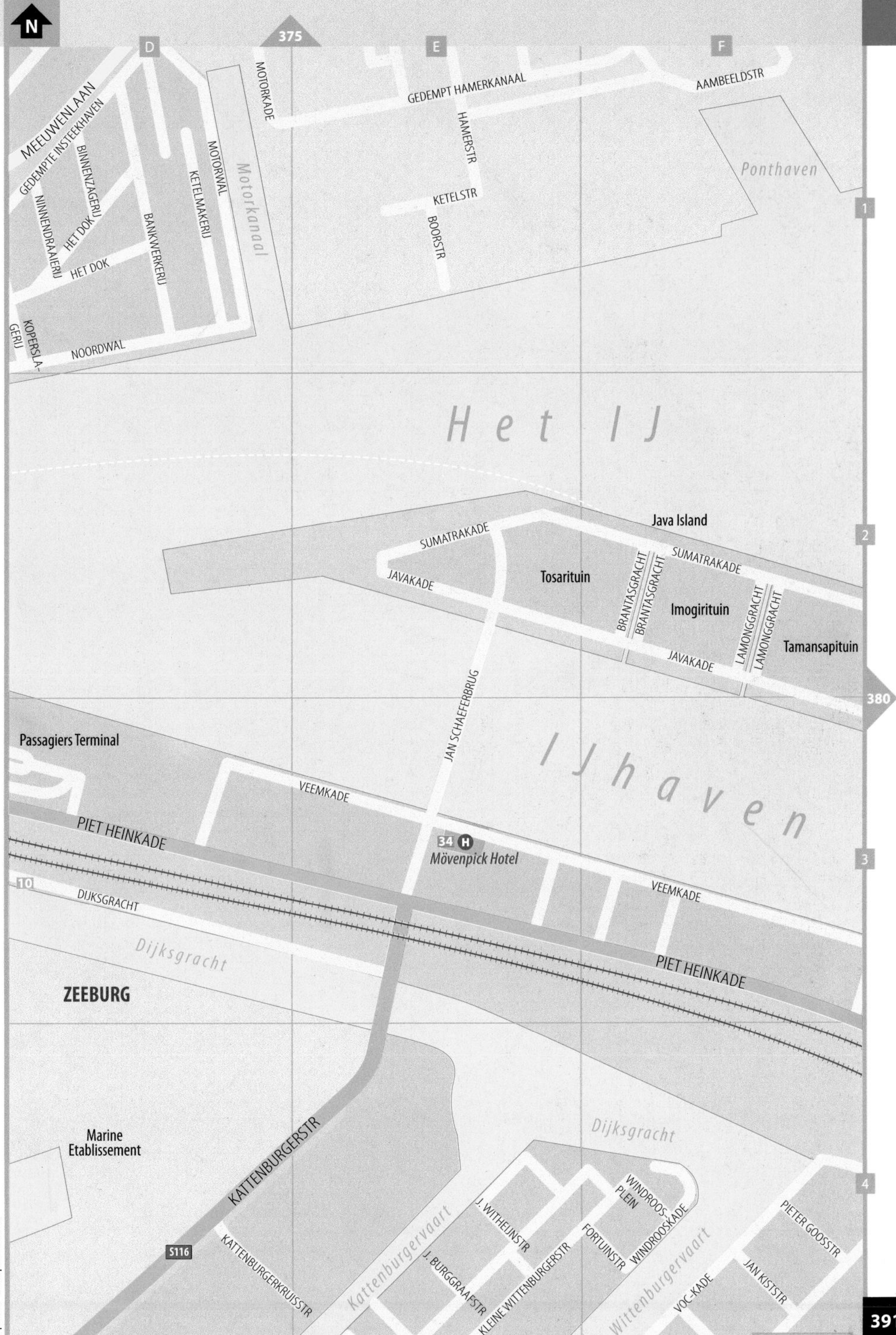
N
375
395
380
D
E
F
1
2
3
4
MEEUWENLAAN
GEDEMPTE INSTEEKHAVEN
BINNENZAGERIJ
NINNENDRAAIERIJ
HET DOK
HET DOK
BANKWERKERIJ
KETELMAKERIJ
MOTORWAL
Motorkanaal
MOTORKADE
KOPERSLA-GERIJ
NOORDWAL
GEDEMPT HAMERKANAAL
HAMERSTR
KETELSTR
BOORSTR
AAMBEELDSTR
Ponthaven
Het IJ
Java Island
SUMATRAKADE
JAVAKADE
Tosarituin
BRANTASGRACHT
BRANTASGRACHT
SUMATRAKADE
Imogirituin
LAMONGGRACHT
LAMONGGRACHT
Tamansapituin
JAVAKADE
JAN SCHAEFERBRUG
IJhaven
Passagiers Terminal
VEEMKADE
PIET HEINKADE
34
Mövenpick Hotel
VEEMKADE
10
DIJKSGRACHT
Dijksgracht
PIET HEINKADE
ZEEBURG
Marine Etablissement
KATTENBURGERSTR
S116
KATTENBURGERKRUISSTR
Kattenburgervaart
Dijksgracht
J. WITHEIJNSTR
J. BURGGRAAFSTR
KLEINE WITTENBURGERSTR
WINDROOS-PLEIN
FORTUINSTR
WINDROOSKADE
Wittenburgervaart
VOC-KADE
PIETER GOOSSTR
JAN KISTSTR
100m

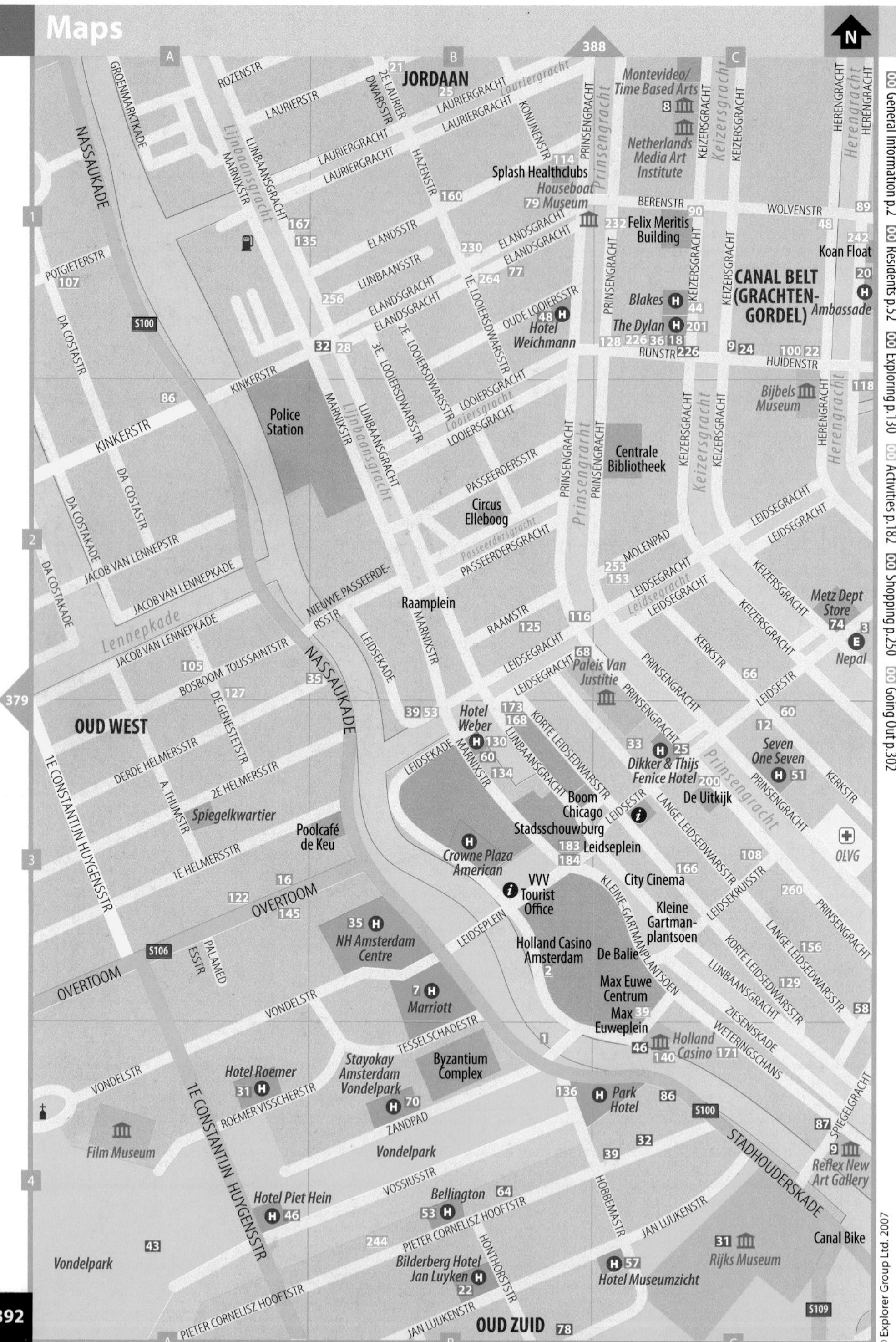

00 General Information p.2 00 Residents p.52 00 Exploring p.130 00 Activities p.182 00 Shopping p.250 00 Going Out p.302

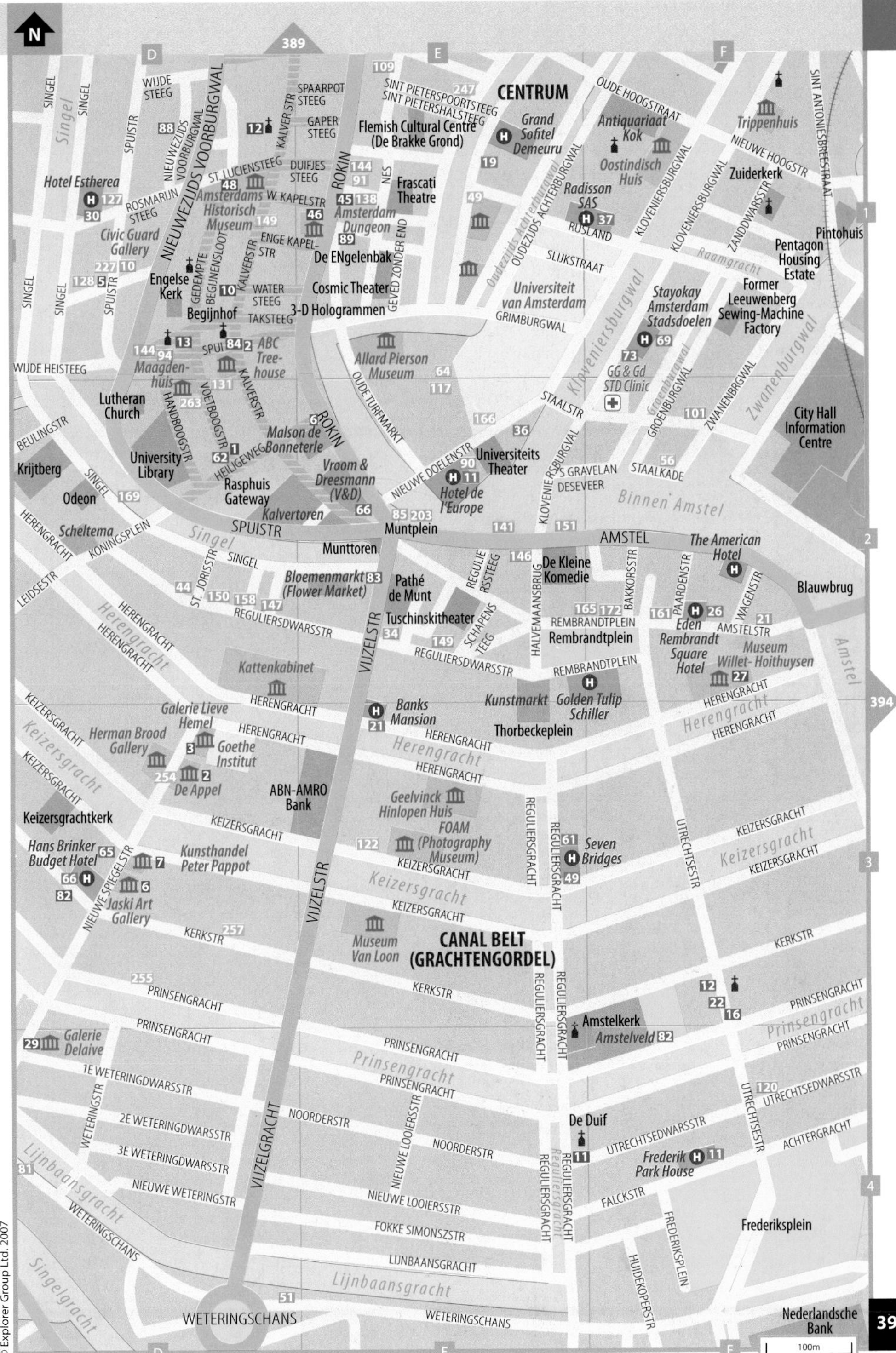
N
389
394
384
CENTRUM
CANAL BELT (GRACHTENGORDEL)
Singel
SINGEL
WIJDE STEEG
SPUISTR
NIEUWEZIJDS VOORBURGWAL
SPAARPOT STEEG
GAPER STEEG
KALVER STR
ROKIN
SINT PIETERSPOORTSTEEG
SINT PIETERSHALSTEEG
OUDE HOOGSTRAAT
SINT ANTONIESBREESTRAAT
Trippenhuis
Grand Sofitel Demeuru
Antiquariaat Kok
Flemish Cultural Centre (De Brakke Grond)
Oostindisch Huis
NIEUWE HOOGSTR
Zuiderkerk
Hotel Estherea
ROSMARIJN STEEG
ST. LUCIENSTEEG
DUIFJES STEEG
NES
Frascati Theatre
Amsterdams Historisch Museum
W. KAPELSTR
Amsterdam Dungeon
Radisson SAS
RUSLAND
OUDEZIJDS ACHTERBURGWAL
Oudezijds Achterburgwal
KLOVENIERSBURGWAL
ZANDDWARSSTR
Raamgracht
Pintohuis
Civic Guard Gallery
ENGE KAPEL-STR
De ENgelenbak
SLIJKSTRAAT
Pentagon Housing Estate
Engelse Kerk
GEDEMPTE BEGIJNENSLOOT
KALVERSTR
WATER STEEG
Cosmic Theater
GEVED ZONDER END
Universiteit van Amsterdam
Stayokay Amsterdam Stadsdoelen
Former Leeuwenberg Sewing-Machine Factory
Begijnhof
TAKSTEEG
3-D Hologrammen
GRIMBURGWAL
Kloveniersburgwal
Zwanenburgwal
SPUI
ABC Tree-house
Allard Pierson Museum
Maagden-huis
WIJDE HEISTEEG
GG & Gd STD Clinic
Groenburgwal
GROENBURGWAL
ZWANENBRGWAL
Lutheran Church
HANDBOOGSTR
VOETBOOGSTR
OUDE TURFMARKT
STAALSTR
City Hall Information Centre
BEULINGSTR
Malson de Bonneterle
Krijtberg
University Library
HEILIGEWEG
Vroom & Dreesmann (V&D)
NIEUWE DOELENSTR
Universiteits Theater
KLOVENIERSBURGWAL
'S GRAVELANDSEVEER
STAALKADE
Odeon
Rasphuis Gateway
Hotel de l'Europe
Binnen Amstel
Kalvertoren
Muntplein
SPUISTR
Scheltema
HERENGRACHT
KONINGSPLEIN
AMSTEL
The American Hotel
Munttoren
REGULIERSSTEEG
De Kleine Komedie
BAKKORSSTR
PAARDENSTR
WAGENSTR
Blauwbrug
LEIDSESTR
ST. JORISSTR
Bloemenmarkt (Flower Market)
Pathé de Munt
HALVEMAANSBRUG
Tuschinskitheater
SCHAPENSTEEG
REMBRANDTPLEIN
Rembrandtplein
Eden Rembrandt Square Hotel
AMSTELSTR
Museum Willet-Hoithuysen
Amstel
Herengracht
REGULIERSDWARSSTR
Kattenkabinet
VIJZELSTR
Kunstmarkt
Golden Tulip Schiller
Galerie Lieve Hemel
Banks Mansion
Thorbeckeplein
KEIZERSGRACHT
Herman Brood Gallery
Goethe Institut
De Appel
ABN-AMRO Bank
Geelvinck Hinlopen Huis
Keizersgracht
Keizersgrachtkerk
FOAM (Photography Museum)
REGULIERSGRACHT
Seven Bridges
UTRECHTSESTR
Hans Brinker Budget Hotel
Kunsthandel Peter Pappot
NIEUWE SPIEGELSTR
Jaski Art Gallery
KERKSTR
Museum Van Loon
PRINSENGRACHT
Amstelkerk
Amstelveld
Prinsengracht
Galerie Delaive
1E WETERINGDWARSSTR
WETERINGSTR
UTRECHTSEDWARSSTR
2E WETERINGDWARSSTR
NOORDERSTR
NIEUWE LOOIERSSTR
De Duif
ACHTERGRACHT
3E WETERINGDWARSSTR
VIJZELGRACHT
Frederik Park House
Lijnbaansgracht
NIEUWE WETERINGSTR
FALCKSTR
FREDERIKSPLEIN
Frederiksplein
WETERINGSCHANS
FOKKE SIMONSZSTR
LIJNBAANSGRACHT
HUIDEKOPERSTR
Singelgracht
Nederlandsche Bank
100m

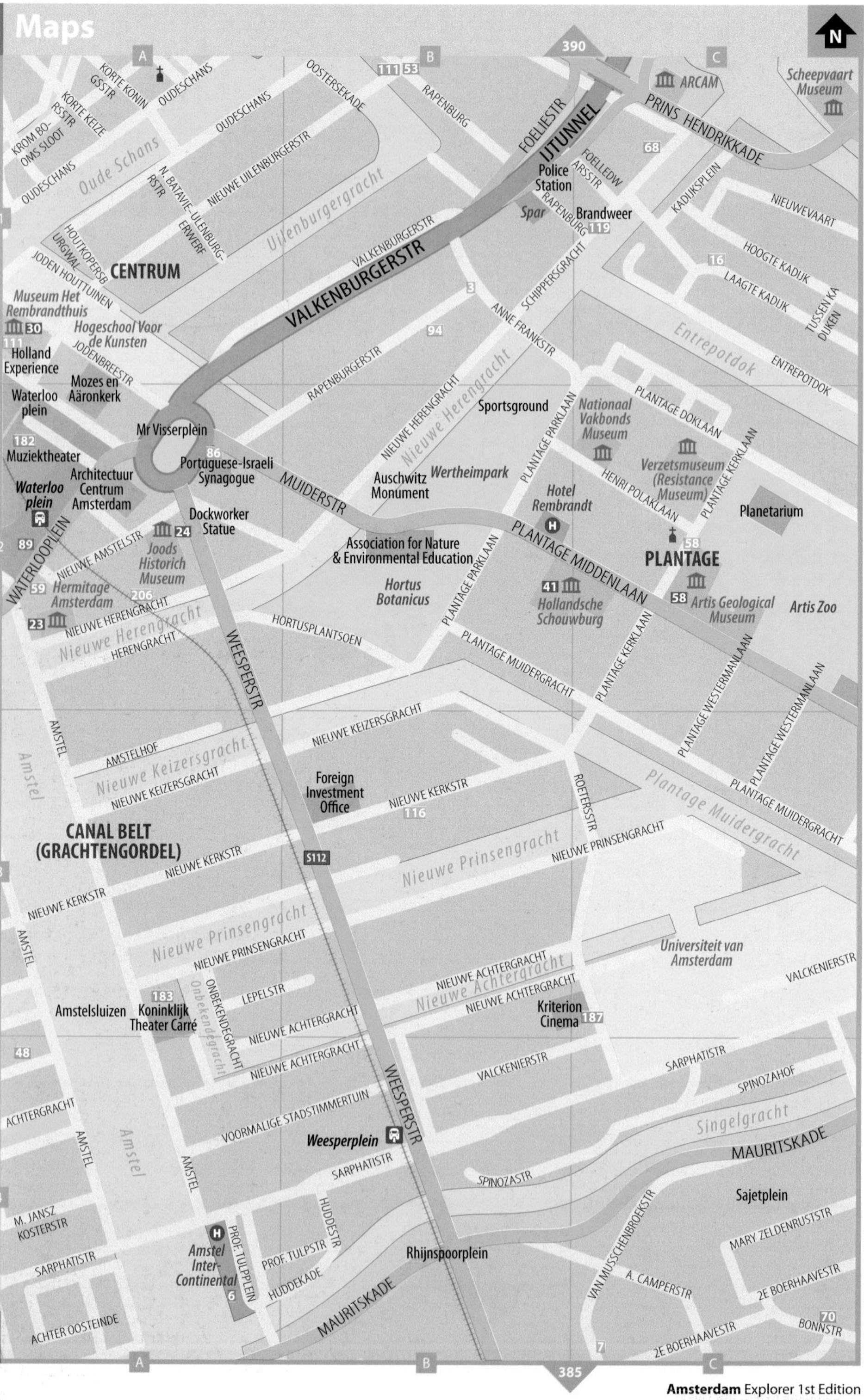

N

390

A B C

KORTE KONIN GSSTR
OUDESCHANS
OOSTERSEKADE
111 53
RAPENBURG
FOELIESTR
IJTUNNEL
ARCAM
Scheepvaart Museum
PRINS HENDRIKKADE
KORTE KEIZE RSSTR
KROM BO-OMS SLOOT
OUDESCHANS
Oude Schans
NIEUWE UILENBURGERSTR
N. BATAVIE-RSTR
ULENBURG-ERWERF
Uilenburgergracht
Police Station
FOELLEDW ARSSTR
68
KADIJKSPLEIN
NIEUWEVAART
Spar
RAPENBURG
Brandweer
119
HOUTKOPERSB URGWAL
JODEN HOUTTUINEN
CENTRUM
VALKENBURGERSTR
VALKENBURGERSTR
SCHIPPERSGRACHT
16
HOOGTE KADIJK
LAAGTE KADIJK
TUSSEN KADIJKEN
Museum Het Rembrandthuis
30
111
Hogeschool Voor de Kunsten
3
ANNE FRANKSTR
94
Entrepotdok
ENTREPOTDOK
Holland Experience
JODENBREESTR
RAPENBURGERSTR
Mozes en Aäronkerk
Waterloo plein
NIEUWE HERENGRACHT
Nieuwe Herengracht
Sportsground
PLANTAGE PARKLAAN
Nationaal Vakbonds Museum
PLANTAGE DOKLAAN
Mr Visserplein
182
Muziektheater
86
Portuguese-Israeli Synagogue
Verzetsmuseum (Resistance Museum)
PLANTAGE KERKLAAN
Architectuur Centrum Amsterdam
Wertheimpark
Auschwitz Monument
HENRI POLAKLAAN
MUIDERSTR
Hotel Rembrandt
Planetarium
Waterloo plein
Dockworker Statue
24
WATERLOOPLEIN
NIEUWE AMSTELSTR
89
Joods Historich Museum
Association for Nature & Environmental Education
PLANTAGE MIDDENLAAN
58
PLANTAGE
59
Hermitage Amsterdam
206
PLANTAGE PARKLAAN
Hortus Botanicus
41
Hollandsche Schouwburg
58
Artis Geological Museum
Artis Zoo
23
NIEUWE HERENGRACHT
Nieuwe Herengracht
HERENGRACHT
HORTUSPLANTSOEN
WEESPERSTR
PLANTAGE MUIDERGRACHT
PLANTAGE KERKLAAN
PLANTAGE WESTERMANLAAN
PLANTAGE WESTERMANLAAN
393
AMSTEL
Amstel
AMSTELHOF
Nieuwe Keizersgracht
NIEUWE KEIZERSGRACHT
NIEUWE KEIZERSGRACHT
Foreign Investment Office
NIEUWE KERKSTR
116
ROETERSSTR
Plantage Muidergracht
PLANTAGE MUIDERGRACHT
CANAL BELT (GRACHTENGORDEL)
NIEUWE KERKSTR
S112
Nieuwe Prinsengracht
NIEUWE PRINSENGRACHT
NIEUWE KERKSTR
AMSTEL
Nieuwe Prinsengracht
NIEUWE PRINSENGRACHT
Universiteit van Amsterdam
VALCKENIERSTR
183
Onbekendegracht
ONBEKENDEGRACHT
LEPELSTR
NIEUWE ACHTERGRACHT
Nieuwe Achtergracht
NIEUWE ACHTERGRACHT
Amstelsluizen
Koninklijk Theater Carré
Kriterion Cinema
187
NIEUWE ACHTERGRACHT
48
NIEUWE ACHTERGRACHT
VALCKENIERSTR
SARPHATISTR
SPINOZAHOF
ACHTERGRACHT
VOORMALIGE STADSTIMMERTUIN
WEESPERSTR
Singelgracht
AMSTEL
Amstel
Weesperplein
MAURITSKADE
AMSTEL
SARPHATISTR
SPINOZASTR
Sajetplein
M. JANSZ KOSTERSTR
HUDDESTR
VAN MUSSCHENBROEKSTR
MARY ZELDENRUSTSTR
Amstel Inter-Continental
PROF. TULPPLEIN
Rhijnspoorplein
SARPHATISTR
PROF. TULPSTR
6
HUDDEKADE
A. CAMPERSTR
2E BOERHAAVESTR
MAURITSKADE
70
ACHTER OOSTEINDE
BONNSTR
7
2E BOERHAAVESTR

1 2 3 4

A B C

385

General Information p.2 Residents p.52 Exploring p.130 Activities p.182 Shopping p.250 Going Out p.302

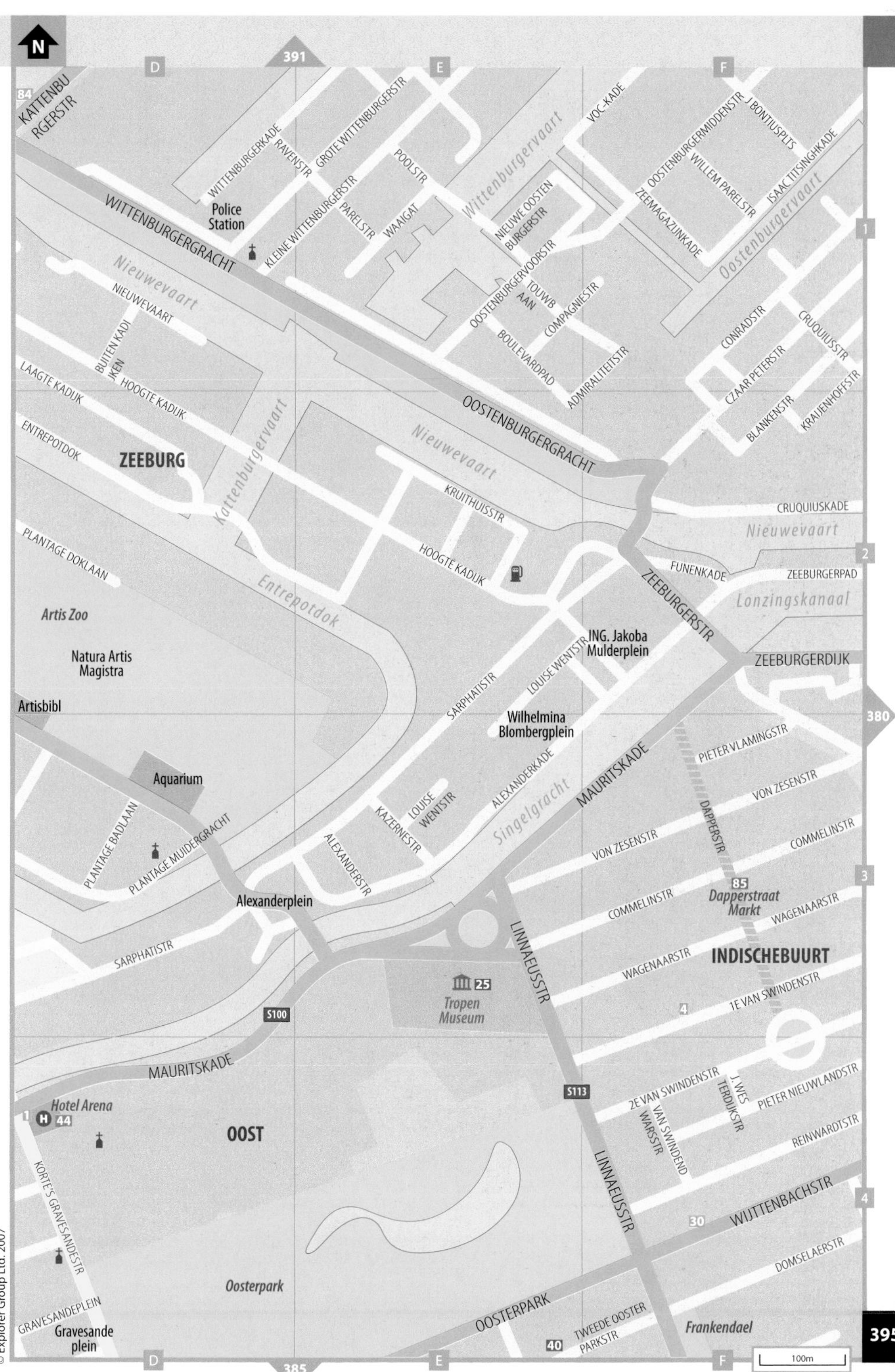
ZEEBURG
Artis Zoo
Natura Artis Magistra
Artisbibl
Aquarium
Police Station
Alexanderplein
Wilhelmina Blombergplein
ING. Jakoba Mulderplein
Tropen Museum
INDISCHEBUURT
Dapperstraat Markt
OOST
Hotel Arena
Oosterpark
Frankendael
Gravesande plein
WITTENBURGERGRACHT
OOSTENBURGERGRACHT
MAURITSKADE
LINNAEUSSTR
ZEEBURGERSTR
ZEEBURGERDIJK
SARPHATISTR
WIJTTENBACHSTR
OOSTERPARK
Nieuwevaart
Entrepotdok
Singelgracht
Lonzingskanaal
Wittenburgervaart
Oostenburgervaart
Kattenburgervaart
100m

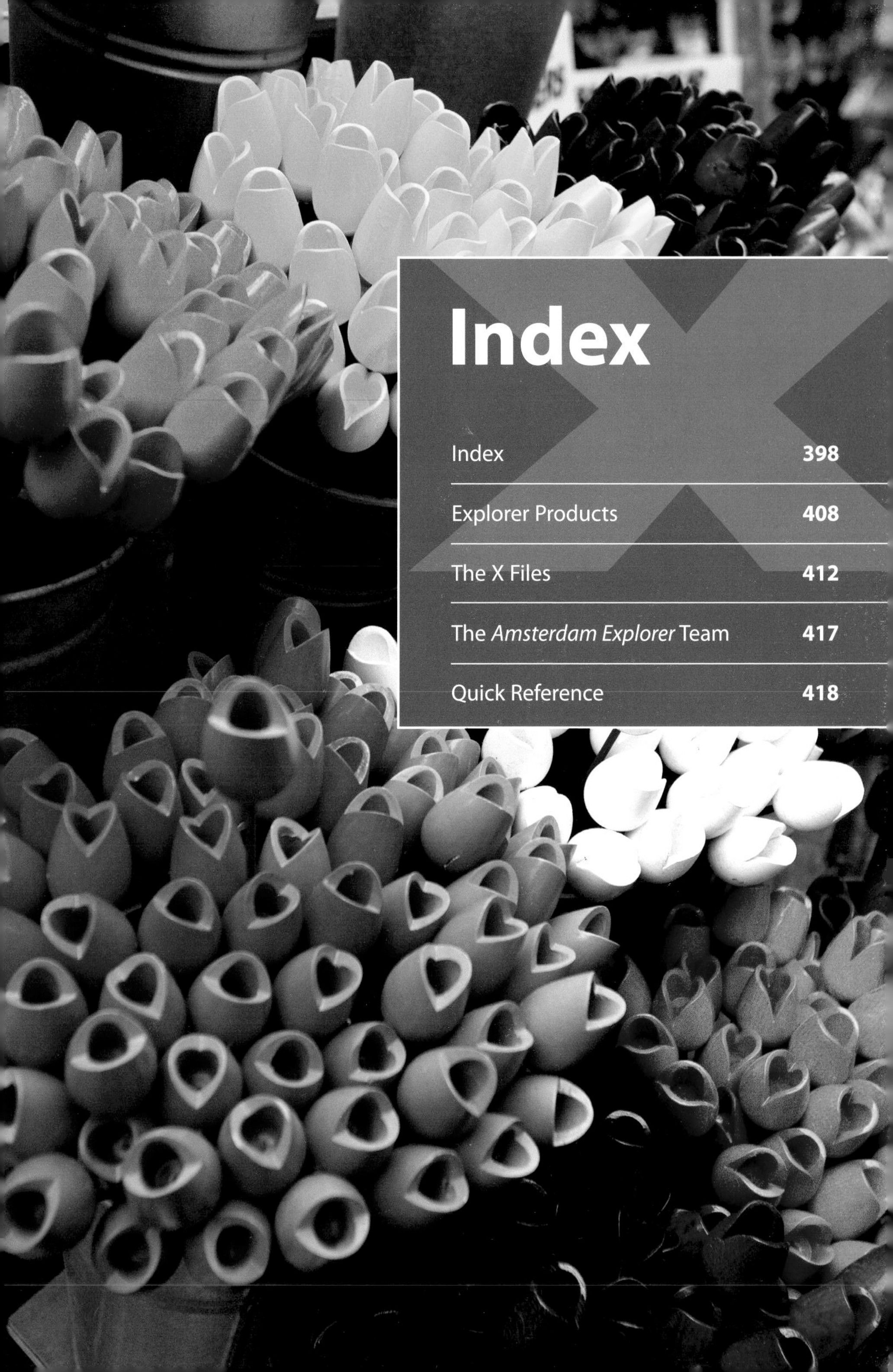

Index

Q

R

S

T

Residents' Guides

All you need to know about living, working and enjoying life in these exciting destinations

*

*

*

Mini Guides

The perfect pocket-sized Visitors' Guides

*

*

*

Mini Maps

Wherever you are, never get lost again

*

*

*

Photography Books

Beautiful cities caught through the lens

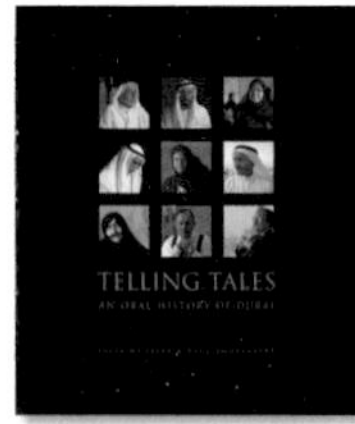

Calendars

The time, the place, and the date

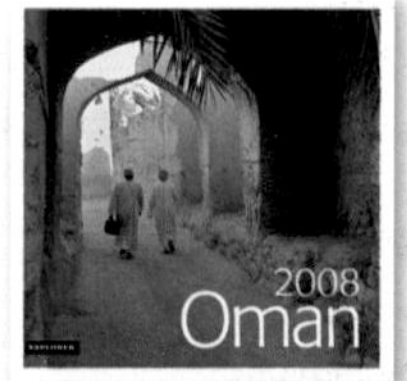

Maps

Wherever you are, never get lost again

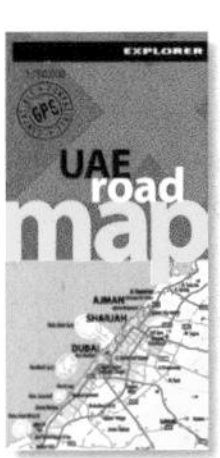

Activity and Lifestyle Guides

Drive, trek, dive and swim... life will never be boring again

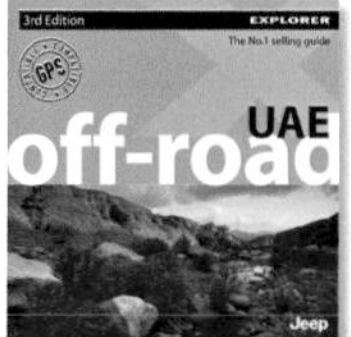

*

*

*

Retail sales

Our books are available in most good bookshops around the world, and are also available online at Amazon.co.uk and Amazon.com. If you would like to enquire about any of our international distributors, please contact retail@explorerpublishing.com

Bulk sales and customisation

All our products are available for bulk sales with customisation options. For discount rates and further information, please contact corporatesales@explorerpublishing.com

Licensing and digital sales

All our content, maps and photography are available for print or digital use. For licensing enquiries please contact licensing@explorerpublishing.com

* Covers not final, titles released second quarter 2008

The X Files

Ahmed Mainodin
AKA: Mystery Man
We can never recognise Ahmed because of his constantly changing facial hair. He waltzes in with big lambchop sideburns one day, a handlebar moustache the next, and a neatly trimmed goatee after that. So far we've had no objections to his hirsute chameleonisms, but we'll definitely draw the line at a monobrow.

Bahrudeen Abdul
AKA: The Stallion
Having tired of creating abstract sculptures out of papier maché and candy canes, Bahrudeen turned to the art of computer programming. After honing his skills in the southern Andes for three years he grew bored of Patagonian winters, and landed a job here, 'The Home of 01010101 Creative Freedom'.

Ajay Krishnan R
AKA: Web Wonder
Ajay's mum and dad knew he was going to be an IT genius when they found him reconfiguring his Commodore 64 at the tender age of 2. He went on to become the technology consultant on all three Matrix films, and counts Keanu as a close personal friend.

Ben Merrett
AKA: Big Ben
After a short (or tall as the case may have been) career as a human statue, Ben tired of the pigeons choosing him, rather than his namesake, as a public convenience and decided to fly the nest to seek his fortune in foreign lands. Not only is he big on personality but he brings in the big bucks with his bulk!

Alex Jeffries
AKA: Easy Rider
Alex is happiest when dressed in leather from head to toe with a humming machine between his thighs – just like any other motorbike enthusiast. Whenever he's not speeding along the Hatta Road at full throttle, he can be found at his beloved Mac, still dressed in leather.

Cherry Enriquez
AKA: Bean Counter
With the team's penchant for sweets and pastries, it's good to know we have Cherry on top of our accounting cake. The local confectioner is always paid on time, so we're guaranteed great gateaux for every special occasion.

Alistair MacKenzie
AKA: Media Mogul
If only Alistair could take the paperless office one step further and achieve the officeless office he would be the happiest publisher alive. Wireless access from a remote spot somewhere in the Hajar Mountains would suit this intrepid explorer – less traffic, lots of fresh air, and wearing sandals all day - the perfect work environment!

Claire England
AKA: Whip Cracker
No longer able to freeload off the fact that she once appeared in a Robbie Williams video, Claire now puts her creative skills to better use – looking up rude words in the dictionary! A child of English nobility, Claire is quite the lady – unless she's down at Jimmy Dix.

Andrea Fust
AKA: Mother Superior
By day Andrea is the most efficient manager in the world and by night she replaces the boardroom for her board and wows the pants off the dudes in Ski Dubai. Literally. Back in the office she definitely wears the trousers!

David Quinn
AKA: Sharp Shooter
After a short stint as a children's TV presenter was robbed from David because he developed an allergy to sticky back plastic, he made his way to sandier pastures. Now that he's thinking outside the box, nothing gets past the man with the sharpest pencil in town.

Derrick Pereira
AKA: The Returnimator
After leaving Explorer in 2003, Derrick's life took a dramatic downturn – his dog ran away, his prized bonsai tree died and he got kicked out of his thrash metal band. Since rejoining us, things are looking up and he just found out he's won $10 million in a Nigerian sweepstakes competition. And he's got the desk by the window!

Iain Young
AKA: 'The Cat'
Iain follows in the fine tradition of Scots with safe hands – Alan Rough, Andy Goram, Jim Leighton on a good day – but breaking into the Explorer XI has proved frustrating. There's no match on a Mac, but that Al Huzaifa ringer doesn't half make himself big.

Enrico Maullon
AKA: The Crooner
Frequently mistaken for his near-namesake Enrique Iglesias, Enrico decided to capitalise and is now a regular stand-in for the Latin heartthrob. If he's ever missing from the office, it usually means he's off performing for millions of adoring fans on another stadium tour of America.

Ieyad Charaf
AKA: Fashion Designer
When we hired Ieyad as a top designer, we didn't realise we'd be getting his designer tops too! By far the snappiest dresser in the office, you'd be hard-pressed to beat his impeccably ironed shirts.

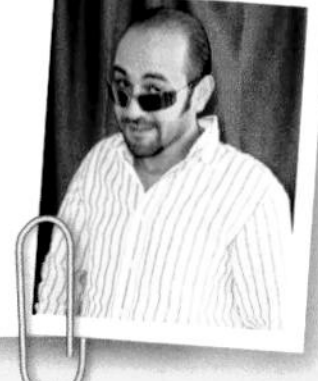

Firos Khan
AKA: Big Smiler
Previously a body double in kung fu movies, including several appearances in close up scenes for Steven Seagal's moustache. He also once tore down a restaurant with his bare hands after they served him a mild curry by mistake.

Ingrid Cupido
AKA: The Karaoke Queen
Ingrid has a voice to match her starlet name. She'll put any Pop Idols to shame once behind the mike, and she's pretty nifty on a keyboard too. She certainly gets our vote if she decides to go pro; just remember you saw her here first.

Hashim MM
AKA: Speedy Gonzales
They don't come much faster than Hashim – he's so speedy with his mouse that scientists are struggling to create a computer that can keep up with him. His nimble fingers leave his keyboard smouldering (he gets through three a week), and his go-faster stripes make him almost invisible to the naked eye when he moves.

Ivan Rodrigues
AKA: The Aviator
After making a mint in the airline market, Ivan came to Explorer where he works for pleasure, not money. That's his story, anyway. We know that he is actually a corporate spy from a rival company and that his multi-level spreadsheets are really elaborate codes designed to confuse us.

Helen Spearman
AKA: Little Miss Sunshine
With her bubbly laugh and permanent smile, Helen is a much-needed ray of sunshine in the office when we're all grumpy and facing harrowing deadlines. It's almost impossible to think that she ever loses her temper or shows a dark side... although put her behind the wheel of a car, and you've got instant road rage.

Jake Marsico
AKA: Don Calzone
Jake spent the last 10 years on the tiny triangular Mediterranean island of Samoza, honing his traditional cooking techniques and perfecting his Italian. Now, whenever he returns to his native America, he impresses his buddies by effortlessly zapping a hot dog to perfection in any microwave, anywhere, anytime.

Henry Hilos
AKA: The Quiet Man
Henry can rarely be seen from behind his large obstructive screen but when you do catch a glimpse you'll be sure to get a smile. Lighthearted Henry keeps all those glossy pages filled with pretty pictures for something to look at when you can't be bothered to read.

Jane Roberts
AKA: The Oracle
After working in an undisclosed role in the government, Jane brought her super sleuth skills to Explorer. Whatever the question, she knows what, where, who, how and when, but her encyclopaedic knowledge is only impressive until you realise she just makes things up randomly.

The X Files

Jayde Fernandes
AKA: Pop Idol
Jayde's idol is Britney Spears, and he recently shaved his head to show solidarity with the troubled star. When he's not checking his dome for stubble, or practising the dance moves to 'Baby One More Time' in front of the bathroom mirror, he actually manages to get some designing done.

Lennie Mangalino
AKA: Shaker Maker
With a giant spring in her step and music in her heart it's hard to not to swing to the beat when Lennie passes by in the office. She loves her Lambada… and Samba… and Salsa and anything else she can get the sales team shaking their hips to.

Johny Mathew
AKA: The Hawker
Caring Johny used to nurse wounded eagles back to health and teach them how to fly again before trying his luck in merchandising. Fortunately his skills in the field have come in handy at Explorer, where his efforts to improve our book sales have been a soaring success.

Mannie Lugtu
AKA: Distribution Demon
When the travelling circus rode into town, their master juggler Mannie decided to leave the Big Top and explore Dubai instead. He may have swapped his balls for our books but his juggling skills still come in handy.

Kate Fox
AKA: Contacts Collector
Kate swooped into the office like the UK equivalent of Wonderwoman, minus the tights of course (it's much too hot for that), but armed with a superhuman marketing brain. Even though she 's just arrived, she is already a regular on the Dubai social scene – she is helping to blast Explorer into the stratosphere, one champagne-soaked networking party at a time.

Maricar Ong
AKA: Pocket Docket
A pint-sized dynamo of ruthless efficiency, Maricar gets the job done before anyone else notices it needed doing. If this most able assistant is absent for a moment, it sends a surge of blind panic through the Explorer ranks.

Katie Drynan
AKA: The Irish Deputy
Katie is a Jumeira Jane in training, and has 35 sisters who take it in turns to work in the Explorer office while she enjoys testing all the beauty treatments available on the Beach Road. This Irish charmer met an oil tycoon in Paris, and they now spend the weekends digging very deep holes in their new garden.

Grace Carnay
AKA: Manila Ice
It's just as well the office is so close to a movie theatre, because Grace is always keen to catch the latest Hollywood offering from Brad Pitt, who she admires purely for his acting ability, of course. Her ice cool exterior conceals a tempestuous passion for jazz, which fuels her frenzied typing speed.

Matt Farquharson
AKA: Hack Hunter
A career of tuppence-a-word hackery ended when Matt arrived in Dubai to cover a maggot wranglers' convention. He misguidedly thinks he's clever because he once wrote for some grown-up English papers.

Kiran Melwani
AKA: Bow Selector
Like a modern-day Robin Hood (right down to the green tights and band of merry men), Kiran's mission in life is to distribute Explorer's wealth of knowledge to the fact-hungry readers of the world. Just make sure you never do anything to upset her – rumour has it she's a pretty mean shot with that bow and arrow.

Matthew Samuel
AKA: Mr Modest
Matt's penchant for the entrepreneurial life began with a pair of red braces and a filofax when still a child. That yearning for the cut and thrust of commerce has brought him to Dubai, where he made a fortune in the sand-selling business before semi-retiring at Explorer.

Michael Samuel
AKA: Gordon Gekko
We have a feeling this mild mannered master of mathematics has a wild side. He hasn't witnessed an Explorer party yet but the office agrees that once the karaoke machine is out, Michael will be the maestro. Watch out Dubai!

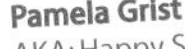

Pamela Grist
AKA: Happy Snapper
If a picture can speak a thousand words then Pam's photos say a lot about her - through her lens she manages to find the beauty in everything – even this motley crew. And when the camera never lies, thankfully Photoshop can.

Mimi Stankova
AKA: Mind Controller
A master of mind control, Mimi's siren-like voice lulls people into doing whatever she asks. Her steely reserve and endless patience mean recalcitrant reporters and persistent PR people are putty in her hands, delivering whatever she wants, whenever she wants it.

Pete Maloney
AKA: Graphic Guru
Image conscious he may be, but when Pete has his designs on something you can bet he's gonna get it! He's the king of chat up lines, ladies – if he ever opens a conversation with 'D'you come here often?' then brace yourself for the Maloney magic.

Mohammed Sameer
AKA: Man in the Van
Known as MS, short for Microsoft, Sameer can pick apart a PC like a thief with a lock, which is why we keep him out of finance and pounding Dubai's roads in the unmissable Explorer van – so we can always spot him coming.

Rafi Jamal
AKA: Soap Star
After a walk on part in The Bold and the Beautiful, Rafi swapped the Hollywood Hills for the Hajar Mountains. Although he left the glitz behind, he still mingles with high society, moonlighting as a male gigolo and impressing Dubai's ladies with his fancy footwork.

Mohammed T
AKA: King of the Castle
T is Explorer's very own Bedouin warehouse dweller; under his caring charge all Explorer stock is kept in masterful order. Arrive uninvited and you'll find T, meditating on a pile of maps, amid an almost eerie sense of calm.

Rafi VP
AKA: Party Trickster
After developing a rare allergy to sunlight in his teens, Rafi started to lose a few centimeters of height every year. He now stands just 30cm tall, and does his best work in our dingy basement wearing a pair of infrared goggles. His favourite party trick is to fold himself into a briefcase, and he was once sick in his hat.

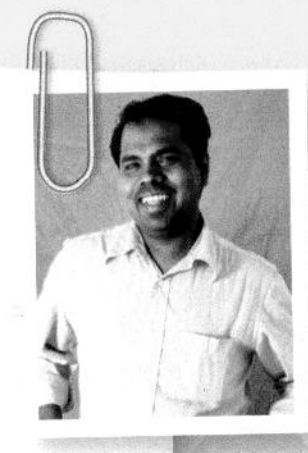

Noushad Madathil
AKA: Map Daddy
Where would Explorer be without the mercurial Madathil brothers? Lost in the Empty Quarter, that's where. Quieter than a mute dormouse, Noushad prefers to let his Photoshop layers, and brother Zain, do all the talking. A true Map Daddy.

Richard Greig
AKA: Sir Lancelot
Chivalrous to the last, Richard's dream of being a mediaeval knight suffered a setback after being born several centuries too late. His stellar parliamentary career remains intact, and he is in the process of creating a new party with the aim of abolishing all onions and onion-related produce.

Roshni Ahuja
AKA: Bright Spark
Never failing to brighten up the office with her colourful get-up, Roshni definitely puts the 'it' in the IT department. She's a perennially pleasant, profound programmer with peerless panache, and she does her job with plenty of pep and piles of pizzazz.

Sunita Lakhiani
AKA: Designlass
Initially suspicious of having a female in their midst, the boys in Designlab now treat Sunita like one of their own. A big shame for her, because they treat each other pretty damn bad!

Sean Kearns
AKA: The Tall Guy
Big Sean, as he's affectionately known, is so laid back he actually spends most of his time lying down (unless he's on a camping trip, when his ridiculously small tent forces him to sleep on his hands and knees). Despite the rest of us constantly tripping over his lanky frame, when the job requires someone who will work flat out, he always rises to the editorial occasion.

Steve Jones
AKA: Golden Boy
Our resident Kiwi lives in a nine-bedroom mansion and is already planning an extension. His winning smile has caused many a knee to weaken in Bur Dubai but sadly for the ladies, he's hopelessly devoted to his clients.

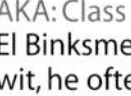

Shabsir M
AKA: Sticky Wicket
Shabsir is a valuable player on the Indian national cricket team, so instead of working you'll usually find him autographing cricket balls for crazed fans around the world. We don't mind though – if ever a retailer is stumped because they run out of stock, he knocks them for six with his speedy delivery.

Tim Binks
AKA: Class Clown
El Binksmeisterooney is such a sharp wit, he often has fellow Explorers gushing tea from their noses in convulsions of mirth. Years spent hiking across the Middle East have given him an encyclopaedic knowledge of rock formations and elaborate hair.

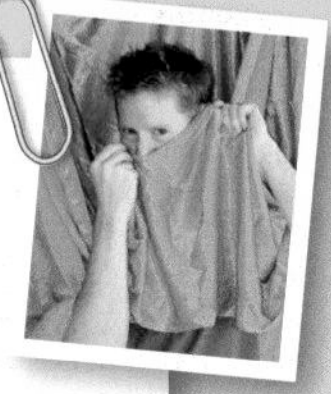

Shawn Jackson Zuzarte
AKA: Paper Plumber
If you thought rocket science was hard, try rearranging the chaotic babble that flows from the editorial team! If it weren't for Shawn, most of our books would require a kaleidoscope to read correctly so we're keeping him and his jazz hands under wraps.

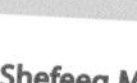

Tom Jordan
AKA: The True Professional
Explorer's resident thesp, Tom delivers lines almost as well as he cuts them. His early promise on the pantomime circuit was rewarded with an all-action role in hit UK drama Heartbeat. He's still living off the royalties – and the fact he shared a sandwich with Kenneth Branagh.

Shefeeq M
AKA: Rapper in Disguise
So new he's still got the wrapper on, Shefeeq was dragged into the Explorer office, and put to work in the design department. The poor chap only stopped by to ask for directions to Wadi Bih, but since we realised how efficient he is, we keep him chained to his desk.

Tracy Fitzgerald
AKA: 'La Dona'
Tracy is a queenpin Catalan mafiosa and ringleader for the 'pescadora' clan, a nefarious group that runs a sushi smuggling operation between the Costa Brava and Ras Al Khaimah. She is not to be crossed. Rival clans will find themselves fed fish, and then fed to the fishes.

Shyrell Tamayo
AKA: Fashion Princess
We've never seen Shyrell wearing the same thing twice – her clothes collection is so large that her husband has to keep all his things in a shoebox. She runs Designlab like clockwork, because being late for deadlines is SO last season.

Zainudheen Madathil
AKA: Map Master
Often confused with retired footballer Zinedine Zidane because of his dexterous displays and a bad head-butting habit, Zain tackles design with the mouse skills of a star striker. Maps are his goal and despite getting red-penned a few times, when he shoots, he scores.

The *Amsterdam Explorer* Team
Lead Editor Tim Binks
Deputy Editor Richard Greig
Editorial Assistant Grace Carnay
Designers Rafi Pullat
Cartographers Sunita Lakhiani, Abdul Hakeem, Fathima Suhra, Mohammed Rafeeq
Photographers Victor Romero, Pamela Grist, Tim Binks
Proofreader Audrey Lee

Publisher
Alistair MacKenzie

Editorial
Managing Editor Claire England
Lead Editors David Quinn, Jane Roberts, Matt Farquharson, Sean Kearns, Tim Binks, Tom Jordan
Deputy Editors Helen Spearman, Jakob Marsico, Katie Drynan, Pamela Afram, Richard Greig, Tracy Fitzgerald
Editorial Assistants Grace Carnay, Ingrid Cupido, Mimi Stankova

Design
Creative Director Pete Maloney
Art Director Ieyad Charaf
Senior Designers Alex Jeffries, Iain Young
Layout Manager Jayde Fernandes
Layouters Hashim Moideen, Rafi Pullat, Shefeeq Marakkatepurath
Junior Layouter Shawn Jackson Zuzarte
Cartography Manager Zainudheen Madathil
Cartographers Noushad Madathil, Sunita Lakhiani
Design Admin Manager Shyrell Tamayo
Production Coordinator Maricar Ong

Photography
Photography Manager Pamela Grist
Photographer Victor Romero
Image Editor Henry Hilos

Sales & Marketing
Area Sales Managers Laura Zuffa, Stephen Jones
Corporate Sales Executive Ben Merrett
Marketing Manager Kate Fox
Marketing Executive Annabel Clough
Retail Sales Manager Ivan Rodrigues
Retail Sales Coordinator Kiran Melwani
Retail Sales Supervisor Matthew Samuel
Merchandiser Johny Mathew
Sales & Marketing Coordinator Lennie Mangalino
Distribution Executives Ahmed Mainodin, Firos Khan, Mannie Lugtu
Warehouse Assistants Mohammed Kunjaymo, Najumudeen K.I.
Drivers Mohammed Sameer, Shabsir Madathil

Finance & Administration
Finance Manager Michael Samuel
HR & Administration Manager Andrea Fust
Accounts Assistant Cherry Enriquez
Administrators Enrico Maullon, Kelly Tesoro
Driver Rafi Jamal

IT
IT Administrator Ajay Krishnan
Software Engineers Bahrudeen Abdul, Roshni Ahuja
Digital Content Manager Derrick Pereira

Contact Us

Reader Response

If you have any comments and suggestions, fill out our online reader response form and you could win prizes. Log on to **www.explorerpublishing.com**

General Enquiries

We'd love to hear your thoughts and answer any questions you have about this book or any other Explorer product. Contact us at **info@explorerpublishing.com**

Careers

If you fancy yourself as an Explorer, send your CV (stating the position you're interested in) to **jobs@explorerpublishing.com**

Designlab & Contract Publishing

For enquiries about Explorer's Contract Publishing arm and design services contact **designlab@explorerpublishing.com**

PR & Marketing

For PR and marketing enquries contact
marketing@explorerpublishing.com
pr@explorerpublishing.com

Corporate Sales

For bulk sales and customisation options, for this book or any Explorer product, contact **sales@explorerpublishing.com**

Advertising & Sponsorship

For advertising and sponsorship, contact **media@explorerpublishing.com**

Explorer Publishing & Distribution
PO Box 34275, Dubai
United Arab Emirates
Phone: +971 (0)4 340 88 05
Fax: +971 (0)4 340 88 06
www.explorerpublishing.com

Main Hotels

Ambassade Hotel	020 555 02 22
Amstel InterContinental Amsterdam	020 622 60 60
The College Hotel	020 571 15 11
The Dylan	020 530 20 10
The Grand Amsterdam	020 555 31 11
Grand Hotel Amrâth Amsterdam	020 552 00 00
Hilton Amsterdam	020 710 60 60
Hotel Okura Amsterdam	020 678 71 11
Hotel Pulitzer	020 523 52 35
Hotel Roemer	020 589 08 00
Lloyd Hotel & Cultural Embassy	020 561 36 36
Mövenpick Hotel Amsterdam	020 519 12 00
NH Grand Hotel Krasnapolsky	020 554 91 11
Qbic WTC Amsterdam	043 321 11 11
Seven One Seven	020 427 07 17

Airport Information

Schiphol Airport (www.schiphol.nl)	
Lost & Found	0900 0141
Airport Medical Services	020 649 2566

Useful Numbers

AMC Academisch Medisch Centrum	020 566 91 11
American Express	020 504 86 66
Apotheek (pharmacy) helpline	0900 7244 7465
BovenIJ Ziekenhuis	020 634 63 46
Bureau Gevonden Vorwerpen (Lost and Found)	020 559 30 05
Diners Club	020 654 55 11
Discrimininatie (Discrimination)	020 638 55 51
Fire, police and ambulance	112
GGD STD Clinic	020 555 58 22
Huisarts (Family Doctors)	020 592 34 34
Huiselijk Geweld (Domestic Violence)	020 611 60 22
M (anonymous crimeline)	0800 7000
Mastercard/Eurocard	030 283 55 55
OLVG	020 599 91 11
Police (non-emergency)	0900 8844
Sint Lucas Ziekenhuis	020 510 89 11
Slachtofferhulp (Victim Support)	020 622 84 41
Slotervaartziekenhuis	020 512 93 33
SOS (24-hour helpline)	020 675 75 75
Tandartsen (Dentists)	0900 821 2230
Visa	0800 022 3110
VU	020 444 44 44

Public Holidays

Ascension (Hemelvaart)	1 May (2008)
Christmas (eerste Kerstdag)	25 Dec
Christmas (tweede Kerstdag)	26 Dec
Easter Monday (tweede Paasdag)	24 Mar
Easter Sunday (Pasen)	23 Mar
Liberation Day (Bevrijdingsdag)	5 May
New Year's Day (Nieuwjaar)	1 Jan
Queen's Day (Koninginnedag)	30 Apr (2008)
Remembrance Day (Dodenherdenking)	4 May
Whitsun (Pinksteren)	11-12 May (2008)

Tourist Information & Service Centres

VVV Centraal Station	020 551 25 25
VVV Leidesestraat	020 551 25 25
VVV Stationsplein	020 551 25 25

Consulates

Albania	070 427 21 01
Argentina	070 360 51 55
Australia	070 310 82 00
Austria	070 324 54 70
Belgium	070 312 34 56
Brazil	070 302 39 59
Canada	070 311 16 00
China	070 306 50 91
Cyprus	070 346 64 99
Czech Republic	070 313 00 31
Denmark	070 302 59 59
Egypt	070 354 20 00
Finland	070 346 97 54
France	070 312 58 00
Germany	070 342 06 00
Ghana	070 338 43 84
Greece	070 363 87 00
Hungary	070 350 04 04
Iceland	020 795 33 34
India	070 346 97 71
Indonesia	070 310 81 00
Ireland	070 363 09 93
Israel	070 376 05 00
Italy	070 302 10 30
Japan	070 346 95 44
Malta	076 520 90 43
Mauritius	020 540 58 20
Mexico	070 360 29 00
Monaco	070 624 52 50
Morocco	070 346 96 17
Nepal	020 624 15 30
New Zealand	070 346 93 24
Norway	070 311 76 11
Portugal	070 363 02 17
Romania	070 354 37 96
Russia	070 346 88 88
Saudi Arabia	070 361 43 91
Senegal	020 693 79 58
Slovakia	070 416 77 77
Slovenia	070 310 86 90
South Africa	070 392 45 01
Spain	070 364 38 14
Sweden	020 301 43 08
Sri Lanka	070 365 59 10
Switzerland	020 364 28 31
Thailand	070 345 20 88
Turkey	070 360 49 12
Uganda	070 538 17 56
United Arab Emirates	070 338 43 70
UK	070 427 04 27
USA	070 310 92 09